1995

1995

Contemporary
Business
Communication

Contemporary Business Communication

SCOT OBER

Ball State University

HOUGHTON MIFFLIN COMPANY   BOSTON   TORONTO
Dallas   Geneva, Illinois   Palo Alto   Princeton, New Jersey

Sponsoring Editor: Mary Jo Southern
Basic Book Editor: Tom Mancuso
Project Editor: Robin Bushnell Hogan
Assistant Design Manager: Pat Mahtani
Cover and Interior Designer: Sandra Gonzalez
Manufacturing Coordinator: Sharon Pearson
Marketing Manager: Diane Gifford

Cover art and photograph: Jerry L. Noe, "JAZZSCAPE #3" neon sculpture

Art Credits: see page 665

Other Credits: see page 665

Library of Congress Catalog Card Number: 91-71968

ISBN: 0-395-51211-5

ABCDEFGHIJ-VH-9987654321

To *my wife, Diana, with love*

Contents

Preface

Students don't have to be convinced of the need for high-level communication skills. By the time they enter business communication classes, they know enough about business to appreciate the critical role communication plays in the contemporary organization and the role it will play in helping them get a job and be successful on the job. To sustain this inherent interest, students need a textbook that is current, fast-paced, and interesting—just like business itself. Thus, the first objective of *Contemporary Business Communication* (CBC) is to present comprehensive coverage of real-world concepts in an interesting and lively manner.

At the same time, we know that many students have difficulty recognizing how to shape communications to meet the needs of a business situation. They need to be guided through the process of analyzing the problem and tailoring the message to their purpose. Thus the second objective of CBC is to provide a guidance approach to developing communication skills.

These two objectives—a real-world emphasis and a guidance approach—distinguish CBC from other mainstream core texts in business communication. This new text, along with a complete package of support materials, will help students enjoy and succeed in business communication.

REAL-WORLD EMPHASIS

One reason for the great success of the business communication course is that it teaches communication skills *in context*. Students learn how to communicate to solve the real-world problems they will face on the job. CBC fosters this "need-to-know" dimension by providing broad, up-to-date coverage of contemporary issues and problems facing business communicators today.

Chapter-opening vignettes illustrate the communication tasks of actual managers at real corporations, such as Digital Equipment, Ben and Jerry's, General Electric, and Keep America Beautiful, Inc. The abundant end-of-chapter exercises and case problems deal with such current real-world problems as environmental concerns, smokers' vs. nonsmokers' rights, Carpal Tunnel Syndrome, job-sharing, AIDS in the workplace, ownership of frequent-flyer flight coupons, and entrepreneurship.

Chapter 2 introduces three contemporary issues that are having an impact on business communication: the increasing international and intercultural nature of business today, technology in the workplace, and the growing emphasis on the legal and technical aspects of business. In the remaining chapters, 17 boxed features, called *Spotlights*, show how these issues affect the specific topic covered.

CONTEMPORARY ISSUES

The size and complexity of the modern organization has increased the need for skill in collaborative communication. Small-group communication (both written and oral) is covered in detail in Chapter 2, with additional coverage in the report and oral-communication chapters. In addition, all 18 chapters in the text contain at least one end-of-chapter collaborative exercise.

In today's fast-paced organization, the ability to locate and analyze data quickly is an increasingly important communication skill. CBC teaches contemporary data-collection and recording techniques (including conducting surveys and interviews), shows how to evaluate the quality of the data received, teaches principles of constructing tables and charts, and provides detailed guidelines on how to analyze and interpret quantitative and qualitative data.

URBAN SYSTEMS: AN ON-GOING CASE STUDY

Every chapter ends with a case study involving Urban Systems (US), a small start-up company whose primary product is Ultra Light, a new paper-thin light source that promises to revolutionize the illumination industry. A company profile is contained in the appendix, and each chapter presents a communication problem faced by one of the managers at US. As students systematically solve these 18 case studies, they face communication problems similar to those typically found in the workplace.

The continuing nature of the case study means that students get to know the managers and the company and are able to use richer contextual clues to solve communication problems than are possible in the short end-of-chapter exercises. In addition, because the same situations often carry over into subsequent chapters, students must face the consequences of their previous decisions.

CONTINUING EXAMPLES

Continuing examples are often used throughout the chapter (or even carried forward to the next chapter) in both the text and in the end-of-chapter exercises. For example, in Chapter 6, students first assume the role of buyer and write a claim letter and later assume the role of seller and answer the claim letter by writing an adjustment letter.

These continuing examples show that communication problems are not solved in a vacuum. They're more realistic because they give a sense of following a problem through to completion; they're more interesting because they provide a continuing thread to the chapter; and they reinforce the concept of audience analysis because students must first assume the role of sender and later the role of receiver for the same communication task.

A GUIDANCE APPROACH

When some students face a writing assignment, they want to get it over with as quickly as possible and often begin composing the final document immediately, thereby compressing all three steps of the writing process (planning, drafting, and revising) into one inefficient effort. These students need to discover that there is much more to writing than *writing* and that the most effective process is one that is long on planning and revising and short on drafting. CBC contains numerous pedagogical features that provide guidance to students to help them succeed in every step of the communication process.

Fourteen chapters in CBC contain microwriting activities—detailed studies of typical communication assignments. Each activity includes the *problem* (a situation that requires a communication task), the *process* (a series of questions with answers that provides step-by-step guidance for accomplishing the communication task), and the *product* (the finished document). Microwriting activities require students to focus their efforts on developing a strategy for the message before beginning to compose the message, and they serve as a step-by-step model for composing the end-of-chapter exercises.

MICROWRITING

Full-page models (more than 60 in all) are shown for each major writing task, with step-by-step composing notes presented in the side margin and grammar and mechanics notes presented in the bottom margin. Each job is shown in complete, ready-to-send format so that students become familiar with the appropriate format for each kind of writing assignment.

FULL-PAGE ANNOTATED MODELS

A student reading with a purpose will learn more than a student wandering aimlessly through the text. Therefore, instructional objectives are presented at the beginning of each chapter to introduce the important outcomes of the chapter. Marginal notations within the chapter connect each objective to the corresponding chapter content. And each end-of-chapter exercise and each item in the test bank is keyed to a specific objective. Thus, students can easily identify the chapter objectives, see where each objective is taught in the chapter, and see how each objective is applied at the end of the chapter. In addition, instructors can easily prepare valid tests that measure the specific objectives they teach.

CONTENT GEARED TO OBJECTIVES

- Part 1—Communicating in Business (Chapters 1–2) presents basic communication theory in a nontechnical manner and introduces four contemporary issues that affect business communication.
- Part 2—Developing Your Writing Skills (Chapters 3–5) introduces and illustrates basic writing principles, with one complete chapter devoted to the writing process.
- Part 3—Basic Correspondence (Chapters 6–9) provides instruction and many annotated, fully formatted models of routine, persuasive, bad-news, and special messages. Audience analysis and legal/ethical implications are discussed throughout.
- Part 4—Report Writing (Chapters 10–14) includes separate chapters on data collection and data analysis. The implications of technology are covered at each stage of the reporting process, including computerized data searches and document design (desktop publishing).
- Part 5—Oral Communication (Chapters 15–16) takes students completely through planning a business presentation. Also covered are business

EFFECTIVE ORGANIZATIONAL PLAN

meetings (including parliamentary procedure), listening skills, telephone communications, dictation, and business etiquette.

· Part 6—Employment Communications (Chapters 17–18) covers every part of the job-search process, including the legal and ethical dimensions of the job campaign.

LABs (LANGUAGE-ARTS BASICS)	Five self-instructional LABs in the appendix cover standard English usage in short, easy-to-manage installments. Each LAB presents the most important rules for that topic, plenty of illustrations of each rule, and exercises to test student mastery. It is recommended that instructors assign one LAB at the end of each of the first five chapters so that students will have covered them all before getting to the first correspondence chapter.

STUDENT AIDS

CBC contains the following additional features to help students master the concepts presented:

· Each chapter is packed with practical, easy-to-understand illustrations of each concept introduced.

· A lively and crisp writing style speaks directly to the student.

· *Key Terms* at the end of each chapter define all technical vocabulary introduced in the chapter.

· Eighteen checklists provide brief, step-by-step outlines for completing specific types of communication tasks. Three of the checklists are unique in that they stress the communication *process* for writing, reporting, and making oral presentations.

· The revision stage of the writing process receives full attention, beginning with detailed instruction in Chapter 5 and reinforced in the report chapters and in every microwriting activity.

· Marginal notes summarize the important points in the chapter.

· Four-color format is used to highlight important points, provide realism, and maintain student interest.

COMPLETE PACKAGE OF SUPPORT MATERIALS

Contemporary Business Communication comes with a complete package of support materials that reinforce the teaching and learning of the concepts in the text:

Study Guide, by Frances Harrington, Business Writing Consultant. This guide provides extra practice in the skills developed in the text. Its lively and engaging exercises include pieces for practice revision, readings for analysis, questions for review, fill-in-the-blank and matching exercises, business vocabulary exercises, and grammar review. The guide is also available as a *Computerized Study Guide* for IBM and Macintosh.

Instructor's Resource Manual, by Harriet Augustin, Southwest Texas State University. This manual contains chapter/lecture notes, answers to all the Review and Discussion questions in the text, answers to the end-of-chapter exercises, and additional microwriting exercises.

Test Bank, by Randy L. Joyner, East Carolina University. For every chapter of the text, the Test Bank includes fifteen true/false questions, fifteen multiple-choice questions, and ten short-answer questions. The questions are keyed to the text page number and chapter objective, and all answers are given. A *Computerized Test Bank*, available for IBM and Macintosh, allows instructors to edit existing questions, add their own questions, create multiple versions of the same test, and store tests.

Transparencies. Forty-eight overhead transparencies summarize key points in the text, with emphasis on the practical aspects of creating messages. Additional microwriting exercises are included.

Business Writing Software. This self-instructional software, available for IBM and MacIntosh, provides interactive practice in basic grammar, punctuation, mechanics, and usage. An on-screen help command gives students access to grammar rules.

ACKNOWLEDGMENTS

During the three-year development of this text, it has been my great pleasure to work with a dedicated and skillful team of professionals. Quality is Job One at Houghton Mifflin, and I gratefully salute the editorial, design, production, and marketing staff at HM for the major contributions they have made to this text.

The author wishes to thank the following reviewers for their thoughtful suggestions:

Barbara Alpern, Walsh College, Troy, Michigan

Deborah S. Bosley, University of North Carolina at Charlotte, Charlotte, North Carolina

William J. Buchholz, Bentley College, Waltham, Massachusetts

David P. Dauwalder, California State University, Los Angeles, California

Kevin W. Dean, University of Maryland, College Park, Maryland

Karen Forrest, Baylor University, Waco, Texas

Frances Harrington, Sauderstown, Rhode Island

Maxine B. Hart, Baylor University, Waco, Texas

Penny Hirsch, Northwestern University, Evanston, Illinois

Carolyn S. Hollman, New Hampshire College, Manchester, New Hampshire

Glenda A. Hudson, California State University, Bakersfield, California

Robert G. Insley, University of North Texas, Denton, Texas

Randy L. Joyner, East Carolina University, Greenville, North Carolina

Judith Kalitzki, University of Washington, Seattle, Washington

Melinda Knight, New York University, New York, New York

Marilyn Lammers, California State University, Northridge, California

Robert F. Litro, Mattutuck Community College, Waterbury, Connecticut

Dan Lupo, Purdue University, West Lafayette, Indiana

Carol D. Lutz, The University of Texas at Austin, Austin, Texas

Rita Noel, West Carolina University, Cullowhee, North Carolina

Joan C. Roderick, Southwest Texas State College, San Marcos, Texas

Jone Rymer, Wayne State University, Detroit, Michigan

Marilyn L. Satterwhite, Danville Area Community College, Danville, Illinois

Marilyn Seguin, Kent State University, Kent, Ohio

Larry R. Smeltzer, Arizona State University, Tempe, Arizona

Joyce Smoot, Virginia Tech, Blacksburg, Virginia

Gary R. Stephens, New York Institute of Technology, New York, New York

Jeremiah Sullivan, University of Washington, Seattle, Washington

James Van Oosting, Southern Illinois University, Carbondale, Illinois

Contemporary
Business
Communication

PART

1

Communicating in Business

CHAPTER 1

Understanding Business Communication

After you have finished this chapter, you will be able to

1. Describe the communication process.

2. Explain the major types of verbal and nonverbal communication.

3. Explain the directions that comprise the formal communication network.

4. List the characteristics of the grapevine, and provide guidelines for managing it.

5. Identify the major verbal, nonverbal, and organizational barriers to communication.

6. List five guidelines for managing organizational communications.

To Deedy Rogers, communication means many things. As Employee Services Manager at the Home Depot, Inc., the largest home hardware store chain in the United States, Rogers is responsible for communicating the company's benefit, wellness, and employee assistance programs to more than 25,000 employees in 100 locations. But to Rogers, communication means more than simply sending relevant information from corporate headquarters in Atlanta to retail stores all over the country. To Rogers, communication means motivating people, breaking down boundaries, and directing the flow of information and ideas that encourage people to think in new ways and to act more effectively.

Communication, the way Rogers sees it, is the lifeblood of the modern business. How well a communication system works determines how easily ideas move through a company and how readily ideas are shared. It's especially important, says Rogers, that employees understand that ideas flow every which way, not just from the top down.

"The key to communicating effectively is to not dictate anything. Since we rely on independent outlets, we are not a hierarchy. Our interactions with the operators of the retail outlets are circular—we work with them, they work with us."

Another key to communicating effectively is knowing when to use which medium to get your message across. Rogers uses many media: letters, telephones, face-to-face contact, and video, and she takes great care to choose the medium that is most appropriate to her particular message.

"The way we pass along information is critical to our employee relations," says Rogers. "We use video in conjunction with more informational media to

Deedy Rogers, Employee
Services Manager
The Home Depot, Inc.,
Atlanta, Georgia

set tones, to deliver feel-good messages that letters don't do as well. But video doesn't tell a whole story; it gives highlights of your message and sends broader messages. For instance, Home Depot uses video to provide employee training seminars on product use and presentation."

In other cases, Rogers says, the appropriate medium is more concrete. To build relationships with company managers, for example, Rogers will write letters, which are more personal and more authoritative. "When we are communicating with managers, we have to excite them," says Rogers. "We want them to go and excite others. This means that we have to ignite the managers' interest with our writing, which is sometimes difficult to do. In the first sentence I tell them what's in it for them. I go on from there to tell them just what the program is that we want them to get behind. The third thing I tell them is that they don't have to do very much at all to make the program a success. Then I tell them how to do it, and give them a contact name if they have any problems or would like any help."

Unfortunately, says Rogers, the most effective form of communication—the face-to-face meeting—is seldom used.

"Many business people make the mistake of avoiding human contact," says Rogers. "Too much is done in writing. The telephone is good, but in-person is preferable. Nothing beats face-to-face communication, even today."

Of course, the constraints of time and space prevent most business people from meeting, however briefly, and so Rogers, like most modern communicators, relies on facsimile machines, modems, or videotapes that can be sent through the mail. However you communicate, says Rogers, the most important thing is to do it constantly, to keep the communication channels open. In a company where communication is poor, people stop communicating. On the other hand, if a company recognizes the value of communication and strives to keep channels open, employees will fill those channels with new ideas; new ideas mean new business. Deedy Rogers knows that. She knows that communication starts even before a word is spoken or read and doesn't stop at the end of the sentence or videotape. Communication starts with thought, which starts with a state of mind that encourages thought.

"When you communicate effectively," says Rogers, "it's intoxicating. It's the greatest feeling in the world. When you mess up, it can be disastrous. That's the risk and excitement of communication." ▼

COMMUNICATING IN ORGANIZATIONS

Walk through the halls of a typical modern organization, and what do you see? Managers reading reports, drafting electronic memos on their computers, attending meetings, conducting interviews, talking on the telephone, conferring with subordinates, holding business lunches, reading mail, dictating correspondence, and making presentations. In short, you see people communicating.

An **organization*** is defined as a group of people working together to achieve a common goal, and communication is a vital part of that process. Indeed, communication must have occurred before a common goal could even be established. And a group of people working together must interact; that is, they must communicate their needs, thoughts, plans, expertise, and so on. In the everyday world of business organizations such as The Home Depot, communication is the means by which information is shared, activities are coordinated, and decision making is enhanced.

Understanding how communication works in business and how to communicate competently within an organization will help you participate more effectively in every aspect of business. Recent surveys of several thousand newly promoted executives in the United States indicated that they ranked communication skills number one in importance in preparing them for business leadership. Another multiyear study of executives found a significant correlation between upward job mobility and high-level communication skills. The researchers concluded that competent communicators were more likely to receive promotions than those with less developed communication skills.[1]

In yet another study, 97% of the CEOs of Fortune 500 companies who were surveyed felt that their skill at communicating had a major influence on employee job satisfaction. In the same group, 84% felt it increased employee job performance. And 71% felt that it had a positive impact on their companies' overall profits.[2]

Communication skills are crucial to your success in the organization. Competent writing and speaking skills will help you get the job, be successful on the job, and enhance your chances for promotion. If you decide to go into business for yourself, writing and speaking skills will help you obtain venture capital, promote your product, and manage your employees. These same skills will also help you achieve your personal and social goals.

THE COMPONENTS OF COMMUNICATION

Since communication is such a vital part of the organizational structure, our study of communication begins with an analysis of its components. **Communication** simply means the process of sending and receiving messages—sometimes through spoken or written words and sometimes through such nonverbal means as facial expressions, gestures, and voice qualities. As illustrated in Figure 1.1, the communication model consists of five components—the stimulus, the filter, the message, the medium, and, finally, the destination.

> Communication is necessary if an organization is to achieve its goals.

> In nearly every survey, effective communication skills are ranked first in importance.

> OBJECTIVE 1: Describe the communication process.

> Communication is the sending and receiving of verbal and nonverbal messages.

---

* Terms shown in boldface are defined at the end of the chapter. Chapter 1 introduces many communication terms that will be used throughout the text.

FIGURE 1.1   Components of Communication

To illustrate the model, let us follow the case of Dave Kaplan, who as a chemical engineer at Dow Chemical in 1982 developed Ultra Light, a flat, electroluminescent sheet of material that serves as a light source. Dave could see the enormous business opportunity offered by a paper-thin light fixture that was bendable and that could be produced in a variety of shapes and sizes as Ultra Light could.

The market for lighting is vast; and Dave, even though at the time an engineer and not a businessman, felt the sting of inventing a device that had great potential but that belonged to somebody else (Dow Chemical). He was disappointed in Dow's eventual decision not to manufacture and market this product. As we learn what happened to Dave Kaplan after Dow's decision, we'll examine the five components of communication, one at a time.

The Stimulus

Step 1: A stimulus creates a need to communicate.

There first must be a **stimulus,** an event that creates within the individual a need to communicate. This stimulus can be internal or external. An internal stimulus is simply an idea that forms within your mind. External sources come to you through your sensory organs—your eyes, ears, nose, mouth, and skin. A stimulus for communicating in business might be a memo you just read, a presentation you heard at a staff meeting, a bit of gossip you heard over lunch, your perception that the general manager has been acting preoccupied lately, or even the cold air that is slipping in from an office window that won't close tightly.

If your response to the stimulus is a desire (or need) to communicate, you will **encode** your response by forming a **verbal message** (written or spoken words), a **nonverbal message** (nonwritten and nonspoken message such as a facial expression, gesture, or voice quality), or a combination of the two.

In the case of Dave Kaplan, the stimulus for communication was a memorandum from the head of the research and development department informing him that Dow would not be developing Ultra Light and would instead be offering the product for sale.

The Filter

If everyone had the same perception of events, your job of communicating would be much easier; you could assume that your perception of reality was accurate and that others would understand your motives and intent. Unfortunately, each person has a unique perception of reality, based on his or her experiences, culture, emotions at the moment, personality, knowledge, socioeconomic status, and a host of other variables. These variables act as a **filter** in shaping everyone's unique impression of reality.

Once your brain receives a message, it begins to interpret, or **decode,** the stimulus, to derive meaning from it so that you will know how to respond or whether any response is even necessary. As the message is filtered through your brain, it is affected by such factors as these:

Step 2: Our knowledge, experience, and viewpoints act as a filter to help us interpret (decode) the stimulus.

- Does the stimulus tend to reinforce or contradict your preconceptions? Stimuli that reinforce preexisting beliefs are likely to create a more lasting impression and to generate a stronger response than those that call into question your beliefs.
- What is your cultural viewpoint on this topic? Everyone belongs to many different groups—categorized by religion, economic status, geography, age, education, and sex, to name but a few. The society within which you live, work, and play determines to a large extent how you perceive reality.
- What is your current emotional and physical frame of reference? An event that might normally cause you to react strongly might not even register if you're suffering from a bad cold or from a lack of sleep. Likewise, a remark made innocently might receive a negative reaction if you're angry or upset about some earlier event.

The memo from R & D simply reinforced what Dave had come to expect at his company, which was firmly committed to pursuing its own predetermined long-range objectives, without the flexibility to exploit the unexpected discoveries such as Ultra Light. Dave's long involvement in the research that led to this product caused him to assume a protective, almost paternalistic, interest in its future. Besides, after so many years in the lab, Dave was ready for a new challenge. These factors, then, acted as a filter through which Dave interpreted the R & D memo and formulated his response—a phone call to his brother in Chicago.

At the time of Dave's call, Marc Kaplan was sitting alone in his office at a Chicago advertising agency sampling five different kinds of cheese pizza. As a marketing manager in charge of a new pizza account, he was preoccupied with finding the competitive edge of his client's product, and his perception of Dave's message was filtered by his current situation.

To hear his scientist brother, the MIT graduate who all his life had preferred to pursue solitary scholarly research, suddenly erupting over the phone with the idea of starting a business contradicted Marc's lifelong preconceptions about Dave and acted as a strong filter resisting Dave's urgent message. Furthermore, Marc's emotional and physical frame of reference—hunkered down as he was over several cheese pizzas—did not put him in a receptive mood for seeing a grand scheme that would take tens of thousands of dollars and many years of hard work. But Marc's cultural background—his economic status, his education, and his current job—added another point of view, a highly favorable filter for taking in Dave's message.

If Dave were good enough at communicating his message, he might be able to persuade Marc to join him in buying the product from Dow and starting a business of their own.

The Message

Step 3: We formulate (encode) a verbal or nonverbal response to the stimulus.

The extent to which your communication effort achieves its desired goal depends very directly on how you construct your message. Success at communicating depends not only on the purpose and content of the message but just as importantly on how skillful you are at communicating, how well you know your audience (the person with whom you're communicating), and how much you share in common with your audience.

As a scientist, Dave Kaplan did not have a good business vocabulary. Nor did he have much practice at oral business presentations and the careful pacing and selective reinforcement required in such circumstances. In effect, Dave was attempting to make an oral business proposal, unfortunately, without much technique or skill.

"You're crazy, Dave. You don't know what you're talking about." This remark from Marc made it clear to Dave his message wasn't getting through. But what Dave lacked in skill, he made up for in knowing his kid brother (his audience) backward and forward.

"You're chicken, Marc," had always gotten Marc's attention and interest in the past, and it worked again. Dave kept challenging Marc, something he knew Marc couldn't resist, and kept recalling out loud what they had in common, all the happy adventures they'd had together as kids and adults.

The Medium

Step 4: We select the form of the message (medium).

Once the sender has encoded a message, the next step in the process is to transmit that message to the receiver. At this point, the sender must choose the form of message to send, or **medium**. Oral messages might be transmitted through a staff meeting, personal conference, telephone conversation, press conference, teleconference, or even through such informal means as the company grapevine. Written messages might be transmitted through a memorandum, report, letter, contract, brochure, bulletin-board notice, electronic mail, company newsletter, press release, or an addition to the

Coca-Cola Foods has approximately 1,000 personal
computers on networks with a groupware program that has
improved communications among workers. Utilizing
electronic mail, employees have virtually eliminated "those
little pink slips" that are used for phone messages.
Source: © Steven Pumphrey

policies and procedures manual. And nonverbal messages might be transmitted through facial expressions, gestures, or body movement.

Since Dave is in the process of talking with Marc over the phone, his medium is a telephone conversation.

The Destination

The message is transmitted and then enters the sensory environment of the receiver, at which point control passes from the sender to the receiver. Once the message reaches its destination, there is no guarantee that communication will actually occur. You are constantly bombarded with stimuli and your sensory organs pick up only part of them. Even assuming your receiver does admit the message, you have no assurance that it will be interpreted (filtered) as you intended. As we shall see, there are numerous barriers to effective communication. The remaining chapters in this text are designed to help you overcome these barriers and to formulate messages that will achieve their goals.

At this point in the communication process, your transmitted message becomes the source, or stimulus, for the next communication episode, and the process begins anew.

After listening to Dave's enthusiastic, one-hour phone call, Marc promised to consider the venture seriously. Marc's message to Dave provided **feedback** to Dave on how accurately his own message had been received; and it led

Step 5: The message reaches its destination and, if successful, is perceived accurately by the receiver.

to many more versions of the communication process, both written and oral, before the two brothers founded Urban Systems, a small, "start-up" company whose primary product is Ultra Light and which employs 178 people at its corporate headquarters in Ann Arbor, Michigan, and in a completely automated manufacturing plant in Charlotte, North Carolina.

The Dynamic Nature of Communication

Our look at the components of communication and the model presented in Figure 1.1 might erroneously imply that communication is a linear, static process—which proceeds orderly from one stage to the next—and that you can easily separate the communicators into senders and receivers. That is not the case.

Two or more people often send and receive messages simultaneously. While you are receiving one message, you may at the same time be sending another message. For example, the look on your face as you are receiving a message may be sending a new message to the sender that you either understand, agree with, or do not understand the message being sent. And the feedback thus given may prompt the sender to modify his or her intended message.

Thus, artificially "freezing" the action by examining each component of the communication process in some ways causes us to lose some of the dynamic richness of that process in terms of both the verbal and nonverbal components.

Urban Systems: A Dynamic Case Study

As we join Urban Systems (US) in its second decade, the 1990s, Dave and Marc's company now has annual sales in the $30 million range, with a net profit last year of $1.4 million. It is considered a progressive company by the investment community, with good management and good earnings potential. The local community considers US to be a good corporate citizen; it is nonpolluting, and its officers are active in community affairs.

You will be seeing more of the Kaplan brothers and Urban Systems in the chapters ahead as communication within the organization serves as an ongoing case study for each of the major areas of business communication— from this model of communication all the way through to the final chapter. You'll have the opportunity to get to know the people in the company and watch from the inside as they handle every type of business communication in concrete terms. Right now you can learn more of the background of Urban Systems by reading in Appendix D about the company's history, its product, its financial data, and its all-too-human personnel.

Verbal communications

OBJECTIVE 2: Explain the major types of verbal and nonverbal communication.

We have defined communication as the process of sending and receiving messages. Verbal messages are made up of words and include oral and written communications. It is the ability to communicate by using words that separates human beings from most of the animal kingdom. Your verbal ability also enables you to learn from the past—to benefit from the experience of others.

Oral Communication

Oral communication is one of the most common functions in business. Consider, for example, how limiting it would be if a manager could not do the following:

- Attend meetings
- Ask questions of colleagues
- Make presentations
- Sell products or services
- Counsel employees
- Give performance appraisals
- Handle customer complaints
- Give instructions

Oral communication is different from written communication in that you have more ways to get your message across to others. You can clear up any questions immediately; use nonverbal clues; provide additional information; and use pauses, accents, and voice tone to stress certain points.

For oral communication to be effective, a second communication skill— listening—must also be present. No matter how well-crafted the content and delivery of an oral presentation, it cannot achieve its goal if the intended audience does not have effective listening skills. It has been found that nearly 60% of all communication problems in business are caused by poor listening.[3]

Written Communication

Writing is often more difficult than speaking because you have to get your message correct the first time; you do not have the advantage of immediate feedback and nonverbal clues such as facial expressions to help you achieve your objective. Examples of typical written communications in industry include the following:

- *Memorandums:* written messages sent to someone working in the same organization; often sent via computer in automated offices
- *Letters:* written messages sent to someone outside the organization; can also be sent by computer via commercial electronic mail networks
- *Reports:* orderly and objective presentations of information that assist in decision making and problem solving, including policies and procedures, status reports, minutes of meetings, financial reports, personnel evaluations, press releases, and computer printouts
- *Contracts:* employee contracts, sales agreements, leases, maintenance agreements, and the like
- *House organs:* brochures, newsletters, bulletin-board notices, and pay-envelope inserts that inform employees of organizational events and news

Writing is of crucial importance to the modern organization because it serves as the major source of documentation; a speech leaves an impression, whereas a memorandum leaves a permanent record for others to refer to in the future in case memory fails or a dispute arises.

For written messages to achieve their goals, they must be read. The skill of efficient reading is becoming more important in today's technological society. The abundance of widespread computing and word processing

BUSINESS READING: *NOT* A SPECTATOR SPORT!

To learn what they need to know to *do* their jobs and to advance their careers, business managers spend 30% of their time reading. That makes reading an important business communication skill, yet reading is not a skill that develops automatically. It requires some attention.

Active or Passive Attitude?

The first thing to do if you want to improve your reading is to examine your attitude toward reading. Do you think of reading as a passive activity, as taking in someone else's ideas the way a cup takes in coffee, say, without noticing or caring whether the coffee's hot or cold, weak or strong, with cream or with sugar? Your reading skills will improve dramatically if your reading is active, if you put your own thinking and ideas, not the writer's, in charge of what you read.

Start with Your Own View—and Keep It

First of all, take a minute to look through the article or report just to get the idea or scope of the topic, no more. Page through the whole thing checking out headings, illustrations, boldface print, and any summary. Then put the reading aside and take up a pen: jot down your own first thoughts about the topic, what you think is important, what other topics it relates to, any questions, big or small, that come to mind. Don't spend a lot of time writing—it's not necessary to think of everything you know or want to know; it's more a matter of getting yourself into position for the next step.

Going through the material a second time, you can read in detail. As you do, keep a sense of independence. Ask yourself questions to help you evaluate, structure, and personalize the writer's ideas. Reading is communication, and that always involves some form of two-way interaction.

Read Faster—It Helps

Unfortunately, most people read no faster than their ancestors did a century ago. Reading experts say that most adults read at 25% of their ability. Reading faster helps you keep an active frame of mind and helps you retain information.

Sources: Business Week, May 14, 1990, pg. 162. *Computer World*, June 1, 1988, pg. C19. *Inc.*, May 1990, pg. 101.

capabilities, along with convenient and economical photocopying, has created more paperwork rather than less. Thus, information overload is one of the unfortunate by-products of our times. These and other implications of technology on business communications are discussed in the next chapter.

NONVERBAL COMMUNICATIONS

A nonverbal message is any message that is not written or spoken. The nonverbal message may accompany a verbal message (smiling as you greet a colleague), or it may occur alone (selecting the back seat when entering the conference room for a staff meeting). Nonverbal messages are typically more spontaneous than verbal messages, but that does not mean that they are any less important. One study has shown that only 7% of the meaning communicated by most messages comes from the verbal portion, with the remaining 93% being conveyed nonverbally.[4]

The most common types of nonverbal communications are discussed in the following sections.

Body Movement

Because so much of your communication is accomplished face-to-face, you must understand the role of facial expressions, gestures, and body stance—both in terms of messages you send and in terms of those you receive. This is as true for business communication as it is for social communication.

By far, the most expressive part of your body is your face—especially your eyes. Research shows that receivers tend to be quite consistent in their reading of facial expressions; and many of these expressions, such as smiling, have the same meaning across different cultures.[5] Eye contact and

Cultures differ in the importance they attach to eye contact.

eye movements tell you a lot about a person, although—as we shall see in Chapter 2—maintaining eye contact with the person with whom you're communicating is not perceived as important (or even polite) in some cultures.

Gestures are hand and upper-body movements that add important information to face-to-face interactions. As the game of charades proves, you can communicate quite a bit without using oral or written signals. You've probably known people who "talk with their hands." Pointing, waving, clapping hands, placing your hands on your hips, and indicating how large something is are all gestures that help to illustrate and reinforce your verbal message.

Body stance (posture, placement of arms and legs, distribution of weight, and the like) is another form of nonverbal communication. For example, leaning slightly toward the person you're communicating with would probably be taken as a sign of interest and involvement in the interaction. Leaning back, arms folded across the chest, on the other hand, might be taken as a sign of disinterest or defiance.

Physical Appearance

Our culture places great value on physical appearance. Television, newspapers, and magazines are filled with advertisements for personal-care products; and the ads typically feature attractive users of these products. Attractive people tend to be seen as more intelligent, more likable, and more persuasive than unattractive people.[6] Your appearance is particularly important for making a good first impression; and although you may not be able to change some of your physical features, understanding the importance of physical appearance can help you to emphasize your strong points.

The articles that you wear or use also provide communication clues. Your clothing, jewelry, and cosmetics, as well as possessions such as automobiles or office furnishings, provide information about your values, taste, heritage, conformity, status, age, sexuality, and group identification.

Voice Qualities

Voice qualities such as volume, speed, pitch, tone, accent, variety, and rhythm supplement the verbal message. No one speaks in a monotone. To illustrate, read the following sentence aloud, each time emphasizing the italicized word. Note how the meaning changes with the word emphasized.

- *You* were late. (*Answers the question, "Who was late?"*)
- You *were* late. (*Responds to the other person's denial of being late.*)
- You were *late*. (*Emphasizes how late the person was.*)

Voice qualities carry both intentional and unintentional messages. When you're nervous, you tend to speak faster and in a higher pitch than normal; when you're angry, you tend to speak louder; and when you're tired, you tend to speak slower and with less enthusiasm. People who constantly speak too softly risk being interrupted or ignored, whereas people who constantly speak too loudly are often seen as being pushy or insecure.

Time

How do you feel when you are late for an appointment? When others are late? The meaning given to time varies drastically by culture, with the North American culture being much more time conscious than South American or Near Eastern cultures.

The concept of time is both culture specific and situation specific.

Time is also related to one's status within the organization. You would be much less likely to keep a superior waiting for an appointment than a subordinate. Time is also very situation specific. Although you normally might not worry about being five minutes late at a staff meeting, you would probably arrive early if you were the first presenter.

Touch

Although touching is a very important form of communication, it is one that most people are unsure how to use appropriately and effectively. The person who never touches anyone in a business setting may be seen as cold and stand-offish, whereas the person who touches too frequently may cause the receiver to feel apprehensive and uncomfortable. Some touches, such as those made by a physician during an examination, are purely physical; others, such as a handshake, are friendly and indicate a willingness to communicate; and still others indicate intimacy.

Space and Territory

Different types of communication occur at different distances.

How do you feel when you're on a crowded elevator? You probably look at the floor indicator, at advertisements, at your feet, or just straight ahead. Most people in our culture are uncomfortable at such close distance with strangers. Psychologists have identified four zones within which people in our culture interact:[7]

1. *Intimate zone.* From physical contact to about 18 inches is where all your body movements occur; this is the area in which you move throughout the day. It is an area normally reserved for close, intimate, protective interactions. Business associates typically enter this space infrequently and only briefly—to shake hands, pat someone on the back, point out something on a computer screen or a sheet of paper, and the like.
2. *Personal zone.* This zone, extending from 18 inches to about 4 feet, is where conversation with close friends and colleagues takes place. Unlike in the intimate zone, normal talking is frequent in the personal zone. Some, but not a great deal of, business interaction occurs here; for example, business lunches typically occur in this zone.
3. *Social zone.* From 4 feet to 12 feet, the social zone is where most business exchanges occur. Informal business conferences and staff meetings occur within this space.
4. *Public zone.* The public zone extends from 12 feet to as far as the eye can see and the ear can hear. This is the most formal zone, and the less significant interactions occur here. Because of the great distance, communication in the public zone is often one way, as from a speaker to a large audience.

These specific zones apply only to the American culture. As Chapter 2 makes clear, the concept of space and territory differs widely among different cultures. Competent communicators recognize their own need for personal space and the needs of others. When communicating with people, perhaps from other cultures, who prefer more or less space, the competent communicator will make the adjustments necessary to facilitate reaching his or her objective.

THE DIRECTIONS OF COMMUNICATION

More than fifty years ago, former AT&T executive Chester Barnard, in his classic *The Functions of the Executive* gave the now familiar advice that "in any exhaustive theory of organization, communication would occupy a central place."[8]

For an organization to be successful, communications must flow freely from superiors to subordinates (downward communication); from subordinates to superiors (upward communication); among people at the same level on the organizational chart (horizontal communication); and among people in different departments within the organization (cross-channel communication.) These four types of communication are illustrated in Figure 1.2. Together, they make up the organization's **formal communication network.**

OBJECTIVE 3: Explain the directions that comprise the formal communication network.

The formal communication network consists of the routes used to transmit prescribed information throughout the organization.

Directions of Communication

FIGURE 1.2

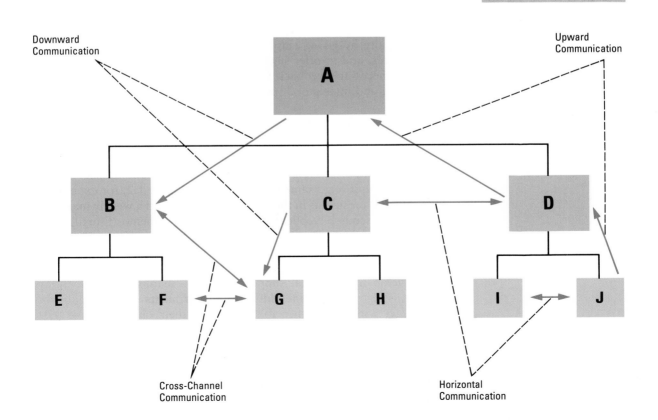

Downward Communication

In most organizations the largest number of vertical communications move downward—from someone of higher authority to someone of lower authority. For example, in Figure 1.2, A sends a memo to B, or C has a conference with G, a subordinate. Through written and oral channels, information regarding job performance, policies and procedures, day-to-day operations, and other organizational information is communicated.

Higher-level management communicates with lower-level employees through such means as memorandums, conferences, telephone conversations, company newsletters, policy manuals, bulletin-board announcements, and videotapes. One of the problems with written downward communication is that management often assumes that what is sent downward is always received and understood. Unfortunately, that is not always the case.

Upward Communication

Upward communication is the flow of information from lower-level employees to upper-level employees. In Figure 1.2, for example, J may complain to D, his superior, about his work schedule; or D may respond to a memo that A, her superior, wrote. Upward communications can take the form of memorandums, reports, suggestion systems, grievance procedures, employee surveys, question boxes, employee round tables, or union publications, among others.

The free flow of communication upward prevents management isolation.

Upward communication is important because it provides higher management with the information needed for decision making. It also cultivates employee loyalty by giving employees an opportunity to be heard, to air their grievances, and to offer suggestions. Finally, upward communication provides the necessary feedback to let supervisors know whether subordinates received and understood messages that were sent downward.

Horizontal Communication

Horizontal communication is the flow of information among peers within the same work unit (e.g., same department). In Figure 1.2, for example, C and D, both vice presidents in the executive suite, attend a weekly manager's meeting; and J sends his colleague, I, an electronic memo (E-mail) about some project on which they are collaborating.

Horizontal communication is important to help coordinate work assignments, to share information on plans and activities, to negotiate differences, and to develop interpersonal support, thereby creating a more cohesive work unit. The more that individuals or departments within a company must interact with each other to accomplish their objectives, the more frequent and intense will be the horizontal communication.

The most common form of horizontal communication is the committee meeting, where most coordination, sharing of information, and problem solving takes place. Other methods include informal interactions during work breaks, lunch, or social functions; phone conversations; and memos.

Intense competition for scarce resources, lack of trust among coworkers, or concerns about job security or promotions can sometimes create barriers to the free flow of horizontal information.

Cross-Channel Communication

Cross-channel communication involves the exchange of information among employees in different work units who are neither subordinate nor superior to each other. In Figure 1.2, for example, G, a payroll clerk, telephones B to inquire about the number of dependents B is claiming on her tax forms; and F, who works in the facility-management department, sends a memo to G, telling him that his new office furniture will arrive shortly.

Staff specialists use cross-channel communications frequently because their responsibilities involve many departments within the organization. Because they lack line authority to direct those with whom they communicate, they must often rely on their persuasive skills, as for instance, when the research department encourages employees to complete a job-satisfaction questionnaire.

The Grapevine

The **informal communication network** (or the *grapevine*, as it is called) is the transmission of information through nonofficial channels within the organization. In the carpool on the way to work, waiting to use the photocopier, jogging at noon, or at a PTA meeting at night—whenever workers come together, they are likely to hear and pass on information they've hear about possible happenings in the organization. One survey found that 50% of the workers said the grapevine was their most frequent source of information on company plans and performance.[9]

These are the common characteristics of the grapevine:[10]

1. Most of the information passed along the grapevine (about 80%) is business related, and most of it (75 to 95%) is accurate.
2. The grapevine is pervasive. It exists at all levels in the organization—from corporate boardroom to the assembly line.
3. Information moves rapidly along the grapevine.
4. The grapevine is most active when change is taking place and when one's need to know or level of fear is highest—during layoffs, plant closings, acquisitions and mergers, legal battles, falling profits, and the like.
5. The grapevine is a normal, often vital, part of every organization.

Rather than trying to eliminate the grapevine (a futile effort), wise managers accept its existence and pay attention to it. They act promptly to counteract false rumors. Most of all, they use the formal communication network (including meetings, memos, newsletters, and bulletin boards) to ensure that all news—positive and negative—gets out to employees as quickly and as completely as possible. The free flow of information within the organization not only stops rumors; it's simply good business.

OBJECTIVE 4: List the characteristics of the grapevine, and provide guidelines for managing it.

▼
OBJECTIVE 5: Identify the major verbal, nonverbal, and organizational barriers to communication.

BARRIERS TO COMMUNICATION

Considering the complex nature of the communication process, you should not be surprised that your messages are not always received exactly as you intended. As a matter of fact, sometimes your messages are not received at all. Other times, they are received incompletely or inaccurately. Some of the obstacles to effective and efficient communication are verbal, some are nonverbal, and some are related to the organizational structure.

Verbal Barriers

Verbal barriers are related to what you write or say. They include inadequate knowledge or vocabulary, differences in interpretation, inappropriate use of expressions, overabstraction and ambiguity, and polarization.

Inadequate Knowledge or Vocabulary   Before you can even begin to think about how you will communicate an idea, you must, first of all, *have* the idea; that is, you must have sufficient knowledge about the topic to know what you want to say. Regardless of your level of expertise, this may not be as simple as it sounds. Assume, for example, that you are a financial consultant who has been asked by the president of a firm to evaluate an investment opportunity. You've completed all the necessary research and are now ready to write your report. Or are you?

You must know enough about both your topic and your audience to express yourself precisely and appropriately.

You must also have adequate knowledge of your audience. Do you know how much the president knows about the investment so that you'll know how much background information to include? Do you know how familiar the president is with investment terminology? Can you safely use the abbreviations "NPV" and "RRR," or will you have to spell out and perhaps define "net present value" and "required rate of return"? Do you know whether the president would prefer to have your conclusions at the beginning of the report, followed by your analysis, or at the end? What tone should the report take? The answer to such questions will be important if you are to achieve your objective in writing your report.

Differences in Interpretation   Sometimes senders and receivers attribute different meanings to the same word or attribute the same meaning to different words. When this happens, miscommunication can occur.

The denotation indicates what a word means; the connotation indicates our associations with that word.

Every word has both a denotative and a connotative meaning. **Denotation** refers to the literal, dictionary meaning of a word. **Connotation** refers to the subjective, emotional meaning that you attach to a word. For example, the denotative meaning of the word *plastic* is a synthetic material that can be easily molded into different forms. For some people, the word has a negative connotative meaning—"cheap or artificial substitute."

Most of the interpretation problems occur because of the personal reactions engendered by the connotative meaning of a word. Do you have a positive, neutral, or negative reaction to the terms *broad, bad, aggressive, hard-hitting, workaholic, corporate raider, head-hunter, gay, golden parachute,* or *wasted*? Would your reactions likely be the same as everyone else's?

The problem with some terms is not only that people assign different meanings to the terms but that the term might engender such an emotional reaction that the receiver is "turned off" to any further communication with the sender.

> Our interpretations of events differ because each of us has a unique mental filter.

Inappropriate Use of Expressions   Expressions are groups of words that have intended meanings that are different from their literal interpretations. Examples include slang, jargon, and euphemisms.

Slang is an expression, often short-lived, that is identified with a specific group of people. Teenagers, construction workers, Vietnamese immigrants, and many other subgroups all have their own sets of slang. Using appropriate slang in everyday speech presents no problem; it conveys precise information and may indicate group membership. Problems arise, however, when the sender uses slang that the receiver doesn't understand or that sends a negative nonverbal message about the sender.

Jargon is the technical terminology used within specialized groups. As with slang, the problem is not in using jargon—it provides a very precise and efficient way of communicating with those familiar with it. The problem comes in using jargon either with someone who doesn't understand it or in using jargon in an effort to impress others.

Euphemisms are inoffensive expressions used in place of words that may offend or suggest something unpleasant. Sensitive writers and speakers use euphemisms occasionally, especially to describe bodily functions. How many ways, for example, can you think of to say that someone has died?

Slang, jargon, and euphemisms all have important roles to play in business communication—so long as they're used with appropriate people, in appropriate contexts. They can, however, prove to be barriers to effective communication when used to impress, when overused, or when used in inappropriate settings. Communicators from different cultures have a special problem in understanding these expressions. How do you think a nonnative speaker might interpret the sentence, "He really blew my mind yesterday"?

Overabstraction and Ambiguity   An **abstract word** identifies an idea or feeling instead of a concrete object. For example *communication* is an abstract word, whereas *memorandum* is a **concrete word**, a word that identifies something that can be perceived by the senses. Abstract words are necessary in order for you to communicate about things you cannot see or touch. However, communication problems result when you use too many abstract words or when you use too high a level of abstraction.

> The word *transportation* is abstract; *automobile* is concrete.

The higher the level of abstraction, the more difficult it is to visualize exactly what the sender has in mind. For example, which sentence communicates more information, "I acquired an asset at a store" or "I purchased a Toshiba 650 at ComputerWorld"?

A similar communication problem results from the use of ambiguous terms, such as *a few, some, several,* and *far away,* which have too broad a meaning for use in much business communication. For example, compare your and your colleagues' answers to the following questions:

> Inappropriate use of pronouns also causes ambiguity, as in "Jan gave Sue her report." (Whose report?)

1. We hold staff meetings regularly. *(How many times are staff meetings held each year?)*

2. The shipping department received a lot of complaints last month? *(How many complaints did the shipping department receive?)*
3. Sheaffer's will close early on Christmas Eve. *(What time will Sheaffer's close?)*
4. Hans took some copies of the long-range plan to the meeting. *(How many copies did he take?)*

Polarization At times, some people act as though every situation is divided into two opposite and distinct poles, with no allowance for a middle ground. Of course, there are some true dichotomies. You are either male or female, and your company either will or will not make a profit this year. But most aspects of life involve more than two alternatives.

For example, you might assume that a speaker is either telling the truth or is lying. In fact, what the speaker actually says may be true, but by selectively omitting some important information, he or she may be giving an inaccurate impression. Is the speaker telling the truth or not? Most likely, the answer lies somewhere in between. Likewise, you are not necessarily either tall or short, rich or poor, smart or dumb. Competent communicators avoid "either/or" logic and make the effort to search for middle-ground words when such words best describe a situation.

Nonverbal Barriers

Not all your communication problems are related to what you write or say. Some are related to how you act. Nonverbal barriers to communication include inappropriate or conflicting signals, differences in perception, inappropriate emotions, and distractions.

Inappropriate or Conflicting Signals As has been made clear, many nonverbal signals vary from culture to culture. Remember also that the United States itself is a multicultural country: a banker from Boston, an art-shop owner from San Francisco, and a farmer from North Dakota might find that they both use and interpret nonverbal signals in quite different ways. What is appropriate in one context might not be appropriate in another.

As has also been made clear, when verbal and nonverbal signals conflict, the receiver tends to put more faith in the nonverbal signals, because nonverbal messages are more difficult to manipulate than verbal messages. Conflicting signals create communication barriers, many of which are related to appearance. For example, note the conflicting signals being transmitted in each of the following situations. Which do you think is the stronger signal?

1. A well-qualified applicant for a secretarial position submits a résumé with a typographical error.
2. A management consultant, who came highly recommended to the bank, shows up for his first client meeting in a leisure suit.
3. The accountant's personal office was in such a state of disorder that she could not find the papers she needed for a meeting with the president.

Communication competence requires that you communicate nonverbal messages that are consistent with your verbal messages and that are appropriate for the context.

Some may feel that having a female boss may lead to a
communication barrier between the boss and male
subordinates. Theo Schwartzkopf, Tulsa, Oklahoma truck
dealer and President of Mid-America Ford Truck Sales,
disagrees. Schwartzkopf believes that barriers develop when
language is not clear, when employees feel no one is willing
to listen, and when you issue orders rather than involve and
motivate.
Source: © Steve Jennings / Picture Group

Differences in Perception   Even when hearing the same speech or when
reading the same document, people of different ages, socioeconomic
backgrounds, cultures, and so forth often form very different perceptions.
We discussed earlier the mental filter by which each communication source
is interpreted. Because each person is unique, with unique experiences,
knowledge, and viewpoints, each person forms different opinions about
what he or she reads and hears.

Some people tend to automatically believe certain people and to automatically distrust other people. For example, when reading a memo from
the company president, one employee may be so intimidated by the president
that he or she tends to believe everything the president says, whereas
another employee may have such negative feelings about the president that
he or she believes nothing the president says.

Inappropriate Emotions   In most cases, a moderate level of emotional
involvement intensifies the communication and makes it more personal.
However, too much emotional involvement can be an obstacle to communication. For example, excessive anger can create such an emotionally
charged environment that reasonable discussion is not possible. Likewise,
prejudice (automatically rejecting certain people or ideas), stereotyping
(placing individuals into categories), and boredom (lack of interest) all
hinder effective communication. Such emotions tend to create a blocked
mind that is closed to reality, rejecting or ignoring information that is
contrary to one's prevailing belief.

Depend on logic—not
emotions—when commu-
nicating orally and in
writing.

Distractions   Any environmental or competing element that restricts one's ability to concentrate on the communication task hinders effective communication. Such distractions are called **noise**. Examples of environmental elements are poor acoustics, extreme temperature, uncomfortable seating, body odor, poor telephone connections, and illegible copy. Examples of competing elements are other important business to attend to, too many meetings, and too many reports to read.

Organizational Barriers

By nature, every organization eventually assumes a culture of its own—with predictable ways of behaving on the job and predictable employee attitudes. In addition, of course, official policies define what should and should not be done, how it should be done, and by whom. It is easy to see, then, how the entire organizational environment can affect communication within that organization. Unfortunately, many of the factors that serve to make the organization more efficient also increase the chance that communications will be distorted.

> Serial messages are more likely to get distorted than are simultaneous messages.

Serial Communications   Messages that are transmitted through channels, one level at a time, are called **serial communications**. For example, the president may ask all vice presidents to relay the message down the line that there is no truth to the rumor of an impending major layoff of personnel. Each vice president, in turn, transmits the president's message to his or her managers who then transmit it to their subordinates, and so on, until, in an ideal environment, the lowest level of worker gets the president's message. (**Simultaneous communications**, on the other hand, are transmitted to all receivers at the same time, thereby minimizing the opportunity for distortion.)

Serial messages are received at each level, interpreted (filtered), and then passed on. Although serial communications enable the sender at each level to personalize the message for his or her own specific work group, **distortion** can occur in such circumstances—distortions involving omissions, additions, and changes to the message during transmission.

> We are more reluctant to convey negative information to our superiors than to our subordinates.

Hierarchical Relationships   Hierarchical, or superior/subordinate, relationships influence the way a person communicates by creating status within the organization. A worker at one level acquires a point of view, value system, and expectations different from a worker at a higher or lower level. Workers at higher levels have greater control over those at lower levels, sometimes making the lower-level workers overly cautious in their communications.

Impersonalization   The formal nature of the organization, with its system of rules and policies, may encourage rigid patterns of communicating. The value of face-to-face interpersonal communication can be neglected, resulting in a lessened awareness of employees' emotions. At the extreme, the organization becomes comprised of individuals who cannot communicate their feelings and who substitute a system of rules for problem-solving and dialogue.

Job Specialization   Although job specialization contributes to increased productivity, it can also be the source of numerous communication problems. Individuals such as systems analysts, accountants, engineers, or researchers often identify with their own areas of expertise, use language unknown to other employees, and may not be able to perceive the total picture and act for the good of either their colleagues or the organization. Their narrow perspective sometimes hinders their ability to understand the problems of others. Lacking a feeling of empathy, they may have difficulty communicating with people outside their specialty.

We have seen that serial communication, hierarchical relationships, impersonalization, and job specialization can sometimes have negative consequences on communication. The solution, however, is not to eliminate these distinctive characteristics of organizations; indeed, these are the characteristics that allow the organization to function productively. Instead, the solution is to ensure that managers are trained in, and sensitive to, the informational and personal needs of their employees.

MANAGING ORGANIZATIONAL COMMUNICATION

Although time and physical resources are costs of communicating even in an ideal environment, an additional cost of poor communication is in the loss of interest and motivation among employees. Where communication has broken down in an organization, employees experience a loss of trust and support, interpersonal conflict increases, and emotional stress becomes common.

OBJECTIVE 6: List five guidelines for managing organizational communications.

Likewise, when accurate and timely information does not flow freely throughout the organization, profitability is adversely affected as deadlines are missed, needed information is unavailable for decision making, and messages are not delivered or interpreted accurately when received. Clearly, communication must be *managed* if the organization is to achieve its goals.

Effective management of organizational communication cannot be reduced to a few principles. Just as in human resources management, production management, or marketing management, a combination of technical skills, human relations skills, and common sense must be applied both to maintain open channels of communication and to deal with those communication problems that do arise. In addition to the necessary general management skills, the following five guidelines apply specifically to managing the communication function effectively.

Develop Written and Oral Communications Carefully

The most important guideline begins with the message origination. You should carefully determine the purpose of your message; analyze the audience for your message to determine their needs, knowledge, and personality; determine the content; and organize these points logically. Beginning with Chapter 3, the remainder of this text is devoted to helping you write and speak effectively in business.

Minimize Distortion

Distortion-free communications are said to have "fidelity."

To the extent possible, you should ensure that complete and objective information travels upward. Sometimes, this will mean establishing more than one source of information as a "check" on the objectivity of the information being received. You can do this by using sources of information outside the organization, including professional publications, colleagues in other organizations, suppliers, and the like. Sometimes you might need to create overlapping areas of responsibility. Then any distortions in one person's reports or memos would be revealed in the reports and memos of others.

Provide for Feedback

Competent managers give and receive feedback.

The major problem with downward communication is that managers often assume that their messages are both received and understood by the receiver. To ensure that this is so, you need to build in some type of formal feedback mechanism. Suggestion systems, employee round tables, breakfast with the manager, a company ombud, and the like have been tried with success in some organizations. Sometimes anonymous feedback is helpful, for example, confidential employee surveys.

Avoid Information Overload

Information overload occurs when a person receives more information than can be processed effectively.

Just as receiving too little information is detrimental, so also is receiving too much. If managers have to spend too much of their time reading information, they won't have enough time to make use of it. Reducing the number of messages sent, reducing the number of people receiving each message, and reducing the number of meetings can send the nonverbal signal that those messages that are received and those meetings that are scheduled are indeed important and therefore deserve close attention.

Train Writers and Speakers

The forward-looking organization values its personnel as its most important resource and constantly looks for ways to enhance the value of that resource. Continuing education in the form of in-house training seminars, attendance at workshops, tuition assistance, and the like are cost-efficient avenues for increasing the communication skills of employees. Communication consultants often conduct a communication audit of the organization to determine the types of communication carried out and the degree of competence with which each communication task is completed. The consultant can then design a training seminar especially tailored to the needs of the organization.

SUMMARY

The study of communication is important because communication is such a pervasive part of the organization. Because it is so critical for achieving organizational goals, most managers spend the vast majority of their workday in some form of verbal communication.

The communication process begins with a stimulus that enters your brain via one of the five senses. Based on your unique knowledge, experience, and viewpoints, you then filter, or interpret, the stimulus and then formulate, or encode, the message you wish to communicate. The next step is to select a medium of transmission for the message. Finally, the message reaches its destination; if it is successful, the receiver picks it up as a source for communication and provides appropriate feedback to the sender.

Verbal communication includes oral (speaking and listening) and written (writing and reading) communication. Nonverbal communication includes body movement, physical appearance, voice qualities, time, touch, and space and territory.

The organization's formal communication network consists of downward communication from superiors to subordinates, upward communication from subordinates to superiors, horizontal communication among people at the same level, and cross-channel communication among people in different departments within the organization. The informal communication network (also called the grapevine) consists of information transmitted through nonofficial channels. Rather than try to eliminate it, managers should accept its existence and pay attention to it.

Sometimes barriers are present that interfere with your ability to communicate effectively. Examples of verbal barriers are inadequate knowledge or vocabulary, differences in interpretation, inappropriate use of expressions, overabstraction and ambiguity, and polarization. Examples of nonverbal barriers are inappropriate or conflicting signals, differences in perception, inappropriate emotions, and distractions. Examples of organizational barriers are serial communications, hierarchical relationships, impersonalization, and job specialization.

The communication function can be managed effectively by developing written and oral communications carefully, providing for feedback, minimizing distortion, avoiding information overload, and training writers and speakers.

KEY TERMS

Abstract word— A word that identifies an idea or feeling as opposed to a concrete object.

Communication— The process of sending and receiving messages.

Concrete word— A word that identifies what the senses can perceive.

Connotation— The subjective or emotional feeling associated with a word.

Decoding— The process of interpreting a message.

Denotation— The literal, dictionary meaning of a word.

Distortion— Omissions, additions, or changes in a message that occur during transmission.

Encoding— The process of formulating a message.

Euphemism— An inoffensive expression used in place of an expression that may offend or suggest something unpleasant.

Feedback— The receiver's reaction or response to a message.

Filter— The mental process of perceiving stimuli based on your knowledge, experience, and viewpoints.

Formal communication network— The transmission of prescribed information through downward, upward, horizontal, and cross-channel routes.

Informal communication network— The transmission of information through nonofficial channels within the organization; also called the grapevine.

Jargon— The technical terminology used within specialized groups.

Letter— A written message sent to someone outside the organization.

Medium— The form of the message; for example, memo or conference.

Memorandum— A written message sent to someone within the organization.

Noise— Environmental or competing elements that distract one's attention when communicating.

Nonverbal message— A nonwritten and nonspoken message comprised of facial expressions, gestures, voice qualities, and the like.

Organization— A group of people working together to achieve a common goal.

Report— An orderly and objective presentation of information that assists in decision making and problem solving.

Serial communication— A message transmitted through channels, one level at a time.

Simultaneous communication— A message transmitted to all receivers at the same time.

Slang— An expression, often short-lived, that is identified with a specific group of people.

Stimulus— An event that creates within the individual a need to communicate.

Verbal message— A message comprised of spoken or written words.

REVIEW AND DISCUSSION

▶ OBJECTIVE 1   1. What are the five components of the communication process?

▶ OBJECTIVE 1   2. What is meant by the statement, "The stimulus is filtered through your brain?"

▶ OBJECTIVE 1   3. Give an example of a medium.

▶ OBJECTIVE 2   4. What are four forms of verbal communication?

▶ OBJECTIVE 2   5. Give an example of a nonverbal message that reinforces a verbal message and one that contradicts a verbal message.

▶ OBJECTIVE 3   6. What four directions comprise the formal communication network?

▶ OBJECTIVE 3   7. Why is it difficult to get objective information flowing upward in the organization?

▶ OBJECTIVE 3   8. What is the difference between horizontal and cross-channel communication?

▶ OBJECTIVE 4   9. What are the characteristics of the grapevine?

▶ OBJECTIVE 5   10. What is the difference between simultaneous and serial communication? Give an example of each.

11. Give an example of the denotation and the connotation of a word.   OBJECTIVE 5 ◀

12. What is the difference between slang and jargon? Give an example of each.   OBJECTIVE 5 ◀

13. Compose a sentence containing an overabstraction. Then revise the sentence to eliminate the overabstraction.   OBJECTIVE 5 ◀

14. What are five guidelines for managing organizational communication?   OBJECTIVE 6 ◀

EXERCISES

1. **Communication Process**—Use an incident from a recent television program to illustrate each of the five components of the communication process.   OBJECTIVE 1 ◀

2. **Collaboration**—Approximately 3,000 words in this chapter were devoted to the discussion of the communication process. Working in small groups, write a 250-word abstract of this discussion. Since this is an informational abstract, you may pick up the exact wording of the original discussion when appropriate. Ensure that all important points are covered, your narrative flows smoothly from one topic to another, and your writing is free from content and English errors.   OBJECTIVE 1 ◀

3. **Entrepreneurship**—Marty Chernov, owner of a small salvage yard employing eighteen people, has an appointment with John Garrison Boyd, IV, vice president of Metropolitan Bank, to discuss his application for a $35,000 business loan. What guidelines can you give Marty regarding his nonverbal behavior at the conference that might benefit him?   OBJECTIVE 2 ◀

4. **Serial Communication**—Divide into groups of four students each: A, B, C, and D. Within each group have A and B leave the room. Then have C read aloud the summary that he or she wrote in Exercise 2 at a normal reading rate and without repeating any of the data, while D takes notes. Have A rejoin the group and take notes while D reads the notes taken of C's oral summary. Then have B rejoin the group and take notes while A reads the notes taken of D's oral notes. Finally, have D reread aloud his or her original summary and B reread aloud his or her notes. What changes, omissions, or additions occurred?   OBJECTIVE 3 ◀

5. **Communication Directions**—Think of a club to which you belong or a business with which you are familiar. Provide a specific illustration of each of the four directions in the formal communication network. Then develop an organizational chart similar to Figure 1.2 showing these four incidents. Label each of the positions in the chart.   OBJECTIVE 3 ◀

6. **Grapevine**—Read a journal article on the company grapevine. Then write a one-page summary of the article. Proofread for content and language errors and revise as needed. Staple a photocopy of the article to your summary, and submit to your instructor.   OBJECTIVE 4 ◀

7. **Meanings Are in People**—Record your personal connotative meaning of each of the following terms: *profit, stress, conservative, alternate lifestyle, Japanese, affirmative action.*   OBJECTIVE 5 ◀

8. **International**—"I'll never understand our people in Pakistan," Eileen said. "I wrote our local agent over there, who's supposedly a financial wizard, this note: 'If your firm wants to play ball with us, we'll need the straight scoop. What's your bottom-line price on the STX model   OBJECTIVE 5 ◀

with all the bells and whistles? Also, if you pull out all the stops, can we get delivery by Xmas?' And you know what he did? He wrote me back a long letter, inquiring about my health and my family, but never answering my questions! If they don't get on the ball, I'm going to recommend that we stop doing business with them." From a communication standpoint, what is happening here? What advice can you give Eileen? Rewrite her message to the Pakistani agent to make it more effective.

OBJECTIVE 5

9. **Technology**—Ralph looked up from his computer, "Fortunately, I do most of my writing via my computer. For example, I send a memo electronically to the other person's computer, where it can be called up and read at his or her convenience. Thus, I don't have to worry about creating any nonverbal barriers." Is Ralph correct? Discuss and give examples of nonverbal barriers that can lessen the effectiveness of Ralph's electronic memos.

OBJECTIVE 6

10. **Managing Communications**—Betty Loomis, an accounting clerk, was complaining to you, the vice president, about the memo she had just received from her boss, Warren Henderson, the head of the accounting department. The memo said, in part:

> In my May 10 memo to all employees in your section, I instructed everyone to begin the 7% extra withholding as of May 15, to reflect the new tax rates. I now learn that you did not make the adjustments until May 18, resulting in an overpayment to each of the 550 employees for whom you are responsible. As you know, company policy requires that during periods of absence, employees are responsible for taking steps to ensure the continued smooth functioning of their office. By copy of this memo, I am informing Personnel of this incident.

"It's just not fair," Betty said. "Mr. Henderson knew I was out of state for three days attending an uncle's funeral. Why didn't he take that into consideration?"

What communication problems were evident in this incident? How could they have been avoided? How should Mr. Henderson have handled the situation?

OBJECTIVES 1–6

C A S E   P R O B L E M ━━━━━━━━━━━

Urban Systems Jumps the Gun

Paul, Wendy, and C. B. entered Marc's office ten minutes late for their meeting. Marc immediately came from behind his desk and ushered them to two comfortable sofas positioned around a coffee table. "Can I have my girl get you a cup of coffee?" he asked. When they all declined, Marc sat down, propped his feet onto the table, and said to C. B., "Now, what seems to be the problem with the advertising schedule?"

"Just as I explained in my memo to you," C. B. replied. "I've committed $18,500 for a full-page four-color ad in next month's *Facilities Management* magazine advertising Ultra Light strips for task lighting with modular furniture. Now Wendy tells me that the new strips won't be available for sale until three weeks after *FM* hits the newsstands.''

"C. B., I did warn you in December that R & D had run into a minor technical problem that would take a little time to fix," Wendy replied.

"A little time! My goodness, they've been working on 'that little technical problem' for over a month. How was I to know that 'a little time' meant two months?" said C. B.

Marc reached over and placed his hand on C. B.'s shoulder and said, "No need to get so upset. How can we fix this problem? Paul, do you have any suggestions?"

Paul replied, "Well, I didn't see a copy of C. B.'s memo to you, so I don't know the details, but it seems to me from reading Wendy's production schedule that C.B. should have known about this problem early enough to hold off on the *FM* advertisement."

"Well, it looks like it's too late to do anything about it this time," said Marc, standing up. "Let's try to have better communication between each group so that we avoid this type of problem in the future. I've got another meeting coming up in fifteen minutes that I have to get ready for. Thanks for stopping by."

1. From what you know about Marc, were his verbal and nonverbal messages consistent with his personality? Give examples.

2. Using Wendy's remarks about the technical problem and C. B.'s response, illustrate the communication process.

3. How helpful was Marc in this incident? Paul?

4. List five negative nonverbal messages that were communicated in this situation.

5. What communication barriers were present in this situation?

CHAPTER 2

Contemporary Issues in Business Communication

After you have finished this chapter, you will be able to

1. Explain the meaning of nonverbal messages communicated in different cultures.

2. Describe strategies for communicating across cultures.

3. Appreciate the intercultural diversity that is present in the United States.

4. Discuss important technological developments that affect business communication.

5. Discuss four implications of technology on communication.

6. Understand the legal and ethical dimensions of communicating.

7. Explain the types of small groups that typically operate in the organization.

8. List four guidelines for communicating collaboratively.

Every country throughout the world has a different way of doing business. This is why Dorothy Manning founded International Business Protocol, a consulting firm that specializes in helping U.S. companies learn about the nuances and correct approaches to conducting business in foreign lands. Manning is also the co-executive producer of a video series called "The Corporate Diplomat," consisting of several 30-minute videos, each focusing on a different country.

From her first-hand experience, Manning has an excellent vantage point from which to compare differences in American business communication practices with those of other cultures. Her clients are business people from both the United States and other countries.

Manning believes that perhaps the most striking difference between American business people and those of other cultures is the American no-nonsense, let's-get-to-it-now approach. "The United States has what we call a monochronic culture, which means that it thinks of time as linear," she explained. "We schedule our time in appointments, in meetings, and in lunches. Those time segments are not supposed to be broken, they're sacred. And so if you have an appointment with your superior, and you have 15 minutes scheduled, you are supposed to have done your homework, come to the appointment with a prepared typewritten statement and all the data and information—if you haven't already sent it ahead of time—so you're wasting no time with social pleasantries. And you get right down to business and deal with the issue."

Dorothy Manning, Founder
International Business
Protocol, Boston,
Massachusetts

Most other cultures, Manning said, approach business with less intensity and "are offended when Americans jump right into business immediately without having established a personal rapport. Perhaps the Dutch are somewhat like us, and maybe the Germans a little bit, but much, much less so."

Generally speaking, Manning noted that the farther south you go in Europe and the Middle East, "the more it is very important for you to establish a human rapport: a personal, social, and emotional bond" before getting down to business. This relationship, she indicated, does not have to be "embarrasingly deep" but enough of a bond to show "that you enjoy being together and that you have a few things in common."

Moreover, many of these cultures are polychronic, Manning said, "which means that several things happen simultaneously." Therefore, an American with a business appointment in another country can "well expect it to be interrupted by anything from a colleague entering to a secretary entering to a call from home. And the meeting will go on until it's finished, however long it takes." This puts an American in the uncomfortable position of being late for his or her next appointment, Manning said, "but the other person waiting for you expects that, doesn't worry about it if you don't show up on time. That kind of thing drives Americans crazy."

Of course, Americans are not without idiosyncrasies that can make members of other cultures feel uneasy. This is particularly true of the expressiveness of Americans' body language. "In Japan and in many oriental countries, you don't touch people," Manning noted. "You don't shake hands. That's why they bow." Bowing, Manning said, is a way of "showing respect to the soul of the other person." Of course, many Japanese people conducting business in a Western country are familiar enough with our ways not to take offense when an American sticks out his hand. However, Manning indicated it would be prudent to let an oriental business person offer his or her hand first.

There's little doubt that technology—facsimile machines and telephones—has made the world smaller and increased business opportunities for American companies. The danger of technology, Manning indicated, is that it provides little time for Americans "to sit, reflect and absorb," and to consider what may be a much different point of view of the person receiving the communications. Americans, Manning said, must understand that not all countries think of business so immediately "in terms of the bottom line." ▼

FOUR ISSUES AFFECTING BUSINESS COMMUNICATION

Because communication is such a pervasive and strategic part of the organization, almost anything that affects the organization and its employees affects the communication function as well. However, four contemporary issues are having a special impact on business communication:

- International and intercultural dimensions
- Technological dimensions
- Legal and ethical considerations
- Collaborative communication

These four topics are introduced and explored briefly in this chapter on contemporary issues. However, we will return to these topics periodically throughout the remainder of this text to discuss their impact on each specific area of business communication.

INTERNATIONAL AND INTERCULTURAL DIMENSIONS

The United States is a major participant in international business—both as a buyer and seller. We are the world's largest importer of goods and services and the world's second largest exporter. The dominant role that the United States thus plays in the global economy does not, however, mean that international business matters are handled "the American way." Some years ago a book called *The Ugly American* condemned Americans abroad for the attitude of "Let 'em do it our way or not at all."

Ethnocentrism is the belief that one's own group is superior. Such an attitude hinders communication, understanding, and goodwill between trading partners. An attitude of arrogance is not only counterproductive but also unrealistic, considering the fact that the U.S. population represents less than 5% of the world population. Moreover, of the world's countries, the United States is currently fourth in population and is expected to drop to seventh place by the year 2100.[1]

Another fact of life in international business is that, comparatively, few Americans speak a foreign language. Although English is the major language for conducting business worldwide, it would be naive to assume that it is the other person's responsibility to learn English. As a matter of fact, only 8.5% of the world's population speaks English. This means that English-only speakers cannot communicate one-to-one with more than 90% of the people in this world.[2]

When we talk about **culture**, we mean the customary traits, attitudes, and behaviors of a group of people. International business depends very heavily on communicating effectively with people of different cultures. Competent communicators are aware of the implications of language differences, they learn to interpret nonverbal messages appropriately, and they recognize the importance of group-oriented behavior in different cultures.

The following discussion provides useful guidance for communicating with people from different cultures. Although it is helpful to be aware of

International business would not be possible without international communication.

cultural differences, you should also recognize that each member of a culture is an individual, with individual needs, perceptions, and experiences, and should be treated as such.

Language Differences

Unless you will actually be located overseas in the same country for an extended period of time, it may not be reasonable for you to learn the host language. Most of the correspondence between American firms and foreign firms is in English; and in other cases, the services of a qualified interpreter may be available. However, even if you do not learn the host language, you should try to learn a few common phrases, such as "Good morning," "Good afternoon," "please," and "thank you." Doing so is a form of courtesy that shows personal interest, respect, and acceptance.

Even with the services of a qualified interpreter, some problems can occur. Consider, for example, the following marketing blunders:[3]

- In Brazil, where Portuguese is spoken, a U.S. airline advertised that its Boeing 747s had "rendezvous lounges," without realizing that *rendezvous* in Portuguese implies prostitution.
- In China, Kentucky Fried Chicken's slogan "Finger-lickin' good" does not have a poetic Chinese translation. The slogan was translated literally: "So good you suck your fingers."
- In Puerto Rico, General Motors had difficulties advertising the Chevrolet Nova automobile because the name sounds like the Spanish phrase "No va," which means "It doesn't go."
- In Thailand, the slogan "Come Alive with Pepsi" was translated, "Bring your ancestors back from the dead with Pepsi."

To ensure that the exact meaning is not lost during translation, legal, technical, and all important documents should be translated into the second language and then retranslated into English.

Interpreting Nonverbal Messages

Even assuming that both parties are fluent in the same language, differences in interpretations will occur, because of the different cultures. Each person interprets events through his or her mental filter, and that filter is based on the receiver's knowledge, experiences, and viewpoints. As a result, several of the nonverbal forms of communication discussed in Chapter 1 have different meanings in different cultures.

Time The language of time is as different between cultures as the language of words. Americans and Germans are very time-conscious and very precise about appointments. As a rule, Japanese are, too (although they will expend much time trying to reach agreement within the group). In Tokyo, it's better to be fifteen minutes early than five minutes late.

South Americans and Arabs, however, are often more casual about time. For example, your Egyptian host would not be considered rude if he made you wait 30 minutes for an appointment while he took care of some family matter. It should be noted, however, that the increasing complexity of

---

> Expressions that make sense in one language often "lose something in the translation."

▼
OBJECTIVE 1: Explain the meaning of nonverbal messages communicated in different cultures.

> Cultures differ not only in their verbal language but also in their nonverbal language. Very few nonverbal messages have universal meanings.

international business is making all countries, including Latin and Arab countries, more time conscious.

Business people in both Asian and South American countries tend to favor long negotiations and slow deliberations. Pleasantries will be exchanged at some length before getting down to business.

Body Language Body language, especially gestures, also varies among cultures. For example, a nod of the head means "yes" to most of us, but in Bulgaria and Greece a nod means "no" and a shake of the head means "yes." Likewise, our sign for "okay"—forming a circle with our forefinger and thumb—means "zero" in France, "money" in Japan, and a vulgarity in Brazil.

Waving or pointing to an Arab business person would be considered rude, because that is how Arabs summon dogs. Folded arms signal pride in Finland but disrespect in Fiji. The number of bows that the Japanese exchange on greeting each other, as well as the length and depth of the bows, signals the social prestige each party feels toward the other. Italians might think you're bored unless you use your hands animatedly during discussions. Many American men sit with their legs crossed, with one ankle resting over the opposite knee. However, such a stance would be considered an insult in Moslem countries, where one would never show the sole of the foot to a guest.

Likewise, Americans consider eye contact very important, often not trusting someone who is "afraid to look you in the eyes." But in Japan and many Latin American countries, keeping the eyes lowered is a sign of respect; to look a partner full in the eye is considered a sign of ill breeding and is felt to be irritating.

> When in doubt about how to act, follow the lead of your host.

Touch Touching behavior is very culture-specific. In Thailand, people do not touch in public, and to touch someone's head would be a major social error. The Chinese are a very reserved people and do not like to be touched, other than a brief handshake on greeting. However, handshakes in much of Europe tend to last much longer than in the United States; pumping the hand five to seven times is normal. Europeans also tend to shake hands every time they see each other, perhaps several times a day. Similarly, in much of Europe, men often kiss each other upon greeting; unless an American businessman is aware of this custom, he might react inappropriately.

Space Our feelings about space are partly an outgrowth of our culture and partly a result of geography and economics. For example, Americans are used to wide-open spaces and tend to move about expansively, using hand and arm motions for emphasis. But in Japan, which has much smaller living and working spaces, such abrupt and extensive body movements are not typical. Likewise, Americans tend to sit face-to-face, so that they can maintain eye contact, whereas the Chinese and Japanese (where eye contact is not considered important) tend to sit side by side during negotiations.

In the United States, office size is related to status, with top executives having the largest offices. In other parts of the world, however, the "bigger is better" mentality gives way to logic: Not much space is needed for thinking and planning, so top executives do not need large offices.

The sense of personal space—the distance from others at which we feel comfortable interacting—also differs among cultures. In the United States, a person's social zone is between 4 and 12 feet, with most business exchanges occurring at about 5 feet. However, in both the Middle East and Latin American countries, this distance is too far. Business people there tend to stand close enough to feel your breath as you speak. Most Americans tend to back away unconsciously from such close contact.

Group-Oriented Behavior

Where unanimous agreement rather than majority rule is the norm, negotiations tend to take longer.

The business environment in a capitalistic society such as the United States places great value on the contributions of the individual toward the success of the organization. Individual effort is often stressed more than group effort, and a competitive atmosphere prevails. In other cultures, however, originality and independence of judgment are not valued as highly as teamwork. There is a frequently quoted Japanese saying, "a nail standing out will be hammered down."[4] Thus, the Japanese go to great lengths to reach decisions through consensus, wherein every participating member, not just a majority, is able to agree.

Closely related to the concept of group-oriented behavior is the concept of saving face. The desire to "save face" simply means that neither party in a given interaction should suffer embarrassment. Human relationships are highly valued in such cultures and are embodied in the concept of *wa*, or the Japanese pursuit of harmony. This concept makes it difficult for the Japanese to say no to a request because it would be impolite. They are very reluctant to offend others—even if they unintentionally mislead them instead. Thus, a "yes" in Japanese might mean "Yes, I understand you" rather than "Yes, I agree." Likewise, a strongly negative reaction to an American proposal might prompt only a mild response, such as "I will try my best." Latin Americans also tend to avoid an outright "no" in their business dealings, preferring a milder, less explicit, response.

One business executive compared negotiating with the Japanese to studying a Japanese ink painting: "Ink painting creates an effect by the use of blank spaces, and unless one is able to read those empty areas, one cannot understand the work. The same is true, they say, of Japanese speech. One always has to figure out the parts that have been left unsaid."[5] In other words, one has to read between the lines, because what is left unsaid or unwritten may be just as important as what was said or written.

OBJECTIVE 2: Describe strategies for communicating across cultures.

Strategies for Communicating Across Cultures

To hasten final acceptance and to enhance your chances for achieving your objectives when communicating with business people abroad, use the following strategies.

Maintain Formality   Much more than the United States, most other countries value and respect a formal approach to business dealings. Call others by their titles and family names unless specifically asked to do otherwise. By both verbal and nonverbal clues, convey an attitude of propriety and decorum. Most other cultures do not equate formality with coldness.

Show Respect Withhold judgment, accepting the premise that attitudes held by an entire culture are probably based on sound reasoning. Listen carefully to what is being communicated, trying to understand the other person's feelings. Learn about your host country—its geography, form of government, largest cities, culture, current events, and the like.

Be Flexible In terms of cultural differences, assume the attitude that there is no right way or wrong way—only different ways. Be adaptable, willing to change your behavior, attitudes, and eating habits. (As one seasoned traveler has said, "Anything tastes like chicken if you slice it thinly and swallow it quickly.") Patience and a sense of humor will help you adapt to your host country.

Communicate Clearly To ensure that your oral and written messages are understood, follow these guidelines:

- Avoid slang, jargon, and other figures of speech. Expressions such as "They'll eat that up," "out in left field," or "a Catch–22 situation" are likely to confuse even a fluent English speaker.
- Be specific and illustrate your points with concrete examples.
- Provide and solicit feedback. Summarize frequently; provide a written summary of the points covered in a meeting; ask your counterpart to paraphrase what has been said; encourage questions.
- Use a variety of media—handouts (distributed before the meeting to allow time for reading), audiovisual aids, models, and the like.
- Avoid attempts at humor; humor is likely to be lost on your counterpart.
- Speak plainly and slowly (but not so slowly as to appear to be condescending), choosing your words carefully.

Intercultural Diversity in the United States

Perhaps the (unintended) implication up to this point has been that you must leave the United States in order to encounter cultures different from the one with which you are comfortable. Nothing could be further from the truth. Consider, for example, the following:[6]

> *Fact*: Today blacks, Asians, and Hispanics make up 21% of the American population. More than 30% of New York City's residents are foreign born. Miami is two-thirds Hispanic. Detroit is 63% black. San Francisco is one-third Asian.
>
> *Projection*: In ten years, minorities will make up 25% of the population of the United States. English will be the second language for the majority of California's population by the year 2000; by 2020, the majority of that state's entry-level workers will be Hispanic. Sometime in the next century, whites will become the minority in the population of the United States.
>
> *Implication*: Diversity will have a profound impact on our lives—and will pose a growing challenge for most human resources managers. Those who view diversity among employees as a source of richness and strength for the company can help bring a wide range of benefits to their organizations.

Showing respect is probably the easiest strategy to exhibit—and one of the most important.

Plan your communications carefully.

OBJECTIVE 3: Appreciate the intercultural diversity that is present in the United States.

The United States is a multicultural nation.

Cultural diversity provides a rich environment for solving problems and for expanding horizons.

Whether you happen to belong to the majority culture or to one of the minority cultures in the United States, you will share your work and leisure hours with people different from yourself—people who have values, mannerisms, and speech habits different from your own. This is true today, and it will be even truer in the future. The same strategies given earlier—showing respect, being flexible, and communicating clearly—apply whether the cultural differences are at home or abroad.

A person who is knowledgeable about, and comfortable with, different cultures is a more effective manager because he or she can avoid misunderstandings, avoid poor performance, and tap into the greater variety of viewpoints a diverse culture provides. In addition, such understanding provides personal satisfaction as well.

TECHNOLOGICAL DIMENSIONS

Communication technology makes international commerce possible.

Considering the different time zones, physical distances, cultural differences, and varying languages of the countries in the international business community, the current high level of international business operations would simply not be possible without the increased communication capabilities brought about through technology.

The written language with the longest continuous history is Chinese, which is more than 6,000 years old. However, it was not until Gutenberg's invention of the printing press with movable type in the fifteenth century that mass communication became possible. And it was not until the 1800s—with the invention of the telegraph, the typewriter, the telephone, and the dictating machine—that major technological changes began to have an effect on communications in business.

Other inventions followed in the first half of the twentieth century, culminating with the development of the first electronic computer in 1946. The ENIAC (electronic numerical integrator and computer) was developed at the University of Pennsylvania, weighed 30 tons, and occupied 1,500 square feet. Today's notebook computers, weighing less than eight pounds, offer many times more computing power than this original behemoth.

Until the advent of word processing, computers were used primarily for large-scale calculations. Word processing was developed in the early 1960s as a means of automating the processing of words, much as computers had automated the processing of numbers.

▼

OBJECTIVE 4: Discuss important technological developments that affect business communication.

Word Processing

Touch keyboarding (typing) skills are important in a word processing environment.

Word processing is the production of letters, memorandums, reports, and other documents through the use of automated electronic equipment. Most word processing today is done through the use of software programs that operate on microcomputers.

Using word processing, a writer can keyboard the message very quickly—without worrying about format or typographical errors. Then, using the various editing functions built into the software, the writer can revise, delete, add, or reposition words and sentences until the final document is ready to be printed. The document is then stored for later retrieval—most often on either a removable floppy disk or on a permanent hard disk.

Sophisticated word processing programs can check spelling, replace a word or phrase throughout a document, automatically insert the current date and page number, generate an index, produce "original" form letters, perform mathematical calculations, copy charts and graphics from other programs (such as spreadsheets), automatically number and position footnotes and endnotes, and arrange text in columns, newspaper-style.

Many word processing systems come with features designed to improve writing. A spelling checker automatically compares each word in a document with a built-in word list to identify words that may be misspelled. An electronic thesaurus provides a list of synonyms for words. A grammar and punctuation checker calls attention to simple errors such as repeated words, numbers in incorrect format (for example, "$5,32"), and sentences not started with a capital letter.

Other features available include an on-line style manual that you can call to the screen to review rules of grammar, punctuation, and usage. Electronic outliners provide a format that the writer can fill in to outline a message. Finally, writing analysis software, now in its infancy but showing great potential, can help analyze the extent to which a document follows the principles of clear writing (Figure 2.1).

Writing-Analysis Software

FIGURE 2.1

Writing analysis software identifies potential problems in the passage and analyzes the overall quality of the writing.

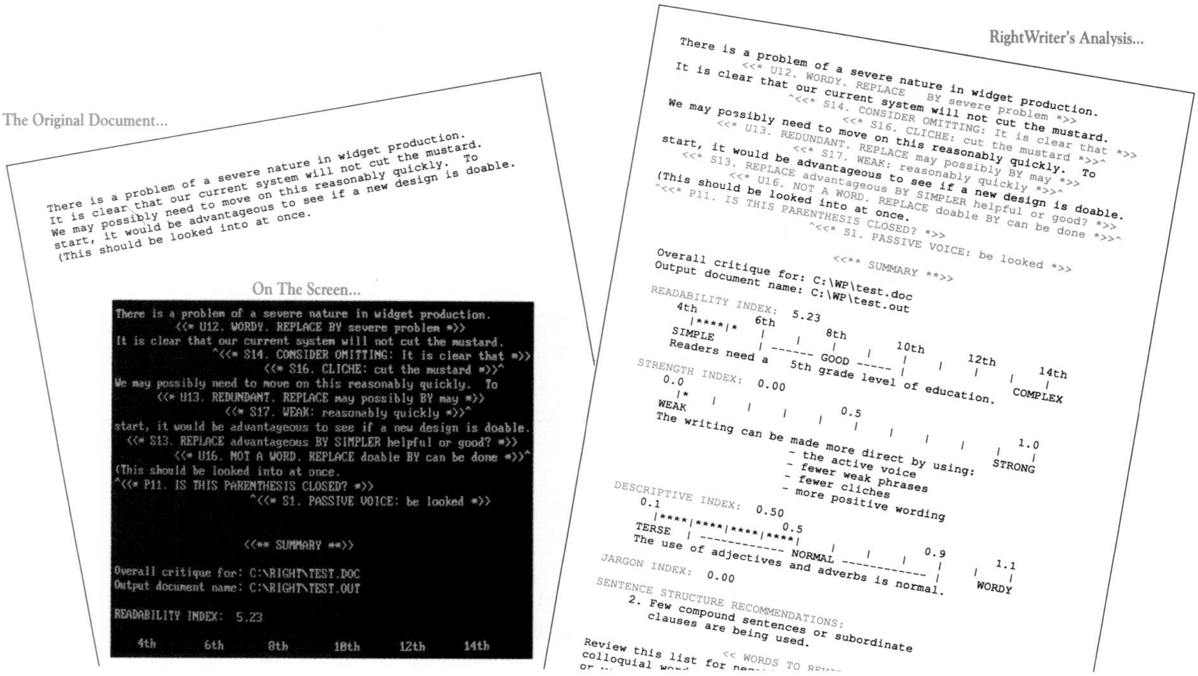

Source: RightSoft, Inc., Sarasota, Florida.

Electronic Communications

In addition to word processing software, many technological developments have affected the way we communicate with others in the workplace. To begin with, a number of recent advances combine features of the telephone and the mail to produce faster, cheaper ways of sending and receiving messages.

In **electronic mail** (or E-mail), messages are composed, transmitted, and usually read on computer screens. Messages travel through cables within the company and through telephone lines outside the company. Although E-mail delivery is almost instantaneous, the receiver knows a message is waiting only when he or she accesses the mail service; if that is only once a week, then the message will have taken a week to arrive.

Voice mail is like a digital answering machine. It allows users to record messages electronically on a computer disk. A **video teleconference** is a meeting held at different sites linked by cameras and microphones that transmit the live voices and images of the participants. A **facsimile machine** (fax, for short) is like a long-distance photocopier—it sends and receives copies of documents over telephone lines.

Electronic bulletin boards are systems that connect computers by telephone to a service for posting messages. Nationwide, many companies are beginning to set up these bulletin boards as inexpensive, speedy message centers for their staff and customers. At General Electric, for instance, an electronic bulletin board helps the sales staff in 30 countries stay current with prices—instead of waiting three weeks for the mail, as in the past.[7] In addition to private bulletin boards, many commercial bulletin boards are available by subscription, allowing customers to obtain information, buy and sell stocks, read newspaper and magazine articles, order plane tickets, and so on.

Besides making it easier for people to send and receive messages, recent advances have improved our ability to prepare written documents. **Desktop publishing** (DTP) permits users to write, assemble, and design such publications as company newsletters, brochures, catalogs, and reports in a business office using a microcomputer. Typically, the text is entered (keyboarded) using word processing software and then copied into the desktop publishing software, where it can be easily manipulated.

Using desktop publishing, text can be set into columns; illustrations and photographs can be inserted and then enlarged or reduced, with the text flowing around the graphic; horizontal and vertical rules and boxes of different weights can be drawn; elaborate headlines can be designed; and the horizontal and vertical spacing around each character can be adjusted. After the document has been designed on the computer, it is typically printed out on a laser printer, which produces high-quality output, and then duplicated.

Desktop publishing is faster and cheaper than using a commercial printing company, and it provides users more flexibility and control of their documents. The disadvantage is that not everyone who knows how to keyboard also knows how to design a document so that the document is both effective and attractive. **Desktop presentation** software is similar to desktop publishing, except it is designed for producing audiovisual aids used in presentations.

Implications of Technology on Communications

We begin our discussion of the implications of technology on communications by refuting one common misconception. Technology will not lead to a "paperless office." The prediction of a paperless office was based on the belief that future offices would store all information on some type of magnetic medium, which could then be filed, retrieved, and disseminated at will. Electronic storage, retrieval, and dissemination is faster and cheaper than manual paper methods.

Nevertheless, the paperless office has not come about, and probably never will. The reason, of course, is that paper is so convenient and portable. It is extremely tiring to read a long document on a computer monitor; it is much easier to first print it out and then read from the "hard copy." In addition, paper documents can be taken and used anywhere—whether a computer is accessible or not.

In addition to making it easier to create, edit, and disseminate information, technology is having the following effects on business communication:

More Information Available   Technology has increased dramatically the amount of information easily available to the manager. Because of the ease with which company data bases can be created, accessed, and manipulated, managers are receiving more computer-generated reports than ever. In addition, the availability of commercial data bases means the manager can easily obtain industry and financial information externally from a variety of published sources. Finally, because sending copies of documents is so easy with electronic mail and high-speed photocopiers, people tend to send each memo or report to more people than in the past. Without careful management, information overload can occur, in which people receive more information than can be intelligently handled.

In such a situation, critical thinking becomes an especially important skill in business communication. Being able to sort through the information and determine what is important and being able to relate ideas to each other becomes crucial for effective communication. Competent communicators carefully assess who legitimately needs the information contained in their messages, and they critically evaluate the information in the messages they receive.

Increased Importance of Abstracting and Early Disclosure   News reporters have always known the importance of "front-loading"—putting the most important information up front, where it receives the most attention. Because of the increased pressures on managers to consume more information (with no increase in time available for reading), managers are seeking ways to get to the main point of each document as early as possible.

Thus, the ability to analyze a mass of data and condense it to a manageable length is becoming more important. Executive summaries, placed at the front of long reports, are now a required part of the reporting process in many organizations. Also, many executives prefer a direct style of writing from their subordinates—with the major ideas presented first, followed by supporting details. Competent communicators carefully analyze their audience and tailor the content and organization of their messages for the specific audience.

OBJECTIVE 5: Discuss four implications of technology on communication.

Paper will continue to be used for temporary storage because it is so convenient and portable.

Busy executives want the important points summarized up front.

FIGURE 2.2   Receiving and Sending Electronic Mail

```
> Mail #309801
> From jthoreson@EMS
> Date Sent: Thu 5 Jan 91 14:20 EST
> To: awilliams@MSA
> Subject: Dec sales

> Al:
>
> The stats on last month's sales don't look rihgt.  Too high,
> I think, esp for West Coast.  Please review asap.  If figures
> are wrong, will need you to fax me the corrected stats.
>
> Joan

MAIL READ MENU
    1  Read memo again          4  Forward memo
    2  Reply to memo            5  Leave memo in inbasket
    3  Delete memo              m  Main menu

Enter a menu option or ? for help: 2
Enter text.  End with a period on a line by itself.

> Joan: Will check the figures tonight and let you know what's
> what tomorrow morning. Al

MAIL SEND MENU
    1  Send memo                4  Edit memo
    2  Copy memo to others      m  Main menu
    3  Clear memo

Enter a menu option or ? for help: 1
Sending . . . Mail 310582 sent.
Return for next, m for menu, or memo number:
```

More Informal Style of Writing   In yesterday's office, the executive dictated a letter, the secretary transcribed it (perhaps doing some minor editing in the process), the executive revised it, and the letter was retyped and mailed. Today, however, many executives do their own keyboarding and often use electronic mail to send the memo directly to the receiver's computer.

This "writing on the fly" is often done in a very abbreviated style—much as someone would jot notes down on a notepad (see Figure 2.2). Typographical errors may not be corrected. The formalities of traditional correspondence may not always be followed. And because many of these messages are never printed on paper, they lack the polished format and appearance of typewritten letters or memos on letterhead stationery. People used to reading such informally written messages tend to overlook the minor errors.

Competent communicators carefully analyze each writing situation to determine what level of formality is expected and desirable. In addition, they always keep their audience and their purpose firmly in mind, regardless of the degree of formality used.

More Collaborative Communications   The increasing quantity and complexity of the information available makes it difficult for any one person to have either the time or the expertise to be able to analyze all the data adequately. The differing skills of several individuals are often needed in a joint effort to analyze the situation and generate proposals or recommendations. Thus, collaborative writing and collaborative oral presentations are becoming quite prevalent in organizations. (As a matter of fact, collaborative communications have always been much more common in organizations than many people realized.)

Competent communicators learn how to work effectively in small groups to gather and analyze data and then to write and revise a written report or prepare an oral presentation. This topic is discussed in more detail later in this chapter.

LEGAL AND ETHICAL CONSIDERATIONS

When writing a business plan, drafting a sales letter, writing a personnel policy, or recruiting a candidate for a job, we make conscious decisions regarding what information to include and what information to exclude from our messages. For the information that is included, we make conscious decisions about how to phrase the language, how much emphasis it should receive, and where it should be positioned in the message. Such decisions have legal and ethical dimensions—both for you as the writer and for the organization.

> OBJECTIVE 6: Understand the legal and ethical dimensions of communicating.

Legal Considerations

Three types of legal considerations are of special relevance to the business communicator: defamation, invasion of privacy, and fraud and misrepresentation.

Defamation   Any false and malicious statement that is communicated to others and that injures a person's good name or reputation may constitute **defamation.** Defamation in a temporary form such as in oral communication is called **slander;** defamation in a permanent form such as in writing or videotape is called **libel.** The three major conditions for defamation are that the statement be false, be communicated to others, and be harmful to a person's good name or reputation. Thus, telling Joe Smith to his face that he is a liar and a crook does not constitute defamation (slander) unless a third person hears the remarks. In addition, truth is generally an acceptable defense to a charge of defamation.

> Oral defamation is slander. Written defamation is libel.

Competent communicators use objective language and verifiable information when communicating about others. For example, instead of saying, "Mr. Baker is a poor credit risk," they might say, "Mr. Baker was at least ten days late in making his payments to us four times during the past six months."

Invasion of Privacy   Any unreasonable intrusion into the private life of another person or denial of a person's right to be left alone may constitute an **invasion of privacy.** Thus, using someone's name or photograph in a sales promotion without that person's permission would be an invasion of privacy. Of particular concern today are the vast amounts of employee and customer information being maintained in corporate data banks. The

> A person's right to reasonable privacy is protected by law. Organizations must ensure that information about its employees and customers is not misused.

proliferation of microcomputers, networks, and electronic mail makes it possible to access large amounts of data about employees and customers very rapidly and easily.

Various state and federal laws, including the Fair Credit Reporting Act and the Privacy Act, now protect the individual's right to privacy. The federal government defines "right to privacy" as "the right of individuals to participate in decisions regarding the collection, use, and disclosure of information personally identifiable to that individual."[8] Thus, someone's right to privacy may be violated if his or her records are read by someone not authorized to examine them.

Competent communicators ensure that they do not misuse information about other people in their communications and that their communications are available only to authorized people.

Fraud and Misrepresentation   A deliberate misrepresentation of the truth that is made to induce someone to give up something of value is called **fraud.** Fraud can occur either when one party actually makes a deliberately false statement (called *active fraud*) or when one party deliberately conceals some information that he or she is required to reveal (*passive fraud*).

To be fraudulent, the statements must involve facts. Opinions and persuasive arguments or exaggerated claims about a product (called *sales puffery*) do not constitute fraud even if they turn out to be false. For example, "The Celeste is the only American-made car that comes with leather seats as standard equipment" is a statement of fact, which, if incorrect, might constitute fraud. However, "The Celeste is the most luxurious car in America" is an opinion; even if most car buyers did not agree with the statement, it would still not be considered fraud.

Misrepresentation is a false statement that is made innocently with no intent to deceive the other party. If misrepresentation is proven, the contract or agreement may be rescinded. If fraud is proven, the contract or agreement may be rescinded and the offended party may collect monetary compensation.

Competent communicators are aware of the relevant laws and ensure that their oral and written messages are accurate—both in terms of what is communicated and in terms of what is left uncommunicated.

Ethical Considerations

Sometimes being legally right is not sufficient justification for our actions. Each of us has our own code of **ethics,** or rules of conduct, that might go beyond legal rules and tell us how to act when the law is silent. In addition, many corporations have developed their own code of ethics to govern employee behavior. For the business communicator, the matter of ethics governs not only one's behavior but also one's communication of behavior; that is, how we use language involves ethical choices.

A message can be true and still be unethical.

When you have doubts about the ethical propriety of your writing, ask yourself these questions:

1. Is this message true?
2. Does it exaggerate?
3. Does it withhold or obscure information that should be communicated?
4. Does it promise something that it cannot deliver?

5. Does it betray a confidence?
6. Does it play unduly on the fears of the reader?
7. Does it reflect the wishes of the organization?

Competent communicators use their knowledge of communication theory to achieve their goals while acting in an ethical manner.

COLLABORATIVE COMMUNICATION

Regardless of the size of the organization, members must periodically divide into small groups to accomplish some objective. In addition, many small groups convene with the purpose of producing a collaboratively written document, such as an organization's five-year plan. Successful collaboration typically requires well-developed communication skills.

> Even in large organizations or large departments, workers tend to come together in small groups to accomplish their goals.

Collaborative Oral Communication

Small-group discussions range from one-time, on-the-spot meetings to permanent committees. Some of the more common types of small-group sessions are as follows:

OBJECTIVE 7: Explain the types of small groups that typically operate in the organization.

- *Operating groups:* Operating groups are the more or less permanent committees within the organization that meet periodically to give and receive information, consult, and reach decisions. Members typically see such groups as very important to success in their present jobs and future promotions. Whether members typically seek to enhance organizational goals or their own personal goals is, to a large extent, determined by the type of communication climate that exists in the organization.
- *Negotiating groups:* Negotiating groups are formed when two groups in conflict meet to work out an agreement. An obvious example is the labor–management team that meets to develop a new contract. The communication climate in such groups may be quite staged, with each side sometimes trying to mislead, confuse, and bluff the other. Also, nonverbal clues, such as a "poker face" and simulated anger, may be used to gain advantage.
- *Creative groups:* Brainstorming sessions are sometimes called to dream up creative ideas and novel solutions. The communication environment encourages freewheeling ideas, with no criticism of ideas being allowed. The quantity of ideas generated, rather than their quality, is emphasized.
- *Training groups:* In-house training sessions are held to help members become more proficient at their jobs. The training leader should encourage an atmosphere of openness, encouraging questions, and soliciting frequent feedback to ensure that the members are following the instruction. A supportive communication environment is necessary to motivate participation and encourage learning.
- *Ad hoc groups:* The Latin term *ad hoc* means "for this special purpose." An ad hoc group is formed to carry out a temporary, special purpose. It may meet once or several times, but it is not a permanent group. Since the group is temporary, there is no team spirit or established way of doing things, and members are usually willing to accept imposed leadership and direction for the short duration of the group.

Representatives from the Republic New York Corporation, the country's 23rd largest banking company, and the Community Preservation Corporation, which devotes itself to the preservation and restoration of buildings in the New York City area, collaborate at the site of a Republic-financed Brooklyn housing rehabilitation project. Such collaboration between different groups is expected and normal in business so that common goals can be achieved.

Source: © William Taufic 1990 / Used by permission of Republic New York Corporation

Collaborative Written Communication

OBJECTIVE 8: List four guidelines for communicating collaboratively.

As a manager, you will write many documents on your own, with minimal supervision or input from others. Memorandums, letters, status reports, and other routine documents are typically written by one person. Many situations, however, require collaborative efforts, as a result of such factors as these:

- Time constraints
- Complexity of the task
- Length of the document
- Importance of the document
- Need to have various viewpoints represented
- Need for consensus

About three-fourths of all professionals write collaboratively on the job, and most of them enjoy the experience.[9] They believe that the benefit of producing a better document through joint effort outweighs the costs of time, energy, and—sometimes—ego. Collaborative experiences permit them to sharpen their managerial skills of building consensus, looking at an issue from different perspectives, listening, and respecting the views of others.

The most interaction among group members typically occurs at the beginning and end of a project. Although the interactions generally occur face-to-face, they may also involve written comments or technological media (electronic mail). In fact, an entirely new class of software, called "groupware," has come into being, which enables numerous people to insert their comments on a draft document directly onto the document via computer.

Typically, the group meets to plan the document jointly. During this phase, the group defines the purpose of the document, identifies the audience, and discusses the content and organization of the document. They may also divide the project into subparts, with individuals assigned to complete each task. Finally, deadlines are set and future meetings are planned.

One of the potential bottlenecks in collaborative writing is the amount of time and effort required for group members to revise the working draft of the document. Scheduling a meeting of the group, having each member present his or her revisions, and then discussing each comment is time-consuming. However, a new class of software, called *groupware*, makes it easy for managers, editors, or other reviewers to edit and comment on the same document at the same time. In fact, anyone you select can make additions, deletions, or corrections to the document—all without altering the original text. Examples of such groupware are *Collaborative Writer* by Research Design Associates, *ForComment:* by Broderbund Software, and *MarkUp* by Mainstay, Inc.

Using *MarkUp*, for example, the author creates a document using his or her favorite word processing program and then copies it into *MarkUp* (thereby leaving the original version intact). The author then sends a copy of the *MarkUp* version of the document to other group members via electronic mail. Each member then keyboards whatever comments he or she wishes onto the image of the document on the computer screen. Short comments are entered directly on the document; longer comments can be entered in a special window on the screen. *MarkUp* also makes the standard proofreading symbols available to the reviewers.

Once all group members have made their comments, the author can then view each comment individually or merge them into one master document. A copy of the marked document with all the individual comments can then be printed for later review by the entire group, or the desired changes can be easily incorporated into the original document. This process can be accomplished individually by the author or collaboratively by using a large projection screen connected to a computer. A copy of an electronically revised document using *MarkUp* is shown below.

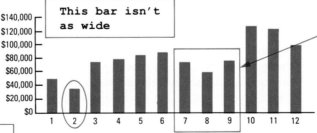

This initial group phase is often followed by a period of relatively independent work, with each individual completing his or her assigned tasks autonomously. Unless the group is especially cohesive, it is frustrating and time-consuming to try to produce a working draft sentence by sentence in a collaborative setting. Typically, instead, each member individually drafts the part of the document that is within his or her area of responsibility, expertise, or interest. Alternately, after extensive planning and discussion by the group, one individual may be assigned to produce a working draft of the whole document.

Regardless of how the draft is prepared, the group then reconvenes for collaborative revision of the first draft. After consensus has been reached regarding the content and organization, one person is typically assigned the task of editing the document to ensure that a consistent tone, voice, and language are used throughout the document and that the document has unity and coherence.

Guidelines for Communicating Collaboratively

Even when the ultimate goal of a group is a written document, collaboration typically requires both oral and written communication skills. The following guidelines will help you achieve your communication goals.

If the group is too large, group members begin to form cliques, or subgroups.

Select an Appropriate Group Size   Two to seven members seems to be the maximum size range for effective work groups; small-group research indicates that five is an ideal size.[10] Smaller groups often do not have enough diversity of skills and interests to function effectively as a group, whereas in larger groups, group interaction often falls off as just a few people dominate the discussions.

Develop a Team Spirit   It is difficult to work effectively as a group if the group members do not know each other well and are not aware of each other's strengths and weaknesses, styles of working, past experiences, attitudes, and the like. Thus, the first task of most new groups is to get to know one another.

For small groups to function effectively, not only the task dimension but also the social dimension must be considered. Some amount of "small talk" about family, friends, current happenings, and the like before and after the meetings is natural and helps to establish a supportive and open environment.

Avoid "Groupthink"   Although group cohesiveness is a necessary condition for successful small-group communication, too much cohesiveness can result in what has been termed **groupthink,** the barrier to communication that results from an overstress on group cohesiveness that stifles opposing ideas and the free flow of information.[11] In groupthink, the pressure to conform is so great that negative information and contrary viewpoints are never even brought out in the open and discussed. Thus, the group loses the advantage of hearing and considering varying perspectives. In effective small-group communications, conflicts, differing opinions, and questions are considered an inevitable and essential part of the collaborative process.

Deal With Conflict Constructively   It is pointless and counterproductive to try to avoid conflict in small-group communication. Indeed, one purpose of collaborating on a project is to ensure that various viewpoints are heard so that a consensus as to the most appropriate course of action can emerge. Thus, conflict is a necessary part of the collaborative experience. If the group has worked on developing cohesiveness, on developing a team spirit or "groupness," it will be able to deal with disagreements as they arise.

Competent communicators welcome all contributions from group members, regardless of whether the members agree or disagree with their own views. They evaluate each contribution objectively and respond in a nonthreatening manner, with comments that are factual, constructive, and goal oriented. If the atmosphere becomes tense, they make a light comment, laugh, compliment, recall previous incidents, or take other helpful actions to defuse the situation and move the group forward. If conflict appears to be developing into a more or less permanent part of the group discussions, the group should put the topic of conflict on its agenda and then devote sufficient meeting time to discussing and working through the conflict.

Groups should avoid the temptation to resolve conflicts by making a scapegoat out of one member; for example, "We'd be finished with this report now if Sam had done his part; you never can depend on him." Rarely is one person solely responsible for the success or failure of a group effort. Because every member's role is a function of both his or her own personality and the group's personality, the group should consider how to help the person contribute more to the group's efforts. Figure 2.4 provides guidelines for dealing with nonproductive group members.

The Ethical Dimensions of Collaborative Communication

Accepting membership in a group implies acceptance of certain standards of ethical behavior. One of the most basic of these is to put the good of the group ahead of personal gain. Just as the successful ball player adopts the tenet "I don't care if I score a home run so long as my team wins," so also should the successful team player in the organization adopt the attitude "I don't care who gets the credit so long as we achieve our goal." Group members should avoid hidden agendas in their group actions and avoid advocating positions that might benefit them personally but that would not be best for the group.

Group members also have an ethical responsibility to respect the integrity and emotional needs of the other group members. Everyone's ideas should be treated with respect, and no action should be taken that results in a loss of self-esteem for a member.

Finally, each member has an ethical responsibility to promote the group's welfare—by contributing his or her best efforts to the group's mission and by refraining from destructive gossip, domination of meetings, and other counterproductive actions.

SUMMARY

International business depends very heavily on communicating effectively with people of different cultures. Language differences can cause problems, especially when translating slang and jargon. The meanings of nonverbal language also depend on the specific culture, especially the language of

FIGURE 2.4   Solving Problems in Small Groups

If a Group Member Creates a Problem		
Symptoms	Reasons	What to do
Member won't participate.	Excessive primary tension. Feels lack of acceptance and status.	Involve him in conversation. Find out about his personal interests. Listen with interest to what he says. Devote some time to him outside the discussion. When he does take part, make a special note of it. "That is a good point, Joe. We haven't been hearing enough from you. We appreciate hearing your position."
		Use questions to draw him out. Ask a direct, open-ended question so that only he can answer. Do not use a question that can be answered "yes" or "no," and, of course, do not ask a question that he might be unable to answer for lack of information.
Member is joker, life of the party.	Feels tension, wants to relieve it. Enjoys spotlight and likes to get laughs.	Encourage him when tensions need release. Laugh, compliment his wit. Ignore him when it is time to go to work and tensions are eased. He will soon learn that his role is the productive release of tensions and that he must not waste time laughing it up when the group should be discussing.
Member monopolizes discussion.	(a) Is involved in a role struggle. Is trying to impress group to achieve high status or leadership.	(a) Encourage her if she is contending for role that will benefit the group the most. If not, interrupt her and move to another discussant. In general, encourage the group to take care of her.

time and space, body language, and touching behavior. Finally, cultures differ in terms of the importance attached to group as opposed to individual behavior. Competent communicators maintain formality, show respect, remain flexible, and write and speak clearly when communicating with people of different cultures. They are also aware of the extent to which cultural diversity is a fundamental part of the American business organization.

Technology has a major effect on the way we communicate, especially word processing with all its related features for improving the writing process. Other forms of electronic communication include electronic mail, voice mail, electronic bulletin boards, facsimile, desktop publishing and presentations, and video teleconferencing. As a result of these developments, more information is becoming available to the manager, abstracting and early disclosure are becoming more important, a more informal style of writing is becoming common in certain situations, and collaborative communications are becoming more prominent.

Solving Problems in Small Groups (*Continued*)   FIGURE 2.4

If a Group Member Creates a Problem

Symptoms	Reasons	What to do
		OR
	(b) Is full of the subject and is sincerely eager to get to work.	(b) Don't embarrass him or be sarcastic. You will need him in this role later. Do not let him monopolize or give long speeches. Interrupt politely and throw the ball to another discussant with a question.
Member is argumentative, obstinate.	(a) Involved in role struggle.	(a) Keep your own temper. Understand she is not inherently obstinate but is so in the context of this discussion. Don't let the group get too tense and excited. Antagonism breeds further antagonism and secondary tension. Remember, the group is partly responsible for her behavior. What can the group do to change it?
		OR
	(b) Has strong personal convictions on topic.	(b) Examine his position carefully. Find merit in it if possible. Do not close your mind to the ideas just because they are expressed in an opinionated way. The group must examine all sides. In an emergency, tell him time is short and you will be glad to talk to him later. Talk to him privately before the next meeting. Explain that his view is important, the group will consider it, but he must not destroy group effectiveness.

Source: Ernest G. Bormann and Nancy C. Bormann, *Effective Small Group Communication,* 4th ed. (Edina, Minn.: Burgess Publishing, 1988), pp. 143–144.

Regardless of the size of the organization, every business writer faces both legal and ethical questions when communicating orally and in writing. Legal questions arise with regard to defamation, invasion of privacy, and fraud or misrepresentation. In choosing what information to convey and which words and sentences to convey that information, we also make ethical choices—moral choices about what is right, even when no question of law is involved.

Within the organization, members periodically form into small groups such as operating, negotiating, creative, training, and ad hoc groups. The end result of many of these small groups is a collaboratively written document. For small groups to function effectively, the group should be of an appropriate size, develop a team spirit, avoid groupthink, and deal with conflict constructively. In addition, each group member should follow high standards of ethical conduct in order to help achieve the group goals.

KEY TERMS

Culture— The customary traits, attitudes, and behaviors of a group of people.

Defamation— A false and malicious statement that is communicated to others and that injures a person's good name or reputation.

Desktop presentation— The production of audiovisual aids such as transparencies, slides, and handouts using a microcomputer.

Desktop publishing— The writing, assembling, and designing of such publications as company newsletters, brochures, catalogs, and reports on a microcomputer.

Electronic bulletin board— An electronic message system accessible by computer connected to a phone line.

Electronic mail— Messages that are composed, transmitted, and usually read using a computer; also called *E-mail.*

Ethnocentrism— The belief that one's own group is superior.

Ethics— Rules of conduct that go beyond legal rules and tell people how to act when the law is silent.

Facsimile machine— A machine that scans a document, converts the data into electronic impulses, and then transmits these impulses over phone lines to a receiving machine that reconverts the impulses into a copy of the original document.

Fraud— A deliberate misrepresentation of the truth that is made to induce someone to give up something of value.

Groupthink— A barrier to communication that results from an overstress on group cohesiveness and that stifles opposing ideas and the free flow of information.

Invasion of privacy— Any unreasonable intrusion into the private life of another person or denial of a person's right to be left alone.

Libel— Defamation in a permanent form such as in writing or videotape.

Misrepresentation— A false statement made innocently with no intent to deceive the other party.

Slander— Defamation in a temporary form such as in oral communication.

Video teleconference— A system using cameras, monitors, and microphones to enable people in different locations to hold meetings that simulate face-to-face meetings.

Voice mail— A communication system that allows users to speak into a phone and have their messages recorded electronically on computer disk.

Word processing— The production of letters, memorandums, reports, and other documents through the use of automated electronic equipment.

REVIEW AND DISCUSSION

▶ OBJECTIVE 1

1. How do cultures differ in terms of time, body language, touch, and space?

▶ OBJECTIVE 1

2. What implications does the Japanese emphasis on the group, rather than on the individual, have for communication?

3. What are four strategies for communicating across cultures? Give an example of each. OBJECTIVE 2 ◀

4. Why is it important for all managers to be knowledgeable about and comfortable with people of different cultures in this country? OBJECTIVE 3 ◀

5. What components of the word processing environment are available to improve writing? OBJECTIVE 4 ◀

6. "Thank goodness I don't have to worry about spelling and typing errors, because I have a spelling checker on my computer." Discuss the validity of this statement. OBJECTIVE 4 ◀

7. What is the difference between desktop publishing and desktop presentations? OBJECTIVE 4 ◀

8. What are four implications of technology on communications? OBJECTIVE 5 ◀

9. Define defamation and describe the two types. OBJECTIVE 6 ◀

10. What is the difference between fraud and misrepresentation? OBJECTIVE 6 ◀

11. "Communicating is an ethical act." Discuss this statement. OBJECTIVE 6 ◀

12. What types of small groups typically operate in the organization? OBJECTIVE 7 ◀

13. Describe the typical process for writing a document collaboratively. OBJECTIVE 8 ◀

EXERCISES

1. **International**—Joe arrived 15 minutes late for his appointment with Itaru Nakamura, sales manager for a small manufacturer to which Joe's firm hoped to sell parts. "Sorry to be late," he apologized, "but you know how Japanese drivers are. At any rate, since I'm late, let's get right down to brass tacks." Joe began to pace back and forth in the small office. "The way I see it, if you and I can come to some agreement this afternoon, we'll be able to get the rest to agree. After all, who knows more about this than you and me?" Joe sat down opposite his colleague and looked him straight in the eye. "So what do you say, can we agree on the basics and let our assistants hammer out the details?" His colleague was silent for a few moments, then said, "Yes." Discuss Joe's intercultural skills. Specifically, what things did he do wrong? What did his Japanese colleague's response probably mean? OBJECTIVES 1–3 ◀

2. **Translations**—Locate two foreign-born people from the same country who speak English as a second language. First, ask one of them to translate literally into his or her native language the following ad slogans, taken from a recent business magazine. Then give the foreign-language translation to the second person and ask that person to retranslate the slogans into English. Compare the original and the retranslated English versions. What are the implications of any mistranslations? OBJECTIVES 1–3 ◀

   - "We took a great idea and made it fly" (Samsonite)
   - "Digital has it now" (Digital)
   - "The heartbeat of America" (General Motors)
   - "Satisfy your lust for power and money" (NEC)
   - "In touch with tomorrow" (Toshiba)

3. **Collaboration**—Working in small groups, interview at least three foreign students or professors, each from a different country. For each OBJECTIVES 1–3, 7–8 ◀

country represented, determine the types of written and oral communications common in business, the extent of technological development, problems with the English language, and examples of slang used in their native language. Prepare a written summary of your findings, proofread, revise as necessary, and submit.

OBJECTIVES 4–5

4. **Technology**—You are the fleet manager for a magazine distributor. You have been asked to write a report on the feasibility of leasing versus purchasing your fleet of delivery vans. Give a specific example of how you might productively make use of each of these technological innovations: electronic mail, voice mail, electronic bulletin board, facsimile machine, desktop publishing, desktop presentation, and video teleconference.

OBJECTIVES 4–5

5. **Telecommuting**—Assume that you are an advertising copywriter for a large pharmaceutical firm in Los Angeles. After the birth of your first child last month, you wish to work out of your home for the next twelve months, staying in contact with the office through electronic communications. Prepare a list of the equipment you will need and how you will use each piece of equipment. What advantages and disadvantages of this arrangement (called *telecommuting*) do you see for yourself? For your company?

OBJECTIVE 6

6. **Legal**—Sam was thinking of hiring Olivia Mason for an open sales territory. Knowing she had previously worked at Kentron, he called his friend there, Barry Kelley, to ask about her performance. "She's very smart, but I wouldn't hire her again, Sam," Barry said. "She's a little lazy. Sometimes she wouldn't begin making her calls until late morning or even after lunch. And she was also sloppy with her paperwork. I assume she's honest, but I never could get her to file receipts for all her expenses. Of course, she was going through a messy divorce then, so maybe that affected her job performance." Sam thanked his friend and notified Olivia that she was not being hired for the job. If Olivia learned of Kelley's comments, would she have the basis for a legal suit? If so, what type and on what grounds? How could Kelley have reworded his comments to convey the information in a legal manner?

OBJECTIVE 6

C A S E   P R O B L E M ───────────

Urban Systems Sees the Light

Marc Kaplan asked Dave to approve the following draft sales letter, which Marc wanted to mail out next month to the 4,200 members of OFA (Office Furniture Association) as the kick-off campaign for Urban System's Ultra Light Strips. Dave had read the letter twice and had still not approved it. Something about the tone of the letter bothered him.

```
Dear Manager:

Would you like us to come visit you in jail?

Now, it's true that you probably won't be put in jail
for requiring your computer operators to sit in front
```

of a monitor eight hours a day, but you just might get slapped with a lawsuit from a disgruntled employee who complains of back problems or failing eyesight. One pregnant employee even won damages by blaming her miscarriage on emotional stress caused by too many hours at her word processor! And two studies published this past year that warn of dangers from long periods of working at a computer don't help the situation any.

Before going to your lawyer, come to US--to Urban Systems--for the answer to your problems. We have just patented a new strip lighting system for modular furniture that will throw precisely the right amount of soft light around the monitor. With Ultra Light Strips, your operators won't have to put up with glare from their monitors, they won't have to position themselves in a certain way just to read the monitor, and they won't have shadows falling on their copy holders.

And if wiring is in place, even your secretary can install Ultra Light Strips. Just order the lengths you need—from one foot to twenty feet long. They are completely flexible, so that you can easily bend them around your modular furniture. And because they attach with Velcro strips, you can move them around and reuse them as your needs change.

We're really the only game in town when it comes to flexible task lighting. For example, the Mod Light by GME produces 200 foot-candles--far too much light to provide the needed contrast between the screen and surrounding light; your operators will soon begin to make careless errors from visual fatigue. And the Light Mite from Tedesco has long had a reputation for poor reliability. In addition, both GME and Tedesco produce their light fixtures abroad, while Ultra Light Strips are 100 percent American-made!

With Ultra Light Strips lighting the way, your operators will be more productive, easily paying the cost of these strips within the first six months of use. Get a jump on the competition. And avoid those costly legal battles. Call us toll-free at 1-800-555-2883 for a free on-site demonstration. We can also show you the many other uses of Ultra Light that will save your company money.

Sincerely,

Marc Kaplan
Vice President--Marketing

1. What is your reaction to this letter? Is it effective or not? Is it ethical?

2. If this letter represented your only knowledge of Urban Systems, what would be your opinion of the company? In other words, what kind of image does the letter portray of US?

3. Does this letter accurately reflect Marc Kaplan's personality? Explain.

4. Without actually rewriting the letter, what revision suggestions can you make for giving this letter a more ethical tone?

WORDWISE

▪ The commonest family name in the world is the Chinese name Chang (Zhang), which is used by at least 104 million people. No Chinese surname has more than one syllable.

▪ The word *automation* did not appear in a dictionary until 1952; however, the word *crummy*, to mean something undesirable, has been around approximately 400 years.

▪ The Bedouin has 160 words for "camel." The Eskimo has more than 100 words for "ice," but no word for "hello" or "goodbye."

PART

*Developing
Your
Writing
Skills*

Writing with Style: Individual Elements

Communication Objectives

After you have finished this chapter, you will be able to

1. Write clearly.

2. Prefer short, simple words.

3. Write with vigor.

4. Write concisely.

5. Prefer positive language.

6. Use a variety of sentence types.

7. Use active and passive voice appropriately.

8. Avoid sentence fragments and run-on sentences.

9. Keep paragraphs unified and coherent.

10. Control paragraph length.

"**D**on't do it right the first time" may sound like a strange piece of advice, but it's exactly what professional writing coach Frank Sanitate tells the lawyers, accountants, and corporate executives who attend his writing seminars. Sanitate thinks that those writers who balk at setting down anything but the perfect word place themselves on the fast track to that dreaded paralysis known as "writer's block." His solution? Write first, think later.

"The way I show people is the *opposite* of what they teach in high school," says Sanitate, who once taught high school English and who worked as an administrator for the American Institute of Certified Public Accountants before he started his consulting company, Sanitate Associates. "I have people just be spontaneous. You can worry about cleaning it up at the editing stage. Self-criticism impedes thinking. It's like having a boss or a teacher looking over your shoulder while you write. That's not conducive to good work."

In offering that advice, Sanitate plays a word game with his clients. The "editing stage," during which writers are supposed to clean up their writing, is just Sanitate's term for writing with good style. This trick helps writers get words on paper. After they do, Sanitate then concentrates on fixing word usage. Wrong verb usage, says Sanitate, is particularly common.

"We do a lot of work on verbs. We stress the active rather than the passive voice. There is a problem, particularly in the legal profession, with the use of

Frank Sanitate, President
Sanitate Associates, Santa
Barbara, California

jargon and technical writing. The way I deal with that comes under the category of 'simplify.' Because we have three vocabularies—reading, writing, and speaking—I first have them *speak* what they want to say. When they speak it, they use simpler words."

Next, says Sanitate, he encourages his writers to use verbs that, while they may be less simple than spoken language, are stronger. He reminds writers that the English language offers many words that can be used to say the same thing. "Some of those words have Latin roots," says Sanitate. "Some have Anglo-Saxon roots. I encourage people to use the Anglo-Saxon rather than the Latin."

Then Sanitate tackles another very common problem: longwindedness. For most writers, says Sanitate, the toughest thing to learn is brevity. "They tend to write to impress rather than express," says Sanitate. They're too wordy, and they're too stuffy. I tell them to get to the point.

"The way I teach unity and coherence is through the concept of accountability. Accountability comes from countability. I tell them to keep track of the ideas. If you have five ideas to get across, show your reader all five ideas clearly. If you have 25 ideas, show all 25. In order for business writing to be effective, it has to either inform or get some kind of action. The object is not to entertain or to please. You have got to be brief and direct. That in itself is a style." ▼

WHAT DO WE MEAN BY STYLE?

If you study the five LAB exercises in Appendix A, you will know how to express yourself *correctly* in most business writing situations. That is, you will know how to avoid major errors in grammar, spelling, punctuation, and word usage. But a technically correct message may still not achieve its objective. For example, consider the following paragraph:

> During the preceding year just past, Oxford Industries operated at a financial deficit. It closed three plants. It laid off many employees. The company's president was recently named Iowa Small Business Executive of the Year. Oxford is now endeavoring to ascertain the causes of its financial exigency.

Your writing can be error-free and still lack style, but it cannot have style unless it is error-free.

This paragraph has no grammatical, mechanical, or usage errors. But it is not clear, vigorous, and coherent. For example, consider the phrase "preceding year just past." "Preceding" *means* "just past." So why use both terms? In the second sentence, was closing the three plants the *cause* or the *result* of the financial deficit? What is the point of the sentence about the president? If you were speaking instead of writing, would you really say, "endeavoring to ascertain," or would you use simpler language, like "trying to find out"? Finally, there is no transition or bridge between the sentences; they don't read smoothly.

Although the paragraph is technically correct, it lacks **style**. By style, we mean the way in which an idea is expressed (not its *substance*). That is, style is the particular words the writer uses and how the writer combines those words into sentences, paragraphs, and complete messages.

Now compare the first-draft paragraph with this revised version:

> Last year Oxford Industries lost money and, as a result, closed three plants and laid off 200 employees. Now the company is trying to determine the causes of its problems. In explaining the situation to stockholders, Oxford's president, who was recently named Iowa Small Business Executive of the Year, said that . . .

The revised version is more direct and readable. It clarifies relationships among the sentences. It uses concise, familiar language. It presents ideas in logical order. In short, it has style.

Chapters 3 and 4 discuss 16 principles of effective writing style for business. Apply these principles of style as you write the letters, memos, and reports that follow in later chapters.

Words:

1. Write clearly.
2. Prefer short, simple words.
3. Write with vigor.
4. Write concisely.
5. Prefer positive language.

> Style is the effectiveness of the words, sentences, paragraphs and tone of your message.

Sentences:

6. Use a variety of sentence types.
7. Use active and passive voice appropriately.
8. Avoid sentence fragments and run-on sentences.

Paragraphs:

9. Keep paragraphs unified and coherent.
10. Control paragraph length.

Overall Tone:

11. Write confidently.
12. Use a courteous and sincere tone.
13. Use appropriate emphasis and subordination.
14. Use nondiscriminatory language.
15. Stress the "you" attitude.
16. Write at an appropriate level of difficulty.

While writing the first draft, you should be more concerned with content than with style. Your major objective should be to get your ideas down in some form, without worrying about style and **mechanics**. (Mechanics are elements in communication that show up only in written form, including spelling, punctuation, abbreviations, capitalization, number expression, and word division.)

The more familiar you are with these basic principles, the easier it will be to write your first draft and the less editing you will need to do later.

So learning these principles first makes your writing process more efficient. You then return to these principles when you revise your writing to make sure that you have followed each guideline.

Principles 1–10 focus on the *parts* of the message (words, sentences, and paragraphs) and are discussed in this chapter. Principles 11–16 focus on the tone of the *whole* message and are discussed in the next chapter. At the end of that chapter, a checklist summarizes these 16 principles. You can use the checklist in evaluating your own writing.

CHOOSING THE RIGHT WORDS

Individual words are our basic units of writing, the bricks with which we build meaningful messages. All writers have access to the same words. The care with which we select and combine words can make the difference between a message that achieves its objective and one that does not. Here are five principles of word choice: write clearly, prefer short and simple words, write with vigor, write concisely, and prefer positive language.

▼

OBJECTIVE 1: Write clearly.

1. Write Clearly.

The basic guideline for writing, the one that must be present in order for any of the other principles to have meaning, is to write clearly—to write messages the reader can understand, depend on, and act on. You can achieve clarity by making your message accurate and complete, by using familiar words, and by avoiding dangling expressions and unnecessary jargon.

Accuracy is *the* most important attribute in business writing. It involves more than freedom from error.

Being Accurate   A writer's credibility is perhaps his or her most important asset, and credibility depends greatly on the accuracy of the message. If, by carelessness, lack of preparation, or a desire to manipulate words, a writer misleads the reader, the damage is immediate and long-lasting. A reader who has been fooled once may not trust the writer again.

Accuracy can take many forms. The most basic is the truth of facts and figures presented. But accuracy involves much more. For example, consider the following sentence from a memo to a firm's financial backers:

> The executive committee of Mitchell Financial Services met on Thursday, May 28, to determine how to resolve the distribution fiasco.

Suppose, on checking, the reader learns that this year May 28 fell on a Wednesday instead of a Thursday. Immediately, the reader may suspect everything else in the message. The reader's thinking might be, "If the writer made this error that I *did* catch, how many other errors that I *didn't* catch are lurking there?"

Now consider more subtle shades of truth. The sentence implies that the committee met, perhaps in an emergency session, for the *sole* purpose of solving the distribution fiasco. But suppose this matter was only one of five agenda items being discussed at a regularly scheduled meeting. Is the statement still accurate? Suppose the actual agenda listed the topic as "Discussion of recent distribution problems." Is "fiasco" the same as "problems"?

The accuracy of a message, then, depends on what is said, how it is said, and what is left unsaid. Each writer must assess the ethical dimensions of his or her writing and use integrity, fairness, and good judgment to make sure communication is ethical.

> Ethical communicators make sure the overall tone of their messages is accurate.

Being Complete   Closely related to accuracy is completeness. A message that lacks important information may create inaccurate impressions. A message is complete when it contains all the information the reader needs— no more and no less—to react appropriately.

As a start, answer the five W's; tell the reader *who, what, when, where,* and *why.* Leaving out any of this information may result either in decisions based on incomplete information or in extra follow-up correspondence to gather the needed information. Answering *why* questions is particularly important when you write persuasive and negative messages. For example, if you tell me that I've been promoted, *why* is not uppermost in my mind. However, if you tell me that my promotion was denied, I'll want to know *why* before I accept the decision. Similarly, if you want to persuade me to do something, you must explain *why.*

Using Familiar Words   Your message must be understood in order for someone to act on it. So you must use words that are both familiar to you (so that you will not misuse the word) and familiar to your readers.

> Use language that you and your reader understand.

A true story illustrates this point. A young soldier, serving in Vietnam as a typist for a general, received a report he thought the general should see. Believing that "for your edification" meant "for your information" (it means "for your *improvement*"), the typist wrote "Sir: For your edification" on the report and sent it to the general. Back came the general's reply: "Private: First, look up the word *edification.* Then see me for *your* edification!"

Don't assume that only long, multisyllabic words cause confusion. Consider the following sentences:

Not: The <u>hexad</u> worked with <u>élan</u> in order to <u>redact</u> their report and <u>eloign</u> their guilt.

But: The group of six vigorously edited their report to conceal their guilt.

The first version consists entirely of short words, with the longest word having just six letters and two syllables. Probably only a crossword puzzle addict, however, would be able to understand the first version; most readers would understand the second.

Long words are sometimes useful in business communication. Could you use each of the following words correctly in a business-related sentence?

acrimony	efficacious	plethora
anomalies	egress	probative
attenuation	halcyon	remandatory
cognizance	parietal	subrogation

Before you decide that such words are unimportant in business writing, you should know that these words came from a word list based on a computer analysis of actual business letters, memos, and reports.[1] The larger your vocabulary and the more you know about your reader, the better equipped you will be to choose and use correctly words that are familiar to your reader.

Avoiding Dangling Expressions   A **dangling expression** is any part of a sentence that doesn't logically fit in with the rest of the sentence. Its relationship with the other parts of the sentence is unclear; it "dangles." To correct dangling expressions, (1) make the subject of the sentence the doer of the action expressed in the introductory clause; (2) move the expression closer to the word that it modifies; (3) make sure that the specific word to which a pronoun refers is clear; or (4) otherwise revise the sentence.

> *Not:* After reading the proposal, a few problems occurred to me. *(As written, the sentence implies that "a few problems" read the proposal.)*
> *But:* After reading the proposal, I noted a few problems.

> *Not:* Dr. Ellis gave a presentation on the use of drugs in our auditorium. *(Are drugs being used in the auditorium?)*
> *But:* Dr. Ellis gave a presentation in our auditorium on the use of drugs.

> *Not:* Robin explained the proposal to Joy, but she was not happy with it. *(Who was not happy—Robin or Joy?)*
> *But:* Although not happy with the proposal, Robin explained it to Joy. *(Robin is not happy.)*
> *Or:* Robin explained the proposal to Joy, but Joy was not happy with it.

> *Not:* You may take your vacation the last week in June or the first week in July; but in that case, you will need to submit your status report early. *(In which case will you have to submit your report early?)*
> *But:* You may take your vacation the last week in June or the first week in July; but if you choose the last week in June, you will need to submit your status report early.

Avoiding Unnecessary Jargon   Jargon is technical vocabulary used within a special group. Every field has its own specialized words, and jargon offers a precise and efficient way of communicating with people in the same field. But problems arise when jargon is used to communicate with someone who does not understand it. For example, to a banker the term *CD* means a certificate of deposit, but to a stereo buff or computer user it means compact disk. Even familiar words can be confusing when given a specialized meaning.

> *Not:* Your incorrect bill was caused by a computer virus, which disabled the error-lockout function, resulting in encrypted data.
> *But:* Your incorrect bill was caused by a temporary software problem, which let unreadable data be entered into the computer.

The original sentence *might* be appropriate when communicating with other information specialists. In this case, a utility company was explaining to a customer why she had received a bill for "$#@a.00." The explanation was probably as unreadable as the bill had been!

Does the field of business communication have jargon? It does—just look at the Key Terms list at the end of each chapter. The word *jargon* itself might be considered business communication jargon. In this text, such terms are first defined and then used to make communication precise and efficient. Competent writers use specialized vocabulary to communicate

Sometimes jargon is appropriate.

with specialists who understand it. And they *avoid* using it when their readers are not specialists.

2. Prefer Short, Simple Words.

Short and simple words are more likely to be understood, less likely to be misused, and less likely to distract the reader. Literary authors often write to *impress*—they select words to achieve a specific reader reaction, such as humor, excitement, or anger. Business writers write to *express;* we want to achieve *comprehension.* We want our readers to focus on our information, not on how we convey it. Using short, simple words helps us achieve this goal.

> *Not:* To recapitulate, the interminable delays were precipitated by our utilization of adulterated water.
>
> *But:* To review, the endless delays were caused by our use of impure water.

It is true, of course, that often no short, simple word is available to convey the precise shade of meaning we want. For example, there is no one-syllable word that means the same thing as *ethnocentrism* (the belief that one's own group is better), a concept introduced in Chapter 2. Our guideline is not to use *only* short and simple words but to *prefer* short and simple words. (As Mark Twain noted, because he was being paid by the word for his writing, "I never write 'metropolis' for seven cents because I can get the same price for 'city.' I never write 'policeman' because I can get the same money for 'cop.'")

Here are some examples of needlessly long words, gleaned from various business documents, with shorter substitutes shown in parentheses:

ascertain	(learn)	initiate	(start)
encompass	(include)	modification	(change)
endeavor	(try)	recapitulate	(review)
enumerate	(list)	reproduction	(copy)
fabricate	(make)	subsequent	(after)
fluctuate	(vary)	substantial	(large)
illustrate	(show)	termination	(end)
indispensable	(vital)	utilization	(use)

You needn't strike these long words totally from your written or spoken vocabulary; any one of these words, used in a clear sentence, would be acceptable. The problem is that a writer may tend to fill his or her writing with very long words when simpler ones could be used. Use long words in moderation.

You've probably heard the advice "Write as you speak." While not universally true, such advice is pretty close to the mark. Of course, if your conversation is peppered with redundancies, excessive jargon, and clichés, you wouldn't want to put such weaknesses on paper. But typical conversation uses mostly short, simple words—the kind you do want on paper. Don't assume that the bigger the words you use, the bigger your intellect. In fact, you need a large vocabulary and a well-developed word sense to select the best word. And more often than not, that word is short and simple. Write to express—not to impress.

OBJECTIVE 2: Prefer short, simple words.

Short, simple words are the building blocks of effective business communications.

── COMMUNICATION **S I D E L I G H T** ──

DANGLING EXPRESSIONS

Can you identify the expressions below that "dangle"? The list was compiled from student papers, accident reports, and newspaper articles.

- Abraham Lincoln wrote the Gettysburg Address while traveling from Washington to Gettysburg on the back of an envelope.
- I was thrown from my car as it left the road. I was later found in a ditch by some stray cows.
- I had been driving for about 40 years when I fell asleep at the wheel and had an accident.
- The license fee for altered dogs with a certificate will be $3; and for pets owned by senior citizens who have not been altered, the fee will be $1.50.

- Safety experts say school bus passengers should be belted.
- Two Sisters Reunited After 18 Years in Checkout Counter
- Two cars were reported stolen by the Groveton police yesterday.
- Guilt, vengeance, and bitterness can be emotionally destructive to you and your children. You must get rid of them.
- Dr. Ruth To Talk About Sex With Newspaper Editors

Source: Compiled by Richard Lederer, *Anguished English: An Anthology of Accidental Assaults Upon Our Language* (Charleston, S. Car.: Wyrick & Co., 1987).

▼

OBJECTIVE 3: Write with vigor.

3. Write with Vigor.

Vigorous language is specific and concrete. Limp language is filled with clichés, slang, and buzz words. Vigorous writing holds your reader's interest. And unless your reader is at least interested enough to read your message, your writing can't possibly achieve its objective.

A second reason for writing with vigor has to do with language itself. Vigorous writing tends to lend vigor to the ideas presented. That is, a good idea looks even better dressed in vigorous language, and a weak idea looks even weaker when dressed in limp language.

Using Specific, Concrete Language   In Chapter 1, we discussed the communication barriers caused by overabstraction and ambiguity. When possible, choose specific words—ones that have a definite, unambiguous meaning. Likewise, choose concrete words—ones that bring a definite picture to your reader's mind.

> *Not:* The <u>vehicle</u> broke down <u>several</u> times.
> *But:* The delivery van broke down three times last week.

In the first version, what does the reader imagine when he or she reads the word *vehicle*—a golf cart? automobile? boat? space shuttle? Likewise, how many times is "several"—two? three? fifteen? The revised version clarifies what is meant. We could build even more meaning into the sentence by adding a modifier or two:

Build as much information as is needed into your sentences.

> The <u>ten-year-old</u> delivery van broke down three times <u>in the blizzard</u> last week.
>
> The <u>new</u> delivery van broke down three times last week <u>even though it was driven less than 50 miles</u>.

Now it is clear that the old van is usually reliable, while the new van may be a lemon.

Sometimes we do not need such specific information. For example, in "The president answered *several* questions from the audience and then adjourned the meeting,'' the specific number of questions is probably not important. But in most situations, watch out for words like *several, recently, a number of, substantial, a few,* and *a lot of.* You may need to be more precise.

Likewise, use the most concrete word that is appropriate; give the reader a specific mental picture of what you mean. Be sure that your terms convey as much meaning as the reader needs to react appropriately. Watch out for terms like *emotional meeting* (anger or gratitude?), *bright color* (red or yellow?), *new equipment* (postage meter or cash register?), and *a change in prices* (increase or decrease?).

> Concrete words present a vivid picture.

Avoiding Clichés, Slang, and Buzz Words   A **cliché** (pronounced *klee shay*) is an expression that has become monotonous through overuse. It lacks freshness and originality and may also send the unintended message that the writer couldn't be bothered to find language geared specifically to the reader.

> *Not:* Enclosed please find an application form that you should return at your earliest convenience.
> *But:* Please return the enclosed application form before the March 15 deadline.

Here are some other expressions that have become overused and that therefore sound trite and boring. Avoid them in your writing.

According to our records	It goes without saying that
Company policy requires/prohibits	Needless to say
Do not hesitate to	Our records indicate that
For your information	Please be advised that
If I can be of further assistance	Take this opportunity to
If you have additional questions	Thank you for your letter
In accordance with your request	Under separate cover
In reference to your letter of	

> Picture a person finding "Thank you for your letter" in all 15 letters he or she reads that day. How sincere and original does it sound?

As noted in Chapter 1, slang is an expression, often short-lived, that is identified with some specific group of people. If you understand each word in an expression but still don't see what it means in context, chances are you're having trouble with a slang expression. For example, read the following sentence:

> It turns my stomach the way you can break your neck and beat your brains out around here, and they still stab you in the back.

To anyone who isn't familiar with American slang (a nonnative speaker, for example), this sentence might seem to be about the body, because it refers to the stomach, neck, brains, and back. The real meaning, of course, is something like this:

> I feel really upset that this company just ignores hard work and loyalty when it makes decisions.

Avoid slang in most business writing, for several reasons. First, it is informal; and much business writing, although not formal, is still *businesslike* and calls for standard word usage. Second, slang is short-lived. A slang phrase used today may not be in use—and thus may not be familiar—in three years, when your letter is retrieved from the files for reference. Third, slang is identified with a specific group of people; and others in the general population may not understand the intended meaning. For these reasons, avoid terms such as the following in business writing:

can of worms	knock it off	sticky fingers
chew out	once-over	use your noodle
clip joint	pay through the nose	wiped out
go for broke	play up to	zonked out
hate one's guts	security blanket	

A **buzz word** is an important-sounding expression used mainly to impress other people. Because buzz words are so often used by government officials and high-ranking businesspeople—people whose comments are newsworthy—these expressions get much media attention. They become instant clichés and then go out of fashion just as quickly. At either end of their short life span, they cause communication problems. If an expression is currently being used by everyone, it sounds monotonous, lacking originality. If it is no longer being used by anyone, readers may not understand the intended meaning. Here are examples of recent "in" expressions:

bottom line	paradigm	scenario
global dimensions	parameter	viable
impact (verb)	pipeline	
interface	prioritize	

Be especially careful of turning nouns and other types of words into verbs by adding *-ize*. Such words as *agendize, prioritize, strategize, utilize,* and *operationalize* quickly become tiresome.

4. Write Concisely.

OBJECTIVE 4: Write concisely.

Businesspeople are busy. The information revolution has created more paperwork, giving businesspeople access to more data. Having more paperwork to analyze (and no extra time), managers want information presented in the fewest possible words. To achieve conciseness, make every word count.

Avoiding Redundancy   A **redundancy** is a word or phrase that needlessly repeats an idea that has already been expressed. Eliminating the repetition contributes to conciseness. Read these two sets of sentences:

Not: Signing both copies of the lease is a <u>necessary requirement</u>.
But: Signing both copies of the lease is necessary.
Or: Signing both copies of the lease is required.
Or: You must sign both copies of the lease.

Not: First <u>combine</u> the ingredients <u>together</u>.
But: First combine the ingredients.

A "requirement" is by definition "necessary," so both words are not needed. And "combine" means to bring "together." Using both words creates a redundancy. Don't confuse redundancy and repetition. Repetition—using the same word more than once—is sometimes used for emphasis. Redundancy, however, serves no purpose and should always be avoided.

Some redundancies are humorous, as in the classic Samuel Goldwyn comment, "Anybody who goes to a psychiatrist ought to have his head examined," or the sign in a jewelry store window, "Ears pierced while you wait," or the statement in an automobile advertisement, "Open seven days a week plus weekends." Most redundancies, however, are simply verbiage—excess words that consume time and space. Avoid them.

Do not use the unnecessary word *together* after such words as *assemble, combine, cooperate, gather, join, merge,* or *mix.* Do not use the unnecessary word *new* before such words as *beginner, discovery, fad, innovation,* or *progress.* And do not use the unnecessary word *up* after such words as *connect, divide, eat, lift, mix,* and *rest.* Also avoid the following common redundancies (use the words in parentheses instead):

| Make every word count.

advance planning   (planning)
any and all   (any *or* all)
basic fundamentals   (basic *or* fundamental)
but nevertheless   (but *or* nevertheless)
consensus of opinion   (consensus *or* opinion)
each and every   (each *or* every)
first and foremost   (first *or* foremost)
free gift   (gift)
good advantage   (advantage)
Jewish rabbi   (rabbi)
over again   (over)
past history   (history)
plan ahead   (plan)
repeat again   (repeat)
rules and regulations   (rules *or* regulations)
sum total   (sum *or* total)
true facts   (facts)
when and if   (when *or* if)

Avoiding Wordy Expressions   Although wordy expressions are not necessarily writing errors (as redundancies are), they do slow down the pace of the communication and should be avoided. For example, try substituting one word for a phrase whenever possible.

| Use the fewest number of words that will achieve your objective.

> *Not:* In view of the fact that the model failed twice during the time that we tested it, we are at this point in time searching for other options.
> *But:* Because the model failed twice when we tested it, we are now searching for other options.

The original sentence contains 28 words; the revised sentence, 16. You've "saved" 12 words. In his delightful book, *Revising Business Prose,* Richard Lanham speaks of a "lard factor": the percentage of words saved by "getting rid of the lard" in the sentence. In this case:

$$28 - 16 = 12; 12 \div 28 = 43\%$$

Thus, 43 percent of the original sentence was "lard," which fattened the sentence without providing any "nutrition." Lanham suggests, "Think of a lard factor (LF) of ⅓ to ½ as normal and don't stop revising until you've removed it."[2]

Here are other wordy phrases and their one-word substitutes.

Wordy	Concise
are of the opinion that	believe
due to the fact that	because
for the purpose of	for
in light of the fact that	since
in order to	to
in the event that	if
pertaining to	about
with regard to	about

Avoiding Hidden Verbs A **hidden verb** is a verb that has been changed into a noun form, weakening the action. Verbs are action words and should convey the main action in the sentence. They provide interest and forward movement. Consider this example:

> Carl made an <u>announcement</u> that he will give <u>consideration</u> to our request.

What is the real action? It is not that Carl "made" something or that he will "give" something. The real action is hiding in the nouns: Carl "announced" and "will consider." These two verb forms should be the main verbs in the sentence:

> Carl <u>announced</u> that he will <u>consider</u> our request.

Notice that the revised sentence is much more direct—and four words shorter (the lard factor was 33 percent). Here are some other examples of action that should be conveyed by verbs instead of being hidden in nouns:

Wordy (Hidden Verb)	Concise (Action Verb)
arrived at the conclusion	concluded
came to an agreement	agreed
gave a demonstration of	demonstrated
gave an explanation	explained
has a requirement for	requires
have a need for	need
held a meeting	met
made a payment	paid
performed an analysis of	analyzed

Using Other Techniques Other means of achieving conciseness are limiting your use of expletives, implying (rather than stating directly), and substituting adjectives for clauses.

An **expletive** is an expression such as *there is* or *it is* that begins a clause or sentence and for which the pronoun has no antecedent. Because the topic of a sentence that begins with an expletive is not immediately clear, use such sentences sparingly in business writing. Avoiding expletives also contributes to conciseness; see the following example:

> *Not:* <u>There has never been</u> any doubt on my part that <u>it is</u> likely that John will attend the meeting.
> *But:* I have never doubted that John will likely attend the meeting.

Changing verbs to nouns produces weak, uninteresting sentences.

The pronoun in an expletive does not stand for any other noun.

Sometimes you do not need to explicitly state some information; you can imply it instead.

Some information need only be implied.

Not: <u>We have received your recent letter</u> and are happy to provide the free samples you requested for your anniversary sale.

But: We are happy to provide the free samples you requested for your anniversary sale.

Finally, you can often use adjectives and adverbs instead of clauses to convey the needed information:

Not: This brochure, <u>which is available free of charge,</u> will answer your questions.

But: This free brochure will answer your questions.

Not: <u>I have enclosed a price list</u> that shows quantity discounts and shipping charges.

But: The enclosed price list shows quantity discounts and shipping charges.

5. Prefer Positive Language.

Words that create a positive image are more likely to help you achieve your objective than negative words. For example, you are more likely to persuade someone to do as you ask if you stress the advantages of doing so rather than the disadvantages of *not* doing so. Positive language also builds goodwill for you and your company and often gives more information than negative language. Note the differences in tone and amount of information given in the following sentences:

OBJECTIVE 5: Prefer positive language.

Negative: The briefcase is not made of cheap imitation leather.
Positive: The briefcase is made of 100-percent belt leather for years of durable service.

Negative: We cannot ship your merchandise until we receive your check.
Positive: As soon as we receive your check, we will ship your merchandise by Federal Express.

Negative: I do not yet have any work experience.
Positive: My two terms as secretary of the Management Club taught me the importance of accurate recordkeeping and gave me experience in working with others.

Not only expressions like *cannot* and *will not* convey negative messages. Other words, like *mistake, damage, failure, refuse,* and *deny* also carry negative connotations and should be avoided when possible.

Avoid negative-*sounding* words.

Negative: Failure to follow the directions may cause the blender to malfunction.
Positive: Following the directions will ensure many years of carefree service from your blender.

Negative: We apologize for this error.
Positive: We appreciate your calling this matter to our attention.

Negative: We close at 7 P.M. on Fridays.
Positive: We're open until 7 P.M. on Fridays to give you enough time for shopping after work.

The subjunctive mood sounds more hopeful than an outright refusal.

Sometimes you can avoid negative language by switching to the subjunctive mood, which uses words like *wish, if,* and *would* to refer to conditions that are impossible or improbable. Such language softens the impact of the negative message, making it more palatable to the reader. Here are two examples:

> *Negative:* I cannot speak at your November meeting.
> *Subjunctive:* I <u>wish it were possible</u> for me to speak at your November meeting.
>
> *Negative:* I cannot release the names of our clients.
> *Subjunctive:* Releasing the names of our clients <u>would</u> violate their privacy.

In short, stress what *is* true and what *can* be done rather than what is not true and what cannot be done. This is not to say that negative language has no place in business writing. Such language is strong and emphatic, and sometimes you may want to use it. But unless the situation clearly calls for negative language, you are more likely to achieve your objective and to build goodwill for yourself and your company by stressing the positive.

Because words are the building blocks for your message, choose them with care. Using short, simple words; writing with clarity, vigor, and conciseness; and using positive language will help you construct effective sentences and paragraphs.

WRITING EFFECTIVE SENTENCES

The sentence is the basic unit of writing. It has a subject and predicate and expresses at least one complete thought. Beyond these simple attributes, however, sentences vary widely in style, length, and effect. They are also very flexible; writers can move sentence parts around, add and delete information, and substitute words in order to express different ideas and emphasize different points. To build effective sentences, use a variety of sentence types, use active and passive voice appropriately, and avoid fragments and run-on sentences.

6. Use a Variety of Sentence Types.

OBJECTIVE 6: Use a variety of sentence types.

There are three basic sentence patterns, all of which are used in business writing.

Simple Sentence   A **simple sentence** contains one independent clause (a clause that can stand alone as a complete thought). Because it presents a single idea and is usually (but not always) short, a simple sentence is often used for emphasis. Although a simple sentence contains only one independent clause, it may have a compound subject or compound verb (or both). All the following are simple sentences:

Use a simple sentence for emphasis and variety.

I quit.

Individual Retirement Accounts are a safe option.

Both Individual Retirement Accounts and Simplified Employee Pension Plans are safe and convenient options as retirement investments for the entrepreneur.

Compound Sentence   A **compound sentence** contains two or more independent clauses. Because each clause presents a complete idea, each idea receives equal emphasis. (If the two ideas are not closely related, they should be presented in two separate sentences.) Here are three compound sentences:

> Stacey listened, but I nodded.
>
> Morris Technologies made a major acquisition last year, and it turned out to be a disaster.
>
> Westmoreland Mines moved its headquarters to Prescott in 1984; however, it stayed there only five years and then moved back to Globe.

Use a compound sentence to show coordinate (equal) relationships.

Complex Sentence   A **complex sentence** contains at least one independent clause and at least one dependent clause. For example, notice the first sentence below. "The scanner will save valuable input time" is the independent clause because it makes sense by itself. "Although it cost $2,150" is the dependent clause because it does not make sense by itself.

> Although it cost $2,150, the scanner will save valuable input time.
>
> George Bosley, who is the new CEO at Hubbell, made the decision.
>
> I will be moving to Austin when I assume my new position.

Use a complex sentence to express subordinate relationships.

The dependent clause provides additional, but subordinate, information related to the independent clause. Sentences that contain two or more independent clauses and one or more dependent clauses are sometimes called *compound-complex sentences.*

Sentence Variety   Using a variety of sentence patterns and sentence lengths helps keep readers interested. Note how simplistic and choppy too many short sentences can be and how boring and difficult too many long sentences can be:

Too Choppy:

Golden Nugget will not purchase the Claridge Hotel. The hotel is 60 years old. The asking price was $110 million. It was not considered too high. Golden Nugget had wanted some commitments from New Jersey regulators. The regulators were unwilling to provide such commitments. Some observers believe that refusal was not the real reason for the decision. They blame the weak Atlantic City economy for the cancelation. Golden Nugget purchased the Stake House in Las Vegas in 1983. It lost money on that purchase. It does not want to repeat its mistake in Atlantic City. *(Average sentence length = 8 words)*

Too Long:

Golden Nugget will not purchase the Claridge Hotel, which is 60 years old, for an asking price of $110 million, which was not considered too high, because the company had wanted some commitments from New Jersey regulators, and the regulators were unwilling to provide such commitments. Some observers believe that refusal was not the real reason for the decision but rather that the weak Atlantic City economy was responsible for the cancelation; and since Golden Nugget purchased the Stake House in Las Vegas in 1983 and lost money on that purchase, it does not want to repeat its mistake in Atlantic City. *(Average sentence length = 50 words)*

The sentences in these paragraphs can be revised to show relationships clearly, to keep readers interested, and to improve readability. Use simple sentences for emphasis and variety, compound sentences for coordinate (equal) relationships, and complex sentences for subordinate relationships.

Golden Nugget will not purchase the 60-year-old Claridge Hotel, even though the $110 million asking price was not considered too high. The company had wanted some commitments from New Jersey regulators, which the regulators were unwilling to provide. However, some observers blame the cancelation on the weak Atlantic City economy. Golden Nugget lost money on its 1983 purchase of the Stake House in Las Vegas, and it does not want to repeat its mistake in Atlantic City. *(Average sentence length = 20 words)*

The first two sentences in the revision are complex, the third sentence is simple, and the last sentence is compound. The length of the four sentences ranges from 12 to 27 words. (In comparison with the revised paragraph, the version with choppy sentences has a lard factor of 17%, and the one with long sentences has a lard factor of 23%.)

To write effective sentences, use different sentence patterns and lengths. Most sentences in good business writing range from 16 to 22 words.

7. Use Active and Passive Voice Appropriately.

OBJECTIVE 7: Use active and passive voice appropriately.

Voice is the aspect of a verb that shows whether the subject of the sentence acts or is acted on. In the **active voice**, the subject does the action expressed by the verb. In the **passive voice**, the subject receives the action.

Active: Inmac offers a full refund on all orders.
Passive: A full refund on all orders is offered by Inmac.

Active: Shoemacher & Doerr audited their books in 1987.
Passive: Their books were audited in 1987 by Shoemacher & Doerr.

In active sentences, the subject performs the action; in passive sentences, the subject receives the action.

Passive sentences use some form of the verb *to be* with the main verb, so passive sentences are always somewhat longer than active sentences. In the first set of sentences just given, for example, compare "offers" in the active sentence with "is offered by" in the passive sentence.

In active sentences, the subject is the doer of the action; in passive sentences, the subject is the receiver of the action. And because the subject gets more emphasis than other nouns in a sentence, active sentences emphasize the doer of the action and passive sentences emphasize the receiver of the action. In the second set of sentences, either version could be considered correct, depending on whether the writer wanted to emphasize the auditor or the books.

Avoid mixing the active voice and the passive voice within the same sentence.

Within the same sentence, it is generally best not to mix active and passive clauses.

Not: At Chemical Bank, we specialize in the needs of small businesses; and credit is made available for expansion.
But: At Chemical Bank, we specialize in the needs of small businesses and make credit available for expansion.

Use active sentences most of the time in business writing, just as you naturally use active sentences in most of your conversations. Note that verb voice has nothing to do with verb *tense,* which shows the time of the action. As the following sentences show, the action in both active and passive sentences can occur in the past, present, or future.

Not: A very logical argument was presented by Harold.
But: Harold presented a very logical argument.

Not: An 18% increase will be reported by the eastern region.
But: The eastern region will report an 18% increase.

Passive sentences are appropriate, however, when you want to emphasize the receiver of the action, when the person doing the action is either unknown or unimportant, or when you want to be tactful in conveying negative information. All the following sentences are correctly stated in the passive voice:

Protective legislation was blamed for the drop in imports.

Transportation will be provided to the construction site.

Several complaints have been received regarding the new policy.

Inappropriate charges are being made against the entertainment budget.

> Passive sentences are sometimes more effective than active sentences.

8. Avoid Fragments and Run-On Sentences.

A **sentence fragment** is a group of words that is not a complete sentence but that has been punctuated as if it were a complete sentence. A complete sentence must have at least one subject and verb and must contain at least one logically complete thought.

> OBJECTIVE 8: Avoid sentence fragments and run-on sentences.

Not: Carolyn spent most of her time in meetings. <u>Although she preferred to be out on the floor talking with customers.</u>
But: Carolyn spent most of her time in meetings, although she preferred to be out on the floor talking with customers.

Not: She found her job very boring. <u>Answering the phone and verifying the sales representatives' expense reports.</u>
But: She found her job of answering the phone and verifying the sales representatives' expense reports very boring.

Sentence fragments *may* be used in résumés—to save space—but not in narrative writing. If you are in doubt about whether a group of words is a complete sentence, first make sure that the expression has both a subject and verb. Then read the expression by itself. If it makes sense (if it contains a complete idea) without reference to the preceding or following sentence, then it is a complete sentence—and not a sentence fragment.

Also avoid using a **run-on sentence,** one that strings together too many ideas without giving the reader needed breaks.

Not: A lease is more beneficial than a purchase for the company's car fleet because it requires less initial cash outlay because only the monthly rental (and not the car's purchase price) needs to be paid yet we would not have to be too concerned about obsolescence because the lease usually runs for only 36 to 48 months also liability insurance is typically included in the monthly rental.

But: A lease is more beneficial than a purchase for the company's car fleet. It requires less initial cash outlay because only the monthly rental (and not the car's purchase price) needs to be paid. Yet we would not have to be too concerned about obsolescence because the lease usually runs for only 36 to 48 months. Also, liability insurance is typically included in the monthly rental.

Words, sentences, and paragraphs are all building blocks of communication. You have seen how using a variety of sentence types, using active and passive voice appropriately, and avoiding fragments and run-on sentences can help make your sentences more effective. Now you can combine sentences to form logical paragraphs.

DEVELOPING LOGICAL PARAGRAPHS

A paragraph is a group of related sentences that focus on one main idea. The main idea is often identified in the first sentence of the paragraph, known as a *topic sentence*. The body of the paragraph supports this main idea by giving more information, analyses, and examples. A paragraph is typically part of a longer message, although one paragraph can hold the entire message, especially in such informal communications as memorandums and electronic mail.

Paragraphs divide the topic into manageable units of information for the reader. Readers need a cue to tell them when they have finished a topic so that they can pause and refocus their attention on the next one. To serve this purpose, paragraphs must be unified and coherent, and they must be of an appropriate length.

9. Keep Paragraphs Unified and Coherent.

OBJECTIVE 9: Keep paragraphs unified and coherent.

Although closely related, unity and coherence are not the same. A paragraph has unity when all its parts work together to develop a single idea consistently and logically. A paragraph has coherence when each sentence links smoothly to the sentences before and after it.

Unity   A unified paragraph gives information that is directly related to the topic, presents this information in a logical order, and leaves out irrelevant details. The following paragraph is a middle paragraph in a memorandum arguing against the proposal that Collins, a baby-food manufacturer, should expand into producing food for adults:

[1] We cannot focus our attention on both ends of the age spectrum. [2] In a recent survey, two-thirds of the under-35 age group named Collins as the first company that came to mind for the category "baby-food products." [3] For more than 50 years we have spent millions of dollars annually to identify our company as *the* baby-food company; and market research shows that we have been successful. [4] Last year, we introduced Peas 'N Pears, our most successful baby-food introduction ever. [5] To now seek to position ourselves as a producer of food for adults would simply be incongruous. [6] Our well-defined image in the marketplace would make producing food for adults risky.

Gary Trudeau, a well-known social and political cartoonist, must always choose the right words. His language must be clear, concise, and vigorous. If it's not, Trudeau's message is sure to be lost.
© *Theo Westenberger/Sygma.*

The paragraph obviously lacks unity. Before reading further, rearrange the sentences to make the sequence of ideas more logical. You would probably decide that the overall topic of the paragraph is Collins's well-defined image as a baby-food producer. So Sentence 6 would be the best topic sentence. You might also decide that Sentence 4 brings in extra information that weakens paragraph unity and should be left out. The most unified paragraph, then, would be sentences 6, 3, 2, 5, and 1, as shown here:

> Our well-defined image in the marketplace would make producing food for adults risky. For more than 50 years we have spent millions of dollars annually to identify our company as *the* baby-food company; and market research shows that we have been successful. In a recent survey, two-thirds of the under-35 age group named Collins as the first company that came to mind for the category "baby-food products." To now seek to position ourselves as a producer of food for adults would simply be incongruous. We cannot focus our attention on both ends of the age spectrum.

A topic sentence is especially helpful for a long paragraph. It is usually put at the beginning of a paragraph. This position helps the writer focus on the topic, so the paragraph will have unity. And it lets the reader know immediately what the topic is.

Sometimes, however, you may want to put the major idea toward the end of the paragraph. For example, if you're communicating negative information, you may want to state your reasons for refusing before you actually make the refusal—which is the topic of the paragraph. Or, if you're trying to persuade someone to do something, you may want to describe the advantages of doing so before before you actually make the request.

Putting the major idea toward the end of the paragraph softens the effect of negative information.

Coherence is achieved by using transitional words, pronouns, repetition, and parallelism.

Coherence   A coherent paragraph weaves sentences together so that the discussion is integrated. The reader never needs to pause to puzzle out the relationships or reread to get the intended meaning. The major ways to achieve coherence are to use transitional words and pronouns, to repeat key words and ideas, and to use parallel structure.

Transitional words help the reader see the relationships between sentences. Such words may be as simple as an indication of sequence, as shown by the underlined words in the following paragraph:

> Ten years ago, Collins tried to overcome market resistance to its new line of baby clothes. <u>First,</u> it mounted a multimillion-dollar ad campaign featuring the Mason quintuplets. <u>Next,</u> it sponsored a Collins Baby look-alike contest. <u>Then</u> it sponsored two network specials featuring Dr. Benjamin Spock. <u>Finally,</u> it brought in the Madison Avenue firm of Morgan & Modine to broaden its image.

The words *first, next, then,* and *finally* clearly signal step-by-step movement. Now note the following logical transitions; the underlined words identify the relationships between sentences:

> I recognize, <u>however,</u> that Collins cannot thrive on baby food alone. <u>To begin with,</u> since we already control 73% of the market, further gains will be difficult. <u>What's more,</u> the current baby boom is slowing. <u>Therefore,</u> we must expand our product line. We must <u>also</u> expand our overseas operations.

These transitional words act as road signs, indicating where the message is heading and letting the reader know what to expect. Here are some commonly used transitional expressions:

Relationship	*Transitional Expression*
addition	also, besides, furthermore, in addition, moreover, too
cause and effect	as a result, because, consequently, hence, so, therefore, thus
comparison	in the same way, likewise, similarly
contrast	although, but, however, in contrast, nevertheless, on the other hand, still, yet
illustration	for example, for instance, in other words, to illustrate
sequence	first, second, third, then, next, finally
summary/conclusion	at last, finally, in conclusion, to summarize
time	after that, before that time, earlier, later, meanwhile, next, since then, soon, then

A second way to achieve coherence is to use pronouns. Because pronouns stand for words already named, using pronouns binds sentences and ideas together. The pronouns and their antecedents are underlined in the following paragraph:

> If Collins branches out with additional food products, one possibility would be a fruit snack for youngsters. <u>Funny Fruits</u> were tested in Columbus last summer, and <u>they</u> were a big hit. <u>Roger Johnson</u>, national marketing manager, says <u>he</u> hopes to build new food categories into a

$200 million business. <u>He</u> is also exploring the possibility of acquiring other established name brands. <u>These</u> acquired <u>brands</u> would let <u>Collins</u> expand faster than if <u>it</u> had to develop a new product of <u>its</u> own.

A third way to achieve coherence is to repeat key words. In a misguided attempt to appear interesting, writers sometimes use different terms for the same idea. For example, in discussing a proposed merger a writer may at different points use *merger, combination, union, association,* and *syndicate.* Or a writer may use the words *administrator, manager, supervisor,* and *executive* all to refer to the same person. Such "elegant variation" only confuses the reader, who has no way of knowing whether the writer is referring to the same concept or to slightly different variations of that concept. Avoid needless repetition, but use purposeful repetition to link ideas and thus to promote paragraph coherence. Here is a good example:

> Collins has taken several <u>steps</u> recently to enhance profits and project a stronger leadership position. One of these <u>steps</u> is streamlining operations. Collins's line of children's clothes was <u>unprofitable</u>, so it discontinued the line. Its four produce farms were likewise <u>unprofitable</u>, so it hired an outside professional <u>team</u> to manage them. This <u>team</u> eventually recommended selling the farms.

> *Purposeful repetition aids coherence; avoid needless repetition.*

The term **parallelism** means using similar grammatical structure for similar ideas; that is, matching adjectives with adjectives, nouns with nouns, infinitives with infinitives, and so on. Much widely quoted writing uses parallelism; for example, Julius Caesar's "I came, I saw, I conquered" and Abraham Lincoln's "government of the people, by the people, and for the people." Parallel structure smoothly links ideas, thereby enhancing coherence.

> *Parallelism refers to consistency.*

Not: The new dispatcher is <u>competent</u> and <u>a fast worker</u>.
But: The new dispatcher is <u>competent</u> and <u>fast</u>.

Not: One management consultant recommended either selling the children's-furniture division or its conversion into a children's-toy division.
But: One management consultant recommended either selling the children's-furniture division or converting it into a children's-toy division.

Not: The new grade of paper is <u>lightweight</u>, <u>nonporous</u>, and <u>it is inexpensive</u>.
But: The new grade of paper is <u>lightweight</u>, <u>nonporous</u>, and <u>inexpensive</u>.

Not: The training program will cover
    1. Vacation and sick leaves
    2. How to resolve grievances
    3. Managing your workstation

But: The training program will cover
    1. Vacation and sick leaves
    2. Grievance resolution
    3. Workstation management

Not: Gladys is not only <u>proficient in word processing</u> but also <u>in desktop publishing</u>.
But: Gladys is proficient not only <u>in word processing</u> but also <u>in desktop publishing</u>.

In the last set of sentences just given, note that correlative conjunctions (such as *both/and, either/or,* and *not only/but also*) must be followed by words in parallel form. Be especially careful to use parallel structure in report headings that have equal weight and in numbered lists.

Ensure paragraph unity by developing only one topic per paragraph and by presenting the information in a logical order. Ensure paragraph coherence by using transitional words and pronouns, repeating key words, and using parallel structure.

10. Control Paragraph Length.

OBJECTIVE 10: Control
paragraph length.

How long should a paragraph of business writing be? As with other considerations, the needs of the reader, rather than the convenience of the writer, should determine length. Paragraphs should help the reader by signaling a new idea as well as by providing a physical break. Long blocks of unbroken text look boring and needlessly complex. And they may unintentionally obscure an important idea buried in the middle (see Figure 3.1). On the other hand, a series of extremely short paragraphs can weaken coherence by obscuring the underlying relationships.

FIGURE 3.1   PARAGRAPH LENGTH

The two memorandums contain identical information. Which one looks more inviting to read? Why?

Essentially, there are no fixed rules for paragraph length, and occasionally one- or ten-sentence paragraphs might be efficient. However, most paragraphs of good business writers fall into the 60- to 80-word range—long enough for a topic sentence and three or four supporting sentences. Although a single paragraph should never discuss more than one major topic, complex topics often need to be divided into several paragraphs. Your purpose and the needs of your reader should ultimately determine paragraph length.

SUMMARY

For business writing to achieve its objectives, it must be clear. Use short, simple, specific, and concrete words, and avoid dangling expressions, clichés, slang, buzz words, and unnecessary jargon. Write concisely: avoid redundancies, wordy expressions, and hidden verbs. Finally, prefer positive language; stress what you *can* do rather than what you cannot do.

To keep reader interest, use a variety of sentence types, including simple, compound, and complex sentences. Make sure your writing is free of fragments and run-on sentences. Use the active voice to emphasize the doer of the action, and use the passive voice to emphasize the receiver.

Your paragraphs should be unified and coherent. Develop only one topic per paragraph, and use transitional words, pronouns, repetition, and parallelism. Although paragraphs of various lengths are desirable, most should range from 60 to 80 words. Help the reader follow your logic by avoiding very long paragraphs and avoiding strings of very short paragraphs.

KEY TERMS

Active voice— The form of a sentence in which the subject performs the action expressed by the verb.

Buzz word— An important-sounding term used mainly to impress people.

Cliché— An expression that has become monotonous through overuse.

Complex sentence— A sentence that has at least one independent clause and at least one dependent clause.

Compound sentence— A sentence that has two or more independent clauses.

Dangling expression— Any part of a sentence that does not logically fit the rest of the sentence.

Expletive— An expression such as *there is* or *it is* that begins a clause and for which the pronoun has no antecedent.

Hidden verb— A verb that has been changed into a noun, weakening the action in the sentence.

Mechanics— Those elements in communication that show up only in written form, including spelling, punctuation, abbreviations, capitalization, number expression, and word division.

Parallelism— Using similar grammatical structure to express similar ideas.

Passive voice— The form of a sentence in which the subject receives the action expressed by the verb.

Redundancy— A word or phrase that needlessly repeats an idea that has already been expressed.

Run-on sentence— A sentence that strings together too many ideas without giving the reader needed breaks.

Sentence fragment— A group of words that is not a complete sentence but that has been punctuated as if it were a complete sentence.

Simple sentence— A sentence that has one independent clause.

Style— The way in which an idea is expressed (rather than the substance of the idea).

REVIEW AND DISCUSSION

▶ OBJECTIVE 1

1. What is meant by the statement "Accuracy involves more than the veracity of facts and figures"?

▶ OBJECTIVES 1, 3, 4

2. Give an example of the following types of expressions (do not repeat any examples given in the text):

buzz word	jargon
cliché	redundancy
expletive	slang
hidden verb	

▶ OBJECTIVE 2

3. Substitute a shorter word for each of the following words:

accordingly	inexhaustible
aggregate	jurisdiction
analogous	materialize
characteristic	perpetuate
commence	stipulate
consequence	transmit
finalize	verification

▶ OBJECTIVE 4

4. Revise the following phrases, getting rid of the redundancies:

and etc.	component part
Easter Sunday	exact same
foreign imports	good benefits
important essentials	mutual cooperation
past experience	personal opinion
refer back	same identical
surrounded on all sides	very unique

▶ OBJECTIVE 4

5. Substitute one word for each of the following wordy expressions:

at the present time	few in number
in the amount of	in most cases
inasmuch as	it would appear that
until such time as	

▶ OBJECTIVE 5

6. Why is positive language more effective than negative language for achieving your objective?

▶ OBJECTIVE 6

7. What are the three sentence patterns? Under what circumstances should each pattern be used for best effect?

8. In business writing, about how long should the typical sentence and paragraph be? Should *all* sentences and paragraphs fall within these ranges? Why or why not?

OBJECTIVE 6 ◀

9. Distinguish between active and passive voice, and discuss when each should be used.

OBJECTIVE 7 ◀

10. Write a paragraph that has both a sentence fragment and a run-on sentence. Then revise to correct these errors.

OBJECTIVE 8 ◀

11. What is the difference between paragraph unity and paragraph coherence?

OBJECTIVE 9 ◀

12. List four ways to make a paragraph coherent.

OBJECTIVE 9 ◀

13. Write a sentence illustrating parallelism.

OBJECTIVE 9 ◀

14. Why should you not write extremely long paragraphs?

OBJECTIVE 10 ◀

EXERCISES

Directions: *Revise the following passages to avoid the writing weaknesses indicated. Do not completely rewrite the passages; just correct any style problems.*

1. **Jargon** *Revise the following paragraph, making it appropriate for a first-year college student who has never taken a communication course. If necessary, refer to the Key Terms section of Chapter 1.*

OBJECTIVE 1 ◀

Regardless of the medium selected, noise that is encountered along the channel during encoding and decoding enters the receiver's filter and affects message fidelity. In addition, distortion is a serious problem during serial communication, especially when it occurs as part of the organization's informal communication network.

2. **Short and Simple Words**

OBJECTIVE 2 ◀

The consultant demonstrated how our aggregate remuneration might be ameliorated by modifications in our propensities to utilize credit for compensating for services. She also endeavored to ascertain which of our characteristics were analogous to those of other entities for which she had fabricated solutions. She recommended we commence to initiate innumerable modifications in our procedures to increase cash flow, which she considers indispensable for facilitating increased corporate health.

3. **Specific and Concrete Words**

OBJECTIVE 3 ◀

In an effort to stimulate sales, Mallmart is lowering prices substantially on its line of consumer items. Sometime soon, it will close most of its stores for several days to provide store personnel time to change prices. Markdowns will range from very little on its line of laundry equipment to a great deal on certain sporting equipment. Mallmart plans to rely on advertising to let people know of these price reductions. In particular, it is considering using a popular television star to publicize the new pricing strategy.

4. **Clichés, Slang, and Buzz Words**

OBJECTIVE 3 ◀

At that point in time the corporate brass were under the gun; they decided to bite the bullet and let the chips fall where they may. They hired a head honcho with some street smarts who would be able to interface with the investment community. Financewise, the new top dog couldn't be beat. He was hard as nails and developed a scenario that would have the company back on its feet within six months. Now it was up to the team players to operationalize his plans.

OBJECTIVE 4

5. **Conciseness**   *(After revising this passage, determine the lard factor of the original version.)*

In spite of the fact that MBE denied wrongdoing, it agreed to a settlement of the patent suit for a price of $6.3 million. Industry sources were surprised at the outcome because the original patent had depreciated in value. In addition to the above, MBE also made an agreement to refrain from the manufacture of similar computers for a period of five years in length. It appears that with the exception of Emerson's new introductions, innovations in workstations will be few in number during the next few years.

OBJECTIVE 5

6. **Positive Language**

We cannot issue a full refund at this time because you did not enclose a receipt or an authorized estimate. I'm sorry that we will have to delay your reimbursement. We are not like those insurance companies that promise you anything but then disappear when you have a claim. As soon as we receive your receipt or estimate, we will not hold up your check. Our refusal to issue reimbursement without proper supporting evidence means that we do not have to charge you outlandish premiums for your automobile insurance.

OBJECTIVE 6

7. **Sentence Patterns**   *For each of the following lettered items, write a simple, a compound, and a complex sentence that incorporates both items of information. For the complex sentences, emphasize the first idea in each item.*

   a. Timothy was given a promotion/Timothy was assigned additional responsibilities
   b. Eileen is our corporate counsel/Eileen will write the letter on our behalf

OBJECTIVES 1, 4, 8, 9

8. **Dangling Expressions, Fragments, Parallel Structure, Redundancies, and Run-On Sentences**   *Edit the following paragraphs to eliminate grammatical errors. Do not completely rewrite the sentences; just correct any weaknesses.*

   a. As a young child, his father took him on business trips both to London and Paris. Before the war, when traveling was cheaper and an enjoyable experience.
   b. First and foremost, Alan Greenspan is a pragmatist. Not an idealist. The favorable advantage of that approach is that he is able to reach a consensus of opinion on most matters. He will announce his latest agreements at a news conference at 3 P.M. in the afternoon.
   c. Although many U.S. businesspeople and politicians agonize over the increasing size of Japanese investment in the United States, in actuality it is the British who continue to outpace all other European and Asian

nations in their eagerness to purchase U.S. companies and to establish a firm foothold in U.S. real estate as one means of helping to protect their domestic investments from the widely fluctuating pound as well as attempting to maximize their long-term investments.

d. The reason that business investment fell at a rate of 4 percent last year and spending for equipment declined, pulled down by a drop in computer purchases. In trying to combat these declines, the Federal Reserve banks maintain excellent relations with the major financial institutions but they are still not doing as much as they had expected.

e. At Hanson we believe that earning stock appreciation for our investors is better than to make temporary profits. In other words, we do not mix up our long- and short-term goals; they are not one and the same. This corporate viewpoint has been in effect for many years; it is not a new innovation.

9. **Sentence Length** *Write a sentence (40–50 words) that attempts to make sense. Then revise the sentence so that it contains 10 or fewer words. Finally, revise the sentence so that it contains 16 to 22 words. Which sentence is the most effective? Why?*

OBJECTIVE 6 ◀

10. **Active and Passive Voice** *For each of the following sentences, first identify whether the sentence is active or passive. Then, if necessary, revise the sentence to use the more effective verb voice.*

OBJECTIVE 7 ◀

a. An out-of-court settlement of the discrimination suit filed by Marjorie Kramer has been agreed to by Morton Industries. The amount of the settlement was not disclosed.

b. We will begin using the new plant in 1993, and the old plant will be converted into a warehouse.

c. A very effective sales letter was written by Paul Mendleson. The letter will be mailed next week.

d. You failed to verify the figures on the quarterly report. As a result, $5,500 was lost by the company.

11. **Coherence** *Put logical transitions in the blanks to give the following paragraph coherence.*

OBJECTIVE 9 ◀

Columbia is widening its lead over Kraft in the computer-magazine war. _____ its revenues increased 27% last year whereas Kraft's increased only 16%. _____ its audited paid circulation increased to 600,000, compared to 450,000 for Kraft. _____ Kraft was able to increase both the ad rate and the number of ad pages last year. One note of worry ____ is Kraft's decision to shut down its independent testing laboratory. Some industry leaders believe much of Kraft's success has been due to its reliable product reviews. _____ Columbia has just announced an agreement whereby Stanford University's world-famous engineering school will perform product testing for Columbia.

▶ OBJECTIVES 1–10   C A S E   P R O B L E M   ——————————————

Stetsky Corrects the Boss

Amy Stetsky opened a new WordPerfect document on her computer and adjusted the headphones of her transcribing unit. She was ready to transcribe some dictation from Mr. Kaplan. The dictation was a first draft for part of a speech on the effects of proper lighting that Kaplan is going to deliver next month at a meeting of the Ann Arbor chapter of the Administrative Management Society. Here's what Stetsky heard:

```
Extensive research shows that lighting has a direct af-
fect on worker productivity and job satisfaction.
Lighting that is of appropriate quantity and quality
provides efficient comfortable illumination and a safe
work environment. They also help to develop a feeling
of visual comfort and an aesthetically attractive work
area. Which increases job satisfaction.

Appropriate lighting makes the task more visible thus
increasing both the speed and the accuracy of the work
performed. Inadequate amounts of light causes poor
workmanship inaccurate work and lowered production. For
example one study conducted by the general industrial
corporation showed that when illumination was temporar-
ily reduced by no more than five percent the output of
word processing operators decreased by twelve percent.
In addition the accuracy of all the operators each of
who were paid according to the number of correct lines
they produced decreased by eight percentage.

An other study at the interstate national bank showed
that errors in processing checks decreased by forty
percent when lighting was increased. The productivity
of the cash register clerks at a large outlet of united
food marts was reduced by twenty eight percent when
they were forced to work in reduced lighting for three
weeks because of store remodeling. According to the re-
searchers we also spoke with several clerks whom com-
plained about headaches and eyestrain and customers
whom complained about slow lines and errors in register
receipts.

As a result of such vision research forward looking fa-
cilities managers human development personnel and labor
unions are all beginning to monitor carefully the qual-
ity and quantity of illumination by which employees
perform their jobs. Farthermore they are looking to
technology to bring more flexibility more efficiency
and to provide higher quality illumination for the
seeing environment. In short they are looking at light
in a new light!
```

Stetsky routinely edits Mr. Kaplan's dictation as she keyboards it, correcting minor grammar and usage errors. As she transcribes, she also uses correct punctuation, capitalization, spelling, and word division. In short, Stetsky is a professional, and her work reflects it. Assuming the role of Stetsky, transcribe this dictation in double-spaced format (leaving one blank line between each line of type), making whatever editing changes are needed to correct errors in grammar, mechanics, punctuation, and usage.

▪ The word *usher* contains four personal pronouns in succession: *us, she, he,* and *her.*

▪ Only two common English words end in *-gry: angry* and *hungry.* Only one word ends in *-sede: supersede.*

▪ Why do we *drive* on a *parkway* but *park* on a *driveway?* Likewise, why is an *economy-sized* box of detergent *large* but an *economy-sized* automobile *small?*

Writing with Style: Overall Tone

After you have finished this chapter, you will be able to

1. Write confidently.

2. Use a courteous and sincere tone.

3. Use appropriate emphasis and subordination.

4. Use nondiscriminatory language.

5. Stress the "you" attitude.

6. Write at an appropriate level of difficulty.

If Mary Snyder, Corporate Communications Manager for Gerry Baby Products Company, painted her correspondences instead of writing them, her paintings would have two different styles. One style, which is used to interest editors of magazines like *Baby Talk, American Baby,* and *Women's Day* in writing about Gerry's products, would use warm colors to depict sweeping landscapes in a loose, semiabstract style. The other style, intended to get a message to people who sell Gerry products, would be less grand, more representational, and would rely heavily on contrasting colors. Writing to editors is different than writing to sales reps, says Snyder, even though you're writing about the same thing. "The idea," she explains, "is to establish the needs of your audience and then to write to those specific concerns, emphasizing what's important to them."

"When you write to consumer magazine editors you need to stay general," says Snyder. "They need what will appeal to their readers, to parent-consumers concerned with basic needs and product categories. A lot of the information you deliver to sales reps, on the other hand, is what's important in order to sell specific products to retail stores. All baby products are soft, warm, and wonderful, so that doesn't matter to the sales reps. The sales reps are into dollars and cents and so we communicate with them in hard facts. We tell them specific product features and we also tell them how to prioritize those features in closing a deal or comparing our product to a competitor's." It's important to be succinct and interesting, says Snyder, because the product that you're presenting isn't the only product the sales rep is selling. "Communications managers from other companies are competing for the same sales rep's attention. If it takes you too long to make a point, you may lose the contest. If

Mary Snyder, Corporate
Communications Manager
Gerry Baby Products
Company, Denver, Colorado

your competitor's writing style is smarter or more entertaining than yours, you may lose again."

"You try to have some spark in the writing," says Snyder. "You want them to pay attention to you. But you have to be specific. If you have something to say to sales reps, then say it. Don't be too 'rah, rah.' These are people who sell all kinds of baby products. They don't have time for 'rah, rah.' Tight, terse, and telegraphic is a good overall tone for writing to sales reps."

Snyder's correspondence to magazine editors, which is designed to initiate news coverage of Gerry products, requires a different strategy as well as a different overall tone; yet the reason for each tone is the same—to write in a way that benefits the particular audience. For magazine editors Snyder suggests an informational, calmly authoritative tone rather than an emphatic, telegraphic one. "Consumer magazines are not there to promote your product," says Snyder. "They are there to provide information to their readers." Their need, therefore, is for information about the whole industry. "Magazine editors pride themselves in separating advertising and editorial functions. They expect you to respect that."

"Acting as a general information source encourages editors and writers to call you rather than the communications manager who can only talk about his or her company's products. They find general-category information helpful. We keep tuned to what is happening in the industry and keep the lines open to the editors. Then when they contact us for something, we provide them with a great deal of information about a particular category. If you make it easier for them to get information, they will start to look to you as their information source."

"The way you fight getting lost among all the other companies," Snyder believes, "is to position yourself as a leader." And being a leader to any particular group is a matter of writing your message in terms that benefit that audience and in an overall tone that appeals to that audience. ▼

WHAT DO WE MEAN BY TONE?

Having chosen the right words to construct effective sentences and then having combined these sentences into logical paragraphs, we now examine the tone of the complete message—the entire letter, memorandum, report, sales brochure, or the like. **Tone** in writing refers to the writer's attitude toward the reader and the subject of the message. The overall tone of a written message affects the reader just as tone of voice affects people in everyday exchanges.

The business writer should strive for an overall tone that is confident, courteous, and sincere; that uses emphasis and subordination appropriately; that contains nondiscriminatory language; that stresses the "you" attitude; and that is written at an appropriate level of difficulty. (Style Principles 1–10 were presented in Chapter 3.)

11. Write Confidently.

Your message should convey the confident attitude that you have done a competent job of communicating and that your reader will do as you ask or will accept your decision. If you believe that your explanation is adequate, that your request is reasonable, or that your decision is based on sound logic, then you are likely to write with confidence. Such confidence has a persuasive effect on your audience.

OBJECTIVE 1: Write confidently.

Avoid using language that makes you look unsure of yourself. Be especially wary of beginning sentences with "I hope," "I trust," "If you agree," and similar self-conscious terms.

> If you believe what you have written, write in such a way that your reader does also.

Doubtful: <u>If</u> you'd like to take advantage of this offer, call our toll-free number.
Confident: To take advantage of this offer, call our toll-free number.

Doubtful: <u>I hope that</u> you will agree that my qualifications match your job needs.
Confident: My qualifications match your job needs in the following ways.

Doubtful: <u>I think that</u> we should proceed with this expansion for three reasons.
Confident: We should proceed with this expansion for three reasons.

Doubtful: <u>Why not</u> take advantage of our three-month trial subscription?
Confident: By taking advantage of our three-month trial subscription, you will experience for yourself the practical tips contained in each issue.

In some situations, the best strategy is simply to omit information. For example, you should not provide the reader with excuses for denying your request, suggest that something might go wrong or intimate that the reader might not be satisfied.

Doubtful: <u>I know you are a busy person, but</u> we would really enjoy hearing you speak.

Confident: The fact that you are involved in so many different enterprises makes your views on small business all the more relevant for our audience.

Doubtful: <u>If you experience any other problems,</u> please let us know.
Confident: Your GrassMaster lawn mower will now give you many years of trouble-free service.

Doubtful: <u>Although some employees have complained that the new uniforms are demeaning,</u> most employees like them.
Confident: Most of our employees like the look and comfort of the new uniforms designed by Bill Blaine.

Modest confidence is the best tactic.

A word of caution: Don't look *overconfident;* that is, presumptuous or arrogant. Be especially wary of using such phrases as "I know that," or "I am sure you will agree that."

Arrogant: <u>I am sure you will agree that</u> our offer is reasonable.
Confident: This solution should enable you to collect the data you need while still protecting the interests of our clients.

Presumptuous: <u>I plan</u> to schedule an interview with you next Thursday to further discuss my qualifications.
Confident: Please let me know when I may meet with you to further discuss my qualifications.

Competent communicators are confident communicators. They write with conviction, yet they avoid appearing to be pushy or presumptuous.

12. Use a Courteous and Sincere Tone.

OBJECTIVE 2: Use a courteous and sincere tone.

A tone of courtesy and sincerity builds goodwill for you and your company and increases the likelihood that your message will achieve its objective. For example, appearing to lecture the reader or filling a letter with **platitudes** (trite, obvious statements) implies a condescending attitude. Likewise, readers are likely to find offensive such expressions as "you failed to," "we find it difficult to believe that," "you surely don't expect," or "your complaint."

A platitude is a statement so obvious that including it in a message insults the reader.

Platitude: Companies like ours cannot survive unless our customers pay their bills on time.
Courteous: By paying your bill before May 30, you will maintain your excellent credit history with our firm.

Blunt: You sent your complaint to the wrong department. We don't handle shipping problems.
Courteous: We have forwarded your letter to the shipping department. You should be hearing from them within the week.

Accusatory: You must not have read the directions that came with your swing set.
Courteous: As discussed on page 13 of the directions that came with your swing set, each swing is designed to support a maximum weight of 150 pounds.

Most readers are sophisticated enough to know when you're being sincere. To achieve a sincere tone, avoid exaggeration (especially using too many modifiers or too strong modifiers), obvious flattery, and expressions of surprise or disbelief.

> *Exaggeration:* Your satisfaction means more to us than making a profit, and we shall work night and day to see that we earn it.
> *Sincere:* We value your goodwill highly and have taken several specific steps to ensure your satisfaction.
>
> *Exaggeration:* The <u>handsome</u> and <u>elegant</u> Queen Anne curio cabinet is made of the <u>very finest</u> mahogany, with a <u>revolutionary</u> adjustable track system designed by our <u>award-winning</u> design studio.
> *Sincere:* The Queen Anne curio cabinet is made of solid mahogany to blend well with your living room furnishings. The adjustable track system enables you to position all your collectibles—from 3-inch miniatures to 15-inch porcelains—for easy viewing.
>
> *Obvious Flattery:* Dear Season Ticket Holder: You are quite obviously a highly educated and refined person, who appreciates the finer things in life.
> *Sincere:* Dear Season Ticket Holder: Remember how exasperated you were when you had to miss a special concert by the New York Philharmonic because you were away on a business trip?
>
> *Surprise:* <u>I am surprised</u> that you would question your raise, considering your overall performance last year.
> *Sincere:* Your raise was based on an evaluation of your performance last year.

Obvious flattery and exaggeration sound insincere.

It is difficult to fake courtesy and sincerity. The best way to achieve the desired tone is to truly assume a courteous and sincere attitude toward your reader.

13. Use Appropriate Emphasis and Subordination.

OBJECTIVE 3: Use appropriate emphasis and subordination.

Not all ideas are created equal. Some are more important and more persuasive than others. Assume, for example, that you have been asked to evaluate and compare the Copy Cat and the Repro 100 photocopiers and then to write a report recommending one for purchase. Assume that the two brands are alike in all important respects except these:

1. Copy Cat produces 65 copies per minute; Repro 100 produces 58 copies per minute.
2. Copy Cat costs $2,750; Repro 100 costs $2,100.
3. Copy Cat has an enlargement/reduction feature; Repro 100 does not.

Copy Cat has greater speed and more features; Repro 100 costs less. Thus, a casual observer might think you should recommend Copy Cat based on its additional advantages.

Suppose, however, that most of your photocopying needs involve fewer than five copies of each original, all of them full size. Therefore, you don't find Copy Cat's higher speed and additional features as important as Repro 100's lower cost; and you decide to recommend purchasing Repro 100. But if you want your recommendation to be credible, you must make sure that your reader sees the relative importance of each feature. To do so, you must use appropriate emphasis and subordination techniques.

Techniques of Emphasis   To emphasize an idea, use any of the following strategies. To subordinate an idea, simply use the opposite strategies:

1. Put the idea in a short, simple sentence. If you need a complex sentence, put the more important idea in the independent clause. (The ideas communicated in each independent clause of a *compound* sentence receive equal emphasis.)

   Simple: Repro 100 is the better photocopier for our purposes.
   Complex: Although Copy Cat is faster, 98% of our copying requires fewer than five copies per original. *(Emphasizes the fact that speed is not a crucial consideration for us.)*

> To subordinate an idea, put it in the dependent clause.

2. Place the major idea first or last. The first paragraph of a message receives the most emphasis, the last paragraph receives less emphasis, and the middle paragraphs receive the least emphasis. Similarly, the middle sentences within a paragraph receive less emphasis than the first sentence in a paragraph.

   The first criterion examined was cost. Copy Cat sells for $2,750, and Repro 100 sells for $2,100, or 24% less than the cost of Copy Cat.

3. Use active voice to emphasize the doer of the action; use passive voice to emphasize the receiver. In other words, use the noun that you want to emphasize as the subject of the sentence.

   Active: Repro 100 costs 24% less than Copy Cat. *(Emphasizes Repro 100 rather than Copy Cat.)*
   Passive: The relative costs of the two models were first compared. *(Emphasizes the relative costs rather than the two models.)*

4. Devote more space to the idea.

   The two models were judged on three criteria. The first two criteria were speed and enlargement/reduction capability, and the third was cost. Total cost is an important consideration for our firm because of the large number of copiers we use and our large volume of copying. Last year our firm used 358 photocopiers and duplicated more than 6.5 million pages. Thus, regardless of the speed or features of a particular model, if it is too expensive to operate, it will not serve our purposes.

> Use language such as "least important" or "a minor point" to subordinate an idea.

5. Use language that directly implies importance, such as "most important," "major," or "primary."

   The most important factor for us is cost.

6. Use repetition (within reason).

   However, Copy Cat is expensive—expensive to purchase and expensive to operate.

7. Use mechanical means—enumeration, underscoring, solid capitals, second color, indenting from left and right margins, and other elements of design—to call attention to your ideas:

But the most important criterion is <u>cost</u>, and Repro 100 costs 24% less than Copy Cat.

The Ethical Dimension   In using emphasis and subordination, your goal is to ensure a common frame of reference between you and your reader; you want your reader to see how important you consider each idea to be. Your goal is *not* to mislead the reader. For example, if you believe that Alternative A is the *slightly* better choice, you would not want to intentionally mislead your reader into concluding that Alternative A is *clearly* the better choice. Such a tactic would not only be unethical but also unwise. Use sound business judgment and a sense of fair play to help you achieve your communication objectives.

> Use language that expresses your honest evaluation; do not mislead the reader.

14. Use Nondiscriminatory Language.

Nondiscriminatory language treats everyone equally, making no unwarranted assumptions about any group of people. Using nondiscriminatory language is smart business because (1) it is the ethical thing to do and because (2) we risk offending others if we do not. Consider the types of bias in this report:

> OBJECTIVE 4: Use nondiscriminatory language.

> The finishing plant was the scene of a confrontation today when two ladies from the morning shift accused a foreman of sexual harassment. Marilyn Humphrey, a black inspector, and Margaret Sawyer, an assembly-line worker, accused Mr. Engerrand of making suggestive comments. Mr. Engerrand, who is 62 years old and an epileptic, denied the charges and said he thought the girls were trying to gyp the company with their demand for a cash award.

Were you able to identify the following instances of bias or discriminatory language?

- The women were referred to as "ladies" and "girls," although it is unlikely that the men in the company are referred to as "gentlemen" and "boys."
- The term *foreman* (and all other *-man* occupational titles) has a sexist connotation.
- The two women were identified by first and last name, without a personal title, whereas the man was identified by a personal title and last name only.
- Humphrey's race was identified, whereas the race of the others was not.
- Engerrand's age is identified, although it is irrelevant to the situation.
- Engerrand's disability is identified, although that too is irrelevant.
- The word *gyp,* derived from *gypsy,* is derogatory.

Competent communicators make sure that their writing is free of sexist language and free of bias based on such factors as race, ethnic background, religion, age, sexual orientation, and disability.

Sexist Language   It makes no business sense to exclude or perhaps offend half the population by using sexist language. To avoid sexism in your writing, follow these strategies:

1. Use neutral job titles that do not imply that a job is held by only men or women.

<table>
<tr><td>*Instead of*</td><td>*Use*</td></tr>
<tr><td>businessmen</td><td>business people (*or use a specific title*)</td></tr>
<tr><td>chairman</td><td>chair, chairperson</td></tr>
<tr><td>fireman</td><td>firefighter</td></tr>
<tr><td>foreman</td><td>supervisor</td></tr>
<tr><td>mailman</td><td>mail carrier, letter carrier</td></tr>
<tr><td>salesman</td><td>sales representative</td></tr>
<tr><td>stewardess</td><td>flight attendant</td></tr>
<tr><td>woman lawyer</td><td>lawyer</td></tr>
<tr><td>workman</td><td>worker, employee</td></tr>
</table>

Be sensitive to your reader's feelings.

2. Avoid words and phrases that unnecessarily imply gender:

<table>
<tr><td>*Instead of*</td><td>*Use*</td></tr>
<tr><td>best man for the job</td><td>best person for the job</td></tr>
<tr><td>executives and their wives</td><td>executives and their spouses</td></tr>
<tr><td>housewife</td><td>homemaker</td></tr>
<tr><td>mankind</td><td>humanity, people</td></tr>
<tr><td>manmade</td><td>artificial, synthetic, manufactured</td></tr>
<tr><td>manpower</td><td>human resources, workforce, personnel</td></tr>
</table>

Males also may be the victims of sexist language.

3. Avoid demeaning or stereotypical terms:

<table>
<tr><td>*Instead of*</td><td>*Use*</td></tr>
<tr><td>My girl will take care of it.</td><td>My secretary will take care of it.</td></tr>
<tr><td>Women are bored with football.</td><td>Some people are bored with football.</td></tr>
<tr><td>Watch your language around the ladies.</td><td>Watch your language.</td></tr>
<tr><td>Housewives like our longer hours.</td><td>Our customers like our longer hours.</td></tr>
<tr><td>He was a real jock.</td><td>He enjoyed all types of sports.</td></tr>
<tr><td>Each nurse supplies her own uniform.</td><td>Nurses supply their own uniforms.</td></tr>
</table>

4. Use parallel language.

<table>
<tr><td>*Instead of*</td><td>*Use*</td></tr>
<tr><td>Joe, a broker, and his wife, a beautiful brunette</td><td>Joe, a broker, and his wife Mary, a lawyer (*or* Mary, a homemaker)</td></tr>
<tr><td>Helen and William Barnwell</td><td>Helen Wyllie and William Barnwell
Or: Helen and William</td></tr>
</table>

Ms. Wyllie and William Barnwell	Ms. Wyllie and Mr. Barnwell
men and ladies	men and women
	Or: gentlemen and ladies
man and wife	husband and wife

5. Use appropriate personal titles and salutations.

- If a woman has a professional title, use it:

Dr. Martha Ralston	The Rev. Deborah Connell

- Follow a woman's preference in being addressed as *Miss, Mrs.,* or *Ms.*
- If a woman's marital status or her preference is unknown, use *Ms.*
- If you do not know the reader's gender, use a nonsexist salutation. (Or use a letter style that omits the salutation; see Chapter 5.)

> Follow the reader's preference to be addressed as *Ms., Miss,* or *Mrs.*

Ladies and Gentlemen:	Dear Friend:
Dear Investor:	Dear Policyholder:

- If you do not know the reader's gender, use the full name in the salutation.

Dear Chris Anderson:	Dear Terry Brooks:

6. Whether it is appropriate to use *he* or *his* as generic pronouns in referring to males or females (e.g., "Each manager must evaluate <u>his</u> subordinates annually") is currently a matter of much debate. Proponents argue that its use is based on tradition and on the fact that no genderless alternative pronoun exists. Opponents argue that its use appears to exclude females. Although many business people would not be offended by such use, some would be. The conservative approach is to avoid such usage when possible, by adopting any of these strategies:

> The generic use of *he* and *him* will offend some readers.

- Use plural nouns and pronouns.

  All managers must evaluate their subordinates annually.
  But not: Each manager must evaluate <u>their</u> subordinates annually.

- Use second-person pronouns (*you, your*).

  You must evaluate your subordinates annually.

- Revise the sentence.

  Each manager must evaluate subordinates annually.

- Use "his or her" (sparingly).

  Each manager must evaluate his or her subordinates annually.

> Excessive use of the term *he or she* or *his or hers* is awkward.

Other Discriminatory Language   We are all members of many different groups, each of which may have different customs, values, and attitudes. If you think of your readers as individuals, rather than as stereotypical members of some particular group, you will avoid bias when communicating about race, ethnic background, religion, age, sexual orientation, and disabilities. Such group memberships should be mentioned only if it is clearly pertinent.

The overall tone of an effective business message utilizes nondiscriminatory language and treats all groups of people fairly and equally. Competent communicators do not make unfounded assumptions about any individual.

(*Source:* © *1991 Taro Yamasaki*)

- Race and ethnic background:

    Not: Richard McKenna, noted black legislator, supported our position.
    But: Richard McKenna, noted legislator, supported our position.

    Not: Juan is not your typical Mexican.
    But: Juan has become one of the most successful bankers in Mexico City.

    Not: Because of rising interest rates, he welshed on the deal.
    But: Because of rising interest rates, he backed out of the deal.

    Not: The city appeared to be an Indian giver in that transaction.
    But: The city lowered property taxes but then increased sales taxes.

Mention group membership only if it is clearly relevant.

- Religion:

    Not: His Jewish mother always stressed the value of a college education.
    But: His mother always stressed the value of a college education.

- Age:

    Not: Anita Voyles performed the job well for her age.
    But: Anita Voyles performed the job well.

- Sexual orientation:

    Not: Patricia Barbour's lesbianism has not affected her job performance.
    But: Patricia Barbour's job performance has been exemplary.

- Disability:

    Not: The blind consultant made two important recommendations.
    But: The consultant made two important recommendations.

    Not: Dennis took his deaf and dumb child to the Mayo Clinic.
    But: Dennis took his hearing- and speech-impaired child to the Mayo Clinic.

Not: Mary, an epileptic, had no trouble passing the medical examination.

But: Mary, who has epilepsy, had no trouble passing the medical examination. *(When the impairment is relevant, separate the impairment from the person.)*

Most of us like to think of ourselves as sensitive, caring people who do not wish to offend others; and our writing (and speaking) should reflect this attitude. Unfortunately, some types of discriminatory language may be so deeply ingrained that using bias-free language may take a concerted effort at first. Bias will not disappear completely from our language until it disappears completely from our lives. Still, competent communicators strive to use language impartially so that readers can focus their attention on *what* is written without being offended by *how* it is written.

15. Stress the "You" Attitude.

Are you more interested in how well you perform in this course or in how well your classmates perform? When you hear a television commercial, are you more interested in how the product will benefit you or how your purchase of the product will benefit the company? If you are like most people reading or hearing a message, your conscious or unconscious reaction is likely to be "What's in it for *me?*" Knowing that this is true provides you with a powerful strategy for structuring your messages to maximize their impact: Stress the "you" attitude, not a "me" attitude.

The **"you" attitude** emphasizes what the *receiver* (either the listener or the reader) wants to know and how he or she will be affected by the message. It requires developing **empathy**—the ability to project yourself into another person's position and to understand that person's situation, feelings, motives, and needs. To avoid sounding selfish and uninterested, stress the reader viewpoint—use the "you" attitude.

I Attitude: I am shipping your order this afternoon.
You Attitude: Your order should arrive by Friday.

I Attitude: We will be open on Sundays from 1 to 5 P.M., beginning May 15.
You Attitude: You will be able to shop on Sundays from 1 to 5 P.M., beginning May 15.

I Attitude: So that I may begin analyzing my data by March 1, I would like to have the completed questionnaire returned by April 15.

You Attitude: So that your views will be included in this study, won't you please return your completed questionnaire by April 15.

Reader Benefits An important component of the "you" attitude is the concept of **reader benefits**—emphasizing how the *reader* will benefit from doing as you ask. Sometimes, especially when asking a favor or refusing a request, the best we can do is to show how *someone* (not necessarily the reader) will benefit. But we should always show how someone *other than ourselves* benefits from our request or from our decision.

I Attitude: We cannot afford to purchase an ad in your organization's directory.

OBJECTIVE 5: Stress the "you" attitude.

Write from the reader's perspective.

Answer the "What's in it for me?" question.

You Attitude: Advertising exclusively on television allows us to offer consumers like yourself the lowest prices on their cosmetics.

I Attitude: Our decorative fireplace has an oak mantel and is portable.

You Attitude: Whether you're entertaining in your living room or den, you can still enjoy the ambience of a blazing fire because our decorative fireplace is portable. Simply take it with you from room to room; its oak mantel will immediately give it a built-in look in any room of your home.

Note that the revised sentences, which stress reader benefits, are longer than the original sentences—because they contain *more information.* Yet they are not wordy; that is, they do not contain unnecessary words. You can add information and still write concisely.

Exceptions Stressing the "you" attitude focuses the attention on the reader, which is right where the attention should be—most of the time. In some situations, however, you want to avoid focusing on the reader; these situations all involve conveying negative information. When you refuse someone's request, disagree with someone, or talk about someone's mistakes or shortcomings, avoid connecting the reader too closely with the negative information. In such situations, avoid second-person pronouns and use passive sentences or other techniques to stress the receiver of the action rather than the doer.

Not: <u>You</u> should have included more supporting evidence in <u>your</u> presentation.
But: Including more supporting evidence would have made the presentation more convincing.

Not: <u>You</u> are mistaken in concluding that San Diego is the best site.
But: Santa Barbara has two advantages over San Diego that have not yet been discussed.

Not: <u>You</u> failed to return the merchandise within the ten-day period.
But: We are happy to give a full refund on all merchandise that is returned within ten days.

Note that none of these revised sentences contains the word *you.* Thus they help separate the reader from the negative information, making the message more tactful and palatable.

16. Write at an Appropriate Level of Difficulty.

The term **readability** refers to the ease of understanding a passage based on its style of writing. Various readability formulas are available that estimate the complexity of a passage based on an analysis of such factors as sentence length, number of syllables per word, and word frequency.

One of the most commonly used readability formulas is the Fog Index, developed by Robert Gunning in 1968 (see Figure 4.1).[1] This formula estimates readability based on average sentence length and the percentage of difficult words. The final product is roughly equal to school grade reading level. Thus, a Fog Index of 8 indicates that someone who is reading at eighth-grade level can be expected to understand the passage easily.

In some situations, you do not *want to focus on the reader.*

OBJECTIVE 6: Write at an appropriate level of difficulty.

The Fog Index estimates the amount of "fog" (complexity) in a passage by considering the length of words and sentences.

Calculating Readability Using the Fog Index   **FIGURE 4.1**

1. Select a passage of at least 100 words. Use complete sentences only. (If the passage is long, take several samples and average the results.) Here is an example:

   The attached *Wall Street Journal* article discusses four large hotel chains that have started frequent-stay plans. The purpose of this memo is to describe such plans and analyze their costs and benefits. Then I will recommend what action, if any, we should take in this regard.

   To gather the needed data, I studied published reports prepared by the Hotel and Restaurant Association; then I interviewed the person in charge of frequent-stay programs at three hotels. Finally, Dr. Kenneth Lowe, professor of hospitality services at Southern Cal, reviewed and commented on my first draft. Thus, this proposal is based on a large body of data collected over two months.

2. Find the average sentence length: $\frac{108}{7} = 15.4$
   a. Count the number of words in the passage. (Count anything with a space before and after as a word.)
   b. Count the number of sentences. (In compound sentences, count each independent clause as a separate sentence.)
   c. Divide the number of words by the number of sentences.

3. Find the percentage of difficult words: $\frac{9}{108} = 8.3$
   a. Count the number of difficult words (containing three or more syllables). Do not include the following:
      ▪ Compound words—unless one of the individual elements is three syllables; for example, *however* and *self-control* are not difficult, but *self-discipline* is difficult.
      ▪ Verbs that become three syllables by adding *-ed* or *-es*.
      ▪ Figures or capitalized words.
   b. Divide the number of difficult words by the total number of words in the passage and multiply by 100.

4. Add the average sentence length (from Step 2) to the percentage of difficult words (from Step 3). 23.7
5. Multiply the resulting number by 0.4 to arrive at the grade level needed to understand the passage. 9.5

Independent research has shown that the Fog Index is accurate to within plus or minus one grade level at all levels up to 13.[2] Accuracy at levels higher than 13 is probably irrelevant, because, as Gunning states, any writing with an index higher than 12 (high school senior level) invites misunderstanding.[3] Most business writing should have a Fog Index of 8–12. In comparison, *Reader's Digest* has an index of 9–10; *Wall Street Journal*, 10–11; and *Scientific American*, 11–12.

Although applying the Fog Index (or any other readability formula) is helpful in judging the readability of your message, you should use the results as a guide only. According to Gunning, "The Fog Index is a tool, not a rule. It is a warning system, not a formula for writing."[4]

You could, for example, artificially lower your Fog Index by using shorter sentences and shorter words. But sometimes a longer word is more precise and more familiar than a shorter word. For example, you know the meaning of such multisyllabic words as *vegetable, unacceptable,* and *veterinarian;* but you might stumble over such one-syllable words as *cade, foss,* and *tael.* Likewise, lowering the index score by using all short sentences (e.g., all simple sentences) might obscure the relationships among ideas because then all ideas would receive equal emphasis.

A further caution with regard to overreliance on readability formulas concerns what they do *not* measure. They do not measure the complexity and organization of the ideas, or the design of the document. Perhaps, more importantly, they do not measure reader interest in the passage. If a reader is intently interested in what you have to say, he or she will plow through even the foggiest writing. But if you have reason to expect low reader interest, make your writing especially easy and inviting to read.

EFFECTIVE BUSINESS WRITING

Writing style goes beyond *correctness.* Although a letter that contains many grammar, mechanical, or usage errors could hardly be considered effective, a letter that contains no such errors might still be ineffective because it lacks style. Style involves choosing the right words, writing effective sentences, developing logical paragraphs, and setting an appropriate overall tone. Checklist 1 summarizes the 16 principles discussed in Chapters 3 and 4.

These principles will help you communicate your ideas clearly and effectively. They provide a solid foundation for the higher-order communication skills you will be developing in the following chapters. At first, you may find it somewhat difficult and time-consuming to constantly assess your writing according to these criteria. Their importance, however, merits that effort. You will soon find that you are beginning to apply these principles automatically as you compose and revise messages.

SUMMARY

Competent communicators achieve their objectives by writing with confidence, courtesy, and sincerity. They recognize that not all ideas are equally important, and they use techniques of emphasis and subordination to develop a common frame of reference between writer and reader. They use nondiscriminatory language in their writing by treating everyone equally and by not making unwarranted assumptions about any group of people.

Effective writing keeps the emphasis on the reader—stressing what the reader needs to know and how the reader will be affected by the message. Effective messages are also written at an appropriate level of difficulty so that the reader can easily understand the passage, based on its style of writing.

Effective Business Writing

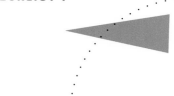

Words

1. *Write clearly:* Be accurate and complete; use familiar words; avoid dangling expressions and unnecessary jargon.

2. *Prefer short, simple words:* They are less likely to be misused and more likely to be understood.

3. *Write with vigor:* Use specific, concrete language; avoid clichés, slang, and buzz words.

4. *Write concisely:* Avoid redundancies, wordy expressions, and hidden verbs.

5. *Prefer positive language:* Stress what you can do or what is true, rather than what you cannot do or what is not true.

Sentences

6. *Use a variety of sentence types:* Use simple sentences for emphasis and variety, compound sentences for coordinate relationships, and complex sentences for subordinate relationships. Most sentences should range from 16 to 22 words.

7. *Use active and passive voice appropriately:* Use active voice to emphasize the doer of the action and passive voice to emphasize the receiver.

8. *Avoid fragments and run-on sentences:* Make sure that each sentence contains at least one logically complete thought but avoid stringing together too many ideas in one sentence.

Paragraphs

9. *Keep paragraphs unified and coherent:* Develop a single idea consistently and logically; use transitional words and pronouns, repetition, and parallelism.

10. *Control paragraph length:* Use a variety of lengths, although most paragraphs should range from 60 to 80 words.

Overall Tone

11. *Write confidently:* Avoid sounding unconfident by overusing such phrases as "I think" and "I hope," but also avoid sounding arrogant or presumptuous.

12. *Use a courteous and sincere tone:* Avoid platitudes, exaggeration, obvious flattery, and expressions of surprise or disbelief.

13. *Use appropriate emphasis and subordination:* Emphasize and subordinate through the use of sentence structure, position, verb voice, amount of space, language, repetition, and mechanical means.

14. *Use nondiscriminatory language:* Avoid bias when communicating about gender, race, ethnic background, religion, age, sexual orientation, and disabilities.

15. *Stress the "you" attitude:* Emphasize what the receiver wants to know and how the receiver will be affected by the message; stress reader benefits.

16. *Write at an appropriate level of difficulty:* A Fog Index score of 8–12 is generally an appropriate readability level in business writing, although many factors other than the Fog measurements of word and sentence length affect readability.

KEY TERMS

Empathy— The ability to project oneself into another person's position and understand that person's situation, feelings, motives, and needs.

Nondiscriminatory language— Language that treats everyone equally, making no unwarranted assumptions about any group of people.

Platitude— A trite, obvious statement.

Readability— The ease with which a passage can be understood, based on its style of writing.

Reader benefits— The advantages a reader would derive from granting the writer's request or from accepting the writer's decision.

Tone— The writer's attitude toward both the reader and the subject of the message.

"You" attitude— A viewpoint that emphasizes what the reader wants to know and how the reader will be affected by the message.

REVIEW AND DISCUSSION

OBJECTIVE 1

1. Give an example of a sentence that sounds too confident and one that doesn't sound confident enough. Then revise both sentences to make them more effective.

OBJECTIVE 2

2. What are three means of achieving sincerity in a message?

OBJECTIVE 3

3. List seven techniques for emphasizing an idea.

OBJECTIVE 3

4. List seven techniques for subordinating an idea.

OBJECTIVE 4

5. Why should discriminatory language be avoided in business writing?

OBJECTIVE 4

6. Do you feel it is appropriate or inappropriate to use the pronoun *he* as a generic pronoun referring to both males and females (e.g., "Each manager must ensure that *he* submits *his* reports on time"). Write a paragraph defending your position.

OBJECTIVE 4

7. List six methods for avoiding sexism in business writing.

OBJECTIVE 5

8. Construct a sentence illustrating the "you" attitude.

OBJECTIVE 5

9. Under what circumstances should the reader *not* be the focus of attention in business writing?

10. Which difficulty factors are included and which ones are not included in the Fog Index? What is an appropriate Fog Index score for most business writing?

OBJECTIVE 6 ◀

EXERCISES

Directions: *For Exercises 1–2 and 4–5, revise the passages to avoid the writing weaknesses indicated. Do not completely rewrite the passages; just correct any style problems.*

1. **Writing Confidently**

OBJECTIVE 1 ◀

If you believe my proposal has merit, I hope that you will allocate $50,000 for a pilot study. It's possible that this pilot study will bear out my profit estimates so that we can proceed on a permanent basis. Even though you have several other worthwhile projects to consider for funding, I know you will agree the proposal should be funded prior to January 1. Please call me before the end of the week to tell me that you've accepted my proposal.

2. **Using a Courteous and Sincere Tone**

OBJECTIVE 2 ◀

You, our loyal and dedicated employees, have always been the most qualified and the most industrious in the industry. Because of your faithful and dependable service, I was quite surprised to learn yesterday that an organizational meeting for union representation was recently held here. You must realize that a company like ours cannot survive unless we hold labor costs down. I cannot believe that you don't appreciate the many benefits of working at Allied. We will immediately have to declare bankruptcy if a union is voted in. Please don't be fooled by empty rhetoric.

3. **Using Appropriate Emphasis and Subordination**   Assume that you have evaluated two candidates for the position of sales assistant. This is what you have learned:

OBJECTIVE 3 ◀

   a. Carl Barteolli has more sales experience.
   b. Elizabeth Larson has more appropriate formal training (college degree in marketing, attendance at several three-week sales seminars, etc.)
   c. Elizabeth Larson's personality appears to mesh more closely with the prevailing corporate culture at your firm.

   You must write a memo to Alan Underwood, the vice president, recommending one of these candidates. First, assume that personality is the most important criterion and write a memo recommending Elizabeth Larson. Secondly, assume that experience is the most important criterion and write a memo recommending Carl Barteolli. Use appropriate emphasis and subordination in each message. You may make up any reasonable information needed to complete this assignment.

4. **Using Nondiscriminatory Language**

OBJECTIVE 4 ◀

Mr. Watkins argued that the 62-year-old Kathy Beviere should be replaced because she doesn't dress appropriately for her receptionist position. However, the human-resources director, who is female, countered that we don't pay any of the girls in clerical positions well enough for them to buy appropriate attire. Mr. Watkins did acknowledge that the receptionist, who is a paraplegic, is well suited for her receptionist job. He added that he just wished she would dress more businesslike instead of wearing the colorful clothes and makeup that reflect her immigrant background.

▶ OBJECTIVE 5

5. **Stressing the "You" Attitude**

We are happy to announce that we are offering for sale an empty parcel of land at the corner of Mission and High Streets. We will be selling this parcel for $62,500, with a minimum down payment of $13,500. We have had the lot rezoned M-2, for student housing. We originally purchased this lot because of its proximity to the University and had planned to erect student housing, but our investment plans have changed. We still feel that our lot would make a profitable site for up to three 12-unit buildings.

▶ OBJECTIVE 6

6. **Writing at an Appropriate Level of Difficulty**   Select an actual paper that you have previously written and submitted for a course grade, either in this course or in some other course. Compute the Fog Index score of an appropriate passage from this paper. What does this score mean? If necessary, revise the passage to adjust the readability level and then recompute your score. Submit both versions to your instructor.

CASE PROBLEM

▶ OBJECTIVES 1–6

Drew Drafts a Drab Memo

See Appendix D for background information on this case.

Here is a first-draft memo written by O. J. Drew to Arnie McNally:

```
MEMO TO: Arnold McNally, Vice President--Manufacturing
FROM:    O. J. Drew, Production Manager
DATE:    October 13, 19--
SUBJECT: Charlotte Expansion

As you will remember, when we opened our Charlotte
plant, we made plans to increase capacity within three
years and we're now approaching the end of our third
year, and even though sales are increasing, I suggest
we delay any expansion plans for another two years.

To begin with, interest rates are heading up across the
board. Last week, North Carolina National Bank and
Wachovia Bank both raised their prime rate quite a bit.
This is the highest it has been in several years. Other
big banks are likely to follow with similar increases.
Both NCNB and Wachovia financed our initial efforts in
Charlotte--at a lower rate. The Wall Street Journal
predicts that interest rates will remain high for at
least the next 18 months. A second reason for my
suggestion is that present capacity is sufficient to
```

support our present level of sales. If sales continue
to grow substantially, we will continue to have sufficient capacity for three more years. We can increase
production for minimal plant cost by simply adding a
third shift. Adding a third shift will lower per-unit
costs and enable us to convert numerous part-time
positions to full-time positions, with a corresponding savings in fringe benefits. Finally, our union
contract expires next year. Although our plant is
automated, we still employ 95 unionized workers. These
men's wage demands are high; and unless we are able to
jew them down a bit, we will simply not be able to
afford an expansion. I predict getting a reasonable
union contract this time will be a hard nut to crack.
In addition, if Neelima believes a strike is at all
possible, we won't even be using the capacity we
presently have--let alone, expanded capacity.

For these reasons, I recommend we delay any expansion
plans for another two years at least. I hope you will
agree with me. Luis Diaz does; and if you desire, Luis
and I can produce a formal report of our recommendation
for you to present to the Board.

juv

1. Analyze each paragraph, using Checklist 1 on pages 103-104 as the basis for your analysis. What effective and ineffective techniques have been used?

2. List each transitional expression that was used in the second paragraph to achieve coherence. Does the paragraph have unity?

3. Revise this memorandum, making whatever changes are necessary to increase its effectiveness. You may make up any needed facts so long as they are reasonable.

- The longest word listed in Webster's Third International Dictionary is *pneumonoultramicroscopicsilicovolcanoconiosises* (47 letters), which is the plural of a lung disease contracted by some miners. The longest words in common use are *interdenominationalism* (22 letters) and *dispropor-tionableness* and *incomprehensibilities* (21 letters).

- The shortest alphabetic sentence that makes sense is "The five boxing wizards jump quickly." This 31-letter sentence incorporates all 26 letters of the alphabet.

CHAPTER 5

The Process
of Writing

After you have finished this chapter, you will be able to

1. Specify the purpose of your message and analyze your audience.

2. Determine what information to include and in what order it should be presented.

3. Compose a first draft of your message.

4. Use a variety of strategies to overcome writer's block.

5. Revise for content, style, and correctness.

6. Format letters, envelopes, and memos in standard format.

7. Proofread a document for content, typographical, and format errors.

John Kazzi is a senior writer at Keep America Beautiful (KAB), a nonprofit, educational organization that has been urging Americans since 1953 not to litter and to respect the environment. Today KAB's agenda includes the national issue of handling and disposing of solid waste, and Kazzi's responsibilities include writing the organization's newsletters, news releases, and educational material. For Kazzi, the writing process boils down to a rewriting process of ideas to organization to words to sentences.

"I start with a big yellow legal pad and write out a list of all the things I want to say," says the senior writer. "Then I sit down at my word processor and work up a first draft. After that, I can get into the meat-and-potatoes of revising it into a finished form. It is very uncommon for me to write something and have it travel up through all the checkpoints without having it returned for revision."

For Kazzi, revision is a process that moves his writing toward greater clarity. His "meat-and-potatoes" effort eliminates rambling sentences and replaces vague language with specific language. And always, *always,* says Kazzi, he strives to stay mindful of two things: who his readers are, and what his goals are.

"It's the same for an organization like ours as it is for anyone who is approaching a major corporation," says Kazzi. "You identify your own organization's goals, then you must point out how helping you is going to help them. The benefit that they derive is just as important as yours."

John Kazzi, Senior Writer
Keep America Beautiful, Inc.
Stamford, Connecticut

To do that well, says Kazzi, a writer has to choose his words carefully, using language that suits his audience rather than himself.

"We are a bit more educated about our topic than some of our audience is because we have to be. But we try not to be overly technical. At the same time we try to give more insight to the reader."

Writing about a subject without being too technical, says Kazzi, is part of the honing process. Kazzi has to edit out technical words and phrases that might come naturally to him or his colleagues but would confuse his audience. That part of the writing process is, in a sense, a translating process.

When the translating is done, Kazzi can move on to another part of writing: organizing. He must decide where to begin and where to end.

"What we'll usually do," says Kazzi, "is begin with a problem, a waste disposal issue. We define it and position that definition as an introduction. Then we go into the more technical aspects of the disposal issue, and we finish with a description of what's being done about the situation. The important thing is not to be overly technical or sophisticated in our presentation of ideas. We don't want people to be unable to understand what we're trying to say."

All of this may sound like a steady and systematic process, but it isn't. Writing, says Kazzi, is periodically frustrating.

"I'm fortunate enough to work across the street from a park, so I can go out for a brisk walk to clear my head. Sometimes the most important thing is to get away from the computer screen. But the reality is that there are times when you simply cannot have writer's block—there is not time for it. In those cases you have to just work through the block. The key is to remain clear, calm, and controlled. The words will come." ▼

AN OVERVIEW OF THE WRITING PROCESS

When faced with a writing task, some people just start writing. They try to do everything at once, figuring out what to say and how to say it, imagining an audience and a goal, keeping watch on spelling and grammar, and choosing their words and building sentences—all at the same time. It's not easy to keep switching back and forth from one of these distinct writing tasks to another and still make headway. In fact, unless you're an expert writer, it's harder and slower than breaking the job up into steps and completing each step in turn.

The idea of writing step by step may at first sound as if it will prolong the job, but it doesn't. The step of planning, for example, gives you a sense

110

of where you want to go and that, in turn, will make getting there faster and easier. The clearer you are about your goals, the more effective your writing is likely to be in accomplishing those goals. And if you save a separate step for proofreading, that job will also go more smoothly and efficiently. (It's difficult to spot a typo if you're still trying to think up the "big ending" for your report.)

Competent communicators, then, follow these steps when faced with a business situation that calls for a written response:

1. *Planning:* Determine what the purpose of your written message is, who the readers will be, what information you need to give these readers to achieve your purpose, and in what order to put that information.
2. *Drafting:* Write a first draft.
3. *Revising:* Revise for content, style, and correctness.
4. *Formatting:* Arrange the document in an appropriate format.
5. *Proofreading:* Reread the document to check for content, typographical, and format errors.

> The writing process consists of planning, drafting, revising, formatting, and proofreading.

The amount of time devoted to each of these steps depends on the complexity, length, and importance of the document. Not all steps may be needed for all writing tasks. Nevertheless, these steps are a good starting point for completing a writing assignment—either in class or on the job.

PLANNING

Planning, the first step in writing, involves making decisions about the purpose, audience, content, and organization of the message.

Purpose

The first decision you must make relates to the purpose of your message. If you don't know *why* you're writing the message (that is, if you don't know what you hope to accomplish), then later you'll have no way of knowing whether you have achieved your goal. In the end, what matters is not how well-crafted your message was or how attractive it looked on the page; what matters is whether you achieved your objective. If you did, your communication was successful; if you did not, it was not.

▼ OBJECTIVE 1 Specify the purpose of your message and analyze your audience.

Most writers find it easier to start with a general purpose and then refine the general purpose into a *specific objective.* The specific objective should indicate the response desired from the reader.

Assume, for example, that you are a marketing manager at Seaside Resorts, a chain of hotels along the California, Oregon, and Washington coasts. You have noted that many of the larger hotel chains have instituted "frequent-stay" plans, which, like the frequent-flier programs they are modeled after, reward repeat customers with free lodging, travel, or merchandise. You want to write a message recommending a similar plan for Seaside Resorts. Your general purpose might be this:

> The purpose should be specific enough to serve as a yardstick for judging the success of the message.

To describe the benefits of a frequent-stay plan at Seaside Resorts.

Such a goal is a good starting point, but it is not specific enough. To begin with, it doesn't identify the intended audience. Are you writing a memo to the vice president of marketing recommending this plan, or are

FIGURE 5.1   The Writing Process

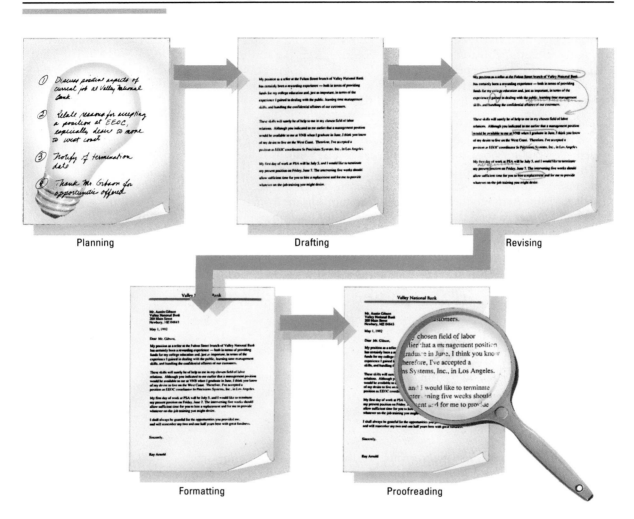

Planning   Drafting   Revising

Formatting   Proofreading

you writing a letter to frequent business travelers recommending that they enroll in this plan? Let's assume, for the moment, that you're writing to the marketing vice president. What is she supposed to *do* as a result of reading your memo? Simply understand what you've written? Agree with you? Commit resources for further research? Agree to implement the plan immediately? How will you know if your message has achieved its objectives? Perhaps you decide that your specific objective is this:

> To persuade the marketing VP to permit you to develop and implement a frequent-stay plan for a 12-month test period in Seaside's three Oregon resorts.

Now you have an objective that's specific enough to guide you as you write the memo and to permit you to judge, in the end, whether your message achieved its goal.

In another situation, your general purpose might be to resolve a problem regarding a shipment of damaged merchandise, and your specific objective might be to persuade the manufacturer to replace the damaged shipment at no cost to you within ten days. Or your general purpose might be to refuse a customer's claim, and your specific objective might be to convince the customer that your refusal is reasonable and to maintain her goodwill.

Having a clear-cut statement of purpose lets you focus on the content and organization, eliminating distracting information and making sure all relevant information is included.

> A clearly stated purpose helps you avoid inserting irrelevant and distracting information.

Audience Analysis

To maximize the effectiveness of your message, you should perform an **audience analysis**; that is, you should identify the interests, needs, and personality of your receiver. Remember our discussion of mental filters in Chapter 1. Each person perceives a message differently, based on his or her unique mental filter. Thus, we need to determine the level of detail, the language used, and the overall tone by answering such questions as the following.

Who Is the Primary Audience? For most letters, the audience is one person, which simplifies the task immensely. It is much easier to personalize a message addressed to one individual than a message addressed to many individuals. Sometimes, however, you have multiple audiences. In this case, you need to identify your **primary audience** (the person whose cooperation is crucial if your message is to achieve its objectives) and your secondary audience (those who will also be affected by the topic of your message). If you can satisfy no one else, try to satisfy the needs of the primary decision-maker. If possible, also satisfy the needs of any secondary audience.

If, for example, you're presenting a proposal that must be approved by the general manager but that will also require the cooperation of your colleagues in other departments, the general manager is the primary audience and your peers the secondary audience. Gear your message—its content, organization, and tone—first to the needs of the general manager. Most often (but not always), the primary audience will be the highest-level person to whom you're addressing your communication.

What Is Your Relationship with the Audience? Does your audience know you? If not, you will first have to establish your credibility by assuming a reasonable tone and giving enough evidence to support your claims. Are you writing to someone inside or outside the company? If outside, your message will typically be a little more formal and will contain more background information and less jargon than when you are writing to someone inside the company.

> Your relationship with the reader determines the tone and content of your message.

What is your status in relation to your audience? Communications to your superior are obviously vital to your success in the organization. Such communications are typically a little more formal, less authoritarian in tone, and more information-filled than communications to peers or subordinates. Study your superior's own messages to get a sense of his or her preferred style and diction, and adapt your own message accordingly.

When you communicate with subordinates, be polite but not patronizing. Try to instill a sense of collaboration and corporate ownership of your proposal. When praising or criticizing, be specific; and criticize the action—

not the person. The standard guideline for subordinate communications is to praise in public and criticize in private.

How Will the Audience React?   If the reader's initial reaction to both you and your topic is likely to be *positive*, your job is relatively easy. You can use a direct approach—beginning with the most important information (for example, your conclusions or recommendations) and then supplying the needed details. If the reader's initial reaction is likely to be *neutral*, use the first few lines of your message to get the reader's attention and convince him or her that what you have to say is important and that your reasoning is sound. Revise carefully to make sure that your message is short and easy to read and that any requested action is easy to take.

> If the expected reader reaction is negative, present lots of evidence and expert testimony.

Suppose, however, that you expect your reader's initial reaction to be *negative*—either to your topic or to you personally. Here you have a real sales job to do. If the reader shows a personal dislike of you, your best strategy is to call on external evidence and expert opinion to bolster your position. Show that others, people whom the reader is likely to know and respect, share your opinions. Use courteous, conservative language, and suggest ways the reader can change his or her mind without appearing to "give in"—perhaps by suggesting that new circumstances and new information call for new strategies.

If you anticipate that your reader will oppose your proposal, your best strategy is to supply extra evidence. Instead of one example, give two or three. Instead of quoting two external sources, quote several. Begin with the areas of agreement, stress reader benefits, and try to anticipate and answer any objections the reader might have. Through logic, evidence, and tone, build your case for the reasonableness of your position.

FIGURE 5.2   Audience Analysis

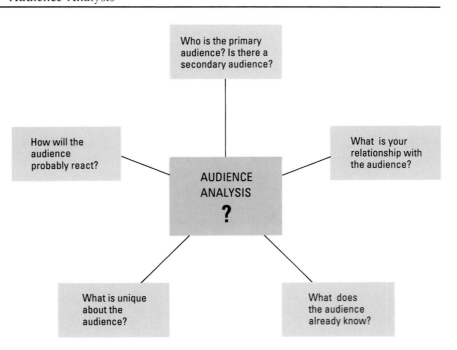

What Does the Audience Already Know?   Understanding the audience's present level of understanding about the topic is crucial to making decisions about content and writing style. You must decide how much background information is necessary, whether the use of jargon is or is not appropriate, and what readability level would, be appropriate. If you are writing to multiple audiences, gear the amount of detail to the level of understanding of the key decision-maker (the primary audience). In general, it is better to provide too much rather than too little information.

Determine how much information the reader needs.

What Is Unique About the Audience?   The success or failure of a message often depends on little things—the extra touches that say to the reader, "You're special, and I've taken the time to learn some things about you."

What can you learn about the personal interests or demographic characteristics of your audience that you can build into your message? Is the reader a "take-charge" kind of person who would prefer to have important information up front—regardless of whether the news is good or bad? What level of formality is expected? Would the reader be flattered or be put off by the use of his or her first name in the salutation? Have good things or bad things happened recently at work or at home that may affect the reader's receptivity to your message? Competent communicators analyze their audience and then use this information to structure the content, organization, and tone of their messages.

Make the reader feel special by personalizing the content.

Example of Audience Analysis   To illustrate the crucial role that audience analysis plays in communication, let's consider different scenarios for the memo to the marketing vice president requesting a pilot test of a frequent-stay incentive program. First, assume that Cynthia Haney, vice president of marketing and your immediate superior, will be the only reader of your memo; that is, she has the authority to approve or reject your proposal. Ms. Haney assumed her position at Seaside Resorts just six months ago, after having served as a regional marketing director for B. Dalton Bookstores for five years. Thus, although she has top-notch managerial skills, she is still "learning the ropes" of the hospitality industry. Up to this point, your relationship with her has been cordial, and you have reason to believe that she has confidence in your skills. That being the case, the first paragraph of your memo to her might be as follows:

> The attached *Wall Street Journal* article discusses four large hotel chains that have started frequent-stay plans. The purpose of this memo is to describe such plans and analyze their costs and benefits. Then I will recommend what action, if any, we should take in this regard.

Now suppose that instead of having confidence in your skills, Haney has given some indication that she *doesn't* yet completely trust your judgment. You might add a second paragraph to establish your credibility:

> To gather the needed data, I studied published reports prepared by the Hotel and Restaurant Association; then I interviewed the person in charge of frequent-stay programs at three hotels. Finally, Dr. Kenneth Lowe, professor of hospitality services at Southern Cal, reviewed and commented on my first draft. Thus, this proposal is based on a large body of data collected over two months.

Establish credibility by showing the basis for your recommendations.

In a third scenario, assume that Haney is an old-hand in the hotel business, having had twenty years of managerial experience, and that she respects your judgment. Assume further that she has made clear that she likes directness in writing and wants the important information up front—so that she can get the major ideas first and then skim, as necessary, the rest of the communication. The first paragraph of your memo might then be as follows:

> The purpose of this memo is to recommend implementing a frequent-stay plan for a 12-month test period in our three Oregon resorts. This recommendation is based on a review of the policies of our competitors and on an analysis of the costs and benefits of instituting such a program. The pertinent data is presented below.

As can be seen, the type of information, the amount, and the organization reflect what we know about our audience.

Some readers like a direct approach, regardless of the purpose of the message.

Content

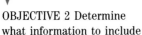

OBJECTIVE 2 Determine what information to include and in what order it should be presented.

Once the purpose of the message has been determined and the needs and interests of the audience identified, the next step is to decide what information to include. For many letters and simple memos, this step presents few problems. However, many communication tasks require numerous decisions about what information to include. How much background information is needed? How much statistical data is needed to support the conclusions? Is expert opinion needed? Would examples, anecdotes, or graphics aid comprehension? Will data-gathering be necessary, or do you have all the needed information at hand?

Include all relevant information. Exclude all irrelevant information.

The trick is to include all the information needed so that you don't lose the reader, yet to avoid including irrelevant material that wastes the reader's time and obscures important data. Different writers use different methods for identifying what information is needed. Some simply jot down notes on the points they plan to cover. For all but the simplest communications, the one thing you should *not* do is start writing immediately, deciding as you write what information to include. Instead, start with at least a rudimentary outline of the essential skeleton of your message—whether it's in your head, in a well-developed outline, or in the form of jotted notes.

Do not start writing until you have planned what you want to say.

One useful strategy is **brainstorming**—jotting down ideas, facts, possible leads, and anything else you think might be helpful in constructing your message. Aim for quantity, not quality. Don't evaluate your output until you've run out of ideas. Then begin to refine, delete, combine, and otherwise revise your ideas to form the basis for your message.

Another possible strategy is **mind mapping**[1] (also called "clustering"), a process that avoids the step-by-step limitations of lists. Instead, you write the objective of your message in the middle of a page and circle it. Then, as you think of possible points to add, simply pencil them in, linking them by a line to either the main objective or to another point. As you think of other points, add them where you think they might fit. This visual outline offers flexibility and encourages free-thinking. Figure 5.3 shows an example of mind mapping for the frequent-stay memo.

Mind Mapping   **FIGURE 5.3**

Organization

The final step in the planning process is to establish the **organization** of the message; that is, to determine in what order to discuss each topic. After you have brainstormed or mapped out your ideas around a main idea, you need to organize them. Using classification, subordination, and sequence, you can organize your ideas in a way that suits your purpose and your audience. The result will be an outline you can use to draft your message in its most effective form.

> To maintain good human relations, base your organization on the expected reader reaction.

Classification—that is, grouping related ideas—is the first step in outlining your message. Once you have grouped your ideas, you'll need to differentiate between the major and minor points. Ranking ideas by their relative importance will let you line up minor ideas and evidence to support the major ideas.

The sequence of the major ideas often depends on the reaction you expect from your audience. If you expect a positive response, use a direct approach in which the conclusion is presented first and the reasons for the conclusion after. If you expect a negative response, use an indirect approach in which the reasons are presented first and the conclusion after. (Because of the importance of the sequence in which topics are discussed, the organization of each type of communication is discussed in the chapters that follow.)

DRAFTING

▼

OBJECTIVE 3 Compose a first draft of your message.

Having finished the planning process, you are ready to begin **drafting**—the process of composing a preliminary version of a message. The success of this second stage of the process depends on the attention you gave to the first stage. The warning given earlier bears repeating—Don't begin writing too early. Some people believe they have weak writing skills, so their first impulse when faced with a writing task is to jump in and get it over with as quickly as possible. Avoid the rush. Follow each of the five steps of the writing process to ease your journey and improve your product.

Do not combine drafting and revising. They involve two separate skills and two separate mindsets.

Probably the most important thing to remember about drafting is to just let go—let your ideas flow as fast as possible onto paper or computer screen, without worrying about style, correctness, or format. Separate the drafting stage from the revising stage. Although some people revise as they create, most find it easier to first get their ideas down on paper in rough-draft form; then revise. It's much easier to polish a page full of writing than a page full of nothing!

As one writing authority noted,

> Writing is art. Rewriting is craft. Mix the two at your peril. If you let your inner editor (who, according to popular theory, lives in the left side of your brain) into the process too early, it's liable to overpower your artist, blocking your creative flow.[2]

So avoid moving from author to editor too quickly. Your first draft is just that—a draft. Don't expect perfection, and don't strive for it. Concentrate, instead, on recording in narrative form all the points you identified in the planning stage. When you have finished and then begin to revise, you will likely discover that a surprising amount of your first draft is usable and will be included in your final draft.

The most efficient way of drafting your message is at the computer because it is easy to revise messages with word processing software. Typing at a typewriter is second most efficient, and handwriting the least efficient. (Dictating, another efficient means of inputting messages, requires special oral communication skills and is discussed in Chapter 16.) Regardless of the way you input your draft, try to edit from typed copy rather than from handwritten copy.

Avoiding Writer's Block

If a report is due in five weeks, some managers (and students) spend four weeks worrying about the task and one week (or one long weekend) actually writing the report. Similarly, when given 45 minutes to write a letter or memo, some people spend 35 minutes worrying or staring at a blank page or blank screen and 10 minutes actually writing.

These people are experiencing **writer's block**—the inability to focus on the writing process and to draft a message. The causes of writer's block are well known:

- *Failure consciousness:* Self-doubts about our ability to write effectively
- *Procrastination:* The tendency to put off what we dislike doing
- *Impatience:* Growing tired of the naturally slow pace of the writing process
- *Perfectionism:* The belief that our draft must be perfect the first time

These factors naturally interfere with creativity and concentration. In addition, they lower the writer's self-image and make him or her even more reluctant to tackle the next writing task. The treatment lies in some or all of the following strategies.

Start with Positive Self-Talk. Recognize that you're probably not much different from your peers with regard to writing—your level of skill is probably similar and perhaps your fear of writing is also similar. Tell yourself that you've successfully made it this far in school or in your career, that you're an intelligent and resourceful person, and that you can do what you put your mind to do. Positive thinking is an important first step.

Choose the Right Environment. The ability to concentrate on the task at hand is one of the most important components of effective writing. The best environment may not be the same desk where you normally do your other work. Even if you can turn off the phones and shut the door to visitors, silent distractions can bother you—a notation on your calendar reminding you of an important upcoming event, notes about a current project, even a photograph of a loved one. Many people write best in a library-type environment—with a low noise level, relative anonymity, and the space to spread out notes and other resources at a large table. Others find a computer room conducive to thinking and writing—with its low level of constant background noise and the presence of other students similarly engaged.

Schedule a Reasonable Block of Time. If the writing task is short, you can block out enough time to plan, draft, and revise the entire message. If the task is long or complex, however, block out no more than two hours or so. After all, writing is hard work. When your time is up or your work completed, give yourself a reward—take a break, get a snack, and so forth.

State Your Purpose in Writing. Having identified your purpose during the planning phase, write it at the top of your blank page or tack it on the bulletin board in front of you. Keep it visible so that it will be uppermost in your consciousness as you compose.

OBJECTIVE 4 Use a variety of strategies to overcome writer's block.

Employ the power of positive thinking: You *can* write an effective message!

Even though Neil Simon writes award-winning plays for a living, he probably has experienced writer's block. Choosing the best environment in which to write is one way to avoid writer's block, and although many people prefer a room with no distractions, Simon's writing environment is filled with mementos and framed posters of his plays.

Source: Photograph of Neil Simon by Sing-Si Schwartz from FROM THE DESK OF, © 1989 by Sid Lerner & hal Drucker, reprinted by permission of Harcourt Brace Jovanovick, Inc.

Engage in Free Writing.   Review your purpose and your audience; then, as a means of releasing your pent-up ideas and getting past the block, begin **free writing.** Write continuously for 10 to 15 minutes, literally without stopping. Don't look back and don't stop writing. If you cannot think of anything to say, simply keep repeating the last word or keep writing some sentence such as, "I'll think of a new idea soon." Resist the temptation to evaluate what you've written. (If you're composing at a computer, darken your screen so you won't be tempted to review what you've written thus far; this is called "invisible writing.") At the end of 10 to 15 minutes, take a breather, stretch and relax, read what you've written, and then start again, if necessary.

Avoid the Perfectionism Syndrome.   Remember that the product you're producing now is a draft—not a final document. Don't worry about style, coherence, spelling or punctuation errors, and the like. The artist must create something before the editor can refine it.

Talk Out Loud.   Think out loud. Some people are more skilled at speaking their thoughts than at writing them. Picture telling a colleague about what you're writing and explain aloud the ideas you're trying to get across. Hearing your ideas will help sharpen and focus them.

You need not write the parts of a message in the order in which they will finally appear. Begin with the easiest parts.

Write the Easiest Parts First.   The opening paragraph of a letter is often the most difficult one to compose. If this is the case for you, skip it and begin in the middle. In a report, the procedures section may be easier for you to write than the recommendations. Getting *something* down on paper will give you a sense of accomplishment, and your writing may generate ideas for other sections.

Try each of these strategies at least once; then build into your writing regimen those that work best for you. Just as different athletes and artists use different strategies for accomplishing their work, so do different writers. There is no one best way, so choose what is effective for you.

REVISING

Revision is the process of modifying a document to increase its effectiveness. Having the raw material—your first draft—available, you can now refine it into the most effective document possible, considering its importance and the time constraints under which you are working. If possible, put your draft away for a period of time—the longer the better. Leaving time between creation and revision helps you distance yourself from your writing. If you revise immediately, the memory of what you "meant to say" rather than what you actually said is too strong and may keep you from seeing weaknesses in logic or diction.

OBJECTIVE 5 Revise for content, style, and correctness.

Three Types of Revision

Although we have discussed revising as the third step of the writing process, in fact it is several steps. Most writers revise first for content, then for style, and finally for correctness. All types of revision are most efficiently done from a typed copy of the draft rather than from a handwritten copy.

Revise for Content.   After an appropriate time lag, first reread the entire draft to get an overview of your message. Ask yourself such questions as these:

Revise for content, style, and correctness.

- Is the content appropriate for the purpose I've identified?
- Will the purpose of the message be clear to the reader?
- Have I been sensitive to the needs of the reader?
- Is all the information necessary?
- Is any needed information missing?
- Is the order of presentation of the topics effective?

Revise for Style.   Now read each paragraph again (aloud, if possible), using the 16 criteria contained in Checklist 1: Effective Business Writing on page 103 as the basis for your evaluation. Reading aloud gives you a feel for the rhythm and flow of your writing. Long sentences that made sense as you wrote them may leave you out of breath when you read them aloud.

If possible, read your message aloud to friends or colleagues, or have them read your draft (after you've revised it as much as possible). Ask them what is clear or unclear. Can they identify the purpose of your message? What kind of image do they get of the writer just from reading the message? Making use of Checklist 1 and securing feedback from colleagues will help you identify areas of your message that need revision.

Make sure the readability of your message is appropriate for the intended audience. Calculating the readability of your draft is often a useful step in the revision process. More importantly, however, is the analysis that follows the calculation. Considering what you know about the interest level, educational level, and knowledge of your audience, revise the readability of your draft as appropriate.

Revise for Correctness.   The final phase of revising is **editing**, the process of ensuring that writing conforms to standard English. Editing involves checking for *correctness;* that is, identifying problems with grammar, spelling, punctuation, and word usage. Editing should follow revision, because there is no need to correct surface errors in passages that may later be revised or deleted.

Writers who fail to check for grammar, mechanical, and usage errors risk losing credibility with their reader. Such errors may distract the reader, delay comprehension, cause misunderstandings, and reflect negatively on the writer's abilities.

Revising on the Computer

You can write faster and revise much faster on a computer than in long-hand.

Using the computer makes nearly every step of the writing process easier and more effective. Even a mediocre typist (using a hunt-and-peck style) can probably write faster at the keyboard than in longhand. (Given the pervasive impact of technology, every student today should develop touch-keyboarding skills of at least 30 words per minute. Considering the amount of time contemporary managers spend using computers, keyboarding must be considered a crucial *communication* skill.) Also, the fact that paragraphs can be moved around so easily lets you write the easiest parts first. Or, if you can't think of what to write in one section, you can simply space down a few lines and begin the next topic.

But the place where computers play their most effective role is during revision. For example, with word processing you can

- move paragraphs around in your document to achieve the most logical organization.
- easily insert, delete, and change wording.
- print drafts quickly (many people find revising on paper easier than revising on a computer screen).
- use the search-and-replace function to make a change throughout the document; for example, in one easy step you could change every occurrence of the abbreviation "SEC" to "Securities and Exchange Commission" in a 10-page document.
- use the thesaurus function to produce a list of synonyms for any highlighted word to help you select the word with the precise meaning that is appropriate for the particular context.
- use the spelling function to help you proofread your document for spelling and typographical errors. The computer does this by comparing each word in the document with its built-in list of perhaps 100,000 words. Any word not on the computer's word list (including most proper names) is highlighted for you to decide whether the word is spelled correctly. Most spelling checkers let the user add a certain number of words to the computer's dictionary. (Note that a spelling checker can only *help* you check for spelling and typographical errors; words that are misused or errors that form a new word are not identified. Thus, most spelling checkers would not identify any problems with even a sentence as silly as "i mint too meat hem at $5 o'clock four a drinks.")

In addition to these features, which are standard on most word processing programs, other software programs are becoming available as writing aids. For example, outline programs help writers easily develop and revise outlines, and grammar and style checkers identify possible problems in these areas.

SPOTLIGHT ON TECHNOLOGY

GRAMMAR AND STYLE CHECKERS

Most of us can use all the help we can get when it comes to writing; and that's where grammar and style checkers come in. These software programs identify possible examples of awkward writing, clichés and jargon, passive voice, mismatched punctuation marks, and the like. They then propose alternatives that you can accept, reject, or mark for subsequent fixing. Some of the best-known programs are *Correct Grammar* (Life Tree Software, Inc.), *Grammatik* (Reference Software Inc.), *RightWriter* (RightSoft Inc.), *MacProof* (Automated Language Processing Systems), and *Sensible Grammar* (Sensible Software, Inc.).

The programs compare words and phrases in a document with built-in lists of words and phrases. Many programs let users add items of their own and delete those they'd rather ignore. A few programs go beyond the compare-and-mark function and actually use artificial intelligence to identify incorrectly used homonyms such as *there*, *their*, and *they're*. For example, *Grammatik*, can not only identify such homonym problems but also can spot many instances of missing words in a sentence, mismatched verb tenses, and subject-verb disagreement.

Here are examples of common problems flagged by these programs, along with the checker's suggestions for revision:

> *Draft:* It is important that we consider this option.
> *Checker:* Avoid beginning sentences with "There is" and "It is."

> *Draft:* Mr. Avery and Ms. Blanchard was at the meeting.
> *Checker:* Consider substituting *were* for *was*.

> *Draft:* We should make some revisions to our manual.
> *Checker:* Replace "make some revisions to" with "revise."

> *Draft:* American National stock was traded at 14½ today.
> *Checker:* Forms of the verb *to be* signal wordy constructions or passive voice.

> *Draft:* Each and every expenditure must be documented.
> *Checker:* Redundant; use *each* or *every*.

In addition to flagging possible grammar and style problems, many programs identify such common punctuation problems as placing a comma after (instead of before) a quotation mark, leaving two spaces between words, or omitting a closing quotation mark or parenthesis. Finally, many programs also provide a word count and readability grade level.

How well do such programs work? Many are rather slow, often taking several minutes to analyze a typical business letter. Also, many of the suggestions are rather nit-picking. A large percentage of the words and phrases that are flagged are, in fact, used appropriately; yet other more serious errors are not identified. And the programs cannot distinguish between the appropriate and inappropriate use of passive voice (the fourth sentence in the preceding illustration, for example, is an appropriate use of passive voice). Nevertheless, as one reviewer noted, "They're far from perfect, but so is most business writing. And every little bit helps."

Sources: William M. Bulkeley, "Improving the Grammar of Computer Users," *Wall Street Journal*, January 25, 1989, B1; Jim Forbes, "Volkswriter Update Includes Grammar Checker," *PC Week*, January 30, 1989, 24; Michael J. Miller, "Perfect Grammar Takes Word Processing One Step Further," *Infoworld*, January 30, 1989, 52; Bob Sillery, "Serious Style Analyzers," *Personal Computing*, December 1988, 240–241; Mark Tebbe, "Grammar Checkers Don't Receive A's But They Do Add Polish to Your Prose," *PC Week*, January 23, 1989, 24.

FORMATTING

Letters are external documents sent to people outside the organization. Memos are internal documents sent to people inside the same organization as the writer. Reports may be either internal or external. No one format for any type of business document is universally accepted as standard; a fair amount of variation is common in industry. This section discusses the most common formatting conventions for letters and memos. Report formats are discussed in Chapter 13.

OBJECTIVE 6 Format letters, envelopes, and memos in standard format.

Formatting Letters and Envelopes

Regardless of who actually types your letters, *you* are the one who signs them, so *you* must accept responsibility for not only the content but also the mechanics, format, and appearance of your documents. In addition, the increasing use of word processing means that executives now keyboard many of their own documents—without the help of a secretary.

Another reason for the importance of formatting standards has to do with efficiency. Formatting documents the same way each time means that decisions do not have to be made for each individual document; thus, a standard format not only saves time but also gives a consistent appearance to the organization's documents. Finally, readers expect to find certain information in certain positions in a document; if it is not there, the reader is unnecessarily distracted. For all these reasons, you should become familiar with the standard conventions for formatting documents.

Letter Styles   The three standard letter styles are shown in Figure 5.4. (*Note:* The down arrows with numbers indicate how many lines to space down before typing the next part. For example, ↓ 15 before the date means you should begin typing the date on line 15; likewise, ↓ 5 after the date means to type the first line of the inside address on the fifth line below the date.)

The *block style* is the simplest letter style to type because all lines begin at the left margin. In the *modified-block style,* the date and closing lines begin at the center point. Offsetting these parts from the left margin enables the reader to locate each part more quickly. In the *simplified style,* which is seldom used, all lines begin at the left margin, the salutation and complimentary closing are omitted, and the subject line and writer's identification are typed in all-capital letters.

The most common punctuation style is a colon after the salutation and a comma after the complimentary closing.

Punctuation Styles   The *standard punctuation* style—the most common format—contains a colon (never a comma) after the salutation and a comma after the complimentary closing. The *open punctuation* style, on the other hand, contains no punctuation after these two lines.

Stationery   Most letters are typed on standard-sized stationery, $8\frac{1}{2}$ by 11 inches. The first page of a business letter is typed on letterhead stationery, which shows company information printed at the top. Subsequent pages of a business letter and all pages of a personal business letter (a letter written to transact one's personal business) are typed on good-quality plain paper.

The letter should look balanced on the page.

Margins   Side and bottom margins should be 1 to $1\frac{1}{2}$ inches (most word processing programs have default margins of 1 inch). Begin the date on line 15. Set a tab at the center if you're formatting a modified-block style letter and 5 spaces from the left margin if you're indenting paragraphs. Leave a 1-inch top margin for the second page.

Required Letter Parts   The required letter parts are as follows:

Date Line   Type the current month (spelled out), day, and year—in that order—on line 15. Begin either at the center point (modified-block) or at the left margin (all other styles).

Inside Address   The inside address shows the name and address of the party to whom you're writing. Include a personal title (e.g., *Mr., Mrs., Miss,* or *Ms.*). The addressee's job title, if included, may be typed either on the same line as the name (separated from the name by a comma) or on the following line by itself. Use the two-letter Postal Service abbreviation, typed in all capitals with no period (see Figure 5.4), and leave one space between the state and Zip Code. Type the inside address at the left margin on the fifth line below the date (leaving four blank lines). For international letters, type the name of the country in all-capital letters on the last line by itself.

Salutation   Use the same name in both the inside address and the salutation. If the letter is addressed to a job position (e.g., *Personnel Manager*) rather than to a person, use a generic, but nonsexist, greeting, such as "Dear Personnel Manager." If the letter is addressed to a company, use a salutation such as "Ladies and Gentlemen." If you typically address the reader in person by first name, use the first name in the salutation (e.g., "Dear Lois:"); otherwise, use a personal title and the surname only (e.g., "Dear Ms. Lane:"). Leave one blank line before and after the salutation.

Body   Single-space the lines of each paragraph and leave one blank line between paragraphs. Follow correct word-division rules (see Appendix A) when dividing a word at the end of a line to make a more even right margin.

Page 2 Heading   Type the addressee's name, the page number, and the date beginning on line 7, blocked at the left margin. Leave two blank lines before continuing with the text. (Carry forward to a second page at least two lines of the body; that is, do not type just the closing lines on a new page.)

Complimentary Closing   Begin the complimentary closing at the same horizontal point as the date line, capitalize the first word only, and leave one blank line before and three blank lines after (to allow room for the signature). If a colon follows the salutation, use a comma after the complimentary closing; otherwise, no punctuation follows.

Signature   Some women insert the personal title they prefer (*Ms., Miss,* or *Mrs.*) in parentheses before their signature. Men never include a personal title.

Writer's Identification   The writer's identification (name or job title, or both) begins on the fourth line immediately below the complimentary closing. Do not use a personal title. The job title may go either on the same line as the typed name, separated from the name by a comma, or on the following line.

Reference Initials   When used, reference initials (the initials of the typist) are typed at the left margin in lowercase letters without periods, with one blank line before. Omit reference initials if you type your own letter.

Do not use reference initials when typing your own correspondence.

FIGURE 5.4   Correspondence Formats

Date Line

Inside Address

Salutation

Body

Complimentary Closing

Writer's Identification

Reference Initials
Notations

THE BOOK MARK   185 SILVER CENTER, BOZEMAN, MT 59715 • Phone (406) 555-3856

↓15

November 18, 19--
↓5

Ms. Ella Shore, Professor
Department of Journalism
Mountainside College
Paseo Canyon Drive
Great Falls, MT 59404 ↓2

Dear Ms. Shore: ↓2

Thank you for thinking of The Book Mark when you were planning
the advertising for next year's yearbook at Mountainside
College. We appreciate the wide acceptance your students and
faculty give our merchandise, and we are proud to be represented in the <u>Mountain Lark</u>. While budget restrictions prevent
us from taking a full-page ad, we are happy to purchase a
quarter-page ad, as follows: ↓2

1. The ad should include our standard trademark and the words
   "Welcome to The Book Mark." Please note that the word "The"
4→ is part of our name and should begin with a capital letter. ↓2

2. We would prefer that our ad appear in the top right corner
   of a right-facing page, if possible. ↓2

Our trademark is enclosed for you to duplicate. I am also
enclosing a check for $275 to cover the cost of the ad. Best
wishes as you prepare the fifty-fifth edition of your yearbook. ↓2

Sincerely,

4↓ *David J. Petrello*

David J. Petrello
Sales Manager
↓2

rmt
Enclosures
c: Advertising Supervisor

Modified-Block Style Letter With Standard Punctuation

Correspondence Formats
FIGURE 5.4

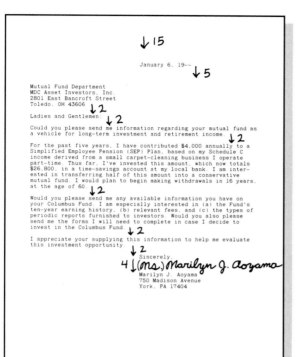

↓15

January 6, 19-- ↓5

Mutual Fund Department
MDC Asset Investors, Inc.
2801 East Bancroft Street
Toledo, OH 43606 ↓2

Ladies and Gentlemen: ↓2

Could you please send me information regarding your mutual fund as
a vehicle for long-term investment and retirement income. ↓2

For the past five years, I have contributed $4,000 annually to a
Simplified Employee Pension (SEP) Plan, based on my Schedule C
income derived from a small carpet-cleaning business I operate
part-time. Thus far, I've invested this amount, which now totals
$26,800, in a time-savings account at my local bank. I am inter-
ested in transferring half of this amount into a conservative
mutual fund. I would plan to begin making withdrawals in 16 years,
at the age of 60. ↓2

Would you please send me any available information you have on
your Columbus Fund. I am especially interested in (a) the Fund's
ten-year earning history, (b) relevant fees, and (c) the types of
periodic reports furnished to investors. Would you also please
send me the forms I will need to complete in case I decide to
invest in the Columbus Fund. ↓2

I appreciate your supplying this information to help me evaluate
this investment opportunity. ↓2
Sincerely,

4 (Ms.) Marilyn J. Aoyama
Marilyn J. Aoyama
750 Madison Avenue
York, PA 17404

Personal-Business Letter in Modified-Block Style

↓13

MEMO TO: Max Dillion, Sales Manager ↓2
FROM: Richard J. Hayes ↓2 (RJH)
DATE: February 25, 19-- ↓2
SUBJECT: New-Venture Proposal ↓3

The purpose of this memorandum is to propose the purchase or lease
of a van to be used as a mobile bookstore. We could then use this
van to generate sales in the outlying towns and villages throughout the state ↓2

We have been aware for quite some time that many small towns
around the state do not have adequate bookstore facilities, but
the economics of the situation are such that we would not be able
to open a comprehensive branch and operate it profitably. However,
we could afford to stock a van with books and operate it for a few
days at a time in various small towns throughout the state. As you
are probably aware, the laws of this state would permit us to acquire a statewide business license fairly easily and inexpensively. ↓2

With the proper advance advertising, we should be able to generate
much interest in this endeavor. It seems to me that this idea has
much merit because of the flexibility it offers us. For example,
we could tailor the length of our stay with the size of the town
and the amount of business generated. Also, we could tailor our
inventory to the needs and interests of the particular locales ↓2

The driver of the van would act as the salesperson; and we would,
of course, have copies of our complete catalog so that mail orders
could be taken as well. Please let me have your reactions to this
proposal. If you wish, I can explore the matter further and generate cost and sales estimates. ↓2

jmc

Memo on Plain Paper

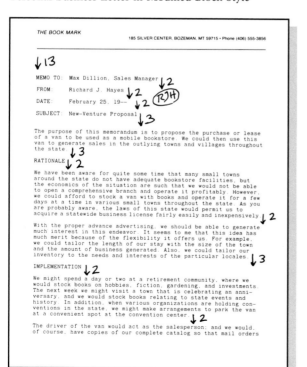

THE BOOK MARK   185 SILVER CENTER, BOZEMAN, MT 59715 • Phone (406) 555-3856

↓13

MEMO TO: Max Dillion, Sales Manager ↓2
FROM: Richard J. Hayes ↓2 (RJH)
DATE: February 25, 19-- ↓2
SUBJECT: New-Venture Proposal ↓3

The purpose of this memorandum is to propose the purchase or lease
of a van to be used as a mobile bookstore. We could then use this
van to generate sales in the outlying towns and villages throughout
the state. ↓3

RATIONALE ↓2

We have been aware for quite some time that many small towns
around the state do not have adequate bookstore facilities, but
the economics of the situation are such that we would not be able
to open a comprehensive branch and operate it profitably. However,
we could afford to stock a van with books and operate it for a few
days at a time in various small towns throughout the state. As you
are probably aware, the laws of this state would permit us to
acquire a statewide business license fairly easily and inexpensively ↓2

With the proper advance advertising, we should be able to generate
much interest in this endeavor. It seems to me that this idea has
much merit because of the flexibility it offers us. For example,
we could tailor the length of our stay with the size of the town
and the amount of business generated. Also, we could tailor our
inventory to the needs and interests of the particular locales ↓3

IMPLEMENTATION ↓2

We might spend a day or two at a retirement community, where we
would stock books on hobbies, fiction, gardening, and investments.
The next week we might visit a town that is celebrating an anniversary, and we would stock books relating to state events and
history. In addition, when various organizations are holding conventions in the state, we might make arrangements to park the van
at a convenient spot at the convention center. ↓2

The driver of the van would act as the salesperson; and we would,
of course, have copies of our complete catalog so that mail orders

Memo on Letterhead Stationery (First Page)

THE BOOK MARK   Memorandum

TO: Max Dillion, Sales Manager
FROM: Richard J. Hayes   (RJH)
DATE: February 25, 19--
SUBJECT: New-Venture Proposal ↓5

The purpose of this memorandum is to propose the purchase or lease of a van to be used as a mobile bookstore. We could then use this van to generate sales in
the outlying towns and villages throughout the state ↓2

We have been aware for quite some time that many small
towns around the state do not have adequate bookstore
facilities, but the economics of the situation are such
that we would not be able to open a comprehensive branch
and operate it profitably. However, we could afford to
stock a van with books and operate it for a few days at
a time in various small towns throughout the state. As
you are probably aware, the laws of this state would
permit us to acquire a statewide business license fairly
easily and inexpensively ↓2

With the proper advance advertising, we should be able
to generate much interest in this endeavor. It seems to
me that this idea has much merit because of the flexibility it offers us. For example, we could tailor the
length of our stay with the size of the town and the
amount of business generated. In addition, we could tailor our inventory to the needs and interests of the particular locales ↓2

The driver of the van would act as the salesperson; and
we would, of course, have copies of our complete catalog
so that mail orders could be taken as well. Please let
me have your reactions to this proposal. If you wish, I
can explore the matter further and generate cost and
sales estimates. ↓2

jmc

Memo on Memorandum Form

FIGURE 5.4   Correspondence Formats

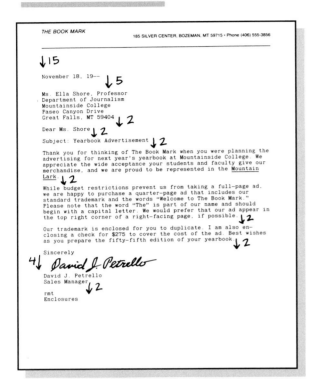

Block-Style Letter With Open Punctuation

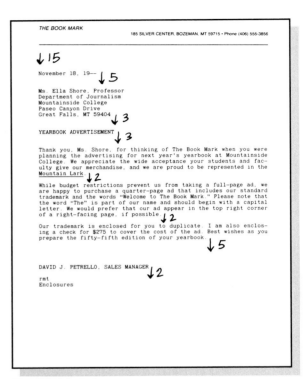

Simplified-Style Letter

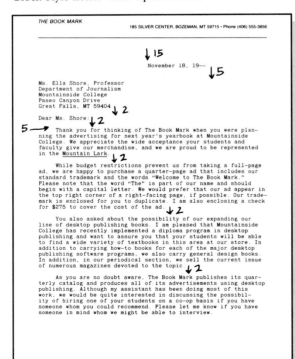

Modified-Block Style Letter With Indented Paragraphs

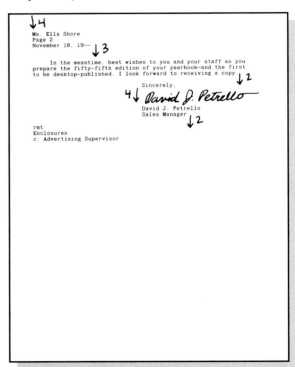

Page 2 of Modified-Block Style Letter

Correspondence Formats   FIGURE 5.4

LARGE (No. 10) ENVELOPES

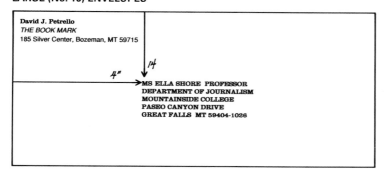

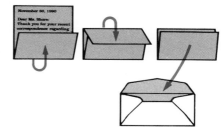

SMALL (No. 6 3/4) ENVELOPES

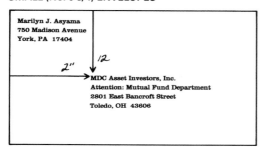

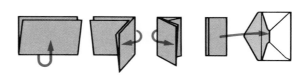

POSTAL SERVICE ABBREVIATIONS

U.S. POSTAL SERVICE ABBREVIATIONS FOR STATES, TERRITORIES, AND CANADIAN PROVINCES

States and Territories					
Alabama	AL	Kansas	KS	North Dakota	ND	Wyoming	WY
Alaska	AK	Kentucky	KY	Ohio	OH		
Arizona	AZ	Louisiana	LA	Oklahoma	OK		
Arkansas	AR	Maine	ME	Oregon	OR		
California	CA	Maryland	MD	Pennsylvania	PA	Canadian Provinces	
Colorado	CO	Massachusetts	MA	Puerto Rico	PR	Alberta	AB
Connecticut	CT	Michigan	MI	Rhode Island	RI	British Columbia	BC
Delaware	DE	Minnesota	MN	South Carolina	SC	Labrador	LB
District of Columbia	DC	Mississippi	MS	South Dakota	SD	Manitoba	MB
Florida	FL	Missouri	MO	Tennessee	TN	New Brunswick	NB
Georgia	GA	Montana	MT	Texas	TX	Newfoundland	NF
Guam	GU	Nebraska	NE	Utah	UT	Northwest Territories	NT
Hawaii	HI	Nevada	NV	Vermont	VT	Nova Scotia	NS
Idaho	ID	New Hampshire	NH	Virgin Islands	VI	Ontario	ON
Illinois	IL	New Jersey	NJ	Virginia	VA	Prince Edward Island	PE
Indiana	IN	New Mexico	NM	Washington	WA	Quebec	PQ
Iowa	IA	New York	NY	West Virginia	WV	Saskatchewan	SK
		North Carolina	NC	Wisconsin	WI	Yukon Territory	YT

Optional Letter Parts   Optional letter parts are as follows:

> Use a subject line when you want the reader to know immediately the purpose of your letter.

Subject Line   A subject line (identified by the words *Subject, Re,* or *In Re* followed by a colon) may be used to identify the topic of the letter. It is typed below the salutation, with one blank line before and one after.

Enumerations in the Body   Begin an enumeration (a numbered list) at the left margin and leave two spaces between the period after the number and the following text. Indent runover lines four spaces. If each item takes up a single line, single-space between items; otherwise, single-space the lines within each item and double-space between items.

Enclosure Notation   Use an enclosure notation if any additional items are to be enclosed in the envelope. Type "Enclosure" on the line immediately below the reference initials, and as an option, add the description of what is enclosed.

Copy Notation   If someone other than the addressee is to receive a copy of the letter, type a copy notation ("c:") immediately below the enclosure notation or reference initials, whichever comes last. Then follow the copy notation with the names of the people who will receive copies.

Postscript   If you add a postscript to a letter, type it as the last item, preceded by one blank line. The heading "P.S.:" is optional. Postscripts are used most often in sales letters.

> You may safely use the same format for domestic and international letters.

International Formatting Styles   In most respects, letters sent to and from a foreign country are formatted similarly. One analysis of business letters received from abroad by U.S. firms found that the majority of such letters were formatted in modified block style, used the American format for the date (month-day-year), used either a title and surname or first name only in the salutation, and "Sincerely," or "Sincerely yours," as the complimentary closing.[3]

Envelopes   Business envelopes have a printed return address. You may type your name above this address. Plain envelopes are used for personal business letters; you should type the return address (your own address) at the upper left corner. Envelopes may either be typed in standard upper- and lowercase style or in all-capital letters without any punctuation. On large (No. 10) envelopes, begin typing the mailing address on line 14 about 4 inches from the left edge. On small (No. 6¾) envelopes, begin typing the mailing address on line 12 about 2 inches from the left edge. Fold envelopes as shown in Figure 5.4.

Formatting Memos

> Memo formats vary widely.

Memos may be typed either on plain paper, on letterhead stationery, or on special memo forms. Although memo formats vary, those shown in Figure 5.4 are typical.

Use side and bottom margins of 1 to 1½ inches and a top margin of 2 inches. When typing a memo on plain paper or letterhead stationery, set a tab 10 spaces from the left margin to align the variable heading information.

Double-space the lines of the heading and leave two blank lines between the heading and body of a memo. Omit the salutation and closing lines, but use special notations such as reference initials, enclosure notation, and copy notation as appropriate.

Single-space the lines of the body of the memo, and double-space between paragraphs. Long memos sometimes contain report-type headings to help the reader along. The heading for the second page of a memo is the same as that for a letter.

PROOFREADING

Proofreading is the final quality-control check for your document. Remember that a reader may not know whether an incorrect word resulted from a simple typo or from the writer's ignorance of correct usage. And even one such error can have adverse effects; being *almost perfect* is not good enough. (Imagine the impact if your telephone directory were only 99% perfect—each page would contain about four wrong numbers!)

Don't depend on having a secretary catch and correct every mistake. To begin with, the increasing use of computers in the workplace means that managers key more of their correspondence themselves, bypassing the secretary. More importantly, it is *your* name that appears on the message; therefore, it is *your* reputation that is at stake. Take responsibility for ensuring the accuracy of your communications, just as you take responsibility for your other managerial tasks.

Proofread for content, typographical errors, and format. First, read through your document quickly, checking for content errors. Was any material omitted unintentionally? Unfortunately, when word processing has been used to move, delete, and insert material, writers sometimes find that passages have been omitted unintentionally or that the same passage shows up in two different places in the document. In short, check to make sure that your document *makes sense*.

Next, read through your document slowly, checking for typographical errors. Watch especially for errors that form a new word; for example, "I took the figures *form* last month's reports." Such errors are difficult to spot. Also be on the lookout for double words, such as "the the report." Double-check all proper names and all figures, using the original source if possible. (Don't overlook the possibility that you may have copied the words or figures incorrectly in your notes or first draft.) Professional proofreaders find that writers overlook errors most often in the titles and headings of reports, in the opening and closing parts of letters, and in the last paragraph of all types of documents.

Finally, visually inspect the document for appropriate format. Are all the parts included and in the correct position? Does the document look attractive on the page? What will be the receiver's first impression before reading the document? Do not consider the proofreading stage complete until you have read the entire document through without making any changes. There is always the possibility that in correcting one error you inadvertently introduced another.

Finally, after planning, writing, revising, formatting, and proofreading your document, transmit it—with the sure knowledge and satisfaction that you've taken all reasonable steps to ensure that it achieves its objectives.

OBJECTIVE 7 Proofread a document for content, typographical, and format errors.

Typographical errors may send a negative nonverbal message about the writer.

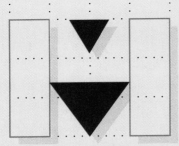

MICROWRITING A SIMPLE MEMO

Microwriting activities are used throughout this text to illustrate important communication concepts. These activities consist of short case studies of typical communication assignments. Each activity includes the *problem*, the *process*, and the *product*. The *problem* defines the situation and discusses the need for a particular communication task. The *process* is a series of questions that provides step-by-step guidance for accomplishing the specific communication task. Finally, the *product* is the key—the finished document.

Microwriting is a practical demonstration of a particular type of communication, shown close-up so you can see the process of writing and not just the results. This model helps you focus on one aspect of writing at a time. Use the microwriting steps as a regular part of your writing process so that your written communications will be easier and more effective.

The Problem

Today is December 3, 19—, and you are Alice R. Stengren, president of the Entrepreneurial Association of Reed Northern College. EARN is the newest of the six student organizations in the School of Business and has 38 members. It was formed two years ago when the Department of Management instituted a major in entrepreneurship. The purposes of EARN are to (1) provide opportunities for members to learn more about entrepreneurship, primarily through monthly meetings that feature guest speakers; (2) provide social interactions for future entrepreneurs; and (3) promote entrepreneurship as a major or minor course of study at the college.

To further the third purpose, the association recently voted to institute a $1,000 EARN scholarship. The scholarship will be awarded on the basis of merit to a junior or senior business student majoring in entrepreneurship at Reed Northern. Funds for the scholarship will be raised by selling coffee and doughnuts each day from 7:30 to 10:30 A.M. in the main lobby of the School of Business building.

As president of EARN, write a memo to Dean Richard Wilhite, asking permission to start this fund-raising project in January.

The Process

1. What is the purpose of your memo?

   ```
   Convince the dean to let EARN sell coffee and doughnuts
   in the main lobby from 7:30 to 10:30 A.M. daily, begin-
   ning in January.
   ```

2. Describe your primary audience.

   ```
   Dean Richard Wilhite:
   — Former president of Wilhite Energy Systems (started
     the company—an entrepreneur himself)
   ```

— 46 years old; has been dean at RNC for six years
  (very familiar with the school and college)
— Nationally known labor expert
— Holds tenure in the Department of Management (same
  department as entrepreneurship major)
— Devotes a great deal of time to lobbying the legis-
  lature and fund-raising (recognizes the need for
  fund-raising)
— Has spoken about the need for increasing the number
  of scholarships in the past (sympathetic to our
  cause)
— Dean does not know me personally but is familiar
  with EARN.

3. Is there a secondary audience for your memo? If so, describe.

   No secondary audience.

4. Considering your purpose, what information should be included in the
   memo? (Either brainstorm, jotting down the topics you might cover, or
   construct a mind map.)

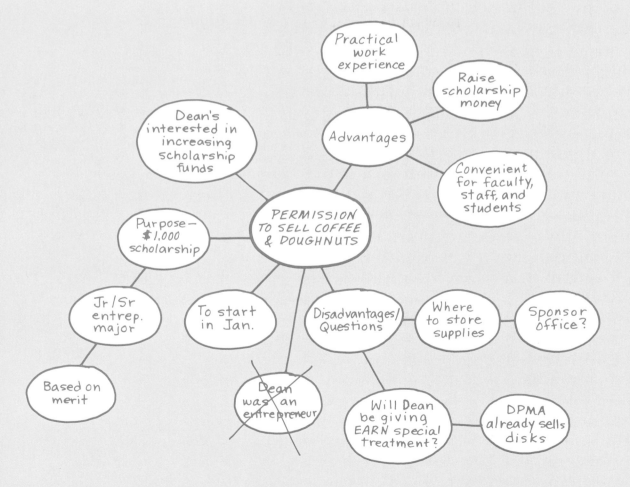

5. List the major topics in the order in which they should be discussed.

   a. Start by tying in with dean's common interest in
      increasing scholarships.
   b. Talk about establishing the scholarship and our fund-
      raising proposal.
   c. Emphasize practical work experience our members will
      gain.
   d. Discuss possible drawbacks—tell how storage problem
      will be solved and address special-treatment question
      (use positive language and subordinate).
   e. Give other details—hope to start in January.
   f. End by emphasizing another advantage—convenience for
      faculty, staff, and students.

6. Using the rough outline developed in Step 5, write your first draft. Concentrate on getting the needed information down. Do not worry about grammar, spelling, punctuation, transition, unity, and the like at this stage.

   The Entrepreneurial Association of Reed Northern
   (EARN) shares your interest in increasing the number of
   scholarships available to business majors. We recently
   voted to establish an annual $1000 scholarship for a
   jr. or sr. student majoring in Entrepreneurship. To
   fund this scholarship, we propose selling doughnuts and
   coffee in the main lobby from 7:30–10:30 A.M. daily. All
   of the profits will be earmarked for the Scholarship
   fund. A secondary benifit of this project is that it
   will provide practical work experience for our club
   members. We will purchase out own supplies and equipment, and keep careful records. When they are not in
   use, the supplies and equipment will be stored in the
   office of Professor Grant Edwards, our Sponsor. DPMA
   follows similar procedures with it's fund raising
   project of selling computer disks in the main lobby.
   We need your approval of this scholarship project in
   time for us to begin in January. This project also
   provides a convenient service for faculty, staff and
   students.

7. Revise your draft for content, style, and correctness. (As needed, refer to Appendix A for grammar, mechanics, punctuation, and usage guidance; refer to Checklist 1 on page 103 for style pointers.)

8. Format your revised draft, using plain paper and a standard memo style. Then proofread.

Revised Draft for Microwriting

FIGURE 5.7

The Entrepreneurial Association of Reed Northern (EARN) shares your interest in increasing the number of scholarships available to business majors. *Toward that end,* We recently voted to establish an annual $1,000 scholarship for a (jr) or (sr) student majoring in Entrepreneurship. To fund this scholarship, we propose selling doughnuts and coffee in the main lobby from 7:30 *to* 10:30 a.m. daily. All ~~of the~~ profits will be earmarked for the scholarship fund. ¶ A secondary benefit of this project is that it will provide practical work experience for our club members. We will purchase ~~out~~ *our* own supplies and equipment, and keep careful records. When ~~they are~~ not in use, the supplies and equipment will be stored in the office of Professor Grant Edwards, our sponsor. *The* (DPMA) follows similar procedures with it's fund-raising project of selling computer disks in the main lobby.

We look forward to receiving ~~We need~~ your approval of this ~~scholarship~~ *fund-raising,* project in time for us to begin in January. ~~This project also provides~~ a convenient service for faculty, staff and students.

In addition to raising new scholarship money and providing work experience for our members, we will also be providing

The Product

Final Memo for Microwriting

APS

MEMO TO: Dean Richard Wilhite

FROM: Alice R. Stengren, President
Entrepreneurial Association of Reed Northern

DATE: December 3, 19—

SUBJECT: Establishment of EARN Scholarship

The Entrepreneurial Association of Reed Northern (EARN) shares your interest in increasing the number of scholarships available to business majors. Toward that end, we recently voted to establish an annual $1,000 scholarship for a junior or senior student majoring in entrepreneurship. To fund this scholarship, we propose selling doughnuts and coffee in the main lobby from 7:30 to 10:30 a.m. daily. All profits will be earmarked for the scholarship fund.

A secondary benefit of this project is that it will provide practical work experience for our club members. We will purchase our own supplies and equipment and keep careful records. When not in use, the supplies and equipment will be stored in the office of Professor Grant Edwards, our sponsor. The Data Processing Management Association follows similar procedures with its fund-raising project of selling computer disks in the main lobby.

We look forward to receiving your approval of this fund-raising project in time for us to begin in January. In addition to raising new scholarship money and providing work experience for our members, we will also be providing a convenient service for faculty, staff, and students.

sma

The Writing Process

Planning

1. Determine the purpose of the message.
   a. Make it as specific as possible.
   b. Indicate the type of response desired from the reader.

2. Analyze the audience.
   a. Identify the primary audience and your relationship with this person.
   b. Determine how the audience will probably react.
   c. Determine how much the audience already knows about the topic.
   d. Determine what is unique about the audience—demographic information, interests, desired level of formality, and the like.

3. Decide what information to include in the message, given its purpose and your analysis of the audience.

4. Organize the information.
   a. Use a direct approach for routine and good-news messages: Present the major idea first, followed by supporting details.
   b. Use an indirect approach for persuasive and bad-news messages: Present the reasons first, followed by the major idea.
   c. Be guided by your knowledge of the audience.

Drafting

5. Choose a productive work environment and schedule a reasonable block of time to devote to the drafting phase.

6. Let your ideas flow as quickly as possible, without worrying about style, correctness, or format. If helpful, write the easiest parts first.

7. Do not expect a perfect first draft, but avoid the urge to revise at this stage.

8. If possible, leave a time gap between writing and revising the draft.

Revising

9. Revise for content: determine whether all information is necessary, whether any needed information has been omitted, and whether the content has been presented in an appropriate order.

10. Revise for style:
    a. Write with clarity, vigor, and conciseness; prefer short and simple words; and use positive language.
    b. Use a variety of sentence types; use active and passive voice appropriately.
    c. Control paragraph length and maintain unity and coherence.
    d. Establish a confident, courteous, and sincere tone; use emphasis and subordination appropriately; stress the "you" attitude; and use nondiscriminatory language.
    e. Ensure that the readability level of the document is appropriate for the intended audience.

11. Revise for correctness: Use correct grammar, mechanics, punctuation, and word choice.

Formatting and Proofreading

12. Format the document according to commonly used standards.
13. Proofread first for content, then for typographical errors, and finally for appropriate format.

The amount of time devoted to each step depends on the complexity, length, and importance of the document. Not all steps may be needed for each document, the steps don't necessarily have to come in order, and one step doesn't necessarily have to be completed before the next one is started. However, you would be well advised to follow each step consciously and carefully in the beginning. Then, after gaining experience and confidence, you can adapt the process to form a writing regimen that is most effective and efficient for you personally.

Summary

The writing process is a series of steps designed to produce written messages in an effective and efficient manner. These steps are summarized in Checklist 2.

The amount of time devoted to each step depends on the complexity, length, and importance of the document. Not all steps may be needed for each document, the steps don't necessarily have to come in order, and one step doesn't necessarily have to be completed before the next one is started. However, you would be well advised to follow each step consciously and carefully in the beginning. Then, after gaining experience and confidence, you can adapt the process to form a writing regimen that is most effective and efficient for you personally.

Key terms

Audience analysis— Identification of the needs, interests, and personality of the receiver of a communication.

Brainstorming— Jotting down ideas, facts, possible leads, and anything else that might be helpful in constructing your message.

Drafting— Composing a preliminary version of a message.

Editing— The stage of revision, which ensures that writing conforms to standard English.

Free writing— Writing continuously for 10–15 minutes without stopping as a means of generating a large quantity of narrative that will later be revised.

Mind mapping— Generating ideas for message content by first writing the purpose of the message in the center of a page and circling it, then writing possible points to include, linking each one to either the purpose or to another point.

Organization— The order in which topics are presented in a message.

Primary audience— The receiver of a communication whose cooperation is most crucial if the message is to achieve its objective.

Revising— Modifying a draft to increase its effectiveness.

Writer's block— The inability to focus one's attention on the writing process and to draft a message.

REVIEW AND DISCUSSION

1. Give an example of a general purpose and a specific objective for a communication task.   OBJECTIVE 1 ◀
2. How does your relationship with the audience affect the content and tone of the message?   OBJECTIVE 1 ◀
3. What strategies should you employ if the expected audience reaction is negative?   OBJECTIVE 1 ◀
4. Distinguish between a direct and an indirect organization plan.   OBJECTIVE 2 ◀
5. What steps should precede the drafting stage? Why?   OBJECTIVE 3 ◀
6. List eight possible strategies for overcoming writer's block.   OBJECTIVE 4 ◀
7. Why should a time gap be left between writing a first draft and revising the draft?   OBJECTIVE 5 ◀
8. Why is it generally not a good idea to combine the writing and the revising stages?   OBJECTIVE 5 ◀
9. Why should executives know how to format common business documents in a standard style?   OBJECTIVE 6 ◀
10. Provide an appropriate salutation for a letter that is addressed to the XYZ Company and directed to the attention of the customer service representative.   OBJECTIVE 6 ◀
11. What three types of errors should you check for when proofreading a document?   OBJECTIVE 7 ◀

EXERCISES

1. **Communication Purpose**   Compose a specific objective for each of the following communication tasks: OBJECTIVE 1 ◀
   a. A memo to a professor asking him to change a grade.
   b. A letter to MasterCard about an incorrect charge.
   c. A letter to the president of a local bank thanking her for speaking at your student organization meeting.
   d. A memo of reprimand to a subordinate for accessing unauthorized files on the company's mainframe computer.

2. **Audience Analysis**   Assume you must write a letter to your current business communication professor, asking him or her to let you take your final examination one week early so that you can attend your cousin's wedding.   OBJECTIVE 1 ◀
   a. Perform an audience analysis of your professor: List everything you know about this professor that might help you compose a more effective letter.
   b. Write two good opening sentences for this letter, the first one assuming that you are an A student who has missed class only once this term, and then one assuming you are a C student who has missed class six times this term.

3. **Free Writing**   As office manager for a small insurance firm, you want to buy a scanner to use with the three IBM Model 70 microcomputers in your office. The scanner would let you input graphics (charts and pictures) into your computer documents and enter data without having to rekeyboard. A scanner operates like a photocopier: You feed a copy of a picture or a page of text into the machine, and the picture or text   OBJECTIVES 1–4 ◀

then appears on your computer screen, where it can be used by your word processing or other software programs.

You must write a memo, the objective of which is to convince the general manager to let you buy a scanner and related software for $2,350. Think for a few moments about ways you could use this equipment. Then free write for 10–15 minutes without stopping and without worrying about the quality of what you're writing. (You may want to reread the discussion of free writing in this chapter.)

Now examine what you have written. If you were actually going to write the memo, how much of your output could actually be used after being revised?

▶ OBJECTIVES 1–7

4. **Collaboration**   You will work in groups of four for this assignment. Assume that a large shopping center is next to your campus, and many day students park there for free while attending classes. The shopping center management is considering closing this lot for student use, citing the need for additional space for customer parking. Four student organizations (a sorority, a fraternity, a business student organization, and a campus service organization) have decided to write a joint letter to the manager of the shopping center, trying to convince him to maintain the status quo.

Following the five-step process outlined in this chapter, compose a 1-page letter to the manager. Brainstorm to generate ideas for the content of the letter; have each member of the group call out possible points to include while one person writes down all the ideas. Don't evaluate any of the ideas until 10–15 minutes are up. Then discuss each point listed and decide which ones to include and in what order.

Format your letter in block style. Address it to Mr. Martin Uthe, executive manager of Fairview Shopping Center, P.O. Box 1083, DeKalb, IL 60115. Type an envelope, fold the letter, and put it in the envelope before submitting it to your instructor.

▶ OBJECTIVE 5

5. **Revising**   Revise the following draft of a memo from Tim White to Jack Presley. White is an assistant vice president and Presley is a vice president (White's superior) at Irving Bank. White believes that initially Presley might be hesitant about approving his request. After revising, format the memo in an appropriate format. Use January 4 as the current date.

```
The purpose of this memo is to request funds and
released time to attend the national convention of
Toastmasters International, which meets February 3–6 in
Honolulu, Hawaii. As you know, I'm required to give
numerous speeches each year for the Irving Bank. During
the past six months I made 18 presentations to outside
groups. I expect to make even more during the next six
months. These presentations were to school groups,
civic clubs, and professional organizations. Attending
this convention will help me to sharpen my speaking
skills. Also, since I chair the continuing education
committee of Toastmasters International, I have
scheduled a meeting of our committee for this
convention. Since I'm not ordinarily very busy at this
time of the year, my work here at Irving will not
suffer during my four day abscence. Also, when I assume
my new position as assistant loan officer next year, I
will be required to make numerous presentations to our
board of directors.
```

6. **Revising**   Bring in one page of a composition you have written in the past—one page of a term paper, essay exam, business letter, or the like. Make sure your name is not on the paper. Exchange papers with a colleague and complete the following revision tasks:

   a. Read the paper once, revising for content. Make sure that all needed information is included, that no unneeded information is included, and that the information is presented in a logical sequence.
   b. Read the paper a second time, revising for style. Make sure that the words, sentences, paragraphs, and overall tone are appropriate.
   c. Read the paper a third time, revising for correctness. Make sure that correct grammar, mechanics, punctuation, and word choice are followed.

   Return the paper to the writer. Then, using the revisions of your paper as a guide only (after all, you are the author), prepare a final version of the page. Submit both the marked-up version and the final version of your paper to your instructor.

7. **Proofreading**   Proofread the following letter, using the line numbers to indicate the position of each error. Proofread for content, typographical errors, and format. For each error, indicate by a "yes" or "no" whether the error would have been identified by using a computer's spelling checker. Assume that the letter is formatted exactly as shown, but on letterhead stationery. (*Hint:* Can you find 29 content, typographical, or format errors?)

OBJECTIVE 5 ◄

OBJECTIVE 7 ◄

```
 1                      April 31, 1993


 2   Mr. Thomas Johnson, Manger
 3   JoAnn @ Friends, Inc.
 4   1323 Charleston Avenue
 5   Minneapolis, MI 55402

 6   Dear Mr. Thomas:

 7   As a writing consultant, I have often aksed aud-
 8   diences to locate all teh errors in this letter.
 9   I am allways surprized if the find all the errors.
10   The result being that we all need more practical
11   advise in how to proof read.

12   To aviod these types of error, you must ensure that
13   that you review your documents carefully. I have
14   preparred the enclosed exercises for each of you
15   to in your efforts at JoAnne & Freinds, Inc.

16     Why not try this out on you own workers.

17                      Sincerly Yours


18                      Mr. Michael Land,
19                      Writing Consultant

20   dcl
```

CASE PROBLEM

Two Heads Are Better Than One

Last year the OIS Department installed a central dictation system, in which users can call over the telephone and dictate their correspondence and reports. All executives below the rank of vice president use the system. Three full-time transcriptionists in the OIS Department then transcribe the dictation using word processing software. Turnaround time is typically less than five hours.

Presently one of the three transcriptionists is a full-time temporary. Yesterday, Angela Harper, one of the other two transcriptionists, told Eric Fox that she really wants to be able to spend more time with her three-year-old son. She asked about the possibility of job-sharing. She has a friend, Barbara Curtis, who has extensive experience as a transcriptionist and who would also like to work half time. Angela could work from 8 A.M. until noon daily, and Barbara Curtis could work from 1 until 5 P.M. daily. Angela would be willing to stay a few minutes late each day, and Barbara would be willing to come a few minutes early so that they could coordinate their work. As much trouble as Eric has had trying to hire a permanent replacement for the temporary worker, he does not want to lose Angela as well.

On the plus side, he would then have two highly qualified employees, if one employee is sick the other may be willing to cover for her, two employees working only half a day would probably be more productive than one employee working the entire day, and any deficiencies in one employee would probably be compensated for by the other employee (e.g., if one employee is better at handling technical vocabulary than the other, such dictation could be saved for her). On the negative side is the fact that there might be some coordination problems (especially in the beginning), and fringe benefits will be increased somewhat (he estimates about 15%).

He decides to write a memo to Neelima Shrikhande recommending the concept of job sharing for this one position. Because this would be a new company policy, he knows that his memo will ultimately be forwarded to David Kaplan, who will make the final decision.

1. Assume the role of Eric Fox. What is the specific objective of your memo?

2. Who are the primary and secondary audiences for this memo? What do you know about the primary audience that will help you write a more effective memo?

3. List the points you should cover in the memo—in the order in which they should be covered.

4. Write a draft of the memo. (You may make up any needed information as long as it is reasonable.)

5. Revise the draft.

6. Format the memo, proofread, and submit.

- The word *sequoia* is the shortest common word that contains all five vowels.
- Can you identify the three grammatical errors in the sentence "Them's them"?
- Can you locate the more than 200 different words in the word *transportation*?

WORD WISE

PART

Basic
Correspondence

Routine Messages

After you have finished this chapter, you will be able to

1. Describe the basic features of a direct organizational plan and specify when it should be used.
2. Compose a routine request.
3. Compose a routine reply to a routine request.
4. Compose a routine claim letter.
5. Compose a routine adjustment letter.

With operations in over 50 countries and territories, Amway Corporation has more distributors than most companies have customers. With each of the million-plus distributors comes a flock of retail customers and, with both distributors and retail customers, come complaints, comments, and service demands.

Amway Corporation has several service departments, each of which specializes in one of the various types of distributor/customer concerns. The Order Services Department answers questions about the delivery and billing of orders. Supervisor Joan Jahr outlined, "In a typical month, Order Services handles 18,000 phone calls and 5,000 letters. The majority of our correspondence is from distributors or customers checking on their orders."

Like the routine messages at most large corporations, much of Order Service's correspondence concerns complaints, always a tricky subject for long-distance communication. "With a complaint, we try to keep out of whose fault it is and just resolve it to the caller's satisfaction. If we hassle them, we lose out. Our goal is to resolve as many concerns on the initial call as we can."

Complicated situations or those requiring extensive research require follow-up. "If we are unable to reach the distributor or customer by phone, or if we feel it is important to have the information in writing for future reference," Jahr said, "we send a letter. Because many of our situations are similar in content, we have 20 or 30 frequently used letters which we use as a base for much

Joan Jahr, Supervisor of Order Services, Amway Corporation, Ada, Michigan

correspondence. We also dictate original letters, send Mailgrams, and communicate over the CompuServe computer network.

"We are more personal than many companies," Jahr suggested. "In our letters, for example, we almost always address the distributor by first name. We make our letters friendly. It's not a business writing to a person, it's a person writing to a person. It's 'What can I do for you,' not 'What can the company do for you.'

"We try to make every situation personal for the distributor," Jahr continued. "We truly care about their welfare. As any good customer service representative does, we try to put ourselves in the distributor's shoes and offer a solution we would want if it was us."

In an organization as large as Amway Corporation, the logistics of routinely personalizing and sending so many messages is formidable. Jahr works closely with the Word Processing, Mail Services and Corporate Communications departments in order to ensure efficient management of communication channels and to remain attuned to the best available technology.

Final phone calls help ensure happy endings. "Often, we will phone the person to follow up on the situation. This gives not only a more personal touch, it also clears up any possible confusion," Jahr said. Apparently, Order Services has a good idea. Jahr added, "We get a lot of thank-you letters from the people we work with. It is really amazing how many take the time to write. We'll never really be satisfied with the level of service we provide, of course. We must continue to strive for improvements and provide the best customer service possible." ▼

▼

OBJECTIVE 1 Describe the basic features of a direct organizational plan and specify when it should be used.

PLANNING THE ROUTINE MESSAGE: SAY IT DIRECTLY

Most of the typical manager's correspondence consists of initiating and responding to routine situations. For example, a small business owner asks for a catalog and credit application from a potential supplier; a manager at a large corporation sends a memo notifying employees of a change in policy; a consumer notifies a company that a product ordered arrived in damaged condition; or a government agency responds to a request for a brochure.

Although routine, such messages are of interest to the reader because the information the message contains is necessary for day-to-day operations.

148

For example, although no company is pleased when a customer is dissatisfied with one of its products, the company *is* interested in learning about such situations so that it can correct the problem and prevent its recurrence.

When the purpose of a message is to convey routine information and our analysis of the audience indicates that the reader will probably be interested in its content, we use a **direct organizational plan**. The main idea is stated first, followed by any needed explanation, then a friendly closing, as illustrated in the following routine memorandum to employees:

> From Memorial Day through Labor Day, office hours will begin and end one-half hour earlier than usual. Thus, from May 29 through September 1, the hours of operation will be from 7:30 A.M. to 4 P.M. Beginning September 5, we will switch back to our regular schedule of 8 A.M. to 4:30 P.M.
>
> As usual, the main entrance to the building will remain unlocked from one hour before to one hour after office hours. At other times, you must sign in at the security entrance on 42nd Street.
>
> We hope you will enjoy having more free time during summer daylight hours.

The advantage of using a direct organizational plan for routine correspondence is that it puts the major news first—where it stands out and gets the most attention. This saves the reader's time because the reader can quickly see what the message is about by scanning the first sentence or two.

As just shown, much routine information is communicated via an interoffice memorandum (called a *memo*, for short), which is a written message from one member of the organization to another. Memos differ in format from business letters (see page 127), primarily in their use of a TO:/FROM:/DATE:/SUBJECT: heading rather than the inside address, salutation, and complimentary closing used in letters.

Memos also differ in content. First, because the communication is between people who work in the same environment, the use of technical jargon, abbreviations, and the like is often appropriate because their meaning will be understood and their use saves time. The writer can typically begin a memo by directly addressing the issue at hand without the need for extensive background explanation; in fact, many memos consist of only a few sentences. Although an informal writing style characterizes many memos, the principles of effective business writing discussed in Chapters 3–5 apply equally to memos and letters.

Before learning how to write routine messages, you should know that many times a letter or memo is not the most efficient means of achieving your objective. Often a quick phone call, a walk down the hall to a colleague's office, or even a postcard will work faster and at less expense than writing a letter or memo. However, when you need a permanent record of your message or when it must go to numerous people, a written response is preferred.

Of course, not all messages are routine, as we will see in the following chapters. Messages that the reader is likely to resist require persuasion and are discussed in Chapter 7, messages that contain bad news are discussed in Chapter 8, and special types of messages are discussed in Chapter 9.

The direct style presents the major idea first, followed by needed details.

Don't use the direct plan if presenting negative news or anticipating reader resistance.

COMMUNICATION **S I D E L I G H T**

THE MEMO: PROS AND CONS

Many executives dislike memos. A recent study showed that four out of five business people think memos are a waste of time, especially in an era when computer communication exists. Many executives also criticize memos for tending to be too self-serving, too long, and distributed to too many people.

Certainly, many memos are written for unworthy reasons, to avoid making decisions or to place blame elsewhere. But even in an age of computers, the beleaguered memo has much to offer. For one thing, it offers its author a chance to carefully organize his or her thoughts and to think through his or her position. If the position is a hostile one, for example, a manager responding to an employee's error, writing a memo gives the writer time to cool off and to compose a criticism that will likely be more constructive than would a verbal tirade.

From a practical standpoint, a memo is still a good way to inform a large number of people without holding a meeting. And a written note of appreciation (a "good job" memo) still carries more weight than a passing remark.

To be effective, however, memos must be written well and used sparingly. Too many memos do more harm than good. Above all, avoid mistaking a memo for action. It's one thing to write about doing something; it's another thing to do it!

Sources: Association Management, "In Defense of the Memo," January 1989, pp. 12–13. *Management World,* Sept.-Oct. 1988, p. 40. *The Wall St. Journal,* Dec 27, 1990, p. B1. "Enemies of Efficiency," by Pamela J. Podger.

▼

OBJECTIVE 2 Compose a routine request.

ROUTINE REQUESTS

A request is routine if you anticipate that the reader will readily do as you ask without having to be persuaded. For example, a request for specific information about an organization's product is routine, because all organizations appreciate the opportunity to promote their products. However, a request for free samples of a company's product to distribute at your store's anniversary sale might not be routine because the company might have concluded that such promotion efforts are not cost-effective; thus, you would have to persuade the reader to grant the request.

Major Idea First

Use a direct question, polite request, or statement to present your request.

When making a routine request, present the major idea—your request—clearly and directly in the first sentence or two. You may use either a direct question, a statement, or a polite request to present the main idea. A polite request is a statement that is phrased as a question out of courtesy and requires a period instead of a question mark, such as "May I please have your answer by May 3." Use a polite request when you expect the reader to respond by *acting* rather than by giving a yes or no answer. Always pose your request clearly and politely, and give any background information needed to set the stage.

Explain why you're making the request.

Direct question: Does Black & Decker offer educational discounts for public institutions making quantity purchases of tools? Blair Junior High School will soon be replacing approximately 50 portable electric drills used by our industrial-arts students.

Statement: I would appreciate your letting me know how I might invest in your deferred money-market fund. As an American currently working in Bangkok, Thailand, I cannot easily take advantage of your automatic monthly deposit plan.

Polite request: Would you please answer several questions about the work performance of Janice Henry. She has applied for the position as industrial safety officer at Inland Steel and has given your name as a reference.

Decide in advance how much detail you are seeking. If you need only a one-sentence response, it would be unfair to word your request in such a way to cause the writer to provide a three-page response. Define clearly the type of response you want and phrase your request to get that response.

Not: Please explain the features of your Interact word processing program.

But: Does your Interact word processing program automatically number lines and paragraphs?

Remember that you are imposing on the goodwill of the reader. Never ask for information that you can reasonably get on your own; that is, ask as few questions as possible. If many questions *are* necessary, number them; most readers will answer questions in the order in which you posed them and will be less likely to skip one. Yes/no questions or short-answer questions are easy for the reader to answer; but when more information is needed, use open-ended questions.

> Do not ask more questions than are necessary. Make the questions easy to answer.

Arrange your questions in logical order (for example, order of importance, chronological order, or simple-to-complex order), word each question clearly and objectively (to avoid bias), and limit the content to one topic per question. If appropriate, assure the reader that the information provided will be treated confidentially.

Explanation and Details

Most of the time you will need to give additional explanation or details about your initial request. Include any needed background information (such as the reason for asking) either immediately before or after making the request. For example, suppose you received the polite request just given asking about Janice Henry's job performance. Unless you were also told that the request came from a potential employer and that Janice Henry had given your name as a reference, you might be reluctant to provide such confidential information.

Or assume that you're writing a former employer or professor to ask for a letter of recommendation. You might need to give some background about yourself to jog the reader's memory. Or you might need to justify or expand on your request. Put yourself in the reader's position. What information would you need to answer the request accurately and completely?

A reader will be more likely to cooperate if you can show how he or she will benefit from your request. In fact, it is often the communication of such benefits that changes a message from being persuasive to being routine:

> If possible, show how others benefit from your having the requested information.

> Will you please help us to serve you better by answering several questions about your banking needs. We're planning to build a branch bank in your neighborhood and would like to make it as convenient for you as possible.

In general, you should stress benefits when they are not obvious to the reader, but you need not belabor the point if such benefits are obvious. For example, a memo asking employees to contribute to the United Way would probably not need to discuss the value of its activities since most readers would already be familiar with its work.

Friendly Closing

In your final paragraph, assume a friendly tone. If you are writing to an individual, enclosing a stamped and addressed reply envelope is a courteous gesture; most businesses, on the other hand, would prefer to use their own preprinted envelopes. Close by expressing appreciation for the assistance to be provided (but without seeming to take his or her cooperation for granted), by stating and justifying any deadlines, or by offering to return the favor. Make your ending friendly and positive.

Close on a friendly note.

> Since I must submit the first draft of my thesis by December 5, I would appreciate hearing from you by November 10.

> Please let me know if I can return the favor.

> We appreciate your providing this information, which will help us make a fairer evaluation of Janice Henry's qualifications for this position.

> May I please have this product information by October 1, when I place my Christmas wholesale orders. That way, I can include Kodak products in my holiday sales.

Figure 6.1 illustrates the guidelines for writing a routine request.

▼

OBJECTIVE 3 Compose a routine reply to a routine request.

ROUTINE REPLIES

Routine replies provide the information requested in the original letter or they otherwise comply with the writer's request. Like the original request letters, they are organized in a direct organizational style, putting the "good news"—the fact that you're complying with the writer's request—up front.

Respond promptly so that the information will arrive in time to be used.

Probably one of the most important guidelines to follow is to answer promptly. If a potential customer asks for product information, ensure that the information arrives before the customer must make a purchase decision. The time it took you to respond will have been wasted if your information arrives so late that it's no longer needed. Also, a delayed response might send the unintentional nonverbal message that you do not want to comply with the writer's request.

Your response should be courteous. If you appear to be acting grudgingly, you will probably lose any goodwill that a gracious response might have earned for you or your organization.

> *Not:* Although we do not like to provide the type of information you requested, we have decided to do so anyway.
> *But:* We are happy to provide the information you requested.

Grant the request or give the requested information early in the message. Doing so not only saves the reader's time but also puts him or her in a

Routine Letter Request

FIGURE 6.1

This letter is from a potential customer to a manufacturer.

```
                              September 3, 19—

Mr. Albert Gleason, Sales Manager
Saito Printers
4480 Thrush Way
El Paso, TX 79922

Dear Mr. Gleason:

Would you please provide me with information regarding your
Saito 150 portable printer. I want to purchase a lightweight      1
printer that I can use with my Toshiba 1200XE portable computer
when I travel.

Specifically, I would like answers to the following four
questions:

1. Does the Saito 150 produce letter-quality print?

2. Is it battery-operated? Since I wish to use the printer for
   traveling, such a feature is important.

3. Does the printer have a 15-inch carriage?

4. Does it come with a six-month guarantee?                        2

I appreciate your providing the information I need to make a
purchase. I would also appreciate receiving ordering informa-
tion.

                     Sincerely,

                     Carolyn J. Ryerson                            3
                     Carolyn J. Ryerson
                     48 Patterson Avenue
                     Columbus, OH 43202

                                                                   4
```

Presents the request in the first sentence, followed by the reason for asking.

Enumerates questions for emphasis and clarity. Questions are easy to answer.

Expresses appreciation; hints at a reader benefit.

Grammar and Mechanics Notes

1. A period follows a polite request.   2. Use the possessive form of a pronoun (*your*) before a gerund.   3. A personal business letter is typed on plain paper; the writer's address may be positioned either immediately above the date or (preferably) immediately below the writer's name.   4. Reference initials are not used in personal business letters.

good state of mind immediately. Although the reader may be pleased to hear that "We have received your letter of June 26," such news is not as eagerly received as telling the reader that "I would be pleased to speak at your Lion's Club meeting on August 8; thanks for thinking of me." Put the good news up front—where it will receive the most emphasis.

Be sure to answer all the questions asked or implied, using objective and clearly understood language. Although it is often helpful to provide additional information or suggestions, you should never fail to at least address all the questions asked—even if your answer is not what the reader hopes to hear. Questions are usually answered in the order in which they were asked, but consider rearranging them if a different order makes more sense. Determining what your reader already knows about the topic should help you to decide what information to include and how to phrase it.

Because the reader will be in a positive mood as the result of your letter, consider either including some sales promotion if appropriate or building goodwill by implying such characteristics about your organization as public spiritedness, quality products, social responsibility, concern for employees, and the like. To be effective, sales promotion and goodwill appeals should be subtle; avoid exaggeration and avoid devoting too much space to such efforts.

Often the writer's questions have been asked many times before; in such a situation, a form letter may be the most appropriate way to respond. (With word processing, it is often difficult to tell the difference between a form letter and a personal letter.) If a stockholder wrote asking why your company conducted business in South Africa, a personal reply would probably be called for; however, if a potential stockholder wrote asking for a copy of your latest annual report, you might simply send an annual report, along with a form letter such as the following:

> We are happy to send you our latest annual report. Also enclosed is a copy of a recent profile of Dennison Industries contained in the June issue of *Fortune* magazine.
>
> As you study our annual report, note the diversity of our product offerings—from men's clothing made by our Kemstran Division, to massive earth movers made by our Clark Equipment Company. This diversity is one of the reasons that we have shown a profit for the past 57 years. Our 5-, 10-, and 15-year income statements and return-on-investment analyses are shown on page 8 of the enclosed report.
>
> Dennison Industries stock is traded on the New York Stock Exchange, listed under "DenIn." Simply call your local broker to join the 275,000 other satisfied investors in Dennison Industries common stock.

In the body of your message, refer to any enclosure and then add an enclosure notation at the bottom of the letter; for example:

Sincerely,

Meredith Marshall

Meredith Marshall, Manager

sjn
Enclosure

Build goodwill and include subtle sales promotion if appropriate.

Consider using form letters for answering frequent requests.

Refer to any enclosures in your letter to make sure they're read.

Referring to a specific page of an enclosed brochure or a particular paragraph of an enclosed document helps ensure that such enclosures are read.

Close your letter on a positive, friendly note. Avoid such clichés as "If you have additional questions, please don't hesitate to let me know." Use original wording, personalized especially for the reader. After all, the reader might receive many letters like yours on the same day; and after reading, "Thank you for your interest in our products," five times, the expression begins to sound trite and insincere.

Figure 6.2 is a routine reply to the request shown in Figure 6.1. The original request asked four questions about the printer, and the answers are as follows: (1) no, the printer does not produce true letter-quality output; (2) no, it is not battery-operated; (3) yes, it does have a 15-inch carriage; and (4) no, it does not come with a six-month warranty. Only one of the questions can be answered with an unqualified "yes," and that is the one the respondent chose to lead off with. Positive language helps soften the impact of the negative responses to the other three questions. Also, reader benefits are stressed throughout the letter; instead of just describing the features, the writer shows how the features can benefit the reader.

Checklist 3 summarizes the points you should consider when writing and responding to routine requests. Use this checklist as a guide in structuring your letter and in evaluating the effectiveness of your first draft.

> Use positive language to create a positive impression.

> OBJECTIVE 4 Compose a routine claim letter.

ROUTINE CLAIM LETTERS

A **claim letter** is written by the buyer to the seller, seeking some type of action to correct a problem with the seller's product or service. The purchaser may be an individual or an organization. A claim letter differs from a simple complaint letter in that some type of adjustment (such as repairing or replacing the product) is requested. As a matter of fact, many complaint letters would probably be more successful if they carried an implied claim that you wanted some adjustment to be made as a result of poor service, unfair practices, or the like. The desired adjustment might be nothing more than an explanation or an apology, but the mere fact that you request some direct action will increase your chances of getting a satisfactory response.

> A claim letter asks a company to fix a problem with its product or service.

A claim letter is routine if the writer can reasonably anticipate that the reader will comply with his or her request. If, for example, you ordered a shipment of shoes for your store that were advertised at $23.50 each and the wholesaler charged you $32.50 instead, you would write a routine claim letter, asking the seller to correct the error. But suppose the wholesaler marked the price down to $19.50 two days after you placed your order. Then instead of writing a routine claim letter, you might want to write a persuasive letter, trying to convince the wholesaler to give you the lower price. (Persuasive letters are discussed in Chapter 7.)

Most companies make a genuine effort to settle claims from customers. They want to know if their customers are dissatisfied with their products so that they can correct the situation. A dissatisfied customer not only refuses to purchase additional products from the offending company but is also likely to tell others about the bad experience. One study of consumers showed that one dissatisfied customer will tell nine or ten others about the

FIGURE 6.2 Routine Reply

This letter responds to the request in Figure 6.1

SAITO PRINTERS

September 12, 19——

Ms. Carolyn J. Ryerson
48 Patterson Avenue
Columbus, OH 43202

Dear Ms. Ryerson:

Begins by answering the "yes" question first.

Yes, our popular Saito 150 portable printer does come with a 15-inch carriage. This longer carriage will enable you to print out even your most complex spreadsheets while on the road. Of course, the pinstops also adjust easily to fit standard 8½ × 11-inch paper.

For quiet operation late at night in your hotel room, the Saito uses ink-jet printing. This technology provides about the same quality output as a good-quality dot-matrix printer at less than half the noise level. Either plain paper or specially coated paper may be used. 1 2

Answers all questions, using positive language and pointing out the reader benefits of each feature. Uses paragraphs instead of enumeration to answer each question, because each answer requires elaboration.

Although many travelers use their laptop computers on a plane or in their automobiles, our research shows that they typically wait until reaching their destination to print out their documents. Thus, the Saito uses AC power only, thereby reducing its weight by nearly a pound. The extra-long 12-foot power cord will let you power-up your printer easily no matter where the electrical outlet is hidden. And our 30-day warranty, standard in the computer industry, ensures you the reliable and trouble-free service that customers have come to expect of all Saito products. 3 4

Gives important purchase information; closes on a forward-looking note.

To purchase the Saito 150, stop by Computerworld at the Eastland Shopping Center in Columbus (phone: 614/555-2188). They will show you how to increase your productivity while increasing your luggage weight by less than four pounds.

Sincerely yours,

Clayton Boyer Jr.
Clayton Boyer, Jr.
Product Information

juc

4480 Thrush Way, El Paso, TX 79922 • telephone: (915) 555-9335

Grammar and Mechanics Notes

1. "ink-jet printing": hyphenate compound adjective before noun.   2. "specially coated paper": no hyphen when first word ends in -*ly*.   3. "its": possessive form requires no apostrophe.   4. "Saito 150,"—comma follows introductory expression.

incident and that each of them will, in turn, tell four or five more people. A satisfied customer, on the other hand, will recommend the product or service to four or five other people.[1]

Write your claim letter promptly—as soon as you've identified a problem. Delaying unnecessarily might not only push you past the warranty date but might also raise suspicions about the validity of your claim; the more recent the purchase, the more valid your claim will appear.

Although some consumer advocates suggest addressing your complaint letter to the company president, common courtesy argues for first giving the company's order department or customer-relations department an opportunity to solve the problem. This or some similar department is designed to handle such problems most efficiently; employees in this department are most knowledgeable about specific company policies and procedures, product history, warranty information, decisions in similar cases, and the like. Only if your claim is not settled satisfactorily at this level should you then appeal to a higher level of management in the company.

Although you may be frustrated or angry as a result of the situation, remember that the person to whom you're writing was not personally responsible for your problem. Be courteous and avoid emotional language. Assume that the company is reasonable and will do as you ask. Avoid any hint of anger, sarcasm, threat, or exaggeration. A reader who becomes angry as a result of the strong language in your claim letter will be unlikely to do as you ask. Instead, using factual and unemotional language, begin your routine letter directly, telling exactly what the problem is:

> *Not:* You should be ashamed at your dishonest advertising for the videotape "Safety Is Job One."
> *But:* The videotape "Safety Is Job One" that I rented for $125 from your company last week lived up to our expectations in every way but one.

> *Not:* I am disgusted at the way United Express cheated me out of $12.50 last week. What a rip-off!
> *But:* An overnight letter that I mailed on December 3 did not arrive the next day, as promised by United Express.

Assume a courteous tone; avoid emotionalism.

After you have identified the problem, begin your explanation. Provide as much background information as necessary—dates, model numbers, amounts, photocopies of canceled checks or correspondence, and the like. Use a confident tone and logic (rather than emotion) to present your case. Write in an impersonal style, avoiding the use of "you" pronouns so as not to link your reader too closely to the negative news.

Provide needed details.

> *Not:* I delivered this letter to <u>you</u> sometime in the early afternoon on December 3. Although <u>you</u> promised to deliver it by 3 P.M. the next day, <u>you</u> failed to do so.
> *But:* As shown on the enclosed copy of my receipt, I delivered this letter to the United Express office on Adams Street at 3:30 P.M. on December 3. According to the sign prominently displayed in the office, any packages delivered by 4 P.M. are guaranteed to arrive by 3 P.M. the following business day.

Tell exactly what went wrong and how you were inconvenienced. If it is true and relevant, mention something good about the company or its products to make your letter appear reasonable.

If possible, mention something positive about the product.

Writing Routine Requests and Routine Replies

Routine Requests

1. Present the major request in the first sentence or two, preceded or followed by reasons for making the request.

2. Provide any needed explanation or details.

3. Phrase each question so that it is clear, easy to answer, and covers only one topic. Ask as few questions as possible, but number them and arrange them in logical order if several questions are necessary.

4. If appropriate, incorporate reader benefits and promise confidentiality of the requested information.

5. Close on a friendly note by expressing appreciation, justifying any necessary deadlines, offering to reciprocate, or otherwise making your ending personal and original.

6. If you are writing to an individual or nonprofit organization, enclose a self-addressed and stamped envelope (SASE) for reply.

Routine Replies

1. Answer promptly and graciously.

2. Grant the request or begin giving the requested information in the first sentence or two.

3. Address all questions asked or implied; include additional information or suggestions if helpful.

4. Include sales promotion if appropriate.

5. Consider developing a form letter for frequent requests.

6. Refer to any items you enclose with your letter, and insert an enclosure notation at the bottom.

7. Close on a positive and friendly note; use original wording, avoiding such clichés as "If you have any further questions, please let me know."

> According to the enclosed receipt, this letter was not delivered until 8:30 A.M. on December 5. Because the letter contained material needed for a dinner meeting on December 4, it arrived too late to be of any use. This is not the type of on-time service I've routinely received from United Express during the eight years I've been using your delivery system.

Finally, tell what type of adjustment you expect. Do you want the company to replace the product, repair it, give you a refund, simply apologize, or what? End the letter on a confident note.

> I would, therefore, appreciate your refunding my $12.50 and thereby reestablishing my confidence in United Express.

In some situations, you may not know what type of adjustment is reasonable; then you would leave it up to the reader to suggest an appropriate course of action. This might be the situation when you suffered no monetary loss but simply wish to avoid an unpleasant situation in the future (e.g., discourteous service, long lines, or ordering the wrong model because of having received incomplete or misleading information).

Please let me know how I might avoid such problems in the future.

Figure 6.3 illustrates a routine claim letter about a defective product, asking for a specific remedy. Figure 6.4 illustrates a routine claim letter about poor service, leaving the type of adjustment up to the reader.

ROUTINE ADJUSTMENT LETTERS

OBJECTIVE 5 Compose a routine adjustment letter.

An **adjustment letter** is written to inform the customer of the action taken in response to the customer's claim letter. The action your organization takes depends on the type of product or service you sell, previous experiences, the circumstances surrounding the particular situation, and, to a certain extent, your company's overall philosophy.

An adjustment letter responds to a claim letter.

Some companies typically accept nearly all claims, believing the few dishonest claims it receives are not worth the time it takes to evaluate each individual claim and the possible loss of goodwill a more stringent policy would risk. Other companies adopt an "all-sales-final" attitude, thereby avoiding the problem of dealing with most claims. Most companies adopt a more middle-of-the-road approach, evaluating each claim on its individual merits.

Few people go to the trouble of writing a claim letter unless they have a real problem. For this reason, the vast majority of claims most companies receive are legitimate and are adjusted according to the individual situation. If the action taken is just what the customer asked for or expected, a routine adjustment letter using the direct organizational plan would be written.

Most claim letters are legitimate.

Overall Tone

A claim represents a possible loss of goodwill and confidence in your company or its products. Because the customer is upset, the overall tone of your adjustment letter is crucial. Since you have already decided to honor the claim, your best strategy is to adopt a gracious, trusting tone. Give your customer the benefit of the doubt. It does not make sense to adopt a grudging or resentful tone and risk losing whatever goodwill you might gain from granting the adjustment.

Adopt a gracious, confident tone for your adjustment letters.

Not: Although our engineers do not understand how this problem could have occurred if the directions had been followed, we are nevertheless willing to repair your generator free of charge.
But: We are happy to repair your generator free of charge. Within ten days, a factory representative will call you to schedule a convenient time to make the repair.

FIGURE 6.3   Routine Claim: Specific Remedy Requested

This claim letter is about a defective product.

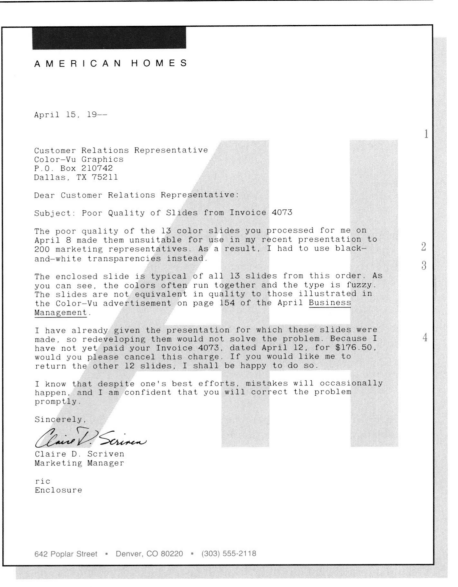

AMERICAN HOMES

April 15, 19—

Customer Relations Representative
Color-Vu Graphics
P.O. Box 210742
Dallas, TX 75211

Dear Customer Relations Representative:

Subject: Poor Quality of Slides from Invoice 4073

The poor quality of the 13 color slides you processed for me on April 8 made them unsuitable for use in my recent presentation to 200 marketing representatives. As a result, I had to use black-and-white transparencies instead.

The enclosed slide is typical of all 13 slides from this order. As you can see, the colors often run together and the type is fuzzy. The slides are not equivalent in quality to those illustrated in the Color-Vu advertisement on page 154 of the April <u>Business Management</u>.

I have already given the presentation for which these slides were made, so redeveloping them would not solve the problem. Because I have not yet paid your Invoice 4073, dated April 12, for $176.50, would you please cancel this charge. If you would like me to return the other 12 slides, I shall be happy to do so.

I know that despite one's best efforts, mistakes will occasionally happen, and I am confident that you will correct the problem promptly.

Sincerely,

Claire D. Scriven
Marketing Manager

ric
Enclosure

642 Poplar Street • Denver, CO 80220 • (303) 555-2118

Identifies the problem immediately and tells how writer was inconvenienced. Provides the needed details in a nonemotional, businesslike manner.

Identifies and justifies the specific remedy requested.

Closes on a confident note.

Grammar and Mechanics Notes

1. If an addressee's name is unknown, a title may be used in both the inside address and salutation.   2. No punctuation is needed before the *and* separating the two independent clauses because the second clause, "the type is fuzzy," is so short.   3. Underline the titles of magazines.   4. "occasionally" has two *c*'s and one *s*.

Routine Claim: Remedy Not Specified

FIGURE 6.4

This claim letter about poor services does not identify a specific remedy.

AMERICAN HOMES

April 15, 19--

Mr. Philip Williams
General Manager
Ambassador Hotel
101 Grant Street
Denver, CO 80203

Dear Mr. Williams:

I feel sure you will want to know about our recent experience at your hotel. Although our 200 marketing representatives who stayed at the Ambassador last week thought your deluxe rooms were beautiful and spacious, they also thought the housekeeping service was substandard.

Presents a balanced view of the problem.

We rented 218 single rooms on April 10-12 for our annual marketing managers' conference. When a few representatives complained about the housekeeping service, I explored the matter further and asked for comments at our closing session. Here's what I learned:

Provides the needed details.

1. Six people commented that at least one lamp in their room had a burned-out light bulb. Because our representatives had to work on projects late each night, the lack of adequate lighting was an inconvenience.

Enumerates specific examples—for credibility—and tells how the people were inconvenienced.

2. Twelve people commented that their rooms sometimes were not cleaned until after 5 p.m., even though they were out of the room all day. They were then disturbed during their evening working hours when the housekeepers showed up to clean the rooms.

3. Others spoke about the general uncleanliness of their rooms, with comments ranging from ice buckets not being emptied to bits of paper and trash not being vacuumed from the corners of the room.

Because our 200 representatives have enjoyed meeting at the Ambassador in the past, won't you please let me know how I can be assured that the housekeeping service will be up to your usual high standards in the future.

Appears reasonable by also presenting positive comments; leaves the specific remedy to the reader; implies a possible future reader benefit.

Sincerely,

Claire D. Scriven

Claire D. Scriven
Marketing Manager

ric

642 Poplar Street • Denver, CO 80220 • (303) 555-2118

Grammar and Mechanics Notes

1. "April 10-12"—Do not space before or after the hyphen. 2. *further* means *to a greater degree* (*farther* refers to distance). 3. "Twelve people"—Spell out a number that begins a sentence.

Your overall tone should show confidence both in the reader's honesty and in the essential worth of your own company and its products. To the extent possible, use neutral or positive language in referring to the claim (for example use, "the situation" instead of "your complaint"). Also avoid appearing to doubt the reader. Instead of saying, "you claim that," use more neutral wording, such as "you state that."

Finally, you should respond promptly. Your customer is already upset; the longer this anger exists, the more difficult it will be to overcome.

Avoid use of negative language in describing the basis for the claim.

Good News First

Nothing that you are likely to tell the reader will be more welcomed than the fact that you are granting the claim, so put this news up front—in the very first sentence if possible. The details and background information will come later.

> A new copy of the *American World Dictionary* is on its way to your office, and I assure you that no pages are missing from this copy. I checked it myself!

> Of course you can depend on Crown Edison's warranty. Simply take the enclosed "no-questions-asked" authorization slip to Pohl Motors, and they will repair your automobile's transmission once and for all at absolutely no cost to you.

> Thanks to you, we have undertaken a new training program for all our housekeepers. Please use the enclosed coupon for two nights' free stay at the Ambassador anytime after July 15 to see for yourself the difference your letter has made.

> The enclosed $12.50 check reimburses you for your company's delayed overnight letter. Thank you for bringing this matter to my attention.

It is appropriate to apologize for serious problems.

It is often appropriate to thank the reader for giving you an opportunity to resolve the situation, but what about apologizing? An apology, which tends to emphasize the negative aspects of the situation, is probably not necessary for small, routine claims that are promptly resolved to the customer's satisfaction. Instead, emphasize the positive aspects and look forward to future transactions. If, however, the customer has been severely inconvenienced or embarrassed and the company is clearly at fault, a sincere apology would be in order. In such a situation, first give the good news, then apologize in a businesslike manner; avoid repeating the apology in the closing lines.

> I have contracted with a local brick mason to rebuild your home's brick chimney, which our driver mistakenly damaged on February 23. I am truly sorry for the inconvenience this situation has caused you and your family and am grateful for your understanding.

Explanation

Explain specifically, but briefly, what went wrong.

After presenting the "good news," you must educate your reader as to why the problem occurred and, if appropriate, what steps you've taken to make sure the problem doesn't recur. Explain the situation in sufficient detail to be believable, but don't belabor the reason for the problem. Emphasize the fact that you stand behind your products. Avoid using negative language, don't pass the buck, and don't hide behind a "mistakes-will-happen" attitude.

> Let me explain what happened. On the morning of December 4, the plane that had your letter in its cargo bay could not land at O'Hare Airport because of a snowstorm and was diverted to Detroit. Although our personnel in Detroit worked overtime to reload the mail onto a delivery truck, which was then driven to Chicago, it did not arrive until early on December 5.

Because the reader's faith in your products has been shaken, you also have a sales job to do. You must build into your letter **resale**; that is, information that reestablishes the customer's confidence in the product purchased or in the company that sells the product. In order to be believable, do not promise that the problem will never happen again; such promises are unrealistic. Do, however, use specific language, including facts and figures when possible.

| Use resale to reassure the customer of the worth of your products. |

> *Not:* We have taken steps to ensure that this situation will not happen again.
> *But:* Fortunately, such incidents are rare. For example, even considering bad weather, airline strikes, and the like, United Express has maintained an on-time delivery record of 97.6% during the past twelve months. According to *Mailroom Digest*, no other delivery service even comes close to this record.

Sometimes you may decide to honor the claim even though the customer is at fault—perhaps because the writer has been a good customer for many years or represents important potential business. In such situations, your beginning paragraph should still convey the news that you're honoring the claim, but you might temper the enthusiasm a bit. And in the explanatory paragraphs, you would communicate to the reader the facts surrounding the case—that the reader is at fault, the product was misused, the warranty has expired, or whatever the situation requires.

| If the customer is at fault, explain in tactful, impersonal language how to avoid such problems in the future. |

It is necessary to inform the reader of the circumstances so that he or she won't keep repeating the problem. On the other hand, if you do so in an insulting manner, you will lose the reader's goodwill. Instead, use impersonal, tactful language, taking special pains not to lecture the reader or sound condescending. For example, in the second paragraph that follows, note that the pronoun *you* is not used at all when explaining the misuse of the equipment.

> Because we value your friendship, we are pleased to repair your Braniff 250 copier free of charge. Our maintenance technician tells me that she took care of the problem on September 15.

> Our technician also told me that the machine's register indicated that 9,832 copies had been made since the copier was installed on July 18. All our advertising states that the Braniff 250 is designed for low-level office use—fewer than 1,500 copies per month. If you find that you will continue to experience high-volume copier usage, may I suggest trading up to the Braniff 300, which will easily handle your needs. We will gladly offer you $1,300 as a trade-in allowance.

Fidelity Investments routes so
many messages through its
mail room (53 million pieces
of mail were dispatched by
the company last year), that
the U.S. Postal Service feels
Fidelity could have as many
as 21 different ZIP codes of
its own!
Source: © John S. Abbott

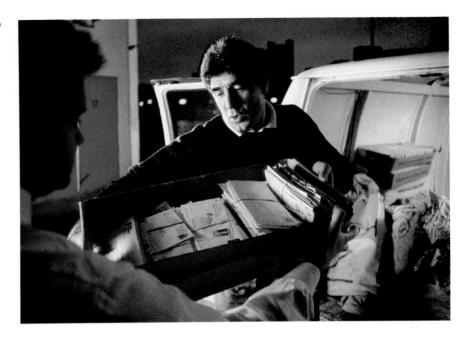

Positive, Forward-Looking Closing

Do not mention the
claim in the closing. In-
stead, look to the future.

End your letter on a positive note. Do not refer to the problem again, do
not apologize again, do not suggest the possibility of future problems, and
do not imply that the reader might still be upset. Instead, use strategies
that imply the expectation of a continued relationship with the customer,
such as including additional resale, a comment about the satisfaction the
reader will receive from the repaired product or improved service, or
appreciation for the reader's interest in your products.

Include sales promotion only if you are confident that your adjustment
has restored the customer's confidence in your product or service; otherwise,
it might backfire. Sales promotion should be subtle and should involve a
new product or accessory rather than promoting a new or improved model
of what the reader has already bought.

> *Not:* Again, I apologize for the delay in delivering your letter. If you
> experience such problems again in the future, please don't hesitate to
> write.
> *But:* We have enjoyed serving your delivery needs for the past eight
> years, Ms. Clarke, and look forward to many more years of service.
> *Or:* If you are the type of person who has frequent crash deadlines, Ms.
> Clarke, you will probably be interested in our eight-hour delivery service.
> It is described in the enclosed brochure.

Figures 6.5 and 6.6 show two versions of an adjustment letter for the
claim letter presented in Figure 6.3. The first version assumes the company
was at fault. The second version assumes the reader was at fault but that
management decided to grant the request for a refund anyway. Although
both letters grant the refund, note the more subdued tone and the "we-
are-not-to-blame" focus of the second letter.

Checklist 4 summarizes the guidelines for writing routine claim and
adjustment letters.

Adjustment Letter—Company at Fault

FIGURE 6.5

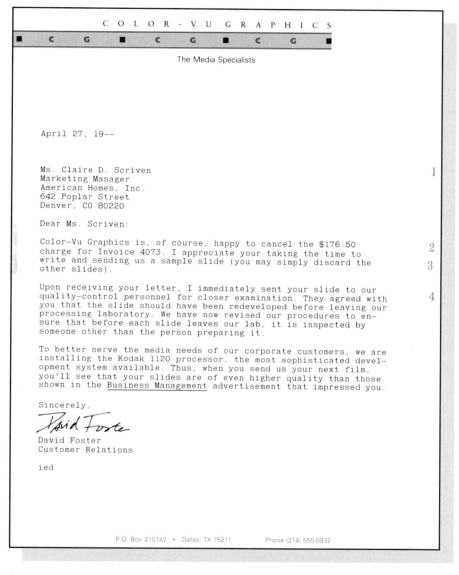

This adjustment letter responds to the claim letter in Figure 6.3.

Tells immediately that the adjustment is being made; thanks the reader.

Explains briefly, but specifically, what happened.

Looks forward to a continuing relationship with the customer; does not refer to the problem.

Grammar and Mechanics Notes

1. The position title can go either on the same line as the person's name or, as here, on a line by itself.   2. "Invoice 4073"—Capitalize a noun that precedes a number.   3. "slides)."—Place the period outside the closing parenthesis unless the entire sentence is in parentheses.   4. "personnel"—employees (*personal*—private).

FIGURE 6.6   Adjustment Letter—Customer at Fault

This adjustment letter responds to the claim letter in Figure 6.3.

Uses subdued language to tell that the adjustment is being made.

In a positive, nonpreachy tone, explains how the problem was caused by the customer.

Includes resale to close on a confident, forward-looking note.

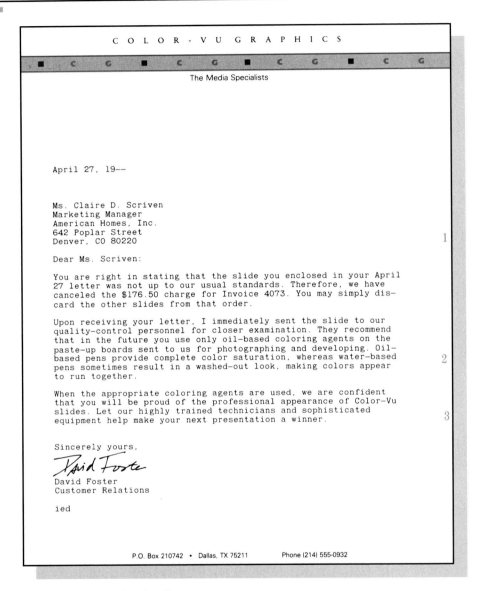

COLOR - VU GRAPHICS

The Media Specialists

April 27, 19—

Ms. Claire D. Scriven
Marketing Manager
American Homes, Inc.
642 Poplar Street
Denver, CO 80220

1

Dear Ms. Scriven:

You are right in stating that the slide you enclosed in your April 27 letter was not up to our usual standards. Therefore, we have canceled the $176.50 charge for Invoice 4073. You may simply discard the other slides from that order.

Upon receiving your letter, I immediately sent the slide to our quality-control personnel for closer examination. They recommend that in the future you use only oil-based coloring agents on the paste-up boards sent to us for photographing and developing. Oil-based pens provide complete color saturation, whereas water-based pens sometimes result in a washed-out look, making colors appear to run together.

2

When the appropriate coloring agents are used, we are confident that you will be proud of the professional appearance of Color-Vu slides. Let our highly trained technicians and sophisticated equipment help make your next presentation a winner.

3

Sincerely yours,

David Foster
Customer Relations

ied

P.O. Box 210742 • Dallas, TX 75211   Phone (214) 555-0932

Grammar and Mechanics Notes

1. Use the two-letter Postal Service abbreviation for state names in addresses.   2. "whereas"—one word.   3. Only the first word in the complimentary closing is capitalized.

Writing Routine Claim and Adjustment Letters

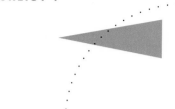

Routine Claim Letters

1. Write your claim letter promptly—as soon as you've identified a problem. Try to determine the name of the appropriate individual to whom to write; if that is not possible, address your letter to the customer-relations department.

2. Strive for an overall tone of courtesy and confidence; avoid anger, sarcasm, threats, and exaggeration. If true and relevant, mention something positive about the company or its products somewhere in the letter.

3. Begin the letter directly, identifying the problem immediately.

4. Provide as much detail as necessary. Using impersonal language, tell specifically what went wrong and how you were inconvenienced.

5. If appropriate, tell what type of adjustment you expect—replacement, repair, refund, apology, and so forth. End on a confident note.

Routine Adjustment Letters

1. Respond promptly; your customer is already upset.

2. Begin the letter directly, telling the reader immediately what adjustment is being made.

3. Adopt a courteous tone. Use neutral or positive language throughout.

4. If appropriate, somewhere in the letter thank the reader for writing, and apologize if the customer has been severely inconvenienced or embarrassed because of the company's actions.

5. In a forthright way and using neutral language, explain the reason for the problem in sufficient detail to be believable, but don't belabor the point. If appropriate, tell what steps you've taken to prevent the problem's recurrence.

6. Provide information that reestablishes your customer's confidence in the product or your company. Be specific.

7. If the customer was at fault, explain in impersonal and tactful language the facts surrounding the case.

8. Close on a positive note; include additional resale, subtle sales promotion, appreciation for the reader's interest in your products, or some other strategy that implies customer satisfaction and the expectation of a future relationship.

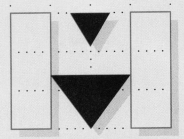

MICROWRITING A ROUTINE ADJUSTMENT LETTER

Microwriting activities guide you step-by-step through a typical writing assignment by posing relevant questions and providing possible responses.

Does this claim letter follow the guidelines presented in Checklist 4?

The Problem

You are Kathryn Smith, a correspondent in the customer-service department of Exciting Interiors, a large home-furnishings store. This morning (May 25, 19—), you received the following letter from an angry customer:

Dear Customer Service Manager:

I am really upset at the poor-quality shades that you sell. Two months ago I purchased two pairs of your pleated fabric shades in Wedgewood Blue at $35.99 each for my two bathroom windows. A copy of my $74.32 bill is enclosed.

The color has already begun to fade from these shades. I couldn't believe it when I checked and found that they now look tie-died! That is not the look I wish for my elegant home.

Since these shades did not provide the type of wear that I paid for, please refund my $74.32.

Sincerely,

Henrietta Daniels

Mrs. Henrietta Daniels
117 Hanley Drive
Grass Valley, CA 95949

You take Mrs. Daniels's itemized bill down to the sales floor and find the model of shades she purchased. You can only conclude that Mrs. Daniels's home has large bathroom windows, because the only size this particular shade comes in is 64 inches long by 32 inches wide. And printed right on the tag attached to the shade is this note: "Warning: The imported fabric in this shade makes them unsuitable for use in areas receiving excessive humidity." Clearly, these shades were not made for bathroom use.

On your computer you call up Mrs. Daniels's account and find that she has been a loyal customer for many years. You decide, therefore, to refund her $74.32, even though she misused the product. Now write the adjustment letter.

The Process

1. What is the purpose of your letter?

   ```
   Refund Mrs. Daniels's money, tactfully explain that you
   were not at fault, and retain her goodwill.
   ```

2. Describe your audience.

   ```
   -- an important customer
   -- angry at you at the present time
   -- now believes your product isn't of high quality
   -- may be the type of person who doesn't read
      instructions carefully
   ```

3. List in the appropriate order the topics you'll include:

   ```
   a. Give the refund.
   b. Explain that the shades weren't intended for bathroom
      use.
   c. Promote your cotton and polyester bathroom curtains.
   ```

4. Write a gracious opening sentence for your letter that tells Mrs. Daniels you're refunding the $74.32. Be warm and positive in granting her request. Remember, however, that she was at fault; therefore, do not be overly enthusiastic.

   ```
   You have been a valued and faithful customer of ours for
   several years, Mrs. Daniels, and we are, therefore,
   refunding your $74.32.
   ```

5. Write the paragraph that explains how the shades were misused. Use tactful, neutral, and impersonal language, avoiding the use of second-person pronouns.

   ```
   As the tag attached to the shades explains, the fine
   imported woven material used in these shades reflects
   sunlight without fading but will not withstand the high
   humidity typically found in bathrooms. When used in such
   rooms as living rooms, dining rooms, and bedrooms, the
   shades provide many years of beautiful and carefree
   service.
   ```

6. Now write your closing paragraph, in which you promote your cotton and polyester bathroom curtains.

   ```
   For the elegant look and durable service you want in
   your bathroom, please consider the cotton and polyester
   bathroom curtains shown in the enclosed brochure. They
   come in Wedgewood Blue and can be custom-ordered in the
   exact size you desire.
   ```

Note that the four stages of the planning component of the writing process are incorporated—purpose, audience analysis, content, and organization.

The Product

Note the minor revisions
made from the individual
sentences composed
earlier.

Dear Mrs. Daniels:

You have been a valued customer of ours for several
years, and we are, therefore, refunding your $74.32. A
check for that amount is enclosed. You can simply
return the blue shades to our customer–service window
the next time you stop by Exciting Interiors.

As the tag attached to the shades explains, the fine
imported woven material used in these shades reflects
sunlight without fading but will not withstand the high
humidity typically found in bathrooms. However, when
these shades are used on windows in living rooms,
dining rooms, and bedrooms, they provide many years of
beautiful and carefree service.

For the elegant look and durable service you want in
your bathroom, please consider the cotton and polyester
bathroom curtains shown on the enclosed brochure. They
come in Wedgewood Blue and can be custom–ordered in the
exact size you require. Please come in and let us show
them to you.

Sincerely,

S P O T L I G H T   ON INTERNATIONAL ISSUES

WHEN IN ROME

The direct organizational style is suggested for use for each type of message presented in this chapter. This style can be summarized in five words: *Present the major idea immediately.* The direct organizational plan generally works best for such routine messages because business executives are busy people; they have little time and patience for needless formalities and "beating around the bush."

Such is not always the case, however, when writing to someone whose culture and experiences are quite different from your own. Natives of some countries may find letters written in the direct style too harsh and abrupt, lacking in courtesy. One study of business letters received from foreign countries, for example, found that 44% contained exaggerated courtesy (superlatives, "esteemed," "great pleasure," etc.), 25% were written in an impersonal tone (formal, passive voice), and 16% contained obvious compliments.[1]

Therefore, adapt your writing style to the expectations of your reader. For example, an American manufacturer sent a form sales letter to many domestic and foreign retail stores, inviting inquiries about stocking its line of fishing tackle. An American businessperson might respond as follows:

> Would you please send me a sample of the fishing tackle you advertised in your October 3 letter, along with price and shipping information. As a long-time retailer of fishing tackle, we would be especially interested in any items you might have for sports fishing.

> Since the trout season starts in six weeks, I would appreciate having this information as soon as possible.

In contrast, what follows is the body of an actual letter received from China in response to this sales letter. Note the language is much less direct and much more formal than its American counterpart.

> It was with great pleasure that we received your letter dated 3 January on 20 January. We send our deepest respects and wish to inform you that Yoon Sung Fishing Tackle Co., Ltd., has been selling fishing items for thirty-eight years.

> We would be pleased to consider your merchandise. May we ask you to please send us samples, price, and shipping information. It will be a great pleasure to conduct business with your company.

The moral is simple: Write as your receiver expects you to write. Take a cue from his or her own writing. If the letters you receive from a foreign associate are written in a direct style, you may safely respond in a similar style. However, if the letters you receive are similar to the one above, you might try a more formal, less direct style when responding. Although you would not want to *adopt* the reader's own style, you might need to *adapt* your own, based on your analysis of the audience.

[1] Retha H. Kilpatrick, "Internationalizing Business Communication Practices," *Journal of Business Communication,* 21 (Fall 1984): 43.

SUMMARY

Most business writing tasks involve routine matters in which the writer conveys either positive or routine information that is of interest to the reader. Such situations call for a direct organizational plan in which the major purpose of the message is presented first. The major idea is followed by any needed background information or additional explanation, and the message ends on a friendly, forward-looking note.

Guidelines for writing routine requests and routine replies are presented in Checklist 3. Guidelines for writing routine claim letters and routine adjustment letters are presented in Checklist 4. Use both checklists in composing such messages and in revising your first drafts.

KEY TERMS

Adjustment letter— A letter written to inform the customer of the action taken in response to the customer's claim letter.

Claim letter— A letter written by the buyer to the seller, seeking some type of action to correct a problem with the seller's product or service.

Direct organizational plan— A plan in which the major purpose of the message is communicated first, followed by any needed explanation.

Resale— Information that reestablishes a customer's confidence in the product purchased or in the company that sold the product.

REVIEW AND DISCUSSION

OBJECTIVE 1

1. Explain the basic parts of the direct organizational plan. For what types of messages is this plan appropriate?

OBJECTIVE 2

2. Assume you need information from a bank about interest rates for a 90-day loan for your small business. Write three versions of the first sentence of your letter, using (a) a direct question, (b) a polite request, and (c) a statement.

OBJECTIVE 2

3. What guidelines should you follow when asking questions in a routine request?

OBJECTIVE 3

4. Why should routine requests be answered promptly?

OBJECTIVE 3

5. Critique each of the following first sentences for a routine reply:

   a. Your letter of November 23 has been referred to me for reply.
   b. Although we will not be able to help you with remodeling your factory, we can provide expert remodeling service for your office area.
   c. Our trained architects and interior designers can provide a complete remodeling plan for your office area.
   d. Thank you for inquiring about our comprehensive remodeling services.

OBJECTIVE 3

6. Compose an appropriate last sentence for your routine reply for the situation described in Number 5 above.

OBJECTIVE 3

7. Under what circumstances is a form letter desirable for answering routine inquiries?

OBJECTIVE 4

8. How does a claim letter differ from a complaint letter?

OBJECTIVE 4

9. Why should claim letters be written promptly? Why should they be answered promptly?

OBJECTIVES 4–5

10. What should be the overall tone of the claim letter? Of the adjustment letter?

OBJECTIVES 4–5

11. Under what circumstances would the direct organizational plan *not* be appropriate for a claim letter? For an adjustment letter?

OBJECTIVE 5

12. Under what circumstances should you apologize in an adjustment letter?

OBJECTIVE 5

13. In what ways does an adjustment letter in which the company is at fault differ from an adjustment letter in which the customer is at fault?

OBJECTIVE 5

14. What is the difference between "resale" and "sales promotion"?

OBJECTIVE 5

15. Assume that you've agreed to replace a customer's broken calculator that has been sent to you for inspection. Compose an appropriate last sentence for this adjustment letter.

EXERCISES

1. **Routine Request—Product Information** Luis St. Jean is a famous design house in France, with annual sales of $2 billion in clothing, perfume, scarves, and other designer items. Each year it prepares more than 150 original designs for its seasonal collection. As head buyer for Cindy's, an upscale women's clothing store in Minneapolis, you think you might like to begin offering LSJ's line of perfume. You need to know what types of perfumes are offered, prices, minimum ordering quantities, and marketing assistance provided by LSJ. Since no other store in the Twin Cities area of Minneapolis/St. Paul now carries LSJ perfumes, you wonder whether the company would be willing to give you exclusive marketing rights. You also need to know if you have to carry LSJ's complete line or if you can be selective. You feel sure that his most expensive perfumes (anything beyond $100 an ounce) would not be a big seller in Minneapolis.

   Write to Mr. Henri Vixier, License Supervisor, Luis St. Jean, 90513 Cergy, Pointoise Cedex, France, seeking answers to your questions.

   OBJECTIVE 2 ◀

2. **Routine Request—Letter of Recommendation** As part of your application papers for a one-semester internship at American Express, you are asked to include a letter of recommendation from one of your management professors. You made your best grade (A−) in MGT 382: Wage and Salary Administration, which you took three semesters ago from Dr. Dennis Thavinet in the Management Department at your university. You liked the course well enough that you missed class only the one week when a family member was ill. Although you were not one of the most vocal members in class, Dr. Thavinet did commend you for your group project, which consisted of planning a comprehensive compensation program for Duffey's Ice Cream Parlor, which has 18 employees. American Express (1850 East Camelback Road, Phoenix, AZ 85017) wants to know especially about your ability to work well with others.

   Write to Dr. Thavinet, asking for a letter of recommendation. You would like him to respond within one week.

   OBJECTIVE 2 ◀

3. **Routine Request—Product Information** Choose an advertisement from a newspaper or magazine for a product about which you have some interest. The ad probably does not have sufficient space to provide all the information you need to make an intelligent purchase decision. Write to the company (if necessary, locate its address using one of the directories available in your library), asking at least three questions about the product. Be sure to mention where you heard about the product. Try to encourage a prompt response.

   Attach a copy of the ad to your letter, and submit both to your instructor. Your instructor may ask you to mail the letter so that you can later compare the types of responses received for different products.

   OBJECTIVE 2 ◀

4. **Routine Response—Product Information** As the business manager for Maison Richard, a 200-seat restaurant in Seattle, you received an inquiry from Chris Shearing, 1926 Second Avenue, Seattle, WA 98101. She had several questions about the type of meat you serve in your restaurant. Here are her questions and the answers:

   a. *Are the cattle from which your beef comes allowed to roam freely*

   OBJECTIVE 3 ◀

instead of being fattened in cramped feedlots? No, allowing free roaming would increase the muscle tissue in the beef, making it less tender. Cattle are instead confined to a 10-foot square pen.

b. *Are the cattle fed antibiotics and hormones?* Yes—to ensure a healthy animal and to promote faster growth. All antibiotics and hormones are approved by the U.S. Department of Agriculture.

c. *Does your trout come from lakes and streams?* No, they're farm-grown, which is more economical and results in less disease.

You purchase only top-quality government-inspected meat, fish, and fowl for your restaurant; and your establishment has received numerous positive reviews in the local press. Ms. Shearing is a well-known community activist and you want to present your case as positively as possible and avoid the loss of her goodwill and any negative publicity that might result. Respond to her letter, supplying whatever other appropriate information you feel is reasonable.

▶ OBJECTIVE 3

5. **Routine Response—Form Letter** You are the executive producer for the Sherry Show, a popular syndicated morning talk show featuring Sherry Baker as the host. The show features interviews and panel discussions on a wide variety of current topics. It is recorded in Chicago and is carried by 356 television stations around the country.

Because Sherry takes questions and comments from the audience, it is important to have a full house each day. When the show first started two years ago, you had trouble filling the 150-seat studio. Now, however, you get many more requests for tickets than you can accommodate. Anyone who wants a ticket must write at least four months ahead of time and can receive no more than four tickets. The tickets are free. The show tapes from 9:30 until 11 A.M. Monday through Friday each week. Tickets are for reserved seats, but any seats not occupied by 9 A.M. are released on a first-come, first-served basis. Because of distractions, the studio doors are closed promptly at 9:15 each morning and are not reopened until after the show ends at 11 A.M. Children under age 12 are not admitted.

Write a form letter telling people how to order tickets and conveying other needed information. The letter will be sent to people who request ticket information.

▶ OBJECTIVE 3

6. **Collaborative Routine Response—Project Information** You are a member of the President's Council, an organization made up of the presidents of each student organization on campus. You just received a memorandum from Dr. Robin H. Hill, dean of students, wanting to know what types of social projects student organizations on campus have been engaged in during the past year. The dean has to make a report to the Board of Trustees on the important role played by student organizations—both in the life of the university and community and in the development of student leadership and social skills. She wants to include such information as student-run programs on drug and alcohol abuse, community service, fund-raising, and the like.

Working in groups of four, identify and summarize the types of social projects that student organizations at your institution have completed this year. Then organize and synthesize your findings into a one-page memo to Dr. Hill. After writing your first draft, have each member review and comment on the draft. Then revise as needed and submit. Use only actual data for this assignment.

7. **Claim Letter—Defective Product** As a purchasing agent for your company, on February 3 you ordered a box of 12 multistrike printer ribbons for your Sampson Model 25 printers at $9.35 each plus $6.85 shipping and handling—total price of $119.05. The catalog description for this ribbon (Part No. 02–8R01656) said, "Fits Diablo and Xerox printers and most compatibles." Since the Sampson is advertised as a Xerox clone printer, you assumed the ribbons would fit. The order arrived on February 12, but you did not get around to trying the ribbons until April 5, when you ran out of your present supply. You then discovered that the ribbons didn't fit your Sampson. Although the ribbon cartridge is the same shape, it's about ¼ inch thicker and won't seat properly on the spindles.

OBJECTIVE 4 ◄

You believe that your supplier's misleading advertising caused you to order the wrong model ribbon. Despite the fact that you've kept the ribbons for two months, you'd like the company to either refund the $119.05 you paid on its Invoice 91–076 or replace the ribbons with ones that do work with your Model 25 printers. You'll be happy to return the entire case of ribbons if the company will give you instructions for doing so.

Write your routine claim letter, addressed to the Customer Service Department of Nationwide Office Supply, which is located at 2640 Kerper Boulevard in Dubuque, IA 52001.

8. **Claim Letter—Inaccurate Reporting** As the chief programmer for *ReSolve*, a basic spreadsheet program for microcomputers, you were pleased that your product was reviewed in the current issue of *Computing Trends*. The review praised your product for its "lightning-fast speed and convenient user interface." You were not pleased, however, that your product was downgraded because it lacked graphics capability. The reviewer compared *ReSolve* with full-featured spreadsheet programs costing, on average, $200 more than your program. No wonder, then, that your program rated a 6.6 out of 10, coming in third out of the five programs reviewed. If your program had been compared with similar low-level programs (such as Alpine's *Professional Calc* or Trius's *As-Easy-As*), you feel certain that *ReSolve* would have easily come out on top.

OBJECTIVE 4 ◄

While you do not want to get the magazine upset with your company (Software Entrepreneurs, Inc.), you do feel that it should compare apples to apples and should conduct another review of your program. Write to Roberta J. Horton, Review Editor, at 200 Public Square, Cleveland, OH 44114, and tell her so.

9. **Claim Letter—Poor Service** As the owner of Parker Central, a small plumbing business, you try to instill in all your employees the "customer-first" attitude. Therefore, you were quite put-off by your treatment yesterday (July 13) at the hands of the receptionist at Englehard Investment Service (231 East 50 Street, Indianapolis, IN 46205). You showed up 20 minutes early for your 2:30 P.M. appointment with Jack Nutley, an investment counselor with the firm. You were meeting with him for the first time to discuss setting up a Simplified Employee Pension plan for your 20 employees.

OBJECTIVE 4 ◄

To begin with, the receptionist (you did not get her name, but she is a woman with short brown hair who appears to be in her early twenties) ignored you for at least five minutes until she finished the last paragraph of a document she was typing. Then, after finding out whom you wanted to see, she did not even call Jack's office to announce your arrival until 2:35 P.M.

Finally, when she did announce your arrival, Jack's secretary came out and said that Jack had just been taken ill and had to go to the doctor. So you wasted half an afternoon and were also insulted by the receptionist's rude treatment.

You decide to write to Jack Nutley about the receptionist's office behavior. Your "claim" is for better service in the future. You want him to know that if you are going to continue to be treated in such a manner, you have no interest in doing business with his firm.

OBJECTIVE 5

10. **Adjustment Letter—Company at Fault** Assume the role of customer service representative at Nationwide Office Supply (see Exercise 7). You've received the letter from Mr. J. R. McCord, purchasing agent for People's Energy Company, Wheatley Road, Old Westbury, NY 11568. You've done some background investigation and have learned that what the customer said is true—the Sampson Model 25 *is* a Xerox clone and your catalog *does* state that this ribbon (Part No. 02-8R01656) fits Xerox printers and most compatibles. The problem came about because the Model 25, Sampson's newest model, was introduced shortly after your catalog went to press. This model uses a slightly shorter spindle than previous Sampson models. You're grateful that the purchasing agent called this problem to your attention so that you can revise the copy for the next printing of your catalog.

Unfortunately, you do not carry in your inventory a ribbon that will fit the Sampson Model 25; you suspect that the purchasing agent will have to order the ribbon directly from Sampson. The customer should return the case of ribbons COD, marking on the address label "Return Authorization 91–076R." In the meantime, you've authorized a refund of $119.05; Mr. McCord should receive the check within ten days. Convey this information to Mr. McCord.

OBJECTIVE 5

11. **Adjustment Letter—Customer at Fault** Assume the role of customer service representative at Nationwide Office Supply (see Exercise 7). You've received the letter from Mr. J. R. McCord, purchasing agent for People's Energy Company, Wheatley Road, Old Westbury, NY 11568. You've done some background investigation and have learned that Mr. McCord was somewhat mistaken in stating that the Sampson Model 25 is a Xerox clone. What Sampson advertises instead is that the Model 25 uses the same character set as Xerox printers; this means that all fonts that are available from Xerox can also be downloaded for the Model 25. Sampson neither states nor implies that Xerox-compatible ribbons or other supplies will fit their machines.

Because the customer made an innocent mistake and because the ribbon ordered in error can be easily resold, you decide to honor his claim anyway. He should return the case of ribbons prepaid, marking on the address label "Return Authorization 91–076R." In the meantime, you're shipping him a dozen ribbons (Part No. 02–9R32732) that *will* work on the Model 25; they should arrive within ten days. You're also enclosing your summer catalog.

OBJECTIVE 5

12. **Adjustment Letter—Form Letter** As the new review editor at *Computing Trends* (see Exercise 8), you've already come to expect that

whenever products are panned in your magazine you can expect a negative reaction from the developers. You're happy to hear from them, however, because they sometimes bring to light additional information that your readers will find helpful. Unless the review contained a factual error, your policy is to edit and publish these letters in the "Feedback" column in a future issue. (In this particular instance, you compared *ReSolve* with the full-featured spreadsheets because that is exactly how Software Entrepreneurs, Inc. advertises the program.)

Most major product categories are reviewed at least once yearly in your magazine. The products are tested extensively in your state-of-the-art computer labs by qualified reviewers. Each product is compared on the basis of criteria established by surveying readers regarding the importance of each feature, and reviewers call the developer directly if they have questions.

Write a form letter to send to product developers who write to complain about the review of their products, giving them this information.

CASE PROBLEM

Big Cabinets and Brief Cases

It was Friday afternoon, and Paul Yu was determined to take care of all correspondence before leaving for the weekend. The first item of business was to request an adjustment for a lateral filing cabinet that had been delivered last week for his office.

OBJECTIVES 1, 4, 5 ◀

On November 18, Paul had ordered the Steelcase 30-inch two-drawer lateral file cabinet in putty color from Edwards Furniture Company, 6434 Lake Lomond Drive, San Diego, CA 92119. Total cost, including shipping, was $389.25 (Invoice 3112, dated November 23, 19—). Because Edwards was temporarily out of stock of the 30-inch file cabinet, they sent instead the more expensive 36-inch model. They attached a note saying it was their policy to upgrade the order at no additional cost to the customer if they were out of stock of the item ordered. The 36-inch model is supposed to sell for $48 more than the 30-inch model.

Although Paul appreciates Edwards's generous gesture, there is a problem. He had intended to put the file cabinet inside a 32-inch closet in his office, and the 36-inch model simply does not fit. He, therefore, wishes to have Edwards pick up the 36-inch model as soon as possible (it's in his way) and ship the 30-inch model when it is back in stock. If the 30-inch model is not expected to be in stock within the next six weeks, he would like his $389.25 refunded.

Paul also has received a memo from Maurice Potts, an Urban Systems sales representative, that said in part:

Last week I made a sales presentation to Albany Electronics and carried two briefcases with me——my regular case plus a second case filled with handouts and brochures. At the conclusion of my presentation, I distributed the handouts and brochures, picked up my

```
regular briefcase and left—completely forgetting my
empty second case. When I discovered what had happened
the following morning, I immediately called Albany
Electronics, but they have been unable to locate the
missing case.

This leather briefcase was two months old and cost
$287.50—see attached sales slip. Since the Urban
Systems policy manual states that employees will be
reimbursed for all reasonable costs of carrying out
their assigned duties, may I please be reimbursed for
the $287.50 lost briefcase.
```

Paul has been thinking about this situation all week; he even discussed it with Marc, but Marc told him to make whatever decision he thought reasonable. On the one hand, Maurice is a good sales representative; although he's only been with the company for a year, he's turned into one of the company's most successful sales reps. He often works late at night and on the weekends exploring leads and learning more about US products. In addition, the policy manual does contain the exact sentence Maurice quoted. On the other hand, Paul does not feel that US should be responsible for such obvious mistakes as this; assuming responsibility for such mistakes would not only be expensive but also might encourage padded expense accounts.

Finally, Paul decides to do two things. First, he'll write a memo to the sales staff, interpreting more fully the company's reimbursement policy. Policy 14.2 is entitled "Reimbursement of Expenses," and Paragraph 14.2.3 states, "With the approval of their supervisors, all full-time employees will be reimbursed for all reasonable costs of carrying out their assigned duties." Paul wants the sales staff to know that in the future he intends to interpret this policy to mean that any personal property that is stolen will be reimbursed at its present value (not its replacement value) if reasonable care has been taken to secure such property, the incident is reported within two days, and the value of the property can be determined. Lost or damaged personal property will normally not be reimbursed, no matter what the reason. Any sales representative may, of course, appeal Paul's decisions to the vice president for marketing.

Second, because the present policy might not have been sufficiently clear, he'll write a memo to Maurice and agree to reimburse him for the $287.50 briefcase. He'll also enclose a copy of the new policy memo he is sending out to the sales staff.

1. How reasonable was Maurice Potts's claim? Was the intent of the policy clear? Should Paul have reimbursed him? Why or why not?

2. How reasonable is Paul's interpretation of company policy?

3. Compose the three documents that Paul intends to write—the letter to Edwards Furniture Company, the memo to the sales staff, and the memo to Maurice Potts. Format them in an appropriate style.

■ The second edition of the *Oxford English Dictionary,* published in 1989, contains 20 volumes, weighs 137 pounds, reaches a height of 3 feet, 9 inches, when stacked in a pile, and costs $2,500.

■ The second edition of this dictionary defines 500,000 words and contains 50 million words of definitions within its 21,728 pages.

■ The second edition contains 5,000 new words not in the original 1928 edition, including *AIDS, fax, Big Apple, desktop publishing, Diner's Club, download, fast track, foxy, ghetto blaster, greenmail, laptop, nose job, palimony, passive smoking,* and *Visa.*

Persuasive Messages

After you have finished this chapter, you will be able to

1. Describe the basic features of an indirect organizational plan and specify when it should be used.

2. Compose a persuasive request that requires selling an idea, requesting a favor, or writing a persuasive claim.

3. Compose a sales letter.

Seva was founded in 1978 as a charitable organization working to combat blindness in the country of Nepal. Since then, it has expanded its efforts to include more sight-related work in India, Native American health projects, village development in Guatemala, support for Guatemalan refugees in Mexico, and homelessness. Seva's goals are ambitious, and expensive. To pay the bills, the organization solicits donations from individuals and corporations. One person charged with encouraging people to give money to Seva is Mirabai Bush, Director of the Central American Project, and former Seva Chairperson.

According to Bush, the task of persuasion begins long before setting pen to paper. Knowing *who* to ask is as important as knowing *how* to ask. "In proposal writing," says Bush, "you look for an organization that is a likely match."

The most likely match, she says, is someone who has already donated money to Seva. Bush contacts them first, but the expanding organization requires an expanding pool of donors. Therefore, Bush uses several lists of people likely to give to such liberal, humane causes. One problem with this method, says Bush, is that other like-minded organizations often work from the same lists and soon end up competing with each other for contributions. When that happens, Bush's task is complicated.

"It becomes a combination of convincing people you are doing good work," says Bush, "and convincing them that what we are doing is as important as what Greenpeace or some other group is doing.

"The key," Bush says, "is pointing out how giving helps them as well as you. You have to figure out the needs and desires of people, then help them underscore how giving benefits them. It's important to project a good return for

Mirabai Bush, Director of
Central American Project
Action Group,
Seva Foundation,
Chelsea, Michigan

what people want to give you. If the results are not measurable, then you have to go into some depth as to what is to be gained."

That, says Bush, is not as easy as it sounds. Because different people are moved by different rewards, Bush tries to tailor persuasive letters for different groups of recipients. That was particularly tricky when Bush received a letter from a group who ran a high-tech operation that used robots to recover wreckages more than 1500 feet below the ocean's surface. The treasure hunters, who had been led to Seva through an interest in author and Seva board member Ram Dass, were very different from Seva's usual contributors.

"They told us: 'We want you to know we're Republicans,'" says Bush. "They had gotten rich very quickly. They found gold off the coast of Florida. They learned that the gold came from Central America, and they wanted to channel some back. So we had to figure out how to help the people of Guatemala and at the same time maintain the integrity of both the donors and us."

And they had to do it quickly. Bush has experienced that people who get rich quick think immediately about giving some away, but change their minds later.

"I wrote about the history of North and Central America," she says. "I talked about how the policies of the North have resulted in what is going on in the South now. The letter itself was condensed—five single-spaced pages—since we were writing to very busy business people. I presented background on the Mayan people, on Guatemala, on Seva's work in Guatemala, and projections for growth."

Bush's letter spoke to the needs of both the benefactors and the beneficiaries, including intangible human factors and more concrete, bottom-line statistics.

"We usually try to communicate at a few levels at once," says Bush. "We keep it short, simple and truthful. The truth doesn't always fit what people want, but always tell the truth." ▼

▼
OBJECTIVE 1 Describe the basic features of an indirect organizational plan and specify when it should be used.

PLANNING THE PERSUASIVE MESSAGE: CONVINCE BEFORE ASKING

Persuasion is the process of motivating someone to take a specific action or to support a particular idea. That is, persuasion gets someone to believe something or to do something that he or she would not have done if you had not asked. During a single day, many people try to persuade you to do certain things or to believe certain ideas. When you watch television, for example, commercials try to persuade you to purchase various products. Likewise, you have many opportunities to persuade others each day.

As an executive, you will also need to persuade others to do as you want. You may need to persuade a superior to adopt a certain proposal. You may want to persuade a supplier to refund the purchase price of defective merchandise. Or you may need to persuade a potential customer to buy some product or service from your company.

In a sense, all business communication involves persuasion. Even if your primary purpose is to inform, you still want your reader to accept your perspective and believe the information you communicate.

The essence of persuasion is overcoming initial resistance. Indeed, if the receiver of your persuasive efforts did not initially resist the suggestion, persuasion would not be necessary. The reader may resist your efforts for any number of reasons. Your proposal may require the reader to spend time or money—at the very least, you're asking for his or her time to read your message. Or the reader may have had bad experiences in the past with similar requests or may have opinions that predispose him or her against your request.

> Persuasion is necessary when the other person initially resists your efforts.

Your job in writing a persuasive message is to talk your readers into something, to convince them that your point of view is right. You'll have the best chance of succeeding if you tailor your message to your audience, provide your readers with reasons they will find convincing, and anticipate their objections. Such tailor-made writing requires careful planning: you need to define your purpose clearly, analyze your audience, determine the content, and organize your message accordingly.

Purpose

The purpose of a persuasive message is to motivate the reader to do as you ask. This chapter provides effective writing strategies when the specific purpose is to sell an idea, request a favor, write a persuasive claim, and sell a product or service. Other types of persuasive messages, including job-application letters, collection letters, and persuasive oral presentations, are covered in later chapters.

Unless you are clear about the specific results you wish to achieve, you won't be able to plan an effective strategy to achieve your goals. Suppose, for example, you want to convince your superior to adopt a complex proposal. The purpose of your memo might be either (1) to get the superior to say "yes" or "no" to your proposal, (2) to permit field-testing as a prelude to a final decision, or even (3) to persuade your superior to schedule a meeting where you can present your proposal in person and answer any questions. Achieving each of these three goals requires a different strategy.

Audience Analysis

To determine the most effective strategies for your message, consider what you know about your reader.

Knowledge and Attitude of the Reader   What does the reader already know about the topic? Determining this will tell you how much background information is needed. What is the reader's predisposition toward the topic? If the reader's predisposition is negative, then where one or two reasons might ordinarily suffice, you will need to give more. Initial resistance also calls for more objective, verifiable evidence than if the reader were initially neutral. You also need to learn *why* the reader is initially resistant so that you can tailor your arguments to those specific objections.

Effect on the Reader How will the reader be affected by your proposal? Is the reader being asked to commit resources (time or money)? If so, discuss the rewards for doing so. Is the reader being asked to endorse some proposal? If so, give enough information to enable the reader to make an informed decision.

The reader always wants to know "What's in it for me?" *You* are already convinced of the wisdom of your proposal. Your job is to inform the reader about the benefits he or she will receive from doing as you ask.

To be persuasive, you must present specific, believable evidence. However, one of the worst mistakes you could make would be simply to describe the features of the product or to list the advantages of doing as you ask. Instead, put yourself in the reader's place. Discuss how the reader will benefit from your proposal. Most of your sentences should emphasize the reader rather than the product or idea you're promoting.

> *Writer Benefits:* The San Diego Accounting Society would like you to speak to us on the topic of expensing versus capitalizing 401-C assets.
> *Reader Benefits:* Speaking to the San Diego Accounting Society would enable you to present your firm's views on the controversial topic of expensing versus capitalizing 401-C assets.

| Discussing indirect benefits prevents your request from sounding selfish. | Sometimes your readers won't directly benefit from doing as you ask. If you are trying to entice your employees to give to the United Way, for example, it would be difficult to discuss direct reader benefits. In such situations, you should discuss the *indirect* benefits of reader participation; that is, you would want to show how someone other than you, the solicitor of the funds, will benefit. |

> *Indirect Benefits:* Your contribution will enable city youngsters, many of whom have never even been outside the city of Columbus, to see pandas living and thriving in their natural habitat.

| A reader who trusts you is more likely to trust your message. | **Writer Credibility** What is your credibility with the reader? The more believable you are, the more believable your message will appear. Credibility comes from many sources. You may be perceived as credible by virtue of the position you hold or by being a well-known authority. Or you may achieve credibility for your proposal by supplying convincing evidence, such as facts and statistics that can be verified. |

Suppose, for example, you have worked in an advertising production department for ten years and have extensive experience with color reproduction. If you are writing a memo to a colleague suggesting that certain photos will not reproduce clearly and should be replaced, you probably don't need to explain your expertise. Your colleague is likely to believe you. But if you are writing a letter to the photographer who does not know you, you should probably discuss past incidents that lead you to conclude the photos should be replaced.

Lobbyists, like the ones shown here waiting by a senate
committee room at the Texas state capitol, spend a great
deal of time writing persuasive messages to motivate,
influence, and convince legislators to pass laws.

Content

Based upon the reader's knowledge about the topic, the effect your proposal
will have on the reader, and the reader's predisposition toward you and
your topic, you must decide what information to include in your message
and what type of appeal to emphasize. Develop an appeal that will overcome
your reader's resistance; that is, convince your reader that what you have
to offer is worthwhile and that what you have to say is true. A variety of
appeals is available.

Logical Versus Emotional Appeals   Logical appeals are directed toward
the reader's rational perceptions and involve such practical concepts as
durability, economy, convenience, safety, and efficiency. Emotional appeals
are directed toward the reader's feelings and involve such concepts as
excitement, glamour, prestige, belonging, and feeling good about oneself.

Logical: Our stationery's 25% rag content means that your correspondence will remain legible even after ten years in the file cabinet.
Emotional: Our stationery's 25% rag content means that your correspondence will make an important statement about you to your colleagues.

Sales letters for consumer goods often emphasize emotional appeals, whereas sales letters for industrial goods often emphasize logical appeals. Likewise, emotional appeals are often used to promote inexpensive or nonessential products, whereas logical appeals are used to promote expensive or essential products. Nonsales persuasive letters and memos may use either logical or emotional appeals, depending on the individual circumstances.

Logical: Adopting this proposal will increase our market share by 1.5% within six months.

Emotional: Adopting this proposal will give our company an international reputation as the leader in Pacific Rim marketing.

Positive Versus Negative Appeals   Most persuasive appeals are positive, stressing the benefits to the reader of accepting the writer's proposal. Negative appeals, in contrast, stress the drawbacks of not accepting the writer's proposal; for example, buying insurance to avoid leaving your family destitute. Negative appeals are used mostly for health and safety issues, such as for antismoking and drug-abuse campaigns. Some products lend themselves to either positive or negative appeals; for example, driving within the legal speed limit can be promoted as either saving gas (positive appeal) or as deterring accidents (negative appeal).

Positive Appeal: By donating a pint of blood next Thursday, you will help ensure a continued supply of plasma for Clifford County residents.

Negative Appeal: To avoid the possibility of facing emergency surgery with an inadequate supply of blood available, please do your part next Thursday.

Unless you have reason to expect that a negative appeal will be effective for your particular audience, most often you're safer to stress the positive benefits of accepting your suggestion.

Self-Interest   The most effective appeals focus on the reader's self-interest and satisfy a need of the reader. Although a persuasive message cannot *create* a need, it can make the reader aware of an existing need. Abraham Maslow[1] has hypothesized that people generally act in order to satisfy certain needs. He identified the following five levels of needs:

1. *Physiological,* such as air, water, food, sleep, and shelter
2. *Safety and security,* such as personal security, financial security, stability, and protection
3. *Social,* such as love, friendship, and group membership
4. *Esteem and status,* such as self-worth, recognition, and respect
5. *Self-actualization,* such as fulfillment and creativity

According to Maslow, people generally satisfy their needs in order from lowest (physiological) to highest (self-actualization), although he recognized that people are sometimes motivated by more than one category of need at once.

One strategy for writing an effective persuasive letter, then, is to decide which level of need your reader is currently trying to satisfy and then appeal to that need. In large measure, the nature of the product or idea determines the type of need it meets. However, you can sometimes position the same product to meet different needs. Assume, for example, that you wanted to persuade your reader to purchase the Elimistress, an isometric exercise device designed to release tension and reduce stress. You might promote the product in a number of ways, depending on the level of need you wished to satisfy:

> *Physiological need:* Using the Elimistress a half hour a day will help your body recover from the stress of the modern executive's typical day.
> *Social need:* Don't let the stress of the day's problems affect your leisure-time enjoyment. Use the Elimistress a half hour a day, and enjoy life again.
> *Self-actualization need:* Is undue stress and anxiety affecting your ability to fulfill your potential? If so, using the Elimistress half an hour a day will help unleash your pent-up creativity.

Your knowledge of the reader and the type of appeal you believe will be most effective will thus determine the content of your message.

Organization

Your audience analysis will help you decide how to organize your message. When presenting a proposal that does not require strong persuasion, use the direct plan of organization; that is, present the main idea (your recommendation) first, followed by the supporting evidence. Such a plan immediately satisfies the reader's curiosity about your purpose. To get readers to accept your proposal when using the direct plan, present your recommendation along with the criteria and brief rationale in the first paragraph.

> *Unsupported:* I recommend we hold our Pittsburgh sales meeting at the Mark-Congress Hotel.
> *Supported:* As you requested, I have evaluated three hotels as possible meeting sites for our Pittsburgh sales conference. Based on the criteria of location, facilities, and cost, I recommend we meet at the Mark-Congress Hotel. It is centrally located, has good meeting rooms, and is moderately priced.

In general, you should use the direct plan when

- Your audience is predisposed to listen objectively to your request. This is often (but not always) the case when you are writing to people within your organization.
- You are writing a long or complex proposal. A reader may become impatient if your main point is buried at the back of your report.
- There are no obvious obstacles to your proposal, so strong persuasion is not necessary.

Unfortunately, life is not always so simple. Many times your reader will resist your suggestions. Your job then is to explain the merits of your proposal and show how the reader will benefit from doing as you ask.

Because a reluctant reader is more likely to agree to something after he or she understands its merits, your plan of organization is to convince the reader before asking for action. Use the **indirect organizational plan,** a plan in which the rationale is presented first, followed by the major idea—the request for action.

Gaining the Reader's Attention When you use the indirect plan, you delay asking for action until after you've presented your reasons. Thus, a subject line is not generally used in persuasive letters. However, if a subject line is a standard part of the heading for an organization's memorandums, use a neutral one; for example, "Analysis of Roper Division Profitability" rather than "Proposal to Sell the Roper Division." Don't announce your purpose immediately but rather lead up to it gradually.

The first test of a good opening sentence in a persuasive request is whether it is interesting enough to catch and keep the reader's attention. It won't matter how much evidence you have marshaled to support your case if the recipient does not bother to continue reading carefully after the first sentence.

A rhetorical question is often effective as an opening sentence. A rhetorical question is asked strictly to get the reader to think about the topic of your message; a literal answer is not expected. To be effective, a rhetorical question must gain the reader's attention. Obvious questions are not effective motivators for further reading and, in fact, may be insulting to the reader's intelligence. Similarly, questions answerable by "yes" or "no" don't make good lead-in questions because answering them doesn't require much thought.

> *Weak:* How would you like to save our department $7,500 yearly?
> *Thought-provoking:* What do you think the labor costs are for changing just one light bulb? $2? $5? More?
>
> *Weak:* Did you know that the Community Fund has been serving Allentown for more than 50 years?
> *Thought-provoking:* What do Tom Selleck and the Allentown Community Fund have in common?

Sometimes an unusual fact or unexpected statement will draw the reader into the letter or memo. Other times, you might want to select some statement about which the reader and writer will agree—to immediately establish some common ground.

> Our company spent more money on janitorial service last year than on research and development.
>
> A five-year-old boy taught me an important lesson last week.
>
> <u>Automotive News</u> calls your 6-year/60,000 mile warranty the best in the business. (*opening for a claim letter*)

| The opening statement must be relevant. |

Your opening statement must also be relevant to the purpose of your message. If your opening is too far off the topic or misleads the reader, you risk losing his or her goodwill, and the reader may simply stop reading. At the very least, the reader will feel confused or deceived, making persuasion more difficult. Consider the following opening to a memo that proposes a new inventory system:

> "The test of courage comes when we are in the minority; the test of tolerance comes when we are in the majority." So said Ralph Sockman. And although the majority of our orders go out on time, a small minority of them are needlessly delayed by our outdated inventory system.

Even though the terms *majority* and *minority* are repeated in the last sentence, the idea introduced in the opening statement is too far off the topic of the real purpose of the memo to achieve its purpose. In addition, Ralph Sockman is never identified, leaving the reader puzzled. A better opening would have been more direct and more relevant:

> Who wouldn't be satisfied with a score of 95%?
> But while such a score might represent an "A" on a test, it represents "failure" when it applies to our on-time delivery of orders. The 5% of our customers who experience late deliveries are not receiving the kind of service they deserve.

Keep your opening statement short. Often an opening paragraph of just one sentence will make the message inviting. Few readers want to wade through a long opening paragraph to figure out the purpose of the message.

In summary, an effective opening for a persuasive message is interesting, relevant, and short.

Creating Interest and Justifying Your Request A good opening helps make sure your reader gets to the body of your message. Then you begin the process of convincing the reader that your request is reasonable. This process may require several paragraphs of discussion, depending on how much evidence you think will be needed to convince the reader.

Because it takes more space to state *why* something should be done than simply to state *that* it should be done, persuasive requests are typically longer than other types of messages. In fact, when trying to persuade someone to adopt a particularly complex proposal, writers often put their proposals in the form of a report rather than in the form of a letter or memorandum. (Proposal reports are covered in Chapter 14.)

To convince your readers, you must be objective, specific, logical, and reasonable. Avoid emotionalism, obvious flattery, insincerity, and exaggeration. Let your evidence carry the weight of your argument.

> *Vague:* Locating our plant in Suffolk instead of in Norfolk would result in considerable savings.
> *Specific:* Locating our plant in Suffolk instead of in Norfolk would result in annual savings of nearly $175,000, as shown in Table 3.
>
> *Exaggeration:* Why should it take a thousand phone calls to convince your computer to credit my account for $38.50?
> *Improved:* Evidently your computer doesn't like me and I don't know why! Even after five phone calls over the past three weeks, I find that $38.50 has still not been credited to my account.

Provide convincing evidence and use a reasonable tone.

The type of evidence you present depends, of course, on the circumstances. The usual types of evidence are these:

- *Facts and statistics:* Facts are objective statements whose truth can be verified; statistics are facts comprised of numbers. Both must be relevant and accurate. For example, statistics that were accurate five years ago may no longer be accurate today.
- *Expert opinion:* Testimony from authorities on the topic might be presented if their testimony is relevant and, if necessary, it is accompanied by a discussion of the experts' credentials.
- *Examples:* Specific cases or incidents used to illustrate the point under discussion should be relevant, representative, and complete.

Present the benefits (either direct or indirect) that will accompany your proposal, and provide enough background and evidence to enable the reader to make an informed decision.

Dealing with Obstacles If there were no obvious obstacles to granting your request, persuasion would not be necessary, and you could use the direct plan of organization. But persuasion is necessary—perhaps because you're asking the reader for time, money, or other resources.

Ignoring the obstacles to your request would provide your reader with a ready excuse to refuse your request. Assume, for example, that you're trying to persuade a supplier to provide an in-store demonstrator of the firm's products—even though you know it's against company policy to do so. If you ignore this factor, you're simply inviting the reader to respond that company policy prohibits granting your request.

Instead, your strategy should be to show that *even considering such obstacles,* your request is still a reasonable one, perhaps as follows:

> Last year we sold 356 Golden Microwave ovens. We believe the extensive publicity our sale will generate (as well as our previous sales performance) justifies your temporarily setting aside your policy and providing an in-store demonstrator. The ease of use and the actual cooked results that your representative will display are sure to increase sales of your microwaves.

Suppose you're asking someone to speak to a professional organization and you're unable to provide an honorarium. In that case, discuss the free publicity the speaker will receive and the impact that the speaker's remarks will have on the audience. Suppose you're asking for confidential information. Let the reader know you recognize this information is confidential, and discuss how you will treat it as such. Suppose you're asking for a large donation. Discuss how the donation can be made on the installment plan or by payroll deduction, and discuss the tax-deductible aspects of the donation.

Even though obstacles should be addressed, don't emphasize them. Subordinate this discussion by devoting relatively little space to it, by discussing obstacles in the same sentence as a reader benefit, and by putting the discussion in the middle of a paragraph. Regardless of how you do it, show the reader that you're aware of the obvious obstacles and that, even considering them, your proposal still has merit.

Note the reader benefits in the last sentence.

Motivating Action   Although your request has been implied earlier, save the direct statement of the request until late in the message—after most of the background information and reader benefits have been thoroughly covered. Make the specific action that you want clear and easy to take. For example, if the reader agrees to do as you ask, how is he or she to let you know? Will a phone call suffice, or is a written reply necessary? If a phone call is adequate, have you provided a phone number? If you're asking for a favor that requires a written response, have you included a stamped, addressed envelope?

Ask for the desired action in a confident tone. If your request or proposal is reasonable, there is no need to apologize, and you surely do not want to supply the reader with excuses. Take whatever steps you can to ensure a prompt reply.

Apologetic: I know you're a busy person, but I would appreciate your completing this questionnaire.

Confident: So that this information will be available for the financial managers attending our fall conference, I would appreciate your returning the questionnaire to me by September 15.

Note the indirect benefit implied.

Hesitant: If you agree that this proposal is worthwhile, please let me know by June 1.

Confident: To enable us to have this plan in place before the opening of our new branch on June 1, simply initial this memo and return it to me.

Note the motivation for a prompt reply.

Checklist 5 summarizes guidelines to use in writing persuasive requests. While you will not be able to use all these suggestions in each persuasive request, you should use them as an overall framework for structuring your message.

WRITING A PERSUASIVE REQUEST

In many ways, writing a persuasive request is more difficult than writing a sales letter because reader benefits are not always as obvious in persuasive requests. This section provides strategies for selling an idea, requesting a favor, and writing a persuasive claim letter. Other types of persuasive requests, such as requesting funds for charity or persuading a supplier to grant credit, would follow the same organizational plan.

OBJECTIVE 2 Compose a persuasive request that requires selling an idea, requesting a favor, or writing a persuasive claim.

Selling an Idea

You will have many opportunities to use your education and your job experience to help solve problems faced by your organization. On the job you will frequently write letters or memorandums proposing one alternative over another, suggesting a new procedure, or in some other way recommending some course of action.

Organize your message logically, showing what the problem is, how you intend to solve the problem, and why your solution is sound. Write in an objective style, avoiding exaggeration. Provide evidence to support your claims.

CHECKLIST 5 | # Writing Persuasive Requests

General Plan (Indirect)

Gain the Reader's Attention

1. Make the first sentence interesting enough to motivate the reader to continue reading. A rhetorical question is often effective; other effective openers include an unusual fact, an unexpected statement, or some statement about which the reader and writer can agree.

2. Keep the opening paragraph short—often just one sentence—to draw the reader into the letter.

3. Make sure that the opening sentence relates to the main topic of the message. Don't mislead the reader.

4. When appropriate, relate the opener to a reader benefit.

Create Interest and Justify Your Request

5. Don't specifically make your request until you've presented some of the reasons.

6. Devote the major part of your message to justifying your request. Give enough background and evidence to enable the reader to make an informed decision.

7. Use facts and statistics, expert opinion, and examples to support your proposal. Ensure that your evidence is accurate, relevant, representative, and complete. Avoid obvious flattery, emotionalism, and exaggeration.

8. Use an objective, logical, reasonable, and sincere tone.

9. Present your evidence in terms of either direct or indirect reader benefits.

Minimize Obstacles

10. Do not ignore obstacles to your request or negative aspects. Instead, show that even considering such obstacles, your request is still reasonable.

11. Subordinate the discussion of obstacles by position and amount of space devoted to the topic.

Ask Confidently for Action

12. Although it may have been implied earlier, save the specific request for late in the message.

13. Make the desired action clear and easy for the reader to take.

14. Ask in a confident tone. Do not apologize and do not supply excuses.

15. End on a forward-looking note, continuing to stress reader benefits.

Alternate Plan (Direct)

1. Use a direct organizational plan when strong persuasion is not necessary (that is, when your audience is predisposed to listen objectively to your request, you are writing a long or complex proposal, or there are no obvious obstacles to your proposal).

2. Present your recommendation, along with the criteria and brief rationale, in the first paragraph.

3. Continue by presenting credible evidence and minimizing obstacles; end on a forward-looking note that continues to stress reader benefits.

The memo in Figure 7.1 illustrates the selling of an idea. In this case, a marketing supervisor for an auto-parts supplier is asking the vice president to reassign parking spaces to give preference for those employees driving American-made cars. Although memos are often written in the direct organizational pattern, this supervisor is new on the job and has not yet earned the automatic trust of the vice president. In addition, the proposed change would affect working conditions, which has union implications. Therefore, the memo requires the use of persuasion and is written in the indirect pattern.

Requesting a Favor

It has been said that the wheels of industry are greased with favors. The mutual giving and receiving of favors makes success more likely and makes life in general more agreeable.

A request for a favor differs from a routine request in that routine requests are granted almost automatically, whereas favors might require some persuasion. For example, asking a colleague to switch places with you on the program for the monthly managers' meeting might be considered a routine request. Asking the same colleague to prepare and give your presentation would more likely be a favor, requiring some persuasion.

> Favors require persuasion because the reader gets nothing tangible in return.

Although friends often do each other favors as a matter of course, in business the granting of a favor might not be so automatic. Here again, you will want to begin your request with an attention-getter and stress the reader benefits from granting the favor.

Suppose, for example, that you were conducting a market survey to determine the feasibility of offering some new consumer product and needed to write a persuasive cover letter to motivate a carefully selected sample of consumers to complete the questionnaire. Your opening paragraphs might be as follows:

If you could change one thing about your hair spray, what would it be? Some consumers don't like the starched feeling it leaves in their hair; others wish their spray would last longer; others have different problems.

Here is your opportunity to talk directly to Lawson Products, the largest maker of beauty aids. We're planning to manufacture a new brand of hair spray, and we'd like you and others like you to help us design a product that meets *your* needs.

> A smooth transition from the opening to the discussion of benefits is easier when the opening relates directly to the topic.

FIGURE 7.1   Selling an Idea

A memorandum is an internal communication from one member of the organization to another.

Subject line does not immediately identify the request.

Opening is interesting, relevant, and short. Provides a smooth transition to the necessary background information.

Cites external testimony.

Makes the recommendation after presenting most of the rationale.

Neutralizes an obvious obstacle.

Closes on a positive, confident note; prompt action is motivated.

**TIMKIN
ELECTRICAL
SYSTEMS, INC.**   1034 York Road,
Baltimore, MD 21204
(301) 555-1086

MEMO TO: Elliott Lamborn, Vice President   *J.P.*

FROM: Jenson Peterson, Marketing Supervisor

DATE: October 3, 19—

SUBJECT: Parking Lots

Our employee parking lots tell our customers a lot about our confidence in our own products.   1

Whenever customers from the auto industry visit our headquarters, they must either drive by or walk through Parking Lots A and B, those nearest the building. When they do, they will see, as our staff did during a recent random inspection, that approximately 32% of our employees drive foreign-made cars—despite the fact that nearly all our business comes from the American auto industry.   2

I recognize, of course, that many factors go into the decision to purchase a particular car. However, as a recent purchasing agent from Embassy told me last week, "How can you expect us to support you when you don't support us?" This executive was not asking us specifically to promote Embassy cars—just American-made cars.   3

The purpose of this memo, then, is to seek your approval to have Parking Lots A and B and Rows 1–5 of the Executive Parking Lot restricted to American-made cars. The Maintenance Department estimates that it will need four weeks and about $500 to make the needed signs.

Our labor contract requires union approval of any changes in working conditions. However, Sally Merritt, our shop steward, has told me that she would be willing to discuss this matter—especially if a similar restriction is made for the executive parking lot.

Since our quarterly marketing manager's meeting will be held on November 8–10, I look forward to being able to announce the new plan to them then. By making this change, we will be sending a powerful positive message to headquarters visitors: Our employees believe in the products we sell.

urs

Grammar and Mechanics Notes

1. "a lot"—two words.   2. Use figures for percentages.   3. "recognize, of course,"—transitional expression.

Note the rhetorical question used as an attention-getter. The reader benefit is the opportunity to have an impact on a product that the reader uses. In many consumer surveys, additional incentives, such as a dollar bill or a free product sample, are included to motivate the reader to complete the questionnaire.

Discuss at least one reader benefit before making your request. Explain why the favor is being asked, and continue to show how the reader will benefit directly or indirectly from granting the favor. Keep a positive, confident tone throughout, and make the action clear and easy to take.

Often the favor is requested because the reader is an expert on some topic. If that is the case, you may legitimately make a complimentary remark about the reader. Make sure, however, that your compliment sounds sincere. Readers are rightfully suspicious, for example, when they read in a form letter that they have been specifically chosen to participate in some project. ("Me and how many thousands of others?" they might wonder.) On the other hand, such a compliment in a letter that is obviously personally typed and signed has much more credibility.

> For a sincere tone, make any flattering comments unique to the reader.

The most important point to remember in asking for a favor has to do with the favor itself rather than with the writing process: keep your request reasonable; don't ask someone else to do something that you can do for yourself.

Figure 7.2 illustrates a persuasive request asking for a favor. The reader and writer do not know each other, which makes persuasion a little more challenging. Reader benefits (the opportunity to promote her firm and the flattering prospect of being the center of attention) are included.

Writing a Persuasive Claim

As discussed in Chapter 6, most claim letters are routine letters and should be written using a direct plan of organization—stating the problem early in the letter. Because it is to the company's benefit to keep its customers satisfied, most reasonable claims are settled to the customer's satisfaction. Therefore, persuasion is not ordinarily necessary.

Suppose, however, that you wrote a routine claim letter and the company, for some reason, denied your claim. If you still feel that your original claim is legitimate, you might then write a persuasive claim letter—using all the techniques discussed earlier in this chapter for writing persuasive requests. Or assume that your new photocopier broke three days after the warranty period expired. The company is not legally obligated to honor your claim, but you may decide to try to persuade them to do so anyway.

Showing anger in your persuasive claim letter would be counterproductive, even if the company turned down your original claim. Remember that the claims adjuster who will read your letter was not responsible for your problem. Also remember that the goal of your letter is not to vent your anger but to solve a problem. And that is more likely to happen when a calm atmosphere prevails.

As in a routine claim letter, you will need to explain in sufficient detail precisely what the problem is, how it came about, and how you want the reader to solve the problem. Use a calm, objective, courteous tone, and avoid anger and exaggeration. Although similar in some respects, the persuasive claim differs from a routine claim letter in the following two important ways.

FIGURE 7.2   Requesting a Favor

**BALTIMORE IBM
USER'S GROUP**

P.O. Box 1038
Baltimore, MD 21204
(301) 555-9879

January 15, 19--

Ms. Tanya Porratt, President
The Office Training Group
1800 Ten Hills Road, Suite B
Boston, MA 02145

Dear Ms. Porratt:

"Desktop publishing has been around for 100 years."

Your comment in a recent interview published in the <u>Boston Globe</u> certainly made me sit up and think. After all, the first desktop publishing software was introduced only in 1986--certainly not 100 years ago.

Members of the Baltimore IBM User's Group would enjoy and benefit from hearing a respected DTP professional who has been actively involved in the field since its inception. As the speaker at our annual banquet at the Baltimore Park Plaza Hotel on April 25, you would be able to present your ideas on DTP to our 200 members. You would, of course, be our guest for the banquet, which begins at 7 p.m. Your 45-minute presentation would begin at 8:30 p.m.

We will reimburse you for air travel and hotel accommodations. Although our nonprofit professional association is unable to offer an honorarium, we do offer you an opportunity to introduce your firm and to present your ideas to representatives of every major company in the Baltimore metropolitan area.

We would like to announce your speech as the lead article in our next newsletter, which goes to press on March 23. Won't you please use the enclosed postal card to let us know that you can come. We will have a large, enthusiastic audience of decision-makers waiting to hear you.

Cordially,

Magda T. P. Lyon

Magda D. Lyon
Banquet Chairperson

jrk
Enclosure

Marginal notes (left column):

Opens with an interesting quotation by the reader, thus complimenting the reader.

Intimates the request.

Provides the necessary background information.

Subordinates a potential obstacle by putting it in the dependent clause of a sentence.
Closes with a restatement of a reader benefit.

Numbered references in letter: 1, 2, 3

Grammar and Mechanics Notes

1. Underline the titles of complete works.   2. "its"—no apostrophe when used to show possession.   3. Use a period after a courteous request.

Writing a Persuasive Claim   **FIGURE 7.3**

June 18, 19—

Customer Services Department
Northern Airlines, Inc.
P.O. Box 6001
Denver, CO 80240

Ladies and Gentlemen:

I think you will agree that a relaxing 90-minute flight on
Northern Airlines is more enjoyable than a grueling six-hour
automobile trip.

Yet on June 2, my wife and I found ourselves doing just that—
driving from Saginaw, Michigan, to Indianapolis, Indiana—in the   1
middle of the night and in the company of three tired children.

We had made reservations on Northern Flight 126 a month earlier   2
and to obtain the cheapest fare ($136 per ticket) had purchased
nonrefundable tickets. When we arrived at the airport, we were
told that Flight 1026, scheduled to depart at 8 p.m., had been
canceled. Your gate agent (Ms. Nixon) had graciously rebooked us
in complimentary first-class seats on the next available flight,
leaving at 9:45 the following morning.

Since the purpose of our trip was to attend a family wedding on
June 3, we had no choice but to cancel our rebooked flight and to
drive to Indianapolis instead. When we tried to turn in our tickets for a refund, Ms. Nixon informed us that because the flight
had been canceled due to inclement weather, she would be unable to
credit my American Express charge card.

As a frequent flier on Northern, I've experienced first-hand the
"Welcome Aboard!" feeling that is the basis for your current
advertising campaign; and I believe you will want to extend that   3
same taken-care-of-feeling to your ticket operations as well.
Please credit my American Express charge card (Account No. 4102
817 171) for the $680 cost of the five tickets, thus putting out
the welcome mat again for my family.

Sincerely,

Oliver J. Arbin

Oliver J. Arbin
518 Thompson Street   4
Saginaw, MI 48607

Begins on a warm and
relevant note.

Provides a smooth
transition from the
opening sentence.

Provides the necessary
background information.

Tells exactly what the
problem is in a neutral,
courteous tone.

Provides a rationale for
granting the claim.

Asks confidently for
specific action; mentions
the reader benefit of
keeping a satisfied
customer.

Grammar and Mechanics Notes

1. To type a dash, type two hyphens with no space before or after.   2. Capitalize
a noun that comes before a number.   3. "taken-care-of-feeling"—Hyphenate a
compound adjective that comes before a noun.   4. For personal business letters
on plain paper, type your address below your name.

Attention-Getting Opening You begin a routine claim letter by stating the problem. This type of opening would not be wise for a persuasive claim, because the reader may infer that the claim is unreasonable until you discuss your rationale. Consider, for example, the following two openings to a persuasive claim letter:

> *Original:* Would you please repair my Marlow 203 copier without charge, even though the 90-day warranty expired last week.
> *Revised:* We took a chance and lost! We bet that the Marlow 203 we purchased from you 93 days ago would prove to be as reliable as the other ten Marlows that our firm has in use.

The original opening gives the reader a ready excuse to deny the claim. The revised version holds off making the request until enough background information has been provided. Note also the personal relationship the writer is beginning to establish with the reader in the revised version—discussing not only that the company owns ten other Marlow copiers but also that the other copiers have all been very reliable. Such an understanding tone will make the reader more likely to grant the request.

In a courteous manner, provide complete details.

More Evidence Because your claim either is nonroutine or has been rejected once, you will need to present as much convincing evidence as possible. Explain fully the basis for your claim in a courteous manner, sticking to the facts; then request a specific adjustment. Leave no doubt as to what action you want taken; for example, do you want the item repaired, do you want it replaced, or do you want a refund?

Figure 7.3 illustrates these guidelines for writing a persuasive claim letter.

OBJECTIVE 3 Compose a sales letter.

WRITING A SALES LETTER

The heart of most business is sales—selling a product or service. Much of a company's sales effort is accomplished through the writing of effective sales letters—either individual letters for individual sales or form letters for large-scale sales.

In large companies, the writing of sales letters is centered in the marketing or advertising department and is a highly specialized task performed by advertising copywriters and marketing consultants. Recently, however, there has been a dramatic increase in the number of people who graduate from college and, within a few years, own their own businesses. These start-up companies are typically quite small, with only one or two employees.

Small-business owners often write their own sales letters.

In such a situation, the company must mount an aggressive sales effort in order to develop business, but the company is often too small to hire a full-time copywriter or marketing consultant. Thus, the owner usually ends up writing these sales letters. So no matter where you intend to work, the chances are that at some point you will need to write a sales letter.

Getting Ready

Because the sales effort is so crucial to a company's success, you should spend an adequate amount of time preparing each sales letter. Doing so is especially important if, as is so often the case, the sales letter will be a form letter, going to perhaps thousands of potential customers. One recent survey indicated that 62 billion pieces of these letters are mailed each year, with the typical household receiving in excess of 10 such letters each week.[2] If you don't want your letters to be considered "junk mail" and dumped in the trash can, you will need to research your product, analyze your audience, select a central selling theme, and plan your campaign.

Research Your Product   "Knowledge is power" and nowhere is this saying truer than in writing a sales letter. In order to write effectively about a product, you must know the product intimately. Some of the facts you'll want to learn about the product are these:

- raw materials and components used to manufacture the product and the manufacturing process (including any environmental issues)
- operation of the product (through first-hand experience if possible)
- its major features
- maintenance, service, and warranties
- pricing structure (e.g., volume discounts)
- means used to market the product (direct mail, retail stores, wholesale outlets, etc.)

You will also need to learn this same information about your competition's products to help you determine the major differences between yours and theirs.

> Know both your product and the competition thoroughly.

Analyze Your Audience   The more you're able to promote the features of your products as satisfying specific needs of your audience, the more persuasive your sales letter will be. This means you must know as much about your audience as possible.

Define your audience first of all in terms of such demographic variables as sex, age, marital status, family size, occupation, income level, home ownership, and educational level. In addition, try to classify your audience according to such nonquantifiable variables as personality, attitudes, and lifestyle. This analysis will help you plan the most appropriate type of appeal to use (for example, logical versus emotional or positive versus negative).

Audience analysis is easier, of course, when you're writing to a single individual. Defining an audience of hundreds requires a little more research. If you discover that your audience is, in fact, a very diverse group, you may want to prepare more than one form of the letter, gearing each one to the interests and needs of a specific subgroup.

> More than one version of your sales letter might be warranted if your audience is diverse.

Suppose, for example, you are promoting a line of men's shoes. A sales letter geared to young professional men might stress "stylish . . . comes in various shades of black and brown . . . a perfect accessory to your business wardrobe." The same line of shoes might be promoted to the middle-aged professional as "perfect detailing . . . 12-hour comfort . . . stays sharp looking through days of traveling." Finally, the retired executive might go for shoes that are "economical . . . comfortable . . . a no-nonsense type of shoe."

The point to remember is to know your audience and to personalize your letter to best meet their needs and interests. Use the "you" attitude to achieve the results you want.

Select a Central Selling Theme   Once you are thoroughly familiar with your product, its competition, and your intended audience, you are then in a position to select a **central selling theme** for your letter. Most products will have numerous features that you will want to introduce and discuss. For your letter to make a real impact, however, you need to have a single theme running through your letter—a major reader benefit that you introduce early and emphasize throughout your letter.

It would be unrealistic to expect your reader to remember five different features that you mention about your product. In any case, you have only a short time period to make a lasting impression on your reader. Use that time wisely to emphasize what you think is the most telling benefit from owning your product. Two means of achieving this emphasis are position and repetition. Introduce your central selling theme early (in the opening sentence if possible), and keep repeating it throughout the letter.

Plan Your Campaign   Decide at the very start how you will use the sales letter you're about to write. Will there be any enclosures in the envelope—brochures, catalogs, order blanks, and so on? How will your letter be duplicated? In what color ink and on what color paper, and in what style of type?

How will you secure an up-to-date mailing list? If you don't maintain your own list of customers and potential customers, there are market-research firms that will provide customized lists of mailing labels for you. All you have to do is tell them what segment of a population you wish to include; for example, a random list of 500 people in Des Moines who are single and earn between $50,000 and $100,000 yearly.

Since all these decisions affect the content and format of the message, make them before you compose your message. Only then are you ready to begin writing. The indirect organizational plan used for sales letters is sometimes called the AIDA plan, because you first gain the reader's *Attention*, then create *Interest* in and *Desire* for the benefits of your proposal, and finally motivate *Action*.

Gaining the Reader's Attention

Review the earlier section on gaining the reader's attention when writing persuasive requests.

A reply to a request for product information from a potential customer is called a **solicited sales letter.** An **unsolicited sales letter,** on the other hand, is a letter promoting a firm's products mailed to a potential customer who has not expressed any interest in the product.

Because most sales letters are unsolicited, you have only a line or two in which to grab the reader's attention. Unless a sales letter is addressed to the reader personally and is obviously not a form letter, the reader is likely to just skim it—either out of curiosity or because the opening sentence got the reader's attention.

Most readers will scan the opening of a form letter, perhaps just to learn what product is being promoted. If you can capture their attention in these first few lines, they may continue reading. Otherwise, all your efforts have been wasted. The following types of opening sentences have proven effective for sales letters:

Many attention-getting openings consist of a one-sentence paragraph.

Rhetorical question: What is the difference between extravagance and luxury? (*promoting a luxury car*)

Thought-provoking statement: Most of what we had to say about business this morning was unprintable! (*promoting early-morning television news program*)

Unusual fact: If your family is typical, you will wash 2,000 pounds of laundry this year. (*promoting a laundry detergent*)

Current event: The new Arrow assembly plant will bring 1,700 new families to White Rock within three years. (*promoting a real-estate company*)

Anecdote: During six years of college, the one experience that helped me the most did not even occur in the classroom. (*promoting a weekly business magazine*)

Direct challenge: Drop the enclosed Pointer pen on the floor, writing tip first, and then sign your name with it. (*promoting a no-blot ball-point pen*)

As in persuasive requests, the opening to a sales letter should be interesting, short, and original. When possible, incorporate the central selling theme in your opening; and avoid irrelevant, obvious, or time-worn statements. Unless your reader is motivated to continue reading, making a sale is unlikely.

If you have received an inquiry from a potential customer about your product, you know that the person is already at least mildly interested in the product. Therefore, when writing solicited sales letters, an attention-getting opening is not as crucial. In such a situation, you might begin by expressing appreciation for the customer's inquiry and then begin introducing the central selling theme.

> Begin a solicited sales letter by expressing appreciation for the inquiry.

Creating Interest and Building Desire

If your opening sentence is directly related to your product, the transition to the discussion of features and reader benefits will be smooth and logical. Make sure that the first sentence of the second paragraph relates directly to the idea introduced in your opening sentence. Unrelated sentences that intervene will make the reader pause and feel puzzled.

Interpreting Features The major part of your letter (several paragraphs) will probably be devoted to creating interest in and building desire for your product. You should not only describe the product and its features but, more importantly, you must *interpret* these features by showing specifically how each will benefit the reader. Make the reader—not the product—the subject of most of your sentences.

> Devote several paragraphs to interpreting the product's features.

Marketers refer to the benefit a user can derive from a product or service as the **derived benefit.** As Charles Revson, founder of Revlon Cosmetics, once said, "In our factory we make lipstick; in our advertising we sell hope."[3]

Product-oriented: The JT Laser II prints at the speed of eight pages per minute.
Reader-oriented: After pushing the print key, you'll barely have time to reach over and retrieve the pages from the bin. The JT Laser II's print speed of eight pages per minute is five times faster than that of the typical dot-matrix printer.

WRITING A PERSONAL LETTER TO 5,000 PEOPLE

Personalizing a form letter is easy using the merge feature of word processing. The software automatically merges the variable data in a secondary file (the information unique to the reader) with the stored paragraphs in a primary file (the text that is included in every copy of the letter). The example below shows the steps involved in creating a merge document using WordPerfect. In this letter, the inside address, salutation, and name and phone number of the local dealer are different in each letter.

Variable Data

```
Mr. Leon Ellis, Manager
Stephen Wyse Wholesalers
1800 East 26 Street
Little Rock, AR 73206^R

Mr. Ellis^R

Comstock Computer Center^R

555-2188^R

^E
```

Stored Data

```
^F1^

Dear ^F2^:

Thank you for requesting information about our Hoskins
2400-baud modem and software. More than 70 of the For-
tune 100 companies now use the Hoskins modem to move
information between their field staff and headquarters.
Why? Ease of use.

The Hoskins unique on-line tutorial will take your users
from novice to expert in just six hours of easy, self-
paced lessons. As shown on page 4 of the enclosed bro-
chure, the $295 price includes modem, software, and ten
hours of toll-free telephone support.

To take a no-risk 30-day test drive, simply call your
local dealer, ^F3^, at ^F4^. They will have a Hoskins
2400-baud modem delivered to your office within the
week. Happy telecommunicating!

Sincerely,



Mary Zimmerman
Sales Manager
```

Product-oriented: Masco binoculars zoom from 3 to 12 power.
Reader-oriented: With Masco binoculars, you can look a ruby-throated hummingbird squarely in the eye at 300 feet and see it blink.

Although emphasizing the derived benefit rather than product features is generally the preferred strategy, there are two situations that call for emphasizing product features instead: promoting a product to experts and promoting expensive equipment. For example, if the car you're promoting to sports-car enthusiasts achieves maximum torque of 138 ft.-lbs. at 3,000 rpm or produces 145 hp at 5,500 rpm, tell the reader that. You would sound condescending to try to interpret what this means to such experts.

Using Vivid Language   Use action-packed verbs when talking about the product's features and benefits. Within reason, use colorful adjectives and adverbs, being careful to avoid a hard-sell approach. Finally, to convey a dynamic image, use positive language, stressing what your product is, rather than what it is not.

Weak: The paper tray is designed to hold 200 sheets.

Improved: The paper tray holds 200 sheets—enough to last the busy executive a full week without reloading.

Negative: The Hercules snowblower is not one of those lightweight models.

HOSKINS ELECTRONICS

November 8, 19--

Mr. Leon Ellis, Manager
Stephen Wyse Wholesalers
1800 East 26 Street
Little Rock, AR 73206

Dear Mr. Ellis:

Thank you for requesting information about our Hoskins 2400-baud
modem and software. More than 70 of the Fortune 100 companies now
use the Hoskins modem to move information between their field
staff and headquarters. Why? Ease of use.

The Hoskins unique on-line tutorial will take your users from
novice to expert in just six hours of easy, self-paced lessons. As
shown on page 4 of the enclosed brochure, the $295 price includes
modem, software, and ten hours of toll-free telephone support.

To take a no-risk 30-day test drive, simply call your local
dealer, Comstock Computer Center, at 555-2188. They will have a
Hoskins 2400-baud modem delivered to your office within the week.
Happy telecommunicating!

Sincerely,

Mary Zimmerman

Mary Zimmerman
Sales Manager

P.O. Box 3824, Rumson, NJ 07760 • Phone: (800) 555-3024, FAX: (201) 555-3842

Positive: The Hercules 4.5 HP engine is 50 percent more powerful than the standard 3.0 HP engine used in most snowblowers.

Using Objective Language   To be convincing, you must present specific, objective evidence. Simply saying that a product is great is not enough. You must provide evidence to show *why* it is great. Here is where you'll use all the data you gathered about your product before you started to write. Avoid generalities, unsupported superlatives and claims, and too many or too strong adjectives and adverbs.

> Maintain credibility by providing specific facts and figures.

Unsupported: At $395, the Sherwood moped is the best buy on the market.
Supported: The May 1991 issue of *Independent Consumer Digest* rated the $395 Sherwood moped as the year's best buy.

Unsupported: We are sure you will enjoy the convenience of our Bread Bakery.
Supported: Our Bread Bakery comes with one feature we don't think you'll ever use: a 30-day, no-questions-asked return policy.

> Positive statements by independent agencies lend powerful support.

Focusing on the Central Selling Theme   By all means, discuss and interpret each product feature that you believe will help persuade your reader. However, there is probably one feature that sets your product apart from the competition, and this feature should be the recurring theme of your letter. If your reader remembers nothing else about your product, this is the one feature you want him or her to remember.

One noted copywriting consultant calls this principle a basic law of direct-mail advertising and labels it "$E^2 = 0$," meaning that when you try to emphasize everything you end up emphasizing nothing.[4]

When possible, unify the features you discuss under one umbrella theme—whether the theme is convenience, ease of use, flexibility, price, or some other distinguishing characteristic around which you can build your case.

Mentioning Price   If price is your central selling theme, introduce it early and emphasize it often. In most cases, however, price is not the central selling theme and should, therefore, be subordinated. In such a situation, introduce the price late in the message, after most of the advantages of owning the product have been discussed. To subordinate price, introduce it in a long, complex, or compound sentence, perhaps in a sentence in which you also mention a reader benefit.

> You'll consider the $250 cost of this spreadsheet seminar repaid in full the very next time your boss asks you to revise the quarterly sales budget—on a Friday afternoon!

Use techniques of subordination when mentioning price.

Sometimes it is helpful to present the price in terms of small units. For example, show how subscribing to a weekly magazine costs less than $1 per week, rather than $50 a year. Compare the price to a familiar object—about what you'd pay for your morning newspaper or for a cup of coffee. Or, when appropriate, compare the price of your product to similar products, using actual figures for believability.

Length of Letter   Discussing and fully interpreting the features of your product will take a considerable amount of space. Most direct-mail experts believe that long sales letters are more effective than shorter ones because longer letters give you the space to provide enough specific evidence and interpretation to be convincing.

Some people may not be willing to read through the long sales letter. However, those who do will be more motivated to respond favorably. The test of an effective sales letter is the number of sales it generates—not the number of people who read the letter.

Enclosures   Sometimes, some of the features of a product or service are best displayed in a brochure that is enclosed with the sales letter. This is especially true when a color photograph or an illustration would help the reader visualize owning and enjoying the product. Subordinate your reference to the enclosure, and refer to some specific item in the enclosure, to increase the likelihood of its being read.

> Note the porcelain robin's detailed coloring on the actual-sized photograph on page 2 of the enclosed brochure.

> Use the enclosed order blank to send us your order today. Within three weeks, you will be enjoying this museum-quality sculpture in your own home.

Motivating Action

Although the purpose of your letter should be apparent right from the start, delay making your specific request until late in the letter—after you have created interest and built desire for your product. Then state the specific action you want.

For many items, the desired action is an actual sale. In such a case, make the action easy to take. Can you offer a toll-free telephone number for placing the order? Can you accept a credit card? Does the customer have to write out a check to send with the order, or will you send a bill?

For high-priced items, it would be unreasonable to expect to make an actual sale by mail. Probably no one has read a sales letter promoting a new automobile and then phoned in an order for the car. For such items, the goal of your letter should be to get the reader to make just a small step toward purchasing—sending for more information, stopping by the dealer for a demonstration, or asking a sales representative to call. Make the step easy for the reader to take.

Provide an incentive for prompt action. Sometimes, you can offer a gift to the first 100 people who respond; other times, you can motivate early action by stressing buying while there is still a good selection, before the holiday rush, or during the three-day sale. Make sure your push for action is *gentle*, however. Any tactic that smacks of high-pressure selling at this point is likely to increase reader resistance.

Use confident language when asking for action, avoiding such hesitant phrases as "If you want to save money" or "I hope you agree that this product will save you time." When asking the reader to part with money, it is always a good idea to mention a reader benefit in the same sentence.

> *Too·weak:* If you agree that this ice cream maker will make your summers more enjoyable, you can place your order by telephone.
>
> *Too strong:* Hurry! Hurry! Hurry! These sale prices won't be in effect long.
>
> *Appropriate:* To have your Jiffy Ice Cream Maker available for use during the upcoming July 4 weekend, simply call our toll-free number today.

| Push confidently, but gently, for prompt action.

Consider putting an important marketing point in a postscript (P.S.). Some marketing studies have shown that a postscript notation is the most often read part of a sales letter.[5] It can be as long or as short as needed, but it should contain new and interesting information.

> P.S. If you stop in for a demonstration before May 1, you'll walk out with a free box of color transparencies (retail value $21.95)—just for trying *Up Front*, the new presentation software program by Acme Products.

Will you be able to use every one of the guidelines just discussed (and summarized in Checklist 6) in every one of your sales letters? Not likely. As always, the test of the effectiveness of a letter is the extent to which it achieves its goal. Use whatever information you have available (especially in terms of audience analysis) to help your letter achieve its goal. An example of an effective sales letter is shown in Figure 7.4.

FIGURE 7.4   Sales Letter

Starts with a rhetorical question.

Central selling theme is feeling secure in your home.

The evidence is convincing because it is specific and is discussed in terms of reader benefits.

Note how many sentences emphasize "you" instead of the product.

Price is subordinated in the middle of a long sentence that discusses benefits.

The desired action is clear and easy to take; letter ends with a reader benefit.

HOME SECURITY PRODUCTS   P.O. Box 302
Edenton, NC 27932
(919) 555-1040

1
2

Dear Homeowner:

Do you view your home as an investment or as your castle? Is it primarily a tax writeoff or a place of refuge—a place where you can find comfort and respite from workday stress?

Most of us view our homes as places where we can feel safe from outside intrusions. Thus, we feel threatened by the latest government statistics showing that 5.3% of all U.S. households were burglarized last year. How can we protect ourselves?

Today, there's a simple and dependable alarm that protects up to 2,500 square feet in your home. Just plug in the Safescan Home Alarm System, adjust the sensitivity to the size of your home, and turn the key. You then have 30 seconds to leave and 15 seconds to switch off the alarm once you return.

Worried that your barking dog might falsely trigger the alarm? You needn't be, because Safescan's microprocessor screens out normal sounds like crying babies, outside traffic, and rain. But hostile noises like breaking glass and splintering wood trigger the alarm. The 105-decibel siren is loud enough to alert neighbors and to drive away even the most determined burglar.

3

What if a smart burglar disconnects the electricity to your home or pulls the plug? No problem: built-in batteries assure that Safescan operates through power failures up to 24 hours, and the batteries recharge automatically. Best of all, installation couldn't be easier. Simply mount the four-pound unit on a wall (we supply the four screws), and plug it in. Nothing could be faster.

Finally, there is a $259 home alarm that you can trust; and the one-year warranty and 30-day return policy ensure your complete satisfaction.

Last year there were 3.2 million burglaries in the U.S. But by taking a few simple precautions, such as locking your doors and installing the Safescan Home Alarm System, you can tip the odds back in your favor. To order, use your credit card and call our operator toll-free at (800) 555-2934. Within ten days, Safescan will be guarding your home, giving you peace of mind.

Sincerely,

Jeffrey Parret
Jeffrey Parret
National Sales Manager

Grammar and Mechanics Notes

1. Mass mailings often do not have a date or inside address.   2. Note the generic salutation.   3. "crying babies, outside traffic, and"—separate items in a series by commas.

Writing Sales Letters

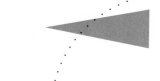

Do Your Homework

1. Learn as much as possible about the product, the competition, and the audience.

2. Select a central selling theme—your product's most distinguishing feature.

3. Plan your campaign. Decide what enclosures to use; what mailing list will be used; and how your message will be formatted, duplicated, and distributed.

Gain the Reader's Attention

4. Make your opening brief, interesting, and original. Avoid obvious, misleading, and irrelevant statements.

5. Use any of the following types of openings: rhetorical question, thought-provoking statement, unusual fact, current event, anecdote, direct challenge, or some similar attention-getting device.

6. Introduce (or at least lead up to) the central selling theme in the opening.

7. If the letter is in response to a customer inquiry, begin by expressing appreciation for the inquiry and introducing the central selling theme.

Create Interest and Build Desire

8. Make the introduction of the product follow naturally from the attention-getter.

9. Interpret the features of the product; instead of just describing the features, show how the reader will benefit from each feature. Let the reader picture owning, using, and enjoying the product.

10. Use action-packed, positive, and objective language. Provide convincing evidence to back up your claims—specific facts and figures, independent product reviews, endorsements, and so on.

11. Continue to stress the central selling theme throughout.

12. Subordinate price, unless price is the central selling theme. State price in small items, in a long sentence, and in a sentence that talks about benefits.

Motivate Action

13. Make the desired action clear and easy to take.

14. Ask confidently, avoiding the hesitant "if you'd like" or "I hope you agree."

15. Motivate prompt action (but avoid a hard-sell approach).

16. End your letter with a reminder of a reader benefit.

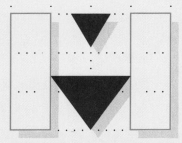

MICROWRITING A SALES LETTER

The Problem

You are the proprietor of Lee's Consumer Products, a small retail store located in the Fiesta Mall, 1200 Dobson Road, Mesa, Arizona 85201. You've recently become the exclusive dealer for Voice Note, a recorder that allows you to record messages to yourself rather than scribbling them on a sheet of paper.

The recorder is 2½ × 1 × ½ inches, weighs 3 ounces, and is made in Japan from sturdy plastic. It records messages up to 30 seconds in length and holds 10 minutes of dictation. A lock button prevents recording over a message. After the message has been played back, the loop-to-loop tape automatically resets for use the next time. The Voice Note is operated by pressing the record button and speaking. It runs on two batteries that are included and comes with a 90-day warranty and a 30-day full-refund policy.

To promote this product, you decide to try a direct-mail campaign directed at the business community. You purchase a mailing list containing the names and addresses of the 800 members of the Phoenix Athletic Club, a downtown facility frequented by business people for lunch, after-work drinks, and social affairs. The club has racquetball and tennis courts, an indoor pool, and separate men's and women's exercise rooms. Its yearly membership fee is $750. You decide to send these 800 members a form letter promoting the Voice Note at a price of $29. You'll include your local phone number (555–2394) for placing credit-card orders by phone; or the readers may stop by the store to purchase the recorder in person.

The Process

1. Describe your audience.

       --Business men and women
       --Active (sports and exercise facilities)
       --Upscale (can afford $750 annual membership)
       --Probably very busy professionally and socially

2. What will be your central selling theme?

       Convenience/portability is the unique benefit of Voice
       Note.

3. Write an attention getter that is original, interesting, and short; that is reader oriented; that relates to the product; and, if possible, introduces the central selling theme.

       You're driving home on the freeway in bumper-to-bumper
       traffic when the solution to a nagging problem facing
       you at work suddenly pops into your head. But by the
       time you get home 30 minutes later, your good idea has
       vanished.

4. Jot down the features you might discuss and the reader benefits associated with these features.

   Size is 2 1/2 × 1 x 1/2 inches, weighs 3 oz.: Smaller and lighter than a microcassette recorder; fits in shirt pocket or purse; easy to use on the go.

   Records 30-second messages--up to 10 minutes' worth: room enough for most "to do" messages--20 different ones.

   Press record button and then speak; lock button prevents overrecording: easy to use, even in car; not a lot of buttons to fiddle with.

   Powered by two batteries (included): real portability.

5. Write the sentence that mentions price. (Since price is not the central selling theme, it should be subordinated.)

   The Voice Note's price of $29 is less than you'd pay for bulky microcassette recorders that are much less convenient for on-the-go use.

6. What action are you seeking from the reader?

   To buy the Voice Note.

7. How can you motivate prompt action?

   Make the action easy to take; offer warranty and guarantee satisfaction. Stress the sooner you buy, the sooner you'll enjoy using it.

> When writing your letter, emphasize the reader benefits and use the features for support.

The Product

Note the minor revisions from the original opening drafted in Step 3.

The letter lets the reader envision owning and enjoying the product.

The notes made in Step 4 are expanded into finished paragraphs.

Dear Club Member:

You leave the Athletic Club and are heading home on the freeway in bumper-to-bumper traffic when the solution to a nagging problem at work suddenly pops into your head. But by the time you get home 30 minutes later, your good idea has vanished.

Next time carry Voice Note, the 3-ounce recorder that allows you to record reminders to yourself on-the-go. Now you can "jot" your ideas as they occur: while jogging, waiting at the bank, or lying in bed at 3 A.M. As you know, inspiration often strikes far from a pad and pencil!

Much smaller than a microcassette (2½ × 1 x ½ inches), Voice Note slips into your shirt pocket or purse. And there aren't a lot of buttons to fiddle with. Just press Record and speak; a Lock button prevents you from recording over your earlier messages.

You can record up to 20 different messages of 30-seconds each—"to--do" messages like "Call Richard about the Hewlett con-tract" or "Place order for 200 shares of SRP stock" or even "Pick up Jenny from soccer practice at 5:30." After playback, the loop-to-loop tape automatically resets for immediate use the next time.

For true portability, the Voice Note is powered by two batteries (included). Your satisfaction is guaranteed by our 90-day warranty and 30-day full-refund policy.

The Voice Note's price of $29 is less than you'd pay for bulky microcassette recorders that are much less convenient for on-the-go use. For credit-card orders, simply call us at 555-2394. Or stop by our retail store at Fiesta Mall for a personal demon-stration. The next time you need to pick up a quart of milk on the way home, make a Voice Note. You won't come home empty-handed.

Sincerely,

Source: Adapted from *The Sharper Image Catalog*, May 1988.

S P O T L I G H T ON LEGAL ISSUES

WHAT MAY YOU LEGALLY SAY IN A SALES LETTER?

May I say that our product is the best on the market?
Yes. You may legally express an opinion about your product; this is called *puffery*. You may not, however, make a claim that can be proven false, such as saying that your product is cheaper than a competing product when, in fact, it is not.

The typist mistakenly typed the price of our product as $19.95, instead of the correct price of $119.95. Do I have to sell it for $19.95?
No. You are not responsible for an honest mistake, so long as your intent was not to deceive the buyer.

May I include a sample of my product with my letter and require the reader to either send payment or return the product at my expense?
No. The readers will not have to pay for or return any unordered goods. They may legally treat them as a gift from you.

Do I have to notify the people who order our furniture that delivery will take up to six weeks?
Yes. Unless you notify them otherwise, they may legally expect delivery within 30 days and may cancel their orders if their goods are not delivered within that time.

I want to send a sales letter promoting our rock music to high school students. May I legally accept orders from minors?
Yes. You may accept their orders and, if you do, you are legally bound to honor the contract. However, until they reach the age of adulthood (18 years in some states and 21 in others), minors may legally cancel a contract and return the merchandise to you.

If I run out of a product I advertise, am I required to give a "rain check"?
Yes. If you advertise an item and run out, you must either take orders for later delivery, give rain checks, or sell a similar product at the same price.

I want to sell the furniture in my showroom that has small knicks and scratches on it. If I state in my sales letter that all sales are final and sale items are marked "as is," do I have to issue refunds to anyone who complains?
No. By using the term "as is," you tell the consumer that you are not promising new merchandise.

Without my knowledge, my assistant wrote a letter in which she promised a customer a 10% price break; such a price reduction is clearly against store policy. Do we have to honor my assistant's price?
Yes. Your assistant was acting as your agent, and her promise is legally binding on your firm.

Sources: Ronald A. Anderson, Ivan Fox, and David P. Twomey, *Business Law and the Legal Environment,* 14th ed. (Cincinnati, OH: South-Western, 1990); Gordon W. Brown, Edward E. Byers, and Mary Ann Lawlor, *Business Law: With UCC Applications,* 7th ed. (New York: McGraw-Hill, 1989); Gordon W. Brown and R. Robert Rosenberg, *Understanding Business and Personal Law,* 7th ed. (New York: McGraw-Hill, 1984); Neil Story and Lynn Ward, *American Business Law and the Regulatory Environment* (Cincinnati, OH: South-Western, 1989).

SUMMARY

The ability to write persuasively is crucial for success in business. In order to write persuasively, you must overcome the reader's initial resistance, establish your own credibility, and develop an appeal that meets a need of the reader. You must also become thoroughly familiar with your reader so that you can translate the advantages of your idea or the features of your product into specific reader benefits.

Get your reader's attention by using an opening paragraph that is relevant, interesting, and short. Effective types of openings include a rhetorical question, a thought-provoking statement, an unusual fact, a current event, an anecdote, or some similar attention-getting device. For persuasive requests (such as selling an idea, requesting a favor, or writing a persuasive claim letter), devote the majority of your message to discussing the merits of your proposal and showing specifically how your proposal meets some need of the reader. Provide evidence (facts and statistics, expert opinion, and examples) that is accurate, relevant, representative, and complete.

Discuss and minimize any obstacles to your proposal. For sales letters, select a central selling theme and introduce that theme early and repeat it often. Devote most of your message to showing how the reader will benefit from owning the product or service. Subordinate the price, unless price is your central selling theme.

For all types of persuasive messages, end on a confident, positive note, making sure the reader knows what action is desired and making that action easy to take. Persuasive messages are often longer than other types of messages because of the need to use specific, objective language and convincing evidence. By taking the space needed to support your statements with specific facts and figures, you'll increase your ability to persuade your reader.

KEY TERMS

Central selling theme— The major reader benefit that is introduced early and emphasized throughout a sales letter.

Derived benefit— The benefit a potential customer would derive from using a product or service.

Indirect organizational plan— A plan in which the rationale is presented first, followed by the major idea—the request for action.

Persuasion— The process of motivating someone to take a specific action or to support a particular idea.

Solicited sales letter— A reply to a request for product information from a potential customer.

Unsolicited sales letter— A letter promoting a firm's products mailed to a potential customer who has not expressed any interest in the product.

REVIEW AND DISCUSSION

OBJECTIVE 1   1. What is meant by the term *persuasion*?

OBJECTIVE 1   2. Why might the reader initially resist your persuasive efforts?

OBJECTIVE 1   3. What are the sources of writer credibility?

OBJECTIVE 1   4. What is the difference between a logical appeal and an emotional appeal? When should each be used?

OBJECTIVE 1   5. Give an example of a direct reader benefit and an indirect benefit.

OBJECTIVE 1   6. What should you know about your reader before beginning to write a persuasive letter?

OBJECTIVE 1   7. What are some criteria for evaluating the effectiveness of an attention getter?

OBJECTIVE 1   8. How should the writer deal with obstacles to his or her proposal?

OBJECTIVE 1   9. Why are persuasive messages often longer than other types of messages?

OBJECTIVE 2   10. Why is showing anger a poor strategy in a persuasive claim letter?

OBJECTIVE 3   11. What is a central selling theme? Why is it important in a sales letter?

12. Why should the reader instead of the product be the focus of attention in a sales letter?

OBJECTIVE 3 ◄

13. What are some techniques for subordinating the price in a sales letter?

OBJECTIVE 3 ◄

EXERCISES

1. **Selling an Idea—Laptop Computers**   You are a sales representative for Midland Medical Supplies. Like most of the other 38 Midland reps, you are on the road three or four days a week, promoting your products to hospitals, clinics, and physicians in private practice. Each evening in your hotel room, you fill out a call report for each office you visit, showing to whom you spoke, their experiences with your products, what they'd like to see changed, and the like. Actual orders are phoned in to headquarters immediately, but these call reports are submitted in handwritten form weekly.

OBJECTIVE 2 ◄

It occurs to you that you could save yourself much time if you had a laptop computer to complete these reports. Then you could simply keyboard the data each evening directly into the computer; and, at the end of the week when you get home, either print them all out and mail them or submit them electronically by using the computer's built-in modem and a telephone. You estimate that a laptop computer would save you three or four hours a week of your own time. In addition, you're sure there are other work uses you would find for the computer, once you actually began using it.

The type of computer you're thinking about (such as the Polaris, which has two disk drives, 1 megabyte of memory, and a built-in modem) would cost about $1,300. Although Midland is not having a great year (thus far, the company is running 8% below sales budget for the year), you still feel this would be a good buy for all the sales reps. Send a memo to Charles J. Redding, National Sales Manager, trying to sell him on the idea.

2. **Selling an Idea—Oversized Dressing Rooms**   You are a merchandising manager at Lordstrom, Inc., a women's clothing store in Seattle. Your firm has decided to open a new store in Fashion Square Mall, an upscale department store on the north side. Retail space is quite expensive in this mall (nearly 50% more expensive than at your other locations), so Lordstrom facility engineers are trying to make every inch of space count.

OBJECTIVE 2 ◄

Despite the costs, you feel that to be competitive in this mall, you will have to offer superior customer service. You already offer a no-questions-asked return policy, abundant inventory to ensure that the right sizes and colors are always available, and a pianist who performs on the main floor from 11 A.M. until 2 P.M. daily. But you feel that the new store should also have oversized dressing rooms—ones large enough to hold a comfortable chair, garment rack, and adjustable three-sided mirrors. You want your customers to be able to make their selections in comfort.

You estimate that adding the additional 20 square feet per dressing room in the new store plus the additional furnishings will add $18,500 to the construction costs plus $155 to the monthly lease. Present your ideas in a memo to Rebecca Lordstrom, Executive Vice President.

▶ OBJECTIVE 2

3. **Requesting a Favor—Field Trip** You are the owner and manager of Jack 'n Jill Preschool. For the next few weeks, you will be discussing food and nutrition with the youngsters; and you want to end the unit by having the children walk to the nearby Salad Haven Restaurant, take a tour of the kitchens, and then make their own salads for lunch from the restaurant's popular salad bar. Of course, each child would pay for his or her own meal. In fact, to help make the visit easier, you'll collect the money beforehand and simply pay the cashier for everyone at once. You will ask several parents to come with you to help supervise the 23 children, ages three through five, although they will probably need some help from the salad-bar attendants. You can come any day during the week of October 10–14. State regulations require that you feed the children lunch between 11 A.M. and 12:30 P.M.

Write to Donna Jo Luse (Manager, Salad Haven Restaurant, 28 Grenvale Road, Westminster, MD 21157) asking for permission to make the field trip.

▶ OBJECTIVE 2

4. **Requesting a Favor—Celebrity Donation** Coming out of the movie theater after watching the Academy Award winning movie *Rocky Mountain Adventure*, starring Robert Forte, you suddenly have an idea. As executive director of the Wilderness Fund, you've been searching for an idea for a raffle prize for your upcoming fund-raiser. You wonder whether you could persuade Robert Forte to donate some item used in the movie (perhaps a small stage prop or some costume item) for this raffle. The Wilderness Fund is an 8,000-member nonprofit agency dedicated to preserving forest lands—the very type of lands photographed so beautifully in Mr. Forte's latest movie. Write to Forte at Century Studios, 590 North Vermont Avenue, Los Angeles, CA 90004.

▶ OBJECTIVE 2

5. **Writing a Persuasive Claim—Azaleas** You are the facilities manager for Public Service Company of Arkansas. In preparation for the recent dedication of your new hydroelectric plant, you spruced up the grounds near the viewing stand. As part of the stage decorations, you ordered ten potted azaleas at $28.50 each (plus $10.50 shipping) from Jackson-Parsons Nurseries (410 Wick Avenue, Youngstown, OH 44555) on February 3. The bushes were guaranteed to arrive in show condition—ready to burst into bloom within three days—or your money would be cheerfully refunded.

The plants arrived in healthy condition but were in the final days (perhaps hours) of flowering—certainly in no shape to display at the dedication. You decided, instead, to plant the azaleas as part of your permanent landscaping. Because the plants arrived only three days before the dedication, you had to purchase substitute azaleas at the local florist—at a much higher price. In fact, you ended up paying $436 for the florist plants—$140.50 more than the Jackson-Parsons price. You feel that the nursery was responsible for your having to incur the additional expenditure, and you write a letter asking Jackson-Parsons to reimburse your company for the $140.50.

▶ OBJECTIVE 2

6. **Writing a Persuasive Claim—Ripped Suit** After a hurried taxi ride from LaGuardia Airport to the Marriott Marquis Hotel on May 15, you barely made it to your 2 P.M. appointment. You did not realize until you sat down at the conference table that you had ripped the

pants of your $350 suit on an exposed spring in the taxi seat. The next day, your tailor tells you there is no way to repair the rip attractively, so the suit is, in effect, now useless. Since you've owned the suit for a year, you don't expect the taxi company to reimburse you for $350, but you do think reimbursement of $150 is reasonable. From your taxi receipt, you learn that you took Taxi 1145 belonging to Empire State Taxi (50 West 77th Street, New York, NY 10024). Since this is a personal claim, write your letter on plain paper, using your own return address.

7. **Writing a Persuasive Claim—Defective Product** Assume the role of purchasing agent at People's Energy Company (see Exercise 7 in Chapter 6). Because Nationwide Office Supply believes you were at fault, it refused your initial routine claim. However, you've been a good customer for many years; last year, in fact, you purchased $5,800 worth of office supplies from Nationwide. In addition, since you've not used the ribbons, they could be resold easily. Thus, you've decided to write Nationwide again, this time, adding persuasion to your claim letter.

OBJECTIVE 2 ◀

8. **Selling a Product—Letter Critique** Select a sales letter that you or a friend has received. Critique the letter, noting the specific ways that it does and does not follow the guidelines discussed in this chapter. Then revise the letter to remedy its weaknesses. Submit the original letter and your revised version, as well as a memo to your instructor explaining the rationale for your revisions.

OBJECTIVE 3 ◀

9. **Selling a Product—Work Boots** As sales manager for Industrial Footwear, Inc., send a form sales letter advertising your Durham work boot to 3,000 members of Local 147 of the Building Trades Union. Local 147 is made up primarily of construction workers on high-rise buildings in Houston, Texas.

OBJECTIVE 3 ◀

The Durham is an 8-inch waterproof insulated boot, made of oil-tanned cowhide. It exceeds the guidelines for steel-toe protection issued by the American National Standards Institute (ANSI). The Durham has an all-rubber heel that provides firm footing, and its steel shanks provide additional support for arches and heels. It comes in sizes 7–13 in black or brown at a price of $79, plus $2.50 shipping. The price is guaranteed through March 1. There is a one-year "no-questions-asked" warranty.

Use the salutation "Dear CWA Member" and no date or inside address. The purpose of your letter is to motivate readers to order the shoe by using the enclosed order blank or by calling your toll-free order number (800) 555-2993.

10. **Writing a Solicited Sales Letter—Realty** As a realtor in the local franchise of National Home Sales, you receive a letter from Ms. Edith Willis (667 Rising Hills Drive, Xenia, OH 45385). Her letter states in part, "I am a single mother of two young children being transferred to your town and wish to purchase a three-bedroom condominium in a nice area in the price range of $75,000–$100,000. I would be able to make a down payment of up to $20,000. Would you please write me, letting me know whether you have any property available that would fit my needs."

OBJECTIVE 3 ◀

Although the housing market in your small town is tight, you do have a condominium available that might suit her needs. It has three bedrooms plus a finished basement, is air-conditioned (important in your part of the country), and is four years old. The neighborhood elementary school is considered the best in town; however, the condominium is next door to a large, but attractive, apartment building. The home is listed for $110,000, although you think the owners would accept $103,000–$106,000.

Send Ms. Willis a photograph and fact sheet on the listing. The purpose of your letter is to encourage her to phone you at (602) 555-3459 to make an appointment to visit your office so that you can personally show her this and perhaps other properties you have available.

OBJECTIVE 3

11. **Collaborative Writing—Selling a Product** Select an ad from a newspaper or journal published within the past month. Working in groups of three or four, write an unsolicited sales letter for this product, to be signed by the sales manager. (You may need to gather additional information about the product.) The audience for your letter will be either the students or the faculty at your institution; identify the intended audience by the type of salutation you use for your form letter. Include only actual data about the product and about the audience. Submit a copy of both the advertisement and your letter.

OBJECTIVE 3

12. **Selling a Service—Small Business** While studying for your bar exams, you decide to start up a part-time business delivering singing telegrams throughout the Atlanta metropolitan area. For a flat fee of $30, you'll personally deliver a greeting card and sing any song (in good taste) of the customer's choice—using either the actual wording of the song or special wording composed by the customer. You promote your company (Musical Messages) for birthdays, anniversaries, graduations, promotions, and other special occasions. Send a form letter to a random sample of Atlanta's residents, promoting your service. The purpose of your letter is to persuade the reader to call you at (404) 555-9831 to order a singing telegram. Orders must be prepaid, and you require seven days' notice. Use the salutation "Dear Friend" and no date or inside address.

OBJECTIVE 2

C A S E   P R O B L E M

Flying High at Urban Systems

Neelima, Jean, and Larry were analyzing the quarterly expense report. "Look at line item 415," Neelima said. "Air-travel expenses have increased 28% from last year. Is there any room for savings there?"

"Jean and I were discussing that earlier," Larry said. "I think we should begin requiring our people to join all the frequent-flyer programs so that after they fly 20,000 to 30,000 miles on any one airline they get a free ticket. Then we should require them to use that free ticket the next time they have to take a business trip for us."

"I disagree," Jean said. "To begin with, there's no easy way to enforce the requirement. Who's going to keep track of how many miles each person flies on each airline and when a free flight coupon is due that person? It would make us appear to be Big Brother, looking over their shoulders all the time.

"In addition, our people put in long hours on the road. If they can get a free ticket and occasionally are able to take their spouses along with them, what's the big deal? They're happier and probably end up doing a better job for us."

"Still," Larry countered, "company resources were used to purchase the original tickets, so logically the free tickets belong to the company. And why should our people who travel get free tickets compliments of the company, when those who don't travel do not get free tickets?"

Jean was ready with a counterargument, but Neelima put an end to the discussion by saying, "Both of you think about the matter some more and let me have a memo by next week giving me your position. Then I'll decide."

1. Jot down all the reasons you can think of for and against the proposition—including any reasons that might not have been discussed at the meeting. What are the benefits associated with each reason?
2. Assume the role of Larry. Write a memo to Neelima trying to persuade her to begin requiring employees to use their free airline tickets for business trips. Knowing that Jean will be writing a memo arguing the opposing viewpoint, try to counteract her arguments.
3. Now assume the role of Jean. Write a memo to Neelima arguing for the status quo. Try to counteract Larry's likely arguments.

Bad-News Messages

After you have finished this chapter, you will be able to

1. Decide when to use a direct and indirect organizational plan for bad-news messages.

2. Describe the four parts of the indirect organizational plan for bad-news messages.

3. Compose a reply that rejects an idea, refuses a favor, or refuses a claim.

4. Compose an announcement that conveys bad news about normal operations as well as about the organization itself.

In 1990, after 30 years of growth, Digital Equipment Corporation felt the pain of a slow economy and an industry-wide slump. When the computer giant found itself in the unfamiliar position of having to report a quarterly loss, it did what it could to soften the news. But to soften the news, Digital's media relations team had to first control it. That meant that they had to get the news out in their own terms before it got out in some other form. In the endless dance with the press, corporate media experts always try to lead, never to follow.

"Any time you start reacting to news, you're playing catch up," says Alan Pike, one of a team responsible for presenting Digital's information to the media. "It's a no-win situation. Of course, we all get caught flatfooted at some point. Anyone in this business who says he doesn't is not telling the truth, but the best defense is a good offense."

Perhaps because the Digital Equipment Corporation is in the computer business, management is keenly aware of the power of information. Digital goes to great lengths to control information about itself. The company employs 135 public relations workers who are assigned to more than 30 groups. Each group disseminates information to a different country. These groups also communicate with each other regularly to ensure that company news in France or Australia doesn't get back to the home office through the newspapers.

Like most public relations professionals, the Digital team communicates with the media with several forms of communication: straight news releases, backgrounders, fact sheets, and white papers. In deciding which means of communication to use, Pike considers three criteria: the amount of influence he wants to exert, the nature of the information, and the nature of the recipient.

Alan Pike, Manager of Corporate Public Relations Center for Expertise, Digital Equipment Corp., Maynard, Massachusetts.

"A press release is formula," says Pike. "But it is a formula on purpose. The idea behind the press release is that the news is timely. The white paper, on the other hand, is research driven, and the fact sheet is just a straightforward list. The backgrounder, though, is almost a narrative. It paints a larger picture of an issue. It is very helpful to news reporters or when we are dealing with a new product."

When the news is bad, Digital's team looks hard for a positive aspect, particularly a positive aspect with staying power. "You can't blanch the numbers," says Pike. "A bad quarter is a bad quarter. So what you have to do is position the report as the beginning of the recovery or the end of the bad times. It's not just to make it palatable, but it's to put it in a greater context, to make the bad news relative. Then it's not as horrendous."

Unfortunately, says Pike, as hard as he looks for a positive aspect, newspapers look for the horrendous. After all, bad news sells papers. So Pike and his team are customarily braced for the worst. What happens then when negative news does leak out?

"Before we get carried away, we get the facts," says Pike. "We can't ignore it or slow it up in bureaucratic red tape. One of the real problems is a tendency for denial. But these things very seldom go away. [For bad news to simply disappear] you have to be the kind of guy who wins the lottery. Usually it just festers. What we are dealing with here is low control and high credibility." ▼

PLANNING THE BAD-NEWS MESSAGE: SOFTEN THE BLOW

At some point in our lives we have all probably been both the bearers and the recipients of bad news. And just as most people find it difficult to accept bad news, they also find it difficult to convey bad news. Therefore, like persuasive messages, bad-news messages require careful planning. How you write your messages won't change the news you have to convey, but it may determine whether your reader accepts your decision as reasonable—or goes away mad.

Purpose

Your objectives are to convey the bad news and retain the reader's good-will.

Your purpose in writing a bad-news message is twofold: first, to say "no" or to convey bad news; and second, to retain the reader's goodwill. To accomplish these goals, you must communicate your message politely, clearly, and firmly. And you must show the reader that you've seriously considered the request and that, as a matter of fairness and good business practice, you must deny the request.

Sometimes you can achieve your purpose better with a phone call or personal visit than with a written message. A phone call is often appropriate when the reader will not be personally disappointed in the outcome, and a personal visit is often called for when you are giving a subordinate negative news of considerable consequence. Often, though, a written message is most appropriate because it lets you more carefully control the wording, sequence, and pace of the ideas presented.

Audience Analysis

The reader's needs, expectations, and personality—as well as the writer's relationship with the reader—will largely determine the content and organization of a bad-news message. Thus you need to put yourself in the place of the reader. As discussed in Chapter 6, many requests are routine; the writer simply wants a yes or no decision and wants it in a direct manner. The direct plan can be justified when

OBJECTIVE 1: Decide when to use a direct and indirect organizational plan for bad-news messages.

- the bad news involves a small, insignificant matter and can be considered routine. If the reader is not likely to be emotionally involved and thus not seriously disappointed in the decision, use the direct approach.
- the reader prefers directness. Superiors often prefer that all messages from subordinates be written in the direct style.
- the reader expects a "no" response. For example, experienced job applicants know that job offers are typically made by phone and job rejections by letter. Thus, upon receiving a letter from the prospective employer, the applicant expects a "no" response; under these circumstances, delaying the inevitable only causes ill will and makes the writer look less than forthright.
- the writer wants to emphasize the negative news. Suppose that you have already refused a request once and the reader writes a second time; under these circumstances, a forceful "no" would be in order. Or, consider the situation where negative information is contained in a form letter—perhaps as an insert in a monthly statement. Because the reader might otherwise discard or only skim an "unimportant-looking" message, you should consider placing the bad news up front—where it will receive immediate attention.
- the reader-writer relationship is either extremely close or extremely poor. Consider using the direct approach if the relationship is either so close that you can assume the continued goodwill of the reader, or so strained and suspicious that the reader may think he or she is being given the runaround if the bad news is buried in the middle.

Because the preceding conditions are *not* true of most bad-news situations, the general rule is to prefer indirect organization, especially when giving bad news to subordinates, customers, or to readers you don't know.[1] In the indirect approach, you present the reasons first, then the negative news. This approach emphasizes the *reasons* for the bad news, rather than the bad news itself.

The general plan for bad-news messages is the indirect pattern.

Suppose, for example, a subordinate expects a "yes" answer upon opening your memo. Putting the negative news in the first sentence might be too harsh and emphatic, and your decision might sound unreasonable until the reader has heard the rationale.

Content and Organization

To decide whether to use the direct or indirect plan for refusing a request, you might check the sender's original message. If the original message was written in the direct style, the sender probably considered it a routine request, and you would be safe in answering in the direct style. If the original message was written in the indirect style, the sender probably considered it a persuasive request, and you should consider answering in the indirect style.

A message organized according to a direct plan is not necessarily shorter than one organized according to an indirect plan. Both types of messages may contain the same basic information but in a different order (see Figure 8.1). Direct messages are often shorter than indirect ones because the direct plan is typically used for *simpler* situations, which require less explanation and background information than do indirect messages.

For example, a memo telling employees that the company cafeteria will be closed for one day to permit installation of new equipment can be told directly and in a paragraph or two. A memo telling employees that from now on the company cafeteria will be reserved for management and that other employees will now have to go outside for lunch (and pay higher prices) will require more explanation and should probably be written in the indirect style.

The direct plan for bad-news messages is basically the same plan used for routine messages discussed in Chapter 6—present the major idea (the bad news) up front, perhaps in the same sentence as a brief rationale. For example,

> The extra time required to resolve the Baton Rouge refinery problem means that our departmental compliance report will be submitted on March 15 rather than on March 1.

Then follow with any needed explanation and a friendly closing. The indirect plan for bad-news messages is a little more complex and has four parts: buffer, reasons, bad news, and closing.

Buffer Begin with a neutral and relevant statement—one that helps establish or strengthen the reader-writer relationship. Such a statement serves as a **buffer** between the reader and the bad news that will follow. Use any of the following types of buffers:

Agreement: We both recognize the promotional possibilities that often accompany big anniversary sales such as yours.

Appreciation: Thanks for letting us know of your success in selling Golden Microwaves. (*However, avoid thanking the reader for asking you to do something that you're refusing to do; such expressions of appreciation sound insincere.*)

Compliment: Congratulations on having served the community of Greenville for ten years.

Complex situations typically call for an indirect pattern and require more explanation than simpler situations.

OBJECTIVE 2: Describe the four parts of the direct organizational plan for bad-news messages.

A buffer lessens the impact of bad news.

Direct vs. Indirect Plan for Bad-News Messages   **FIGURE 8.1**

Situation: The program chairman of the Downtown Marketing Club has written to ask you to be the luncheon speaker at their March 8 meeting. Because of a prior commitment, you must decline.

October 26, 19--

Dear Mr. Caine:

As a long-time member of the Downtown Marketing Club, I've enjoyed and benefited from the luncheon speakers the Club sponsors each month. Monica Foote's December talk on the pitfalls of international marketing was especially interesting.

As you may have read in the newspaper, Hansdorf Industries is opening an outlet in Nogales, Mexico, and I'll be there March 7-14 interviewing marketing representatives and setting up sales territories. Thus, you will need to select another speaker for your March 8 meeting.

If you find yourself in need of a speaker during the summer months, Mr. Caine, please keep me in mind. My travel schedule thus far is quite light during June, July, and August.

Sincerely,

Indirect Version (Assumes no
reader/writer relationship):

October 26, 19--

Dear Roger:

Except for the fact that I'll be in Mexico on March 8, I would have enjoyed speaking to the Downtown Marketing Club. As you know, Hansdorf Industries is opening an outlet in Nogales, and I'll be there March 7-14 interviewing marketing representatives and setting up sales territories.

If, however, you find yourself in need of a speaker during the summer months, please keep me in mind. My travel schedule thus far is quite light during June, July, and August.

As a long-time member of the Downtown Marketing Club, I've enjoyed and benefited from the luncheon speakers the Club sponsors each month. Best wishes, Roger, for a successful year as program chairperson.

Sincerely,

Direct Version (Assumes a close
reader/writer relationsip):

Letters written in a direct pattern are not necessarily shorter than those written in an indirect pattern.

Facts: Nearly three-fourths of the Golden distributors who held anniversary sales last year reported a 5–10 percent annual increase in the sale of our home products.

General Principle: We believe in furnishing Golden distributors a wide range of support in promoting our products.

Good News: Golden's upcoming 20%-off sale will be heavily advertised and will certainly provide increased traffic for your February anniversary sale.

Understanding: I wish to assure you of Golden's desire to help make your anniversary sale successful.

Note these characteristics of an effective opening buffer:

A buffer should be neutral, relevant, supportive, interesting, and short.

1. It is *neutral*. To serve as a true buffer, the opening must not convey the negative news immediately. But guard against implying that the request will be granted, thus building the reader up for a big letdown.

   Not neutral: Stores like Parker Brothers benefit from Golden's policy of not providing in-store demonstrators for our line of microwave ovens.

   Misleading: Your tenth anniversary sale would be a great opportunity for Golden to promote its products.

2. It is *relevant*. The danger with starting *too* far from the topic is that the reader might not recognize the letter is in response to his or her request; in addition, an irrelevant opening seems to avoid the issue, thus sounding insincere or self-serving. To show relevance and to personalize the opening, you might include some reference to the reader's letter in your opening sentence. A relevant opening provides a smooth transition to the reasons that follow.

   Irrelevant: Golden's new apartment-sized microwave oven means that young couples, retirees, even students, can enjoy the convenience of microwave cooking.

3. It is *supportive*. The purpose of the opening is to help establish compatibility between the reader and writer. If the opening is controversial or seems to lecture the reader, it will not achieve its purpose.

   Not supportive: You must realize how expensive it would be to supply an in-house demonstrator for anniversary sales such as yours.

4. It is *interesting*. Although buffer openings do not require the strong attention-getter that is used in persuasive messages, they should be interesting enough to motivate the recipient to continue reading. Therefore, avoid giving obvious information.

   Obvious: We have received your letter requesting an in-store demonstrator for your upcoming tenth-anniversary sale.

5. It is *short*. Readers get impatient if they have to wait too long to get to the major point of the message.

   Too Long: As you may remember, for many years Golden provided in-store demonstrators for our line of microwave ovens. We were happy to do this because we felt that customers needed to see the spectacular results of our new browning element, which made microwaved food look as if it had just come from a regular oven. We discontinued this practice five years ago because . . .

Competent communicators use a buffer, not in an attempt to manipulate or confuse the reader, but in a sincere effort to help the reader accept the information in an objective manner.

Reasons   Presumably, you reached your negative decision by analyzing all the relevant information. Explaining your analysis will help convince the reader that your decision is reasonable. The major part of your message should thus focus on the reasons rather than on the bad news itself.

Provide a smooth transition from the opening buffer and present the reasons honestly and convincingly. If possible, explain how the reasons benefit the reader or, at least, benefit someone other than the writer. Thus, refusing to exchange a worn garment might enable you to offer better merchandise to your customers, raising the price might enable you to switch to nonpolluting energy for manufacturing your product, and refusing to provide copies of company documents might protect the confidentiality of customer transactions. Presenting reader benefits keeps your decision from sounding selfish.

If your buffer is relevant, the transition from buffer to reasons is smooth.

Sometimes, granting the request is simply not in the company's own best interests. In such situations, don't "manufacture" reader benefits; instead, just provide whatever short explanation you can and let it go at that.

> Because this data would be of strategic importance to our competitors, we treat it as confidential. Similar information about our entire industry (SIC Code 1473), however, is collected in the annual U.S. census of manufacturing. These census reports are available in most public and university libraries.

Show the reader that your decision was a business decision—not a personal one. Show that the request was taken seriously; don't hide behind company policy. If the policy is a good one, it was established for good reason; therefore, explain the rationale for the policy.

> *Weak:* Company policy prohibits our providing an in-store demonstrator for your tenth-anniversary sale.

> *Improved:* A survey of our dealers three years ago indicated they felt the space taken up by in-store demonstrators and the resulting traffic problems were not worth the effort; they were also somewhat concerned about the legal implications of having someone cooking in their stores.

The reasons justifying your decision should take up the major part of the message, but be concise or your readers may become impatient. Do not belabor a point and do not provide more background than is necessary. If you have several reasons for refusing a request, present the most positive ones first—where they will receive the most emphasis. If you have several good reasons, avoid including any weak ones. If the reader feels he or she can effectively rebut even one of the reasons, you're simply raising false hopes and inviting needless correspondence.

Bad News   If you have done a convincing job of explaining the reasons, the bad news itself will come as no surprise; the decision will appear logical

The reader should be able to infer the bad news before it is presented.

S P O T L I G H T ON LEGAL ISSUES

TEN REASONS TO CONSULT LEGAL COUNSEL

Because memos, letters, and corporate communications may be used against you or your organization in a court of law, it is often wise to check with a lawyer to make sure that what you write doesn't violate state or federal law. You should consult legal counsel when a document that you have written

1. commits you to a legally binding contract.
2. commits you to a warranty or guarantee of a product or service.
3. makes an advertising claim.
4. amends or modifies corporate policy.
5. requests documents from an attorney.
6. makes a statement to an insurance adjuster, the police, or a government agency.
7. reports on an accident involving a product, service, or an employee.
8. concerns the termination of an employee.
9. concerns workers compensation or insurance matters.
10. concerns any product or process that will effect the environment.

---

and reasonable—indeed the *only* logical and reasonable decision that could have been made under the circumstances.

To retain the reader's goodwill, state the bad news in positive language, stressing what you *are* able to do rather than what you are not able to do. Avoid, for example, such phrases as "cannot," "are not able to," "impossible," "unfortunately," "sorry," and "must refuse." To subordinate the bad news, put it in the middle of a paragraph (never in a paragraph by itself); and include in the same sentence (or immediately afterward) additional discussion of reasons.

> In response to these dealer concerns, we eliminated in-store demonstrators and now advertise exclusively in the print media. Doing so has enabled us to begin featuring a two-page spread in each major Sunday newspaper, including the *Greenville Courier*.

The bad news should be phrased in impersonal language, avoiding the use of "you" and "your." The objective is to distance the reader from the bad news so that it will not be perceived as a personal rejection. So as not to point out the bad news that lies ahead, also avoid the use of "but" and "however" to introduce the bad news. Such transitional words say to the reader, "Stop. Turn in another direction." Most readers won't remember what was written before the "but"—only what was written after it.

You do not need to apologize for making a rational business decision.

Avoid any temptation to apologize for your decision. You may reasonably assume that if the reader were faced with the same decision and had the same information available, he or she would have made a similar decision. There is no reason to apologize for any reasonable business decision.

In many situations, the refusal can be implied, making a direct statement of refusal unnecessary. But don't be evasive. If you think a positive, subordinated refusal might be misunderstood, go ahead and state it directly. However, even under these circumstances, you should use impersonal language and include reader benefits.

Do not refer to the bad news in the closing.

Closing Any refusal, even when handled skillfully, has negative overtones. Therefore, you need to end your message on a more pleasant note. Make your closing original, friendly, and positive by using any of the following techniques. Avoid referring back to the bad news.

Best wishes: Best wishes for success with your tenth-anniversary sale. We have certainly enjoyed our ten-year relationship with Parker Brothers and look forward to continuing to serve your needs in the future.

Counterproposal: To provide increased publicity for your tenth-anniversary sale, we would be happy to include a special 2″ × 6″ boxed notice of your sale in the *Greenville Courier* edition of our ad on Sunday, February 8. Just send us your camera-ready copy by January 26.

Other sources of help: A dealer in South Carolina switched from using in-store demonstrators to showing a video continuously during his microwave sale. He used the 10-minute film, "Twenty-Minute Dinners with Pizzazz" (available for $45 from the Microwave Research Institute, P.O. Box 800, Chicago, IL 60625), and reported a very favorable reaction from customers.

Resale or subtle sales promotion: You can be sure that the new Golden Mini-Micro we're introducing in January will draw many customers to your store during your anniversary sale.

To sound sincere and helpful, make your ending original. If you provide a counteroffer or offer other sources of help, provide all the information the reader needs to follow through. Likewise, if you include sales promotion, make it subtle and reader-oriented. Avoid statements such as the following:

If you run into any problems, please write me directly. (*Do not anticipate problems.*)

Again, I am sorry that we were unable to grant this request. (*Do not apologize.*)

If you have any further questions, please let me know. (*Do not invite needless communication.*)

Although we are unable to supply an in-store demonstrator, we do wish you much success in your tenth-anniversary sale. (*Do not refer back to the bad news.*)

If we can be of any further help, please let us know. (*Do not repeat a cliché.*)

I trust that you now understand why we made this decision. (*Do not reveal doubt.*)

Don't forget to feature Golden microwaves prominently in your anniversary display. (*Do not sound selfish.*)

In short, the last idea the audience hears from you should be positive, friendly, and helpful. Checklist 7 summarizes guidelines for writing bad-news letters. The rest of this chapter discusses strategies for writing both bad-news replies and bad-news announcements.

BAD-NEWS REPLIES

Despite the skill with which a persuasive message is written, circumstances of which the reader is unaware may require a negative response. The organization's (and your own) well-being depends on the skill with which you are able to refuse a request and maintain the goodwill of the writer.

OBJECTIVE 3: Compose a reply that rejects an idea, refuses a favor, or refuses a claim.

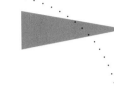

CHECKLIST 7   # Writing Bad-News Messages

Indirect Plan

Buffer

1. Remember the purpose: to establish a common ground with the reader.

2. Select an opening statement that is neutral, relevant, supportive, interesting, and short.

3. Consider establishing a point of agreement, expressing appreciation, giving a sincere compliment, presenting a fact or general principle, giving good news, or showing understanding.

4. Provide a smooth transition from the buffer to the reasons that follow.

Reasons

5. If possible, stress reasons that are for the benefit of someone other than yourself.

6. State reasons in positive language.

7. Avoid relying on "company policy"; instead, explain the reason for the policy.

8. State reasons concisely to avoid reader impatience. Do not overexplain.

9. Present the strongest and most positive reasons first; avoid discussing weak reasons.

Bad News

10. Present the bad news as a logical outcome of the reasons given.

11. State the bad news in positive and impersonal language. Avoid terms such as *cannot* and *your* request.

12. Do not apologize.

13. Subordinate the bad news—in a compound or complex sentence that talks about reader benefits, in the middle of a paragraph, followed by another reason, or so on.

14. Make the refusal definite—by implication if possible; otherwise, by stating it directly.

Closing

15. Make your closing original, friendly, off the topic of the bad news, and positive.

16. Consider expressing best wishes, offering a counterproposal, providing other sources of help, or building in resale or subtle sales promotion.

17. Avoid anticipating problems, apologizing, inviting needless communication, referring to the bad news, repeating a cliché, revealing doubt, or sounding selfish.

Direct Plan

1. Present the bad news in the first paragraph, perhaps preceded or followed by a short buffer or reason. State the bad news in a friendly, positive manner and do not apologize.

2. Discuss the reasons for the decision, including reader benefits as appropriate.

3. Close on a friendly and positive note. (See Steps 15–17.)

Rejecting an Idea

Perhaps one of the more challenging bad-news messages to write is one that rejects someone's idea or proposal. Put yourself in the role of the person making the suggestion. He or she has probably spent a considerable amount of time in developing the idea, studying its feasibility, perhaps doing some research, and, of course, writing the original persuasive message.

Consider, for example, the persuasive memo shown in Figure 7.1, in which Jenson Peterson tried to persuade Elliott Lamborn to restrict nearby parking lots to American-made automobiles. Peterson obviously thinks his idea has merit. He went to the trouble of having his staff count the number of foreign-made automobiles in the lots, getting a cost estimate for making the change, and contacting the union representative to get the union's position. Finally, he organized all his information into an effectively written memorandum.

Having invested that much time and energy into the proposal, Peterson probably feels quite strongly that his proposal is valid, and he likely expects Lamborn to approve it. If his proposal is rejected, Peterson will be surprised—and disappointed.

Because Lamborn is Peterson's superior, he could send Peterson a directly written memo saying in effect, "I have considered your proposal and must reject it." But Peterson is obviously intelligent and enterprising, and Lamborn does not want to discourage future initiatives on his part. As with all such messages, then, Lamborn's twin objectives are to refuse the proposal and retain Peterson's goodwill.

To be successful, Lamborn has an educating job to do. He must give Peterson the reasons for the rejection, reasons of which Peterson is evidently unaware. He must show that Peterson's proposal was carefully considered, and that the rejection is based on business—not personal—considerations.

Considering the amount of effort Peterson has put into this project, Lamborn's memo will be most effective if written in the indirect pattern, following the steps given earlier. This pattern will let Lamborn move his subordinate gradually into agreeing that the proposal is not in the best interests of the firm.

Lamborn's memo rejecting Peterson's proposal is shown in Figure 8.2. Although we label this memo a bad-news message, actually it is a *persuasive* message as well. Like all bad-news messages written in the indirect pattern, the memo seeks to persuade the reader that the writer's position is reasonable.

FIGURE 8.2   Rejecting an Idea

This memo responds to
the personal request
in Figure 7.1

TIMKIN
ELECTRICAL
SYSTEMS, INC.

1034 York Road,
Baltimore, MD 21204
(301) 555-1086

MEMO TO: Jenson Peterson, Marketing Supervisor

FROM: Elliott Lamborn, Vice President

DATE: October 15, 19——

SUBJECT: Parking Lot Proposal

A neutral subject line is
used.

Supportive buffer opening.
Second sentence provides a
smooth transition to the
reason.

Begins discussion of the
reason.

Last sentence of this paragraph presents the refusal
in positive and impersonal
language.

Forward-looking, off-the-
topic closing.

Your October 3 memo certainly enlightened me regarding the automobile buying habits of our employees. I had no idea that one-
third of our workers drive foreign made cars.

The increasing popularity of foreign-made cars recently led Timkin
management to conclude that we should expand our promotional
thrust to take advantage of this expanding market. President Wrede
has appointed a task force to determine how we might enter the
Japanese, German, and English auto market. In fact, our newest
long-range plan, which will be presented to the board next week,
estimates that within five years, international sales will account
for 15% to 18% of Timkin's sales.

Our successful entry into the international automotive market will
mean that many of the foreign-made automobiles Timkin employees
drive will have Timkin electrical systems. Thus, our firm will
benefit from the continuing presence of these cars in all our
lots.

Your memo got me to thinking, Jenson, that we might be missing an
opportunity to promote our products to headquarters visitors.
Would you please develop some type of awareness campaign (perhaps
a bumper sticker for employee cars that have Timkin electrical
systems or some type of billboard) that shows our employees support the products we sell. I would appreciate having a memo from
you with your ideas by November 3 so that I might include this
project in next year's marketing campaign.

emc

1

2

3

Grammar and Mechanics Notes

1. "one-third": Spell out and hyphenate fractions.   2. "thinking, Jenson, that"—
Use commas for direct address.   3. "year's"—singular possessive.

Refusing a Favor

Many favors are asked and granted almost automatically. Doing routine favors for others in the organization shows a cooperative spirit, and a spirit of reciprocity often prevails—we recognize that the person asking us for a favor today may be the person from whom we'll need a favor next week. Sometimes, however, for business or personal reasons, we are not able to accommodate the other person and must decline an invitation or request for a favor.

The type of message written to refuse a favor depends on the particular circumstances. Occasionally, someone asks a "big" favor—perhaps one involving a major investment of time or resources. In that case, the person has probably written a thoughtful, reasoned message trying to persuade you to do as he or she asked. If you must refuse such a big request, you should probably present your refusal indirectly, following the guidelines given earlier.

Most favor requests, however, are routine, and a routine request should receive a routine response; that is, a response written in the direct organizational plan. A colleague asking you to attend a meeting in her place, an organization asking you to serve on a committee, or a business associate inviting you to lunch is not going to be deeply disappointed if you decline. The writer has probably not spent a great deal of energy composing the request; the main thing he or she wants to know from you is "yes" or "no."

For routine requests, give the refusal in the first paragraph.

In such situations, give your refusal in the first paragraph, but avoid curtness and coldness. Common courtesy demands that you buffer the bad news somewhat and that you at least give a quick, reasonable rationale for declining. Although the refusal itself might not lose the reader's goodwill, a poorly written refusal message might! The memo in Figure 8.3 declines a request to serve on a corporate committee and is written utilizing the direct plan.

Assume for a moment that we had decided, instead, that our best strategy would be to write this memo in the indirect pattern, explaining our rationale before refusing. Our opening buffer might then have been as follows:

> Like you, I believe our new Executive-in-Residence program will prove to be effective for both Utah State and for our executives who participate.

Refusing a Claim

The indirect plan is almost always used when refusing an adjustment request because the reader is emotionally involved in the situation. The customer is already upset by the failure of the product to live up to expectations. If you refuse the claim immediately, you would risk losing the customer's goodwill. And, as noted previously, every dissatisfied customer tells nine or ten people about the bad experience and they, in turn, tell four or five others. Clearly, you want to avoid such situations.

The tone of your refusal must convey respect and consideration for the customer—even when the customer is at fault. To separate the reader from

FIGURE 8.3   Refusing a Favor

KEMPERER MANUFACTURING

May 18, 19—

TO: Wanda K. Berenson
          Personnel Department   1

FROM: Peter R. Carmichael
          Accounting Department *PRC*

SUBJECT: Your Memo of May 9, 19—

Gives a quick reason, immediately followed by the refusal.

You did such a good job of explaining the merits of our new Executive-in-Residence program that I've tentatively decided to apply for the program myself. To keep my options open, then, I must ask you to select someone else to serve on the evaluation committee.

Provides additional details.

Since I may be an applicant myself, I believe it would be inappropriate for me to suggest an alternate committee member.

Closes on a helpful note.

I will know by July 1 whether my workload for the fall semester will allow me to apply. If I decide not to apply, I shall be back in touch with you then to see if there is some way I can assist you in getting this important program off to a successful start.   2

iem

c: Fay Lee, Director of Accounting   3

24 South 500 East • Salt Lake City, Utah 84102 • Phone: (801) 555-3061

Grammar and Mechanics Notes

1. Many different formats for memos are acceptable.   2. Do not use a comma after an incomplete date ("July 1").   3. The copy notation indicates who else received a copy of this document.

the refusal, begin with a buffer, using one of the techniques presented earlier.

> Frequent travelers like you depend on luggage that "can take it"— luggage that will hold up for many years under normal use.

When explaining the reasons for denying the claim, do not accuse or lecture the reader. At the same time, however, don't appear to accept responsibility for the problem. In impersonal, neutral language, explain why you are denying the claim.

> *Not:* The reason the handles ripped off your Sebastian luggage is that you overloaded it. The tag on the luggage clearly states that you should use the luggage only for clothing, with a maximum of 40 pounds. However, our engineers concluded that you had put at least 65 pounds of items in the luggage.

> *But:* On receiving the piece of Sebastian luggage that you returned to us, we sent it to our testing department. The engineers there found stretch marks on the leather at the top of the luggage and frayed nylon stitching cord. They concluded that such wear could only have been caused by contents weighing substantially more than the 40 pounds maximum weight that is stated on the luggage tag. Such use is beyond the "normal wear and tear" covered in our warranty.

Use impersonal, neutral language to explain the basis for the refusal.

Note that in the second example, the pronoun *you* is not used at all when discussing the bad news. By using third-person pronouns and the passive voice, the example avoids directly accusing the reader of misusing the product. The actual refusal, given in the last sentence, is conveyed in neutral language.

As with other bad-news messages, close on a friendly, forward-looking note. If you can offer a compromise, it will take the sting out of the rejection and show the customer that you are reasonable. It will also help the customer save face. Be careful, however, that your offer does not imply any assumption of responsibility on your part. The compromise can either come before, or be a part of, the closing. For example,

An offer of a compromise, however small, helps retain the reader's goodwill.

> Although we replace luggage only when it is damaged in normal use, our repair shop tells me the damaged handle can easily be replaced. We would be happy to do so free of charge. If you will simply initial this letter and return it to us in the enclosed addressed envelope, we will return your repaired luggage within four weeks.

Somewhere in your letter you might also include a pitch for resale. The customer has had a negative experience with your product. If you want your reader to continue to be a customer, you might restate some of the benefits that led him or her to buy the product in the first place. But use this technique carefully; a strong pitch may simply annoy an already unhappy customer.

Consider the persuasive request written by Oliver Arbin (Figure 7.3). Mr. Arbin, as you may remember, was upset that his flight to Indianapolis was canceled, which caused him to have to make a six-hour drive instead. He wanted a refund of the $680 cost of his five nonrefundable tickets. It appears, on further investigation, that Mr. Arbin was not completely forthright. The letter refusing his claim request is shown in Figure 8.4.

FIGURE 8.4   Refusing a Claim—Indirect Pattern

This letter responds
to the personal
claim in Figure
7.3

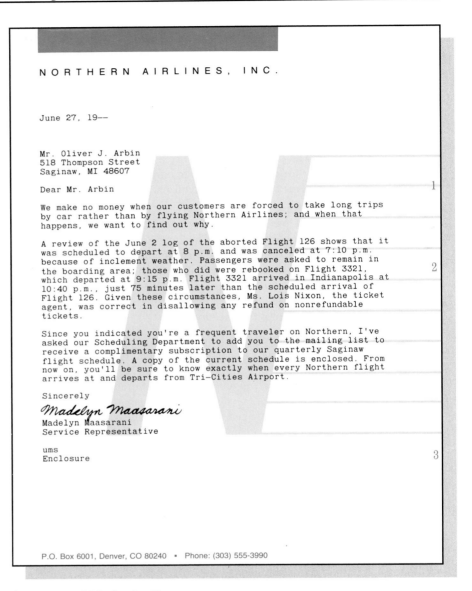

NORTHERN AIRLINES, INC.

June 27, 19—

Mr. Oliver J. Arbin
518 Thompson Street
Saginaw, MI 48607

Dear Mr. Arbin   1

Agreeable and relevant
opening.

We make no money when our customers are forced to take long trips
by car rather than by flying Northern Airlines; and when that
happens, we want to find out why.

Begins the explanation;
presents the refusal in impersonal language.

A review of the June 2 log of the aborted Flight 126 shows that it
was scheduled to depart at 8 p.m. and was canceled at 7:10 p.m.
because of inclement weather. Passengers were asked to remain in
the boarding area; those who did were rebooked on Flight 3321,   2
which departed at 9:15 p.m. Flight 3321 arrived in Indianapolis at
10:40 p.m., just 75 minutes later than the scheduled arrival of
Flight 126. Given these circumstances, Ms. Lois Nixon, the ticket
agent, was correct in disallowing any refund on nonrefundable
tickets.

Helpful closing; implies
that reader will continue to
fly with Northern.

Since you indicated you're a frequent traveler on Northern, I've
asked our Scheduling Department to add you to the mailing list to
receive a complimentary subscription to our quarterly Saginaw
flight schedule. A copy of the current schedule is enclosed. From
now on, you'll be sure to know exactly when every Northern flight
arrives at and departs from Tri-Cities Airport.

Sincerely

Madelyn Maasarani
Madelyn Maasarani
Service Representative

ums
Enclosure   3

P.O. Box 6001, Denver, CO 80240 • Phone: (303) 555-3990

Grammar and Mechanics Notes

1. Open punctuation is used: no punctuation after the salutation or
complimentary closing.   2. "boarding area;"—Use a semicolon between
independent clauses that are not joined by a coordinate conjunction.   3. Use an
enclosure notation to remind the recipient to look for some enclosed material.

BAD-NEWS ANNOUNCEMENTS

The previous section discussed strategies for writing negative replies. Often, however, the bad news we have to present involves a new situation; that is, it is not in response to another message. And quite often, these messages go to a large audience, as, for example, when you're announcing a major price increase, new rules and regulations, and the like. Such announcements may be either internal (addressed to employees) or external (addressed to customers, news media, stockholders, or the like).

As with other bad-news messages, you must decide whether to use the direct or indirect pattern of organization. Be guided by the effect the bad news will have on the recipients and your relationship with them.

Bad News About Normal Operations

Assume that management has decided that a price increase of 10% is justified on the Danforth cabin tent you manufacture. To notify the order department of the price change, a routine matter, you send a memo written in the direct pattern:

> Effective March 1, the regular price of our Danforth cabin tent (Item R-885) changes from $149.99 to $164.99, an increase of 10%. Any order postmarked before March 1 should be billed at the lower price, regardless of when the order is actually shipped.
>
> The new price will be shown in our spring catalog, and a notice is being sent immediately to all wholesalers. If you receive orders postmarked after March 1 with the old price, please notify the wholesaler before filling the order.

The preceding message reflects the fact that the price increase will have little or no negative consequences to the order department. Therefore, the news is given directly—in the first sentence, followed by the details. Because the person receiving this memorandum will not be personally disappointed in the news, you don't need to explain the price increase.

You also need to notify your wholesalers of this price increase. What will be their reaction? They will probably not be personally disappointed because price increases are common in business and come as no surprise; thus a direct message is called for. But wholesalers do have a choice about where to buy tents for resale, so you need to justify your price increase.

> Because of the prolonged strike in South African mines, we now must purchase the chrome used in our Danforth cabin tent elsewhere at a higher cost. Thus, effective March 1, the regular price of the Danforth tent (Item R-885) will change from $149.99 to $164.99.
>
> As a courtesy to our wholesalers, however, we are billing any orders postmarked prior to March 1 at the old price of $149.99. Use the enclosed form or call our toll-free number (1-800-555-9843) to place your order for what *American Camper* calls the "sock-it-to-me" tent.

Note how the bad news is cushioned by (1) presenting the reason first, a reason that is clearly beyond your control; (2) selling at the old price until March 1; and (3) including resale in the closing.

OBJECTIVE 4: Compose an announcement that conveys bad news about normal operations as well as about the organization itself.

Bad-news announcements are not in response to any request.

If the reader will not be disappointed, present the bad news directly.

A reason may be presented first—even in a message written in a direct pattern.

Bad-news messages require careful planning to control the wording, sequence, and pace of the ideas you present. Your organization's (and your own) well-being may depend on the skill with which you construct the bad-news message.

Source: Howard Grey / © Tonystone Worldwide

Finally, you need to write a third message about the price increase. For the past two years, you have had an exclusive marketing agreement with the Association for Backpackers and Campers. They promote the Danforth cabin tent in each issue of *Field News,* their quarterly magazine, at no cost to you in exchange for your offering their members the wholesale price of $149.99 (instead of the retail price, which is about 35% higher).

ABC selected the Danforth tent both because of its quality and because of its attractive price, and you want to make sure that your price increase does not endanger this agreement. Thus, you write an indirect-pattern letter, in which your major emphasis is on the reasons.

If the reader will need to be persuaded of the reasonableness of your decision, use the indirect approach.

The popularity of the Danforth cabin tent that you feature in each issue of *Field News* is based on our exclusive use of a chrome frame. Chrome is twice as strong as aluminum, yet weighs about the same.

Because of the prolonged strike in South African mines, we were faced with the choice of either switching to aluminum or securing the needed chrome elsewhere at a higher cost. We elected to continue using chrome in our tent. This decision to maintain quality has resulted in a change in the price of the Danforth cabin tent (Item R-885) from $149.99 to $164.99.

The Danforth tent promotion in the spring issue of *Field News* should be changed to reflect this new price. Since the spring issue usually arrives the last week of February, we will bill any orders postmarked before March 1 at the lower price of $149.99.

We have enjoyed the opportunity to serve ABC members and extend best wishes to your organization for another successful year of providing such valuable service to American backpackers and campers.

Another situation that calls for indirect organization is one in which a change in organizational policy will adversely affect employees. It is just as important, of course, to retain the goodwill of employees as it is of customers. Acceptance of a new policy depends not only on the reasons for the policy but also on the skill with which the reasons are communicated. An example of such a situation is shown in Figure 8.5.

When dealing with issues that are of such personal interest to the reader, don't hurry your discussion. Take as much space as necessary to show the reader that your decision was not made in haste, that you considered all options, and that the reader's interests were taken into account.

> Explain thoroughly the basis for your decision.

Note, especially, the use of personal and impersonal language throughout the memo. When discussing insurance programs that will be retained (third paragraph), "you" and "your" are used extensively. When discussing the program that will be dropped (fourth paragraph), impersonal language is used instead. The purpose is to closely associate the readers with the good news and to separate them from the bad news. Such deliberate use of language does not manipulate the reader; it simply uses good human relations to bring the reader to an understanding and appreciation of the writer's position.

Bad News About the Organization

If your organization is experiencing serious problems, your employees, customers, and stockholders should hear the news from you—not from newspaper accounts or rumors. For extremely serious problems that receive widespread attention (for example, product recalls, unexpected operating deficits, or legal problems), the company's public-relations department will probably issue a news release.

Often, some type of correspondence is also necessary. For example, owners of recalled products must be notified, customers must be notified if an impending strike will affect delivery dates, and employees must be notified if they will be affected by plant closings or layoffs. To show that these situations are receiving attention from top management, such messages should generally come from the president or other high-level official.

> Show that the situation is receiving top-management attention.

If the situation about which you are writing has news value, assume that your communication may find its way to a reporter's desk. Thus, make sure not only that the overall tone of the letter is appropriate but also that individual sentences of the letter cannot be misinterpreted if they are lifted out of context. Effective communication techniques can help you control the emphasis, subordination, and tone of your own message; however, you cannot do so for a news item that quotes individual parts of your message.

> Write in such a way as not to be misinterpreted.

> *News Item:* Although other drilling companies in the area erect eight-foot fences around their excavation sites, Owens-Ohio President Robert Leach admitted in a letter to stockholders yesterday that "our company does not require fences around these sites."

> *Actual Paragraph from President's Letter:* Unlike several other firms in the area, we have always had a strict policy of not allowing any digging in residential areas. In fact, all our excavation sites are at least two miles from any paved road and are well marked by ten-foot signs. Because these sites are so isolated, our company does not require fences around these sites.

FIGURE 8.5   Bad-News Announcement—Indirect Pattern

Uses a neutral subject line. Uses a compliment as the buffer.

Provides a smooth transition to the explanation; uses figures for believability.

The reader benefit used is the overall welfare of all employees.

Presents the good news before the bad.

Implies that fairness demands a change.

Subordinates the bad news in the middle of the long paragraph.

Ending moves on to a different, but related, topic.

 Danforth Recreational Industries

M E M O

TO: All Danforth Employees
FROM: Mary Louise Lytle, Vice President *MLL*
DATE: July 8, 19—
RE: Change in Insurance Coverage   1

Thanks to you, President Adams will announce a 13% increase in sales   2
for the year that ended June 30. Six of the seven divisions met or
exceeded their sales quota for the year. What an example of the
Danforth spirit!

Our pleasure at the 13% increase in sales is somewhat tempered by a
corresponding 14.5% increase in expenditures for the year. In studying the reasons for this increase, we found that fringe benefits, especially insurance, were the largest contributor. Medical
insurance costs increased 23% last year and have risen 58% in the
past three years.

In order to continue providing needed coverage for our employees and
their families and at the same time hold costs to a reasonable level,
we've analyzed the use and cost of each component of our program. We
learned that last year 89% of you used your health insurance at least
once, with the average being 12 family-member consultations per year.
Clearly, your health insurance (which covers 80% of the cost of doctor's visits and prescription medicine) is important to you, and,
therefore, to us. Similarly, although only 6% of you used your major
medical insurance for hospital care last year, protecting our employees from devastating health-care costs remains a top priority for us.

The other major component of our medical insurance program is dental.
Here we found that only 9% of our employees used this coverage last
year, yet dental insurance contributed 19% of our total medical
insurance costs. We believe the funds now being used for dental care
for a small minority of our employees can better be used to pay the
escalating costs of health and major-medical coverage for all our
employees. Thus, effective January 1, your company-paid insurance
program will include only health and major-medical coverage. Although
dental coverage will be discontinued at that time, all requests for
reimbursement for dental bills submitted on or before December 31
will be paid at the normal rates.

The Benefits Office will hold an open forum on July 28, from 2 to 3   3
p.m. in the second-floor auditorium to solicit your input and views
on all areas of employee benefits. Please come prepared with questions and comments on pensions, vacations, medical insurance, stock-
option plans, and other areas of interest. Your input will enable us
to continue to provide our family of employees the kind of protection
and options you deserve.

sma

Grammar and Mechanics Notes

1. "Re:" is sometimes used instead of "Subject:". 2. "President Adams"—Capitalize a title that is used before a name. 3. Use figures to express time; type the abbreviation "p.m." in lowercase letters, with no space after the internal period.

The last sentence of the president's paragraph would have been more effective had it been worded in positive, impersonal language:

> Fences are unnecessary in such isolated sites and, in fact, can cause safety hazards of their own. For example, . . .

Throughout your message, choose each word with care. In general, avoid the use of words with negative connotations and emphasize those with positive connotations.

Avoid Words Such As:	*Emphasize Words Such As:*
accident	care
catastrophe	concern
discrimination	cooperation
layoffs	equal opportunity
liability	joint efforts
negligence	open discussions
strike	progressive
unsafe	safety

If the reader has already learned about the situation from other sources, your best strategy is to use a direct organizational pattern. In a spirit of helpfulness and forthrightness, confirm the bad news quickly and begin immediately to provide the necessary information to help the reader understand the situation. For example,

> As you entered the building this morning, you saw the evidence of a burglary last night. The purpose of this memo is to let you know exactly what happened and to outline steps we are taking to ensure the continued safety of our employees who work during the evening hours.

If the reader is hearing the news for the first time, your best strategy is to use the indirect pattern, using a buffer opening and stressing the most positive aspects of the situation (in this case, the steps you're taking to prevent a recurrence of the problem).

> Employees in data processing, maintenance, and other departments who work at night perform a valuable service for Martin Company, and their safety and well-being are of prime concern to us. In that spirit, I would like to discuss with you several steps we are taking . . .

Figure 8.6 shows a letter written to alert customers about a possible demonstration to be held outside the site of a meeting announcing a new product. By showing a respectful attitude toward the demonstrators and by avoiding emotional language, the writer is able to convey the bad news with a minimum of fuss. And the fact that each customer received a personally typed letter from the president is in itself reassuring.

This letter also illustrates another common aspect of bad-news messages: Occasionally you may have to defend positions with which you personally disagree. Your disagreement may be strategic (it's not a smart move at this time) or philosophical (we shouldn't be selling this product). The issue, of course, goes much deeper than communicating. If your and your organization's philosophies consistently do not mesh, you would be happier finding employment in a more hospitable environment. Having made the decision to stay, however, you should have no qualms about defending the organization's positions so long as they are legal and ethical.

> Being a part of the management team sometimes requires that you support decisions with which you personally disagree.

FIGURE 8.6   Bad-News Announcement: Personal Letter

A personal letter from the president draws the needed attention.

PACIFIC LABORATORIES

November 8, 19——   1

Ms. Michelle Loftis
Planning Department
Crosslanes Pharmacies
3842 Le Purc Boulevard
El Toro, CA 92630

Dear Ms. Loftis:

Sales promotion is used for the opening buffer.

The breakthrough in over-the-counter birth control that Pacific Laboratories will announce at 3 p.m. on December 5 at the Park Inn will present a very substantial marketing opportunity for Crosslanes Pharmacies. I'm pleased you can be with us for the announcement.

The reasoned and even-handed discussion presents the company in a favorable light.

Like many scientific breakthroughs, our new product is generating quite a bit of interest in the media. Already, twelve newspapers and television stations have requested and been granted permission to cover this product announcement. We welcome such coverage and believe that an open discussion of such products will lead to more informed decisions by consumers.   2

News of the expected demonstrations (the bad news) is treated objectively and unemotionally.

In the same spirit, we have taken no steps to prevent any demonstrations outside the Park Inn on that day. It is likely that some pro-life and anti-abortion groups will march and distribute leaflets. So long as they do so peacefully, they are perfectly within their rights. We also are within our rights to hold a meeting without disruption, and there will be adequate security personnel on hand to ensure that everything runs smoothly. We do ask that you bring your original invitation (or this letter) to identify yourself, and we suggest that you use the Broad Street entrance to the hotel.   3

Closes with additional sales promotion and reader benefits.

We look forward to showing off the efforts of five years of research by our staff. The safety, convenience, and ease of use of this product will make it a very popular item on your pharmacy shelves.

Sincerely,

Stephen Lynch
President

iud

924 Ninth Street, Santa Monica, CA 90403 • telephone: (415) 555-2389

Grammar and Mechanics Notes

1. This letter is shown in the modified block style, with the date and closing lines beginning at the center point.   2. "coverage and"—No comma is necessary because what follows is not an independent clause.   3. "personnel"—means staff (*personal*—means private).

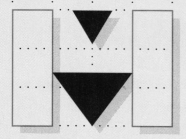

MICROWRITING   A BAD-NEWS MESSAGE

The Problem

You are the owner and president of Hudson Research Services. Your firm recently constructed a new headquarters building on a five-acre lot, and you've landscaped the unused four acres with lighted walkways, fountains, and ponds for employees to enjoy during their lunch hours and before and after work. Your lovely, campus-like site is one of the few such locations within the city limits.

Joan Bradley, the mayor of your city, is running for reelection. She has written to you asking permission to hold a fund-raiser on your grounds on July 7 from 8 P.M. until midnight. This event will be for heavy contributors; up to 150 people, each paying $500, are expected. Her campaign will take care of all catering, security, and cleanup.

You do not want to become involved in this event for several reasons. First, you are not a supporter of the mayor. Second, if the present mayor loses, you don't want to risk offending the new mayor. Third, if you allow this event, you will probably receive many similar requests by other candidates, nonprofit organizations, and the like. Despite their best efforts, so many people gathered outside at night are likely to damage the lawn and plants, frighten the animals, and cause other problems.

You decide to write to the mayor (The Honorable Joan Bradley, Mayor of Hudson, Hudson, OH 44236) and decline her request.

> Note the political implications of this situation.

The Process

1. Describe your audience.

   —Very important person (don't want to offend her)
   —Holds political views different from my own
   —Possibility of her losing the election (don't want to appear to be backing a loser)
   —Secondary audience: the 150 big contributors (what will be their reaction to my refusal?)
   —Secondary audience: other candidates (do not wish to offend anyone who might become the next mayor)

2. Should you use a direct or indirect organization? Why?

   —Indirect; considering the political implications of the situation, a direct refusal would be too blunt.

3. Brainstorm: List as many reasons as you can think of as to why you might refuse her request. Then, after you've thought of several, determine which one will be most effective. Underline that reason.

   —Other sites in the city offer a more suitable environment for the event.
   —Would have to provide the same favor to every other candidate.
   —<u>Possible harm to lawn, plants, and animals</u>.
   —Company policy prohibits outside use.

4. Write your buffer opening—neutral, relevant, supportive, interesting, and short.

   Thank you for your kind comments about our lovely grounds. With much effort, our staff has been able to

> Note how the second sentence provides a smooth transition to the following explanation.

create an environment in which plants and animals not
normally found in the Midwest are able to thrive here.

5. Now skip to the actual refusal itself. Write the statement in which you refuse the request—making it positive, subordinated, unselfish.

To protect this delicate environment, we now restrict
the use of these grounds to company employees.

6. Write the closing for your letter—original, friendly, off the topic of the refusal, and positive (Suggestions: best wishes, counterproposal, other sources of help, or subtle resale).

Another source of help is offered.

As an alternative, may I suggest the beautiful grounds
at the Ohio Educational Consortium on Lapeer Street.
They were designed with an Ohio motif by Larry Miller,
the designer for our grounds.

The Product

Dear Mayor Bradley:

Thank you for your kind comments about our lovely grounds. Our
staff has been able to create an environment here in which plants
and animals not normally found in the Midwest are able to thrive.

For example, after much effort, we have finally been able to
attract a family of Eastern Bluebirds to our site. At this very
moment, the female is sitting on three eggs, and various members
of our staff unobtrusively check on her progress each day.

Similar efforts have resulted in the successful introduction of
beautiful, but sensitive, flowers, shrubs, and marsh grasses. To
protect this delicate environment, we restrict the use of these
grounds to company employees, many of whom have contributed ideas,
plants, and time in developing the grounds.

As an alternative, may I suggest the beautiful grounds at the Ohio
Educational Consortium on Lapeer Street. They were designed with
an Ohio motif by Larry Miller, the designer for our grounds.
Various public events have been held there without damage to the
environment. Susan Siebold, their executive director, can be
reached at 555-9832 if you wish to contact her about using their
facilities.

Sincerely,

SUMMARY

When writing bad-news messages, your goal is to convey the bad news and, at the same time, keep the reader's goodwill. A direct pattern is recommended when (1) the bad news involves a small, insignificant matter; (2) the reader prefers directness or expects a negative answer; (3) the writer wants to emphasize the bad news; or (4) the reader-writer relationship is very good or very bad.

In the absence of such conditions, use the indirect plan. This approach begins with a buffer—a neutral and relevant statement that helps establish or strengthen the reader-writer relationship. Then follows the explanation of or reasons for the bad news. The reasons should be logical and, when possible, should identify a reader benefit. The bad news should be subordinated, using positive language and impersonal language; apologies are not necessary. The closing should be friendly, positive, and off the topic.

When using the direct plan, state the bad news in positive language in the first paragraph, perhaps preceded or followed by a short buffer and/or a reason for the decision. Then present the explanation or reasons, and close on a friendly and positive note.

Depending on the circumstances, either the direct or indirect pattern may be used to reject an idea, refuse a favor, refuse a claim, or present bad news about normal operations or about the organization itself.

KEY TERM

Buffer— A neutral and supportive opening statement designed to lessen the impact of negative news.

REVIEW AND DISCUSSION

1. What are the two objectives when writing a bad-news message?   OBJECTIVE 1 ◄
2. Under what conditions should a direct plan of organization be used for bad-news messages?   OBJECTIVE 1 ◄
3. Why are direct messages often shorter than indirect messages?   OBJECTIVE 1 ◄
4. Would a direct or indirect message be more effective under the following circumstances?   OBJECTIVE 1 ◄
   a. You're writing to a colleague, refusing her offer of a free ride to your upcoming sales conference, because you have to go a day early.
   b. You're writing to employees, telling them that for the first time no vacations may be scheduled during July and August.
   c. You're writing to your superior, informing him that the quarterly employee newsletter will be three days late because the offset machine broke down.
   d. You're writing to the sales staff, informing them that their sales quotas will be increased by 8 percent for the coming year.
   e. You're writing to stockholders, informing them of an impending federal investigation of your vice chairperson.

▶ OBJECTIVE 2 5. Why is the opening sentence called a *buffer*?

▶ OBJECTIVE 2 6. What are the five characteristics of an effective buffer?

▶ OBJECTIVE 2 7. Critique each of the following buffers; then revise to correct the weaknesses.

    a. Thank you so much for asking me to serve on the employee-relations committee.

    b. You can always depend on Meyers to honor claims for damaged merchandise.

    c. I wish I could grant your request to mail your organization's newsletter from our mailroom.

▶ OBJECTIVE 2 8. Critique each of the following reasons or explanations for refusing; then revise to correct the weaknesses.

    a. Unfortunately, the cost of participating in this project is prohibitive; furthermore, . . .

    b. You can surely understand that participating in this project would be prohibitively expensive.

    c. That is why company policy prohibits all such endeavors.

▶ OBJECTIVE 2 9. You wish to refuse a worker's request to use the microcomputer at her desk after hours to compose a newsletter for a charitable organization to which she belongs. Write the statement in which you actually refuse the request.

▶ OBJECTIVE 2 10. What techniques are effective to use in the closing of a bad-news message? What techniques should be avoided?

▶ OBJECTIVE 2 11. Write an effective closing sentence for a letter in which you refused to honor a claim for a damaged dress because it was improperly laundered.

EXERCISES

▶ OBJECTIVE 3 1. **Rejecting an Idea—Laptop Computers** You are Charles J. Redding, and you have received the memo written by O. B. Presley in Exercise 1 of Chapter 7). You have, of course, considered all kinds of options to make the sales representatives more productive—laptop computers, cellular telephones in their cars, telephone answering machines, and the like. The fact is that your firm simply cannot afford them for every sales representative. And some of the less-energetic representatives clearly do not need them. Instead, your company's philosophy is to pay your representatives top salary and commission and then have them purchase out of their commission earnings whatever "extra" devices or services are deemed worthwhile. You have checked with the Purchasing Department, however, and find that your corporate price for the Polaris is $950 rather than the $1,300 Presley quoted. You would be happy to have the company purchase this machine for Presley and deduct the cost from his commission check. Even though Presley will be quite disappointed in what you have to say, send him a memo conveying this information.

▶ OBJECTIVE 3 2. **Refusing an Application—McDonald's Franchise** As the director of franchise operations for McDonald's, Inc., you must evaluate the hundreds of applications you receive for franchises each month. Today you received an application from Maxine Denton, who is developing a large shopping center complex in Austin, Texas. Her corporation wants to open a McDonald's restaurant in her shopping center. Of course, they will have no trouble coming up with the initial investment. And they will select a qualified manager who will then go through McDonald's extensive training and orientation course.

But McDonald's has a policy against granting franchises to corporations, real-estate developers, or other absentee owners. They want their owners to manage their stores personally. They prefer high-energy types who will devote their careers to their restaurant and not be involved in numerous other business ventures. Write to Ms. Denton (she's the president of Lone Star Development Corporation, P.O. Box 1086, Houston, TX 77001), turning down her application.

3. **Refusing an Idea—Oversized Dressing Rooms**   You are Rebecca Lordstrom (see Exercise 2 of Chapter 7), and you certainly appreciate Robert Kilcline's memo recommending oversized dressing rooms for your new store in Fashion Square Mall. Robert has always been very customer conscious, a trait you try to instill and nourish in all your employees.

OBJECTIVE 3 ◄

After checking with the facility planner for the new store, you find that the Fashion Square Mall management has available only a certain amount of space for your store. Thus, any space taken up by the dressing rooms would have to be at the expense of the public store areas. The high rent for the mall site has already caused you to cut your store size down to what you consider to be an absolute minimum. Further cuts would endanger the store's profitability.

Write a memo to Robert, giving him this information. Perhaps there are other things you can do instead to offer better customer service.

4. **Refusing a Favor—Field Trip**   You are Donna Jo Luse and you have received the letter written by David Pearson in Exercise 3 of Chapter 7. Lunch is, of course, your busiest time, and no one has the time then (or the patience) to provide a tour of the kitchens and help 23 youngsters make their salads. Perhaps they could come for a tour and snack midmorning or midafternoon—anytime before 11 A.M. or after 1:30 P.M. Write Mr. Pearson (Jack 'n Jill Preschool, 113 Grenvale Road, Westminster, MD 21157) refusing his request.

OBJECTIVE 3 ◄

5. **Refusing Business—Hotel Reservation**   You are the manager of the Daytona 100, a 100-room hotel in Daytona, Florida, that caters to business people. You've received a reservation from Alpha Kappa Psi Fraternity at Illinois State University to rent 24 double rooms during their spring break (April 6–13). They have offered to send a $1,000 deposit to guarantee the rooms if necessary.

OBJECTIVE 3 ◄

As a former AKPsi yourself, you know that these are responsible students who would cause no problems. You also recognize that when these students graduate and assume positions in industry, they are the very type of people you hope will use your hotel. However, because of previous bad experiences, you now have a strict policy against accepting reservations from all student groups. Write to their treasurer (Scott Rovan, 40 Cypress Grove Court, No. 25, Normal, IL 61761-1142) conveying this information.

6. **Refusing a Claim—Azaleas**   You are the customer-service representative for Jackson-Parsons Nurseries and have received the letter written by Vera Malcolm in Exercise 5 of Chapter 7. Jackson-Parsons goes to

OBJECTIVE 3 ◄

great expense to use only the highest-quality patented stock and to ship each order packed in dampened sphagnum moss. However, there is no way that any nursery can control the care that plants receive on reaching their destination. Your obligation in this matter clearly ended when Ms. Malcolm did not notify you of any problems immediately. If she had, you would have cheerfully refunded her money. But evidently the azaleas are now thriving where they were planted, and you feel you have no further obligation. Tell this to Ms. Malcolm in a letter (189 Blackwood Lane, Stamford, CT 06903).

▶ OBJECTIVE 3

7. **Collaborative Writing—AIDS Policy** Working in groups of three or four, assume the role of the grievance committee of your union. Your company has its first known case of an employee with AIDS. The employee, an assistant manager (nonunion employee), has indicated that she intends to continue working as long as she is physically able. The company has upheld her right to do so.

    You've received a memo signed by six union members who work in her department, objecting to her continued presence at work. They are worried about the risks of contracting the disease from a coworker. Although they have compassion for the assistant manager, they want the union to step in and require that she either resign or be reassigned so that union members do not have to interact with her in the course of completing their work.

    Your committee does some research on the topic and based on your findings, decides not to intervene in this matter. Write a memo to Katherine Kellendorf, chair of the Committee of Concerned Workers, giving her this information.

▶ OBJECTIVE 3

8. **Declining an Invitation—Luncheon** You are the purchasing manager at your firm and have received a letter from Barbara Sorrels, one of your firm's major suppliers. She will be in town on October 13 and would like to take you out to dinner that evening. However, you have an early-morning flight on October 14 to Kansas City and will need to pack and make last-minute preparations on the evening of October 13. Write to Ms. Sorrels (P.O. Box 20, Johnson City, TN 37614), declining her invitation.

▶ OBJECTIVE 4

9. **Bad-News Announcement—Undercharge** The Wade & Roe law firm is an important customer of your delicatessen. Each day, you receive a large lunch order from their receptionist, which you deliver to their premises. They pay their bill monthly. In recording their January payment of $348.50, you discover you made an error in billing them. You sent them a bill for $348.50, when, in fact, their charges totaled $438.50. Write them a letter, explaining the matter and requesting payment of the remaining $90 (Fred Walsh, Office Manager, Wade & Roe, Suite 350, North Serrano Place, Los Angeles, CA 90004).

▶ OBJECTIVE 4

10. **Bad-News Announcement—Accounting** As budget specialist, send a memo to all departments telling them that beginning July 1, all unused balances in their departmental budgets will revert to the organization's central fund. Previously, departments were permitted to carry forward unspent funds to the new year. However, this caused problems in budgeting and forecasting. Any purchase orders processed by June 10 will be charged against this year's budget; those processed after that date will be charged against the new budget.

11. **Bad-News Announcement—Fringe Benefits** When your organization moved to its new building in Dallas three years ago, you negotiated a contract with the Universal Self-Parking garage a half block away to provide free parking to all employees at Grade Level 11 or above. Your rationale was that these managerial employees often work long hours and having easily accessible and free parking was a justifiable fringe benefit.

OBJECTIVE 4 ◄

Universal has just notified you that when your contract expires in three months, the monthly fee will increase by 15%. Given the state of the economy and your organization's declining profits, you feel that not only can you not afford the 15% increase but that you must, reluctantly, discontinue the free parking altogether.

Therefore, beginning January 1, all employees must locate and pay for their own parking. Your organization continues to promote ride sharing; employees can call Extension 4245 to have the computer locate employees living in the same area who are interested in carpooling. And the receptionist has copies of the city bus schedule, which stops one-half block from your building. Write a memo to these managerial employees giving them the information.

12. **Bad-News Announcement—Product Recall** You have received two reports that users of your ten-stitch portable sewing machine have been injured when the needle broke off while sewing. One person was sewing lined denim and the other was sewing drapery fabric—neither of which should have been used on this small machine. Fortunately, neither injury was serious. Although your firm accepts no responsibility for these injuries, you decide to recall all these machines to have a stronger needle installed.

OBJECTIVE 4 ◄

The purchasers of this machine (Model 4532-A; the model number is shown on a metal plate right below the light) should take their machines to the store where they purchased them. These stores have been notified and already have a supply of the replacement needles. The needle can be replaced while the customer waits. Or users can ship their machines to you prepaid (Dancer Sewing Machine Company, 168 West 17 Avenue, Columbus, OH 43210). Other than shipping, there is no cost to the user.

Prepare a form letter that will go out to the 1,750 purchasers of this machine. Customers can call your toll-free number (1-800-555-9821) if they have questions.

CASE PROBLEM

OBJECTIVES 3–4 ◄

No Such Thing as a Free Flight

Neelima has now received the memos she requested from Jean and Larry regarding the frequent-flyer program (see "Flying High at Urban Systems" on page 216). She has thought about the issue quite a bit and discussed it with Marc, Arnie, and Dave.

It seems to her that Larry has the more convincing argument: Company funds *were* used to purchase the tickets; therefore, the company logically owns the free tickets its employees earned. In addition, allowing traveling employees to keep their free tickets in effect amounts to an additional fringe benefit that nontraveling employees do not receive. So Neelima decides to begin requiring US employees to use their frequent-flyer free tickets for business travel rather than personal travel.

Now she needs to write to Jean and Larry to communicate her decision. Larry, of course, will be pleased; Jean will be extremely disappointed—not only because she believes her position to be correct but because she will feel threatened by being turned down by her superior. Jean was promoted to her present position only several months ago and is still a little unsure of her abilities.

Neelima also needs to issue a policy memo to all employees outlining the new program. The system will have to be built on trust; she does not intend to act as "Big Brother," policing the program and verifying mileage. Each employee will be required to join the frequent-flyer program for any airline he or she uses in connection with business travel. Employees can use different versions of their name if they also have a frequent-flyer number for their nonbusiness travel; for example, "John Q. Doe" and a home address for nonbusiness travel and "J. Q. Doe" and a business address for business travel.

The expense report form will be revised to have a check-off question that asks, in effect, "Did you have your frequent-flyer mileage recorded for this flight? If not, please explain." The clerk in OIS who makes all flight reservations will be instructed to ask each manager requesting tickets if he or she has accumulated enough miles on any airline to receive a free flight. Other details can be worked out.

Although many employees, especially those in marketing and R & D who travel extensively, will be upset, Neelima is confident her decision is reasonable and in the best interests of Urban Systems.

1. Should Neelima send Jean and Larry a joint memo or separate memos? Why or why not?
2. Write the needed memos: to Jean and Larry (either a joint memo or separate memos, depending on your response to the preceding question) and to the staff.
3. Assume that Urban System employees do not travel extensively and that Neelima's memo outlining the new restrictions will be considered a routine policy announcement. Write a second version of this memo using the direct pattern.

■ An *aptonym* is a person's name that is especially appropriate for his or   W O R D   W I S E
her actual profession. Below are some documented examples:

Dick Tracy, police chief
Solomon Gemorah, lecturer on morality
Stanford Schwimer, a swimmer at Stanford University
I. Doctor, optometrist
Jack Taylor, president, Tailors' Council of America
Will Pearce, acupuncturist

■ An *antinym* is a person's name that is especially inappropriate for his or
her actual profession. Below are two documented examples:

Bernard Crook, police chief
Jaime Sin, cardinal of Manila

9

Special Messages

After you have finished this chapter, you will be able to

1. Compose mixed-news messages—messages with more than one purpose.

2. Recognize the legal implications of personnel, credit, and collection messages.

3. Compose personnel messages, including letters of recommendation, job-rejection letters, and personnel evaluations.

4. Compose letters that approve and deny credit.

5. Compose letters written during the inquiry, appeal, and ultimatum stages of the collection process.

6. Compose goodwill messages, including congratulatory, thank-you, and sympathy notes.

Many manufacturers of luxury cars have the good business sense to thank customers with a "fulfillment letter," but few companies go so far as to include the telephone number of the company president. Range Rover of North America, a four-year-old distributor of high-line, British-made luxury sport utility vehicles, provides not only the president's number, but the name and number of the selling dealership owner as well as the area field manager responsible for service. Why? Because, explains Manager of Sales Steve McKnight, courtesies like that persuade the public that the company is serious about customer service.

"The fulfillment letter first says thank you for buying the Range Rover," says McKnight. "Then it tells customers that the dealer is committed to taking care of them. Finally, it tells them if things are not going as they should, they should call Range Rover corporate headquarters."

And call they do. "If someone calls the president, he will acknowledge the call," says McKnight. "If the president is not there to take the call himself, you can expect to hear from him or his office within twenty-four hours. For general owner concerns we usually just give the customer a call back after contacting the selling dealing first. If the problem is extraordinary, we have field engineers available to personally solve it."

At Range Rover, the fulfillment letter is just the first of three initial after-sale contacts with customers. Next comes a telephone call to check customer satisfaction. "An outside firm handles phone and mail surveys," says McKnight.

Steve McKnight,
Manager of Sales
Range Rover of
North America, Inc.,
Lanham, Maryland

"Range Rover purchasers have proven to be very receptive to questioning. They appreciate our follow-up."

If, in the telephone interview, the customer mentions a problem or complaint, specific information is forwarded to an appropriate manager who promptly responds by mail. The manufacturers' letters typically say "Dear so-and-so, we are sorry about the difficulty. Your complaint has been passed along to _____. You will hear from him shortly," says McKnight.

"Our letters make it clear that we will jump through hoops to investigate any problems, and we do. We also send along something such as a Ranger Rover umbrella, not as an attempt to mollify the customer, but as an indication of our genuine determination that things be put right."

"We want to be the best car company in the eyes of our customers. We believe quality treatment is essential and key to Range Rover's relationship with our customers." According to McKnight, Range Rover tries to support all customers in the highest possible manner. Typically, most owners are high profile, successful people who expect personal treatment.

Range Rover dealers expect the same high quality and personal treatment as Range Rover customers do. A recent survey shows that dealers' satisfaction with Ranger Rover of North America, Inc., is second only to that of Lexus dealers. ▼

PLANNING THE SPECIAL MESSAGE: CONSIDER YOUR OBJECTIVES

Up to this point, we have considered strategies for writing routine, persuasive, and bad-news messages. Although the suggested organizational plan differs for each type of message, each type has a single business objective—to convey routine information, to persuade the reader to do as you wish, or to convey bad news.

The messages discussed in this chapter are a little more complex. For example, some business messages have more than one objective, as when the same message must convey both good and bad news. Other types of messages require special consideration because they have legal implications that determine in part what you may or may not say. And the primary objective of some messages is simply goodwill, as when conveying sympathy, for example.

No one organizational pattern will serve the needs of each of these special types of messages. Instead, you must first identify your audience and objective and then organize each message in such a way that will help you achieve that objective.

MIXED-NEWS MESSAGES

Complex business operations often generate complex writing situations, and many of these writing situations involve more than one objective. You may need to combine good news with bad news or combine bad news with persuasion.

OBJECTIVE 1: Compose mixed-news messages— messages with more than one purpose.

Good News and Bad News

Sometimes you have both good news and bad news to convey. Perhaps an angry customer wrote a claim letter asking you not only to refund the $39.95 she paid for an electric coffee maker but also to reimburse her for the $87.50 damage that occurred when the electrical element came loose and burned her countertop. You might be willing to give a $39.95 refund for the coffee maker but not an $87.50 reimbursement for the damaged countertop. As with bad-news messages, your objectives here are to communicate the needed information clearly while at the same time retaining the reader's goodwill.

Messages that convey both good news and bad news should present the good news (the most favorable aspect of the message) first, where it will receive the most attention; explain the basis for the decision, using neutral and impersonal language; subordinate the bad news, presenting it as positively as possible; and end on a friendly note.

Figure 9.1 shows a mixed-news message. The good news is that the reader has been accepted for graduate study. The bad news is that he will not be admitted for the fall semester but must wait until the spring semester.

> Emphasize the good news, explain before presenting the bad news, and stress reader benefits.

Bad News and Persuasion

Suppose a customer orders a product you no longer sell. You might write, giving the bad news that you cannot fill the order and then trying to persuade the customer to accept a substitute product that you do sell. In such a situation, organize your message as follows:

Use a Buffer Opening   Begin with a neutral, relevant, and supportive opening. If you're trying to persuade the reader to accept a substitute product, for example, your opening might be as follows:

> I was pleased to learn that your Arco cellular telephone has served you so well for the past five years. For someone who travels as much as you do, a cellular telephone provides portable communication at an economical price.

Explain the Situation   Explain the reason for the bad news, present the bad news, and discuss why the reader should adopt your alternative suggestion. The first two purposes should be accomplished quickly, with the major discussion centered on the benefits of doing as you suggest. Avoid using the word *substitute,* and avoid negative comments about the original idea or product. Instead, concentrate on the positive aspects of the alternative you're proposing, as follows:

> When you purchased your Arco, it was the most technologically advanced cellular telephone available. In the five years since, however,

FIGURE 9.1   Mixed-News Message

Presents the good news first.

Begins presenting the reasons for the bad news.

Presents the bad news in the same sentence as a reader benefit.

Closes on a positive note.

C O A S T A L   S T A T E   C O L L E G E

Graduate School of Business Administration

March 3, 19——

Mr. Perry Mack
1048 Continental Way
Belmont, CA 94002

Dear Mr. Mack:

Congratulations on being accepted into Coastal State's Master of Business Administration program. We notified the Graduate Division last week that you have been granted regular admission.

The latest Board of Regents figures show that our MBA program has the third largest enrollment in the state. Students benefit from this increased enrollment because all the major corporations now actively recruit on campus each semester. And because many of our new enrollees are full-time executives, our students also develop a wide network of friends and professional contacts throughout the state.   1

To better manage our increased enrollments and to continue providing the quality of education that California business has come to expect of our graduates, we have staggered our enrollments, admitting some students for the fall semester and others for the spring semester. You are scheduled to start your MBA program in January 19——. If a vacancy opens up for the fall semester, you will be notified prior to July 1. Otherwise, you should assume that your classes will begin on January 8. Course registration procedures are outlined in the enclosed packet of information.   2

We look forward to having you join our program, Mr. Mack. We will benefit from your insights and experiences and feel sure that you will benefit from and enjoy our unique approach to management education.   3

Sincerely,

Georgia E. Grumann
Director of Admissions

plw
Enclosure

Berkeley, California 94720

Grammar and Mechanics Notes

1. "MBA"—Some abbreviations are written solid, without periods.   2. "fall semester"—Do not capitalize the names of seasons.   3. "experiences _and"—Do not use a comma between parts of a compound predicate.

major advances have been made in cellular technology that have not been incorporated into the Arco line. Thus, a year ago, we began offering the Zoom cellular telephone exclusively.

The Zoom comes with an exclusive snap-on battery pack that makes it an ideal unit for portable use. For example, no longer will you be tied to your car for emergency communications. Even if your car battery fails, you can still call for help. Its small 2- × 1- × 7-inch size means you can slip it into your briefcase for true portable use anywhere—up to three hours of continuous use without recharging.

Other features unique to the Zoom are explained in the enclosed brochure. Despite its smaller size, battery pack, and greater number of features, the Zoom cellular telephone costs only a few dollars more than the Arco—$314.99 for the Zoom compared to $279.99 for the Arco.

Ask for the Desired Action   Clearly explain what action you want the reader to take. Write confidently, but avoid making decisions for the reader; for example, do not automatically send the substitute product without first getting the reader's approval. Close with a final reference to a reader benefit.

Please let us know your wishes by completing the enclosed card and returning it to us. Within three days, you can be enjoying the convenience of true portability that only today's Zoom cellular telephone can provide.

MESSAGES WITH LEGAL IMPLICATIONS

All written messages have certain legal implications. For example, if you knowingly write something false about a company that results in damages to that company's reputation or financial well-being, you are guilty of libel. Three types of messages have special legal implications: letters and memos about personnel matters, credit letters, and collection letters.

Messages About Personnel Matters

Various laws and regulations limit what you may say, write, and do with regard to personnel matters. Therefore, in addition to conveying the needed information and maintaining goodwill, you must also be concerned with legal implications when writing letters of recommendation (also called "letters of reference"), rejecting job applicants, and writing personnel evaluations.

Writing a Letter of Recommendation   Writing a letter of recommendation presents not only legal but also ethical considerations. The overriding guideline is that you must be fair—fair to your own conscience, fair to the prospective employer, and fair to the applicants—including those for whom you are *not* writing a letter of recommendation.

To be fair to yourself, you must act in good faith. If you are satisfied in your own mind that you have written an honest and objective appraisal of the person's qualifications, you should have no concerns about the applicant's ultimate fate. That decision is the responsibility of the prospective employer.

▼ OBJECTIVE 2: Recognize the legal implications of personnel, credit, and collection messages.

▼ OBJECTIVE 3: Compose personnel messages, including letters of recommendation, job-rejection letters, and personnel evaluations.

S P O T L I G H T   ON LEGAL ISSUES

LEGAL IMPLICATIONS OF PERSONNEL MESSAGES

I refused to write a letter of recommendation for a former employee, and he did not get the position. Now he's threatening to sue me. Does he have a legal case against me?

No. You are not required to give a reference for a former employee. In fact, some employers now provide only factual information about former employees (name, starting and stopping work dates, positions, salary, and the like) because of their concern for legal problems.

Our company has no policy allowing my subordinates to see the evaluations I write and place in their personnel files. Do they have such a legal right?

All federal employees have the right to review and photocopy their personnel files. But only a few states have passed laws that allow business employees to review their files.

In my termination letter to an employee, I gave as one reason for his termination the aggravation of always having to rearrange his work schedule to permit him to observe the Sabbath on Saturdays. Was this a legitimate reason?

No. The law requires you to make reasonable accommodations to enable your employees to practice their religious beliefs—including rearranging schedules. You would have to show that doing so created an undue hardship on your firm.

Another department head has asked for my opinion about one of my employees for a management position. However, I believe she is too old for the position. Should I say so in my recommendation?

No. It is illegal to discriminate based on age. You would first have to have evidence that most people at that age would not be able to perform the new job competently.

I declined to give a reason for terminating an unsatisfactory worker. Was I within my legal rights?

Yes, in most states. Only a few states require an employer to tell an employee why he or she has been fired. Most employees are classified as "at-will" employees and can be fired for any reason or for no reason at the will of the employer. The exception is that they may not be fired for discriminatory reasons.

I wrote in a letter of recommendation that a former employee was chronically late for work. As a result, he did not get the job and threatens to sue me for libel. Will he win?

No, so long as you can document that, in fact, the worker was chronically late. You may provide the prospective employer any factual evidence that has a direct bearing on job performance so long as such information was solicited.

Sources: Ronald A. Anderson, Ivan Fox, and David P. Twomey, *Business Law and the Legal Environment,* 14th ed. (Cincinnati, OH: South-Western, 1990); Gordon W. Brown, Edward E. Byers, and Mary Ann Lawlor, *Business Law: With UCC Applications,* 7th ed. (New York: McGraw-Hill, 1989); Gordon W. Brown and R. Robert Rosenberg, *Understanding Business and Personal Law,* 7th ed. (New York: McGraw-Hill, 1984); Neil Story and Lynn Ward, *American Business Law and the Regulatory Environment* (Cincinnati, OH: South-Western, 1989).

You must also be fair to the employer because he or she is relying on your honest observations to make an appropriate hiring decision. There is also an implied reciprocity at work: If you do not give honest evaluations, how can you expect others to do so when you need their input in making hiring decisions?

Finally, you must be fair to the applicants. You are not doing anyone a favor by helping him or her get a job for which he or she is not qualified. Similarly, if an unqualified person you recommend does get the job, your recommendation may have helped deny the job to a better-qualified candidate. Thus, neither the unqualified person who got the job nor the qualified person who was denied the job was treated fairly.

Letters of recommendation may be of two types—general or specific. General letters are often requested by students as part of the personnel record they file with their college placement office. Sometimes a form is provided; otherwise, you should use a generic salutation, such as "Dear

Prospective Employer." Specific letters require your evaluation of a candidate's fitness for a specific position. Gear your comments to the specific job, making sure that you answer completely each specific question that is asked.

Regardless of whether you're writing a general or specific letter, begin by providing certain standard information:

- The full name of the job applicant (may be given in a subject line)
- The position the applicant is seeking
- The nature and length of your relationship with the applicant

A good legal safeguard is to label the information "confidential" and to state that you are providing this information at the specific request of either the applicant or the prospective employer. Because state laws differ, assume that whatever you write may, at some time, be seen by the applicant.

> Mr. Chung Kuang Chao, who has applied for the position of systems analyst at your firm, has asked me to write a letter on his behalf, and I am happy to provide this confidential information. Chao worked for me part time from February 1990 until April 1991 as a computer programmer while he was a full-time undergraduate student. He left when the special project for which he was hired was completed.

The major part of your recommendation will, of course, be your comments on the applicant's performance and potential. From the employer's viewpoint, the most helpful comments are those that are reinforced with examples and specific factual information. Include only relevant information—information that will help the prospective employer evaluate the candidate's qualifications. Be especially careful to avoid mentioning any factors that might later become the basis for a discrimination lawsuit, such as age, race, religion, handicaps, and the like.

Include only relevant information, and document each general comment with examples or factual data.

> I would evaluate Chao's programming skills as excellent. He designed, wrote, debugged, and ran four complex computer programs for me, each consisting of between 750 and 1,000 lines of COBOL code. His programs were innovative, efficient, and well documented.

Most people do not ask someone to write a letter of recommendation unless they have had pleasant relations with that person. Thus, most such letters are primarily positive in tone. No one is perfect, however. If the negative trait is either irrelevant to the applicant's performance on the job or if you are unable to document the deficiency, simply avoid mentioning it.

Occasionally you will need to include some negative aspect regarding the applicant's qualifications for a particular job. When doing so, avoid value judgments and opinions and simply relate the specific facts.

> *Not:* The one problem I had with Chao was that he was somewhat lazy and undependable.
>
> *But:* Regarding his work attendance, Chao was absent from work an average of twice a month. A few of these absences were unexpected in that he never called to report that he would be unable to come to work.

Because so much of what typically goes into a letter of recommendation is positive, any negative information tends to stand out and receive, perhaps, more attention than it deserves. You are the best judge of how to use emphasis and subordination appropriately to present the negative information fairly. The point is not to downplay the negative information but rather to make sure the reader perceives it with the same degree of importance with which you perceive it.

For example, if you believe Chao's attendance problems were fairly unimportant, you might either omit them altogether or subordinate them by placing them in the dependent part of a sentence, using the independent part of a sentence to explain the negative aspect or present more favorable information:

> Although Chao was absent from work an average of twice a month, he was able to complete all his assigned work competently and on schedule. Furthermore, . . .

End your letter by making some summary overall evaluation of the candidate. If your evaluation of the candidate has raised some questions about which the prospective employer might need more information, offer to provide more information if necessary. Under such circumstances, offering to answer further questions would be a genuine offer of help—not a cliché.

> Based on my observation of Chao's performance, I recommend him highly for the position of systems analyst. If I can provide additional confidential information, please call me at (571) 555-3220.

Figure 9.2 shows a letter of recommendation that contains mostly positive information but that also contains a minor bit of negative information, which the writer believes to be relatively unimportant.

To protect themselves from possible lawsuits, some companies refuse to provide any personal information about former employees. In fact, one survey of human-resources executives indicated that 41% of the companies have such a policy.[1] Other companies provide only oral evaluations, preferring not to provide any written record of their comments.

If you honestly feel that you should not recommend a candidate, you should decline to do so. A letter to the prospective employer declining to evaluate a job applicant should be straightforward, providing whatever factual information about the applicant that you feel is appropriate.

> Ms. Susan Buehler, about whom you inquired on May 3, worked for us as a teller from January 1988 until May 1990. Because of the legal implications, we no longer provide evaluations of former employees. This policy was in existence before Ms. Buehler was hired and should not be taken as a negative reflection on her performance.

Your letter to the applicant, telling him or her of your refusal to write a letter of recommendation, should be more indirect, stating the refusal as tactfully and as friendly as possible. If the reason for not providing a recommendation is related to company policy, explain that the decision had nothing to do with the applicant personally. However, if you simply prefer not to recommend this particular applicant, you need not provide a reason.

> Congratulations on your recent marriage and on your move to San Francisco. I was pleased to learn that you had found temporary employment in the Bay area and are now seeking a permanent position.

If possible, provide an overall summary evaluation of the candidate.

Letters to the prospective employer declining to write a recommendation are written in the direct pattern.

Letters to the applicant declining to write a recommendation are written in the indirect pattern.

Letter of Recommendation

FIGURE 9.2

W H E A T O N   P R O D U C T S

The Breakfast-Food Company

July 3, 19—

Mr. Foster B. Clark
Human Resources Department
Eastern Engelhard
3524 Water Street, N.W.
Washington, DC 20007

RECOMMENDATION FOR SHEILA J. YATES   1

I am pleased to recommend Sheila Yates for the position of assistant advertising manager with your company. I was Miss Yates's
immediate supervisor when she worked for Wheaton as an advertising   2
copywriter from September 1987 until March 1991 and am providing
this confidential information at her request.

Miss Yates's writing skills are superior. During her employment
here, she composed the narrative for all our print ads, sales
letters, and radio spots. We credit much of our marketing success
to her efforts. One of her sales letters won second place in the
statewide Eddy Award competition in 1989. Our Public Relations
Department routinely asked her to edit our annual report for
clarity, organization, and readability.

Her position required that she interact extensively with higher
management, outside suppliers, and two subordinates. In her
dealings with management and outside personnel, she was always
tactful, articulate, and cooperative. Although she had some problems in supervising her two assistants (a secretary and a copy
editor), I'm confident she will improve in this area with more
experience. She has always impressed me as a person who is quick
to recognize her own limitations and to work toward remedying
them. For example, she availed herself of every opportunity to
attend work-related seminars and was an active member of several
professional associations.

I have a very high regard for Miss Yates and recommend her to you.
You will find that she is an intelligent, experienced, and moti-   3
vated manager.

Anne Bryant
ANNE BRYANT, MARKETING DIRECTOR

uce

600 Grant Avenue   •   Pittsburgh, PA 15219   Phone (412) 555-2747

Starts by giving the applicant's name, position ap-
plied for, and nature and
length of relationship.

Reinforces general
comments with specific
examples and factual
information.

Presents negative news so
that it will be perceived as
intended.

Ends by giving a summary
overall evaluation of the
candidate.

Grammar and Mechanics Notes

1. This letter is shown in the simplified style, with no salutation or
complimentary closing.   2. "September 1987"—No comma is needed if only the
month and year are given.   3. Use a comma before the conjunction connecting
items in a series.

Because your most recent employer will be able to provide more current and more relevant information about you than I can, I suggest asking him or her to write a letter of recommendation for you instead.

Best wishes as you prepare for the future.

Rejecting a Job Applicant   People would not apply for a job with your firm unless they believed your organization would be a good place to work; they flatter your firm by applying. It is only right, then, to treat all applicants with courtesy and respect—even those who are not chosen.

The large number of applications received by some firms requires that a form letter be used for rejecting an application. However, regardless of the firm's size, if the applicant passed the initial screening and was interviewed, a personal letter is required. The most effective pattern for a rejection letter is a modification of the indirect approach: a buffer, refusal and explanation, and friendly closing. The refusal letter should be short because the reader is anxious to learn your decision.

> It was a genuine pleasure to meet you on August 15 and to interview you for the position of assistant advertising manager with our firm. I enjoyed hearing your reactions to the recent changes in our industry.
>
> We received nearly 50 high-quality applications for this position and finally filled it with a person from New York who has had extensive experience in supervising a large staff of artists and copywriters.
>
> I appreciate your interest in Eastern Engelhard, Ms. Yates, and wish you success in your search for a position in the Washington, D.C., area.

Writing a Personnel Evaluation   In most organizations, superiors evaluate their subordinates periodically. Such evaluations are typically first reported orally to the subordinate and then written for the employee's personnel file. Superiors also evaluate their employees at other times, as when a manager sends a memo to a subordinate discussing a specific problem with the employee's job performance.

In many ways, a personnel evaluation is like a letter of recommendation. You want to be fair both to the employee and to the organization, and you want to document any praise or criticism with specific examples. A personnel evaluation differs, however, in that its emphasis is on *improvement*. Both the employee and the organization have a vested interest in seeing that any weaknesses are understood by the employee and that an improvement plan is developed and implemented.

The message (typically a memo) should end on a friendly, helpful, and forward-looking note. A typical personnel evaluation memo is shown in Figure 9.3. The evaluation discusses both strong and weak points of the employee's performance. Use Checklist 8 as a guide to writing personnel messages.

Credit Letters

Credit represents the confidence that a business has in a customer's ability and intention to pay his or her debts. Allowing individuals and businesses to buy on credit has become the accepted way of doing business in America.

Margin notes:

Keep a job-rejection letter short and friendly.

The emphasis in a personnel evaluation is on ways to improve performance.

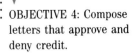
OBJECTIVE 4: Compose letters that approve and deny credit.

Personnel Evaluation

FIGURE 9.3

MEMORANDUM

DATE: July 15, 19--
TO: Robert Plachta, Mailroom Supervisor
FROM: Sharon Northcutt, Administrative Office Manager *SN*
SUBJECT: Semiannual Performance Review

The purpose of this memorandum is to review the points we discussed at our July 9 meeting regarding your performance for the
first six months of the year.

As shown on the enclosed Personnel Rating Form, I evaluate your
technical skills as excellent. You continue to stay abreast of the
latest technology in mail management, and your recent efforts to
further automate the mailroom will likely save the organization
$15,000-$20,000 yearly in labor costs. More importantly, the
organization will benefit from more timely mail delivery.

I discussed with you in some detail the fact that two female managers in other departments have complained to me recently of
inappropriate remarks you have made to them. They wished to remain
anonymous, so I am not exploring the matter further. We agreed,
however, that within the next month, you will schedule a one-hour
conference with Ms. Arelia Gomez in Personnel. She will outline
for you the types of actions and comments that are and that are
not permissible legally or according to company policy. You will
write me a memo summarizing the outcome of that conference. I am
confident that once you learn the corporate and legal implications
of your remarks, no further action will be necessary and we can
then simply forget about the matter.

I continue to be highly satisfied with your management skills.
Your reports are well written and on schedule, and your subordinates are quite happy with your supervision. In addition, you
maintain a safe and pleasant work enviroment--an especially noteworthy achievement, considering the large amount of equipment and
traffic in your department.

My overall evaluation of your performance, Bob, is that you are an
above-average manager. I'm pleased to have you as a member of my
staff and look forward to continuing to work with you as you seek
to increase the effectiveness and efficiency of our mailroom
operations.

weo
Enclosure
c: Personnel File--Robert Plachta

1   Documents each general
    comment.

2   Presents negative informa-
    tion objectively; outlines
    an improvement plan.

    Continues with positive
    comments to subordi-
    nate the earlier negative
    discussion.

3   Ends with an overall
    evaluation.

Grammar and Mechanics Notes

1. "$15,000–$20,000"—Do not space before or after a hyphen.   2. "well
written"—Do not hyphenate compound adjectives that come after a
noun.   3. "c:"—Type the copy notation with a lowercase *c* followed by a colon
and two spaces.

CHECKLIST 8

Writing Personnel Messages

Note: For *all* personnel messages, ensure that the information is accurate and that your message follows all federal and state laws regarding employment practices.

Writing a Letter of Recommendation

1. Be fair—to yourself, to the prospective employer, to the applicant whom you're recommending, and to other applicants for the same position.

2. Begin by giving the name of the applicant, the position for which the applicant is applying, and the nature and length of your relationship with the applicant.

3. Label the information "Confidential," and state that you were asked to provide this information.

4. Discuss only job-related traits and behaviors, be as objective as possible, and support your statements with specific examples.

5. If writing a recommendation for a specific position, answer all questions asked and gear your comments to the applicant's qualifications for the particular job.

6. Present any negative information in such a way that the reader will perceive it with the same degree of importance that you do.

7. Close by giving an overall summary of your evaluation.

Rejecting a Job Applicant

1. Keep the letter short; the candidate is anxious to learn what your answer is, "yes" or "no."

2. Provide a short, supportive buffer, perhaps mentioning some specific positive comment about the candidate's résumé or interview.

3. Say that another candidate was chosen (not that the reader was *not* chosen), and briefly explain why.

4. Close on an off-the-topic note, perhaps thanking the reader for applying or extending best wishes.

Writing a Personnel Evaluation

1. Be fair—to yourself, to the employee, and to the organization.

2. Discuss only job-related behaviors and traits.

3. Document any praise or criticism with specific examples and avoid exaggeration.

4. Ensure that any negative information receives only the appropriate amount of emphasis.

5. Emphasize the improvement aspect of the evaluation—specifically, what steps should be taken to improve any negative aspects.

6. End on a friendly, helpful, and forward-looking note.

Typically, requesting credit or checking references does not require writing a letter; however, approving or denying credit does. The customer applies for credit by filling out a credit-application form. Most cities have a credit bureau, which is an association of stores, banks, credit unions, and the like, that collects information about customers' borrowing and bill-paying habits. The bureau provides a credit history, for a fee, to firms requesting such information about an individual or business.

Legal Implications   Because an individual's or business's credit reputation is so important, a variety of federal and state legislation has been enacted to ensure that the rights of consumers are protected. For these reasons, as well as for ethical considerations, you must make sure that both your credit decisions and your communication of such decisions are based on a thorough and objective analysis of all the relevant data. Irrelevant data must not be considered. Because letters approving and denying credit are legal documents, check them carefully for accuracy and clarity.

> Consumer legislation protects the rights of creditors and would-be creditors.

Approving Credit   Because of the volume of credit requests received, most firms use form letters for approving credit, often personalizing them through the use of word processing. The decision is good news, so the use of a form letter is not likely to create ill will.

> Use a direct pattern for approving credit.

Like all good-news messages, credit-approval letters should be written in the direct pattern. Begin by telling the reader that credit has been approved. Then provide the needed explanation, primarily the credit arrangements: the maximum amount of credit, the date bills are sent, the date payment is due, interest charges for unpaid balances, and the like. A clear and complete presentation of this information now will help avoid misinterpretation and collection problems later.

> A full discussion of the credit arrangements sends the message that you take these commitments seriously.

If the credit arrangements are long and complex, consider putting them in an enclosure, to keep the letter itself relatively short. Once you've made the decision to grant the line of credit, avoid a heavy-handed, distrusting approach. Instead, be gracious and use impersonal language when discussing repayment terms.

Not: You are required to pay your bills by the 15th of each month.
But: Payment is due by the 15th of each month.

End your letter on a forward-looking note. Discuss how the customer will benefit from doing business with your firm, and use sales promotion or resale to encourage your customer to use his or her new credit.

> Encourage use of the new line of credit.

Figure 9.4 shows a form letter granting a customer credit. The mail-merge feature of word processing software permits the use of a personal inside address, salutation, and maximum credit amount.

Denying Credit   Credit may be denied for any number of legitimate business reasons: insufficient information, excessive obligations, irregular employment record, and poor payment history, among others.

> Use an indirect pattern for refusing credit.

Because purchasing on credit has become such a widespread way of conducting both business and personal affairs, a credit denial is especially serious for the applicant. Individual applicants often take it as a personal affront calling into question the person's character and integrity. For business applicants, a credit denial limits the firm's ability to stock sufficient

FIGURE 9.4   Credit Approval

James River Enterprises

November 8, 19—

Ms. Jill Boyer, Vice President
The Home Builder, Inc.
1001 Main Street
Houston, TX 77002

Dear Ms. Boyer:

Begins by giving the good news.

The Home Builder's fine credit history certainly merits credit privileges with our firm. Beginning immediately, you may charge purchases up to $3,000. When you mail or phone in your next order simply say, "Charge it."   1
                                                                                                    2
Explains the credit arrangements.

Bills are mailed on the 15th of each month and include all charges for the preceding month. Bills paid by the 25th of each month qualify for a 2% prompt-payment discount. Otherwise, the net amount is due by the 15th of the following month. A monthly finance charge of 1.5% (18% annually) is added to any balance unpaid within 30 days.   3

Includes sales promotion.

As one of our valued credit customers, you will not only enjoy credit privileges but also receive our quarterly sales brochures (in addition to the annual catalog you already receive). These brochures describe new products added to our growing inventory of insulation products as well as sale items at discounts of 15% to 35% off our regular low prices.

Encourages use of new credit privileges.

Use your new line of credit today, Ms. Boyer, to order some of the specials advertised in our winter sales brochure that is enclosed. As usual, your purchases will reach you within three days and are backed by our unconditional 30-day return policy.

Cordially,

L. P. Ewald
Credit Manager

pwc
Enc.   4

1251 Avenue of the Americas
New York, NY 10020

(212) 555-1000

Grammar and Mechanics Notes

1. "Builder's"—Add an apostrophe plus <u>s</u> to show possession of nouns not ending in <u>s</u>.   2. "Charge it."—The closing quotation mark goes after the period.
3. "15th of the month"—Use ordinal numbers (1st, 2d, etc.) only when the day comes before the month.   4. "Enc."—The enclosure notation may be abbreviated.

Like all banks across the country, Ohio-based Star Banc processes thousands of credit applications every year. Even though requesting credit or checking an applicant's references usually does not require writing a letter, approving or denying credit does, and to be effective, each type of letter requires a specific format.
(Star Banc Corporation / Tom Rogowski, photographer)

inventory or supplies. Damage to a person's reputation or to the profit-making ability of a business might result in a lawsuit. For these reasons, you need to use good judgment in refusing credit and in communicating your refusal.

Form letters for denying credit are often used by large firms. Although the volume of credit requests may make such a step necessary, it is difficult to personalize such refusal letters and retain goodwill with form letters. Retaining the goodwill of a rejected applicant is important because you want to retain the customer's business—on a cash basis now, but perhaps on a credit basis at some point in the future if the applicant's financial condition improves.

Thus, the overall tone of the refusal letter (whether a form or individual letter) should be one of respect, thoughtfulness, and helpfulness. Given the serious nature of the refusal, such letters should be written in an indirect pattern, beginning with a buffer opening.

> Your request for a line of credit with Bateman's shows that you appreciate the profit-making potential of our line of fine jewelry and our extensive national advertising efforts.

The buffer should provide a smooth transition to the explanation that follows. The extent of the explanation given depends on the individual circumstances. Occasionally, you may receive a credit request from someone whose credit history is grossly deficient—for example, an applicant with a long history of not paying bills on time. Such an applicant will not be surprised by a refusal and will know the reasons without your recounting them. Good human relations require that you avoid embarrassing the applicant. Instead, give a general statement of explanation, or forgo any explanation and immediately give the refusal.

Sometimes the reasons for denying credit may be omitted for human-relations reasons.

> Our review of the credit history provided by Dun & Bradstreet indicates that we can best serve you by continuing to sell on a cash basis only.

In the absence of such a clear-cut basis for denial of credit, courtesy demands that you explain the reason for your decision. And because the Fair Credit Reporting Act permits rejected applicants to request an explanation for the credit refusal, specifying the reasons helps avoid needless correspondence.

Explain the reasons factually and impersonally. Use a sincere tone, being especially careful not to sound patronizing. Then state the refusal positively, avoiding such negative terms as "must refuse," "does not meet," and "poor financial position." Because your decision was based on an objective analysis of the evidence, no apology is needed.

> Our experience, and the experience of others in our industry, shows that at least a 2-to-1 ratio of current assets to current liabilities is desirable to enable firms to pay their bills without undue hardship. As soon as your firm meets this ratio, we will be happy to extend credit to you.

Discuss the advantages of cash transactions.

After giving the refusal, move quickly to a forward-looking closing. If you can offer a counterproposal, do so. If you can realistically offer hope for a positive decision at some point in the near future, do so. At a minimum, discuss the advantages of continuing to do business with your firm on a cash basis. End on an optimistic note, without referring back to the refusal.

> In the meantime, we look forward to continuing to serve you on a cash basis. And you can look forward to continuing to receive the 2% discount we offer for cash purchases.

> Our fall national advertising campaign will feature *Vogue* cover girl Cheryl Alan. We expect the new creations she will model to be very popular with the type of clientele your store attracts.

Figure 9.5 shows a credit-denial letter that follows these guidelines. It is a refusal version of the approval letter shown in Figure 9.4.

Collection Letters

OBJECTIVE 5: Compose letters written during the inquiry, appeal, and ultimatum stages of the collection process.

The primary purpose of collection messages is to collect past-due accounts. The secondary purpose is to retain the debtor's goodwill. Although letters are the most commonly used medium for collection messages, the telephone can be used either instead of or in conjunction with letters. Some companies have also been successful in using ExpressMail, Mailgrams, and, increasingly, fax (facsimile) messages to emphasize the urgency of the situation.

Legal Implications   In addition to various state laws, the federal Fair Debt Collection Practices Act prescribes the types of actions you may and may not take in your efforts to collect legal debts. You may not, for example:

You may not use unreasonable actions or language in trying to collect debts.

- Use abusive, obscene, or defamatory language.
- Communicate with the debtor's employer, relatives, or friends about the unpaid debt (you may, however, communicate the facts to credit bureaus, collection agencies, and attorneys).
- Harass the debtor or intentionally cause mental distress (e.g., you may not telephone the debtor before 8 A.M. or after 9 P.M. unless he or she agrees).

Begins with a supportive

Credit Denial   **FIGURE 9.5**

James River Enterprises

November 8, 19—

Ms. Jill Boyer, Vice President
The Home Builder, Inc.
1001 Main Street
Houston, TX 77002

Dear Ms. Boyer:

I appreciate both your recent cash order and the confidence you
have shown in us by your credit application. I sincerely hope the
grand opening of your new home-improvement center was both enjoyable and successful.

The National Small Business Council estimates that 75% of new
firms such as yours that achieve profitability within three months   1
will have a secure future. Given the current interest in home
remodeling, I feel sure The Home Builder will reach this mile-
stone, at which time we will be pleased to reconsider your
application for credit.

During this critical three-month period, your continued purchases
for cash will enable you to take advantage of our 2% cash discount, thus contributing to profitability. Also, our overnight   2
delivery system will enable you to maintain smaller inventories.

Because we want to do everything we reasonably can to help you
succeed, I am asking Mr. Willard Perkins, our national sales   3
manager, to telephone you. Mr. Perkins has had extensive experience in display management and will be able to provide some
valuable tips that should help you promote all of your merchandise
more effectively.

Cordially,

L. P. Ewald
L. P. Ewald
Credit Manager

pwc

1251 Avenue of the Americas
New York, NY 10020

(212) 555-1000

Begins with a supportive
buffer.

First, gives reason for
the refusal; then presents
the refusal in positive
language.

Gives advantages of con-
tinuing to purchase for
cash.

Closes by making a gen-
uine offer of assistance.

Grammar and Mechanics Notes

1. "yours"—Do not use an apostrophe to show possession with personal
pronouns.   2. "overnight"—one word.   3. "national sales manager"—Do not
capitalize job titles unless they are used in place of a personal title (e.g.,
"President Smith").

CHECKLIST 9   # Writing Credit Letters

Note: For *all* credit letters, ensure that the information is accurate and that your message follows all federal and state laws regarding credit practices.

Approving Credit

1. Use a form letter if necessary.

2. Write in the direct pattern; begin by telling the reader that credit has been approved.

3. In the middle section, provide the needed information about the credit arrangements, using impersonal language and a gracious tone.

4. End on a forward-looking note, perhaps by including resale about your firm or sales promotion to encourage use of credit.

Denying Credit

1. Use a form letter if necessary.

2. Use an overall tone of respect, thoughtfulness, and helpfulness. Stress the goodwill aspects, because you want to keep the reader as a cash customer.

3. Begin with a relevant, supportive, and neutral buffer, perhaps an expression of appreciation or subtle resale.

4. Give only as many reasons as the specific situation warrants. Do not embarrass the reader.

5. Use impersonal and objective language in presenting the reasons. Discuss only relevant information and stick to the facts.

6. Present the refusal in positive language; do not apologize.

7. Close on an optimistic, off-the-topic note. Stress the benefits of continuing to buy for cash.

- Misrepresent your messages (e.g., you may not send anonymous messages, disguise your message as a letter from the IRS, or *falsely* imply that you have filed a lawsuit).

In communicating directly with the debtor, you are usually on sound legal ground so long as you stick to the facts. For example, you may tell a debtor that you will sue him or her if payment is not received by a certain date—if that is exactly what you intend to do.

Features of Collection Letters   Because more than one letter is often needed to collect past-due accounts, most companies use a series of collection letters. The most successful collection series have these features in common:

- *Understanding:* Show understanding by adopting a tone of reasonableness and helpfulness. Avoid anger; the reader is your customer—not your enemy. The most successful messages are those specifically adapted to the reader. For example, your best customers should be given more opportunities to pay their delinquent bills, with longer intervals between letters, than should your less creditworthy customers.
- *Timeliness:* Delinquent debtors will take as much time to pay as you give them. Therefore, you need to have a prompt and systematic procedure for notifying people of delinquent accounts—beginning a few days after the account is due. The letters should ordinarily come no more than two weeks apart. This gives enough time in between for debtors to pay without receiving another collection letter but never lets them forget about the debt.
- *Increasing urgency:* Most people typically pay their bills on time. Therefore, your first letters should be rather routine, increasing in urgency with each message. Poor credit risks will tend to pay first those debts that seem the most pressing.
- *Completeness:* Each letter should contain the reader's account number (perhaps in a subject line or at the bottom of the letter), the amount owed, and a postpaid envelope (to encourage prompt action).

The collection process usually begins with the mailing of the monthly statement; and the vast majority of accounts are paid within the due date. For those that are not, a four-stage series (reminder, inquiry, appeal, and ultimatum) is used, although more than one message may be sent at any one of these stages.

Reminder   At the reminder stage, you assume that the reader has simply overlooked paying and will pay when reminded. Make the reminder appear routine. Some of your very best customers will occasionally forget to send in a payment or be away when bills come due. You want to avoid insulting or embarrassing them. Thus, an individually typed letter would be much too personal at this stage; it might appear that you are questioning the customer's personal integrity.

Often, the notification is simply a second copy of the bill, perhaps on colored paper for emphasis or containing either a stamp or a sticker with a phrase such as "Friendly Reminder," "Please Remit," or "Second Notice" on it. Or you might use a computer-generated note, with a short message such as the following:

| Avoid personal letters at the reminder stage. |

> This note is a friendly reminder of the balance of $875.26 that was due on your account on October 15. Many thanks in advance for both your payment and your continued patronage. We sincerely appreciate both.

Depending on your analysis of the situation, you may send several reminder notices before moving to the next stage.

Inquiry   Once you can reasonably assume the customer has not merely forgotten to pay, you should move to the next stage. The assumption at this stage is that payment is being withheld because of some unusual circumstance.

The purpose of inquiry letters is to determine why payment hasn't been made and to arrange for either payment or an explanation. These letters

| The goal of the inquiry stage is to get *some* response from the debtor. |

are typically short and are considered routine; thus, they are written in the direct pattern. The assumption is still that the customer will pay, and retaining the reader's goodwill is still a major consideration. Personalizing the letter at this stage is appropriate.

> Dear Ms. Wheeler:
>
> Your October 15 account balance of $875.26 is now two months past due. Since this is the first time that you have been as much as a day late, I wonder whether something unusual has happened. Can I be of help?
>
> Won't you please either pay the full balance immediately or give me a call so that I can arrange a special repayment plan that will suit your particular circumstances.
>
> Sincerely,

At the inquiry stage, you can no longer assume the reader has merely overlooked paying. The reader is *consciously* withholding payment.

The tone of this letter is one of understanding and helpfulness. The aim is to get *some* action from the reader—preferably a check for the full amount or a partial payment or, at a minimum, an explanation and plan for repayment. Don't provide excuses, such as asking whether there was some problem with the product or service. If there were, the delinquent debtor would already have used that as an excuse for deferring payment. Likewise, do not mention that you believe the customer has merely overlooked paying. That was the tactic used in the reminder stage and it didn't work. In other words, once you leave one stage, do not backtrack.

Send only one inquiry letter. If it doesn't result in payment, move directly to the appeal stage. Some firms skip the inquiry stage altogether for new customers or for those with poor payment records and go immediately to the third stage.

Appeal   The appeal stage assumes the reader must now be persuaded to pay. Consider the situation: these debtors know they owe you the money, and they are not pleased to receive your letters because they know what the letters are about before reading them. Thus, you have an uphill battle to get them to do as you ask, and that calls for persuasion and an indirect approach.

Just as you develop a central selling theme for your persuasive sales letters, you should develop a central appeal for your collection letters at this stage. These letters must not be unduly long if you want the delinquent debtor to read them; you do not have time to develop numerous appeals. The more effective strategy is to select one appeal, based on your analysis of the individual situation, and then to emphasize that appeal throughout the letter, beginning with the attention getter.

Five common types of appeal, in increasing order of forcefulness, are resale, fair play, pride, self-interest, and fear. The first letter in the appeal stage typically uses one of the milder appeals; if that is not successful, one of the more forceful ones is used in subsequent letters.

1. *Resale:* Stresses the enjoyment or benefit the reader is receiving from using the product—a product he or she has not yet paid for.

   > Your Signet fax machine's ability to send and receive documents across the country in seconds is surely a profit-enhancing strategy for construction companies such as yours.

2. *Fair Play:* Stresses the fact that you've lived up to your part of the bargain by providing the goods or services; now it's the reader's turn to live up to his or her part. This appeal thus strives for a sense of closure.

   When you ordered the Signet fax machine, we were happy to deliver it, set it up, program ten telephone numbers for you, and train you in its use—even though this machine is typically an item the customer picks up. We even threw in a free 100-foot roll of thermal paper.

3. *Pride:* Stresses the reader's sense of pride—pride in a good credit rating, fine reputation, integrity, and the like.

   The pride that you have in Ellsworth Construction Company's fine reputation is shared by others. Congratulations on the positive write-up in last Sunday's <u>Dispatch</u>.

4. *Self-interest:* Stresses the financial advantages of maintaining a good credit reputation.

   How many months of having to pay cash for all your purchases did it take for you to secure the A-1 credit rating you have enjoyed up to this point?

5. *Fear:* Stresses the negative aspects of not paying—repossession, turning the account over to a collection agency, reporting the delinquent account to the credit bureau, bringing a lawsuit, and the like. It is the most forceful of all appeals and should not be used except as a last resort.

   > Use negative appeals only when all else fails.

   What will be the effect on your profits next quarter if suddenly you are forced to pay cash for all your purchases?

As illustrated in Examples 4 and 5, a rhetorical question is often effective in gaining the reader's attention. Your opening statement must introduce the appeal you intend to use and your subsequent paragraphs should develop this theme further—politely, but clearly and forcefully. In no uncertain language, explain the consequences of not paying, and ask for payment directly, forgoing subtlety. Stress the reader benefits of doing as you ask.

Letters at this stage are typically signed by a high-level official within the firm to stress their urgency. Figure 9.6 shows an appeal letter that uses self-interest as the central appeal. An earlier appeal letter that used resale as its theme was not effective in securing payment.

Ultimatum   The ultimatum stage assumes the reader has no intention of paying. In effect, this letter tells the reader either to pay or you'll use every legal means at your disposal to secure payment. In a polite and businesslike manner, discuss the steps you've taken thus far and the steps you intend to take if payment is not forthcoming. Do not issue idle threats, do not get angry, and do not defame the reader.

At this point, maintaining the goodwill of the reader is of minor importance; securing payment is paramount. Give the reader one last opportunity to pay, setting a deadline for receipt of payment. Because letters written in the direct pattern are more forceful, get to the point immediately in the ultimatum stage.

> The ultimatum letter gives the reader one last chance to pay before you take action.

FIGURE 9.6   Collection Letter

This persuasive letter is written during the appeal stage.

Uses a subject line to identify account.

Begins with a rhetorical question.

Presents the advantages of continued credit privileges.

Closes with a direct request for payment, coupled with another reader benefit.

Letter is signed by a high-level official.

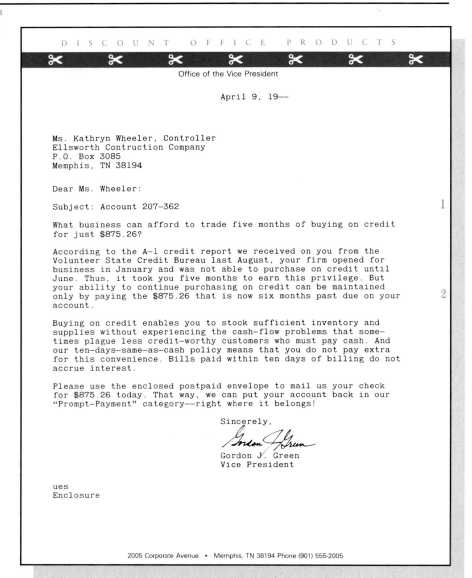

DISCOUNT   OFFICE   PRODUCTS

Office of the Vice President

April 9, 19—

Ms. Kathryn Wheeler, Controller
Ellsworth Contruction Company
P.O. Box 3085
Memphis, TN 38194

Dear Ms. Wheeler:

Subject: Account 207-362   1

What business can afford to trade five months of buying on credit for just $875.26?

According to the A-1 credit report we received on you from the Volunteer State Credit Bureau last August, your firm opened for business in January and was not able to purchase on credit until June. Thus, it took you five months to earn this privilege. But your ability to continue purchasing on credit can be maintained only by paying the $875.26 that is now six months past due on your account.   2

Buying on credit enables you to stock sufficient inventory and supplies without experiencing the cash-flow problems that sometimes plague less credit-worthy customers who must pay cash. And our ten-days-same-as-cash policy means that you do not pay extra for this convenience. Bills paid within ten days of billing do not accrue interest.

Please use the enclosed postpaid envelope to mail us your check for $875.26 today. That way, we can put your account back in our "Prompt-Payment" category—right where it belongs!

Sincerely,

Gordon J. Green
Vice President

ues
Enclosure

2005 Corporate Avenue • Memphis, TN 38194 Phone (901) 555-2005

Grammar and Mechanics Notes

1. Type the subject line immediately below the salutation, with double spacing before and after.   2. "six months"—Spell out numbers one through ten.

Dear Ms. Wheeler:

Despite eight letters and four phone calls, we have been unable to secure payment of the $945.63 ($875.26 balance plus interest of $70.37) that you owe us. Your failure to pay leaves us no choice but to turn this matter over to our attorneys to institute legal proceedings against your firm.

This is a drastic step that we'd sincerely like to avoid. The embarrassment that your firm would suffer, the almost-certain loss of all credit privileges, and the legal and court costs you will have to pay will have a serious negative effect on your firm's ability to remain profitable. Surely refusing to pay a legal debt of $945.63 is not worth such dire consequences.

If we have not received a check from you for $945.63 by 5 p.m. on June 23, we will ask our attorney to institute legal proceedings against your firm immediately. Please do not make this action necessary.

Sincerely,

Use Checklist 10 as a guide to writing collection letters.

GOODWILL MESSAGES

OBJECTIVE 6: Compose goodwill messages, including congratulatory, thank-you, and sympathy notes.

A **goodwill message** is one that is sent strictly out of a sense of kindness and friendliness. Examples include messages conveying congratulations, appreciation, and sympathy. These messages achieve their goodwill objective precisely because they have no true business objective. To include sales promotion, no matter how subtle, in such messages would defeat their purpose. Recipients are quick to see through such efforts. Letters that include sales promotion or resale are sales letters, as might be expected, and are covered elsewhere in this text.

That is not to say, however, that business advantages do not accrue from such efforts. People naturally like to deal with businesses and with people who are friendly and who take the time to comment on noteworthy occasions. The point is that such business advantages are strictly incidental to the real purpose of extending a friendly gesture.

Often the gesture could be accomplished by telephoning instead of by writing—especially for minor occasions. But a written message is more thoughtful, more appreciated, and more permanent. And because it requires extra effort and the recipient will receive fewer of them, a written message is much more meaningful than a telephone message.

General Guidelines

Five guidelines for good-will message:
· Be prompt.
· Be sincere.
· Be specific.
· Be brief.
· Be direct.

If you want your goodwill messages to achieve the desired effect, follow these five guidelines:

1. *Be prompt.* Too often, people consider writing a goodwill message but then put it off until it is too late. The most meaningful messages are those received while the reason for them is still fresh in the reader's mind.

CHECKLIST 10 Writing Collection Letters

For All Collection Letters

1. Ensure that the information is accurate and that your message follows all federal and state laws regarding collection practices.

2. Adopt a tone of reasonableness and helpfulness; avoid anger.

3. Send letters promptly and—if payment doesn't result—in systematic intervals, so that the debt is never out of the reader's mind.

4. In every letter include the reader's account number, the amount owed, and a postpaid envelope.

Reminder Stage

1. Assume the reader has simply overlooked paying.

2. Avoid embarrassing your customers; do not send a personal letter.

3. Send a second copy of the bill or an impersonal form letter.

Inquiry Stage

1. Assume the reader is deliberately not paying because of some unusual circumstance.

2. Send a short, personalized letter, written in the direct pattern.

3. Remind the reader that payment is late, find out why the account hasn't been paid, and solicit either payment or a plan for payment.

4. Don't provide excuses, and don't suggest that the reader has merely overlooked payment.

Appeal Stage

1. Assume the reader must be persuaded to pay.

2. Write a persuasive letter—in the indirect pattern.

3. Select one central appeal to use and stress it throughout the letter. The most effective appeals (in increasing order of forcefulness) are resale, fair play, pride, self-interest, and fear.

4. Make the opening attention-getter interesting, short, and related to the central appeal.

5. In the middle section, continue to stress the central appeal, using reader benefits and positive language to motivate payment.

6. Close by directly asking for payment, combining your request with another reader benefit.

Ultimatum Stage

1. Assume the reader has no intention of paying.

2. Write in a direct pattern; at this point, maintaining goodwill is much less important than securing payment.

3. In a polite and businesslike manner, explain exactly what you intend to do if the bill is not paid. Review the efforts you've already made to collect.

4. Give the reader one last opportunity to pay, setting a specific deadline.

---

2. *Be sincere.* For your message to sound sincere, avoid using language that is too strong or too flowery. Use a conversational tone, writing as if you were speaking to the person directly, and focus on the reader—not on yourself. Take special care to spell names correctly and to make sure your facts are correct.

3. *Be specific.* If you are thanking or complimenting someone, mention a specific incident or anecdote. Personalize your message to avoid having it sound like a form letter.

4. *Be brief.* You do not need two pages (or even likely one full page) to get your point across. Often a personal note card is more appropriate than full-sized business stationery.

5. *Be direct.* State the major idea in the first sentence or two—where it will receive the most emphasis. This is true even for sympathy notes; since the reader already knows the bad news, you don't need to shelter him or her from it.

Congratulatory Messages

Congratulatory notes should be sent for major business achievements—a promotion, retirement, winning a competition, opening a new branch, celebrating an anniversary, and the like. Such notes are also appropriate for personal milestones—engagements, weddings, births, graduations, and other noteworthy occasions. Congratulatory notes should be written both to employees within the company and to customers, suppliers, and others outside the firm with whom you have a relationship.

> Congratulations, Tom, on your election to the presidency of the United Way of Alberta County. I was happy to see the announcement in this morning's newspaper and to learn of your plans for the upcoming campaign.
>
> Best wishes for a successful fund drive. This important community effort surely deserves everyone's full support.

Thank-You Notes

A note of thanks or appreciation is often more valued than a monetary reward. A handwritten thank-you note is especially appreciated today, when people routinely receive so many "personalized" computer-generated messages. A handwritten note assures the reader that you are offering sincere and genuine thanks, rather than simply sending out a form letter.

Thank-you notes are expected in some situations; they are unexpected (but much appreciated) in others.

The more personal approach of a handwritten note must, however, be weighed against the major advantage of a typed note. You can send a copy of a typed note to the person's supervisor, so the person is twice blessed.

Thank-you notes (either typed or handwritten) should be sent whenever someone does you a favor—gives you a gift, writes a letter of recommendation for you, comes to your support unexpectedly, gives a speech or appears on a panel, and other similar occasions. Don't forget that customers and suppliers like to be recognized as well. The unexpected thank you's are often the most appreciated—to the salesperson, instructor, secretary, copy center operator, waiter or waitress, or anyone else who provided service beyond the call of duty.

> Thank you so much, John, for serving on the panel of suppliers for our new-employee orientation program. Your comments on scheduling problems and your suggestions for alleviating them were especially helpful. They were the kind of information that only an old pro like yourself could give.
>
> I think you could tell from the comments and many questions that your remarks were well received by our new employees. Thanks again for your professional contributions.

Sympathy Notes

Expressions of sympathy or condolence to a person who has experienced pain, grief, or misfortune are especially difficult to write but also are especially appreciated. People who have experienced serious health problems, a serious business setback, or the death of a loved one need to know that others are thinking of them and that they are not alone.

The most difficult messages to write are those expressing sympathy about the death of someone. These notes should be handwritten and should strike a balance in not artificially avoiding the negative aspect of the death, yet not dwelling on it unnecessarily. Most sympathy notes are short, perhaps even a sympathy card with a handwritten note. Begin with an expression of sympathy, mention some specific quality or personal reminiscence about the deceased, and then close with some expression of comfort and affection. An offer to help, if genuine, would be appropriate. (See Figure 9.7.)

Begin by expressing sympathy, offer some personal memory of the deceased, and close by offering comfort.

Other Goodwill Messages

The variety of types of goodwill messages is great indeed. Many organizations send out welcome messages to new employees and new customers—even to new members of the community. Others send out holiday messages. Even invitations to company-sponsored events can be considered a goodwill message.

The important point to remember is to concentrate on the goodwill aspect of such messages, forgoing any urge to blatantly promote your products or services. There is, of course, a place for such messages, but your goodwill message will most likely achieve its objective if it is written solely out of a sense of kindness and friendliness.

Sympathy Note

FIGURE 9.7

Robert B. Meyers

Dear Jane,

I was deeply saddened to learn of Ralph's sudden death. It was certainly a great shock to his many friends and colleagues.

Ralph had a well-earned reputation here for his top-notch negotiating skills and for his endearing sense of humor. He was an accomplished manager and a good friend, and I shall miss him greatly.

If I can help smooth the way in your dealings with our personnel office, I would be honored to help. Please call me on my private line (555-1036) if there is anything I can do.

Affectionately
Bob

Begin with an expression of sympathy.

Mention some specific quality or personal reminiscence.

Close with an expression of comfort and affection or a genuine offer of help.

Grammar and Mechanics Note:
Sympathy notes should be handwritten.

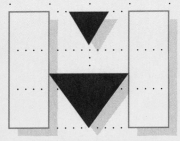

MICROWRITING A RECOMMENDATION LETTER

The Problem

Roger Brannen worked as your secretary for three years before quitting work to return to college to finish his degree. His secretarial skills were only adequate (he had some trouble adjusting to any new computer program). However, his organizational skills were top-notch; thus, he was always able to complete his work in a timely and competent manner.

Roger had an engaging personality and got along well with his coworkers and with people at higher levels of management with whom he had to deal. Twenty-four and single, he also had somewhat of a playboy reputation among the female staff at your company. However, he always behaved appropriately to everyone during working hours; you figured what he did on his own time was his own concern.

Roger is graduating this spring with a degree in business education and has, with your permission, used your name as a reference. Today you received the following letter from Susan Archie, assistant superintendent for personnel for the Atlanta, Georgia, public school system.

> Would you please provide some information on Roger Brannen? Mr. Brannen has applied for the position of cooperative office educator with one of our inner-city schools and has given your name as a work reference.
>
> Since this position requires supervising student interns in clerical and secretarial positions, the person holding this position must have excellent technical skills. How would you rate Mr. Brannen's technical skills?
>
> This position also requires frequent and close contact with members of the business community. How successful do you think Mr. Brannen would be in interacting with business executives?
>
> I appreciate your providing this confidential information, which will help us evaluate Mr. Brannen's qualifications for this position.

You sit down to plan and write the requested letter of recommendation to Ms. Archie.

The Process

1. Describe your audience.

> --Assistant superintendent for personnel for a large school system in a major metropolitan area
> --No vested interest in the outcome
> --Will make hiring decision based partly on the written evaluation provided

2. Who (if anyone) is the secondary audience?

   ```
   --Roger Brannen
   --Other applicants for the same position
   --The student interns
   --The business executives hiring the interns
   ```

3. Write the first paragraph of your letter.

   ```
   I am happy to provide the confidential information you
   requested on Mr. Roger Brannen, who has applied for the
   position of cooperative office educator with the Atlanta
   public school system. Roger worked as my full-time
   secretary from 1987 until 1990.
   ```

4. Should you discuss Roger's difficulties in adjusting to new computer programs?

   ```
   Yes, these skills are relevant to success in this posi-
   tion. However, they should be placed in appropriate
   context--he was able to compensate, and overall job
   performance is what counts.
   ```

5. Write the sentence in which you discuss this aspect of Roger's performance.

   ```
   Although it took Roger longer than most other secre-
   taries to learn new software programs, he eventually
   developed competence in each new program. And his top-
   level organizational skills enabled him to handle all
   tasks assigned to him in an efficient and competent
   manner.
   ```

6. Should you discuss Roger's playboy image?

   ```
   No, not relevant to his job performance and too many
   legal implications.
   ```

7. Write the last paragraph of your letter.

   ```
   I enjoyed knowing Roger, appreciated the competent work
   he did for me, and would, if I had the opportunity,
   rehire him. Please call me if I can provide additional
   information to help you in the evaluation process.
   ```

The Product

Note the minor editing
from the original drafts
of some of these
sentences.

Dear Ms. Archie:

I am happy to provide the information you requested on Mr. Roger Brannen, who has applied for the position of cooperative office educator with the Atlanta public school system. Roger worked as my full-time secretary from 1987 until 1990 and left to return to college full-time to complete his degree.

Roger's overall technical skills were competent. Although it took him longer than most other secretaries to learn new software programs, he eventually mastered each new program. More importantly, his top-level organizational skills enabled him to handle all tasks assigned to him in an efficient and competent manner.

Roger's human-relations skills were superb. He had an outgoing personality and cooperative attitude. He got along well with everyone, including high-level executives similar to those with whom your student interns work. If he had stayed with us for another year, I suspect he would have been promoted to be the administrative assistant for the executive vice president.

I enjoyed knowing Roger; I appreciated the competent work he did for me; and if I had the opportunity, I would gladly rehire him. Please call me if I can provide additional confidential information to help you in the evaluation process.

Sincerely,

Summary

When writing a message containing both good news and bad news, present the good news first, explain the rationale for the bad news, present the bad news, and then close on a positive and friendly note. When writing a message that contains both bad news and persuasion (e.g., getting the reader to accept an alternative to his or her original request), use an indirect approach: start with a buffer opening, explain the reason for the bad news, present the bad news, and present reasons for adopting your alternative suggestion; then close by asking for the desired action.

Letters of recommendation should be fair to all concerned, should discuss and illustrate only job-related behaviors and traits, and should use appropriate emphasis and subordination in presenting negative traits. Job-rejection letters should be short, written in the indirect pattern, and contain a brief explanation of why another person was chosen. All comments on a personnel evaluation should be fair, job-related, and documented with specific examples. The emphasis should be on job improvement.

When approving a request for credit, give the good news in the first sentence, follow it with the needed details about credit arrangements, and close with resale or sales promotion. When denying a request for credit, adopt the indirect pattern (beginning with a buffer), use impersonal and objective language to present the reasons, and give the refusal in positive language. End on an optimistic, off-the-topic note.

The collection series of letters should show understanding, timeliness, increasing urgency, and completeness. The reminder stage is very routine and impersonal—often simply a second copy of the bill. The inquiry stage requires a direct-pattern letter that seeks to determine why payment hasn't been made and to arrange for either payment or an explanation. The appeal stage requires a persuasive, indirect-pattern letter, using as a central appeal either resale, fair play, pride, self-interest, or fear. The final stage (ultimatum) is a direct-pattern letter that tells the reader that unless payment is received by a specified date, certain serious actions will be taken immediately.

Goodwill messages include congratulatory messages, thank-you notes, and sympathy notes. The important points to remember for all of these are to write promptly, using a direct pattern, and to be sincere, specific, and brief. Rather than serving an overt business purpose, these notes are written out of a sense of kindness and friendliness.

Key terms

Credit— The confidence that a business has in a customer's ability and intention to pay his or her debts.

Goodwill message— A message (such as a congratulatory, thank-you, or sympathy note) sent strictly out of a sense of kindness and friendliness.

Review and discussion

1. Assume that a subordinate wrote you a persuasive memo, proposing that the company set up a new branch in Altoona and name the

OBJECTIVE 1 ◄

subordinate as the branch manager. You decide that a new branch should be opened but you decide to name someone else as the branch manager.

a. Jot down an outline for conveying this information to your subordinate (i.e., in what order will it be presented).

b. Write the first sentence of this memo.

c. Write the last sentence.

OBJECTIVE 1

2. Suppose in the preceding situation, that you decide the new branch should be located in Grand Valley instead of in Altoona and that your subordinate should be named as the branch manager.

a. Jot down an outline for conveying this information.

b. Write the first sentence of this memo.

c. Write the last sentence.

OBJECTIVES 2–3

3. In writing a letter of recommendation, to whom should you be fair? Why?

OBJECTIVES 2–3

4. Give three bits of information about yourself that would be irrelevant to a prospective employer and that should, therefore, not be included in anyone's letter of recommendation.

OBJECTIVES 2–3

5. Should negative traits of a candidate always be subordinated? Why or why not?

OBJECTIVES 2–3

6. Assume you want to decline to write a letter of recommendation for someone. Should your letter conveying this decision to the prospective employer be written in the direct or the indirect pattern? How about your letter conveying this decision to the candidate?

OBJECTIVE 4

7. What effects do the Equal Credit Opportunity Act, the Truth in Lending Act, and the Fair Credit Reporting Act have on what should and should not be included in letters approving and denying credit?

OBJECTIVE 4

8. What should go in the first sentence or two of a letter approving credit? Of one denying credit?

OBJECTIVE 4

9. Why is it important to retain the goodwill of those people or businesses to whom you deny credit?

OBJECTIVE 4

10. Under what circumstances do many businesses refrain from stating a reason for denying credit?

OBJECTIVE 5

11. What are the primary and secondary purposes of collection letters?

OBJECTIVE 5

12. One of Paul's customers failed to pay a large account on time; as a result, Paul doesn't have enough cash to make his quarterly estimated-tax payment to the federal government. May Paul stamp on the envelope of his collection letter "Federal Tax Information Inside" to motivate the debtor to pay more attention to his letter? Why or why not?

OBJECTIVE 5

13. What is the disadvantage of providing too much or too little time between collection letters?

OBJECTIVE 5

14. Why is a personal letter inappropriate for the reminder stage?

OBJECTIVE 5

15. Name the assumptions for each of the four stages of the collection process.

OBJECTIVE 5

16. Which letters in the collection process are written in the direct and which in the indirect pattern?

OBJECTIVE 6

17. Why is it typically not appropriate to include sales promotion in goodwill letters?

EXERCISES

1. **Mixed-News Message—Bad News and Persuasion**   Assume that you are director of resurfacing for the Wyoming Department of Transportation. Jim Wycliff, one of your engineers, has requested permission to attend a two-week seminar offered by the University of Wyoming entitled "Load Constraints and Surface Technology." The course costs $1,350 and would require Jim's absence from work for two weeks.

OBJECTIVE 1 ◀

   Although continuing education is an important part of your engineers' schedule, you feel that your department would benefit more from having Jim attend a one-week course entitled "Grading Innovations for Erosion Control." Even though this course, also taught at the University of Wyoming, is offered the same week that Jim usually schedules his summer vacation (July 6–10), you feel that he will enjoy the course, that it will help your department achieve its objectives, and that it will make Jim more useful to the department. Send Jim a memo, denying his request to attend the load-constraint seminar and try to persuade him to attend the grading seminar instead. Your department will, of course, pay all expenses associated with the seminar.

2. **Mixed-News Message—Good News and Bad News**   Assume that you're the editor of a business communication textbook. Previous editions of your textbook have been published in two colors—black and a second color for headings, illustrations, and the like. In order to attract a larger share of the market, you would like to publish the upcoming edition in four colors. A four-color book permits full-color photographs, charts, and other illustrations. You believe such an added feature will dramatically increase sales and increase student interest, thereby aiding the learning process.

OBJECTIVE 1 ◀

   But four-color books are quite expensive. To help defray the cost of a four-color book, you must ask the author to take a smaller royalty percentage—going from 16% on the present edition to 13% on the upcoming edition. The author's contract permits such an arrangement. Write the author (Dr. Judith J. Kondler, College of Business, University of Minnesota, St. Paul, MN 55108) and announce this news.

3. **Letter of Recommendation—Willingness to Write**   Frances Kinchelow worked for your medium-priced restaurant for two years as the sous chef. The customers raved about her soup creations; she revised your somewhat bland soup menu by adding numerous new soups and making the others more appealing and more delicious; and she kept a clean and safe kitchen. When she decided to seek employment as a sous chef at a well-known restaurant in a nearby resort, you were surprised (after all, she is 63 years old) and also disappointed.

OBJECTIVES 2–3 ◀

   Frances's only fault was that you never could get her to watch expenses. If the recipe called for fresh ingredients, she was unwilling to use the cheaper canned or frozen substitutes. Often the leftover ingredients spoiled because they could not be used in other recipes. When you spoke to her about this, she promised to do better, but soon reverted to her old ways. You finally decided that these were her personal standards, and you reluctantly raised the soup prices to accommodate her.

The hotel manager where Frances has applied has written, asking you for a recommendation for Frances. Write the requested letter of recommendation (Mr. Jean Lefiere, Manager; Twin Oaks; 111 East Madison Street, Tampa, FL 33602).

▶ OBJECTIVES 2–3

4. **Letter of Recommendation—Unwillingness to Write** Despite your letter, Frances Kinchelow (187 Second Street, Tampa, FL 33620-5650) didn't get the sous chef job (see Exercise 3 above). She then quit her position with you suddenly, without giving any notice, and, according to your other workers, began drinking heavily. Three months later, you receive a letter from Frances, requesting that a letter of recommendation for her be sent to the Luau Ladle (165 South King Street, Honolulu, HI 96813). She sent a copy of her letter to the Luau Ladle manager. You decide not to write the letter.

   a. Write to the Luau Ladle, declining to give any subjective evaluation; you may provide a brief factual summary of Frances's employment history with you.

   b. Write to Frances, telling her of your decision.

▶ OBJECTIVES 2–3

5. **Rejecting a Job Applicant—Collaborative Writing** You are the proprietor of Knight Galleries, a major Manhattan gallery dealing in the purchase and sale of fine contemporary art. Traditionally, most of your sales have been to private collectors or to museums. However, noting the trend for business firms to purchase fine art for display and investment purposes, you've decided to expand into this market. You advertised in two gallery magazines for an art-marketing consultant, who would serve as your primary contact with business firms. Your ad stated qualifications as five years of art-consulting experience and a college degree in fine arts. Much to your surprise, you received nearly 100 applications. By studying the résumés and checking references, you narrowed the list to five candidates, whom you will bring in to New York for interviews. Working in groups of three to five members, do the following:

   a. Write a form letter that will go to the 95 rejected candidates, telling them that they were not selected.

   b. After the five interviews, you had much difficulty choosing between Ryan McNeil and Marie Durmond. Both impressed you during their interviews. Ryan had a degree in art history and had served as an art-marketing representative for a small Santa Fe gallery for seven years. Marie had a BFA degree in art from Simmons College, had worked as art curator for First National Bank in Manhattan for three years, and had been a working painter for the past three years. Assume that you finally chose Ryan, and he accepted the position. Write to Marie, giving her the news (Apt. 14-C, 226 Avenue of the Americas, New York, NY 10020).

   c. As a group, review and edit the two letters, proofread, and submit to your instructor.

▶ OBJECTIVES 2–3

6. **Personnel Evaluation** As chief of the three-person legal staff of a manufacturing concern, you prepare for the semiannual performance evaluation of Arthur Rodin, a legal assistant on your staff. As you reflect on his performance, you note these items:

   a. He is a good researcher—always able to locate opinions, precedents, and journal articles.

b. His writing skills are excellent.

c. His oral skills are satisfactory, especially considering the fact that he has a slight lisp.

d. He gets along well with everyone on the staff.

e. He sometimes volunteers for more work than he can handle; as a result, he occasionally misses an important deadline, causing extra work for the attorneys.

f. He's quite computer-literate, using word processing and such on-line computerized legal databases as Lexus and Dialog.

g. The other two attorneys have told you they often can use entire paragraphs that Art has written for their legal briefs, without changing a word.

Although you will present this information to Art in a face-to-face meeting, company policy also requires that a written memorandum be placed in each employee's personnel file. Write the memo to Art, adding whatever other reasonable information you feel is appropriate.

The following information applies to Exercises 7–10

You are the credit manager for Reginald's, an exclusive men's clothing store on Rodeo Drive. Your line of merchandise ranges from $50 ties to $800 silk suits. Your most popular items (and the items with the biggest markup) are Alex Henry sports jackets, which average $400 each. These back-pleated jackets are carried by only ten stores in the entire country; they've received much publicity lately because the president of the United States, who golfs frequently in Palm Springs, often wears jackets with the distinctive AH pocket crest.

You sell on credit exclusively through the use of the Reginald Card. There is no interest charge on any outstanding balance paid within ten days of the statement date. After ten days, interest accrues at the rate of 18% yearly.

7. **Credit Letter—Approval**   Pat Brody, a film editor (8025 Briar Summit Drive, Los Angeles, CA 90046), has applied to you for credit. You checked out his credit history with the local credit bureau and found that he has a solid history of paying his bills on time. You hear from industry sources that he is very proud of his good reputation within the financial community. You therefore approve him for a Reginald Card. Write a letter, giving the needed information.

OBJECTIVE 4 ◄

8. **Credit Letter—Denial**   The Prop Shop is a specialty store that supplies props to the television and movie industry. They have been in business for two years and have made several cash purchases of various items of clothing from you during that period. When they applied for credit, you made your usual inquiry to the local credit bureau and found that their history of payment has been erratic. Some months (when they were on contract to supply props for a production), they paid all bills immediately; at other times, they were as much as six months late in paying bills; and two rather substantial bills were finally written off as uncollectible.

You decide that Reginald's should not offer credit to the Prop Shop at this time. However, because you would like to see the AH label featured in more movie and television scenes, you wish to retain them as a cash customer. In fact, as soon as their credit history improves,

OBJECTIVE 4 ◄

you would be happy to issue them a Reginald Card. Write them (515 South Flower Street, Los Angeles, CA 90071), and deny the owners a card for now.

OBJECTIVE 5

9. **Collection Letter—Appeal Stage** It was just your luck—the Prop Shop is prospering; meanwhile Pat Brody has had a run of bad luck and cannot find steady work. As a result, his account is now $1,863.45 in arrears and has been for four months. You have already sent him three reminder letters and one inquiry letter—to no avail. Write the first letter in the appeal stage of the collection process.

OBJECTIVE 5

10. **Collection Letter—Ultimatum Stage** Despite your two well-written appeal letters, Pat has still not paid his bill; in fact, you've not heard from him. With interest, the unpaid balance is now $2,030.67 and is six months past due. If you do not receive his check for this amount no later than two weeks from today, you will (a) institute a lawsuit against him, and (b) report the incident to the Greater Los Angeles Credit Bureau. Write him, giving him one final chance to pay before you take these drastic steps.

OBJECTIVE 6

11. **Goodwill Letter—Letter of Appreciation** Think of a recent speech you heard and enjoyed—perhaps a speaker at a student organization meeting, a speaker sponsored by your university, a guest speaker in class, or some similar presentation. If necessary, do some research to locate a correct mailing address for this person. Then write this person a letter of appreciation, letting him or her know how much you enjoyed and benefited from his or her remarks. (If you have not heard a speech you enjoyed lately, write a former professor, expressing appreciation for what you learned in his or her class). Use only actual data for this assignment.

OBJECTIVE 6

12. **Goodwill Letter—Letter of Sympathy** Assume the role of national marketing manager of your organization. You have just learned that the mother of John Statler, your West Coast manager, died this morning. Although you did not know her personally, you learn that she was 87 years of age and died instantly of a massive stroke. She was a widow and had lived alone in apparent good health, tending her small garden, and enjoying life. Since John has already left for his mother's home and you cannot reach him by phone, send him a handwritten sympathy note.

OBJECTIVE 1

CASE PROBLEM

The Good, the Bad, and the Persuaded

Neelima Shrikhande has received a three-page memo from Eric Fox on the topic of word processing software. From the start, Urban Systems has taken a laissez-faire approach to the purchase of most software—leaving the decision as to which programs to purchase (and to support) at the departmental level. As a result, at least five different word processing programs are presently being used at US.

Eric feels that having to support so many different systems is inefficient, time-consuming, and costly. He wants Neelima to standardize on one word

CHAPTER 10

The Report Process

After you have finished this chapter, you will be able to

1. Discuss the important role that reports play in the contemporary organization.

2. Describe six common types of business reports.

3. Distinguish among informational, analytical, and recommendation reports.

4. Describe five common characteristics of business reports.

5. Explain each step of the report process.

6. Discuss the need for managing reports in the organization.

Several times a year, George Bollan sits down at his desk and carefully reads final proposals to sell jet engines to Pacific Rim governments. It's no easy task: These proposals, when finished, are often *hundreds* of pages in length, and each can take as long as three months to prepare. The proposals contain a mixture of financial, contractual, and technical language, and Bollan must be sure each aspect of a proposal is examined in painstaking detail in order to avoid complications down the road.

Bollan is Manager of Advanced Military Programs for Massachusetts-based General Electric Aircraft Engines—Lynn. He is one of thousands of U.S. executives who are, with increasing frequency, doing business with Korea, Taiwan, Japan, the Philippines, and the Peoples' Republic of China. For G.E. Aircraft Engines, the Pacific Rim business is worth quite a bit; the Korea fighter program is worth $500 million in initial sales alone.

The rules for doing business in the Pacific Rim vary with each country, but there is one constant: The reports must be written in such a way that those who speak English as a second language will not have problems understanding them.

"We obviously avoid using language that's only known to a small select group of people in the United States," said Bollan, specifically referring to acronyms that are casually used throughout the military supply business. Bollan must also make sure the language is kept simple, that "flowery" descriptions are simplified. When Bollan spots something in a report, presentation, or proposal that has the slightest chance of being misunderstood, he makes sure the sentence is rewritten.

The need for uncomplicated language in these reports is vital. Bollan has learned from his verbal dealings with businesspeople in the Pacific Rim that "the more words you're talking about, the more chance there is for confusion.

George Bollan, Manager of
Advanced Military Programs
General Electric Aircraft
Engines, Lynn, Massachusetts

And language we consider very flowery is sometimes hard [for Pacific Rim business people] to focus on." Bollan has transferred this lesson to the written word, especially since proposals are often translated by customers into summary reports for members of their upper management. Flowery prose, said Bollan, simply doesn't translate well and can lead to costly misinterpretations.

Without a near perfect report, the company would have a hard time doing business in the Pacific Rim. And since most military programs "don't happen more than once, say, every 15 years in a given country," a misunderstanding or losing a competition could cost the company millions of dollars. "Selling aircraft engines," said Bollan "is not like selling consumer electronics or other commodities."

The entire proposal writing process involves a lot of initial planning, then preliminary proposals are created, followed up by the final report and, usually, a number of revisions. Throughout the creation of the proposal, there's plenty of letter writing back and forth—and there, too, the language must be kept simple. Even after the contract is signed, the reporting process still goes on, Bollan said. Progress reports have to be made and any change in the production schedule has to be noted and approved.

Has the company ever had a deal fall through because of a language slip up? "No," said Bollan emphatically. And it's clear that he has every intention of keeping it that way. ▼

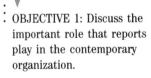

OBJECTIVE 1: Discuss the important role that reports play in the contemporary organization.

WHO READS AND WRITES REPORTS?

Consider the following informational needs of management in a large, complex, and perhaps multinational organization:

- A sales manager at headquarters uses information provided by the field representatives to make sales projections.
- A busy vice president asks subordinates to gather and analyze information needed to make an operational decision.
- A personnel supervisor relies on the firm's legal staff to interpret government requirements for completing a compliance report.
- A supervisor thinks up a cost-cutting procedure and prepares a proposal for management.
- An administrator informs all subordinates about a new company policy on hiring temporary personnel.

These common situations show why a wide variety of reports have become such a basic part of the typical management information system (MIS). Because constraints are imposed by geographical separation, lack of time, and lack of technical expertise, managers must rely on others to provide the information, analysis, and recommendations they need for making decisions and solving problems. Because reports travel upward, downward, and laterally within the organization, reading and writing reports are a typical part of nearly every manager's duties.

Reports can range from a fill-in form to a one-page letter or memo to a multivolume manuscript. For our purposes, we define a business report as an orderly and objective presentation of information that helps in decision-making and problem-solving. The report must be *orderly* so that the reader can locate the needed information quickly. It must be *objective* because the reader will use the report to make decisions that affect the health and welfare of the organization. And it must present *information*—facts, data. Where subjective judgments are required, as in drawing conclusions and making recommendations, they must be presented ethically and be based squarely on the information presented in the report.

Finally, the report must aid in *decision-making* and *problem-solving*. There is a "need-to-know" dimension in business reports that is sometimes missing in scientific and academic reports. Business reports must provide the specific information that management needs to make a decision or solve a problem. This goal should be uppermost in the writer's mind during all phases of the reporting process.

A wide variety of reports helps managers solve problems.

COMMON TYPES AND PURPOSES OF REPORTS

Management needs comprehensive, up-to-date, accurate, and understandable information to achieve the organization's goals. Much of this information is communicated in the form of reports. Although reports vary widely in terms of type and purpose, the most common are discussed in the following section.

OBJECTIVE 2: Describe six common types of business reports.

Report Types

The six most common types of business reports are routine management reports, policies and procedures, compliance reports, proposals, progress reports, and situational reports.

Routine Management Reports   Every organization requires its own set of recurring reports to provide the knowledge base from which decisions are made and problems are solved. Some reports are statistical in nature; others are primarily narrative. Routine management reports range from accounting, financial, and sales reports to various personnel and equipment reports.

Policies and Procedures   Most organizations establish policies and procedures for guiding action in recurring situations. For example, an organization may have a policy on accepting gifts from customers or a procedure for completing monthly expense reports. Writing policies and procedures requires careful organization, clarity, and a careful analysis of audience needs, so that the report is neither so general that it is of little practical use nor so specific that the resulting document is cumbersome and voluminous.

Compliance Reports   Many state and federal government agencies require companies doing business with them to file reports showing that they are complying with regulations in such areas as affirmative action, contacts with foreign firms, labor relations, occupational safety, and financial dealings. Completing compliance reports is often mostly a matter of gathering the needed data and reporting it honestly and completely. Typically, very little analysis of the data is required.

Proposals   A proposal is a written presentation that attempts to persuade someone to take some action—for example, to accept a bid for a project, approve a request for a loan, or make an investment. Proposals must use evidence and persuasion to convince the reader to do as the writer wants. All proposals have legal implications and must be prepared with care.

Progress Reports   Interim progress reports are often used to report the status of long-term projects. These reports are submitted periodically to management for internal projects, to the customer for external projects, or to the investor for an accounting of venture capital expenditures. Typically, these narrative reports tell what work has been accomplished since the last progress report, how well the project is adhering to the schedule and budget, any problems encountered and how they were solved, and future plans.

Situational Reports   In any organization, unique problems and opportunities appear that require one-time-only reports. Many of these situations call for information to be gathered and analyzed and for recommendations to be made.

Situational reports are perhaps the most challenging for the report writer. Because they involve a one-of-a-kind event, the writer has no previous reports to use as a guide. And because the situation is unique, the writer must decide what types and how much information is needed and how best to organize and present the findings.

▼
OBJECTIVE 3: Distinguish among informational, analytical, and recommendation reports.

Report Purposes

Business reports generally aim to inform, to analyze, or to recommend.

Informational reports present information without analyzing it.

Informing   Informational reports relate objectively the facts and events surrounding a particular situation. No attempt is made to analyze and interpret the data, draw conclusions, or recommend a course of action. An example is a progress report, which documents the status of a project. Figure 10.1 illustrates an informational report written in letter format.

Analytical reports interpret the information.

Analyzing   One step above the informational report is the analytical report, which not only presents the information but also analyzes it. Data by itself may be meaningless; it must be put into some context before we can make use of it. As social forecaster John Naisbitt has remarked, "We are drowning in information but starved for knowledge."[1]

Consider, for example, this statement: "Sales for the quarter ending June 30 were $780,000." Was this performance good or bad? You cannot possibly know unless the writer interprets the information. Here are two possible interpretations of this statement:

Sales for the quarter ending June 30 were $780,000, up 7% from the previous quarter. This strong showing was achieved despite an industry-wide slump and may be attributed to the new "Tell One-Sell One" campaign we introduced in January.

S P O T L I G H T   ON TECHNOLOGY

OVERCOMING INFORMATION ANXIETY

The ability to analyze pages of data, glean the important points, and present this information in a clearly written report is becoming increasingly important. Executives, like nearly everyone else in this information-laden society, are being bombarded by more data than they can absorb.

The Black Hole

According to Richard Wurman, author of *Information Anxiety,* in order to function in business we are forced to assimilate a body of knowledge that is expanding by the minute. Trying to process all this information can induce "information anxiety"—apprehension about the ever-widening gap between what we understand and what we think we *should* understand. In other words, it is the black hole between data and knowledge.

Here are some symptoms of information anxiety as Wurman describes them:

- Nodding your head knowingly when someone mentions a book, artist, or news story that you have actually never heard of before.
- Feeling guilty about that ever-higher stack of periodicals waiting to be read.
- Blaming yourself for not being able to follow the instructions for putting a bike together.
- Feeling depressed because you don't know what all the buttons are for on your VCR.

Wurman believes that "the System" is at fault—too many people putting out too much data. For example, about 9,600 periodicals are published in the United States each year. In addition, today's newspapers are more than twice as big as they were in 1970—up from 145 pages in 1970 to 351 pages today on average.

Too Many Choices

Wurman believes it is a myth that the more choices you have, the more freedom you enjoy. More choices produce more anxiety. So as you decrease them, you decrease your fear of having made a wrong choice.

Nobody Knows It All

The first step in overcoming information anxiety is to accept that there is much you won't understand. Use your ignorance as an inspiration to learn instead of something to conceal. Wurman recommends standing in front of a mirror and practice saying, "Could you clarify that?" or "I'm not sure I understand what you're talking about" instead of pretending to understand what you do not.

Other suggestions include the following:

- Separate what you are really interested in from what you merely think you should be interested in.
- Moderate your use of technology.
- Minimize the time you spend reading or watching news that isn't germane to your life.
- Reduce your pile of office reading.

Source: Richard Saul Wurman, *Information Anxiety* (New York: Doubleday, 1989).

Sales for the quarter ending June 30 were $780,000, a decline of 5.5% from the same quarter last year. All regions experienced a 3 to 5% increase except for the western region, which experienced an 18% *decrease* in sales. John Manilow, western regional manager, attributes his sharp drop in sales to the budgetary problems now being experienced by the state governments in California and Arizona. Three-fourths of his sales are to governmental units.

The report writer must be careful to make sure that any conclusions drawn are reasonable and valid and fully supported by the data presented. Figure 10.2 illustrates an analytical report written in memorandum format.

Can you tell which is factual data and which is the writer's analysis of this data—her conclusions? Do the conclusions seem to be based directly on the evidence presented? Was the writer careful to avoid inserting her own biases or preexisting opinions into the report?

Analysis and interpretation can never be completely objective. The report writer makes numerous decisions that call for subjective evaluations. For

FIGURE 10.1   Informational Report

This progress report is shown in letter format.

Davenport Construction Company

May 9, 19—

Mr. Ellis Shepherd, Chief
Manufacturing Department
Columbia-Collins, Inc.
680 Fourth Avenue
Louisville, KY 40202

Dear Mr. Shepherd:

This letter brings you up to date on the status of the construction of your new warehouse on Lafayette Street. As you will see, construction is on schedule and within budget, with no major problems foreseen.

Background: On January 3, 19—, Columbia-Collins contracted with Davenport Construction Company to construct a 48′ × 96′ frame warehouse at 136 Lafayette Street. Turn-key price was $76,500, with construction to begin on March 10 and to be completed no later than July 20. We agreed to provide interim progress reports on April 10, May 10, and June 10.

Work Completed to Date: We have now completed the following jobs:

1. By February 20, all of the plans had been approved by the appropriate regulatory agencies.   1
2. The foundation was poured on March 27.
3. The exterior of the building, including asphalt roofing and aluminum siding, was completed on April 23.

Work in Progress: The following work has been started but has not yet been completed: 2

1. The dry-wallers are installing the interior walls and partitions; they should be finished by the end of next week.
2. The electricians are installing the lighting, alarm system, outlets, and other electrical requirements.
3. The plumbers have installed the necessary fixtures in the washrooms and are installing the Amana high-energy-efficient heating/cooling unit.

    3

134 North Limestone
Lexington, Kentucky 40507
(606) 555-9935

Begins by giving the purpose and an overall summary.

Provides a brief history of the project.

Identifies the work completed, in progress, and still to be done.

Uses enumerations to make the items stand out.

Grammar and Mechanics Notes

1. Double-space between enumerations unless every item is just one line.
2. "been started but"—no comma needed between parts of a compound predicate.   3. Leave at least a 1-inch bottom margin.

Informational Report   **FIGURE 10.1**

```
Mr. Ellis Shepherd                                          4
Page 2
May 9, 19--

Work To Be Completed: From now until July 20, we will be complet-
ing these tasks:
1. The vinyl flooring will be installed by June 23.
2. The painters are scheduled to paint the interior on July 1-3.
3. The modular rack storage system is scheduled to be installed by
   July 15.
4. The landscaper will install all landscaping by July 15, includ-
   ing exterior lighting and a sprinkler system.
5. The city inspector and fire marshall will perform a final
   inspection on July 17.

Anticipated Problems or Decisions to Be Made: Listed below is a     5
minor problem regarding a shipment delay and a decision that we
need from you:
1. The modular rack storage system was ordered on April 3 and
   should have been delivered two weeks ago. I've spoken with our
   supplier and she assures me that the system will be delivered
   by May 12. If so, we should have no problems installing it on
   schedule.
2. By June 25, you will need to make a final color selection for
   the interior walls. The plan calls for one color. In making
   your selection, you might want to remember that the exterior
   of the warehouse is Colonial blue (a pale blue), and the metal
   storage system is putty.
We appreciate the opportunity to build this facility for you and
are sure you will enjoy using it. I will write you again in June
with another update.

                              Sincerely,

                              Mark Handorf

                              Mark Handorf
                              Project Supervisor

ked
```

Uses first- and second-person pronouns (in a letter or memo report).

Identifies problems and needed decisions.

Closes on a goodwill note.

Grammar and Mechanics Notes

4. Type the second page on plain paper, with a 1-inch top margin and a heading that identifies the recipient, page number, and date.   5. When underlining a phrase, underline the spaces between the words but do not underline the punctuation that follows (for example, the colon).

instance, look at the last paragraph of Figure 10.2. Would the reader receive a different message if the order of the two clauses had been switched?

Original order: Although it is too early to determine the effectiveness of Roger's efforts, he believes the steps he is taking will bring the absentee rate at Limerick down to the industry average of 3.6% by the end of the year.

Reversed order: Roger believes the steps he is taking will bring the absentee rate at Limerick down to the industry average of 3.6% by the end of the year. However, it is too early to determine the effectiveness of Roger's efforts.

The original order leaves a confident impression of the probable success of the steps taken, whereas the reversed order leaves a much more negative impression—especially since it is the last point in the memo.

Recommending   Recommendation reports add the element of endorsing a specific course of action. The writer presents the relevant information, interprets it, and then suggests a plan of attack. For example, a situational report might identify the causes of a problem, evaluate the possible solutions, and then recommend one specific solution. Or a feasibility report might evaluate the merits of entering a new market and recommend a go/no-go decision. Figure 10.3 illustrates a recommendation report written in manuscript format.

Study the first three headings in this report. Can you tell from reading only the headings what the conclusion will be? Headings that identify not only the topic of the section but also the major conclusion are especially useful for business reports, where they can serve as a preview or executive summary of the entire report.

> Recommendation reports propose a course of action.

CHARACTERISTICS OF REPORTS

To better understand your role as a reporter of business information, consider the following characteristics of business reports:

1. They vary widely in length, complexity, formality, and format.
2. Most reports are requested by higher-level management.
3. The quality of the process affects the quality of the final product.
4. Reports are often a collaborative effort.
5. Accuracy is the most important trait of a report.

Let's examine each of these characteristics further.

> OBJECTIVE 4: Describe five common characteristics of business reports.

Reports Vary Widely

There is no such document as a standard report—in length, complexity, formality, or format. The sales representative who spends five minutes completing a half-page call report showing which customers were contacted has completed a report. Likewise, the team of designers, engineers, and marketing personnel who spend six months preparing a six-volume proposal to submit to the U.S. Department of Defense has completed a report. The typical report lies somewhere in between. One analysis of 383 actual business reports found that 36% were one page, 37% were two to three pages, and 27% were four or more pages.[2]

> The typical report is 1–3 pages long and written in narrative format.

Analytical Report **FIGURE 10.2**

This analytical report is shown in memo format.

MEMO TO: James Van Oosterhoot, Vice President
FROM: Sarah J. Burke, Assistant Vice President *S.J.B.*
DATE: July 26, 19—
SUBJECT: Absenteeism at the Limerick Generating Station

As you requested in your June 28 memo, I've analyzed the absentee-ism of our union personnel at the Limerick Generating Station. I studied the attendance reports and met twice with Roger Chesin, the station manager. I found that the station's absentee rate of 4.7% is much higher than in previous years and somewhat higher than the industry average. However, Roger believes the steps he is taking will bring the station's average down to 3.6% by year's end.

Begins by providing the background, procedures, and an overall summary.

ABSENTEEISM RATE   1

During the first six months of this year, Limerick had an absentee rate of 4.7%, meaning that 8 of the 170 workers were typically ab-sent on each workday. Absenteeism at the station increased 5% dur-ing the past year and nearly 14% during the past three years.

George Bonner, assistant executive director of the Energy Industry Research Institute, told me last month that the industry average is 3.6% and has remained fairly steady over the past several years.

Discusses the extent of the problem. Presents and *interprets* the information.

CAUSES OF ABSENTEEISM

According to each employee's attendance report, the most common reason for absence is employee sickness, accounting for just over half of the self-reported reasons given. The bargaining agreement permits 12 no-penalty sick days yearly, with 6 days available for carryover from one year to the next. The typical employee took 10 sick days last year and carried over 2 days.   2

Mondays and Fridays present the most problems. These two days rep-resent only 40% of the workweek but account for nearly 60% of all absences. Sickness remains the Number 1 self-reported reason for absence on Mondays and Fridays.

Discusses the causes of the problem.

MANAGEMENT RESPONSES

Roger Chesin, the station manager, recently met with all the work-ers in groups of 25–30. He informed them that beginning August, written evidence of a doctor's visit will be required for any Mon-day or Friday absence reported as sickness. This requirement is an option permitted by the bargaining agreement.

Roger has also instituted a monthly recognition program in which the section with the lowest absentee rate will be publicly recog-nized each month in the newsletter. Their group photograph will also be displayed for that month in the display case in the em-ployee break room.

Discusses solutions being tried.

Although it's too early to determine the effectiveness of Roger's efforts, he believes the steps he's taking will bring Limerick's absentee rate down to the industry average of 3.6% by December.

kiv   3

Closes by discussing the desired results.

Grammar and Mechanics Notes

1. Although the spacing around the report headings may be adjusted based on the needs of the individual report, two blank lines before and one after is standard.   2. Use figures for all related numbers (both above and below ten) in the same sentence.   3. Leave one blank line before the reference initials (typist's initials).

FIGURE 10.3   Recommendation Report

This recommendation report is shown in manuscript format.

Begins by introducing the topic and discussing the procedures used. This report follows the indirect plan, saving the recommendations until the end.

Report is organized by subproblems.

Uses the author-and-date method for citing references (see Chapter 13).

Uses talking headings to identify the topic and major conclusion of each section.

Closes by making a recommendation based on the findings presented.

THE FEASIBILITY OF A MIXED-USE DEVELOPMENT IN PHOENIX

David M. Beall

Mixed-use development (MXD) is a form of real estate that integrates three or more land uses (e.g., office, retail, hotel, residential, and recreation) in a high-density configuration with uninterrupted circulation from one component to another. Interviews with seven local real estate developers and bankers and documents available from the Urban Land Institute and from the Greater Phoenix Chamber of Commerce provided information on the feasibility of constructing a mixed-use development in Phoenix.   1

LOW LAND PRICES WEAKEN MXD POTENTIAL

Land prices are a key economic factor in real estate development. High prices force developers to develop land with highly intensive uses (such as MXDs) to justify land costs. The much more expensive cost of an MXD makes economic sense only when high land prices justify the investment. Land prices in Phoenix, however, are relatively low compared to prices in other major U.S. cities.

The Galleria in Houston (a mixed-use development) and the Metrocenter in Phoenix (the city's largest shopping center) are similar-sized developments that offer an excellent comparison of how land prices dictate development intensity. The Galleria site cost   2
$85,000 per acre in 1964; six years later, in 1970, the Metrocenter site cost only $10,000 per acre (ULI 1986, 148).

LOW-DENSITY POPULATION LIMITS POTENTIAL BUSINESS

Successful MXDs tend to be located in high-density urban cores, where sufficient traffic is generated. The Phoenix market, on the other hand, is a low-density environment, as reflected by its horizontal urban form. Approximately 67% of the Phoenix housing stock is single-family homes and few commercial buildings reach over four stories high ("Inside Phoenix" 1990).

FINANCING WOULD BE DIFFICULT

The area bankers interviewed are reluctant to become involved with a new type of large-scale commercial development. Instead, they prefer to sponsor the types of projects with which they have had experience. According to one banker, "A bank is only as successful as its last loan" (Wyss 1991).

The bankers believe the economic risks associated with developing an MXD outweigh the rewards. They cited such adverse factors as high development costs, complexity, and lack of expertise (Allen 1991; Gorman 1991; Oaks 1991).

RECOMMENDATION: DAVENPORT SHOULD DELAY MXD PROJECT

Because of Phoenix's relative low land costs and low-density population and the difficulty of securing financing, Davenport should not pursue a mixed-use development in the Phoenix area now. However, because the Southwest is growing so rapidly, Davenport should reevaluate the Phoenix market in five years.

Grammar and Mechanics Notes

1. "real estate developers—Do not hyphenate compound nouns that come before another noun.   2. "site"—location ("cite": to quote; "sight": to view).

Most reports are written using a standard narrative (manuscript) format, but reports may also be in the form of letters, memos, or preprinted forms. In addition to the body, a report may include such preliminary (prefatory) parts as a cover letter, title page, table of contents, and executive summary. Supplemental parts may include a list of references, appendixes, and index.

Although reports may be either oral or written, most important reports are written; and even most oral reports are written initially. In other words, many reports are first written and then presented orally. Having the report available in written format is important because the written report provides a permanent record, it can be read and reread as needed, and the reader can control the pace—rereading the complex parts, marking the important points, and skipping some sections.

Most Reports Are Requested by Higher-Level Management

Because managers use reports to help make decisions and solve problems and because they are often busy, managers typically ask their subordinates to gather and report the information needed to aid in their deliberations. Likewise, these same managers are often asked by their own superiors to provide input for higher-level decisions. In fact, reports prepared at one level of management are often combined into a single integrated report that then goes to the next level, and so on.

> Most reports travel upward in the organization, although much routine information is transmitted downward in report form.

Because your report will be read by your superior and, quite often, by your superior's superior, your report-writing skills can have a major effect (positive or negative) on your career. Unlike most letters and memos, reports are often read and reread, studied at length, discussed, and used as the basis for achieving the organization's goals. Thus, the quality of the thinking, the research, and the writing that goes into a report can have major career implications.

Because most reports are requested by higher authority, reports typically travel upward in the organization—from your subordinates to you and from you to your superior. The types of reports that do travel downward in the organization are most often information reports that communicate decisions that have already been made that affect the organization (e.g., mergers, promotions, and profitability results) or policies and procedures that employees need to know to perform their jobs or take advantage of benefits (e.g., policies regarding smoking in the workplace, procedures for completing the monthly expense report, and announcements of changes in the pension plan).

The Quality of the Process Affects the Quality of the Product

Writing a report involves much more than writing a report. As contradictory as this statement might seem, consider a fairly routine report assignment—determining whether to recommend the purchase of Brand A, B, or C electronic typewriter. Before you can begin to write your report recommending one brand, you must do your homework. At a minimum, you must (1) determine what technical features are most important to the users of the machines; (2) evaluate each brand in terms of these features;

> A report may be well written and still contain faulty data.

(3) compare the brands on such characteristics as cost, maintenance, reliability, ease of use, and the like; and (4) draw a conclusion about which brand to recommend.

If at any step of the way you make a mistake, your report will be worse than useless; it will contain erroneous information that the reader will then rely on to make a decision. Suppose, for instance, that you interviewed only two typists out of the 50 who will be using the new machine. The needs of these two typists may not be typical of the needs of the other 48. Or suppose you failed to consider the amount of down time expected from each brand. Regardless of its features, no machine can meet the needs of its users when it is inoperable.

As such situations show, your report itself (the end product of your efforts) can be well written and well designed, with lots of appropriate charts and tables; yet if the process by which the information was assembled and analyzed was defective, erroneous, or incomplete, the report will be also. The final product can be only as good as the weakest link in the chain of events leading up to the report.

Reports Are Often a Collaborative Effort

Complex reports require the talents of many people.

Short, informal reports are typically a one-person effort. But many recurring reports in an organization are multiperson efforts. It is not likely, for example, that general management would ask just one person to study the feasibility of entering the generic-product market. Instead, a combination of talents would be needed—marketing, manufacturing, personnel, and the like.

As discussed in Chapter 2, such joint efforts require well-defined organizational skills, time management, close coordination, and a real spirit of cooperation. Although perhaps more difficult to manage than individually written reports, collaborative reports draw on the diverse experiences and talents of many members, help develop important networking contacts, increase each manager's awareness of other viewpoints, and, in general, result in higher-quality output than might be the case if a single person worked alone on a complex assignment. In addition, joint efforts can produce a final product in less time than would be possible otherwise.

Accuracy Is the Most Important Trait of a Report

Your most important job is to ensure that the information you transmit is correct.

No report weakness—including making major grammatical mistakes, misspelling the name of the report reader, or missing the deadline for submitting the report—is as serious as communicating inaccurate information. It's a basic tenet of management that bad information leads to bad decisions. And in such situations, the bearer of the "bad" news will surely suffer the consequences.

Suppose in the notes you made while conducting the research for the typewriter report you inadvertently wrote down that the ribbons for Brand A have a 10,000-character yield when, in fact, they have a 100,000-character yield. If operating costs were a major criterion, your final recommendation might be incorrect based on this simple careless error. It doesn't even matter how the error occurred—whether you made it or whether the typist made it. You are responsible for the project, and the praise or criticism of the results of your efforts will fall on you.

At Motorola's Communication, or Comm, Sector, employees and managers brainstorm to develop improvements for two-way radios. This scene is typical in business where a combination of talents joins to produce a collaborative report.
(© *Michael L. Abramson*)

To achieve accuracy, follow these guidelines:

1. Report *all the relevant facts*. Errors of omission are just as serious as errors of commission. Don't mislead the reader by reporting just those facts that tend to support your position.

   Misleading: During the two-year period of 1990–1991, our return on investment averaged 13%.
   Accurate: Our return on investment was 34% in 1990 and –8% in 1991, for an average of 13%.

2. *Use emphasis and subordination appropriately.* Your goal is to help the reader see the relative importance of the points you discuss. If you honestly think Point A is of minor importance, subordinate it—regardless of whether it reinforces or weakens your ultimate conclusion. Don't emphasize a point simply because it reinforces your position, and don't subordinate a point simply because it weakens your position.

3. *Give enough evidence to support your conclusions.* Make sure that your sources are accurate, reliable, and objective and that there is enough evidence to support your position. Sometimes your evidence (the data you gather) may be so sparse or of such questionable quality that you are unable to draw a valid conclusion. If so, simply present the findings and don't draw a conclusion. To give the reader confidence in your statements, provide plenty of documentation—discuss your procedures thoroughly and cite all your sources.

4. *Avoid letting personal biases and unfounded opinions influence your interpretation and presentation of the data.* Sometimes you will be asked to draw conclusions and to make recommendations, and such acts inherently involve a certain amount of subjectivity. But you should

make a special effort to look at the data objectively and to base your conclusions solely on the data. Avoid letting your personal feelings influence the outcomes. Sometimes the use of a single word will convey an unintended bias; for example,

Biased: The accounting supervisor <u>claimed</u> the error was unintentional.
Neutral: The accounting supervisor <u>stated</u> the error was unintentional.

THE PROCESS OF BUSINESS REPORTING

OBJECTIVE 5: Explain each step of the report process.

Chapter 5 presented the general process of business writing. Because business reporting involves so much more than just writing, we now expand that process to encompass all the steps in preparing a business report:

Planning

1. Become aware that a problem exists.
2. Define the purpose of the report.
3. Define the audience for the report.
4. Develop hypotheses regarding causes or solutions for the problem.

Data Gathering

5. Determine what data will be required.
6. Decide which methods to use to collect the needed data.
7. Collect the data.

Report Writing

8. Analyze the data.
9. Write the report.

It is not necessary to follow all nine steps for every report-writing project. For example, if you return from a meeting and want to summarize what happened, you might simply be able to write a memo report immediately, without collecting further data. However, even then, thinking through each of these steps will help to ensure that your memo achieves your objectives.

To illustrate each step of the reporting process, we'll use the case of Just Pool Supplies, a small firm in San Antonio, Texas, owned and operated by Joe Cox. Joe has asked Martha Halpern, his assistant store manager, to research a problem and write a report recommending a solution.

1. Become Aware That a Problem Exists.

The basis for a report may be an obvious problem or a proposal for taking advantage of new opportunities.

If your report has been authorized by your superior, you become aware of the problem to be solved by discussing it with your superior. In other situations, becoming aware that a problem exists may not be as easy as it sounds. The problem may not be in the form of an obvious breakdown in normal operational efficiency. Many "problems" that forward-looking managers recognize are really questions about opportunities—the opportunity to perform an assigned function better or more efficiently, to increase revenues, to perform greater service, and the like.

The problem that Joe Cox faces is a cyclical workload: His store is quite busy and profitable during the hot summer months when home pools are heavily used. But during the winter months, his business is extremely light— he sells only enough pool chemicals for homeowners to maintain their

— COMMUNICATION **S I D E L I G H T** —

CHOOSING A REPORT TOPIC

In business, of course, the needs of the organization will determine the topics of your research reports. As a student, however, you might be given the option of selecting your own report topic. Some students find this one of the most difficult parts of the report assignment. Using the following three criteria will get you off to a good start.

The Problem Must Be of Interest

Conducting a formal report project requires a bit of effort. You'll spend a great deal of time gathering and analyzing data and writing the final report. Thus, you should select a topic that will hold your interest throughout the process. Curiosity is a powerful motivator.

Although you should be curious about the topic, you should not have such a biased interest that it would be difficult for you to accept the outcome if it contradicts your preconceived ideas. You must be able to approach the topic with an open mind—with no axes to grind. But that doesn't mean that you should have no clues as to what the outcome will be. Indeed, a fundamental part of the report process is to pose hypotheses—hunches about possible causes or solutions, so that you will then know what data to collect.

The Topic Must Be Circumscribed

The topic you select must be limited enough to be feasible—in time, money, expertise of the researcher, and availability of valid data. Because a research paper is often relatively long, students sometimes have a tendency to select a big topic. And it is true that the broader the topic you select, the easier it is to find data on that topic. However, the criterion of a good research

paper is whether or not the writer answers completely and accurately the problem statement that was posed. Within the time and length constraints of typical college papers, you would not be able to provide a thorough answer to a broad problem statement.

In addition, data are not available to explore some topics—at least not without extraordinary efforts and expertise. For example, it takes experienced and trained researchers to elicit from people honest responses to controversial questions. Whether a given topic is too technical or too difficult depends on your education and experience and on the amount of time you have available to devote to the project.

Topics that are too controversial pose two problems. First, it is often difficult to locate valid and reliable information because the sources may be strongly biased. Second, you yourself may feel so strongly about the topic that it will be difficult for you to write about it with an open mind.

The Problem Must Possess a Degree of Originality

Your study should expand your (and your reader's) horizons; that is, it should contribute new knowledge, not just repeat the already known. You do not need to reinvent the wheel. You want your study to provide new insights into the topic—both for yourself and for your reader.

Findings based on primary data are original because the data was gathered specifically for the paper. If your paper is based exclusively on secondary data, be sure to synthesize and integrate (not just summarize) the findings from all your sources. Ensure that the whole is greater than the sum of its parts.

---

unused pools. Joe is looking for a way to even out his workload and asks his assistant store manager, Martha Halpern, to research the problem and write a report recommending a course of action.

2. Define the Purpose of the Report.

At the outset you need to determine why you are writing the report, what the report is supposed to accomplish, and what will be the outcome. To help you develop a realistic statement of the problem or purpose of your study, make sure that you understand the full dimensions of the assignment:

Identify what you hope to accomplish with your report.

- Why is this issue important?
- How much detail is requested?
- What are the time and resource constraints?
- What use will be made of the report?

You will remember that the three major purposes of business reports are to inform, to analyze, or to recommend. In our example, Joe will use Martha's report to help resolve the problem of uneven workload at Just Pool Supplies. That, then, is the purpose of her study.

3. Define the Audience for the Report.

Identify the needs of your report readers.

The audience for a report—the reader or readers—is typically very homogeneous. Many times, of course, the audience is one person; but even when it is not, the audience usually consists of people with similar levels of expertise, background knowledge, and the like. Thus, you can, and should, develop your report to take into account the needs of your reader. In doing so, you will need to consider the following elements.

Internal Versus External

Internal reports are written for readers within the organization and are usually less formal than external reports, where the reader might be a customer, potential customer, or government agency. Internal reports also typically require less background information and can safely use more technical vocabulary than external reports, which are often more sensitive to public relations.

Internal reports are also directional, aimed either at the writer's superiors, peers, or subordinates. The strategy used must be appropriate for the audience's position. For example, reports usually have a costs-and-profits tone when directed to superiors, a conversational tone when directed to peers, and an emphatic tone when directed to subordinates.

Authorized Versus Voluntary   Authorized reports are written at the specific request of some higher authority. Thus the reader has some inherent interest in the report. Voluntary reports, on the other hand, are prepared on the writer's own initiative. Therefore, the reader needs more background information and frequently more persuasive evidence than do readers of authorized reports.

Authorized reports may be either periodic or special. Periodic reports are submitted on a recurring, systematic basis. Very often they are form reports, with space provided for specific items of information. Readers of periodic reports need little introductory or background information because of the report's recurring nature. Readers of special one-time reports, on the other hand, need more explanatory material because of the uniqueness of the report.

Level of Knowledge and Interest   Is the reader already familiar with the topic? Will he or she understand the terms used, or will the terms need to be defined? If you have a heterogeneous audience for your report, striking an appropriate balance in level of detail given will require careful planning.

As stated earlier, most reports are written in the direct pattern, with the major conclusions and recommendations given up front. This is especially true when you know the reader is interested in your project or will likely agree with your conclusions and recommendations. Reports that make a recommendation with which the reader may disagree are often written in the indirect pattern because you want the reader to study the reasons for the recommendation first. The reader will be more likely to believe the recommendation is reasonable if he or she has first had an opportunity to study the rationale.

In our Just Pool Supplies situation, the reader of Martha's report will be Joe Cox, the owner and operator of the store. This will be an internal authorized report, and the reader has a high level of interest in and a high level of knowledge about the subject.

4. Develop Hypotheses Regarding Causes or Solutions for the Problem.

A **hypothesis** is a tentative explanation that can be tested by further investigation. Sometimes a hypothesis involves no more than a hunch or guess about what factors might be causing a problem, what the possible solutions might be, or what the best course of action would be.

> Identify possible causes and solutions to the problem.

The more the writer knows about the topic, the better able he or she will be to develop realistic hypotheses. Thus, sometimes preliminary research is necessary. Before forming a hypothesis, the writer may need to talk with people knowledgeable about the problem, study company records, and perhaps read industry reports or journal articles on the topic.

It is important to develop logical hypotheses because these hypotheses determine what types of data will be collected and analyzed. If your hunches turn out to be incorrect, not only will you have wasted much time and effort but your problem will remain unsolved. Taking the time at this stage to think through the problem and generate possible causes or solutions will help ensure an efficient and successful report.

After doing some preliminary research, Martha Halpern hypothesizes that Joe's problem might be solved by expanding into spa (hot tub) supplies. The store could then concentrate on selling pool supplies in the summer and on selling spa supplies in the winter.

After consulting with Joe Cox, Martha decides that the question she will seek to answer in her report (that is, her problem statement) is this: What is the feasibility of Just Pool Supplies' expanding into the spa-supply business?

Notice how this step has narrowed the focus of the report project. She has now ruled out, for example, trying to develop more business from firms with in-house pools (such as hotels, resorts, and health clubs) that keep their pools open year-round. Nor will she explore expanding into product lines other than spa supplies. If, in reality, one of these solutions would have been a better solution than her proposed solution, she will never know without doing further research and writing another report.

Note also that the problem statement (which is often developed as part of the purpose in Step 2) is stated in neutral form. It does not imply any bias on the part of the writer. A problem statement such as "to show why Just Pool Supplies should expand into the spa-supply business" might bring the writer's credibility into question.

5. Determine What Data Will Be Required.

Having developed some ideas about the causes or solutions for the problem, you now need to determine what data is needed to test your ideas. This step depends directly on your hypotheses, and all later steps in the report process depend on this step. Sometimes the data needed will be in your

> Divide the problem into logical components in order to determine what information is needed.

mind or in documents you already have at hand, sometimes it will be in documents located elsewhere, and sometimes the data is not available at all but must be generated by you.

To determine what data is needed, you should **factor** the problem statement; that is, you break it down into its component parts. Most often, it is easiest to state subproblems as questions. The answers to these subproblems will ultimately provide the answer to the general problem statement.

In our example, Martha decides she needs information that will answer the following questions:

1. What has been the experience of other stores that have sold both pool and spa supplies?
2. Does Just Pool Supplies have the space, expertise, and working capital to expand into the spa-supply business?
3. Are there a sufficient number of potential customers to make the expansion profitable?

6. Decide Which Methods to Use to Collect the Needed Data.

You may use secondary data collected by others or primary data that you collect yourself.

Research and report writing are a cost, just like any other corporate expense. Thus, you should use data-collection methods that will provide the needed data with the least expenditure of time and money at a level of completeness, accuracy, and precision needed to solve your problem. In other words, there is a break-even point to data collection. You do not want to provide a $100 answer to a $5 question, but neither do you want to provide a $5 answer to a $100 question.

The two major types of data you will collect are secondary and primary data. You should choose the type that will solve your problem most efficiently.

Secondary data is collected by someone else for some other purpose; it may be published or unpublished. Published data includes journal, magazine, and newspaper articles; books; brochures and pamphlets; technical reports; and any other material that is widely disseminated.   Unpublished secondary data includes company records (such as financial records, personnel data, and previous correspondence and reports), legal documents (such as court records, regulatory hearings, and legislative acts), personal records (such as diaries, receipts, and checkbook registers), and medical records.

Primary data is collected by the researcher to solve the specific problem at hand. Because you are collecting the data yourself, you have more control over its accuracy, completeness, objectivity, and relevance. The three main types of primary data collection are through surveys (questionnaires and interviews), observation, and experimentation. These three methods are discussed in Chapter 11.

Martha will need to collect both primary and secondary data to answer the three subproblems she posed in Step 5:

1. What has been the experience of other stores? Most likely, Martha will use published secondary data to answer this question. For example, the magazine *Pool and Spa News* would likely contain news items and features that might answer this question. Martha would probably not

use a questionnaire or interview to question other store owners directly because they might be reluctant to provide such information to a possible competitor.

2. Does Just Pool Supplies have the space, expertise, and working capital? Here, Martha will probably use both secondary data and primary data. For example, she might study the store layout and dimensions (observation) to evaluate space; question store employees (interview) to evaluate expertise; and peruse company financial records (unpublished secondary data) to evaluate working capital requirements.

3. Are there enough potential customers? Here again, both primary and secondary data might be used. It is likely that secondary data in the form of government census records or local business studies available from the Chamber of Commerce or from a local university would show the number of households with pools and spas and also the extent of the competition. Also, a survey of Just Pool Supplies' present customers would indicate how many of them would also be likely spa customers.

7. Collect the Data.

Before beginning to collect the needed data, you should know exactly what data you need. Otherwise, you will find yourself backtracking, having to reread secondary sources because you failed to glean all the necessary information, or having to call back interviewees to ask additional questions.

Gathering more data than is needed—either too much relevant data or any irrelevant data—wastes time and resources. Yet gathering insufficient data will likely result in faulty decisions. Do not make the common mistake of not allowing enough time for data collection. Because the end result of your efforts (indeed, the only visible product of your labors) is the final written report, many writers want to begin writing as soon as possible. They soon find, unfortunately, that they have nothing of substance to say unless they've done the necessary background work.

Because of the important role that data collection plays in the reporting process, Chapter 11 explores this topic in greater detail.

> Collect the needed data as efficiently as possible and interpret it for the reader.

8. Analyze the Data.

Your raw data might be in the form of handwritten notes, copies of various documents, completed questionnaires, tapes of interviews, or computer printouts, as well as mental observations you've made up to this point. You must now begin to make sense of it.

First, you must compile your data in a systematic and logical form. At least initially, you should organize the data according to the subproblems you identified in Step 5. This first step toward analysis might mean, for example, that some information from a journal article or interview should be placed in one pile, so to speak, and other information from the same article or interview placed in another pile.

Once you've compiled your data this way, the true analysis and interpretation begin. Some of your **findings** (data that has been collected and analyzed) will be obvious immediately; others will not become apparent until you've studied the data in more detail and begin to see trends, contradictions, items for additional exploration, and the like. Some findings will likely support your preexisting opinions, others may contradict them, still others you may not know how to interpret. Techniques of analysis are discussed in Chapter 12.

The important point is that you should let the data be the basis for any conclusions you draw. You want to analyze and present your data so that the truth, the whole truth, and nothing but the truth emerges. If your findings do not support any of your original hypotheses, you may need to begin the entire process anew.

9. Write the Report.

The written report is the only evidence the reader has of the work you've done.

The writing step includes the component steps of drafting, revising, formatting, and proofreading. Your final report must be clearly written, complete, scholarly, objective, and credible. The organization, length, formality, format, and complexity of the report will depend on the nature of the problem you investigated and the needs of the readers. You must provide enough information to give the reader a full understanding and appreciation of the procedures followed and of the findings presented.

In a sense, the final report is only the tip of the iceberg. However, it is a very visible tip—in fact the only visible part of the entire report process. All the steps you've taken thus far lead to this one step, so you will want to bring all your writing skills to bear in making the report as clear and as useful to the reader as possible. You will typically write a first draft, revise the draft, arrange the report in an acceptable format, and finally proofread the final report before submitting it. These steps are discussed in more detail in Chapter 13.

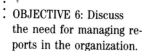

OBJECTIVE 6: Discuss the need for managing reports in the organization.

MANAGING REPORTS

Throughout this chapter, a strong case has been made for the increasingly important role that business reports play in the successful management of the contemporary organization. However, too much of a good thing is a bad thing. Without proper management, reports, especially computer printouts, can become a nuisance and contribute to information overload.

With the increasing availability of data and the ease with which that data can be manipulated, managers sometimes tend to generate every type of report possible and then submit them all to higher-level management. These managers seem to devote more attention to generating reports than to analyzing their contents.

Thus, someone in the organization—preferably someone in higher management—should be assigned the task of controlling reports. Periodically (typically annually) an inventory should be made of all recurring reports, and the continuing usefulness of each report should be determined. Some reports may be eliminated altogether, some may be modified, others merged, and, where justified, new reports authorized.

This review process will ensure that business reports continue to serve management rather than vice versa. With or without such controls,

The Reporting Process

Planning

1. Become aware that a problem exists.
   a. Explore details with your superior if the report is authorized.
   b. Study problems or opportunities if the report is voluntary.

2. Define the purpose of the report.
   a. Determine why the issue is important; what use will be made of the report; and what the time, resource, and length constraints are.
   b. Decide whether the purpose is to inform, analyze, or recommend.
   c. Using neutral language, construct a one-sentence problem statement, perhaps in question form.

3. Define the audience for the report.
   a. Is the report for an internal or external reader?
   b. Did the reader authorize the report or is it voluntary?
   c. What is the level of knowledge and interest of the reader?

4. Develop hypotheses regarding causes or solutions for the problem.
   a. Conduct preliminary research if necessary.
   b. Generate a list of possible causes or solutions.

Data Gathering

5. Determine what data will be required.
   a. Factor the problem statement into its component parts, perhaps stating each subproblem as a question.
   b. Determine what data will be needed to answer each subproblem.

6. Decide which methods to use to collect the needed data.
   a. Ensure that any secondary data used is current, accurate, complete, free from author bias and misinterpretation, and relevant.
   b. If secondary data is not available, generate primary data through survey, observation, or experimentation.
   c. Obtain the needed data as efficiently as possible.

7. Collect the data.
   a. Ensure that all informational needs have been identified.
   b. Allot sufficient time to gather the needed data.

Report Writing

8. Analyze the data.
   a. Compile the data in a systematic and logical form, organizing it according to the subproblems.
   b. Analyze each bit of data individually at first and then in conjunction with each other bit of data. Finally, look at all the data together to try to discern trends, contradictions, unexpected findings, areas for further investigation, and the like.

9. Write the report.
   a. Consider the needs of the reader and the nature of the problem in determining the organization, length, formality, and format of the report.
   b. Make sure the report is clearly written, complete, scholarly, objective, and credible.

---

individual managers should ensure that the reports they write serve some actual purpose, stick to that purpose, and avoid including extraneous computer data just because it's easily available.

SUMMARY

Reading and writing reports are a typical part of nearly every manager's duties. The most common types of reports are routine management reports, policies and procedures, compliance reports, proposals, progress reports, and situational reports. The purpose of each type of report may be either to inform, to analyze, or to recommend.

Although reports vary widely in length, complexity, formality, and format, most are requested by higher-level management, and many are collaborative efforts. Accuracy is the most important trait of all reports, and the quality of the process affects the quality of the final product.

Planning a report requires becoming aware that a problem exists, defining the purpose and the intended audience, and developing hypotheses regarding causes or solutions for the problem. Data gathering requires identifying what data will be needed, determining how to collect the data, and then actually collecting the data. Report writing requires that the raw data be analyzed and a final report written to bring out the full meaning of the data.

Because reports can become a drain on the organization's resources if they are not controlled, management should periodically inventory and review all reports to ensure that only needed reports are being generated and that they contain the information to help solve problems and make decisions.

KEY TERMS

Factoring— Breaking the problem of a report down into its component subparts; dividing the problem statement into subproblems.

Findings— Data that has been collected and analyzed.

Hypothesis— A tentative explanation that can be tested by further investigation.

Primary data— Data that is collected by the researcher to solve the specific problem at hand.

Secondary data— Data that is collected by someone else for some other purpose.

REVIEW AND DISCUSSION

1. Why do business reports play such an important role in the contemporary organization?   OBJECTIVE 1 ◀
2. Define and give an example of each of the six types of common business reports.   OBJECTIVE 2 ◀
3. What is meant by the statement, "There is no such document as a standard report"?   OBJECTIVE 3 ◀
4. What is meant by the statement, "Writing a report involves much more than writing a report"?   OBJECTIVE 3 ◀
5. What are the advantages of collaboratively written reports?   OBJECTIVE 3 ◀
6. Give four guidelines for achieving accuracy in a report.   OBJECTIVE 3 ◀
7. What is the difference between an informational, analytical, and recommendation report?   OBJECTIVE
8. In what ways do internal and external reports differ? Authorized and voluntary?   OBJECTIVE 5 ◀
9. Assume you wish to determine whether your clerical staff would be more productive if you switched from electronic typewriters to microcomputers with word processing software. Write a hypothesis for this problem and break it into subproblems.   OBJECTIVE 5 ◀
10. List two types of secondary data, and give an example of each.   OBJECTIVE 5 ◀
11. List three types of primary data, and give an example of each.   OBJECTIVE 5 ◀
12. Why should reports be controlled?   OBJECTIVE 6 ◀

EXERCISES

1. **Small Business: Reporting Needs**—Interview the owner-operator of a small business in your area—someone with 10–50 employees. Determine the extent and types of reports written and received by employees in this firm. Write a memo report to your instructor summarizing your findings.   OBJECTIVES 1–2 ◀

2. **Collaborative Writing: Common Report Types**—Six types of business reports were identified in this chapter. Working in groups of three to five students, obtain a sample of at least three of these report types, perhaps from someone at the university or where you work. Analyze these reports based on such factors as the following: OBJECTIVES 1–4 ◀

   a. Purpose (to inform, analyze, or recommend)
   b. Target audience
   c. Length, format, and degree of formality
   d. Clarity, completeness, and accuracy of the information
   e. Authorship (individual or collaborative)

   Write a two-page memo report to your instructor summarizing your findings.

3. **Planning a Report: Data Collection**—Given the following problem statement and subproblems, develop a data-collection plan that will collect the needed data to answer each subproblem. Identify specifically what data needs to be collected and how it will be collected.   OBJECTIVE 5 ◀

   Problem statement: How effective would an eight-hour course on letter writing be for mid-level executives at Best Western Hotels?

Subproblems:

a. To what extent do mid-level executives at Best Western need to know how to write effective business letters?

b. What are the letter-writing skills of mid-level executives at Best Western at the present time?

c. What should be included in a letter-writing seminar?

d. What improvement, if any, in letter-writing skills would result from attending a letter-writing seminar.

▶ OBJECTIVE 5

4. **Planning a Report: Evaluating Business Communication Textbooks—** You have been assigned the task of evaluating five business communication textbooks for possible use at your institution. You are to review each book, evaluate its appropriateness for your institution, and write a report recommending a specific text.

Write a problem statement, and then divide the statement into its component subproblems. Use a question format for each. (See Exercise 3 for an example.)

▶ OBJECTIVE 5

5. **Audience Analysis: Curriculum—**The provost (or academic vice president) of your institution has asked you, as president of the leading business honorary society on campus, to write a report evaluating the advantages and disadvantages of adding another required English course to the curriculum for all students.

Write out what you know (or can learn) about the provost that will help make your report more effective. Include such considerations as internal versus external audience, authorized versus voluntary report, and level of knowledge and interest of reader. Discuss specifically how each item of information will be used in your decisions about content, format, organization, and the like.

▶ OBJECTIVE 6

6. **Large Business: Report Management—**Interview the records manager at a large business in your area (personally or by phone). Determine what policies the organization has to control reports, especially recurring reports, in terms of need, frequency, length, readers, and the like. Write a memo to your instructor summarizing your findings.

C A S E P R O B L E M

Reporting for Duty

▶ OBJECTIVE 5

Arnie McNally was catching up on some of his professional reading when he came across the following paragraph in an article entitled "The Benefits of Good Lighting":

> Errors erode productivity because additional time and energy must be spent to redo what should have been done properly the first time. But that cost is minor compared to the expense that can result when an error is not detected: soured customer relations, damaged image, and even lawsuits. Better lighting can help minimize errors while also improving the effectiveness of quality control. In some instances, just a small investment in better lighting can save hundreds of thousands of dollars annually.*

It occurred to Arnie that data-entry operators, who spend up to eight hours a day inputting data into computer terminals, might especially benefit from adequate lighting—specifically from the installation of Ultra Light task lighting. If he could produce some actual data showing that data-entry operators make fewer errors when using Ultra Light than when using conventional fluorescent or incandescent light, this information just might give Urban Systems the advantage it needed to crack a very lucrative market.

He called Mary Lyons into his office, showed her the article, and asked her to write him a memo outlining how this study might be conducted. Eventually, he wants Mary to supervise the study and write up the final report presenting the results of the study.

1. Assume the role of Mary Lyons. What questions would you ask Arnie in order to understand the assignment better?
2. For the final report that you will write later, will there be a primary audience as well as a secondary audience? Explain.
3. What do you know about the reader(s) of your ultimate report that will help you in planning this study and writing the report? (See Exercise 5 for factors to consider.)
4. Write the planning memo to Arnie. Organize your memo as follows:
   a. *Introduction:* Explain the purpose of the memo and why the study needs to be done.
   b. *Purpose of the study:* Include the problem statement and subproblems.
   c. *Procedures:* Identify what data should be collected to answer each subproblem and how it will be collected.
   d. *Closing:* State when the study can be conducted and provide an estimate of the resources needed.

* Office Lighting and Productivity (Washington, DC: National Lighting Bureau, 1988), p. 3.

With its 23,000 workers, the Pentagon is a hothouse for jargon and acronyms. Here are some examples, along with their meanings:*   **W O R D W I S E**

▪ *Analysis paralysis:* result of excessive study
▪ *BFO:* blazing flash of the obvious
▪ *Face time:* time spent near the boss in an attempt to impress
▪ *Fudge Factory* (also *Fort Fumble*): the Pentagon itself
▪ *Mushroom treatment:* being kept in the dark and fed on manure

* "Just Call It 'Brass-Speak,' " *USA Today*, May 23, 1989, p. 4A.

Collecting the Data

Communication Objectives

After you have finished this chapter, you will be able to

1. Evaluate the quality of secondary data.

2. Develop an efficient search strategy.

3. Use print indexes and directories efficiently.

4. Take notes in an efficient, accurate, and helpful manner.

5. Collect secondary data via computer searching.

6. Develop an effective questionnaire.

7. Construct an appropriate cover letter to accompany a questionnaire.

8. Select an appropriate sample for a survey.

9. Conduct a data-gathering interview.

10. Discuss the appropriate use of observation, telephone inquiries, and experimentation.

Mary Hall oversees research at the New York-based advertising agency, Della Femina McNamee. Her research helps determine who is likely to buy a product, what kind of advertising will sell it, and whether or not the advertising has been effective. Therefore, when Mary Hall sees an advertisement on television that appeals to her, she knows that before the commercial appeared on the air, someone did a lot of research and collected a lot of data to persuade her—and other women like her—to buy the product.

Hall, who has seventeen years of marketing experience, noted the first step in creating advertising is to research the product category, "so that you're very well educated about what's going on, what the product's about, what the trends are, what the regulatory situation is, and what the advertising history is." It's important, she added, "to understand what marketers in that category have been through already, what they're familiar with and not familiar with."

Say, for example, the agency has been asked to sell a new cookie. Hall's staff would use several on-line databases, which can retrieve major newspaper and magazine articles about virtually anything, including cookies and the companies that make them. The information will tell the agency what types of advertising campaigns have worked with what kinds of cookies in the past and

Mary Hall, Senior Vice
President, Director of
Research
Della Femina McNamee,
New York, New York

which have failed. In addition to on-line database services, the agency can also rely on its physical library that includes periodicals and books.

But, Hall cautioned, researching a product category is "really an imperfect science. And [the information] is best used in a relative way." In other words, the information she gathers is a tool that helps shape a campaign—not an answer to what will *absolutely* work or fail. Moreover, common sense should not be overlooked when it comes to advertising: For instance, it probably would not be a good idea to run perfume commercials during a football game.

Once a product's history is understood, Hall indicated, "You need to discover who your target audience is. You want to know what the various segments of the target are." If the product is not new to the market, but a new account for the agency, Hall needs to find out if people "use it and like it, or use it occasionally, or if they have used it and rejected it, or if they've ever heard of it at all, or if they've heard of it and haven't tried it."

But that, she said speaking quickly, is still just the beginning: "Then you need to know the demographic characteristics of [each of] these groups." To gather this information, questionnaires are developed and given to focus groups. One basic rule of questionnaires, Hall said, is that they begin with the general and end with the specific, which helps the advertiser determine who is likely to buy a product. The questionnaires are designed to teach the agency about a person's lifestyle, the products they use, and whether they're likely to spend money in a given category. "You need that to design any kind of primary research, to make it pertinent and relevant, and also to make it efficient, because you may decide that some of those segments aren't going to be useful, and you don't want to waste time and money selling to people who are least likely to buy a product."

When you break it all down, Hall indicated, the most important part of her research is based on one question: "Who am I going to talk to? But," she added, " 'who am I going to talk to' has all of those things to think about." ▼

318

Workers at Wisconsin-based Larsen's research lab (shown
here) prepare primary data from a comparative product
test. Secondary data will be then created from Larsen's
results. Both types of data collection are important sources
for business reports.
(Source: Dean Foods Company)

THE DATA-COLLECTION PHASE

As noted in Chapter 10, collecting the data is by no means the first step in
the reporting process. Before collecting any data, you must define the report
purpose and audience, determine possible causes or solutions, and factor
the problem into subproblems to determine what data is needed and how
to collect it. Only then are you ready to begin collecting the data (Step 7
of the nine-step process).

As discussed earlier, primary data is collected by the researcher to solve
the specific problem at hand, whereas secondary data is collected by
someone else for some other purpose. Although both types of data are
important sources for business reports, we usually start our data collection
by reviewing the data that is already available. Not all report assignments
require collecting new (primary) data, but it would be unusual to write a
report that did not use some type of secondary data.

Studying what is already known about a topic and what remains to be
learned makes the reporting process more efficient because the report writer
can then concentrate scarce resources on generating new information rather
than rediscovering existing information. Also, studying secondary data can
provide sources for additional information, suggest methods of primary
research, or give clues for questionnaire items—that is, provide guidance
for primary research.

For these reasons, this discussion of data collection begins with secondary sources.

> Nearly all reporting tasks
> use secondary data.

COLLECTING SECONDARY DATA

Secondary data includes traditional books and journal* articles as well as government reports, industry studies, company records, and the like. Such data is sometimes a substitute for and sometimes a supplement to primary data.

Secondary and primary data are of equal importance.

Secondary data is neither better than nor worse than primary data; it's simply different. The source of the data is not as important as the data's quality and relevance for your particular purpose. The major advantages of using secondary data are economic: using secondary data is less costly and less time consuming than collecting primary data. The disadvantages relate not only to the availability of sufficient secondary data but also to the quality of the data that is available. No data should be used without first evaluating its appropriateness for the intended purpose.

Evaluating Secondary Data

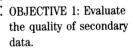

OBJECTIVE 1: Evaluate the quality of secondary data.

By definition, secondary data was gathered for some purpose other than your own. Therefore, the categories used, the population sampled, and the analyses reported might not be appropriate for your own use. Ask yourself the following five questions about any secondary sources you're contemplating incorporating into your report.

What Was the Purpose of the Study? If the study was undertaken to genuinely find the answer to a question or problem, you can have more confidence about the accuracy and objectivity of the results than if, for example, the study was undertaken merely to prove a point. People seeking honest answers to honest questions are more likely to select their samples carefully, to ask clear and unbiased questions, and to analyze the data appropriately.

Be wary of secondary data if the researcher had a vested interest in the outcome of the study. For example, you would probably have more faith in a study that extols the merits of the Hubbard automobile if that study were conducted by *Consumer Reports* than if it were conducted by the makers of Hubbard automobiles.

How Was the Data Collected? Were appropriate procedures used? Although you may not be an experienced researcher yourself, your reading of secondary data (including this chapter of your textbook) will likely alert you to certain standard research procedures that should be followed. For example, common sense tells you that if you are interested in learning the

---

* A journal is a scholarly periodical typically published by a professional association or university; its articles, which are written by professionals (usually university professors or professional researchers), are accepted for publication only after being reviewed by other professionals; and it contains few, if any, advertisements. A magazine, on the other hand, is a general-interest publication typically published by a commercial organization, its articles are written by staff members, and it contains many advertisements. Thus, the *Journal of Marketing* is a journal, and *Business Week* is a magazine. Journals are generally considered to be more reliable sources of data, although numerous magazines also contain much useful information, especially for business research. Although the distinction between journals and magazines is useful in evaluating secondary sources, the two terms are used interchangeably in this chapter to refer to any periodical publication.

reactions of all factory workers in your organization to a particular proposal, you would not gather data from just the newly hired workers. Likewise, if a questionnaire were sent to all the factory workers and only 10% responded, you would probably not be able to conclude that the opinions of these respondents represent the views of all the workers.

How Was the Data Analyzed?   As we shall see in Chapter 12, different types of data lend themselves to different types of analyses. Survey data, for example, is analyzed differently from experimental data. Sometimes the low number of responses to a particular question or ambiguity in the question itself prevent us from drawing any valid conclusions.

In some situations, even though the analysis was appropriate for the original study, it may not be appropriate for your purposes. For example, suppose you are interested in the reactions of teenagers and the secondary data used the category "under 21 years of age." You would not know whether the responses came mostly from those younger than 13 years old, those 13 to 19 years old (your target group), or those older than 19 years old.

How Consistent Is the Data with That from Other Studies?   When you find the same general conclusions in several independent sources, you can have greater confidence in the data. On the other hand, if five studies of a particular topic reached one conclusion and a sixth study reached an opposite conclusion, you would need to scrutinize the sixth study carefully before accepting its findings.

> Generally, the more consensus you find in secondary data, the more trustworthy the data.

Avoid accepting something as true simply because you read it someplace. Because the reader of your report will be making decisions based on the data you present, take care that the data in your report is accurate.

How Old Is the Data?   Data that was true at the time it was collected might not be true today. A job satisfaction study completed at your organization last year may have yielded accurate data then. But if in the meantime your organization has merged with another company, moved its headquarters, or been torn by a strike, the job-satisfaction data may have no relevance today. Yet some data may still be accurate years after its collection. For example, a study of the origins of the labor movement in the United States may have almost permanent relevance.

Your data must pass these five tests, whether it comes from company records or published sources. Data that fails even one of these tests should probably be discarded and not used in your report. At the very least, such data requires extra scrutiny and perhaps extra explanation in the report itself if it is used.

Planning the Search Strategy

In the business world, much of the data you use in your reports will come from company records—financial records, personnel data, correspondence, reports, and the like.

Increasingly, however, business decisions are affected by factors outside the organization for which internal data may not be sufficient. Government regulation, the international business climate, technological developments,

> OBJECTIVE 2: Develop an efficient search strategy.

and other factors often affect organizational decisions. Because these factors change so rapidly, the smart report writer will ensure that his or her report sources are comprehensive and up to date.

Consider the negative consequences, for example, of recommending that your firm market a certain product when, in fact, the government has just banned the manufacture of that product or has banned trade with the only country that makes a key component of the product. Only a thorough search for the relevant secondary data would reveal such information.

Your search for published secondary data may take place at your company library or at a city or university library using traditional print resources, or it may take place at your own desk using a computer. Wherever it takes place, you will save yourself time and get better results if you spend some time planning what to look for.

Develop a List of Key Terms   Begin your search for secondary data by developing a list of key terms by which you will search the directories and indexes for secondary sources. At this stage of your search, your list of key terms should be long and quite general. Don't just select the obvious terms; try to think of related topics that might be of interest to you. As you continue your search, undoubtedly other terms will come to mind.

Consult Directories and Indexes   Begin your search with the major directories and indexes for business, government, education, and the like. Each of these sources contains an alphabetized list of subject headings, which you will search using your list of key terms.

Under each subject heading are one or more **citations** (references to relevant books, journal articles, newspaper articles, or similar sources). A citation for a book identifies the author or editor, book title, name and location of the publisher, and the year of publication. A citation for a journal article identifies the author, title of the article, title of the journal, and volume, date, and page numbers of the specific issue in which the article appeared.

If your topic relates primarily to business, the *Business Periodicals Index* is a good starting point; if it relates primarily to education, try the *Education Index*. And for any topic, the *Monthly Catalog* is the basic source for locating data compiled by the federal government.

Some report writers neglect searching for government data, perhaps because government data is typically not cataloged like other books or periodicals and they are not sure how to locate government sources. This neglect is a serious mistake because the U.S. government is the world's largest collector of information, and the quality of the data it gathers is excellent.

Be sure to check the card catalog (or its equivalent). Someone somewhere has probably written a book that is directly or indirectly related to your topic. Whereas journal articles often contain ·the most current statistics, books and monographs often provide more detailed background information and sources of additional information.

The terms you use to identify your topic might not be the ones used by the indexes and directories you use to locate source documents. If you cannot locate any citations using your term, try a related term or synonym. Some indexes come with a thesaurus that identifies the headings used in the index.

You locate secondary sources by using key terms, or subject headings.

▼
OBJECTIVE 3: Use print indexes and directories efficiently.

Do not neglect government sources in your search for secondary data.

If you're having trouble locating sources, you may be using inappropriate headings.

Because so many library collections and all government documents use the Library of Congress classifications, start by using the terms identified in the reference work *Library of Congress Subject Headings* (or *LCSH*). Suppose, for example, that you've been asked to write a report on the feasibility of opening a frozen yogurt store in Provo, Utah. If you look under the subject heading "yogurt" in the *LCSH*, you find the following:

> Yogurt, Frozen
>   Use Frozen Yogurt

The notation "use" (also called "see" in some indexes) tells you that this topic is cataloged under "Frozen" instead of under "Yogurt." If you look up "Frozen Yogurt" in the *LCSH*, you find the following:

> Frozen Yogurt
>   UF Yogurt, Frozen
>   BT Frozen Desserts
>   Yogurt

The "UF" stands for "used for" and tells you that you are now looking under the correct heading. "BT" stands for "broader term" and tells you that if you wish to expand your search, you might use the headings "Frozen Desserts" or "Yogurt." Other *LCSH* abbreviations are "NT—narrower term" (to narrow your search) and "RT—related term" (to broaden your search). A "see" notation tells you that you're looking under the wrong heading, and a "see also" notation leads to additional related topics.

If you were to look up "Frozen Yogurt" in one of the editions of *Business Periodicals Index,* you would find the following citations:

> **Frozen yogurt**
>   *See also*
>   Frozen yogurt stores
> Market segment report: premium ice cream. J. W. Kochak. graphs il tabs *Restaur Bus* 86:241–2 + Jl 1 '87
> A yogurt named Zack's [S. Holt and H. Watts] D. Marth. pors *Nations Bus* 75:52 Ag '87
>
> **Frozen yogurt stores**
>   *See also*
>   Penguin's Place Frozen Yogurt
>   Zack's Famous Frozen Yogurt, Inc.
>   **Chain and franchise operations**
>   The frozen yogurt race is red-hot. T. Carson. il tab *Bus Week* p67 Mr 7 '88

Immediately, you have identified three additional headings to search— the three "see also" headings given. You can also see that the first article listed, "Market Segment Report: Premium Ice Cream" by J. W. Kochak, is published in the July 1, 1987, issue of *Restaurant Business* and that it contains graphs, illustrations, and tables.

Other directories and indexes are read similarly. The front matter or appendix in each directory explains the meaning of any abbreviations used in the citations and provides additional information about the publications listed. (Don't just guess about the meaning of abbreviated titles—look them up!)

Most printed directories and indexes are compiled annually. Based on how fast changes occur in your subject area, you will have to decide how many years' worth of literature you need to search.

Evaluate your sources for their appropriateness for your specific purposes.

Compile and Review the Literature   Some report writers like to locate sources, scan them quickly to determine if they are relevant for their purposes, and, if so, photocopy the articles for later study. Other report writers prefer to make their notes immediately (see the following section). Regardless of your work habits, once you've gathered your initial data you should review it with the following questions in mind:

1. How relevant is each source for your specific needs?
2. Does each source meet the five requirements discussed earlier?
3. Are there some areas for which you have not gathered sufficient data? If so, continue your data collection.
4. Are there bibliographies and reference lists included with any of the articles that provide leads for additional sources?

You may decide you need to expand your search by revising or adding to your list of key terms or by searching a few more years' worth of directories and indexes. If you have trouble locating sources, the *Encyclopedia of Business Information Sources* is an excellent reference for identifying sources of information on approximately 1,000 business topics. When necessary, consult a reference librarian.

If, after an exhaustive search, you have not been able to locate sufficient sources, you have several options. You can collect the data yourself through primary research; you can write the report using the sources that are available, ensuring that your conclusions are appropriate for the amount of data available; or you can consult with the person who requested the report for additional direction.

OBJECTIVE 4: Take notes in an efficient, accurate, and helpful manner.

TAKING NOTES

Once you've identified a relevant source, you're ready to take notes. If you're working from a photocopy, quickly read through the article, highlighting the information that is relevant for your purposes. Doing this will enable you to take notes efficiently.

The specific method for recording notes is a highly individual matter. Whether you record your notes on index cards or sheets of paper or whether you handwrite them or compose them at a keyboard is not important. The point that is important is that you must record notes somewhere. Do not stop with the preliminary step of highlighting relevant material on the photocopy.

Writing out your notes serves several purposes. First, the act of rereading the article and putting the information in your own words fixes the information more firmly in your mind, making the later task of writing the report easier. Secondly, it is much more efficient to work from your notes, which contain only information that is relevant to your needs, than to have to constantly scan an entire document, searching for what you need.

Write on one side of the paper only.

The traditional suggestion for note taking has been to use index cards, placing one major point on each card. The advantage of this system is that you can easily shuffle your cards to fit your final outline. However, the same flexibility can be achieved when using a full sheet of paper *if you write on one side of the paper only*. You can later cut each note and assemble the notes in whatever "piles" are appropriate.

On a computer, you can easily use a word processing program to arrange and rearrange your notes on the page or use an outlining software program to expand your notes into narrative copy and assemble the final report without having to retype the notes. Figure 11.1 shows a journal article with the relevant points underlined and examples of notes taken manually and on a computer.

Information to Include

Regardless of the format you use for taking notes, include the following information from each source:

Call Numbers   Recording library call numbers will save you time if you need to find the document again later.

Bibliographic Information   Record the complete bibliographic information—either on a separate bibliographic card or at the top of the sheet of paper if you're taking notes on paper. Record the information in the order and style you'll use in your bibliography so that you can later type your bibliography directly from these notes. (Chapter 13 discusses different methods for documenting your sources.) If you compile your references on separate index cards or sheets of paper, you can easily insert and delete sources and keep them in alphabetical order.

Source Numbers   It is not necessary to arrange your sources in alphabetical order, but you should number each source as you locate it. Then make sure that each note you take from that source is labeled with that number. That way, you avoid having to write out the complete citation on each note but can always identify the source of each note later.

Headings   Assign a topic heading to each note. If you've already scanned the entire article, you should be able to organize the important points into groups. Note, for example, in the computer notes shown in Figure 11.1 that even though the article itself does not contain any headings, the reader grouped the relevant information into three headings—"Overview of the Firm," "Competition," and "Miscellaneous."

Labeling each important topic lets you include more than one note on each card or section of your sheet of paper and makes compiling and analyzing of your data easier. Sometimes these headings will refer to one of the subproblems you identified when planning your report; other times, a more detailed heading will be appropriate.

Page Numbers   Unless the source document is only one page in length, record the page number for every note you take, whether the notes are in your own words or in the words of the original author. You will need the page numbers for each note later for documenting your sources.

FIGURE 11.1　　　　Taking Notes—Part A: Original Journal Article

from, Eric Schumuckler, *Forbes*, June 26, 1989, p. 133.

TCBY's frozen yogurt is low-fat, but its stock price could give you a heart attack.

A fatty stock

TO JUDGE FROM the action in TCBY Enterprises, the stock is getting a little ripe around the edges. Based in Little Rock, Ark, TCBY is the nation's largest chain of franchised frozen yogurt shops. (TCBY stands for The Country's Best Yogurt.) As Americans look for low-calorie, low-fat alternatives to ice cream, a lot in investors have jumped on the TCBY bandwagon. As a result, the chain's shares have shot up 150% this year. The recent price is 26 1/8 valuing the company at nearly $700 million. To put that figure in perspective, TCBY's shareholders' equity is $72 million, sales last year were $98 million, and profits were $20 million. So the stock sells at 7 times sales, almost 10 times book value and 35 times earnings. The yogurt may be low-fat, but the stock looks downright obese.

The stock, incidentally, trades on the New York—not Vancouver — Stock Exchange.

You have to hand it to Frank Hickingbotham, TCBY's 52-year old founder and chairman. He has performed something close to a miracle. A born salesman and former lay Baptist minister, Hickingbotham opened the first TCBY store in 1981, after selling a deep-dish pie business. Today he and his son Herren preside over more than 1,300 stores, all but 125 franchised. Systemwide sales last year were $210 million, with $300 million expected in 1989. Its largest competitor is I Can't Believe It's Yogurt, with 215 stores and a projected $58 million in 1989 systemwide sales. "We don't feel we've scratched the surface in developing this," says Hickingbotham.

But, as far as the stock market is concerned, Forbes would bet that TCBY has done more than scratch the surface; it has dug a hole for itself. The stock has gotten so rich that is growth falters even for a moment the market will likely seek revenge. In 1986 the company lost one-third of its market value in a single day. Today, the company is not as overvalued as it was then. Still, TCBY again looks like an accident waiting to happen.

Like a farmer expanding onto less productive soil, Hickingbothamwill have to work much harder for future growth. The yogurt market continues to expand. But TCBY's competitors are multiplying.

TCBY is strongest in the Southeast and Midwest; there are 75 TCBY stores in Chicago alone. In other regions, however, things aren't going as well.

In California, for example, the big name is Penguin's, with its snazzy black-and-white stores. Penguin's was acquired last summer by Bongrain, a multibillion-dollar French food outfit that also owns Columbo yogurt. Penguin's already has 125 stores and systemwide 1988 sales of $35 million. With the new Bongrain's backing, Penguin's is eyeing Florida, one of TCBY's biggest markets.

Another strong regional chain is Everything Yogurt, which has 220 stores and projects systemwide sales of $43 million this year. In the New York area, where TCBY has just 37 stores, Everthing Yogurt has 66. Meanwhile, hard-charging I Can't Believe It's Yogurt has ambitions to challangeTCBY nationwide, and is said to be about to announce a codevelopment plan with Blockbuster Video.

That isn't the end of people wanting a bite out of TCBY's

growth. The ice cream chains could become tough competition. Already, 1,000 of Baskin Robbins' franchises have gone so far as to add "& Yogurt" to their signs. Dairy Queen, with 5,000 franchised stores, is considering rolling out frozen yogurt nationwide.

There are other weaknesses in the TCBY story. The company grew by keeping the cost of opening a new TCBY store low. Even now, opening a new TCBY store costs about $140,000 depending on location, as compared with around $200,000 for the typical Everything Yogurt and Penguin's stores. To keep costs low, Hickingbotham often allows TCBY stores to open in areas with relatively light traffic. And the construction and design of a basic TCBY outlet looks chintzy compared with some other chains' stores. Sniffs competitor Stephen Beninati, presidnet of Everything Yogurt: "Those stores wouldn't survive ten years of heavy traffic."

In the past, much of TCBY's profits came from selling franchises. But now, the bulk of its business is selling yogurt to franchisees. TCBY's franchises pay about $7 a gallon for their yogurt, versus $5 a gallon for Penguin's franchises, according to one Penguin Franchisee. Should TCBY's franchises demand more favorable prices—a classic conflict in the franchising industry— TCBY's margins would suffer accordingly.

Woody Whyte, an analyst at Stephens Inc., thinks TCBY is still a good buy. The company, he says, is modeling itself after McDonald's in many key ways. But has anyone ever countered the number of fast-food franchise chains that flourished briefly, then died while trying to follow the McDonald's formula? ∎

Taking Notes—Part B: Taking Notes Manually **FIGURE 11.1**

Bibliography Card

> HF 5001. F6 ④
>
> E. Schumuckler. (1989, June 26).
> A fatty stock. *Forbes*, p. 133.

Note Card

> *Competition* ④
>
> 1- I Can't Believe It's Yogurt —
>   215 stores; $58 million sales (1989)
> 2- Everything Yogurt —
>   220 stores; $38 million sales (1989)
> 3- Penguins —
>   125 stores; $35 million sales (1988)
>
> Dairy Queen is considering adding yogurt.
>
> 1,000 Baskin-Robbins have added
> " & Yogurt " to their names.

FIGURE 11.1   Taking Notes—Part C: Taking Notes on a Computer

```
4.  HF 5001.56
    E. Schumuckler, (1989, June 26). A fatty
    stock. Forbes, p.133.

(4) Overview of Firm:
TCBY (The Country's Best Yogurt) is the largest
chain of franchised frozen yogurt stores, with
more than 1,300 stores. All but 125 are
franchised.
Net profit for the firm was $20 million in
1988, with systemwide sales of $210 million;
$300 million in sales are expected in 1989.
(Most of the profit is generated by sales of
yogurt to the franchises—not from sales of
franchises.)

(4) Competition:
Strongest competitor is I Can't Believe It's
Yogurt, with 125 stores and $58 million sales
in 1989.
Everything Yogurt has 220 stores and $43 million
sales in 1989.
Penguin's has 125 stores and $35 million sales
in 1988.
Dairy stores are also beginning to compete.
Dairy Queen is considering adding yogurt, and
1,000 Baskin-Robbins stores have added
"& Yogurt" to their signs.

(4) Miscellaneous:
Opening a new TCBY store costs $140,000—compared
to $200,000 for opening an Everything Yogurt or
Penguin's store.

(4) Note: Forbes believes the stock is over-
valued: "The yogurt may be low-fat, but the
stock looks downright obese." However, USA
Today (June 23, 1989, p.3B) recommends the
stock to investors
```

Paraphrases Versus Direct Quotations

Paraphrase most data;
use direct quotations
sparingly.

Paraphrase and quote appropriately. Avoid the temptation to become lazy and copy everything in the author's exact words. It is unlikely that the problem you're trying to solve and the problem discussed by the author mesh exactly. More than likely, you will need to takes bits and pieces of information from numerous sources and integrate them into a context appropriate for your own purposes.

Your notes can be of two types—paraphrases or direct quotations—and each should be readily identifiable in your notes. A **paraphrase** is a summary or restatement of a passage in your own words. Paraphrasing involves more than rearranging the words or leaving out a word or two. It requires, instead, that you understand the writer's idea and then restate it in your own language. Most of your notes should be paraphrases from the original document.

The second type of note is a **direct quotation**—the exact words of another. Use direct quotations only for definitions or for text that is so precise, clear, or otherwise noteworthy that it cannot be improved on. Enclose all direct quotations in quotation marks in your notes. Check immediately that you've written the quotation down accurately and completely, with the appropriate page number(s).

With either paraphrased or directly quoted notes, you may add a personal comment—a note that you make to yourself to help later in analyzing the data and writing the report. Label your personal comments in some distinctive manner. For example, the last item in the computer notes in Figure 11.1 labels a personal comment with the heading "Note" and indicates that another source presents an opposing viewpoint. As you're reading and making notes of a secondary source, don't risk forgetting any insights that come to mind—write them down immediately. But make sure they are clearly labeled as your own ideas to avoid confusing them later with your published sources.

> Write down personal comments, questions, and the like as they occur to you.

USING THE COMPUTER TO COLLECT SECONDARY DATA

In the past, researchers seeking secondary data had no choice but to slowly and systematically search manually through card catalogs and through several years' worth of relevant directories and indexes. They then had to locate the books and periodicals and scan them to determine if they were relevant.

> OBJECTIVE 5: Collect secondary data via computer searching.

Today, most university libraries and many public libraries can perform computer-assisted data searches. An entire knowledge industry has evolved in which organizations store huge amounts of statistical, financial, and bibliographic information in the memory banks of their mainframe computers or on computer disks and then make this information available to users nationwide for a fee.

An electronic **data base** is a computer-searchable collection of information on a particular topic. You can access numerous databases within the broad topics of business, education, psychology, and the like. Electronic data bases are fast: a user can typically collect more data electronically in one hour than would be possible in one day of traditional library research.

> You can conduct a comprehensive search for secondary data without ever leaving your office via on-line computer searching.

In addition, electronic data bases are typically more current than printed data bases; most are updated weekly or monthly. Also, each contains several years' worth of citations, whereas manual indexes require searching through individual annual volumes of indexes. Finally, electronic data bases are extremely flexible. You can use different search terms, combine them, and modify your search at every step.

Although you may not write another academic report after graduating from college, you *will* continue to need to locate information—for business, political, or personal reasons. Computer-assisted information retrieval has now become so widely available, economical, and easy to use that it is fast becoming a powerful new tool helping managers solve problems and make decisions.

Types of Data Bases

Data bases can be of three types—bibliographic, numeric, or full-text. Most data bases provide only bibliographic information and sometimes a brief abstract of documents. Some data bases, such as Disclosure, are numeric, providing comprehensive financial and other statistical information. And some data bases provide the full text of the documents they contain; for example, the Dow Jones News/Retrieval Service contains the complete contents of each issue of the *Wall Street Journal*. These data bases are available either as *on-line* or as *CD-ROM* data bases.

Unlike CD-ROM data bases, on-line data bases require that you be electronically connected to a remote mainframe computer.

On-Line Data Bases   An **on-line data base** is a collection of information stored in a mainframe computer that is accessible by a microcomputer or terminal and a telephone hookup. A user in Bangor, Maine, for example, could use his or her computer and modem to access the ABI/Inform data base by dialing up the DIALOG Information Services mainframe computer in Palo Alto, California.* The user could then instruct the computer to print out a list of articles on a particular topic from its data base of citations from 800 business and management journals.

The main advantage of using an on-line data base is that it can be accessed anywhere a microcomputer, modem, and telephone line are available. The user can print out citations, abstracts, and sometimes even the full text of the articles. If the full text is not available, information is provided for ordering photocopies of the articles.

The user pays a fee for each search, usually $50 to $100 per connect hour. Several services (e.g., BRS/After Dark and Knowledge Index) offer nonprime-time rates, some as low as $12 an hour. DIALOG, one of the major data-base vendors, estimates that a typical search during normal business hours lasts about 10 minutes and costs from $5 to $16.50.[1]

CD-ROM Data Bases   The second major type of computer collection is the **CD-ROM data base,** a collection of information stored on a high-capacity disk that is accessible by a specially adapted microcomputer. One CD-ROM (compact disk—read-only memory) disk can hold up to 250,000 pages of text—the equivalent of 1,500 floppy disks. The advantage of using a CD-ROM data base is that the collection is stored on a disk connected directly to the computer you're using. Rather than pay for a telephone hookup to the remote mainframe computer, the library purchases the CD-ROM collection and periodic updates; individual computer searches are typically free to the user. Many of the directories and indexes available in print format (and nearly all the major ones) are also available in computer format, although sometimes under a different name.

*The two vendors of on-line data bases most useful for business researchers are (1) BRS (Bibliographic Retrieval Services, 1200 Route 7, Latham, New York 12110; Phone 800/345-4277), which offers BRS and BRS/After Dark and (2) DIALOG Information Services (3460 Hillview Avenue, Palo Alto, CA 94304; Phone 800/334-2564) which offers DIALOG and Knowledge Index.

Accessing On-Line and CD-ROM Data Bases

Both on-line and CD-ROM data bases are accessed similarly. Each citation in the data base contains a list of **descriptors**—subject headings that describe the contents of the document stored in the computer. For example, an article on purchasing a TCBY franchise might have as descriptors "franchising," "frozen desserts," "frozen yogurt," and "TCBY." The user enters relevant key words, and the computer then identifies all citations in its collection that contain those key words.

The success of your search will depend on how skillfully you choose these key words, or **search terms.** The principles that guide your choice are similar to those we discussed earlier for searches of card catalogs, indexes, and directories, but there's one important difference. The computer makes a very literal search; it will find exactly what you ask for—and nothing more.

If you use the search term "secretaries," the computer will not find citations for the words "secretary" or "secretarial." Most data bases have a feature known as *truncation*, which allows you to search for the root of a term. A search for "secre/" would retrieve "secretariat," "secretarial," "secretaries," "secretary," "secretion," and so on. You then choose the entries that are appropriate for your purpose.

One real advantage of electronic data bases is that they allow you to combine concepts to broaden or restrict your search. Using the **logical operator** "or" between terms will find all citations using either *or* both terms. Using "and" will find only those citations that include both terms. Using "not" will exclude a term; for example, you could retrieve only those citations that include the term "secretaries" and that do not include the term "unions." Finally, using parentheses lets you group terms that you want the computer to treat together.

Using logical operators can help you make your search quite precise. But your success will always depend on how thoughtfully you choose your terms. Suppose, for example, you wished to identify citations relating to the unionization of secretaries. First, you have to think of the different ways this topic might be addressed in the literature. For example, how would you design a search statement that would retrieve all the following journal articles?

"Office Workers Organize for Better Working Conditions"
"Is There a Secretarial Union in Your Future?"
"Unionization Moves into the Office"
"NEA Leads Effort to Organize Clerical Workers"

The statement "Secretaries and Unions" would not likely retrieve all four documents; neither would "Secretar/ and Union/." Your best option would probably be to use a search statement such as "(Secretar/ or Cler/ or Office) and (Union/ or Organiz/)," which would, in fact, retrieve all four articles.

Regardless of the precision of your search statement, you are still likely to miss some relevant articles, and you are even more likely to retrieve many articles that have no relevance at all to your study. One of the great advantages of many electronic data bases is that you can search interactively—that is, you can begin with a broad category and a large number of search terms just to see how many citations would be retrieved for each.

The search terms used in a computer search correspond to the key words used in a manual search.

The term "or" increases the number of citations found; "and" and "not" decrease the number of citations found.

Because many data bases charge on a per-citation basis, take care in writing your search statement.

S P O T L I G H T   ON TECHNOLOGY

SAMPLE ON-LINE SEARCH SESSION

User dials an information-retrieval service and is connected to the data base.

```
SIGN ON      7:18:23       07/02/91
(1/74-3/91)
SEARCH MODE-ENTER QUERY

    No.    Request              Documents
```

Steps 1–3: User asks the computer to search for three terms. Computer responds by telling how many documents contain that term.

```
    1      banking-industry.de    8394

    2      management.de          61847

    3      women.de               2994
```

Step 4: User asks for all documents containing all three terms; computer locates 21 such documents.

```
    4      1 and 2 and 3          21
```

Step 5: User asks computer to print (P) the first document (1/1) from the 4th search (4). Computer lists author (AU), title (TI), source (SO), descriptors (DE), abstract (AB), service that sells a photocopy of the document (AV), and the accession number (AC)—the number used to identify the document.

```
    5      p 4 1/1
AU:    Shinar-Eva-H.
TI:    Sexual Stereotypes of Occupations
SO:    J. Voc. Behavior. VOL: v20n8. PAG: 102-110, 9 pages.
       Aug 1988.
DE:    Role-stereotypes.   Personnel-management.   Women.
       Banking-industry.   Manufacturing-industry.   Retail-
       industry.
AB:    The strength of sexual stereotypes attached to 129
       occupations was measured by having 60 male and 60
       female subjects rank these jobs as masculine,
       feminine, or neutral. An extremely high correlation
       between male and female subjects' mean ratings of
       the sex appropriateness of the given occupations
       indicates that sex labeling of occupations is a
       deeply ingrained feature in attitudes toward the
       world of work. The results showed that those
       occupations stereotypically associated with high
       levels of competence, rationality, and assertion are
       viewed as masculine while those associated with
       dependency, passivity, nurturance, and interpersonal
       warmth are perceived as feminine occupations. For
       example, bank tellers, elementary school teachers,
       and librarians had high feminine ratings whereas
       bankers, doctors, politicians, and professional
       athletes had high masculine ratings. The notion that
       males continue to stereotype while females have more
       liberated views is not supported.
AV:    ABI/INFORM
AC:    0120-5582

END OF REQUEST
```

User signs off. Computer shows search took 8 minutes and 26 seconds, or 0.141 of an hour.

```
SEARCH MODE-ENTER QUERY
    bye

*CONNECT TIME:  0:08:26  HH:MM:SS    0.141 DEC HRS
SESSION 17208
```

Then you can easily combine the categories using the logical operators "and," "or," and "not" until you gradually narrow your topic appropriately.

Many data bases not only indicate the number of citations for each search statement but also let you view the first few citations to get an idea of their relevance for your purposes. If many appear to be irrelevant, you can further restrict your search through the use of "and" and "not" commands. The Spotlight on page 332 shows the interactive nature of computer-assisted data collection, in this case on the topic of women managers in the banking industry.

COLLECTING PRIMARY DATA
THROUGH QUESTIONNAIRES

Despite your best efforts, you will sometimes find that not enough high-quality secondary data is available to solve your problem. In such a situation, you will need to collect primary data. The main types of primary data collection are through surveys, observation, and experimentation.

OBJECTIVE 6: Develop an effective questionnaire.

A **survey** is a data-collection method that gathers information through questionnaires, telephone inquiries, and interviews. The **questionnaire** (an instrument containing questions designed to obtain information from the individual being surveyed) is the most frequently used method in business research. The researcher can economically get a representative sampling over a large geographical area. After all, it costs no more to send a questionnaire across the country than across the street.

Also, the anonymity of a questionnaire increases the validity of the responses. Certain personal and economic data may be given more completely and honestly when the respondent remains unidentified. In addition, no interviewer is present to possibly bias the results. Finally, respondents can answer at a time convenient for them, which is not true with telephone or interview studies.

The big disadvantage of mail questionnaires is the low response rate; and those who do respond may not be representative (typical) of the population. Indeed, extensive research has shown that respondents tend to be better educated, have higher social status, be more intelligent, have higher need for social approval, and be more sociable than those who choose not to respond.[2]

Thus mail questionnaires should be used only under certain conditions:

- *When the desired information can be answered easily and quickly.* Questionnaires should contain yes-or-no questions, check-off alternatives, or a one- to two-word fill-in response. People tend not to return questionnaires that call for lengthy or complex responses or tend simply to leave such questions blank.
- *When the relevant group of people is homogeneous.* To ensure a high response rate, your study must interest the respondents and you must use language they understand. It is very difficult to construct a questionnaire that would be clearly and uniformly understood by people with widely differing interests, education, and socioeconomic standards.
- *When sufficient time is available.* Three to four weeks is generally required from the time a questionnaire is mailed to final returns—including follow-ups of the nonrespondents. (A telephone survey, on the other hand, can often be completed in one day.)

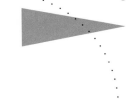

Constructing a Questionnaire

Content

1. Do not ask for information that is easily available elsewhere.

2. Make sure that all questions are necessary—that they directly help you to solve your problem. Do not ask for unimportant or merely "interesting" information. Have a purpose for each question.

3. Use precise wording so that no question can possibly be misunderstood. Use clear, simple language, and define any terms that may be unfamiliar to the respondent or that are used in a special way.

4. Use neutrally worded questions and deal with only one topic per question. Loaded, leading, or multifaceted questions may bias the responses or confuse the respondent.

5. Make sure the response choices are both exhaustive and mutually exclusive (i.e., that there is an appropriate response for everyone and no overlapping categories).

6. Be especially careful when asking sensitive questions, such as questions about age, salary, or morals. Using broad categories (rather than narrow, more specific categories) for responses will often increase response rate and response accuracy.

7. Pilot-test your questionnaire on a few people to ensure that all questions function as intended. Revise as necessary.

Organization

8. Arrange the responses in some logical order—numerical, chronological, alphabetical, and so forth. Avoid possibly biasing the responses by placing the responses in what you consider to be the most popular or most reasonable order.

9. Arrange the questions in some logical order. Group together all questions that deal with a particular topic. If your questionnaire is long, divide it into sections.

10. Give the questionnaire a descriptive title, provide whatever directions are necessary, and give your name and address somewhere on the questionnaire.

Format

11. Use an easy-to-answer format. Check-off questions draw the most responses and are easiest to answer and tabulate. Use free-response items only when absolutely necessary; for example, when the number of possible responses is unmanageably long; when the possible responses are unknown; or when subjective or detailed information, such as motives or personal experiences, is desired.

12. To increase the likelihood that your target audience will cooperate and take your study seriously, ensure that your questionnaire has a professional appearance:

- Use a simple and attractive format, allowing for plenty of white space.
- Ensure that the questionnaire is free from errors in grammar, spelling, and the like.
- Use a good-quality typewriter or printer and make good-quality photocopies.

Constructing the Questionnaire

Because the target audience's time is valuable, you should ensure that every question you ask is necessary—that it is essential to help you solve your problem and that you cannot acquire the information from other sources (such as through library research). Guidelines for constructing a questionnaire are given in Checklist 12. Some of the more important points are illustrated in the following paragraphs.

Your language must be clear, precise, and understandable so that the questionnaire yields valid and reliable data. **Validity** is the extent to which the questionnaire measures what it is supposed to measure. Suppose your questionnaire on consumer buying habits is written at a readability level of Grade 14 and the respondents have a reading level of Grade 10. This questionnaire might actually be measuring reading ability and would thus be an invalid measure of consumer buying habits.

> An instrument can be reliable and still not be valid—it can consistently yield incorrect results.

The term **reliability** refers to the extent to which the questionnaire yields consistent results. Suppose, for instance, your questionnaire asked the respondent to rank 15 criteria for selecting a particular brand, from 1 (most important) to 15 (least important). Because it is nearly impossible to differentiate 15 levels of importance, if the same respondents answered this question on two different occasions, their answers would probably vary somewhat; that is, their responses would be inconsistent and, therefore, unreliable.

Each question must also be neutral (unbiased). Consider the following question:

> The question should not yield clues to the "correct" answer.

```
Do you think our company should open an on-site child-
care center as a means of ensuring the welfare of our
employees' small children?
_____ yes     _____ no
```

This question obviously presents only one side (the "pro" side) of the issue, thereby biasing the responses toward a "yes." A more neutral question is needed if valid responses are to result:

```
Which one of the following possible additional fringe ben-
efits would you most prefer?

_____ a dental insurance plan

_____ an on-site child-care center

_____ three personal-leave days annually

_____ other (please specify _____ )
```

Note several things about this question. First, it is more neutral than the original version; no "right" answer is apparent. Second, the alternatives are arranged in alphabetical order. To avoid possibly biasing the responses, always arrange the responses in some logical order—alphabetical, numeric, chronological, and the like.

Finally, note that an "other" category is provided (and it always goes last and is accompanied by the request to "please specify"). Suppose the one fringe benefit that the vast majority of employees wanted most was to increase the company's pension contributions. If the "other" category were missing, the researcher would never learn that important information.

Ask only one question in each item.

Ensure that your categories are exhaustive (that is, that they include all possible alternatives), by including an "other" category if necessary. Also ensure that each question contains a single idea. Note the following question:

```
Our company should spend less money on advertising and
more money on research and development.

_____ agree        _____ disagree
```

Suppose the respondent believes that the company should spend more (or less) money on both advertising and on research and development. How is he or she supposed to answer? The solution is to put the two different ideas into two different questions.

Finally, ensure that your categories are mutually exclusive; that is, that there are no overlapping categories.

```
In your opinion, what is the major cause of high em-
ployee turnover?

_____ lack of air-conditioning

_____ noncompetitive financial package

_____ poor fringe benefits

_____ poor working conditions

_____ weak management
```

The problem, of course, is that the "lack of air-conditioning" category overlaps with the "poor working conditions" category, and "noncompetitive financial package" overlaps with "poor fringe benefits." And all four of these probably overlap with "weak management." Such intermingling of categories will thoroughly confuse the respondent.

Recognize that respondents may be hesitant to answer sensitive questions (regarding age, salary, morals, and the like). Even worse, they may provide inaccurate responses. When it is necessary to gather such data, ensure that the respondent understands that the questionnaire is anonymous (by prominently discussing that fact in the cover letter).

Simply checking a broad range of figures might be less threatening than writing in an exact figure.

Respondents also tend to be more cooperative in answering such questions when broad categories are used. Accurate estimates provided by broad categories are preferable to precise data that is, nevertheless, incorrect.

```
Not: What is your annual gross salary? $_____

But: Please check the category that best describes your
     annual salary:

_____ less than $15,000      _____ $25,001–$50,000

_____ $15,000–$25,000        _____ more than $50,000
```

Note that the use of the number "$25,00<u>1</u>" in the third category is necessary to avoid overlap with the figure "$25,000" in the second category—the categories must be mutually exclusive.

Even experienced researchers find it difficult to spot ambiguities or other problems in their own questionnaires. If time permits, administer the draft questionnaire to a small sample of potential respondents and then revise it as necessary. At a minimum, ask a colleague to edit your instrument with a critical eye.

The sample questionnaire in Figure 11.2 shows a variety of question types: check-off responses (Q. 1), fill-in-the-blank (Q. 4), ranking (Q. 8), complex check-off response (Q. 9), scale (Q. 10–15), and open-ended (Q. 16). This questionnaire also illustrates good design: lots of white space, clear directions, and attractive appearance.

For the attitude questions (Q. 10–15), note that a combination of positive and negative statements is used rather than all positive or all negative statements. The open-ended question (Q. 16) is presented last; if it were one of the first questions, the respondent might erroneously believe that completing the questionnaire would require too much time.

> When composing attitude items, use both pro and con statements.

Writing the Cover Letter

Unless you intend to distribute the questionnaires personally, include a cover letter. The cover letter should be written as a regular persuasive letter; your job is to convince the reader that it's worth taking the time to respond (see Chapter 7):

> **OBJECTIVE 7:** Construct an appropriate cover letter to accompany a questionnaire.

```
Dear Fellow Student:

Have you ever thought, "Oh no--not another computer
project!" Or has your experience been more like, "Why
is the instructor making us do this project manually
when it would be so much easier to do on a computer?"

Either way, here is your chance to provide the CMU
administration with your views on computer use. This
research project is a class project for ADS 360
(Business Communication); the results will be shared
with Dr. Dan Rulong, Vice President for Academic Com-
puting.

If you are a full-time junior or senior student, at-
tended CMU during the Spring 1992 semester, and have
declared a major, please take five minutes to complete
this questionnaire. Then simply return it in the en-
closed envelope. You'll be doing yourself and your
fellow students a big favor.

Sincerely,
```

Selecting a Sample

The **population** of a study is every member of a group about whom you're trying to find information. The population for our sample questionnaire in Figure 11.2 would be all the students at Central Metropolitan University. But it isn't necessary to survey all 15,000 students at the university in order to be able to predict their views. When a cook takes a single sip from the kettle and decides the soup needs more salt, he or she makes a judgment based on a sample; the cook does not need to consume the entire pot of

> **OBJECTIVE 8:** Select an appropriate sample for a survey.

FIGURE 11.2 Sample Questionnaire

STUDENT USE OF COMPUTERS AT CMU

This survey is being conducted as part of a research project for
ADS 360 (Business Communication). Please complete this questionnaire only if you (1) are a junior or senior full-time student at
CMU, (2) attended CMU during the Spring 1992 semester, and (3)
have declared a major. Please return the completed questionnaire
in the enclosed addressed envelope to Pat Jones, 105 Woldt, Phone
555-1086.

A. DESCRIPTIVE INFORMATION

1. Grade level: 2. Sex: 3. Age:
   ___ junior   ___ female   ___ 20 or younger
   ___ senior   ___ male   ___ 21-24
                                    ___ 25 or older

4. Are you pursuing a nonteaching or teaching major?
   ___ nonteaching (Please write in name of major: _____)
   ___ teaching (Please write in name of major: _____)

5. School/College where major is located:
   ___ Arts and Sciences
   ___ Business Administration
   ___ Education, Health, and Human Services

6. Have you used a computer at CMU either as a course requirement
   or for personal use since January 1990?
   ___ yes (Please continue with Question 7.)
   ___ no (Please disregard the following questions and return
   the questionnaire to the researcher.)

B. TYPE AND EXTENT OF COMPUTER USE

7. During the Spring 1990 semester, which type of computer did
   you use most frequently?
   ___ Apple (II, C, or GS)
   ___ IBM or compatible
   ___ Macintosh (Plus, SE, or II)
   ___ Other (please specify: _____)

8. Please rank from 1 (most convenient) to 4 (least convenient)
   the convenience of each of the on-campus computer labs for
   completing your out-of-class computer assignments. Write the
   appropriate number beside each lab.
   ___ computer labs in dormitories
   ___ Grawn computer lab
   ___ Ronan computer lab
   ___ University Center computer lab

9. Listed on the next page are different types of computer software. For each, check the type of use you made of this
   software at any time during the Spring 1990 semester; check both

Sample Questionnaire (*Cont'd*)   **FIGURE11.2**

Required and Personal if appropriate. (An example of personal use
would be typing a term paper using word processing software if
such use were not required.) Then, if you did use this type of
software, check the total number of hours of use, including both
in-class and out-of-class, and both required and personal.

TYPE OF SOFTWARE	None	TYPE OF USE		AMOUNT OF USE		
		Re-quired	Per-sonal	>5 hrs	5-10 hrs	<10 hrs
Accounting or payroll	——	——	——	——	——	——
Database	——	——	——	——	——	——
Educational (tutorial)	——	——	——	——	——	——
Graphics or charting	——	——	——	——	——	——
Programming	——	——	——	——	——	——
Spreadsheet	——	——	——	——	——	——
Word processing	——	——	——	——	——	——
Other (please specify)	——	——	——	——	——	——

C. STUDENT OPINIONS

Please indicate whether you agree with, have no opinion about, or
disagree with each of the following statements.

	Agree	No Opinion	Disagree
10. Considering my major, I am receiving adequate training in computer use.	——	——	——
11. The computer equipment at CMU is not up to date.	——	——	——
12. I have to wait an unreasonable length of time to get onto a computer in the lab.	——	——	——
13. I enjoy working with computers.	——	——	——
14. Most instructors provide adequate instruction in the use of the software they require.	——	——	——
15. Lab attendants are not as helpful as they should be.	——	——	——

D. IMPROVEMENTS NEEDED

16. If you could make one suggestion to the University administra-
    tion to improve computer usage at CMU, what would it be?

_____

_____

_____

soup to make a judgment. Similarly, we can select a **sample** of students—the part of the population that will actually participate in the study.

Types of Samples For a sample to be accurate, it must reflect the makeup of the entire population. One way to achieve this is to select a random sample—a sample drawn in such a way that each individual in the population has an equal and independent chance of being selected. A **random sample** might be selected by putting the names of all members of the population on a slip of paper and then randomly selecting the number of participants needed for the study.

Alternately, if the members of the population are available on a list, a table of random numbers from a statistics textbook could be used to determine which members to select. Suppose the first four numbers in the random-number table were 14763, 10332, 23045, and 00928, and you wish to randomly select 150 names from your population. You would select the 147th, 103rd (skip 23045 because 230 is higher than your 150 cut-off), and the 9th names on your list as the first three sample members.

Sometimes the business researcher believes that responses from people in different subgroups may differ. In such situations, stratifying the sample will yield more accurate estimates than when using a simple random sample. In a **stratified sample,** subgroups are represented in the sample in proportion to their numbers in the population. If you are conducting a consumer survey, for example, you might divide your population into high, medium, and low incomes in order to be able to tell whether groups with different buying power hold different views.

Avoid using a **convenience sample**—a sample that uses whatever subjects happen to be available. Since you cannot be sure that the respondents are representative of the population, you cannot draw any valid conclusions about the population from such data. At best, projects using convenience samples should be considered preliminary research, rather than a final solution.

Sample Size Despite widespread belief, large samples are not needed in order to draw valid conclusions. Small samples can be very precise if they are representative of the population. And, as you can see in Table 11.1, the size of the population has only a small bearing on the needed sample size. For example, if your population size is 10,000, you need a sample size of 370; however, if your population size increases to 1 million, the sample size increases by only 14 (to 384).

The percentage of people responding to your survey (response rate) typically has more effect on the accuracy of your findings than does the initial size of your sample. It is much better to get a 90% response from a random sample of 350 than it is to get a 50% response from a sample of 5,000—even though the smaller study yields only 315 responses whereas the larger study yields 2,500 responses. The reason, of course, is that with a 90% response rate, you can have more assurance that your respondents are typical of the population.

Thus, it is better to devote your efforts to motivating those who did not respond to your initial mailing to respond (through follow-up postcards, telephone calls, and the like) rather than making an excessively large initial mailout.

Although only simple random and stratified samples are discussed here, there are many variations to each.

The response rate is usually more important than the sample size.

TABLE 11.1   Maximum Sample Size Needed for a Given Population
Size (With a 95% probability that the sample statistics
will be within ±5% of the population parameters)

Population	Sample
100[a]	80
150	108
200	132
250	152
300	169
500	217
750	260
1,000	285
1,500	306
2,000	322
3,000	341
5,000	357
10,000	370
15,000	375
30,000	379
50,000	381
75,000	382
1,000,000	384

Interpretation: 95 times out of 100, the findings based on this sample study would vary by no more than five percentage points—plus or minus—from the results that would have been obtained if every member of the population had been studied.

[a] When the population is less than 100, the entire population should be studied.

COLLECTING PRIMARY DATA THROUGH INTERVIEWS

Personal interviews are generally considered to be the most valid method of survey research. In a personal interview, the interviewer can probe, ask for clarification, clear up any misunderstandings immediately, ensure that all questions are answered completely, and pursue unexpected avenues. Thus, the quality of data resulting from an interview is often higher than data resulting from a questionnaire.

Personal interviews are most appropriate when in-depth information is desired. The interview permits open-ended questions and gives the respondent free rein to answer as he or she desires. Respondents are typically likely to say more than they will write. Research into topics such as motives, deeply held feelings, complex issues, and the like simply does not lend itself to the objective questions found in most questionnaires.

There are, however, several problems with interviews. First of all, interview research is very expensive; it is very time consuming to schedule the interviews, conduct them, and analyze the subjective data that flows from interviews. In addition, in-depth interviewing requires specially trained and experienced interviewers.

Secondly, the interviewer can consciously or unconsciously bias the results—by not recording the answers exactly, showing a favorable or

OBJECTIVE 9: Conduct a
data-gathering interview.

Although expensive to
conduct, personal inter-
views are most appropri-
ate for gathering in-
depth or complex data.

unfavorable reaction to a response, hurrying through parts of the interview, and the like. Different interviewers may experience the same situation and "see" different things. Thus, analyzing interview data is sometimes more difficult than analyzing questionnaire data. The subjective nature of the data being given and of the data being received affect the validity of the research.

Finally, a personal interview is not appropriate for eliciting information of a sensitive nature. Questions about age, salary, personal beliefs, and the like should not be used in face-to-face questioning where anonymity is not possible. (The alert interviewer can, however, sometimes get an estimate of these variables by carefully observing the interviewee and his or her environment.)

In most situations, the sample for a questionnaire study is selected so that each member is typical of the population. However, interviewees are often selected for just the opposite reason: They may have unique expertise or experiences to share, and the data they provide will serve as "expert testimony" and not be tabulated and generalized to the population.

Types of Questions

In many ways, your interview questions should follow the same guidelines given in Checklist 12 for questionnaire items: they should be clear and unbiased and deal with only one topic per question. However, because of the increased complexity of many interview questions, you now have other choices to make.

Both open-ended and closed questions are typically used.

Open Versus Closed Questions Open-ended questions allow the interviewee flexibility in responding, whereas closed questions limit the subject matter of the response:

Open: What is your view of the impending foreign-trade legislation?
Closed: How much of your firm's business is attributable to international sales?

Open questions expose the interviewee's priorities and frame of reference. If you ask an employee, "Tell me about your job," whatever aspect (duties, importance, salary, and the like) is mentioned first is probably what the employee considers most important or significant about the job. Open questions also may uncover information that the interviewer may never have thought to ask. Finally, interviewees like open questions because they are easy to answer (there is no wrong answer) and they give recognition to the interviewee—by letting him or her talk through ideas while the interviewer listens intently. The drawback to open questions is that they are time consuming, and the responses may be rambling, difficult to record, and difficult to tabulate later.

Closed questions save time and are very useful when you know exactly what type of information you want, when you intend to tabulate the responses, and when the responses don't require elaborate explanation by the interviewee. The amount of interview information that can be obtained by closed questions, however, is fairly restricted; if all your questions lend themselves to the closed format, a questionnaire would probably yield just as valid results at a great saving in money.

In actual practice, the interviewer usually uses both open and closed questions, often following up a closed question with an open one:

> *Closed:* Do you agree or disagree with the proposal?
> *Open:* Why?
>
> *Closed:* Will it have any effect on your own firm?
> *Open:* In what way?

Direct Versus Indirect Questions   Most questions may be asked directly. In threatening or sensitive situations, however, you may want to resort to indirect questions, which are less threatening because they let the interviewee camouflage his or her response.

> *Not:* How would you evaluate your boss's people skills?
> *But:* How do you think most people in this department would evaluate the boss's people skills?

Conducting the Interview

As an interviewer, you must wear two hats—that of an observer and that of a participant. You participate by asking questions, but you must also analyze the responses to ensure that the interviewee is answering the question asked and to determine if follow-up questions are needed. Fulfilling this demanding role requires concentration, preparation, and flexibility.

To secure the greatest cooperation from the interviewee, you should make him or her feel comfortable and important. The first few minutes of the interview are crucial for establishing rapport. Begin with a warm greeting, reintroduce yourself, and explain again the purpose of the interview, how the information will be used, and how much time will be required.

One of the barriers to effective listening during an interview is the need for note taking. Keep note taking to a minimum by using a small portable cassette recorder when possible. Always get permission first, assuring the interviewee that the purpose is to make certain that he or she is not misquoted and to let you give his or her responses your full attention. Keep the recorder out of sight (perhaps on the floor beside you) so that the interviewee is not constantly reminded that his or her remarks are being recorded. Test the recording level beforehand to ensure that the responses will be audible.

Always use an **interview guide**—a list of questions to ask, with suggested wording and possible follow-up questions. Mark off each question as it is asked (and answered—don't assume that just because a question was asked, it was answered!). Nothing is more embarrassing than repeating a question that has already been answered, and nothing is more frustrating than learning after the interview is over that you failed to ask an important question.

> Listening in an interview involves much more than simply hearing what is being said.

> It is difficult to listen actively if you are busy taking notes.

Provide smooth transitions when moving from topic to topic by using periodic summaries and previews of what will be covered next; for example,

> We've covered the start-up and initial funding for your firm. Next I'd like to investigate any problems your firm experienced during its early years.

> Now that I know why you chose banking as a career, I'd like to discuss any problems you may have experienced as a female banker. Specifically, . . .

> So you do feel the proposal has some merit. Now I'd like to explore how it might be implemented.

Follow up a point if the interviewee's response is inadequate in some way; for example, the interviewee may have consciously or unconsciously failed to answer all or part of a question, given inaccurate information, or given a response you did not understand completely. When the response needs amplification, you can probe by asking for more information, by asking for clarification, or by simply repeating the question (either verbatim or paraphrasing).

> *Elaboration:* Can you tell me more about that?

> *Clarification:* Exactly what do you mean by that?

> *Repetition:*

> > *Interviewer:* What do you think should be done to curb inflation?

> > *Interviewee:* Well, that's a difficult question, and there are a lot of suggestions that ought to be considered. We've got to stop it, that's for certain, or we're going to have some real problems.

> > *Interviewer:* And what do you think should be done to reduce it?

Indicate when the interview is over—either by a direct statement or by such nonverbal gestures as putting your papers away or standing up. Experienced interviewers often end an interview by asking two standard questions:

> "Is there some question you think I should have asked that I didn't ask?" (to uncover unexpected information).

> "May I call you back if I need to verify some information?" (to enable the checking of some fact or spelling or to ask a quick follow-up question).

Leave the interviewee with a sense of accomplishment by quickly summarizing the important points you've gathered (to show that you've listened) or by restating how the information will be used. Finally, express appreciation once more for the time granted.

COLLECTING PRIMARY DATA THROUGH OTHER METHODS

OBJECTIVE 10: Discuss the appropriate use of observation, telephone inquiries, and experimentation.

Although mail surveys and interviews are the major means for collecting primary information for business purposes, the executive has many other research methods at his or her disposal, including observation, telephone inquiries, and experiments.

Observation is often used in market research. For example, the researcher can measure the amount of display space devoted to the firm's product in a sample of retail stores, record people's facial expressions as they watch a sample television commercial, or count the number of coupons redeemed for a company's product.

Telephone inquiries are an increasingly popular way to obtain information quickly and inexpensively. The information desired must be simple and short. Questions should be answerable with yes or no or in a few words, and the entire call should require no more than two or three minutes of the respondent's time. There is, however, an increasing public resistance to this form of data-gathering. Some people view it as an invasion of privacy; and some view it with distrust, fearing that the questions are merely a prelude to a sales pitch.

One new development is computer-assisted telephone interviewing (CATI), which lets interviewers enter answers directly into the computer, without using paper and pencil. Each question appears on a computer screen in turn, the interviewer reads it, the respondent answers, and the interviewer types in the appropriate letter or number representing the response. Doing so triggers the next question on the computer screen, and the process continues.

Experimental studies are extremely useful for determining cause-and-effect outcomes. Assume, for example, that you wish to find out whether production workers would produce more when working in a brightly lit as opposed to a moderately lit factory. You might randomly select 200 of your production workers and randomly assign 100 of them to the brightly lit workroom and 100 to the moderately lit workroom.

During the experiment, all other conditions should be held constant—the employees should be exposed to similar working conditions, similar levels of management, and the like. The only factor that is different should be the level of lighting. At the end of the experiment, you would compare the average production of each group and then determine which type of lighting caused the higher productivity. Because experiments require very careful planning and control, organizations typically call on the services of research consultants to conduct formal experiments.

> Observations can be either personal (visual) or mechanical (e.g., using a counter).

> The major advantage of experiments is that they enable you to conclude that one event caused a certain outcome.

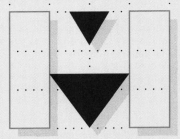

MICROWRITING A QUESTIONNAIRE

The Problem

You are Martha Halpern, assistant store manager for Just Pool Supplies, a small firm in San Antonio, Texas. You have been asked by Joe Cox, store owner, to determine the feasibility of expanding into the spa-supply business (see Chapter 10). To help answer your third subproblem ("Is there a sufficient number of potential customers to make the expansion profitable?"), you decide to develop and administer a short questionnaire.

The Process

1. What is the purpose of your questionnaire?

   To determine whether there are enough potential customers to make it profitable for us to expand into the spa-supply business.

2. Who is your audience?

   The theoretical population for my study would be all spa owners in the San Antonio area. However, because my major business will still be pool supplies, I'll assume that most of my spa-supply business would come from my present pool-supply customers.

   Thus, the real population for my survey will be the approximately 1,500 present customers that I have on my mailing list. Table 11.1 tells me that I should select 306 of these for my sample. Thus, I'll have my database program generate address labels for every fifth customer. I can also use my word processing program to generate personal letters to each of the customers selected.

3. What information do you need from these customers?

   a. Whether they presently own a spa or intend to purchase one in the near future
   b. Where they typically purchase their spa supplies
   c. How much money they typically spend on spa supplies
   d. How satisfied they are with their suppliers
   e. What the likelihood is that they'd switch their spa-supply business to us

4. Is all this information necessary? Can any of it be found elsewhere?

   All the information is needed, and none of it can be obtained elsewhere. I know from secondary sources how many spa-supply firms are located in the area and their volume of business. However, I don't know which firms my customers use.

5. Do any of these questions ask for sensitive information, or are any of them difficult to answer?

   No. The question asking about the amount of money spent on spa supplies depends a little on memory; but since most people buy spa supplies only four or five times a

year, respondents should be able to provide a fairly
accurate estimate.

6. Is there any logical order to the questions in Item 3?

The question about spa ownership must come first,
because respondents cannot answer the other questions
unless they own a spa. In reviewing the other questions, the logical order appears to be c, b, d, and e.

7. Will the questionnaire require a cover letter?

Yes, and since the questionnaire contains several
questions, the cover letter and questionnaire should be
typed on separate sheets of paper.

The Product

Dear Mr. Diehl:

We miss you during the winter!

Although you're a frequent shopper at Just Pool Supplies during
the summer months when you're using your pool, we miss having the
opportunity to serve you during the rest of the year. Therefore,
we're considering adding a complete line of spa supplies to our
inventory.

Would you please help us make this decision by answering the
following five questions and then returning this form to us in the
enclosed stamped envelope.

Thanks for sharing your views with us. We look forward to seeing
you during our traditional Pool Party Sale in March.

Sincerely,

Joe Cox, Manager

1. Do you presently own a spa?
   ____ yes
   ____ no (Please skip the other questions and return this form to us in the enclosed envelope.)

2. Considering the number of times you purchased spa supplies last year and the average amount of each purchase, how much do you estimate you spent on spa supplies last year (include all types of purchases—chemicals, accessories, decorative items, and the like)?
   ____ less than $100
   ____ $100–$300
   ____ $301–$500
   ____ more than $500

3. Where did you purchase the majority of your spa supplies last year? (Please check only one.)
   ____ at a general-merchandise store (e.g., K-Mart or Sears)
   ____ at a pool- or spa-supply store
   ____ from a mail-order firm
   ____ other (please specify _____)

4. How satisfied were you with each of the following factors at the store where you purchased most of your spa supplies?

	Very Satisfied	Satisfied	Very Dissatisfied
Customer service	____	____	____
Hours of operation	____	____	____
Location of store	____	____	____
Prices	____	____	____
Quality of products	____	____	____
Quantity of products	____	____	____

5. If Just Pool Supplies were to sell spa supplies, how likely would you be to purchase most of your spa supplies here? (Assume that the quality, selection, and pricing would be similar to that in effect for our pool supplies.)
   ____ very likely
   ____ somewhat likely
   ____ don't know
   ____ somewhat unlikely
   ____ very unlikely

SUMMARY

Secondary data is data collected by others for their own specific purposes. Therefore, the researcher who wants to use secondary data for his or her own study must first evaluate it in terms of why and how the data was collected, how it was analyzed, how consistent the data is with that found in other studies, and how old the data is.

The strategy to use for locating relevant secondary sources consists of developing a list of key terms, consulting directories and indexes, and then compiling and reviewing the literature. Sources can be searched using either traditional print indexes and directories or by making a computer search using either on-line or CD-ROM data bases. The format of these computer data bases is either bibliographic, numeric, or full-text.

Notes should be taken of each relevant article, using either index cards or full sheets of paper. Record the call numbers, bibliographic information, source numbers, headings, and page numbers for your notes. Most notes should be in the form of paraphrases, with direct quotations used sparingly.

Mail questionnaires are an economical and convenient way to gather primary data when the desired information can be answered easily and quickly. Care should be taken to ensure that all questions are necessary, clearly worded, complete, and unbiased. The questions and their alternatives should be organized in a logical order, the directions should be clear, and the overall format should be attractive. The cover letter should be a persuasive letter explaining why it is in the reader's interest to answer the survey.

Some type of random or stratified sample should be used for most survey research. Even small sample sizes can yield reliable results if most people respond to the questionnaire.

Personal interviews are preferable to questionnaires when the information desired is complex or requires extensive explanation or elaboration. The interviewer must determine whether to use open or closed questions and whether to use direct or indirect questions. The use of a cassette recorder will enable the interviewer to minimize note-taking, thereby enabling him or her to listen more attentively.

Other types of primary data collection often used in business include personal observation, telephone inquiries, and experimental studies.

KEY TERMS

CD-ROM (compact disk—read-only memory) data base— A collection of information stored on a high-capacity disk that is accessible by a specially adapted microcomputer.

Citation— A reference to a relevant book, journal article, newspaper article, or similar source.

Convenience sample— A nonrepresentative sample that uses whatever subjects happen to be available.

Data base— A computer-searchable collection of information on a particular topic.

Descriptor— A subject heading that describes the contents of a document stored in a computer.

Direct quotation— The use of the exact words of another.

Interview guide— A list of questions to ask during an interview, with suggested wording and possible follow-up questions.

Logical operators— The terms "and," "or," and "not" that permit the combining of concepts to broaden or restrict a computer search.

On-line data base— A collection of information stored in a mainframe computer that is accessible by a microcomputer or terminal and telephone hookup.

Paraphrase— A summary or restatement of a passage in another form.

Population— Every member of a group about which information is being sought.

Questionnaire— An instrument that contains questions designed to obtain information from the individual being surveyed.

Random sample— A sample drawn in such a way that each individual in the population has an equal and independent chance of being selected.

Reliability— The extent to which an instrument yields consistent results.

Sample— The part of the population chosen to participate in a study.

Search term— The words or phrases entered by the user that the computer tries to match with its list of descriptors for each citation.

Stratified sample— A sample drawn in such a way that certain subgroups are represented in the sample in proportion to their numbers in the population.

Survey— A data-collection method that gathers information through questionnaires, telephone inquiries, and interviews.

Validity— The extent to which an instrument measures what it is supposed to measure.

REVIEW AND DISCUSSION

▶ OBJECTIVE 1
1. Why is secondary data an important part of most research?

▶ OBJECTIVE 1
2. What criteria should be used to evaluate the quality of secondary data?

▶ OBJECTIVE 2
3. How can government data be searched? Why is it important to do so?

▶ OBJECTIVE 2
4. Consult the *Library of Congress Subject Headings.* Locate one or more headings that include the terms "Use," "See," "See Also," "UF," "BT," "NT," and "RT." What do these terms mean?

▶ OBJECTIVES 3, 5
5. List at least two print indexes or directories and at least two computerized data bases that would be appropriate for researching the following topics:
   a. The use of robots in the automotive industry
   b. The need for elementary school students to learn touch keyboarding
   c. Managing intercultural diversity among workers

▶ OBJECTIVE 2
6. For the three preceding topics, develop a list of key words to use as descriptors. Make sure your terms are compatible with the *Library of Congress Subject Headings.*

▶ OBJECTIVE 4
7. Describe your own system for taking notes from secondary sources.

▶ OBJECTIVE 4
8. Under what circumstances should a direct quotation as opposed to a paraphrase be used?

9. Give an example of a search statement using the terms "and," "or," and "not." What does the statement mean? OBJECTIVE 5 ◄

10. Compose a questionnaire item using each of the following formats: OBJECTIVE 6 ◄
    a. Check-off response   d. Scale
    b. Fill-in-the-blank   e. Open-ended
    c. Ranking

11. Assume that you want to survey local rental-unit owners regarding the market for student housing. Compose the first sentence of the cover letter that will accompany your questionnaire. OBJECTIVE 7 ◄

12. "The larger the sample, the more valid the data." Is this statement true or false? Explain. OBJECTIVE 8 ◄

13. Under what circumstances is it better to use a personal interview instead of a questionnaire? OBJECTIVE 9 ◄

14. Assume you wish to interview the vice president for student affairs at your university regarding the adequacy of student housing on campus. Compose an interview question in each of the following formats: OBJECTIVE 9 ◄
    a. Open   c. Direct
    b. Closed   d. Indirect
    Under what circumstances should each of these formats be used?

15. Why is probing sometimes necessary during an interview? How can it be accomplished? OBJECTIVE 9 ◄

16. Briefly describe how you might gather information through the use of observation, telephone inquiries, and experimentation to determine whether living on-campus is more or less expensive than living off-campus. OBJECTIVE 10 ◄

EXERCISES

Note: For each of the following exercises, assume that you have been asked to write a report on the feasibility of opening a frozen yogurt store in Provo, Utah.

1. **Secondary Data—Evaluation and Notetaking** Using whatever indexes would be appropriate, locate and photocopy three journal articles related to this topic. Make notes of each article. In a memo to your instructor, identify and evaluate these articles using the criteria given in this chapter. Submit photocopies of the articles, your notes, and your memo to your instructor. OBJECTIVES 1, 4 ◄

2. **Secondary Data—Locating Specific Information** Answer the following questions, using the latest figures available. Provide a citation for each source. OBJECTIVES 2–3 ◄
   a. What was the number of establishments and total sales last year for Everything Yogurt, a frozen-yogurt franchise?
   b. What is the population of Provo, Utah? What percentage of this population is between the ages of 18 and 24?
   c. What is the per capita income of residents of Provo?

d. Who is the chief executive officer of TCBY, a frozen-yogurt franchise? What is his or her address?

e. What is the climate of Provo, Utah?

f. How many students are enrolled at Brigham Young University?

g. What is the market outlook for frozen yogurt stores nationwide?

h. What is the most current journal or newspaper article you can find on this topic?

OBJECTIVES 2, 5

3. **Secondary Data—Computer Search**   Assume that you had funds to conduct a search using two different computer data bases. Select the two data bases that you think would be most helpful and design an appropriate search statement for each. (*Note:* Use two different types of data bases and two different subtopics in order to identify the most sources.) If feasible, conduct the two computer searches and report on your results.

OBJECTIVES 6–7

4. **Collaborative Writing—Questionnaire**   Since Brigham Young University would provide the major source of potential customers for your yogurt store, you decide to survey BYU students to gather relevant data. Working in groups of four or five, develop a two-page questionnaire and a cover letter that you will mail to a sample of these students.

Ensure that the questionnaire follows the guidelines given in Checklist 12 in content and appearance. Pilot-test your questionnaire and cover letter on a small sample of students; then revise as necessary and submit to your instructor.

OBJECTIVE 8

5. **Survey Research—Selecting a Sample**   Assume that you wish to send the questionnaire you developed in Exercise 4 to a sample of BYU students. Determine from secondary data the current size of the BYU student body, determine the appropriate sample size, and develop a plan for identifying a simple random sample of these students.

OBJECTIVE 9

6. **Primary Data—Interview**   You decide to get some first-hand information from the owner-manager of a premium ice cream or frozen yogurt store in your area (e.g., Dairy Queen, Baskin-Robbins, TCBY, or I Can't Believe It's Yogurt). Think of the type of information he or she might be able to provide that would help you solve your problem. Then prepare an interview guide, listing the possible questions in a logical order and possible follow-up questions.

Schedule an interview with the owner/manager and conduct the interview, recording it on tape. Write up your findings in a one- or two-page memo report to your instructor. Retain your tape of the interview until after this assignment has been returned to you.

CASE   PROBLEM

The Keyboard Strikes Back

OBJECTIVES 1–6

The manufacturing facility in Charlotte employs three data-entry operators who work full-time keyboarding production, personnel, and inventory data into a terminal. This data is then sent over telephone lines to the Urban

Systems mainframe computer, where it becomes part of the corporate data base used for financial, production, and personnel management.

As required by the labor agreement, these three operators receive two 15-minute breaks daily; they may take them at any convenient time, once in the morning and once in the afternoon. Otherwise, they generally work full time at their keyboards all day.

Last year, Arlene Berkowitz, one of the operators, was absent from work for two weeks for a condition diagnosed as carpal tunnel syndrome, a neuromuscular disorder of the tendons and tissue in the wrists caused by repeated hand motions. Her symptoms included a dull ache in the wrist and excruciating pain in the shoulder and neck. Her doctor treated her with antiinflammatory medicine and a cortisone injection, and she has had no further problems. However, just last week a second data-entry operator experienced similar symptoms; her doctor diagnosed her ailment as "repeated-motion illness" and referred to it informally as the "VDT disease."

Because the company anticipates further automation in the future, with more data-entry operators to be hired, Jean Tate asked her assistant, Pat Robbins, to gather additional information on this condition. In fact, Jean wants Pat to survey all workers at US who use a computer or typewriter to determine the type and extent of their use and to identify any health problems. Once the extent of the problems are known, she wants Pat to make any appropriate recommendations regarding the work environment—posture, furniture, work habits, rest breaks, and the like—that will alleviate this problem.

1. Assume the role of Pat Robbins. Compose a problem statement and the component subproblems for this study.
2. Search the appropriate indexes and identify five relevant journal articles on this topic. Photocopy each article and save for a future assignment. Evaluate each article using the criteria given in this chapter; write a one-paragraph summary of your evaluation for each article. Using the guidelines given in this chapter, make notes of these articles.
3. Develop an employee questionnaire that elicits the information Jean asked for, plus whatever additional information you believe would be helpful, based on your reading of the journal articles you located. In lieu of a cover letter, include a short introductory paragraph at the top of the questionnaire explaining the purpose of the study and giving any needed directions.

■ **Food for Thought**[3] — Each of the following words or phrases describes an item of food. For example, a "complaint" is a "beef" and a "meek person" is a "lamb." See how many you can recognize.

WORDWISE

1. Easy to do
2. Rosy complexion
3. Bronx cheer
4. Grouchy person
5. Salute with a drink
6. Term of endearment
7. Money
8. Tall and lanky person
9. Musical session
10. Goad
11. Overly demonstrative
12. Lousy automobile

Answers: 1. piece of cake; 2. peaches and cream; 3. raspberry; 4. crab; 5. toast; 6. honey or sugar; 7. bread; 8. string bean; 9. jam; 10. egg; 11. ham; 12. lemon

12

Analyzing the Data and Preparing Visual Aids

After you have finished this chapter, you will be able to

1. Perform a preliminary analysis to edit and evaluate the data collected.

2. Construct clear, concise, and accurate tables.

3. Determine the most effective chart form and construct any needed charts.

4. Interpret the data for the reader.

5. Avoid misrepresentation when presenting and analyzing data.

How data is presented in a report can have an influence on the direction a company takes. Just ask Jim Solum, Manager of Business Systems Development for Wisconsin-based Oshkosh B'Gosh, a company that specializes in children's clothing.

"Resources are often committed to certain areas of a corporation based upon those that represent the highest percentage contribution to total revenue," Solum said.

Reports that are full of charts, numbers, and graphs, which divide each segment of the company's business into percentages, may not tell the whole story. "You have to take a look at the other aspect: How many dollars does it represent? This is where your numbers come in." Twenty percent of a $300+ million business, Solum noted, actually translates into $60 million of revenues. How data is presented affects how it is interpreted, and it is important to choose the type of presentation that suits the problem.

That $60 million figure can be overlooked when shown merely as a percentage of company business.

"If you start talking percentages, that's one thing, but you have to know when to use percentages and when to use raw data." When a company is looking at a $60 million segment of business, he noted, the people dedicated to preserving that market share should be given the tools needed to expand and maintain it. Further digging may show that the overhead costs of maintaining the line may be small in comparison to the line's returns.

"In that particular case, graphics wouldn't give you an accurate representation. I felt that if you start talking to people about $60 million, that's a big hunk of change, with a much bigger impact than the figure, *20%*." In fact, this $60 million "is almost as big as our company used to be just six years ago."

"The thing is, it's always been a *percentage* throughout the years. And the percentage usually stays about the same. The idea, if the percentage stays the same, is to look at the dollars involved. In a company such as ours, constant percentages still represent a growing dollar revenue."

Too often, a small successful segment of a company can be overlooked, especially if it is looked at in the wrong light. "I believe Senator Dirkson said, 'A billion here, a billion there, next thing you know you're talking real dollars.'" ▼

Jim Solum, Manager, Business Systems Development, Oshkosh B'Gosh, Oshkosh, Wisconsin

Analysis and interpretation turn data into information.

CONVERTING DATA INTO INFORMATION

At this point in the reporting process, you have presumably gathered enough data from your secondary and primary sources to enable you to solve your problem. (It is always possible, of course, that at any point during the data analysis and writing of your report you may find that you need additional information on a topic.)

Your job at this point, then, is to convert your raw data, which might be represented by your notes, photocopies of journal articles, completed questionnaires, audiotapes of interviews, computer printouts, and the like, into *information*—meaningful facts, statistics, and conclusions—that will help the reader of your report make a decision. In addition to interpreting your findings in narrative form, you will also likely prepare some **visual aids**—tables, charts, photographs, or other graphic materials to add interest and aid comprehension.

Data analysis is not a step that can be accomplished at one sitting. The more familiar you become with the data and the more you pore over it, the more things you will see. Data analysis is usually the part of the report process that requires the most time as well as the most skill. The more insight you can provide the reader about the *meaning* of the data you've collected and presented, the more helpful will be your report.

PRELIMINARY ANALYSIS

Preliminary analysis involves editing the data for accuracy and completeness and then evaluating the data to see if it solves the problem; that is, if it gives the reader the information needed to make a decision.

Editing

OBJECTIVE 1: Perform a preliminary analysis to edit and evaluate the data collected.

In an ideal world, every respondent would do exactly as he or she were asked, and there would be no need to edit raw data. But that's not what happens. For example, you might get a response like this:

356

8. Number of full-time employees in your company:
   ___X___ fewer than 500
   _____ 500–1,000
   ___X___ more than 1,000

The respondent has checked two different categories and written in the margin, "We have 350 employees in our parent organization but more than 1,000 including our overseas subsidiaries." Now the researcher must make a decision and then edit the questionnaire accordingly.

Similarly, respondents may record an impossible answer (giving a birth date of 1845, for example) or give an obviously contradictory response (checking the age category "less than 25 years old" for one question and the category "Medicare" as the major insurance provider in another question, for example). Because of such problems, never send your completed questionnaires directly to the computer center for analysis before editing them. Even if you find no errors to correct, you will often find other tidbits of information or insight that you would have missed had your data "never been touched by human hands."

Data editing is the process of reviewing the data for accuracy and completeness before data analysis. Sometimes you must try to determine the respondent's intentions or predict how the respondent *would have* answered the question. Doing so sometimes requires that you change a respondent's response or fill in a blank response. Obviously, good judgment and honest intentions should be the hallmarks of editing.

> Editing sometimes requires that you guess the respondent's intentions.

Today, most survey data is tabulated by microcomputer. The survey is coded—that is, numbers or symbols are assigned to each question—and responses are fed into the computer with those codes. Numerous microcomputer software programs are available for entering and analyzing data and printing tables and charts of the results. The researcher can edit the data as it's entered into the computer, correcting respondent or keyboarding errors, combining categories, and performing other analyses "on the fly" so to speak. The convenience and flexibility of microcomputer software programs have made computer data analysis a very personalized process.

> Statistical-analysis software gives the researcher more flexibility and control over the data analysis.

In addition to these specialized statistical analysis programs, most full-featured spreadsheet or database programs can also analyze survey data and produce tables and charts, which can then be copied directly into a word processing program for producing the final report.

Evaluating the Data

Recall from Chapter 10 that Step 4 of the research process is to develop hypotheses regarding causes or solutions for the problem; this step in turn determines what types of data you collect. In analyzing the resulting data, you must first determine whether it does, in fact, solve your problem. It would make no sense to prepare elaborate tables and other visual aids if your data is irrelevant, incomplete, or inaccurate.

> Determine the meaning of each finding by itself, in conjunction with each other finding, and in conjunction with all other findings.

To help you make this initial evaluation of your data, assume for the sake of simplification that you have gathered only three points of information and are now ready to analyze the data (see Figure 12.1). First, look at each piece of data individually (Step 1). If Finding A were the only piece of data you collected, what would that mean in terms of solving the problem? What conclusions could you draw from this bit of information? Follow the

FIGURE 12.1   Analyzing the Data

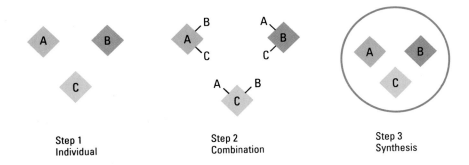

| | Step 1 | Step 2 | Step 3 |
| | Individual | Combination | Synthesis |

same process for Findings B and C, looking at each in isolation, without considering any other data.

Then look at each piece of data in combination with the other bits (Step 2). For example, by itself Finding A might lead to one conclusion, but when viewed in conjunction with Findings B and C, it might assume a different shade of meaning. In other words, does knowing Findings B and C *reinforce* your initial conclusion? If so, you can use stronger language in drawing your conclusion. Or does it *weaken* your initial conclusion? If so, you might wish to use less certain language or refrain from drawing any conclusion at all.

Finally, synthesize all the information you've collected (Step 3). When all the facts are considered together, what do they mean? For example, if Findings A, B, and C all point in the same direction, you might be able to define a trend. More importantly, you must determine whether all the data taken together provides an accurate and complete answer to your problem statement. If it does, you're ready to begin the detailed analysis and presentation that will help the reader understand your findings. If it does not, you must backtrack and start the research process again.

CONSTRUCTING TABLES

OBJECTIVE 2: Construct clear, concise, and accurate tables.

A **table** is an orderly arrangement of data in columnar form. It represents the most basic form of statistical analysis and is useful for showing a large amount of numerical data in a small space. A table presents numerical data more economically and more interestingly than narrative text and provides more information than a graph, though it lacks the visual impact of a graph. Because of its orderly arrangement of information into vertical columns and horizontal rows, a table also permits easy comparison of figures. However, trends are more obvious when presented in graphs.

Figure 12.2 shows an example of a computer printout of an attitude-scale item (Question 9) on a questionnaire and the corresponding table constructed from this printout. Apex, a manufacturer of consumer products headquartered in Cleveland, Ohio, is considering building a major addition to its factory there and wants to gauge local opinion before making a commitment.

Consider first the computer printout at the top of Figure 12.2. The "Value-Label" column simply lists the five alternatives given on the questionnaire. The "Value" column lists the code used for each of these

Example of Computer Printout and Corresponding Table   **FIGURE 12.2**

```
-------------------------------------------------------------------

Q.9 "Apex Company is an asset to our community."


       VALUE LABEL        VALUE   FREQUENCY   PCT   VALID PCT  CUM PCT
    Strongly agree          1        41       15.0    15.1     15.1
    Agree                   2       175       63.8    64.6     79.7
    No opinion              3        34       12.4    12.6     92.3
    Disagree                4        15        5.5     5.5     97.8
    Strongly disagree       5         6        2.2     2.2    100.0
                            •         3        1.1   MISSING
                          -----   -------    -----   ------   -----
    TOTAL                            274      100.0  100.0    100.0

    VALID CASES          271            MISSING CASES 3
-------------------------------------------------------------------
```

TABLE 4. RESPONSE TO STATEMENT "APEX COMPANY IS AN
          ASSET TO OUR COMMUNITY"

Response	No.	Pct.
Strongly agree	41	15.1
Agree	175	64.6
No opinion	34	12.6
Disagree	15	5.5
Strongly disagree	6	2.2
Total	271	100.0

five alternatives. The "Frequency" column shows the number of respondents who checked each alternative. The "Pct" column shows the percentage of each response, based on the total number of respondents, including those who left this item blank ($N = 274$). The "Valid Pct" column shows the percentage of each response, based on the total number of respondents who answered this question ($N = 271$). The "Cum Pct" column gives the cumulative percentage—that is, the sum of this response plus those above it (e.g., 79.7% of the respondents either agreed or strongly agreed with this statement).

The researcher must determine whether the "Pct" or "Valid Pct" column is more appropriate for the analysis. In most cases, the "Valid Pct" column, which ignores any blank responses, would be the one chosen. That is the case in the Table 4 shown in the lower half of Figure 12.2.

Your reader must be able to understand each table on its own, without reading the surrounding text. Thus, at a minimum, each table should contain a table number, a descriptive but concise title, column headings, and body (the items under each column heading). If you need footnotes to explain individual items within the table, put them immediately below the body. Similarly, if the table is based on secondary data, type a source note below the body, giving the appropriate citation. Common abbreviations and symbols are acceptable in tables.

> The reader should be able to understand the table without having to refer to the text.

FIGURE 12.3   Example of Cross-Tabulation Analysis

TABLE 4.   RESPONSE TO STATEMENT "APEX COMPANY IS AN ASSET TO OUR COMMUNITY"

Response	Total		Marital Status		Sex		Age			
	Total	Pct.	Married	Single	Male	Female	Under 21	21–35	36–50	Over 50
Strongly agree	41	15.1	14.0%	17.6%	15.7%	10.4%	21.7%	8.4%	12.0%	28.4%
Agree	175	64.6	67.5%	58.8%	67.6%	46.3%	47.8%	65.1%	69.1%	61.0%
No opinion	34	12.6	11.2%	15.4%	11.4%	20.9%	17.5%	13.0%	14.3%	9.2%
Disagree	15	5.5	5.1%	5.5%	4.0%	13.4%	13.0%	8.4%	4.0%	0.7%
Strongly disagree	6	2.2	2.2%	2.7%	1.3%	9.0%	0.0%	5.1%	0.6%	0.7%
Total	271	100.0	100.0%	100.0%	100.0%	100.0%	100.0%	100.0%	100.0%	100.0%

Cross-Tabulation Analysis

Cross-tab analysis enables you to look at two or more groups of data simultaneously.

In some cases, the simple question-by-question tabulation illustrated in Table 4 of Figure 12.2 would be sufficient analysis for the reader's purpose. However, in most cases such simple tabulations would not yield all the "secrets" the data holds. Most data can be further analyzed through **cross-tabulation**, a process by which two or more pieces of data are analyzed together. For example, because of the type of products Apex manufactures, you might suspect that different subgroups of respondents might hold different views of the company. Therefore, you can combine Question 9 with the questions about marital status, sex, and age, as shown in Figure 12.3.

This table shows not only the total responses (both the number and the percentages) but also the percentage responses for the subgroups according to marital status, sex, and age. A quick "eye-balling" of the table shows that there do not seem to be any major differences in the perceptions of married versus single respondents. However, there does seem to be a fairly sizable difference between male and female respondents: males have a much more positive view of the company than do females.

If the table in Figure 12.3 were one of only a few tables in your report, it would be just fine the way it is shown. However, suppose the statement "Apex Company is an asset to our community" is one of a dozen attitude items, each of which requires a similar table. It is probably too much to expect the reader to study a dozen similar tables; in such a situation, you might consider simplifying the table.

Sometimes tabular data needs to be condensed for easier and faster comprehension.

There are a number of ways to simplify a table. You should recognize right from the start, however, that whenever you simplify a table (that is, whenever you combine rows or columns or simply delete data), your table loses some of its detail. The goal is to ensure that you gain more in comprehensibility than you lose in specificity. Your knowledge of the reader and his or her needs will help you determine how much detail to present.

With that in mind, consider the simplified version of this table shown in Figure 12.4. The two positive responses ("strongly agree" and "agree") have been combined into one "agree" row, as have the two negative responses. Combining not only simplifies the table but also prevents some possible interpretation problems. Given the original table in Figure 12.3, for example, would this statement be accurate: "Less than half of the

Example of Simplified Table   **FIGURE 12.4**

TABLE 4.   RESPONSE TO STATEMENT "APEX COMPANY IS AN ASSET TO OUR COMMUNITY"

Response	Total		Marital Status		Sex		Age		
	Total	Pct.	Married	Single	Male	Female	Under 21	21–50	Over 50
Agree	216	79.7	81.5%	76.4%	83.3%	56.7%	69.5%	77.3%	89.4%
No opinion	34	12.6	11.2%	15.4%	11.4%	20.9%	17.5%	13.7%	9.2%
Disagree	21	7.7	7.3%	8.2%	5.3%	22.4%	13.0%	9.0%	1.4%
Total	271	100.0	100.0%	100.0%	100.0%	100.0%	100.0%	100.0%	100.0%

females agree that Apex Company is an asset to their community"? Technically, the statement is accurate, since the 46.3% who "agree" is less than half. However, the statement leaves an incorrect impression because more than half of the females (57%—those who "agree" and who "strongly agree") believe Apex Company is an asset to their community. This conclusion is made clear in Figure 12.4.

Note also that the two middle age groups ("21–35" and "36–50") have been combined into one age group ("21–50"). Because the company's products are geared mainly to this large middle group, the company wanted to compare the responses of this important group with the less important younger and older groups.

This simplification deleted one of the ten columns and two of the five rows—for a net decrease of 46% in the number of individual bits of data presented. When this reduction is multiplied by the number of similar tables, the net effect is rather dramatic. The simplification could have been taken a step further by rounding each percentage to the nearest whole—which would have made each table "appear" much simpler, with little loss of precision.

> More data is not always better than less data.

An alternative method of presenting this and similar scale data would be to use a weighted average. The weighted average for the question shown in the original computer printout would be calculated as follows:

Response	Freq.	× Weight	= Total
Strongly agree	41	1	41
Agree	175	2	350
No opinion	34	3	102
Disagree	15	4	60
Strongly disagree	6	5	30
	271		583 $583 / 271 = 2.15$

The resulting weighted average of 2.15 would be interpreted this way: On a scale of 1 to 5 (where 1 = "strongly agree" and 5 = "strongly disagree"), the average response to this question was 2.15.

Arranging Data in Tables

As discussed earlier, the check-off alternatives in your questionnaire items should be arranged in some logical order, most often either numerical or alphabetical, to avoid possibly biasing the responses. Once you have the

> Arrange the data in logical format—usually from high to low.

FIGURE 12.5   Arranging Data in Tables

From This:

6. In which of the following categories of clerical workers do you expect to hire additional
   workers within the next three years? (Check all
   that apply.)

   _211_ bookkeepers and accounting clerks
   _31_ computer operators
   _30_ data-entry keyers
   _24_ file clerks
   _247_ general office clerks
   _78_ receptionists and information clerks
   _323_ secretaries
   _7_ statistical clerks
   _107_ typists and word processors

To This:

TABLE 2.   COMPANIES PLANNING TO HIRE
           ADDITIONAL CLERICAL WORKERS

Category	No. of Co's	Pct.[a]
Secretaries	323	99.1
General office clerks	247	75.8
Bookkeepers and accounting clerks	211	64.7
Typists and word processors	107	32.8
Receptionists and information clerks	78	23.9
Miscellaneous	92	28.2
Total	326	

[a]Answers total more than 100% because of multiple
responses.

data in hand, however, it is often a help to the reader to rearrange the data
from high to low.

In Figure 12.5, for example, the categories have been rearranged from
their original alphabetical order in the questionnaire to high-to-low order
in the report table. Note also that the four smallest categories have been
combined into a miscellaneous category, which always goes last, regardless
of its size. Finally, note the position and format of the table footnote, which
is used to explain an entry in the table.

PREPARING CHARTS

OBJECTIVE 3: Determine
the most effective chart
form and construct any
needed charts.

The appropriate use of well-designed charts and graphs (although, technically, graphs are shown on graph paper, the two terms are commonly used
interchangeably) can aid in reader comprehension, emphasize certain data,
create interest, and save time and space, since the essential meaning of large
masses of statistical data can be perceived immediately.

Because of their visual impact, charts receive more emphasis than tables or narrative text. Therefore, you should save them for presenting information that is important and that can best be grasped visually, for example, when the overall picture is more important than the individual numbers. Also recognize that the more charts your report contains, the less impact each individual chart will have.

The cardinal rule for designing charts is to keep them simple. Trying to cram too much information into one chart will only confuse the reader and lessen the impact of the graphic. Well-designed charts have only one interpretation, and that interpretation should be clear immediately; the reader shouldn't have to study the chart at length or refer to the surrounding text.

> Keep charts simple. Immediate comprehension is the goal.

Regardless of their type, label all your charts as figures, and assign them consecutive numbers, separate from table numbers. Although tables are captioned at the top, charts may be captioned at the top or bottom. Charts used alone (for example, as an overhead transparency or slide) are typically captioned at the top. Charts preceded or followed by text or that contain an explanatory paragraph are typically captioned at the bottom (see Figure 12.12). As with tables, commonly understood abbreviations may be used.

Today, many microcomputer software programs are available to generate special charts automatically from data already contained in spreadsheets or from data entered at the keyboard. The professional appearance and ready availability of such charts often make up for the loss of flexibility in designing the chart precisely to your wishes.

> Many software programs can generate high-quality charts with little effort.

The main types of charts used in business presentations are line charts, bar charts, pie charts, and pictorial charts. Each of these types has numerous variations, as illustrated in Figure 12.6.

Line Charts

A **line chart** is a graph with rectangular grids, with the vertical grid representing values and the horizontal grid representing time. Line charts are very useful for showing changes in data over long periods of time and for emphasizing the movement of the data—the trends—rather than the individual amounts. Both grids should be marked off in equal intervals and clearly labeled. The vertical grid should begin with zero, even when all the amounts are quite large. In some situations, it may be desirable to show a break in the intervals—as illustrated in the first and second line charts in Figure 12.6A.

> Line charts show trends over long periods of time.

Fluctuations of the line over time indicate variations in the trend, whereas the distance of the line from the horizontal axis indicates quantity. More than one variable may be plotted on the same chart; for example, both sales and net profits can be plotted on one chart, with either different-colored lines or different types of lines (for example, one solid and one broken) used to avoid confusion. Each line should be clearly labeled.

A variation of the line chart is the surface chart, which uses shading to emphasize the overall picture of the trend. A second variation is the divided surface chart, which contains several bands that depict the components of the total trend. Because the individual components cannot be read accurately, the divided surface chart should be used only to give an overall picture.

FIGURE 12.6A The Line Chart

Simple Line Chart

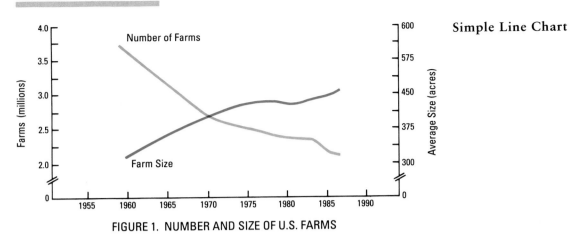

FIGURE 1. NUMBER AND SIZE OF U.S. FARMS

SOURCE: Department of Labor, *Occupational Outlook Handbook, 1988-89 ed.,* (Washington, DC: Government Printing Office, 1989), p. 332.

Surface Chart

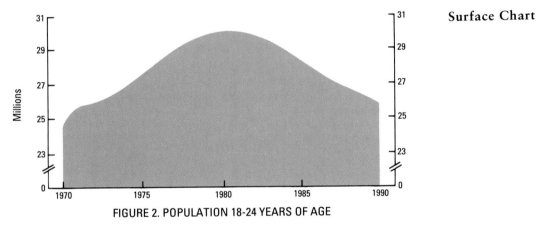

FIGURE 2. POPULATION 18-24 YEARS OF AGE

SOURCE: Department of Labor, *Occupational Outlook Handbook, 1988-89 ed.,* (Washington, DC: Government Printing Office, 1989), p. 218.

Divided Surface Chart

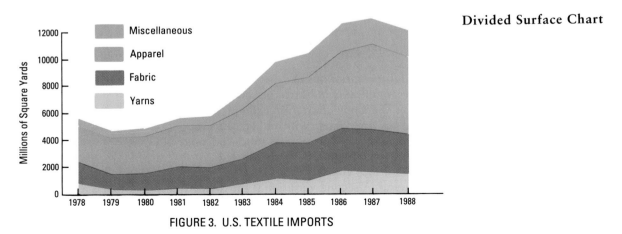

FIGURE 3. U.S. TEXTILE IMPORTS

SOURCE: Standard & Poor's, *Standard & Poor's Industry Surveys, 1989, Vol 2* (New York: Standard & Poor's, 1989), p. T64.

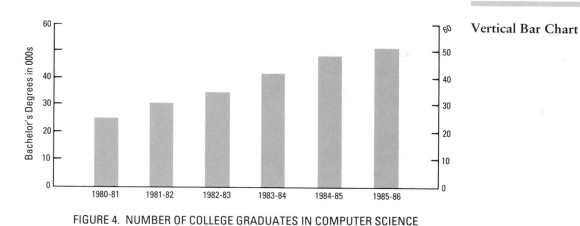

Vertical Bar Chart

FIGURE 4. NUMBER OF COLLEGE GRADUATES IN COMPUTER SCIENCE

SOURCE: Department of Labor, *Occupational Outlook Handbook, 1988-89 ed.*,
(Washington, DC: Government Printing Office, 1989), p. 192.

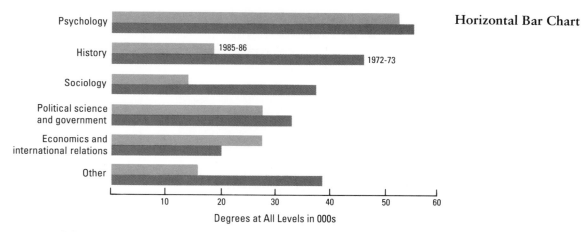

Horizontal Bar Chart

FIGURE 5. NUMBER OF COLLEGE GRADUATES IN SOCIAL SCIENCE

SOURCE: Department of Labor, *Occupational Outlook Handbook, 1988-89 ed.*,
(Washington, DC: Government Printing Office, 1989), p. 89.

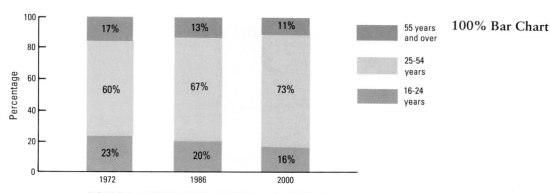

100% Bar Chart

FIGURE 6. DISTRIBUTION OF THE LABOR FORCE BY AGE

SOURCE: Department of Labor, *Occupational Outlook Handbook, 1988-89 ed.*,
(Washington, DC: Government Printing Office, 1989), p. 9.

FIGURE 12.6C

Miscellaneous Charts

Pie Chart

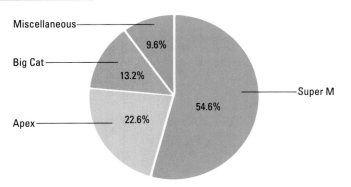

FIGURE 7. MARKET SHARE FOR PERSONAL-CARE PRODUCTS
(1990 data)

Pictogram

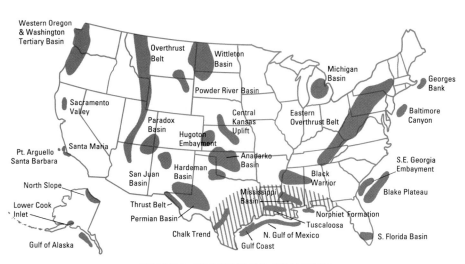

FIGURE 8. RESIDENTIAL HALL POPULATION — FALL 1991
(Each symbol represents 50 residents)

Map Chart

FIGURE 9. PRINCIPAL U.S. OIL BASINS

SOURCE: Standard & Poor's, *Standard & Poor's Industry Surveys, 1989, Vol 2*
(New York: Standard & Poor's, 1989), p. U-20.

FIGURE 12.6D

Line Chart

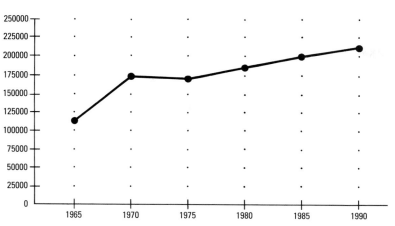

FIGURE 10. SALES BY YEAR: 1965 — 1990

Bar Chart

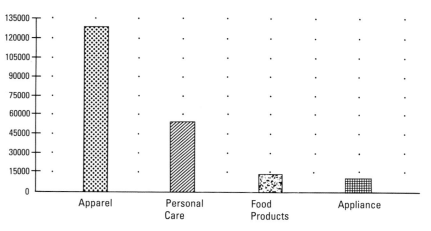

FIGURE 11. COMPONENT SALES FOR 1990

Pie Chart

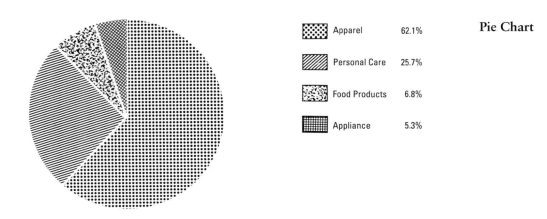

FIGURE 12. COMPONENT SALES FOR 1990

FIGURE 12.6E   Informal Pictorial Charts

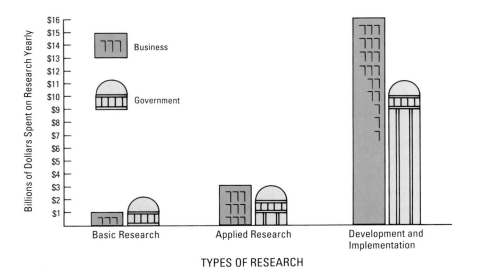

TYPES OF RESEARCH

Sole Proprietorships—
506 billion
7%

Partnerships—
292 billion
4%

Corporations—
6.4 trillion
89%

TOTAL SALES RECEIPTS EARNED BY AMERICAN BUSINESSES IN 1980.

SOURCE: Adapted from *Statistical Abstract of the United States*, 1984 U.S. Bureau of the Census.

GROWTH IN CONVENIENCE STORES

Bar Charts

A **bar chart** is a graph with horizontal or vertical bars representing values. Bar charts are one of the most useful, simple, and popular graphic techniques. They are particularly appropriate for comparing the magnitude or size of items, either at a specified time or over a period of time. The vertical bar chart (sometimes called a *column chart*) is typically used for portraying a time series when the emphasis is on the individual amounts rather than on the trends.

The bars should all be the same width, with the length changing to reflect the value of each item. The spacing between the bars should generally be about one-half the width of the bars. Bars may be grouped to compare several variables over a period of time or to show component parts of several variables.

As with tables, the bars should be arranged in some logical order. If space permits, the actual value of each bar may be included for quicker comprehension.

> Bar charts compare the magnitude of items. Use vertical bars for comparing items over time.

Pie Charts

A **pie chart** is a circle graph whose area is divided into component wedges. It compares the relative parts that make up a whole. Some software charting programs permit you to "drag out" a particular wedge of the pie chart for special emphasis.

Although pie charts rank very high in popular appeal, they are held in somewhat lower esteem by graphic specialists because of the difficulty in differentiating many categories, the lack of precision, and the difficulty of comparing component values across several pie charts. However, pie charts are useful for showing how component parts add up to make a total when between three and five component parts are used. A chart is generally not needed for presenting only two component parts; more than five can present visual difficulties in perceiving the relative value of each wedge.

It is common to begin slicing the pie at the 12 o'clock position and move clockwise in some logical order (often in order of descending size). If there is room, the labels should be placed inside each wedge; otherwise, they may go outside the wedge, with an arrow pointing to the wedge, or be labeled in a legend or key.

It is customary to letter in the percentages or other values represented by each wedge and to distinguish each wedge by shading, cross-hatched lines, different colors, or some similar device. Use a protractor to construct a pie chart manually. For example, to show a slice making up 25% of the whole, use the protractor to mark off 90 degrees (25% of the 360-degree circle).

> Pie charts show the parts that make up a whole.

> Pie charts are effective for giving a general impression—not for communicating actual amounts.

Pictorial Charts

A **pictorial chart** is a graph with relevant symbols representing values. Pictorial charts add emphasis and interest to the presentation of data and are often more expressive than words. Because of their attention-getting qualities, they are often used in reports directed to mass audiences, such as

> Pictorial charts add interest to mass-audience communications.

Show different amounts
by varying the number—
not the size—of the
pictograms.

annual reports. They are less frequently used in formal business reports or in academic reports.

For the chart to be effective, the pictogram (the symbol representing the item being presented) must have a close and immediate association with the item being presented. In most cases, it is difficult to portray quantities by drawing them in proportion to the values represented. Note, for example, in Figure 12.7, the problems with trying to show that Symbol B represents twice as much as Symbol A. No matter how the sailor is drawn, an inaccurate picture emerges.

The most effective types of pictorial charts treat each symbol as one unit of measure and show the value by the number of symbols rather than by their size. Thus, one sailor might represent 1,000 enlisted personnel, one garbage can might represent five tons of trash, or one dollar mark might

FIGURE 12.7   Avoid Varying the Size of Pictograms

Pictorial Charts

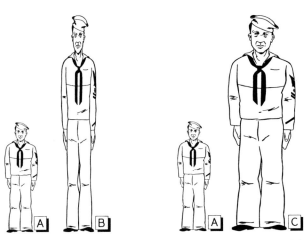

Figure 137. **Comparison of Sizes of Pictorial Symbols.** *A,* Original symbol. *B,* Original symbol doubled in height only. *C,* Original symbol doubled in both height and width. It will be observed that this symbol is four times as large in area and eight times as large in volume as the original symbol.

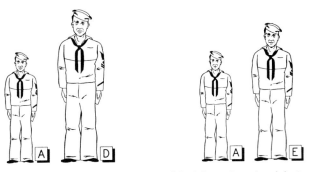

Figure 138. **Comparison of Sizes of Pictorial Symbols.** *A,* Original symbol. *D,* Symbol made twice the area of original symbol. *E,* Symbol is twice the volume of original symbol.

Source: Calvin F. Schmid, *Handbook of Graphic Presentation* (New York: Ronald Press, 1954), p. 225.

represent $10 million. Instead of bars, these symbols would be used to show amounts. Sometimes symbols cut in half must be used to give an accurate representation.

Other Types of Charts

The number of different types of visual aids that can be incorporated into a business report is limited only by the report writer's imagination. The vast array of devices available can only be mentioned here.

Map charts show state-by-state or other geographical comparisons. Flow charts present the steps in a process or the progress of events; the PERT (Program Evaluation Review Technique) chart is a specialized flow chart that shows the management of a project. Organizational charts show the overall structural plan of a group or organization. Diagrams can be used to show the component parts of an item, to illustrate a process (for example, assembling a metal storage case), or to represent a model (for example, the data-analysis model in Figure 12.1). Finally, photographs or drawings can be used to illustrate and clarify the meaning of many business concepts.

> Many types of visual aids can be productively used in business communications.

A Word of Caution

As the name "visual aid" implies, charts act as a *help*—not a substitute—for the narrative presentation and interpretation. Never use visual aids simply to make your report look "prettier."

Although such publications as *USA Today* and other popular newspapers and magazines make extensive use of three-dimensional graphics and elaborately illustrated charts (often called "chartoons") to show statistical information, their use in business should be limited to general-interest audiences. Such graphics are quite effective for gaining attention and providing a general impression but are less effective for conveying the precise meanings typically needed in business communications.

Three-dimensional graphics, although attention-grabbing, are difficult to interpret because they are often used to display only two-dimensional data (horizontal and vertical), with the third dimension (depth) having no meaning. Similarly, three-dimensional pie charts (shown slanted away from the viewer rather than vertically) are difficult to interpret because of perspective—the slices farthest away appear smaller than they actually are.

Recent research indicates that the format of the data (tables versus graphs) has little or no effect on the quality of the decisions made when the task requires a thorough analysis of financial data; both formats are judged to be equally effective. Managers appear to have more confidence in their decisions when such decisions are based on data from tables alone as opposed to data from graphs alone; but managers have the most confidence when both formats are used.[1]

These research findings indicate that graphic devices should be used as an adjunct to textual and tabular presentations. Although most numerical data can more efficiently be presented in tables, the competent business communicator uses charts to call attention to particular findings. Rarely should the same data be presented in both tabular and graphic formats.

In *The Visual Display of Quantitative Information*, Edward Tufte warns against "chartjunk"—charts that call attention to themselves instead of to

> Do not overuse visual aids; they'll detract from your message.

> Research shows that managers make effective use of both tables and charts.

the information they contain.[2] Others have labeled these overly elaborate charts "graphics garbage."

With the ready availability and ease of use of computer graphics, the temptation might be to "overvisualize" your report. Avoid using too many, too large, too garish, or too complicated charts. If the impact is not immediate or if interpretations vary, the chart loses its effectiveness. As with all other aspects of your report project, the visual aids must contribute directly to telling your story more effectively. Avoid chartjunk: strive to *express*—not to *impress*.

INTERPRETING DATA

OBJECTIVE 4: Interpret the data for the reader.

In some situations, the numerical data is so simple or the reader is so attuned to the problem that merely presenting the percentages in tabular form is all that is needed to "tell the story." Such might be the case for a recurring report, where the same quantitative data is presented in the same format month after month. The more typical situation, however, requires the report writer to perform a more in-depth analysis of the quantitative data.

Selecting and Calculating Statistics

Statistics is the branch of mathematics dealing with the collection, organization, and interpretation of numerical data. We use statistics every day, as illustrated by the following comments:

- "My GPA last semester was 2.8."
- "We outsold DeVry last month 3 to 2."
- "Our typical customer is a married female in her early twenties."
- "Sales picked up 9% when we offered consumers a $2 rebate."

Even when statistics are not mentioned in a statement (for example, "The Detroit Pistons are going to kill the Chicago Bulls in the playoffs"), they are often implied. For example, the preceding prediction was probably based on a knowledge of such team statistics as player heights, percentage of shots made, and percentage of games won.

Although the study of statistics is beyond the scope of this text, we can usefully review some elementary statistical concepts to help us analyze the data we collect. The most common descriptive statistics used to summarize a mass of data are the mean, median, mode, and range.

Use the mean to describe a group of numbers unless there are one or two extreme values.

Mean   The arithmetic average of a group of numbers is called the **mean**; it is computed by dividing the sum of the figures by the number of figures in the group. Assume that the ages of the ten respondents to your survey are as follows:

24	28	30	33	60
26	30	33	35	63

The mean age of your respondents is 362/10 or 36.2 years. The mean is the value we generally intend when we talk about an average. It is the most important descriptive statistic because it is takes into account the numerical value of all the scores in a group. Because the mean is strongly affected by extreme values, it should not be used when one or two of the figures are so dramatically different from the others that they might result in an inaccurate representation of the data.

Median   The middle value (or midpoint) in a group of numbers arranged from low to high (or vice versa) is called the **median**. The median divides the group into two equal groups. Assume that your ten respondents purchased the following volume of products from you last year:

$5,600	$22,500	$25,800	$31,000	$95,000
$17,800	$24,700	$26,000	$34,000	$175,000

The median sales volume of your ten respondents is half-way between the fifth and sixth responses, or $25,900 (computing the midpoint is not necessary if there is an odd number of figures). In this example, the median of $25,900 is a more accurate representation of the group of figures than would be the mean value of $43,270, because of the effect on the mean of the one extreme value of $175,000.

Mode   The value in a group of numbers that occurs most frequently is called the **mode**. Assume you surveyed ten users regarding their favorite container size of the cheese spread that you manufacture, with the following responses:

4 oz.	4 oz.	8 oz.	12 oz.	16 oz.
4 oz.	4 oz.	8 oz.	16 oz.	32 oz.

The mode of this distribution is 4 ounces; that is, the 4-ounce size is the most popular size with the respondents. The chief advantage of using the mode to describe a group of figures is that it is easy to obtain, easy to interpret, and not affected by extreme values in the group of figures. Sometimes it is also the only logical choice. For instance, it would not have made sense in this example to say that the most popular sized container for cheese spread was 10.8 ounces (the mean), because you don't manufacture that size. (How could a container that doesn't even exist be the most popular one?)

However, because the mode is based on only part of the data, it is often not representative of the entire group. Suppose in a group of 12 people there are 10 adults, each of a different age, and two children each of whom is a year old. The mode of one year (the most common age) would not be an accurate way to describe this group.

Range   Whereas the mean, median, and mode tell how the scores tend to be similar (and are called *measures of central tendency*), the **range** is a *measure of variability* and tells how the scores tend to be different. It is computed by subtracting the highest and lowest figures in a group and then adding 1 (in order to include both the highest and lowest figure). Thus, the respondents above had an age range of 40 years (63 − 24 + 1); or, to put it another way, the respondents ranged in age from 24 to 63 years.

The range is easily computed, easily understood, and quite helpful in presenting a general interpretation of the data. But because it includes only two figures in the group (the highest and the lowest), it is a fairly crude measure and is greatly affected by extreme values. (The computation for a more precise measure of variability, the standard deviation, is covered in

Use the range to indicate how scores differ.

any standard statistics textbook.) Taken together, the range and one of the measures of central tendency (mean, median, or mode) often provide a clear interpretation of a group of figures.

As should be evident, each of these statistics is useful in its own way in helping the reader understand a mass of data. Other methods of statistical analysis (especially correlation, trend analysis, and tests of inference) are often helpful in interpreting the raw data but are beyond the scope of this course and may be beyond the comprehension of some general business readers. The competent communicator selects those statistics that are most helpful to the reader and that provide the most accurate picture of the raw data.

Making Sense of the Data

Don't just present tables and figures. Interpret their important points.

As a report writer, you cannot simply present the raw data without interpreting it. The data in your tables and charts helps to solve a problem, and the report writer must make the connection between that data and the solution to the problem. You need not discuss all the data in the tables and charts; that would be boring and insulting to the reader. But you must determine what you think the important implications of your data are, and then identify and discuss them for the reader.

At a minimum, discuss the overall response.

What types of important points do you look for? Almost always, the most important finding is the overall response to a question (rather than the responses of the cross-tabulation subgroups). And almost always the category within the question that receives the largest response is the most important point. So discuss this question and this category first.

In Table 4 in Figure 12.2, for example, the major finding is this: four-fifths of the respondents believe that Apex Company is an asset to their community. Note that if you have the exact figures given in the table, you can use less precise language in the narrative—"four-fifths," "one in four," "a slight majority," and the like. Doing so helps prevent you from presenting facts and figures too quickly. Pace your analysis because the reader will not be able to comprehend data that is presented too quickly or in too concentrated a format.

Discuss any important cross-tab findings.

Once you've discussed the overall finding, you should begin discussing the cross-tabulation data as necessary. Look for trends, unexpected findings, data that reinforces or contradicts other tables, extreme values, data that raises questions, and the like. If these are important, discuss them. In our example, there were no major differences in the responses by marital status, so you would probably not need to discuss them. However, you would need to discuss the big difference in responses between males and females. If possible, present data or draw any valid conclusions regarding the reasons for these differences.

Finally, point out the trend that is evident with regard to age: the older the respondent, the more positive the response. If it's important enough, this trend could be displayed in a graph for more visual effect.

Sometimes you will want to include descriptive statistics (such as the mean, median, range, and standard deviation). At other times, the nature of your data will necessitate the use of significance testing—to determine whether the differences found in your sample data are also likely to exist in the population. These topics are beyond the scope of this text but are covered in depth in any basic statistics textbook.

Once you have gathered and analyzed the data for a report,
you will likely prepare visual aids. Charts, like the bar chart
shown here, have a greater visual impact for the reader
than do tables or narrative text. Keep in mind, however,
that the more charts a report contains, the less impact
individual charts will have.
(Source: Superstock, Inc.)

You now probably know more about the topic on which you're writing
than will the reader. Assist the reader, then, by pointing out the important
implications, findings, and relationships of your data. Help your reader
reach the same conclusions you have.

AVOIDING MISREPRESENTATION

*In preparation for selecting the next sales manager, Roger Davis sent his
three assistant sales managers to an intensive one-week seminar sponsored
by the National Sales Management Association. He needed a fast learner
for the job and figured the test results from this seminar would tell him
who has the most growth potential. Roger asked you, his assistant, to
analyze the test results and write him a memo report recommending one
of the three for the promotion, based on their growth potential. Before
reading the discussion that follows, study the following test scores and
decide whom you will recommend.*

OBJECTIVE 5: Avoid
misrepresentation when presenting and analyzing data.

	Pretest Score	Posttest Score
Marilyn Driskill	*30*	*50*
Donald Malone	*50*	*70*
Pat Scheiber	*70*	*90*

*Marilyn argues that she should be selected. After all, she improved from
a beginning score of 30 to an ending score of 50; her 20-point improvement
represents a 67% increase whereas Donald increased only 40% and Pat,
29%.*

*Donald argues that he should be selected. Since all three candidates
showed the same growth (20 points), he believes the decision should be*

based on other factors—such as that he's the most experienced of the three candidates.

Pat argues that he should be selected. Since the maximum score on the test was 100 points, he began with only 30 possible points that he could improve, and he actually improved 20 points—or 67% of the maximum. Marilyn, on the other hand, improved only 29% of the points available to her, and Don improved only 40% of the points available to him.

Whom will you recommend?

As this vignette makes clear, during the analysis and subsequent write-up of your data, you will have many decisions to make. How much data should you present? In most cases, you will not be able to present all the data you gathered. Do you have enough data on which to base a conclusion? If so, how definite should you make that conclusion? Which of your findings should you emphasize and which should you subordinate?

| Misrepresentation includes not only making factual misstatements but also leaving incorrect impressions. |

Unfortunately (as in the preceding example), in many cases there is no one right answer. Instead, the answer depends on the purpose of your report and the needs of your reader. Having acknowledged that, however, we can productively discuss some of the more common dilemmas the report writer faces.

Distortion in Charts

| Chart distortion can result from varying the grid, skipping intervals, or using unequal time intervals. |

There are many ways to consciously or unconsciously distort graphic data, or to engage in "cheating by charting."[3] First of all, consider the different visual impact that can result from simply varying the scale of the grid. The three charts in the first row of Figure 12.8 all show the same numbers; yet notice the different visual impact of each.

Charts can also be distorted by skipping intervals. As noted earlier, all charts should begin at the zero point. In Figure 12.8, note how the third bar in the distorted chart appears to be about half the size of the first bar; in actuality, it is only slightly smaller.

Finally, the use of unequal time intervals can cause distortion. If some data points are missing, indicate that fact by varying the size of the intervals, as in the first chart on the third row of Figure 12.8. Notice how much steeper the trend line is in the distorted chart, when different time intervals are incorrectly treated as equal.

Distortion in Statistics

| Use statistics to help you communicate your story more effectively—not to support a biased viewpoint. |

Assume that XYZ Company has 27 employees. The president earns $200,000 yearly, the vice president earns $150,000, and each of the 25 factory workers earns $20,000, for a total annual payroll of $850,000. Would it be accurate for the president to brag that the average employee at XYZ earns $31,481 a year ($850,000/27)? Of course not. In this case, the mean does not give an accurate portrayal for any of the employees—not for the president, the vice president, or the factory workers. Either the mode ($20,000) or the median ($20,000) would have been a more accurate figure.

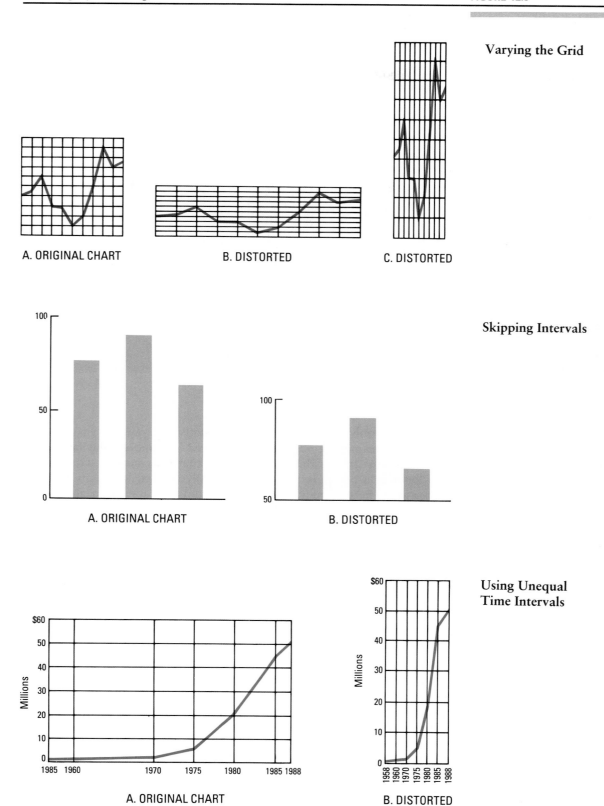

Varying the Grid

A. ORIGINAL CHART   B. DISTORTED   C. DISTORTED

Skipping Intervals

A. ORIGINAL CHART   B. DISTORTED

Using Unequal
Time Intervals

A. ORIGINAL CHART   B. DISTORTED

Source: Adapted from Mary Eleanor Spear, *Practical Charting Techniques* (New York: McGraw-Hill, 1969), pp. 56–59.

FIGURE 12.9 Misuse of Statistics

This pond is safe because the average depth of water is only 2 feet.

A similar problem exists when giving statistics from too small a data base. If a department of 30 people experienced only one sick day last month and had two sick days this month, saying that their number of sick days had doubled in one month, while technically correct, leaves an incorrect impression. The one additional sick day could have been an aberration; and at any rate, the statement disguises the fact that even two sick days a month is a very commendable record indeed.

The situation is similar to the apocryphal report of an athletic meet in which the United States team soundly defeated the Soviet team. The Soviet press proudly proclaimed, "USSR comes in second in international athletic meet while the United States team was next to last!" Beware of using statistics inappropriately.

Distortion by Omission

It is unethical to leave an inaccurate impression, even when what you report is true. Sins of omission are as serious as sins of commission. Distortion by omission can occur when using quotations out of context, when omitting some relevant background information, or when including only the most extreme or most interesting data.

Do not use quotations out of context.

It would be inappropriate, for example, to quote extensively from a survey that was conducted 15 years ago without first establishing for the reader that the findings were still valid. Likewise, it would be inappropriate to quote a finding from one study and not discuss the fact that four similar studies reached opposite conclusions.

Be especially careful to quote and paraphrase accurately from interview sources. Provide enough information to ensure that the passage reflects the interviewee's *intention*. Here is an example of possible distortions:

Johnson's original quotation: "I think the Lancelot is an excellent car for anyone who does not need to worry about fuel economy."

Distortion: Johnson thinks the Lancelot is "an excellent car."

Worse distortion: Johnson thinks the Lancelot is "an excellent car for anyone."

Worst distortion: Johnson thinks the Lancelot is "an excellent car <u>for anyone</u>!"

The Ethical Dimension

In gathering, analyzing, reporting, and disseminating data, everyone involved has both rights and obligations. For example, the researcher (1) has the right to expect that respondents will be truthful in their responses and (2) has an obligation not to deceive the respondent. Similarly, the organization that is paying for the research (1) has the right to expect that the researcher will provide valid and reliable information and (2) has an obligation not to misuse that data. The American Association for Public Opinion Research has adopted guidelines that are useful for all researchers. Its Code of Professional Ethics and Practices[4] requires researchers to

- Disclose who sponsored and conducted the research, the exact wording of questions and instructions, the population and sample used, and the location and dates of data collection.
- Avoid methods that may harm, humiliate, or seriously mislead survey respondents.
- Hold as confidential all information that might identify a respondent with his or her responses.
- Neither make interpretations nor allow others to make interpretations that are misleading or inconsistent with the findings.
- Take vigorous steps to publicly correct anyone else's distortions of their research data.

If your research and corresponding report are to help solve problems and aid in decision-making, all parties involved must use common sense, good judgment, and goodwill to make the project successful.

> Everyone involved in the reporting situation has a responsibility to act in an ethical manner.

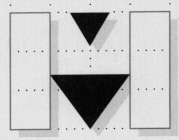

MICROWRITING ANALYZING DATA

The Problem

You are a manager at a software-development house that publishes communication software for the HAL and Pear microcomputers. Together, these two computers comprise about 90% of the business market. In 1990, you were asked to survey users of communication software. (You conducted a similar study in 1985.)

You conducted the survey using the same questionnaire and same procedures from the 1985 study. Now you've gathered the data, along with the comparable data collected in 1985, and have organized it roughly into draft tables, one of which is shown in Figure 12.10. You're now ready to put this table into final report format and analyze its contents.

FIGURE 12.10   Draft Table

Q. From what source did you obtain your last software program?

Source	1985 Total N	%	HAL N	%	Pear N	%	1990 Total N	%	HAL N	%	Pear N	%
Mail-order company	28	21.2	24	26.1	4	10.0	60	41.1	25	30.9	35	53.9
On-line bulletin board	3	2.3	2	2.2	1	2.5	4	2.7	2	2.5	2	3.1
Retail outlet	70	53.0	46	50.0	24	60.0	63	43.2	44	54.3	19	29.2
Software publisher	9	6.8	4	4.3	5	12.5	10	6.8	4	4.9	6	9.2
Unauthorized copy	21	15.9	15	16.3	6	15.0	6	4.1	3	3.7	3	4.6
Other	1	.8	1	1.1	0	0.0	3	2.1	3	3.7	0	0.0
Total	132	100.0	92	100.0	40	100.0	146	100.0	81	100.0	65	100.0

The Process

1. TABLE FORMAT

a. Examine the format of your draft table—the arrangement of columns and rows. Should anything be changed for the final table?

First, the year columns (1985 and 1990) should be reversed. The new data is more important than the old data, so it should be emphasized.

Second, the rows need to be rearranged. They're now in alphabetical order but should be rearranged in descending order according to the first amount column—the 1990 total column. Doing this will put the most important data first in the table.

b. Assuming that you will have many tables in your final report, is there some way to condense the information in this table without undue loss of precision or detail?

```
Although the number of respondents is important, the
readers of my report will be much more interested in
the percentages. Therefore, I'll give only the total
number of respondents for each column and put that
figure immediately under each column heading.

Also, I see immediately that very few people obtained
their software from on-line bulletin boards either in
1985 or 1990, so I'll combine that category with the
"other" category.

These changes are shown in Figure 12.11.
```

2. TABLE INTERPRETATION

a. Study the table in Figure 12.11. If you had space to make only one statement about this table, what would it be?

```
Retail outlets and mail-order companies are equally
important sources for obtaining software, together
accounting for more than four-fifths of all sources.
```

b. What other 1990 data should you discuss in your narrative?

```
HAL and Pear users obtain their software in different
ways: the majority of HAL users obtain theirs from
retail outlets whereas the majority of Pear users
obtain theirs from mail-order firms.
```

c. What should you point out in comparing 1990 data with that of 1985?

```
Retail outlets have decreased in popularity (down 10%)
while mail-order companies have dramatically increased
in popularity (up 20%).

Also, the use of unauthorized copies appears to be
decreasing (although the actual figure is probably
somewhat higher than these self-reported figures).
```

3. VISUAL AIDS

If you wanted to show graphically the change in the popularity of retail outlets versus mail-order companies, what type of chart would you use?

```
Two years' worth of data would not be enough data
points for a line chart, and it would be difficult to
compare the relative sizes of pie wedges between two
pie charts. Therefore, a bar chart would be best
because the relative sizes of the bars would emphasize
the magnitude of the differences that have occurred
since 1985 (see Figure 12.12).
```

The Product

FIGURE 12.11   Report Table

TABLE 8. Source of Last Software Program (in percentages)

Source	1990			1985		
	Total (N = 146)	HAL (N = 81)	Pear (N = 65)	Total (N = 132)	HAL (N = 92)	Pear (N = 40)
Retail outlet	43.2	54.3	29.2	53.0	50.0	60.0
Mail-order company	41.1	30.9	53.9	21.2	26.1	10.0
Software publisher	6.8	4.9	9.2	6.8	4.3	12.5
Unauthorized copy	4.1	3.7	4.6	15.9	16.3	15.0
Other	4.8	6.2	3.1	3.1	3.3	2.5
Total	100.0	100.0	100.0	100.0	100.0	100.0

FIGURE 12.12   Bar Chart

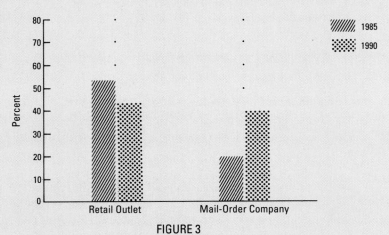

FIGURE 3
Retail outlets decreased 10% in popularity from 1985 to
1990 while mail-order companies increased 20%.

SUMMARY

Raw data becomes information only after it has been organized, analyzed, and interpreted so as to point out meaningful facts, statistics, and conclusions that help solve a problem. The first step in the process is to perform a preliminary analysis by editing the data for accuracy and completeness and evaluating the data to see if it solves the report problem.

Each table you construct from the data should be interpretable by itself, without reference to the text. Often you will want to analyze two or more fields of data together in the same table to help identify relationships. Include only as much data in a table as is helpful, keeping the table as simple as possible. Arrange the data in logical order, most often in order of descending value. Do not analyze every figure from the table in your narrative. Instead, interpret the important points from the table, pointing out the major findings, trends, contradictions, and the like.

Use well-designed line, bar, pie, and pictorial charts to aid in reader comprehension, emphasize certain data, create interest, and save time and space. Avoid using too many, too large, too garish, or too complicated charts. Also avoid misrepresenting your information—through distorting charts or statistics or omitting relevant information. Recognize the rights and obligations of all parties involved—the researcher, the respondent, and the organization.

KEY TERMS

Bar chart— A graph with horizontal or vertical bars representing values.

Cross-tabulation— The process by which two or more pieces of data are analyzed together.

Data editing— The process of reviewing the data for accuracy and completeness before data analysis.

Line chart— A graph containing rectangular grids, with the vertical grid representing values and the horizontal grid representing time.

Mean— The arithmetic average of a group of numbers.

Median— The middle value (or midpoint) in a group of numbers arranged from low to high (or vice versa).

Mode— The value in a group of numbers that occurs most frequently.

Pictorial chart— A graph with relevant symbols representing values.

Pie chart— A circle graph whose area is divided into component wedges.

Range— A measure of variability computed by subtracting the highest and lowest figures in a group and adding 1.

Statistics— The branch of mathematics dealing with the collection, organization, and interpretation of numerical data.

Table— An orderly arrangement of data in columnar form.

Visual aids— Tables, charts, photographs, and other graphic materials used to add interest and aid comprehension in communications.

REVIEW AND DISCUSSION

▶ OBJECTIVE 1

1. Give an example of a specific incident in which editing of research data might be necessary.

▶ OBJECTIVE 2

2. What are the advantages of presenting numerical data in tables as opposed to presenting the data in narrative form?

▶ OBJECTIVE 2

3. Assume you have surveyed a sample of students at your institution to determine their career objectives and expectations. List three possible cross-tabulation analyses that might be appropriate for this study.

▶ OBJECTIVE 2

4. In what order should data be arranged in tables?

▶ OBJECTIVE 3

5. What type of visual aid would probably be most appropriate for each of the following situations? Explain your decisions.

   a. Data showing the percentage breakdown of employees by ethnic background.
   b. Data showing the state-by-state analysis of market share for the company's major product.
   c. A news release announcing the appointment of a new executive vice president.
   d. Data showing the number of employees by year from 1980 to 1990.
   e. An explanation of how to replace the cartridge in a laser printer.
   f. Data showing the average number of employees per department last year.

▶ OBJECTIVE 4

6. What material from a table should be discussed in the text? What material need not be discussed?

▶ OBJECTIVE 4

7. What is meant by "overvisualizing" data? Why should this be avoided?

▶ OBJECTIVE 4

8. What is the difference between the mean, median, and mode?

▶ OBJECTIVE 5

9. What are the major types of misrepresentation that can occur in analysis of business data?

▶ OBJECTIVE 5

10. List two rights and two obligations of each of the major parties involved in a primary research project—the researcher, the respondent, and the user of the research.

EXERCISES

Collaborative Research: Exercises 1–3 below are based on the survey results shown in Figure 12.13. Next year Combustion Industries will move its headquarters from Manhattan to Stamford, Connecticut, in the building where Tri-City Bank occupies the first floor. The bank hopes to secure many Combustion Industries employees as customers and conducted a survey to determine their banking habits. The handwritten figures on the questionnaire give the number of respondents who checked each alternative.

▶ OBJECTIVE 2

1. **Constructing Tables**

   a. Is a table needed to present the information in Question 1?
   b. Would any cross-tabulation analyses help readers understand the data in this questionnaire? Explain.
   c. Construct a table that presents the important information from Question 4 of the questionnaire in a logical, helpful, and efficient manner. Give the table an appropriate title and arrange it in final report format.

Survey Results

FIGURE 12.13

COMBUSTION INDUSTRY SURVEY

1. Do you currently have an account at Tri-City Bank?
   _58_ yes
   _170_ no

2. At which of the following institutions do you currently have an account? (Please check all institutions that apply.)
   _201_ commercial bank
   _52_ employee credit union
   _75_ savings and loan association
   _6_ other (please specify _____)
   _18_ None

3. In terms of location, which one of the following bank locations do you consider most important in selecting your main bank?
   _70_ near home
   _102_ near office
   _12_ near shopping
   _31_ on way to and from work
   _13_ other (please specify _____)

4. How important do you consider each of the following banking services?

	Very Important	Somewhat Important	Not Important
Bank credit card	88	132	8
Check-guarantee card	74	32	122
Convenient installment loans	143	56	29
Drive-in service	148	47	33
Free checking	219	9	0
Overdrawing privileges	20	187	21
Personal banker	40	32	156
Telephone transfer	6	20	202
Trust department	13	45	170

5. If you have changed banks within the past three years, what was the major reason for the change?
   _33_ relocation of residence
   _4_ relocation of bank
   _18_ dissatisfaction with bank service
   _7_ Other (please specify _____)

Thank you so much for your cooperation. Please return this questionnaire in the enclosed envelope to Customer Service Department, Tri-City Bank, P.O. Box 1086, Stamford, CT 06902.

2. **Interpreting Data**

OBJECTIVE 3 ◄

   a. Give a one- or two-sentence interpretation of the data for each of the five questions.
   b. Assume you need to present the important information from this questionnaire in one paragraph of no more than fifty or sixty words. Construct the paragraph.

3. **Constructing Charts**

OBJECTIVE 4 ◄

   a. Construct a chart that would most effectively present the important information in Question 2.
   b. For Question 3, construct both a bar chart and a pie chart. Which do you think is more effective? Why?

▶ OBJECTIVE 5

4. **Misrepresenting Data: Interpreting a Table—** The following sentences interpret the table in Figure 12.4. Analyze each sentence to determine whether it represents the data in the table accurately.

  a. Males and females alike believe Apex is an asset to the community.

  b. More than one-fifth of the females (22.4%) did not respond.

  c. Age and the generation gap bring about different beliefs.

  d. Married males over age 50 had the most positive opinions.

  e. Females disagree more than males—probably because most of the workers at Apex are male.

  f. Female respondents tend to disagree with the statement.

  g. Apex should be proud of the fact that four-fifths of the residents believe the company is an asset to the community.

  h. Thirteen percent of the younger residents have doubts about whether Apex is an asset to the community.

  i. More single than married residents didn't care or had no opinion about the topic.

  j. Overall, the residents believe that 8% of the company is not an asset to the community.

▶ OBJECTIVE 5

5. **Misrepresenting Data: Use of Statistics—** Politicians, business people, and others love to quote statistics to support their viewpoints. Locate three news stories of someone quoting statistics to support a particular case. Then find an unbiased source that either confirms or refutes those statistics. Write a memo to your instructor discussing your findings. Include a photocopy of both the original news articles and your supporting statistics.

CASE PROBLEM

Light at the End of the Carpal Tunnel

▶ OBJECTIVES 2–5

Review the case problem at the end of Chapter 11, in which Jean Tate asked Pat Robbins to write a report on carpal tunnel syndrome. As part of her data gathering, Pat interviewed Terry Vaughn, executive director of the National Right-to-Safety Task Force. The NRSTF has been active in seeking a safer work environment for office workers. The following transcript shows part of this interview. (Note: "ER" stands for "Interviewer," and "EE" stands for "Interviewee.")

```
    ER: What is the extent of the problem? How many people
are afflicted with CTS each year?
    EE: CTS is the largest of several injuries that are
classified as cumulative trauma disorders. NIOSH esti-
mates that 73,000 employees suffered from one of these
disorders in 1987, up from 45,000 the year before, when
the disorders accounted for a third of all occupational
illnesses. The Bureau of Labor Standards estimates that
for the years 1981 through 1987, these repeated trauma
disorders accounted for 18, 21, 25, 28, 29, 33, and 38%
of all occupational injuries, respectively. So it's a
major problem, that's for sure.
    ER: What is NIOSH?
    EE: The National Institute for Occupational Safety and
Health--or maybe it's "of" instead of "for." Anyway,
it's a government agency located in Cincinnati, Ohio.
```

```
NIOSH is also heavily involved in studying the effect
of smoking in the workplace. One recent study showed
that 25% of all U.S. firms have now imposed an across-
the-board ban on workplace smoking and fully 60% have
set up some form of smoking policy.
     ER: Do VDT operators represent most of the CTS cases?
     EE: No, but they do represent a growing percentage.
Victims are still most likely to be physical laborers,
such as meat packers and jack-hammer operators. Inter-
estingly, musicians also suffer inordinately from this
disorder. I personally believe that women are most
often the victim of this disease.
     ER: Do you have any data to back that up?
     EE: I don't need data; I just know it. When you have
75,000 people who suffered from this painful disorder
in 1987, you just know it's a major problem for every-
one. I know if I ever experienced that problem, I'd
quit on the spot and sue the company.
     ER: What can be done to alleviate the problem?
     EE: In the office, you need wrist rests for each key-
board and rest breaks each hour, and also the furniture
needs to be designed to eliminate awkward posture and
the use of needless force.
     ER: What is the government doing to help victims of
this disorder?
     EE: Not enough. The American Academy of Orthopedic
Surgeons reports that lost earnings and expenses for
medical costs and treatment for this disorder cost more
than $27 billion annually.
```

1. How skillful was Pat in conducting this interview? Give some examples of both positive and negative aspects of the interview, especially in terms of probing.
2. What specific part(s) of the interview should you *not* use? Why?
3. Write one or two paragraphs analyzing part of this interview; include both a paraphrase and a direct quotation.
4. Assume that you have verified the Bureau of Labor Standards figures given in the interview. Construct both a table and a chart to communicate this information. Which one would you probably use in your report to Jean? Why?

WORD WISE

▪ **Places We Call Home*** With 60,809 places to live, why would you want to live in Hell, Michigan, when you can live in Nice, California, instead? Other interesting place names:

▪ Fairview is the most popular city name; there are 66 Fairviews in 31 states. Midway is second most popular, with 52.

▪ Jefferson is the most popular presidential city (28 of them), followed by Lincoln and Washington (27 each).

▪ Folks actually live in Belcher, New York; Boring, Maryland; Gross, Kansas; Little Hope, Tennessee; Odd, West Virginia; Pitts, Georgia; and Tightwad, Missouri.

▪ However, the more fortunate live in Carefree or Paradise, Arizona; Friendly, Maryland; Happy, Texas; Ideal, Georgia; Joy, Illinois; Okay, Oklahoma; Plush, Oregon; Rich, Mississippi; or Thankful, North Carolina.

* "Places We Call Home: Nice to Pitts," *USA Today,* July 12, 1989, p. 7A.

Writing the Report

Communication Objectives

After you have finished this chapter, you will be able to

1. Determine the report's format and general traits based on the needs of the reader and the nature of the report problem.

2. Organize the report in a logical manner.

3. Develop an effective report outline.

4. Write each part of the report body and all supplementary pages.

5. Use an effective writing style.

6. Provide appropriate documentation when quoting, paraphrasing, or summarizing someone else's work.

7. Revise a report for content, style, and correctness.

8. Format a document for consistency and readability.

9. Proofread a report to ensure that it reflects pride of authorship.

10. Use document-design techniques for maximum report effectiveness and impact.

Often a business report outlines and recommends a course of action. No one understands this better than Jay Abraham, the 34-year-old General Manager of Marketing in the Packaged Goods Division of Heinz Company. Abraham oversees the marketing strategies for several Heinz products including rice cakes, pickles, and relish. This job, Abraham said, requires a continual amount of reporting to both upper management and to the sales force responsible for making sure the product ends up on the supermarket shelves.

Every year, Abraham's team starts off "with a very detailed business review, which is probably anywhere from a 30- to 75-page document" depending on the product, he said. The report states what has been learned from the previous year's sales effort—including such things as how consumer trends toward health and nutrition affect the movement of a particular product. In addition, the report suggests ways to put this knowledge to practical use when it comes to actually selling the product.

Abraham's experience with business reviews puts him in a good position to give advice on how to organize and write a report. To help organize a report in a way that best gets the point across, Abraham first asks his staff "to step

Jay Abraham, General
Manager of Marketing
Heinz Company, Pittsburgh,
Pennsylvania

back and think of who their audience is, whom are they talking to, and what they are trying to sell to that audience." The audience, he notes, could be top management who has to "buy" a marketing plan, or it could be the sales staff who has to implement it. "And then," Abraham said, "we try to talk through what it is we're trying to communicate to those people. Once we've come to an agreement, then writing the document becomes fairly easy."

How a report is organized often depends on the preference of the company or the manager. Abraham likes his staff members to start off their reports with a conclusion. "For instance, on our Chico San rice cake business, *New Products Drive Category Growth* might be the conclusion," he explained. "Then I would expect some data that would support the conclusion." The supporting information might include "some sales data, some distribution data, competitive information, share gain information, or whatever analysis needs to be done to support the fact that new products do drive category growth within the rice cake segment." After the analysis, a statement or two follows that explains what all this implies for the company. In the case of Chico San rice cakes, Abraham said, the implication could be that the company should introduce new products on a routine basis.

Throughout this report, Abraham noted, there can be dozens of conclusions about a single product, ranging from product packaging to the effectiveness of different advertising campaigns, each followed by analysis and an implication for the company.

Over all, what does Abraham think is the most important part of presenting a well-organized report? "Solid pre-report planning," he said, which means the basics: good ideas and a good plan. "If it's a good, clear, believable concept," he added, "then you can usually deliver a good, clear, believable document." But if ideas are vague, the report will often end up being complex and difficult to read—a condition almost guaranteed not to help a product sell. And selling, Abraham noted, is ultimately what all business reports are about. ▼

Planning

As we have seen throughout our study of business communication, the writing process consists of planning, writing, revising, formatting, and proofreading. You follow this same process when writing a report.

As Chapter 10 explains, the planning portion of the report process consists of determining that a problem exists, defining the purpose and the audience for the report, and developing hypotheses regarding causes or solutions for the problem. The data-gathering portion of the report process (Chapter 11) involves determining what data is needed, deciding what methods to use to collect the data, and then collecting the data. The needed data—computer printouts, correspondence, previous reports, journal articles, interview data, survey results, and the like—is then interpreted and analyzed (Chapter 12).

Now you're ready to begin writing the report. Although much of the planning in the report process is done before collecting data, the written presentation of the results requires its own stage of planning. Decisions about the format of the report, the organization of the content, and the heading structure need to be made before and as you write.

Format and General Traits

The format of the report and such general traits as complexity, degree of formality, and length depend on the audience for the report and also on the nature of the problem that the report addresses.

The three most common formats for a report are manuscript, memorandum, and letter format. Manuscript reports, the most formal of the three, are formatted in narrative (paragraph) style, with headings and subheadings separating the different sections. Memorandum and letter reports contain the standard correspondence parts presented in Chapter 5 (for example, lines identifying the names of the sender and receiver) and may or may not contain headings and subheadings.

If the problem that the report addresses is complex and has serious consequences, the report will likely follow a manuscript format and a formal writing style. If the purpose of the report is not only to provide information but also to make a recommendation, the complexity and length of the report will probably increase.

Decisions on format also depend directly on your analysis of the audience. What is the reader's preference—formal or informal? If the reader's preference is formal, that calls for a manuscript format and the use of a formal writing style. The more formal the report, the more parts are included (such as table of contents, executive summary, appendixes, and the like) and, therefore, the longer the report. If the reader's preference is informal, the report may be formatted in letter or memo format, using a more informal writing style.

Is the reader an internal audience (calling for a memo report) or an external audience (calling for a letter report)? How much does the reader already know? How much does the reader need or want to know? Answers to these questions are part of planning your written presentation, and they affect the length and complexity of your report.

Figure 13.1 compares an informal, simple, and short report in memo format with a formal, complex, and long report (first page only) in

OBJECTIVE 1: Determine the report's format and general traits based on the needs of the reader and the nature of the report problem.

Most reports are formatted as manuscripts, memos, or letters.

FIGURE 13.1A   What Report Structure Works Best?

The memo format indicates the reader is someone within the firm.

All Systems Go Moving Company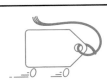

MEMO TO: Hiram Cooper, Director of Marketing
FROM: Barbara Novak, Sales Assistant *BN*
DATE: August 9, 1990
SUBJECT: Yellow Pages Advertising

Hiram, I believe that All Systems Go should continue purchasing a quarter-page ad in the Mountain Bell Yellow Pages. My recommendation is based on the conclusion that Yellow Pages advertising produced more inquiries than any other method of advertising and increased net profits, especially in the local residential market.

A PILOT TEST WAS SET UP
On March 1 you asked me to conduct a three-month test of the effectiveness of Yellow Pages advertising. I subsequently purchased a quarter-page ad for the edition of the Yellow Pages that was distributed the week of June 2-6. For six weeks thereafter, we queried all telephone and walk-in customers to determine how they had learned about our company. I also compared the percentage of signed contracts resulting from each source. Precise before-and-after sales data could not be generated because of other factors that affected sales for each period (e.g., time of year and other promotional campaigns).

THE RESULTS WERE POSITIVE
My analysis of the data shows that 38% of the callers after June 2-6 heard of our company from the Yellow Pages; the next highest source was referrals and repeat business, which accounted for 26% of the calls. In addition, 21% of the Yellow Pages inquiries resulted in signed contracts, as compared with our 19% overall average.

The new business that resulted from Yellow Pages advertising substantially affects the local residential market (11%-12% increase), has some effect on the commercial market (5%-6% increase), and has little or no effect on the long-haul or large-job market (0-2% increase). Your last quarterly sales report indicated that the residential market accounts for 78% of our total sales.

Based on the $258 monthly cost of our quarter-page ad, each dollar of ad cost is producing $3.77 in sales revenue and $0.938 toward product margin. These results clearly support the continuation of our Yellow Pages advertising. I would be happy to discuss the results of this research with you in more detail and to provide the supporting statistical data if you wish.

jeo

2443 South Canton

Mesa, AZ 85202

(602) 555-0143

The organizational style is direct: the recommendation and conclusions are given first, followed by the supporting evidence.

The use of talking headings supports the direct plan.

Note the informal language—extensive use of first- and second-person pronouns such as *I*, *we*, *you*, and *me*.

The detailed statistical information is not included—but is available if needed.

Report Structure

Short report; informal style; simple content; direct organizational plan; memo format.

What Report Structure Works Best? (*cont'd*)

FIGURE 13.1B

THE EFFECTIVENESS OF YELLOW-PAGES ADVERTISING

FOR ALL SYSTEMS GO

Barbara Novak, Sales Assistant

According to Mountain Bell, display advertising typically accounts for 55% of total sales for a firm in the residential moving business. So Hiram Cooper, director of marketing, requested that a three-month test be conducted of the effectiveness of Yellow Pages advertising for All Systems Go.

This report describes the procedures used to gather the data and the results obtained. Based on the data, a recommendation is made regarding the continuation of Yellow Pages advertising.

Procedures

A quarter-page ad was purchased in the edition of the Mountain Bell Yellow Pages that was distributed the week of June 2-6. For the six-week period encompassing June 9-July 17, all telephone and walk-in customers were queried to determine how they had learned about the company. Comparisons were made of the percentage of signed contracts resulting from each source.

One delimitation of this study was that precise before-and-after sales data could not be generated because of other factors that affected sales for each period (e.g., time of year and other promotional campaigns).

Findings

The findings of this study are reported in terms of the sources of information for learning about All Systems Go, the amount of new business generated, and a cost-benefits comparison for Yellow Pages advertising.

Sources of Information

As shown in Table 1, 38% of the callers during the test period first learned about All Systems Go from the Yellow Pages display.

The manuscript format is used for this formal report. (Only the first page is shown here.)

An indirect organizational plan is used. The conclusions and recommendations will be given after the supporting data is presented.

The use of generic report headings supports the indirect plan.

Formal language is used. Note the absence of first- and second-person pronouns.

The use of visual aids and multilevel headings increases the complexity of the report.

Report Structure

Long report; formal style; complex content; indirect organizational plan; manuscript format.

manuscript format. So that your written presentation will have an overall sense of proportion and unity, decide beforehand on the complexity, formality, length, and format of the report. The "right" decision depends on the needs and desires of the reader.

Organization of the Report

OBJECTIVE 2: Organize the report in a logical manner.

A sculptor creating a statue of someone doesn't start at the head and work down to the feet in lock-step fashion. Instead, he or she may first create part of the torso, then part of the head, then another part of the torso, and so on. Similarly, a movie director films segments of the film out of narrative order. But in the end, both creations are put together in such a way as to show unity, order, logic, and beauty.

Similarly, you may have organized the collecting of data in a way that suited the investigation of various subtopics of the problem. But now that it is time to put the results together in a written presentation, you may need a new organization, one that assembles the whole and takes into account what you have learned through your research.

Planning your written presentation to show unity, order, logic, and, yes, even beauty involves selecting an organizational basis for the findings and developing an outline. You must decide in what order to present each piece of the puzzle and when to "spill the beans"—when to present your overall conclusions (the answers to the research questions raised in the introduction) and any recommendations you may wish to make.

Most reports are organized by time, location, importance, or criteria.

Organizational Basis   As shown in Figure 13.2, the four most common bases for organizing your findings are time, location, importance, and criteria. There are, of course, many other methods of organizing data; for example, moving from the known to the unknown, or moving from the simple to the complex. The purpose of the report (information, analysis, or recommendation), the nature of the problem, and your knowledge of the reader will help you select the organizational pattern that will be most useful.

Time   The use of chronology, or time sequence, is appropriate for agendas, minutes of meetings, programs, some status reports, and similar projects. Discussing events in the order in which they occurred or in which they will or should occur is an efficient way to organize many informational reports—those whose purpose is simply to inform.

Despite its usefulness and simplicity, time sequence should not be overused. Because events occur naturally, one thing after another, chronology is often the most efficient way to *record* data, but often it is not the most efficient way to *present* that data to management. Assume, for example, that you are writing a progress report on a recruiting trip you made to four college campuses. Each day you interviewed candidates for three positions you have open. The first passage, given in time sequence, requires too much work of the reader.

> *Not:* On Monday morning, I interviewed a candidate for the budget-analyst position and two candidates for the junior-accountant position. Then, in the afternoon, I interviewed two candidates for the asset-manager position and another for the budget-analyst position. Finally, on

Tuesday, I interviewed another candidate for budget analyst and two for junior accountant.

But: On Monday and Tuesday, I interviewed three candidates for the budget-analyst position, four for the junior-accountant position, and two for the asset-manager position.

The point is that a blow-by-blow description is often not the most efficient means of communicating information to the reader—sometimes it forces the reader to do too much work. Organize your information in time sequence only when it is important for the reader to know the sequence in which events either did occur or should or will occur.

Location   Like the use of time sequence, the use of location as the basis for organizing a report is often appropriate for simple informational reports. Discussing topics according to their physical (for example, describing an office layout) or geographical location may be the most efficient way to present the data. Again, however, be sure that such an organizational plan helps the reader process the information most efficiently and that it is not merely the easiest way to report the data. Decisions should be based on reader needs rather than on writer convenience.

Importance   For the busy reader, the most efficient organizational plan may be to have the most important topic discussed first, followed in order by topics of decreasing importance. The reader then gets the major idea up front and can skim the less important information as needed. This organizational plan is routinely used by newspapers, where the most important points are discussed in the first paragraph.

For some types of reports, especially recommendation reports, the opposite plan might be used effectively. If you've analyzed four alternatives and will recommend the implementation of Alternative 4, you might first present each of the other alternatives in turn and show why they're *not* feasible. Then, you save your "trump card" until last, thus making the alternative you're recommending the freshest in the reader's mind because it is the last thing read. If you use this option, make sure that you effectively "slay all the dragons" except your own and that the reader will agree your recommendation is the most logical one.

Criteria   For most analytical and recommendation reports, where the purpose is to analyze the data and possibly recommend a solution, the most logical arrangement is to organize the data by criteria. One of the important steps in the reporting process is to develop hypotheses regarding causes or solutions for the problem you're exploring. This process requires factoring, or breaking down, your problem into its component subproblems. These factors, or criteria, then become the basis for organizing the report.

In Example D in Figure 13.2, for instance, the three factors presented—professional training, work experience, and written work samples—are the bases on which you will evaluate each candidate. Thus, they should also form the bases for presenting the data. By focusing attention on the criteria, you help lead the reader to the same conclusion you reached. Thus, organizing data by criteria is an especially effective organizational plan when the reader might be initially resistant to your recommendations.

If you're evaluating three sites for a new facility, for example, avoid the temptation to use the locations of these sites as the report headings. Such

FIGURE 13.2   How Should You Organize the Data?

Factor / Format

By Time / Noun Phrases

A. EASTERN ELECTRONICS: A CASE STUDY

1. Start-up of firm: 1984
2. Rapid expansion: 1985–87
3. Industry-wide slowdown: 1988
4. Retrenchment: 1989–90
5. Return to profitability: 1991

By Location / Participial Phrases

B. RENOVATION NEEDS

1. Expanding the Mailroom
2. Modernizing the reception area
3. Installing a humidity system in warehouse C
4. Repaving the north parking lot

By Importance / Partial Statements

C. PROGRESS REPORT ON AUTOMATION PROJECT

1. Conversion on budget
2. Time schedule slipped one month
3. Branch offices added to project
4. Software programs upgraded

By Criteria / Statements

D. EVALUATION OF APPLICANTS FOR COMMUNICATIONS
   DIRECTOR

1. Sefcik has higher professional training
2. Jenson has more relevant work experience
3. Jenson's written work samples are more effective

By Criteria / Questions

E. ESTABLISHING A POLICY ON AIDS IN THE WORKPLACE

1. What are the firm's legal and social responsibilities?
2. What policies have other firms established?
3. What policies are needed to deal with the needs of AIDS-
   infected employees?
4. What policies are needed to deal with the concerns of non-
   AIDS-infected employees?
5. How should these policies be implemented?

an organizational plan focuses attention on the sites themselves instead of on the criteria by which you judged the sites and on which your recommendation is based. Instead, use the criteria as the headings. Similarly, avoid using "Advantages" and "Disadvantages" as headings. Keep your reader in step with you by having the reader focus on the same topics—the criteria—that you focused on during the research and analysis phase of your project.

In actual practice, you might use a combination of these organizational plans. For instance, you might organize your first-degree headings by criteria but your second-degree headings in simple-to-complex order. Or you might organize your first-degree headings by criteria but present these criteria in their order of importance. Competent communicators select an organizational plan with a view toward helping the reader comprehend and appreciate the information and viewpoints being presented in the most efficient manner possible.

Presenting Conclusions and Recommendations   Once you've decided how to organize the findings of your study, you must decide where to present the conclusions and/or recommendations that emanate from these findings. The differences among findings, conclusions, and recommendations can be illustrated by the following examples:

> *Finding:* The computer monitor sometimes goes blank during operation.
> *Finding:* Garbage sometimes prints out on the screen for no reason.
> *Conclusion:* The computer is broken.
> *Recommendation:* The computer should be repaired before May 3, when we begin processing payroll records.

> In general, you should prefer the direct plan (conclusions and recommendations first) for business reports.

Academic reports and many business reports have traditionally presented the conclusions and recommendations of a study at the end of the report, the rationale being that conclusions cannot logically be drawn until the data has been presented and analyzed; similarly, recommendations cannot be made until conclusions have been drawn.

Figure 13.1 presented earlier illustrates the two approaches. The informal memo report presents the conclusions and recommendations in the first paragraph; the formal manuscript report delays such presentation until after the findings have been presented and analyzed.

> The **conclusions** answer the research questions raised in the introduction.

Although hard-and-fast rules cannot be given for when to use the direct and indirect organizational plans in reports, some guidance can be given. Generally, it is best to use the direct organizational pattern, in which the conclusions and recommendations are presented at the beginning of the report, when

1. The reader prefers the direct plan for reports.
2. The reader will be receptive to your conclusions and recommendations.
3. The reader can evaluate the information in the report more efficiently if the conclusions and recommendations are given up front.
4. You have no specific reason to prefer the indirect pattern.

Similarly, the indirect plan (in which the evidence is presented first, followed by conclusions and recommendations) is most appropriate when

1. The reader prefers the indirect plan for reports.
2. The reader will be initially disinterested in or resistant to the conclusions and recommendations.

3. The topic is so complex that detailed explanations and discussion are needed in order for the conclusions and recommendations to be understood and accepted.

The decision isn't necessarily an either/or situation. Instead of putting all the conclusions and recommendations either first or last, you may choose to split them up, discussing each in the appropriate subsection of your report. Similarly, even though the report may be written in an indirect pattern, an executive summary or letter of transmittal may communicate the conclusions and recommendations to the reader before the report itself has been read.

Outlining the Report

▼
OBJECTIVE 3: Develop an effective report outline.

Although we've not used the term *outlining* thus far, whenever we've talked about organizing, we've actually been talking about outlining as well. For example, early in the report process you organized your problem statement into its component subproblems. Thus, your problem statement and subproblems served as your first working outline.

Many business writers find it useful at this point in the report process to construct a more formal outline. A formal outline provides an orderly visual representation of the report, showing clearly which points are to be covered, in what order they are to be covered, and what their relationship is to the rest of the report. The purpose of the outline is to guide you, the writer, in structuring your report logically and efficiently. Consider it a working draft, subject to being revised as you compose the report.

Begin your outline by identifying your problem statement. Then use uppercase roman numerals for your major headings, uppercase alphabet letters for first-level subheadings, arabic numerals for second-level subheadings, and lowercase alphabet letters for third-degree subheadings. Only rarely will you need to use all four levels of headings. Figure 13.3 shows the outline for the report illustrated later in this chapter.

As part of the process of developing a formal outline, you should compose the actual wording for your headings and decide how many headings are needed. Headings play an important role in helping to focus the reader's attention and in helping your report achieve unity and coherence, so plan them carefully, and revise them as needed as you work toward a final version of your report.

Use descriptive and parallel headings for unity and coherence.

Talking Versus Generic Headings   **Talking headings** identify not only the topic of the section but also the major conclusion. For instance, Example C of Figure 13.2 uses talking headings to indicate not only that the first section of this report is about the budget for the conversion project but also that the conversion is proceeding on budget.

Talking headings, which are always used in newspapers and magazines, are often also useful for business reports, where they can serve as a preview or executive summary of the entire report. They are especially useful when directness is desired—the reader can simply skim the headings in the report (or in the table of contents) and get an overview of the topics covered and the conclusions reached for each topic.

Generic headings, on the other hand, identify only the topic of the section, without giving the conclusion. Most formal reports and any report written

Outline for a Report

FIGURE 13.3

```
                         OUTLINE

PROBLEM:  What are the opinions of staff employees at Atlantic
          State University regarding their employee benefits?

  I.  Introduction                                              1
      A. Purpose and Scope
      B. Procedures

 II.  Findings
      A. Communication of Benefits
         1. Employees' Knowledge of Benefits
            a. Familiarity with Benefits
            b. Suggestions for Improving Communication          2
         2. Present Methods of Communication
         3. Preferred Methods of Communication
      B. Opinions of Present Benefits
         1. Importance of Benefits
         2. Satisfaction with Benefits
      C. Desirability of Additional Benefits

III.  Summary, Conclusions, and Recommendations
      A. Summary of the Findings
      B. Conclusions and Recommendations
Appendix
      A. Cover Letter                                           3
      B. Questionnaire
```

Identify the problem statement or report thesis.

These findings are organized by criteria.

Noun phrases are used for each heading and subheading.

Each subdivision must contain at least two items.

Mechanics Notes

1. Align the roman numerals vertically under the decimals.   2. Type each entry in upper- and lowercase letters.   3. Identify each appendix item by letter.

in an indirect pattern would use generic headings, similar to the headings used for Examples A and B in Figure 13.2 and in Figure 13.3.

Parallelism   As shown in Figure 13.2, you have wide leeway in selecting the formats of headings you wish to use in your report. Noun phrases are probably the most common form of heading, but you may also choose participial phrases, partial statements (in which a verb is missing—the kind often used in newspaper headlines), statements, or questions. Perhaps, there are other forms you might choose as well.

Regardless of the form of heading you select, be consistent within each level of heading. That is, if the first major heading (a first-level heading) is a noun phrase, all first-level headings should be noun phrases. If the first major heading is a talking heading, so should the others. As you move from level to level, you may switch to another form of heading if it would be more appropriate. Again, however, you must keep parallel the headings within the same level.

Length and Number of Headings   Headings that are too long lose some of their effectiveness; the shorter the heading, the more emphasis it receives. Yet headings that are too short are ineffective because they do not convey enough meaning. Four to eight words are about the right length for most headings.

Similarly, choose an appropriate number of headings. Too many headings weaken the unity of a report—they chop the report up too much, making it look more like an outline than a discussion. Too few headings, however, confront the reader with page after page of solid copy, without the chance to stop periodically and refocus attention on the topic.

In general, have at least one heading or visual aid to break up one single-spaced page or two consecutive double-spaced pages. Make your report inviting to read.

Balance   Maintain a sense of balance within and among sections. It would be unusual to give one section of a report eight subsections (eight second-level headings) and give the following section none. Similarly, it would be unusual to have one section ten pages long and another section only half a page long. Finally, ensure that the most important ideas are in the highest levels of headings. If you're discussing four criteria for a topic, for example, all four of these should be in the same level of heading—presumably in first-level headings.

When you do divide a section into subsections, break it into at least two subsections. You cannot logically have just one second-level heading within a section, for example, because if you divide something, it logically must be divided into more than one "piece."

WRITING

Although it is only the last step of a long and sometimes complex process, the written presentation of your research is the only evidence the reader has of the effort that has gone into the project. The success or failure of all your work depends directly on this physical evidence. Prepare the written report carefully to bring out the full significance of your data and to help the reader reach a decision and solve a problem.

Everything that you learned in Chapter 5 about the writing process applies directly to report writing—choosing a productive work environment; scheduling a reasonable block of time to devote to the drafting phase; letting ideas flow quickly during the drafting stage, without worrying about style, correctness, or format; and revising for content, style, correctness, and readability. However, report writing requires several other considerations as well.

Writing the Body of the Report

The report body consists of the introduction, the findings, and the summary, conclusions, and recommendations. As stated earlier, the conclusions may go first or last in the report. Each part may be a separate chapter in long reports or a major section in shorter reports.

OBJECTIVE 4: Write each part of the report body and all supplementary pages.

Introduction   The introduction sets the stage for understanding the findings that follow. In this section, present such information as the following:

- Background of the problem
- Need for the study
- Authorization for the report
- Hypothesis or problem statement and subproblems
- Definition of terms (if needed)
- Procedures used to gather and analyze the data

If you present the conclusions and recommendations in the introduction, provide a smooth transition to the background information that follows, such as "These conclusions and recommendations resulted from a detailed study of . . ." If the report is long or complex, preview the organization of the report for the reader; that is, discuss what information will be presented and in what order.

Findings   The findings of the study represent the major contribution of the report and comprise the largest section of the report. Discuss and interpret any primary and secondary data you gathered. Organize this section using one of the plans discussed earlier (for example, by time, location, importance, or criteria). Using objective language, present the information clearly, concisely, and accurately.

Don't just present your findings; analyze and interpret them for the reader.

Many reports will display numerical information in tables and figures (such as bar, line, or pie charts). The information in such displays should be self-explanatory; that is, it should be understandable without having to refer to the text. Nevertheless, all tables and figures must be mentioned and explained in the text so that the text, too, is self-explanatory. All text references should be by number (e.g., "as shown in Table 4")—never by a phrase such as "as shown below."

Summarize the important information from the display. Give enough interpretation to help the reader comprehend the table or figure, but don't repeat all the information it contains. Discussing display information in the narrative emphasizes that information, so discuss only what merits such emphasis.

The table or figure should be placed immediately below the first paragraph of text in which the reference to the display occurs. (Of course, if the display contains supplementary information, it may be placed in an appendix rather than in the body of the report itself.) Avoid splitting a table or figure between two pages. If not enough space is available on the page for the display, continue with the text to the bottom of the page and then place the display at the very top of the following page.

For all primary and secondary data, point out important items, implications, trends, contradictions, unexpected findings, similarities and contradictions, and the like. Use emphasis, subordination, preview, summary, and transition to make the report read clearly and smoothly. Keep the reader's needs and desires uppermost in your mind as you organize, present, and discuss the information.

Findings lead to conclusions; conclusions lead to recommendations.

Summary, Conclusions, and Recommendations   A one- or two-page report may need only a one-sentence or one-paragraph summary. Longer or complex reports, however, should include a more extensive summary. Briefly review the problem and procedures used to solve the problem, and provide an overview of the major findings. Repeating the main points or arguments immediately before presenting the conclusions and recommendations reinforces the reasonableness of those conclusions and recommendations. To avoid monotony when summarizing, use wording that is different from the original presentation.

If your report only analyzes the information presented and does not make recommendations, the final section of analytical reports might be labeled "Summary" or "Summary and Conclusions," as appropriate. If your report includes both conclusions and recommendations, ensure that the conclusions stem directly from your findings and that the recommendations stem directly from the conclusions. Provide ample evidence to support all your conclusions and recommendations.

Writing the Supplementary Sections

The length, formality, and complexity of the report, as well as the needs of the reader, affect the number of report parts that precede and follow the body of the report. Use any of the following report parts that will help you achieve your report objectives.

Title Page   A title page is typically used for reports typed in manuscript (as opposed to letter or memo) format. It shows such information as the title of the report, the names (and perhaps titles and departments) of the reader and writer, and the date the report was transmitted to the reader. Other information may be included at the writer's discretion. The information on the title page should be arranged attractively (see Figure 13.5A).

Transmittal Document   Formal reports and all reports that are not hand-delivered to the reader should be accompanied by a transmittal document. As its name implies, a **transmittal document** conveys the report to the reader. If the reader is from outside the organization, you would use a transmittal letter; if the reader is within the organization, you would typically use a transmittal memo. Whether the report is written in formal or informal style, use a conversational, personal style of writing for the transmittal document.

Since the completion of the report assignment is good news (whether the information it contains is good or bad news), use the direct organizational plan. Begin by actually transmitting the report; for example, "Here is the report you requested on May 15." Briefly discuss any needed background information, and perhaps give an overview of the conclusions and major recommendations of the report (unless you want the reader to first read the evidence supporting these conclusions and recommendations). Include any other information that will help the reader understand, appreciate, and make use of the information presented in the report.

The transmittal document often ends with such goodwill features as an expression of appreciation for being given the report assignment, an offer of willingness to discuss the report further, or perhaps an offer of assistance in the future. The letter or memo may simply be transmitted along with the report or it may be a part of the report. In the latter case, it is placed immediately after the title page but before the executive summary or table of contents (see Figure 13.5B).

Executive Summary   An **executive summary**, also called an *abstract* or *synopsis*, is a condensed version of the body of the report (including introduction, findings, and any conclusions or recommendations). Although some readers may simply scan the report itself, most will read the executive summary carefully. Like the transmittal document, the executive summary is an optional part of the report. It is especially appropriate when the conclusions and recommendations will be welcomed by the reader, when the report is long, or when you know your reader appreciates having such information up front.

> The report summary may be read more carefully than the report itself.

Because the purpose of the executive summary is to save the reader time, the summary should be short, generally about 10% to 15% of the length of the report. The summary should contain the same emphasis as the report itself and should be independent of the report; that is, don't refer to the report itself in the summary. Assume that the person reading the summary will not have a chance to read the report, so include as much useful information as possible.

Use the same writing style for the summary as that used in the report. The summary goes immediately before the table of contents (see Figure 13.5C).

Table of Contents   Long reports with many headings and subheadings usually benefit from a table of contents. The headings used in the table of contents must be identical to the wording used in the headings in the body of the report. Typically, only two or three levels of headings are included in the table of contents—even if more levels are used in the body of the report. The page numbers identify the page on which the section heading appears—even though the section itself may comprise many pages (see Figure 13.5D). Obviously, the table of contents must be written after the report itself has been typed. The table of contents and any pages that precede it are numbered with lowercase roman numerals; those that follow, including supplementary pages (such as appendixes) are numbered with arabic numerals.

Appendix   The appendix is an optional report part that contains supplementary information or documents. For example, in an appendix you might include a copy of the questionnaire and cover letter used to collect data, supplementary tables, forms, or computer printouts that might be helpful

> An appendix might include supplementary reference material not important enough to go in the body of the report.

to the reader but that are not important enough to include in the body of the report. Label each appendix separately, by letter; for example, "Appendix A: Questionnaire" or "Appendix B: Cover Letter." In the body of the report, you should refer to any items placed in the appendix.

References The reference list contains the complete listing of any secondary sources cited to in the report. Different disciplines use different formats for citing these references; whichever you choose, be consistent and include enough information that the reader can easily locate any source if he or she wants to.

A good indication of a researcher's scholarship is the accuracy of the reference list—both in terms of content and format, so proofread this part of your report carefully. The reference list is the very last part of the report (see Figure 13.5J).

Writing Style

OBJECTIVE 5: Use an effective writing style.

The effectiveness of a written report can be enhanced by paying attention to appropriate tone, pronouns, verb tenses, and emphasis and subordination.

Tone Regardless of the structure of your report, the writing style used is typically more objective and less conversational than, for example, an informal memorandum. Avoid colloquial expressions, attempts at humor, subjectivity, and exaggeration.

> *Weak:* The company hit the jackpot with its new MRP program.
> *Better:* The new MRP program saved the company $125,000 the first year.
>
> *Weak:* He claimed that half of his projects involved name-brand advertising.
> *Better:* He stated that half of his projects involved name-brand advertising.

Pronouns For most business reports, the use of first- and second-person pronouns is not only acceptable but also quite helpful for achieving an effective, informal writing style. Formal language, however, focuses attention on the information being conveyed instead of on the writer; therefore, reports written in the formal style should use third-person pronouns and avoid using *I*, *we*, *you*, and the like.

You can avoid the awkward substitute "the writer" by recasting the sentence. Most often, it is evident that the writer was the person doing the action communicated.

> *Informal:* I recommend that the project be canceled.
> *Awkward:* The writer recommends that the project be canceled.
> *Formal:* The project should be canceled.

Using the passive voice is a common device for avoiding the use of *I* in formal reports, but doing so weakens the report. Recast the sentence to avoid undue use of the passive voice.

Informal: I interviewed Jan Smith.
Passive: Jan Smith was interviewed.
Formal: In a personal interview, Jan Smith stated . . .

Also avoid using *he* as a generic pronoun when referring to an indefinite person. Chapter 4 discusses many ways to avoid such discriminatory language.

Verb Tense   Use the verb tense (past, present, or future) that is appropriate at the time the reader reads the report—not necessarily at the time you wrote the report. Use past tense to describe procedures and to describe the findings of a particular study already completed, but use present tense for conclusions from that study. When possible, use the stronger present tense to present the data from your study. The rationale for doing so is that we assume our findings continue to be true; thus, the use of the present·tense is justified. (If we cannot assume the continuing truth of our findings, they should probably not be used in the study.)

> Verb tenses should reflect the *reader's* (not the writer's) time frame.

Weak: These findings <u>will be discussed</u> later in this report.
Better: These findings <u>are discussed</u> later in this report.
But: These findings <u>were discussed</u> earlier in this report.

Weak: Three-fourths of the managers <u>responded</u> that they <u>believed</u> quality circles were effective at the plant.
Better: Three-fourths of the managers <u>believe</u> that quality circles <u>are</u> effective at the plant.

Procedure: Nearly 500 people <u>responded</u> to the survey, which <u>represents</u> a response rate of 61%.
Finding: Only 11% of the managers <u>had received</u> any specific training on the new procedure.
Conclusion: Most managers <u>do not receive</u> any specific training on the new procedure.

Emphasis and Subordination   Only rarely does all the data consistently point to one decision. More likely, you will have a mixed bag of data from which you will have to evaluate the relative merits of each point. For your report to achieve its objective, the reader must evaluate the importance of each point the same way you do. At the very least, your reader must be *aware* of the importance you attached to each point. Therefore, you should employ the emphasis and subordination techniques learned in Chapter 4 when discussing your findings.

> Use emphasis and subordination ethically—not to pressure the reader.

Through such techniques as the amount of space devoted to a topic, the position of that topic (first, last, or in the middle), the use of wording that directly tells what is more and less important, and other techniques presented in Chapter 4, you can help ensure that your reader is on the same wavelength as you in analyzing the data.

Use emphasis and subordination to let the reader know what you consider most and least important—not to unduly sway the reader. If the data honestly leads to a strong, definite conclusion, then by all means make your conclusion strong and definite. But if the data permits only a tentative conclusion, then draw such a conclusion.

Use previews, summaries, and transitions to achieve coherence and unity.

Coherence   One of the difficulties of writing any long document—especially when the document is drafted in sections and then put together—is in making the finished product read smoothly and coherently, like a unified presentation rather than a cut-and-paste job.

One effective way to achieve coherence in a report is to use previews, summaries, and transitions regularly. At the beginning of each major section, preview what is discussed in that section. At the conclusion of each section, summarize what was presented and provide a smooth transition to the following section. For long sections, the preview, summary, and transition might each comprise a separate paragraph; for short sections, a sentence might suffice. Note how these devices are used in the following illustration of a report section:

<u>Training of System Users</u>

The training program can be evaluated in terms of the opinions of the users and in terms of the cost of training in proportion to the cost of the system itself. *(After this topic lead-in, several paragraphs follow that discuss the opinions of the users and the cost of the training program.)*

Even though a slight majority of users now feel competent in using the system, the training provided falls far short of the 20% of total system cost recommended by experts. This low level of training may have affected the precision of the data generated by the MRP system. *(The first sentence contains the summary of this section; the second sentence contains the transition to the next section.)*

Data Accuracy

Don't depend on your heading structure for coherence. Your report should read smoothly and coherently without the headings. Avoid repeating the exact words of the heading in the following narrative, and avoid using the heading as part of the narrative. (The following underlined passages represent the heading for each section.)

Not: <u>The Two Departments Should Be Merged.</u> The two departments should be merged. The reason is that there is a duplication of services.

Not: <u>The Two Departments Should Be Merged.</u> The reason is that there is a duplication of services.

But: <u>The Two Departments Should Be Merged.</u> Merging the two departments will eliminate the duplication of services.

Always introduce a topic before dividing it into subtopics. Thus, you should never have two headings coming together without some intervening text. Preview for the reader how the topic will be divided before you actually make the division.

OBJECTIVE 6: Provide appropriate documentation when quoting, paraphrasing, or summarizing someone else's work.

Documentation

Documentation is the identifying of one's sources by giving credit to another person, either in the text or in the reference list, for using his or her words or ideas. You may, of course, use the words and ideas of others, provided that use is properly documented. In fact, for many business reports such

S P O T L I G H T   ON ETHICS

WHO SAID SO?

Plagiarism is a potential problem for anyone who writes. For example, the head of Harvard University's psychiatric hospital resigned when it was found he had committed plagiarism in four papers he published. A nationally known minister was accused of plagiarizing numerous sections from someone else's book to include in his own popular book. A director of the Cooley Law School resigned immediately after admitting he used "substantial unattributed quotations" in a law-review article. Problems of dishonesty in research have become so serious, in fact, that the federal government has issued new rules designed to police scientific fraud by researchers.

Business writers have also been guilty of shoddy scholarship. In *Pacific Rim Trade*, a book published by the American Management Association, the writers stated that Lakewood Industries, a small Minnesota firm, sells the most chopsticks in Japan. *Forbes* magazine investigated and found that the company doesn't sell the most chopsticks in Japan, never did, and never will. In fact, the three-year-old firm went bankrupt trying to perfect a technique for manufacturing the chopsticks.

You can, of course, go too far in the other direction and provide excessive documentation. Such a practice not only is distracting but also leaves the impression that the writer is not an original thinker. As an example of excessive documentation, one in-depth study of criminal procedure in the *Georgetown Law Journal* was accompanied by 3,917 footnotes!

In addition to citing your sources, you should also verify any information you include in a report, regardless of who said it. For example, according to the book *They Never Said It*, despite widespread belief Voltaire never said, "I disapprove of what you say, but I will defend to the death your right to say it"; Leo Durocher never said, "Nice guys finish last"; and W. C. Fields never said, "Anybody who hates children and dogs can't be all bad." Similarly, James Cagney never used the line

"You Dirty Rat" nor Humphrey Bogart, "Play it again, Sam" in any of their films. And Sherlock Holmes never uttered "Elementary, my dear Watson," in any of A. Conan Doyle's novels.

Creating inaccurate impressions is just as unethical as giving inaccurate information. For example, with electronic technology, a picture may no longer be worth a thousand words. The magazine *TV Guide* once featured talk-show host Oprah Winfrey on its cover. Only after the designer of the dress she was wearing complained did the magazine admit that the body shown was really not that of Oprah Winfrey—but rather Ann Margaret! Even the venerable *National Geographic* magazine once used electronic retouching to move two pyramids closer together so that they would fit on the magazine's cover. Thus, photographs and charts may no longer be a reliable source of information.

As a competent communicator, you must give appropriate credit to your sources and ensure the accuracy of your data. Make certain that you have answered completely and fairly the question "Who said so?" Your organization's reputation and welfare—not to mention your own—demand no less.

Sources: Kenneth H. Bacon, "U.S. Issues Rules Aimed at Policing Fraud in Research," *Wall Street Journal*, August 9, 1989, p. B3; Paul M. Barrett, "To Read This Story in Full, Don't Forget to See the Footnotes," *Wall Street Journal*, May 10, 1988, p. 1; Paul Boller and John George, *They Never Said It* (Oxford, England: Oxford University Press, 1989); Christopher Cook, "Judge Reportedly Plagiarized in Article," *Detroit Free Press*, March 19, 1989, p. 3A; John Harris, "Chop-Stuck," *Forbes*, August 21, 1989, p. 14; "Minister Accused," *Morning Sun*, August 19, 1989, p. 6; Patty Rhuie, "TV Guide Snatches a Body," *USA Today*, August 29, 1989, p. 1A; Bill Slapin, "Publisher's Memo," *Presentation Products*, August 1989, p. 6; Rob Stein, "Plagiarism Charges End in Departure at Harvard," *Detroit Free Press*, November 29, 1988, p. 8A.

secondary information is the only data used. You must, however, provide appropriate documentation whenever you quote, paraphrase, or summarize someone else's work.

Plagiarism is the using of another person's words or ideas without giving proper credit. One's writings are considered legal property; someone else who wrongfully uses such property is guilty of theft. Plagiarism, therefore, carries stiff penalties. In the classroom, the penalty ranges from failure in a course to expulsion from school. On the job, the penalty for plagiarism ranges from loss of credibility to loss of employment.

Provide a reference for material that came from others, unless that material is common knowledge or can be verified easily.

What Needs to Be Documented Except as noted, all material in your report that comes from secondary sources must be documented; that is, enough information about the source must be given to enable the reader to locate the source if he or she so desires. If the secondary source is published (for example, a journal article), the documentation should appear as a reference citation. If the source is unpublished, enough documentation can generally be given in the narrative, making a formal citation unnecessary, as follows:

> According to Board Policy 91-18b, all position vacancies above the level of C-3 must be posted internally at least two weeks prior to being advertised.

> The contractor's letter of May 23, 1991, stated, "We hereby agree to modify Blueprint 3884 by widening the Southeast entrance from 10 feet to 12 feet 6 inches for a total additional charge of $273.50."

Occasionally, enough information can be given in the narrative so that a formal citation is unnecessary even for published sources. This format is most appropriate when only one or two sources are used in a report:

> Widmark made this very argument in a guest editorial entitled "Here We Go Again" in the May 4, 1989, Wall Street Journal (p. A12).

Once a study has been cited, it may be mentioned again in continuous discussion on the same page or even on the next pages without further citation if no ambiguity results. If several pages intervene or if ambiguity might result, the citation should be given again.

What Does Not Need to Be Documented Two types of material by others do not need to be documented: (1) facts that are common knowledge to the readers of your report; or (2) facts that can be verified easily.

> Apple Computer is a large manufacturer of microcomputers.

> The stock market closed at 2,506 on November 8.

But statements such as "Sales of the original Macintosh were disappointing" and "Only 4,000 Macintosh computers were sold in 1984" would need to be documented. If in doubt about whether documentation is needed, provide the citation.

Standard citation formats are footnotes, endnotes, and author–year citations.

Forms of Documentation The three major forms for documenting the ideas, information, and quotations of other people in a report are endnotes, footnotes, and author–date references (see Figure 13.4). Let the nature of the report and the needs of the reader dictate the documentation method used. Regardless of the method you select, ensure that the citations are accurate, complete, and consistently formatted and that your bibliography format is compatible with your documentation format.

Word processing has simplified the generation of endnotes and footnotes.

Endnotes The endnote format uses superscript (raised) numbers to identify secondary sources in the text and then provides the actual citations in a numbered list entitled "Notes" at the end of the report. The endnotes are

Three Documentation Formats

FIGURE 13.4A

Endnotes:

Other organizations have found Yellow Pages display advertising to be extremely important. One out of ten adults nationwide inquires about moving or storage every year, and a slight majority of these people turn to the Yellow Pages for guidance.[1] Approximately 40% of the time, consumers in general do not have a specific company in mind when they begin searching the Yellow Pages for a particular product or service.[2]

Size appears to be the single most important factor in a Yellow Pages display ad because "the eye focuses first on a large ad and later on the smaller ads."[3] Color, design, and illustrations seem to be much less important than size.

Endnotes are numbered consecutively throughout the report, using superior numbers. The actual citations are given on a separate Notes page at the back of the report.

Footnotes:

Other organizations have found Yellow Pages display advertising to be extremely important. One out of ten adults nationwide inquires about moving or storage every year, and a slight majority of these people turn to the Yellow Pages for guidance.[1] Approximately 40% of the time, consumers in general do not have a specific company in mind when they begin searching the Yellow Pages for a particular product or service.[2]

Size appears to be the single most important factor in a Yellow Pages display ad because "the eye focuses first on a large ad and later on the smaller ads."[3] Color, design, and illustrations seem to be much less important than size.

Footnotes are numbered starting with "1" on each page. The actual citations appear at the bottom of the same page as the text references. Each part of a footnote is separated by a comma.

[1]Max Voight, Marketing Techniques for the Moving and Storage Industry (Chicago: Midwest Publishing Co., 1987), 54.

[2]Lisa Poston, "Eye-Perception Research: A Marketing Tool," Journal of Telecommunications, 15 (May 1989): 75.

[3]Larry R. Chilton and Harry M. Raines, "Who Really Reads the Yellow Pages?" Business Monthly, 23 October 1990, 13.

Author-Date Method:

Other organizations have found Yellow Pages display advertising to be extremely important. One out of ten adults nationwide inquires about moving or storage every year, and a slight majority of these people turn to the Yellow Pages for guidance (Voight 1987). Approximately 40% of the time, consumers in general do not have a specific company in mind when they begin searching the Yellow Pages for a particular product or service (Poston 1989).

Size appears to be the single most important factor in a Yellow Pages display ad because "the eye focuses first on a large ad and later on the smaller ads" (Chilton and Raines 1990, p. 13). Color, design, and illustrations appear to be much less important than size.

The author-year method puts the author's name and the publication date in parentheses. If the author's name is given in the narrative, only the year goes in parentheses. Page numbers are given for direct quotations.

Mechanics Notes

1. Type the superior numbers immediately after punctuation and after closing quotation marks.   2. Single-space before and double-space after the two-inch divider line.   3. Single-space the lines within a citation; double-space between citations.   4. Type the parenthetical reference before any punctuation but after the closing quotation mark.

FIGURE 13.4B   Three Bibliographic Formats

The same format is used for the notes as for the footnote citations except that numbers followed by periods are used instead of superior numbers. Arrange the entries in the order in which they appear in the body of the report.

Only the last name of the first author is shown in reverse order. Initial capital letters are used for publication titles. Each part of the citation is separated by a period. Arrange the entries in alphabetical order.

Only the first word, proper nouns, and the first word following a colon or dash are capitalized in titles of journal and magazine articles and of books. Do not use quotation marks around article titles. The year of publication immediately follows the name.

For Endnotes:

NOTES   1

  1. Max Voight, Marketing Techniques for the Moving and Storage Industry (Chicago: Midwest Publishing Co., 1987), 54.   2
  2. Lisa Poston, "Eye-Perception Research: A Marketing Tool," Journal of Telecommunications, 15 (May 1989): 75.
  3. Larry R. Chilton and Harry M. Raines, "Who Really Reads the Yellow Pages?" Business Monthly, 23 October 1990, 13.

For Footnotes:

BIBLIOGRAPHY

Chilton, Larry R., and Harry M. Raines. "Who Really Reads the   3
  Yellow Pages?" Business Monthly 23 October 1990, 12–17.
Poston, Lisa. "Eye-Perception Research: A Marketing Tool." Journal of Telecommunications 15 (May 1989): 75–77.
Voight, Max. Marketing Techniques for the Moving and Storage Industry. Chicago: Midwest Publishing Co., 1987.

For Author–Date References:

REFERENCES

Chilton, Larry R., and Harry M. Raines 1990. Who really reads the Yellow Pages? Business Monthly 23 October, 12–17.
Poston, Lisa. 1989. Eye-perception research: A marketing tool. Journal of Telecommunications 15 (May): 75–77.
Voight, Max. 1987. Marketing techniques for the moving and storage industry. Chicago: Midwest Publishing Co.

Mechanics Notes

1. Whichever of the three formats is used, begin the list on a separate page, leaving a 2-inch top margin.   2. Indent the first line of each citation five spaces.   Single-space the lines of each citation but double-space between citations.   3. Begin the first line at the left margin, and indent runover lines five spaces.

numbered consecutively throughout the report. Some readers prefer the endnote format because it avoids the clutter of footnotes and because it's easy to use.

In the past, however, using endnotes for a long or complex report was somewhat risky because of the possibility of introducing errors when revising text. Every time text with a reference was inserted, deleted, or moved, all following endnote references in the text and in the list at the back of the report had to be renumbered. Today, however, most word processors have an endnote feature that automatically numbers and keeps track of endnote references. Still, some readers prefer one of the other formats because endnotes provide no clues in the text regarding the source.

Footnotes   For years, footnotes were the traditional way of citing sources, especially in scholarly reports. A bibliographic footnote provides the complete reference at the bottom of the page on which the citation occurs in the text. Thus, a reader interested in exploring the source wouldn't have to turn to the back of the report. Today's word processors can format footnotes almost painlessly—automatically numbering and positioning each note correctly. Some readers, however, find the presence of footnotes on the text page distracting.

Author–Date Format   Many business report readers prefer the author–date format of documentation because they feel the method is a reasonable compromise between endnotes (which provide no reference information on the text page) and footnotes (which provide all the reference information on the text page). Because of the popularity of the author–date format for business reports, detailed information about this method follows.

> The author–date format is preferred by many users of business reports.

To use the author–date format, insert at an appropriate point in the text the last name of the author and the year of publication. If the author's name appears in the text, only the year of publication is given in parentheses; otherwise, both name and year appear in parentheses, with no intervening comma.

Place the parenthetical citation just before (not after) a mark of punctuation if possible or at some other logical place in the sentence (for example, immediately after the author's name if the name appears in the text). Use the following styles:

1. *One Author:*

   Ray (1989) compared the productivity of union and nonunion workers. (*author's name in text*)

   A recent study found no differences in the productivity of union and nonunion workers (Ray 1989). (*author's name in reference*)

2. *Two or Three Authors:*

   As shown by Lee and Day (1988), institutional selling was the major cause of the October drop.

   As has been documented (Turner, Miller, and Lynch 1987), the October drop had been predicted.

3. *More than Three Authors:* Use the Latin abbreviation *et al.* (meaning "and others") in the text citation; however, list all authors (in the order shown in the original source) in the reference list.

> Roscoe et al. (1988) believe that increasing international trade is one solution.

> Increasing international trade has been proposed as one solution (Roscoe et al. 1988).

4. *No Author:* Use the first two or three words of the title of the article (not the title of the journal or newspaper) enclosed in quotation marks.

> One study ("Wiped Out" 1991) found a strong correlation between profitability and workplace safety.

5. *Multiple Citations:* Arrange multiple citations by the same author in chronological order, separating the years by commas; do not repeat the author's name. In citing multiple works by the same author in the same year, add the suffixes *a*, *b*, and so forth to the year both in the text citation and in the reference list. Arrange multiple citations by different authors in alphabetical order, separated by semicolons.

> Several economists (Brown 1987a, 1987b, 1989; Jones and Williams 1990; Thomas 1989) argue that more stringent measures are needed.

6. *Authors with the Same Surname:* Include initials to avoid confusion, even if the year of publication differs.

> The frozen-yogurt market is projected to increase 10% to 15% yearly for the next five years (J. Smith 1988; T. Smith 1990).

Include page numbers for references to statistics or direct quotations.	**Documentation of a Part of a Source** If an entire study is being referred to in the text, use the author–date method as just described. If only part of a source is being cited (for example, a particular statistic from a study or a direct quotation), include the page number of the source. Insert a comma between the year and the page number and omit "p." or "pp."

> Using this method, the company had a loss of $74.5 million (Jones 1986, 384).

> Jones (1986, 392–398) found this was a paper loss only.

Direct Quotations For direct quotations, always provide the name of the writer or speaker and the source page numbers. A short quotation (fewer than four typed lines) should be incorporated into the text and enclosed in double quotation marks. The parenthetical reference goes after the closing quotation mark but before any sentence punctuation.

> Campbell et al. state that "a direct quotation . . . is appropriate when you need to provide authority, originality of wording, or accuracy" (1982, 53).

As just shown, three ellipsis points (periods with spaces before and after each) are used to indicate omitted material within a sentence. Four such points indicate any omission between two sentences within a quotation. Ellipsis points are not needed at the beginning or end of a quotation.

A long quotation (four or more typed lines) should be set off from the text, single-spaced, without quotation marks, and indented five spaces from the left margin. Double-space before and after the quoted block. The parenthetical reference goes after the concluding punctuation mark of the quotation. Here is an example:

The *MLA Handbook for Writers of Research Papers* makes this observation about the use of direct quotations:

> While quotations are a common and often effective feature of a research paper, use them selectively. Quote only words, phrases, lines, and passages that are particularly interesting, vivid, unique, or apt, and keep all quotations as brief as possible. Overquotation can bore your readers and might lead them to conclude that you are neither an original thinker nor a skillful writer. (Gibaldi and Achtert 1984, 136)

The only permissible changes from the original quotation are that the first letter of the first word may be changed to a capital or small letter and the punctuation mark at the end of a sentence may be changed to fit the syntax. Any other changes to the original quotation must be explicitly indicated by brackets.

REVISING

Once you have produced a first draft of your report, put it away for a few days. Doing so will enable you to view the draft with a fresh perspective and perhaps find a more effective means of communicating your ideas to the reader. Don't try to correct all problems in one review. Instead, look at this process as having three steps—revising first for content, then for style, and finally for correctness.

Revise first for content. Make sure you've included sufficient information to support each point, that you've included no extraneous information (regardless of how interesting it might be), that all the information is accurate, and that it is presented in an efficient and logical sequence. Keep the purpose of the report and the reader's needs and desires in mind as you review for content.

Once you're satisfied with the content of the report, revise for style (see Checklist 1 "Effective Business Writing"). Ensure that your writing has clarity and that you have used short, simple, vigorous, and concise words. Check to see that you have used a variety of sentence types and have used active and passive voice appropriately. Do your paragraphs have unity and coherence, and are they of reasonable length? Have you maintained an overall tone of confidence, courtesy, sincerity, and objectivity? Finally, review your draft to ensure that you have used nondiscriminatory language and appropriate emphasis and subordination.

After you're confident about the content and style of your draft, revise once more for correctness. This revision step is known as *editing* and identifies any problems with grammar, spelling, punctuation, and word usage—the topics covered in Chapter 4. Do not risk losing credibility with the reader by careless English usage. If possible, have a colleague review your draft to catch any errors you may have overlooked.

OBJECTIVE 7: Revise a report for content, style, and correctness.

Edit for grammar, spelling, punctuation, and word usage.

FORMATTING

The physical format of your report (margins, spacing, and the like) depends to a certain extent on the length and complexity of the report and the formats preferred by either the organization or the reader. Consistency and readability are the hallmarks of an effective format. For example, ensure that your first-degree headings are all formatted consistently; if they are not, the reader may not be able to tell which headings are superior or subordinate to other headings.

General Formatting Guidelines

Adopt a consistent, logical format, keeping the needs of the reader in mind.

If the reader or the organization has a preferred format style, use it. Otherwise, the sections that follow present generally accepted guidelines for formatting business reports. Also make use of any automatic or formatting features of your computer to enhance the appearance and readability of your report and to increase the efficiency of the process.

Margins Memo and letter reports (see Figures 10.1 and 10.2) use regular correspondence margins as discussed in Chapter 5. For reports typed in manuscript (formal report) format, use a 2-inch top margin (begin typing on line 13, thus leaving 12 blank lines) for the first page of each special part (e.g., the table of contents, the executive summary, the first page of the body of the report, and the first page of the reference list). Leave a 1-inch top margin (begin typing on line 7) for all other pages and at least a 1-inch bottom margin on all pages. If the report is to be bound at the left, set a 1½-inch left margin and a 1-inch right margin. If the report is to be unbound, set 1-inch side margins on both the left and right.

Spacing Memo and letter reports are typed single-spaced. Manuscript reports may be either single- or double-spaced. Double-spacing is preferred if the reader will likely make many comments on the pages. Note that double-spacing leaves one blank line between each line of type; do not confuse double-spacing with 1½ spacing, which leaves only half a blank line between lines of type.

Regardless of the spacing used for the body of the report, single-spacing is typically used for the table of contents, the executive summary, block quotes, tables, and the reference list. Use a 5-space paragraph indention for double-spaced paragraphs. Do not indent single-spaced paragraphs; instead, double-space between them.

Too many headings are disruptive; too few headings weaken coherence.

Report Headings The number of levels of headings used will vary from report to report. Memo reports may have only first-level headings—with no part titles or other headings. Long reports may have all four levels of headings. One standard format for the various levels is given here. Recognize, however, that the format presented here is only one of several that might be used. Again, consistency and readability are the major goals. Regardless of the format used, make sure that the reader can instantly tell which are major headings and which are subordinate headings.

Part Title   Center a part title (e.g., "Contents" or "References") in all capitals on a new page, leaving a 2-inch top margin. Leave two blank lines after a part title. Double-space titles of two or more lines, using an inverted-pyramid style. Begin the text on the third line below the title.

First-Level Subheading   Center and underline the first-level subheading, and capitalize the first and last words and all other words except articles, short prepositions, and conjunctions. Leave two blank lines before and one blank line after.

Second-Level Subheading   Begin the second-level subheading at the left margin. Underscore and capitalize as in first-level subheadings. Leave two blank lines before and one blank line after.

Third-Level Subheading   Type the third-level subheading a double space below the preceding paragraph, beginning at the paragraph indention. Leave a period and two spaces after the subheading, and begin typing the text on the same line. Capitalize only the first word and underline the entire subheading (but not the period).

Pagination   Number the preliminary pages, such as the table of contents, with lowercase roman numerals centered on line 4 from the bottom of the page. The title page is counted as "page i," but no page number is shown. Page numbers appear on all other preliminary pages. For example, the executive summary might be "page ii" and the table of contents "page iii."

Number all pages beginning with the first page of the body of the report with arabic numerals. *Note:* The following guidelines should be followed when possible. If you're using a word processing program that does not easily permit such formatting, it is acceptable to type the page number at the top right of every page, beginning with the first page of the body.

1. The first page of the body is counted as page 1, but no page number is typed. Beginning with page 2 of the body and continuing through the appendix pages, number all pages consecutively.
2. Type the page number on line 4 from the top at the right margin on every page except those that begin a part, such as the first page of the reference list or an appendix. Type the page number only; do not use the word *page* and do not surround the page number with punctuation. After typing the page number, triple-space and begin typing the first line of the text on line 7.
3. Center the page number for all part pages on line 4 from the bottom of the page.

Sample Report   Figure 13.5 shows the various types of features common to business reports. Study these pages for content, organization, writing style, and format, and refer to them as necessary when writing and formatting a report. Although any individual report you write may not contain every feature shown on these pages, over time you will probably need to know how to format each of these report parts.

FIGURE 13.5A Sample Report

Center each line; type the
title in all capitals. Double-
space and use inverted-
pyramid style for two-line
titles.

Use upper- and lowercase
letters for all other lines.

Leave the same amount of
blank space between each
section.

Leave equal top and bot-
tom margins.

```
           STAFF EMPLOYEES' EVALUATION OF THE BENEFIT PROGRAM

                     AT ATLANTIC STATE UNIVERSITY




                              Prepared for

                             David Riggins
                          Director of Personnel
                         Atlantic State University




                              Prepared by

                              Lyn Santos
                      Assistant Director of Personnel
                         Atlantic State University

                           December 8, 1991
```

Title Page

A title page is typically used for manuscript reports but not for memo or letter
reports. The report title, reader's name, writer's name, and submission date are
required; other information is optional. An academic report might also contain a
section with this wording (diagonals indicate line breaks): "A Research Report /
Submitted in Partial Fulfillment / of the Requirements for the Course / *Course
Number and Name*."

Sample Report

FIGURE 13.5B

MEMO TO: David Riggins, Director of Personnel
     FROM: Lyn Santos, Assistant Director of Personnel *LS*
     DATE: December 8, 1991
  SUBJECT: Staff Employees' Evaluation of the Benefit Program at At-
           lantic State University

Here is the report evaluating our staff benefits program
that you requested on October 15.

The report shows that overall, the staff is familiar with
and values most of the benefits we offer. At the end of
the report, I've made several recommendations regarding
issuing individualized benefit statements annually and
determining the usefulness of the automobile-insurance
benefit, the feasibility of offering compensation for unused sick leave, and the competitiveness of our retirement program.

I enjoyed working on this assignment, Dave, and learned
quite a bit from my analysis of the problem that will
help me during the upcoming labor negotiations. Please
let me know if you have any questions about the report.

emc

ii

Use a memo format for an internal reader and a letter format for an external reader.

The date on the title page should agree with the date on the memo.

Triple-space.

Use standard correspondence margins and format

Type the page number on line 4 from the bottom.

Transmittal Document

The transmittal document is an optional part of a report. Use a direct organizational pattern and informal language, even if the report itself uses formal language. Give a brief overview of the major conclusions and recommendations if you expect the reader to be receptive or neutral to such information. Close with goodwill comments.

FIGURE 13.5C   Sample Report

Start on line 13.

Use an inverse-pyramid
form for multiline titles.

Triple-space
Single-space the body, with
double-spacing between
paragraphs.

Margins:
  2″ top
  1½″ left (for bound
    reports)
  1″ right
  1″ bottom

Type the page number on
line 4 from the bottom.

EXECUTIVE SUMMARY

STAFF EMPLOYEES' EVALUATION OF THE BENEFIT PROGRAM

AT ATLANTIC STATE UNIVERSITY

Lyn Santos
December 8, 1991

Employee benefits now account for over a third of all payroll costs. Thus, on the basis of cost alone, an organization's benefit program must be carefully monitored and evaluated.

The problem in this study was to determine the opinions of the nearly 2,500 staff employees at Atlantic State University regarding the employee benefit program. Specifically, the investigation included determining the employees' present level of knowledge about the benefit program, their opinions of the benefits presently offered, and their preferences for additional benefits. A survey of 206 staff employees and interviews with three managers familiar with the ASU employee benefit program provided the primary data for this study.

Overall, nearly 70% of the employees feel the benefit program has been explained adequately to them. However, a majority of the employees would prefer to have an individualized benefit statement instead of the brochures now used to explain the benefit program.

Employees are most familiar with the benefits having to do with paid time off; more than 90% of the employees are familiar with ASU policies concerning vacation, holidays, and sick leave. Similarly, more than 95% of the employees rank these three benefits as most important to them; auto insurance and bookstore discounts are considered the least important. Employees are most satisfied with the ASU vacation policy (90% satisfied) and least satisfied with the retirement policy (20% dissatisfied).

The only additional benefit that a majority of the staff employees would like to see added is compensation for unused sick leave; this potential benefit was endorsed by 82% of the employees. Other research has shown that in the long run, paying employees for unused sick leave is generally cost effective.

The University should study further the offering of individualized benefit statements, automobile insurance, compensation for unused sick leave, and retirement benefits. This employee assessment of the ASU employee benefit program should help the university administration in ensuring that the program operates as effectively as possible.

iii

Executive Summary

The executive summary, also called an *abstract* or *synopsis,* is an optional part of a report. If used, it goes immediately before the table of contents. If a transmittal document is not included, the summary page would be numbered "ii."

Sample Report

FIGURE 13.5D

```
                      CONTENTS

MEMO OF TRANSMITTAL  . . . . . . . . . . . . . . . . . . . . . . . . . .  ii

EXECUTIVE SUMMARY  . . . . . . . . . . . . . . . . . . . . . . . . .  iii

INTRODUCTION  . . . . . . . . . . . . . . . . . . . . . . . . . . . . .  1
    Purpose and Scope of the Study  . . . . . . . . . . . . . . .  1
    Procedures  . . . . . . . . . . . . . . . . . . . . . . . . . . . .  2

FINDINGS  . . . . . . . . . . . . . . . . . . . . . . . . . . . . . . .  2
    Communication of Benefits  . . . . . . . . . . . . . . . . .  2
        Employees' Knowledge of Benefits  . . . . . . . . .  2
        Present Methods of Communication  . . . . . . . . .  5
        Preferred Methods of Communication  . . . . . . . .  6
    Opinions of Present Benefits  . . . . . . . . . . . . . . . .  8
        Importance of Benefits  . . . . . . . . . . . . . . . . .  8
        Satisfaction with Benefits  . . . . . . . . . . . . . .  10
    Desirability of Additional Benefits  . . . . . . . . . . .  12

SUMMARY, CONCLUSIONS, AND RECOMMENDATIONS  . . . . . . . . . . .  13
    Summary of the Problem and Procedures  . . . . . . . . . .  13
    Summary of the Findings  . . . . . . . . . . . . . . . . . .  13
    Conclusions and Recommendations  . . . . . . . . . . . . .  14

APPENDIX
    A. Cover Letter  . . . . . . . . . . . . . . . . . . . . . . . .  15
    B. Questionnaire  . . . . . . . . . . . . . . . . . . . . . . .  16

REFERENCES  . . . . . . . . . . . . . . . . . . . . . . . . . . . . .  18




                        iv
```

Start on line 13.
Triple-space before part titles.
Numbers align at the right.

Double-space after part titles.

Indent each lower-level heading 3 spaces.

Use either leaders or spaced leaders (period, space, period) between the headings and page numbers.

Margins:
  2″ top
  1½″ left (for bound reports)
  1″ right
  1″ bottom

Table of Contents

Use a table of contents for long reports with numerous headings. The wording in the headings on the contents page must be identical with that used in the report itself. (Exception: The heading "Introduction" is identified on the contents page but not in the report itself.) Identify only the page on which each heading is located, even though the section may comprise several pages. Generic headings (noun phrases) are used here.

FIGURE 13.5E   Sample Report

Start on line 13.

Triple-space.

The heading "Introduction" is not used since it is obvious that the first section introduces the report.

The introduction begins by giving background information and establishing a need for the study.

The author–date method is used for documenting sources.

Margins:
2″ top (first page)
1″ top (other pages)
1½″ left (for bound
  reports)
1″ right
1″ bottom

The scope (also called *delimitations*) of the study is explained.

STAFF EMPLOYEES' EVALUATION OF THE BENEFIT PROGRAM

AT ATLANTIC STATE UNIVERSITY

Employee benefits are a rapidly growing and an increasingly important form of employee compensation for both profit and nonprofit organizations. According to a recent U.S. Chamber of Commerce survey, benefits now comprise 37% of all payroll costs, costing an average of $7,832 a year for each employee (Berelson, Lazarsfield, and Connell 1989, 183). Thus, on the basis of cost alone, an organization's benefit program must be carefully monitored and evaluated.

Atlantic State University employs nearly 2,500 staff personnel, and they have not received a cost-of-living increase in two years. As a result, staff salaries may not have kept pace with private industry, and the University's employee benefits program may become more important in attracting and retaining good workers. In addition, the contracts of three of the four staff unions expire next year; and the benefits program is typically a major area of bargaining.

Purpose and Scope of the Study

As has been noted by one management consultant, "The success of employee benefit programs depends directly on whether employees need, understand, and appreciate the value of the benefits provided" (Egan 1989, 220). Thus, to help ensure that the benefit program is operating as effectively as possible, David Riggins, director of personnel, authorized this report on October 15, 1991.

Specifically, the following problem was addressed in this study: What are the opinions of staff employees at Atlantic State University regarding their employee benefits? To answer this question, the following subproblems were addressed:

1. How knowledgeable are the employees about the benefit program?

2. What are the employees' opinions of the value of the benefits presently available?

3. What benefits, if any, would the employees like to have added to the program?

This study explored the attitudes of the staff employees at Atlantic State University. Although staff employees at all three state universities receive the same benefits, no attempt has been made to generalize the findings beyond Atlantic State University because the communication of the benefits may be different, different geographical areas may make some benefits of more use at one

Body of the Report

This recommendation report is written in formal style (note the absence of first- and second-person pronouns) and in manuscript format. An indirect organizational pattern with generic headings is used.

Sample Report (*cont'd*)   **FIGURE 13.5F**

2

institution than at another, and similar considerations. In addition, this study attempted to determine employee preferences only. The question of whether employee preferences are economically feasible is not within the scope of this study.

Procedures

A list of the 2,489 staff employees who are eligible for benefits (i.e., those who are employed at least 20 hours a week) was generated from the October 15 payroll run. Using a 10% systematic sample, 250 employees were selected for the survey. On November 3, each of the selected employees was sent the cover letter and questionnaire shown in Appendixes A and B via campus mail. A total of 206 employees completed usable questionnaires, for a response rate of 82%.

In addition to the questionnaire data, personal interviews were held with Lois White, compensation specialist at ASU; Roger Ray, chair of the Staff Personnel Committee at ASU; and Lewis Rigby, director of the State Personnel Board. The primary data provided by the survey and personal interviews was then analyzed and compared with findings from secondary sources to determine the staff employees' opinions of the benefits program at ASU.

Findings

For a benefits program to achieve its goals, employees must be aware of the benefits provided. Thus, the first section that follows discusses the effectiveness of the University's present method of communicating benefits as well as those methods that employees would prefer. An effective benefit package must also include benefits that are relevant to employee needs. Thus, the employees' opinions of the importance of and satisfaction with each benefit offered are discussed next. The section concludes with a discussion of those benefits employees would like to see added to the benefits program at ASU.

Knowledge of Benefits

Several studies (Egan 1989; Ignatio 1990; Meany 1988) have shown that employee satisfaction with benefits is directly correlated with their knowledge of such benefits. Thus, an indication of the staff employees' level of familiarity with their benefits and suggestions for improving communication were solicited.

Familiarity with benefits. The staff employees were asked to rate their level of familiarity with each benefit. As shown in Table 1, most staff employees believe that most benefits have been adequately communicated to them.

At least three-fourths of the employees are familiar with all major benefits except for long-term disability insurance, which is familiar to only a slight majority. The low level of knowledge

---

Type the page number on line 4; begin the text on line 7.

This report is shown in single-spaced format with blocked paragraphs. A five-space paragraph indention could have been used instead.

First-level subheading: Leave two blank lines before, one after.

Second-level subheading: Leave two blank lines before, one after.

Third-level subheading: Leave one blank line before. Only the first word is capitalized. Do not underline the period.

The findings (also called *results*) section begins by giving an overview of the organization of this section. Each of the subsections that follow discusses one of the subproblems; thus the organizational basis used in this report is the criteria identified earlier for solving this problem.

FIGURE 13.5G   Sample Report

Table 1. Atlantic State University Staff Employees' Level of Familiarity with the
Benefit Program

| Benefit | Level of Familiarity | | | | Total |
	Familiar	Unfamiliar	Undecided	No response	
Sick leave	94%	4%	1%	1%	100%
Vacation	94%	4%	1%	1%	100%
Paid holidays	92%	4%	3%	1%	100%
Hospital/medical ins.	90%	7%	2%	0%	100%
Life insurance	84%	10%	5%	1%	100%
Retirement	84%	11%	4%	1%	100%
Long-term disability ins.	55%	33%	12%	1%	100%
Auto insurance*	36%	57%	6%	15%	100%

* This benefit started six weeks before the survey was taken.

In general, benefit familiarity is not related to length of employment at ASU. Most
employees are familiar with most benefits, regardless of their length of employment.
However, as shown in Figure 1, the one benefit for which this is not true is life
insurance. The longer a person has been employed at ASU, the more likely he or she
is to know about this benefit.

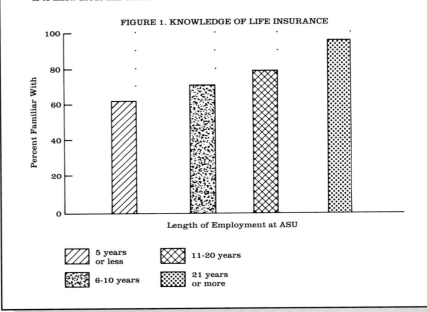

FIGURE 1. KNOWLEDGE OF LIFE INSURANCE

Each visual aid (table or chart, for example) is introduced before it is presented.
Only the most important data from each is discussed in the narrative. Tables may
be presented in any standard table format. Charts should be of an appropriate
size and kept simple. Be consistent in formatting tables and charts throughout
the report.

Sample Report

FIGURE 13.5H

14

compensated for unused sick leave. Previous research was reviewed that showed that such compensation has been cost effective over the long run for companies in the manufacturing and service industries.

Conclusions and Recommendations

These findings show that staff employees at Atlantic State University are extremely knowledgeable about all benefits except long-term disability and automobile insurance; however, a majority would prefer to have an individualized benefits statement instead of the brochures now used to explain the benefits program. They consider paid time off as the most important benefit and automobile insurance as the least important. A majority are satisfied with all benefits, although retirement benefits generated substantial dissatisfaction. The only additional benefit desired by a majority of the employees is compensation for unused sick leave.

The following recommendations are based on these conclusions:

1. Determine the feasibility of generating for each staff employee an annual individualized benefits statement.

2. Reevaluate the attractiveness of the automobile-insurance benefit in one year to determine staff employees' knowledge about, use of, and desire for this benefit. Consider the feasibility of substituting compensation for unused sick leave for the automobile-insurance benefit.

3. Conduct a follow-up study of the retirement benefits at ASU to determine how competitive they are with comparable public and private institutions.

These recommendations, as well as the findings of this study, should help the university administration assure that its benefit program is accomplishing its stated objectives of attracting and retaining high-quality employees and meeting their needs once employed.

Conclusions are drawn based on each of the three subproblems.

Note the format for a numbered list.

The ending paragraph provides a sense of completion for the report.

This is the last page of the report. Ensure that the conclusions and recommendations stem directly from the findings and that ample supporting evidence has been presented. Avoid extreme or exaggerated language. Provide an appropriate concluding paragraph.

FIGURE 13.5l   Sample Report

3

Type the page number on line 4; begin the text on line 7.

First-degree heading: Leave two blank lines before, one after.

Second-degree heading: Leave two blank lines before, one after.

Third-degree heading: Leave one blank line before and indent. Only the first word is capitalized. Do not underline the period.

Margins:
  2" top (first page)
  1" top (other pages)
  1½" left (for bound reports)
  1" right
  1" bottom

and Lewis Rigby, director of the State Personnel Board. The primary data provided by the survey and personal interviews was then analyzed and compared with findings from secondary sources to determine the staff employees' opinions of the benefits program at ASU.

Findings
For a benefits program to achieve its goals, employees must be aware of the benefits provided. Thus, the first section that follows discusses the effectiveness of the university's present method of communicating benefits as well as those methods that employees would prefer. An effective benefits package must also include benefits that are relevant to employee needs. Thus, the employees' opinions of the importance of and satisfaction with each benefit offered are discussed next. The section concludes with a discussion of those benefits employees would like to see added to the benefits program at ASU.

Knowledge of Benefits
Several studies (Egan 1989; Ignatio 1990; Meany 1988) have shown that employee satisfaction with benefits is directly correlated with their knowledge of such benefits. Thus, an indication of the staff employees' level of familiarity with their benefits and suggestions for improving communication were solicited.

   Familiarity with benefits. The staff employees were asked to rate their level of familiarity with each benefit. As shown in Table 1, most staff employees believe that most benefits have been adequately communicated to them.

   At least three-fourths of the employees are familiar with all major benefits except for long-term disability insurance, which is familiar to only a slight majority. The low level of knowledge about automobile insurance can be explained by the fact that this benefit

Alternate Double-Spaced Format
Double-space the body of the report when you expect the reader to make comments (either for personal use or for someone else's use). Quadruple spacing (two double spaces) may be left before first- and second-degree headings instead of the triple-spacing shown.

Sample Report   **FIGURE 13.5J**

REFERENCES

Adams, J. B. 1990. Compensation systems. Boston: Benson and Bacon, Inc.

Adams, John M., and G. Robert Stearns. 1987. Personnel administration. Cambridge: All-State Press.

Berelson, Barnard R., Paul F. Lazarsfield, and William Connell, Jr. 1989. Managing your fringe-benefit program. 2nd. ed. Chicago: Novak-Siebold.

Corporate Libraries Association. 1991. Directory of business and financial services, New York: Corporate Libraries Association.

Egan, J. D., ed. 1989. Human resources management. London: Varsity Press.

Gowens, Jo Anne. 1991. Cafeteria-style benefits. In Personnel management, ed. Ruth Anshen, 661-72. New York: Gump Bros.

Ignatio, Earl. 1990. Flexible benefits are the key to compensation. Personnel Quarterly 61:113-25.

————. 1991. Employee benefits in transition: managers look to the past to move employee benefits into the future. Supervisory Management in the 21st Century 28: 36-39.

Kean, Thomas J. III. 1989. Employee benefits: Then and now. Business Monthly, 19 November, 39-41.

Letting employees determine their own benefits. 1991. New City Times, 12 January, E21.

Meany, Grant. 1986. Employee benefits at American universities. Ph.D. dissertation, Atlantic State University.

Potts' Ron. 1989. Tuition reimbursement in government. Paper presented at the National Mayors' Conference, Atlantic City, N.J., 14 August.

Rigby, Lewis, director of State Personnel Board. 1991. Personal interview, 20 October.

Tri Star Publishing. 1991. Trademark search database. DIALOG, File 305, Item 0119 473.

U.S. Department of Commerce. Bureau of the Census. 1982. United States census of the population: 1980, vol. 1: Characteristics of the population. Washington, D.C.: GPO.

18

Start on line 13.
Triple-space.
Book—one author

Book—two authors

Book—three or more authors

Book—organization as author

Book—editor as author

Book—component part

Journal article

Second work by same author (8-space underscore in chronological order
Magazine article

Unsigned newspaper article

Thesis or dissertation

Paper presented at a meeting

Interview

Computerized data base

Government document

Type the page number on line 4 from the bottom.

References

Arrange all entries (including journal articles, books, and the like) in one alphabetical listing according to the author's last name. Include only those sources actually cited in the report—not every source read. Begin the first line of each entry at the left margin and indent subsequent lines five spaces. Single-space the lines within each entry and double-space between entries. Type magazine, journal, and newspaper titles in upper- and lowercase letters. Type book and article titles sentence style: Capitalize only the first word, proper nouns, and the first word after a colon. Do not enclose articles in quotation marks.

PROOFREADING

First impressions are important. Even before reading the first line of your report, the reader will have formed an initial impression of the report—and of *you*. Make this impression a positive one by ensuring that the report carries with it a professional appearance.

After making all your revisions and formatting the various pages, give each page one final proofreading. Check closely for typographical errors. Check for appearance. Have you arranged the pages in correct order and stapled them neatly? If you're submitting a photocopy, are all the copies legible and of even darkness? Is each page free of wrinkles and smudges?

If you formatted the report on a computer, ensure that in moving passages about, you did not inadvertently delete a line or two or repeat a passage unintentionally. Run the spelling checker a final time after all changes have been made. If you have a grammar software program available, evaluate your writing electronically. The grammar checker will check for use of passive voice, sentence length, misuse of words, unmatched punctuation (e.g., an opening parenthesis not followed by a closing parenthesis), and readability. Use every aid at your disposal to ensure that report reflects the highest standards of scholarship, critical thinking, and care.

In short, let your pride of authorship show through in every facet of your report. Appearances count. Review your entire document to ensure that you can answer yes to every question contained in Checklist 13, "Reviewing Your Report Draft."

ENHANCING REPORTS THROUGH DOCUMENT DESIGN

The advent of desktop publishing (DTP) software such as *Pagemaker* and word processing software with DTP features such as *WordPerfect* makes it easy for writers to take the report process one step further; that is, to *design* their business reports for maximum impact and effectiveness. Although the product is always more important than the packaging, there is no denying the fact that an attractively formatted document, with legible type and plenty of white space, will help you achieve your report objectives.

With that in mind, consider the following ten guidelines when designing your documents. These guidelines are illustrated in the Spotlight on Technology. The version of the report page on the left was formatted in WordPerfect using the principles of document design. Compare it with the typewritten version of the same page on the right for impact and readability.

1. Keep It Simple.

The most important guideline is to use a simple, clean, and consistent design. Just because you have access to many DTP features doesn't mean that you have to use all of them. As with the language you select, strive to *express*, not to *impress*.

It would be distracting to use many different type styles and sizes in the same document. Instead, select one serif typeface (*serifs* are the small strokes at the tops and bottoms of characters, such as the "feet" at the bottom of

Reviewing Your Report Draft

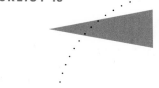

Introduction

1. Is the report title accurate, descriptive, and honest?

2. Is the research problem or purpose of the study stated clearly and accurately?

3. Is the scope of the study made clear?

4. Are any unusual terms, or any terms used in a special way, defined?

5. Were appropriate procedures used to solve the problem?

6. Are the procedures specified in sufficient detail?

7. Are any questionable decisions justified?

Findings

8. Is the data analyzed completely, accurately, and appropriately?

9. Is the analysis free from bias and misrepresentation?

10. Is the data interpreted (its importance and implications discussed) rather than just presented?

11. Are all calculations correct?

12. Is all the data included relevant and all relevant data included?

13. Does the analysis reflect appropriate reader knowledge of secondary data relevant to the topic?

14. Are visual aids correct, needed, clear, appropriately positioned, and labeled correctly?

Summary, Conclusions, and Recommendations

15. Is the wording used in the summary different from that used earlier to present the data initially?

16. Are the conclusions drawn supported by ample credible evidence?

17. Do the conclusions answer the questions or issues raised in the introduction?

18. Are the recommendations reasonable in light of the conclusions?

19. Does the report end with a sense of completion?

Supplementary Pages

20. Is the executive summary short, descriptive, in proportion to the report itself?

21. Is the table of contents accurate, with appropriate page numbers and wording that is identical to that used in the report?

22. Is any appended material properly labeled and referred to in the body of the report?

23. Is the reference list accurate, complete, and in an appropriate format?

Writing Style and Format

24. Does the overall report take into account the needs and desires of the reader?

25. Is the material properly organized?

26. Are the headings used descriptive, parallel, and appropriate in quantity?

27. Is emphasis and subordination used effectively?

28. Does each major section contain a preview, summary, and transition?

29. Has proper verb tense been used throughout?

30. Has an appropriate level of formality been used?

31. Are all references to secondary sources properly documented?

32. Is each needed report part included and in an appropriate format?

33. Is the length of the report appropriate?

34. Are the paragraphs of an appropriate length?

35. If the report is formatted on a computer, have the principles of document design been used to enhance the report's effectiveness?

36. Is the report free from spelling, grammar, and punctuation errors?

37. Does the overall appearance of the report provide a positive first impression?

38. Does the entire project reflect care, neatness, and scholarship?

a *T*; sans serif typefaces have no such ornamental strokes) for the body of your report and one sans serif typeface for headings and subheadings. Thus, a good choice would be to use Times Roman (also called Dutch) for your body type and Helvetica (also called Swiss) for special treatments such as headings, subheadings, and captions for figures.

This is an example of Times Roman in 12-point type. Because the serifs aid in readability, Times Roman is a good choice for the body of your report.

This is an example of Helvetica in 12-point type. Because it contrasts nicely with Times Roman, Helvetica is a good choice for headings.

As an aid to readability, strive for consistency in your document. For example, if a reader is accustomed to seeing lists arranged in a certain

S P O T L I G H T   ON TECHNOLOGY

ENHANCING REPORTS THROUGH DOCUMENT DESIGN

Staff Employees' Evaluation Of the Benefit Program At Atlantic State University

EMPLOYEE BENEFITS ARE a rapidly growing and an increasingly important form of employee compensation for both profit and nonprofit organizations. According to a recent U.S. Chamber of Commerce survey, benefits now comprise 37% of all payroll costs, costing an average of $7,832 a year for each employee (Berelson, Lazarsfield, and Connell 1989, p. 183). Thus, on the basis of cost alone, an organization's benefit program must be carefully monitored and evaluated.

Atlantic State University employs nearly 2,500 staff personnel, and they have not received a cost-of-living increase in two years. As a result, staff salaries may not have kept pace with private industry, and the university's employee benefits program may become more important in attracting and retaining desirable personnel. In addition, the contracts of three of the four staff unions expire next year; and the benefits program is typically a major area of bargaining.

Purpose and Scope of the Study

As has been noted by one management consultant, "The success of employee benefits programs depends directly on whether employees need, understand, and appreciate the value of the benefits provided" (Egan 1989, p. 220). Thus, to help ensure that the benefits program is operating as effectively as possible, David Riggins, director of personnel, authorized this report on October 15, 1991.

Specifically, the following problem was addressed in this study: What are the opinions of staff employees at Atlantic State University regarding their employee benefits? To answer this question, the following subproblems were addressed:

• How knowledgeable are the employees about the benefits program?

Document-Designed Version

STAFF EMPLOYEES' EVALUATION OF THE BENEFIT PROGRAM AT ATLANTIC STATE UNIVERSITY

Employee benefits are a rapidly growing and an increasingly important form of employee compensation for both profit and nonprofit organizations. According to a recent U.S. Chamber of Commerce survey, benefits now comprise 37% of all payroll costs, costing an average of $7,832 a year for each employee (Berelson, Lazarsfield, and Connell 1989, p. 183). Thus, on the basis of cost alone, an organization's benefit program must be carefully monitored and evaluated.

Atlantic State University employs nearly 2,500 staff personnel, and they have not received a cost-of-living increase in two years. As a result, staff salaries may not have kept pace with private industry, and the university's employee benefits program may become more important in attracting and retaining desirable personnel. In addition, the contracts of three of the four staff unions expire next year; and the benefits program is typically a major area of bargaining.

Purpose and Scope of the Study

As has been noted by one management consultant, "The success of employee benefits programs depends directly on whether employees need, understand, and appreciate the value of the benefits provided" (Egan 1989, p. 220). Thus, to help ensure that the benefits program is operating as effectively as possible, David Riggins, director of personnel, authorized this report on October 15, 1991.

Specifically, the following problem was addressed in this study: What are the opinions of staff employees at Atlantic State University regarding their employee benefits? To answer this question, the following subproblems were addressed:

1. How knowledgeable are the employees about the benefits program?
2. What are the employees' opinions of the value of the benefits presently available?
3. What benefits, if any, would the employees like to have added to the program?

This study explored the attitudes of the staff employees at Atlantic State University. Although staff employees at all three state universities receive the same benefits, no attempt has been made to generalize the findings beyond Atlantic State University because the communication of the benefits may be different.

Typewritten Version   1

format in your report, it would then be distracting to encounter a list formatted differently. The reader must pause to figure out what was different, and why. Make sure that whatever decisions you initially make about margins, spacing, headings, and the like are followed consistently throughout your report.

2. Use White Space to Advantage.

Use generous top, bottom, and side margins to make your report inviting to read. Consider white space (the blank sections of the page) as part of

The empty space on a page also communicates.

your overall design. Break up long paragraphs into shorter ones, and leave generous space before and after headings.

Also separate lengthy areas of text with subheadings. Subheadings not only break up solid blocks of type but also enhance readability by periodically providing signals for the reader. Always leave more space before a subheading than after it; that is, make sure the subheading is closer to the text it relates to than to the preceding text.

3. Select a Suitable Line Length and Type Size.

Line length can have a major impact on the readability of a document. Lines that are too short weaken coherence because they needlessly disrupt the normal horizontal pattern of reading. Lines that are too long cause readers to lose their place when they have to return to the left-hand edge of the next line.

Using too many columns on a page will result in line lengths that are so short they are difficult to read. The line length is partially a function of the size and style of typeface you select. Larger typefaces should be formatted on longer lines than smaller typefaces.

Lines that are too long for the size of type used cause the reader to lose his or her place too easily. Using long line lengths simply to get more information on the page is counterproductive if it results in a less readable document. Format the report for the convenience of the reader—not the writer.

The first line of the first column above contains only 14 characters and spaces; it is too short. The first line of the second paragraph contains 85 characters and spaces; it is too long for easy readability. In general, use a line no shorter than 25 characters and no longer than 65 characters for business documents. Although one column is standard for business reports, any business document can also be typed in two or three columns on a standard-sized page.

For the body of most business reports, use a type size between 10 points (elite size) and 12 points (pica size); 1 point equals 1/72 of an inch. Proportionately larger type should be used for headings and subheadings.

4. Determine an Appropriate Justification Format.

Use full justification for a formal appearance and an uneven right margin for an informal appearance.

All lines in the body of your report should be left-justified; that is, they should all begin at the left margin (with the exceptions, of course, of an optional indention for the first line of each paragraph or indented material such as block quotes). However, the end of each line may either be right-justified (sometimes called simply, "justified") or ragged-right.

This is an example of a justified column, which produces even left and right margins. Always have the hyphenation feature of your word processor turned on when justifying your lines.

This is an example of a column with a ragged right margin; that is, one where the lines end unevenly. Ragged-right lines do not typically require as many distracting hyphenations as do justified lines of type.

To force each line of justified type to end evenly, a word processor inserts extra spaces between each word and, if the printer permits, between each letter as well. If your printer does not permit letter spacing, avoid using justified type because the "rivers" of extra space between each word are distracting. In general, a justified line presents a clean, formal look, while a ragged-right line gives an informal, casual appearance.

5. Use a Contemporary Punctuation Style.

In monospaced type (where each character is the same size, as in most typewriter type), you were accustomed to leaving two spaces after a period at the end of a sentence and after a colon. DTP uses proportional type, where the width of each letter varies according to the shape of the letter (in proportional type, an *m*, for example, is much wider than an *i*). In DTP, it is customary to leave only one space after each punctuation mark instead of two.

```
This is typewriter type.  Leave two spaces after a
period at the end of a sentence.
```

This is proportional type. Leave one space after a period at the end of a sentence.

Also, in typewriter type, you are accustomed to using generic quotation marks; that is, to using the same character for both the opening and closing quotation mark. DTP uses different marks for each.

```
Use "generic" quotation marks on a typewriter.
```
Use "differentiated" quotation marks in desktop publishing.

Finally, in typewriter type, you make a dash by typing two hyphens with no space before or after. DTP provides a special character for the dash.

```
Type a dash--two hyphens--like this on a typewriter.
```
Type a dash—a special character—like this in desktop publishing.

Oryx Energy, a Texas-based oil and natural gas exploration and drilling company, has interests all over the world. Furthermore, the company often expands their interests by acquiring additional oil and gas fields. To clarify their findings and recommendations to company employees and stockholders, members of Oryx's acquisition evaluation and financing team (shown here) often utilize charts; when used in moderation, graphics enhance a report by adding interest and comprehension.

Source: Oryx Energy Company

6. Format Paragraphs Correctly.

Business reports prepared on a typewriter may be single- or double-spaced. DTP uses only single-spacing. New paragraphs are indicated either by leaving a blank line (or half line) before or by indenting the first line of the paragraph. Do not, however, both indent *and* leave a blank line; that would be too much. Even when paragraphs are indented, DTP typically does not indent the first line of a paragraph that immediately follows a heading or subheading; it is obvious that what follows a heading is a new paragraph.

Various techniques are sometimes used at the start of a document to engage the reader immediately—using an extra-large, decorative letter to begin the first word of the document, typing the first three or four words in solid capitals, or setting the first paragraph in larger type than the rest of the document.

7. Emphasize Words and Ideas Appropriately.

Use special emphasis techniques sparingly.

On a typewriter, underlining and solid capitals are about the only way to emphasize an idea. Thus, report headings and subheadings have traditionally been formatted in one of these two styles.

DTP, however, has a variety of techniques readily available—larger type size, boldface, and italic type, for example, or some combination of these. Any of these techniques is preferable to underlining and solid capitals. Solid capitals are appropriate only for very short headings. Unlike lowercase letters, capital letters are all the same size, making them more difficult to comprehend. Also avoid using nonstandard type styles such as outline or shadow type in business reports; they provide visual clutter and are distracting.

Use boldface for strong emphasis and italics for medium emphasis in the body of a report. Both boldface and italic type, along with a larger type size, may be used for headings and subheadings; just be sure that your main headings stand out more than your subheadings. When headings are displayed prominently, they may be typed in upper- and lowercase letters or with only the first word and proper names in uppercase. Any of the following three styles would be appropriate for a report heading:

Opinions of Present Benefits

Opinions of Present Benefits

Opinions of present benefits

8. Format Lists for Readability.

Because lists or enumerations are surrounded by white space, with each item by itself on a separate line, they tend to stand out more than when the same material is presented in narrative form. DTP users have the choice of using either numbered lists or bulleted lists. Number your lists when order is important ("Here are the five steps for requesting temporary help") or when the list is long and numbering will help when referring to a specific point. When order is not important and the list is short, use bullets (small filled-in circles or squares) to call attention to each item. Keep the bullets small and close to the items they relate to. For both numbered and bulleted lists, either a hanging style or a first-line-indented style may be used. Both of the following lists are formatted appropriately:

> Use numbered lists when order is important; otherwise, use bulleted lists.

To insert a chart into your report file:
1. Create the chart using a graphics or spreadsheet program, such as *Harvard Graphics* or *Lotus 1–2–3*.
2. Open your report file.
3. Use your word processor's command to insert the graphic.
4. Resize the graphic so that it is in proper scale and position it below the paragraph where it is introduced.

Each typeface can vary in a number of important ways:
- *Posture:* Roman (vertical) and italic (oblique)
- *Weight:* Hairline, thin, light, book, regular, medium, demibold, bold, heavy, black, and ultra
- *Width:* Condensed, regular, and expanded
- *Size:* Text (all type sizes up to 12 points) and display (type sizes larger than 12 points)

9. Use Graphics in Moderation.

Use graphics only when they help you achieve your report objectives.

When used in moderation, graphics add interest and aid comprehension. This is especially the case when using charts and tables. In addition, writers today can make use of files of computerized drawings, called "clip art," which they can electronically insert into their documents.

 **New Labor Agreement**

To be effective, such clip art must be used sparingly and be well drawn, relevant, and in proper scale. Unless you are certain that a particular piece of clip art will help you tell your story better, save clip art for more informal communications such as company newsletters and advertising documents. Most business reports should have a dignified, businesslike appearance.

Tables can be formatted directly in your word processing or DTP report, and charts can be created in a graphics or spreadsheet program and then imported (copied) into your report file. Although you can also electronically scan and then import illustrations and photographs, you'll generally get better (and faster) results by simply leaving a "hole" in your page and pasting in the illustration or photograph by hand later, and then submitting a good-quality photocopy of your report.

Horizontal and vertical lines (called *rules*), another graphic device, can also be used in moderation to separate different elements of the document. Horizontal rules can be narrow or wide; vertical rules (sometimes used to separate columns) should be very narrow. If horizontal rules are used at the top and bottom of a page, the top rule is generally wider than the bottom.

10. Have Fun!

Just as the arrival of the personal computer gave non-data-processing managers easy access to strategic information, so also has the arrival of desktop publishing given the average business person more control over the documents he or she produces. You don't have to be a designer to use DTP. Buy a book or two on basic design, and perhaps subscribe to one of the many desktop or personal publishing magazines. Begin to pay attention to the layout and design of professionally prepared documents, and learn from them. Be creative and don't be afraid to experiment. And, most importantly, have fun! Desktop publishing is empowering—to you and your ideas.

SUMMARY

The most common report formats are manuscript (for formal reports) and letter or memorandum (for informal reports). The most common plans for organizing the findings of a study are by time, location, importance, and criteria. Conclusions should be presented at the beginning of the report unless the reader prefers the indirect plan, the reader will not be receptive toward the conclusions, or the topic is complex. Report headings should be composed carefully—in terms of their type, parallelism, length, number, and balance.

The body of the report consists of the introduction, findings (the major part of the report), and, as needed, the summary, conclusions, and recommendations. Long, formal reports might require such supplementary pages as a title page, transmittal document, executive summary, table of contents, appendix, and reference list.

Use an objective writing style, appropriate pronouns, and verb tenses that reflect the reader's time frame. Emphasis and subordination techniques help alert the reader to what you consider important; and preview, summary, and transitional devices help maintain coherence. Provide appropriate documentation whenever you quote, paraphrase, or summarize someone else's work by using either endnotes, footnotes, or the author–date method of citation.

Delay revising the report until a few days after completing the first draft. Revise in three distinct steps: first for content, then for style, and finally for correctness.

The report's format should enhance the report's appearance and readability and should be based on the organization's and reader's preferences. Unless directed otherwise, follow generally accepted formatting guidelines for margins, report headings, and pagination. Use a simple, consistent design and make generous use of white space. Select an appropriate line length, type size, justification format, and punctuation style; format paragraphs and lists correctly; use graphics in moderation; and emphasize words and ideas appropriately.

After all revisions and formatting have been done, give each page one final proofreading. Make sure the final report reflects the highest standards of scholarship, critical thinking, and care.

KEY TERMS

Conclusions— The answers to the research questions raised in the introduction.

Documentation— Giving credit to another person for his or her words or ideas that you have used.

Executive summary— A condensed version of the report body (An executive summary is also called an *abstract* or *synopsis*).

Plagiarism— Using another person's words or ideas without giving proper credit.

Talking heading— A report heading that identifies not only the topic of the section but also the major conclusion.

Transmittal document— A letter or memorandum that conveys the finished report to the reader.

REVIEW AND DISCUSSION

▶ OBJECTIVE 1   1. What factors influence the format and general traits of a report?

▶ OBJECTIVE 2   2. Give an example of a report topic for which it would be most logical to organize the findings by (a) time, (b) location, (c) importance, and (d) criteria.

▶ OBJECTIVE 2   3. Under what circumstances should a direct versus an indirect organizational pattern be used for presenting conclusions and recommendations?

▶ OBJECTIVE 3   4. Assume that your report evaluating three business texts discusses the following topics (the book that rated highest in each category is shown in parentheses):

   a. Content and organization (Book B)

   b. What types of supplementary aids (such as transparencies and a student guide) are available (Book B)

   c. How much the book costs (Book A)

   d. What kind of national reputation the author has (Book B)

   e. Whether the book is up to date—copyright date (Book C)

   Compose the headings for these five sections, first using generic headings, then talking headings. Make sure each set of headings is parallel.

▶ OBJECTIVE 4   5. What is the difference between merely presenting data and analyzing data? Give an example.

▶ OBJECTIVE 5   6. What verb tense (past, present, future) should be used for presenting the following information from a study on the effectiveness of a new accounting software program?

   a. A preview of the topics covered in the following section

   b. The procedures of this study

   c. The conclusion regarding the effectiveness of the program

   d. Recommendations for conducting a follow-up study

   e. A discussion of the product reviews contained in computer magazines

▶ OBJECTIVE 5   7. Assume you surveyed your firm's 50 sales representatives in April. Your survey results showed that they felt left out of the product-planning phase. As a result, you're recommending that the sales manager (the reader of your report) include a two-hour session on this topic at the next sales conference. Write a paragraph presenting this information, first using an informal writing style and then using a formal writing style.

▶ OBJECTIVE 5   8. Describe some techniques that can be used to emphasize and subordinate findings in a report. What is the appropriate use of such techniques?

▶ OBJECTIVE 6   9. Give an example of a fact that does and one that does not need to be documented by a citation.

▶ OBJECTIVE 6   10. What are the advantages and disadvantages of each of the three documentation methods discussed in this chapter?

▶ OBJECTIVE 7   11. Why should a report not be revised immediately after it is written?

▶ OBJECTIVE 8   12. Under what circumstances should a report be single-spaced? Double-spaced?

▶ OBJECTIVE 9   13. What special proofreading steps should you take if you formatted your report on a computer?

▶ OBJECTIVE 10 14. Why is white space important in a document?

EXERCISES

1. **Short, Formal Report—Primary and Secondary Statistical Data**   OBJECTIVES 1–10 ◀
Furnished   North Star is a producer of consumer products with annual
sales of $47.2 million. It has 4.5% of the consumer market for its six
consumer products (soap, deodorant, ammonia, chili, canned ham,
and frozen vegetables).

On July 8 of this year, Paul Gettisfield, sales manager, asked you, a
product manager, to study the feasibility of North Star's entering the
generic-products market. Generic products are products that do not
have brand names and that typically carry a plain generic label, such
as "Paper Towels." Generic products are typically not advertised; they
involve less packaging, less processing, and cheaper ingredients than
brand names; and they compete both with private brands (those
distributed solely by individual store chains such as A&P and Kroger)
and national brands (those available for sale at all grocery stores and
advertised nationally).

At the present time, North Star produces only national brands. Paul
specifically asked you not to explore whether North Star had the plant
capacity. He wanted you only to provide up-to-date information on
the generic market in general and to explore likely consumer acceptance
of generic brands for the products North Star produces. He is quite
interested in learning the results of your research.

You conducted a mail survey of 1,500 consumers in the three states
(California, Texas, and Arizona) that comprise your largest market in
August. Responses were received from 832 consumers to the following
questions:

Have you purchased a food generic product (e.g., canned fruit or vegetables)
in the last month?

	Yes	No
All consumers	36%	64%
Consumers doing 51–100% of household shopping	29%	71%

Was this the first time you had purchased a food generic product?

	Yes	No
All consumers	18%	82%
Consumers doing 51–100% of household shopping	20%	80%

Have you purchased a nonfood generic product (e.g., paper towels or soap)
in the last month?

	Yes	No
All consumers	60%	40%
Consumers doing 51–100% of household shopping	59%	41%

Was this the first time you had purchased a nonfood generic product?

	Yes	No
All consumers	5%	95%
Consumers doing 51–100% of household shopping	7%	93%

<u>If you could save at least 30% by purchasing a generic brand rather than a national brand, would you purchase a generic brand of each of the following products?</u>

	Yes	*No*	*Do Not Use This Product*
Bar of soap	43%	57%	0%
Deodorant	31	67	2
Ammonia	80	10	10
Chili	34	52	14
Canned ham	19	44	37
Frozen vegetables	54	30	16

You also asked the local North Star sales representative to audit 20 randomly selected chain supermarkets in each of these three states in August. Personal observation showed that 39 of the stores stocked generic brands, 37 of these 39 stocked 100 or more generic items, and 15 had separate generic sections. All but 3 of the 60 stores stocked all six products that North Star produces.

In gathering your data, you also made the following notes from three secondary sources:

1. *Hammond's Market Reports* (Gary, Indiana, 1990), pp. 1027–1030: This annual index lists various information for more than 2,000 consumer products. The percentages of market share for the six products North Star produces are as follows:

	1980	*1985*	*1990*
Generic brands	1.5%	2.6%	7.3%
Private labels	31.6	30.7	27.8
National brands	66.9	66.7	64.9

2. H. R. Nolan, "No-Name Brands: An Update," *Supermarket Management* (April 1991), pp. 31–37.

   a. Generic brands are typically priced 30–50% below national brands. (p. 31)

   b. Consumers require a 36% saving on a bar of soap and 40% savings on deodorants to motivate them to switch to a generic. (p. 32)

   c. Consumer awareness of generics has tripled since 1978. (p. 33)

   d. "The easiest way to become a no-name store is to ignore no-name brands." (direct quotation from p. 33)

   e. Many leading brand manufacturers feel compelled to produce the lower-profit generic brands because either the market has grown too big to ignore or the inroads generic brands have made on their own brands have left them with idle capacity.

3. Edward J. Rauch and Pamela G. McCleary, "National Brands to Play a Bit Part in the Future," *Grocery Business* (Fall 1990), pp. 118–120.

   a. Eight out of ten food-chain officers believe their costs will rise more than their prices this year. (p. 118)

   b. Generics are now available in 74% of the stores nationwide and account for about 2% of the store space. (p. 118)

   c. "Supermarket executives foresee a drop in shelf space allocated to brand products and an increase in the space allocated to generics and private labels. Many experts predict that supermarkets will ultimately carry no more than the top two brands in a category plus a private label and a generic label." (direct quotation from p. 119)

d. Today, 37% of the grocery stores have switched from paper bags to the less expensive plastic bags for packaging customer purchases, even though the plastic bags are nonbiodegradable. (p. 119)

e. Starting from nearly zero in 1977, generics have acquired 5% of the $250-billion grocery market. Many observers predict they will go up to 25% by the turn of the century. (p. 120)

Analyze the data, prepare whatever visual aids would be helpful, and then write a formal report for Gettisfield. Include any supplementary report pages you feel would be helpful. If your instructor approves, you may supplement the preceding data with additional secondary sources.

2. **Memorandum Report—Primary Statistical Data Furnished** You are a systems analyst, reporting to Hilda Brandt, vice president of information services at General Resources, Inc. The executive vice president of GRI has asked Brandt to develop a style and procedures manual for all internally produced office documents.

OBJECTIVES 1–6, 8–10 ◄

In preparation for this task, Brandt has asked you to analyze the documents prepared at GRI offices to determine the kinds of documents typed, the input source for these documents, the amount of time required to type each document, and the number of copies made of each. She then asked you to prepare an informal memorandum report, summarizing your findings.

For a period of one week, you asked a random sample of 100 office workers to make an extra copy of the first item they typed either at their typewriters or computers after 9 A.M., 11 A.M., and 2 P.M. each day and to complete a short form answering several questions about the document. A total of 531 documents were submitted for analysis— 173 letters, 77 memos, 21 reports, 222 forms, and 18 miscellaneous other items.

Analyze the data contained in Figure 13.6, prepare whatever visual aids would be helpful (keep them simple for this memo report), and then write the requested analytical report.

3. **Short Memorandum Report—Nonstatistical Data Furnished** You are the research assistant for Congressman Alton Murray. A constituent has written him asking that he introduce legislation to ban telephone call identification. Congressman Murray sent you a note with this handwritten message attached to the letter: "I really don't know anything about this telephone service. Please research it and prepare a short informal report (no tables, charts, or footnotes, please) so that I can make an informed decision about this matter. Should I or should I not support legislation to ban this new telephone service?"

OBJECTIVES 1–6, 8–10 ◄

You've talked to numerous people at the telephone company and have read brochures, magazine articles, and editorials about this topic. You've jotted down the following notes—in no particular order:

a. Automatic number identification (ANI): A telephone service that displays the phone number of the person calling you.

FIGURE 13.6   Data for Exercise 2

Origin of Typing Tasks, Classified by Kind of Item

Origin		Forms	Letters	Memos	Reports	Tables	Other	Totals
Handwritten—	No.	66	44	17	8	12	9	156
not on same form	%	29.7%	25.4%	22.1%	38.1%	60.0%	50.0%	29.4%
Handwritten on same form	No.	56	2	4		3		65
	%	25.2%	1.2%	5.2%		15.0%		12.2%
Typed and handwritten	No.	16	15	7	3	2	3	46
	%	7.2%	8.7%	9.1%	14.3%	10.0%	16.7%	8.7%
All typed	No.	21	35	15	6		4	81
	%	9.5%	20.2%	19.5%	28.6%		22.2%	15.3%
Shorthand dictation	No.	4	36	16	1			57
	%	1.8%	20.8%	20.8%	4.8%			10.7%
Machine dictation	No.	3	8	12	3			26
	%	1.4%	4.6%	15.6%	14.3%			4.9%
Self-composed	No.	29	33	6			2	70
	%	13.1%	19.1%	7.8%			11.1%	13.2%
Other	No.	27				3		30
	%	12.2%				15.0%		5.6%
Totals	No.	222	173	77	21	20	18	531
	%	41.8%	32.6%	14.5%	4.0%	3.8%	3.4%	100.0%

Amount of Time Required by Office Workers to Type Items, Classified by Kind of Item

Minutes required		Forms	Letters	Memos	Reports	Tables	Other	Totals
Less than 5	No.	144	72	40	2		4	262
	%	64.9%	41.6%	51.9%	9.5%		22.2%	49.3%
5–9	No.	37	77	17	4	9	5	149
	%	16.7%	44.5%	22.1%	19.0%	45.0%	27.8%	28.1%
10 or more	No.	41	24	20	15	11	9	120
	%	18.5%	13.9%	26.0%	71.4%	55.0%	50.0%	22.6%
Totals	No.	222	173	77	21	20	18	531
	%	41.8%	32.6%	14.5%	4.0%	3.8%	3.4%	100.0%

Number of Copies of Typed Items Required (Including Original), Classified by Kind of Item

Number of copies (including original)		Forms	Letters	Memos	Reports	Tables	Other	Totals
1 (original only)	No.	27	9	5	1	2	4	48
	%	12.2%	5.2%	6.5%	4.8%	10.0%	22.2%	9.0%
2	No.	35	88	15	5	6		149
	%	15.8%	50.9%	19.5%	23.8%	30.0%		28.1%
3–4	No.	82	56	22	4	1	6	171
	%	36.9%	32.4%	28.6%	19.0%	5.0%	33.3%	32.2%
5 or more	No.	78	20	35	11	11	8	163
	%	35.1%	11.6%	45.5%	52.4%	55.0%	44.4%	30.7%
Totals	No.	222	173	77	21	20	18	531
	%	41.8%	32.6%	14.5%	4.0%	3.8%	3.4%	100.0%

b. You can use ANI to decide which calls you want to answer and simply ignore the others.

c. It can threaten the privacy and personal safety of users.

d. Every caller's number would be displayed—even those with unpublished numbers who have paid extra for their privacy.

e. Delivery businesses (taxis and pizzerias, for example) can use ANI to ensure that telephone orders are legitimate.

f. The device that displays the callers' numbers costs up to $80.

g. Emergency services can use the number to dispatch help quickly for people who may be too panicky to give an address.

h. Customer-service agents at your local utility or your stockbroker can immediately call up your file when you call to serve you more efficiently. A computer can even be programmed to do this automatically as soon as your call goes through.

i. ANI allows businesses to record the number of every caller—and perhaps even to sell your number to telemarketers.

j. New Jersey Bell Telephone Co. began the service after learning that a whopping 1.2 million of their customers had received threatening or obscene calls.

k. If you receive a threatening, obscene, or harassing call, you can record the number to notify the police or phone company without their having to tap your phone. (You can even call the person back yourself, although that might not be wise.)

l. People who make calls from their home may have legitimate reasons for not wanting their private numbers revealed—law enforcement officers, doctors, psychiatrists, or social workers.

m. New Jersey Bell reported that phone-trace requests in Hudson County dropped 49% after ANI was established—even though only 2.3% of its customers used it.

n. It's now available in a growing number of states.

o. You can even program ANI to prevent your phone from receiving calls from a specified number, thus preventing harassers from repeatedly calling your number from the same phone.

p. Runaway children might be scared to call home for fear of being traced.

q. There's no provision for callers to prevent their numbers from being displayed. (That would defeat the whole purpose of the service.)

r. New Jersey Bell says complaints about obscene or harassing phone calls have dropped nearly 50% since it began offering ANI.

s. You can refuse to answer telephone sales pitches that come in the middle of dinner.

t. It threatens the privacy of individuals who call suicide-prevention, drug-treatment, AIDS, and abortion-counseling hotlines.

u. It took 23 years to catch and convict Bobby Gene Stice, who used the telephone for two decades to terrorize thousands of California women. ANI could have stopped it in a day.

v. The service charge for the ANI feature is as much as $8.50 monthly.

Organize and analyze the data, and then write the requested recommendation report. Use whatever report headings would be helpful.

4. **Letter Report—Primary Statistical Data Supplied**   Review the Combustion Industries Survey exercises at the end of Chapter 12, including

OBJECTIVES 1–6, 8–10 ◄

the completed questionnaire. Assume that you are a management consultant for Banking Services, Inc., and were hired by Carol J. Green, vice president of Tri-City Bank (65 Washington Avenue, Stamford, CT 06902) to conduct this survey.

Write a letter report presenting the information you gathered and analyzed. Include any appropriate visual aids and headings in your report that would be helpful. You may assume any reasonable data needed.

OBJECTIVES 2, 4–10

5. **Collaborative Writing—Long Formal Report Requiring Library Research** Assume that your group of four has been asked by Jim Miller, executive vice president of Jefferson Industries, to write an exploratory report on the feasibility of Jefferson's opening a frozen yogurt store in Provo, Utah. If the preliminary data your group gathers warrants further exploration of this project, a professional venture-consultant group will be hired to conduct an in-depth "dollars-and-cents" study. Your job, then, is to recommend whether such an expensive in-depth study is warranted. Assume that Jefferson has the financial resources to support such a venture if it looks promising.

You can immediately think of several areas you'll want to explore: the general market outlook for frozen yogurt stores, the demographic makeup of Provo, Utah (home of Brigham Young University), the local economic climate, franchise opportunities in the industry, and the like. Undoubtedly, other topics (or criteria) will surface as you brainstorm the problem.

Working as a group, carry through the entire research process for this project—planning the study, collecting the data, organizing and analyzing the data, and writing the report. (*Note:* If you gathered any data by completing the exercises at the end of Chapter 11, integrate that data into your study.)

Write the body of the report using formal language, organize the study by criteria, and place the conclusions and recommendations at the end. Include a title page, transmittal memo (addressed to James H. Miller), executive summary, table of contents, and reference list (use the author–date method of citation).

Regardless of how your group decides to divide up the work, everyone should review and comment on the draft of the final report. If different members wrote different parts, edit as needed to ensure that the report reads smoothly and coherently.

Note: *For each of the following projects, follow the desires of your instructor (the reader) in terms of length, format, degree of formality, number of report parts, and the like.*

OBJECTIVES 1–10

6. **Secondary Data—The Female Manager** Using the appropriate business indexes, identify three women who are presidents or CEOs of companies listed on the New York Stock Exchange. Provide information on their backgrounds. Did they make it to the top by coming up through the ranks, by starting the firm, by taking over from another family member, or in some other manner?

Analyze the effectiveness of these three individuals. How profitable are the firms they head in relation to others in the industry? Are their firms more or less profitable now than when they assumed the top job? Finally, try to uncover data regarding their management styles—how they see their role, how they relate to their employees, problems they've experienced, and the like.

From your study of these three individuals, are there any valid conclusions that can be drawn? Write a report objectively presenting and analyzing the information you've gathered.

7. **Secondary Data—Keyboarding Skills**   You are the director of training for an aerospace firm located in Seattle, Washington. Your superior, Charles R. Underwood, personnel manager, is concerned that so many of the firm's 2,000 white-collar employees use their computers for hours a day but still do not know how to touch-keyboard. He believes the hunt-and-peck method is inefficient and increases the possibility of making errors when inputting data, thus lowering the reliability of the data.

OBJECTIVES 1–10 ◀

He has asked you to recommend a software program that teaches the user how to type. He is specifically interested in a program that is IBM-compatible, that is geared to adults, that is educationally sound, and that can be learned on an individual basis without an instructor present.

Identify and evaluate three to five keyboarding software programs that meet these criteria, and write a report recommending the best one to Underwood. Fully justify your choice.

8. **Primary Data—Career Choices**   Explore a career in which you are interested. Determine the job outlook, present level of employment, salary trends, typical duties, working conditions, educational or experience requirements, and the like. If possible, interview someone holding this position to gain first-hand impressions. Then write up your findings in a report to your instructor. Include at least one table or visual aid in your report.

OBJECTIVES 1–6, 8–10 ◀

9. **Primary Data—Intercultural Dimensions**   To what extent does network and cable television accurately portray members of cultural, ethnic, and racial minorities? To what extent are they portrayed at all during prime time (8–11 P.M. nightly)? In what types of roles are they shown, and what is their relationship with the nonminority characters?

OBJECTIVES 1–6, 8–10 ◀

Locate and review at least two journal articles on this topic. Then develop a definition of what you mean by *minority*. Randomly select at least ten prime-time television shows, and develop a form to help you record the needed data on minority representation as you watch these shows. As part of your research, compare the proportion of minority members in this country with their representation on prime-time television. Integrate your primary and secondary data into a report. Use objective language, being careful to present ample data to support any conclusions or recommendations you may make.

10. **Primary Data—Student Living Arrangements**   Darlene Anderson, a real estate developer and president of Anderson and Associates, is exploring the feasibility of building a large student-apartment complex on a lot her firm owns two blocks from campus. Even though the city planning commission believes there is already enough student housing, Anderson believes she can succeed if she addresses specific problems of present housing.

OBJECTIVES 1–6, 8–10 ◀

She has asked you, her executive assistant, to survey students to determine their views of off-campus living. Specifically, she wants you to develop a ranked listing of the most important attributes of student housing. How important to students are such criteria as price, location (nearness to campus, shopping, and the like), space and layout, furnishings (furnished versus unfurnished), social activities, parking, pets policy, and the like?

In addition, the architect has drawn a plan that features the following living options: a private hotel-like room (sleeping and sitting area and private bath but no kitchen); a private one-room efficiency apartment; a one-bedroom, two-person apartment; and a four-bedroom, four-person apartment. Considering their present economic situations, which of these arrangements would students most likely rent?

Develop a questionnaire and administer it to a sample of students. Then analyze the data and write a report to Anderson.

CASE PROBLEM

Reporting—A Pain in the Wrist

▶ OBJECTIVES 2, 4–10

Review the case problem at the end of Chapters 11 and 12 in which Jean Tate asked Pat Robbins to write a report on carpal tunnel syndrome, a neuromuscular wrist ailment caused by repeated hand motions as in typing.

1. Administer the questionnaire you developed in Chapter 11 to a sample of at least 30 clerical workers at your institution, where you work, or at some other office. For the purposes of this assignment, assume that the responses you receive were actually those from Urban Systems clerical workers.
2. Analyze the questionnaire data carefully. Construct whatever tables and charts would be helpful to the reader.
3. Integrate the findings from your questionnaire, interview of Terry Vaughn, and secondary sources. Taken together, what does all this information mean in terms of your problem statement?
4. For each subproblem you specified (see Chapter 11), what conclusion can you draw? Considering each of these individual conclusions, what overall conclusion is merited? Considering your individual and overall conclusions, what recommendations are appropriate?
5. Prepare a recommendation report in manuscript format for Tate. Write the body of the report using formal language, organize the study by criteria, and place the conclusions and recommendations at the end. Include a title page, transmittal memo, executive summary, table of contents, abstract (copy of the questionnaire), and reference list (use the author–date method of citation).

- The best-selling book of all time is the Bible, with more than 2.5 billion copies sold. *The Guinness Book of World Records*, with cumulative sales of 60 million copies, is in second place.
- The best-selling living author is romance novelist Barbara Cartland (500 million copies); the best-selling deceased author is mystery writer Erle Stanley Gardner (319 million copies).
- The most expensive book published is *The Birds of America*, which contains a full set of Audubon reproductions and costs $15,000.

WORD WISE

Specialized Reports

After you have finished this chapter, you will be able to

1. Prepare a proposal using techniques of persuasion and audience analysis.

2. Prepare a business plan that is complete, persuasive, objective, and market-oriented.

3. Emphasize a particular goal, stress reader needs, and present the facts honestly when writing promotional reports.

4. Compose promotional reports such as news releases, presentation brochures, and annual reports.

5. Compose policies and procedures using simple language, practical content, and logical organization.

Richard Manning sat down at his desk and began to open his mail. In front of him were envelopes of various sizes and shapes stacked in a pile seven inches tall. Nearly every envelope contained a press release. Quickly, Manning cut open an envelope, removed its contents, glanced at it briefly, and then threw it in the trash can. Manning goes through a huge stack of mail every work day, especially on Monday, when Saturday's mail is also heaped on his desk.

The press—often considered a two-edged sword—can provide an enormous boost for a company. A positive story about an enterprising firm with new ideas and good products can work as effectively as advertising but without the expense, which is why Manning gets so much mail.

Manning is the editor of *New England Business Magazine,* a monthly periodical that focuses on companies and businesses in New England. He is also the former editor of the weekly newspaper the *Boston Business Journal,* and before that a correspondent for *Newsweek.* Throughout his career, the 40-year-old Manning has read thousands of press releases trying to entice him to write or assign a story about a company or product.

Sometimes Manning will pick up an envelope, glance at it, and throw it into the trash without opening it. "When I get press releases from some companies, I don't bother opening them because I get something from them virtually every day," he explained. "What can be so earth shattering that you have to get something every single day?"

Richard Manning, Editor
New England Business
Magazine, Boston,
Massachusetts

Manning noted that he's more inclined to open an envelope with interest that has been hand-typed, rather than an envelope that has a computer-generated address label. The latter tells him that in all likelihood every publication in the area, including the daily papers, has received the same press release. While some publications do sum up a week's or a month's news, *New England Business* tries to stay away from events that have already been covered. In addition, many of the press releases are simply announcements of promotions—something the magazine doesn't publish. "The people who write these things have to do a little bit of research," he said, shaking his head.

When Manning sees a press release that interests him, he puts it aside to give to his writers. At best, maybe one in twenty is put in the save pile.

If you really want to annoy Manning, send him a release in an envelope that is made from plastic and cannot be torn open. "They have to be cut open. If you want somebody to open your envelope it has to be an envelope that is openable; it's as simple as that." Another good way to annoy an editor is to write "personal and confidential" on the envelope. No doubt the envelope will be opened by an editor, but when he or she discovers that it contains yet another press release, the deceit will just about guarantee that the press release ends up in the garbage.

After several minutes, Manning found a press release that he liked. " 'Dear Editor," he read aloud. " 'The following is the latest national office and industrial vacancy data prepared by Coldwell Banker Real Estate.' It's short, to the point, and it doesn't say 'I've spotted a new trend in footware' or something like that."

"Any press release that's two pages long is probably not going to be worth anything. What I want in a press release is something that is short, quick, and to the point. What I don't like is the long, very verbose thing that just goes on and on and mentions your name three times in the body of the text. It's not a press release, per se, it's sort of a pitch letter on doing a story."

A press release, he indicated, has "life expectancy of about two seconds—and that's stretching it a little bit. You have to be able to say, 'Look, this is what's happening and here's why we think it's important.' "

"But really," he said with a smile, "they have to stay away from the plastic envelopes." ▼

COMMON REPORTS VERSUS SPECIALIZED REPORTS

As discussed earlier, common reports (such as routine management reports or one-time situational reports) are usually written with one of three purposes: to inform, to analyze, or to recommend. Chapters 10–13 presented the principles for writing reports with these purposes.

Specialized reports often have additional purposes; for example, to persuade or to teach. Proposals, business plans, promotional reports (such as news releases or brochures), and policies and procedures are specialized reports that are discussed in this chapter.

PROPOSALS

A **proposal** is a written report that seeks to persuade a reader from outside the organization to do as the writer wishes. For example, a manager may write a proposal that seeks to persuade a potential customer to purchase goods or services from the writer's firm, persuade the federal government to locate a new research facility in the headquarters city of the writer's firm, or persuade a foundation to fund a project to be undertaken by the writer or the writer's firm.

OBJECTIVE 1: Prepare a proposal using techniques of persuasion and audience analysis.

Proposals may be solicited or unsolicited. Government agencies and many large commercial firms routinely solicit proposals from potential suppliers. For example, the government might publish an RFP (request for proposal) stating its intention to purchase 5,000 microcomputers and giving detailed specifications regarding the features it needs on these computers. Similarly, the computer manufacturer that submits the successful bid might itself publish an RFP to invite a parts manufacturer to bid on some component the manufacturer needs for these computers.

The unsolicited proposal differs from the solicited proposal in that it typically requires more background information and more persuasion. Because the reader may not be familiar with the project, the writer must provide more detail, must explain the rationale for the proposal, and must present more evidence to convince the reader of the merits of the proposal.

The proposal reader is typically outside the organization (internal proposals, or justification reports, are a form of situational report; see Chapter 10). The format for these external documents may be a letter report, a manuscript report, or even a form report, with the form supplied by the soliciting organization. If the soliciting organization does not supply a form, it will likely specify in detailed language the specific format for the proposal. Obviously, the reader's desires should be followed explicitly. Despite the merits of a proposal, failure to follow such guidelines may be sufficient reason for rejecting the proposal.

When writing a proposal, the writer must keep in mind that the proposal may become legally binding on the writer and his or her organization. In spelling out exactly what the writer or organization will provide, when, under what circumstances, and at what price, the proposal report writer creates the offer portion of a contract that, if accepted, becomes binding on the writer's organization.

Both solicited and unsolicited proposals are persuasive reports.

Audience analysis is a key ingredient for the successful proposal.

Proposals are persuasive documents, and all the techniques you learned about persuasion and argumentation in letter and memo writing apply equally here. When writing a proposal give ample, credible evidence for all statements. Do not exaggerate. Provide examples, expert testimony, and specific facts and figures to support your statements. Use simple, straightforward, and direct language, preferring simple sentences and the active voice.

In addition, throughout your proposal, keep the reader's needs and desires firmly in mind. What level of formality is expected or desired? How much does the reader know about the topic (which determines how much background information is needed and how much jargon can safely be used)? What will the reader gain from accepting your proposal? Stress reader benefits (the "you" attitude) throughout. Remember that you are asking for something—usually a commitment of money. Let the reader know what he or she will get in return.

As can be seen, having a good idea is not enough. You must be able to present that idea clearly and convincingly so that it will be accepted. The benefits of clear and persuasive writing go far beyond the immediate goal of securing approval for your current project. A well-written proposal increases both your visibility and your credibility with the reader and with the company on whose behalf you wrote the proposal.

Although proposals vary in length, organization, complexity, and format, the following sections are common:

1. *Background:* Introduce the problem you're addressing and discuss why it merits the reader's consideration. Provide enough background information to show that a problem exists and that you have a viable solution to the problem. Be guided in the amount of detail provided by your knowledge of the reader.

2. *Objectives of the project:* Provide specific information about what the outcomes of the project will be. Be specific and honest in discussing what the reader will get for his or her commitment of resources. Keep the tone factual and low key, and stress reader benefits.

3. *Procedures:* Discuss in detail exactly how you will achieve these objectives. Include a step-by-step discussion of what will be done, when, and how much it will cost. The budget or cost schedule should include all costs, including time commitments, overhead, an allowance for inflation, and all other likely monetary requirements. Keep in mind that if your proposal is accepted, you are legally bound to deliver what you promise.

4. *Personnel or organizational qualifications:* Show how you, your organization, and any others who would be involved in conducting this project are qualified to do so. Discuss previous similar projects completed successfully, the training of the principals involved, and the resources available. If appropriate, include testimonials or other external evidence to support your claims.

5. *Request for approval:* Directly ask for approval of your proposal, perhaps including an additional reader benefit or restating a particularly strong benefit introduced earlier. Depending on the reader's needs, this request could come either at the beginning or at the end of the proposal.

6. *Supporting information:* Include as an appendix to your proposal any relevant, but supplementary information that might bolster your arguments. Be sure to refer to any attachments in the body of your proposal to increase the likelihood of their being read.

As with all persuasive writing, the use of clear and objective language, ample evidence, and a logical organization of the ideas presented will help you achieve your goals. An example of a proposal for a small project is shown in Figure 14.1.

BUSINESS PLANS

A **business plan** is a written report that describes a proposed for-profit venture and often solicits financing for that venture. It can be considered a proposal in that it seeks to persuade an external reader to do as the writer wishes. Although most business plans are written to secure outside funding, the preparation of such a plan also helps the entrepreneur focus attention on every aspect of the proposed venture, thereby increasing its chances for success.

Because of its crucial role in the success of the start-up firm, developing a business plan requires much thought and assistance from accountants, business consultants, bankers, other entrepreneurs, and others able to help plan, collect, and analyze the needed information. The discussion that follows concentrates on the written presentation, which typically has these sections:

OBJECTIVE 2: Prepare a business plan that is complete, persuasive, objective, and market-oriented.

Business plans are written primarily to secure funding for a new venture.

1. *Executive summary:* Highlight the important points made throughout the report. Although written last, the executive summary is the only part of your entire report that you can be fairly assured will be read carefully, so plan it carefully. In a typical 30- to 50-page business plan, the summary should be no longer than two or three pages.
2. *Description of the company:* Outline the background of the company and discuss its size and organization. Describe the new product or service you will provide, including how it will be produced, and show how it fulfills a unique need in the market. Discuss the skills and background of each principal in the organization. Finally, discuss future directions and plans.
3. *Market analysis:* Discuss the target market you intend to serve, describing its size, growth rate, characteristics, expected changes, and the like. Be forthright in discussing the strengths and weaknesses of the competition within that market. The focus of attention throughout the business plan should be on the market rather than on your product or service; that is, show that you are a market-driven company.

Show the reader that you've thought through your plans carefully.

4. *Marketing plan:* Outline how you intend to promote, sell, distribute, and service your new product. Be realistic in discussing specific strategies and in projecting results in dollars-and-cents figures.
5. *Financial statements:* Include such financial statements as an income statement, balance sheet, cash-flow statement, and a break-even analysis. Provide historical data as well as projections for several years ahead.

FIGURE 14.1   Proposal

The proposal is in the format
of a letter report.

Begins by identifying the
purpose of the letter.

Shows that a need exists,
by providing specific examples.

Suggests a reasonable solution.

Tells exactly what the proposal should accomplish.

T H E   W R I T I N G   D O C T O R

Anne Skarzinski, President

September 16, 19—

Ms. Carolyn Soule, Employee Manager
Everglades National Corporation
1407 Lincoln Road, Suite 15
Miami, FL 33139
Dear Ms. Soule:

Subject: Proposal for an In-House Workshop on Business Writing   1
I enjoyed discussing with you the business writing workshops you intend to sponsor for the engineering staff at Everglades National Corporation. As you requested, I am submitting this proposal to conduct
a two-day workshop.

Background

On September 4–5, I interviewed engineers at your organization and
analyzed samples of their writing. My research indicates that your
engineers are typical of many highly trained specialists who know exactly what they want to say but sometimes do not structure their com-   2
munications in the most effective manner. Problems with audience
analysis, organization, and overall writing style were especially apparent when they were communicating with nonspecialists either inside
or outside the organization.

Because your engineers devote much of their time to written communications, a workshop that teaches writing as a process should prove
especially helpful. Thus, I propose that you sponsor a two-day writing workshop that I will develop entitled "The Process of Business   3
Writing." The workshop could be held during any two days between November 26 and December 10; the two dates need not be consecutive.

Objectives

The workshop would help your engineers achieve these objectives:

1. Specify the purpose of a message and perform an audience analysis.
2. Determine what information to include and in what order to present
   it.
3. Choose the right words for a message and construct effective sentences and logical paragraphs.
4. Set an appropriate overall tone by using confident, courteous, and   4
   sincere language; using appropriate emphasis and subordination;
   and stressing the "you" attitude.
5. Revise a draft for content, style, correctness, and readability.
6. Format written communications in an efficient standard format.
7. Proofread a document for content, typing errors, and format.

P.O. Box 1036 • West Palm Beach, FL 33402 Phone (813) 555-1036

Grammar and Mechanics Notes

1. Subject line is optional; leave one blank line before and after.   2. "highly
trained specialists"—compound adjective is not hyphenated because the first
word ends in -*ly*.   3. "Business Writing."—the period goes inside the closing
quotation mark.   4. Semicolons separate these items in a series because the
first item contains internal commas; note that all three items are in parallel
format.

Proposal (*cont'd*)

FIGURE 14.1

Ms. Carolyn Soule, Employee Manager
Page 2
September 16, 19—

Procedures

The enclosed outline shows the coverage of the course. The workshop would require a meeting room with participants seated at tables, an overhead projector, and a chalkboard or some other writing surface.

The program would be divided into four half-day segments, each comprising three hours. The first two hours would be devoted to discussing the topics listed, followed by a 15-minute break. The final hour would consist of group and individual writing assignments, with appropriate guidance, discussion, and feedback provided.

My fee for teaching the two-day workshop would be $2,000 plus expenses (including photocopying handouts, automobile mileage, and lunch on the workshop days). Your organization would be responsible for arranging and providing the morning and afternoon refreshments and lunch for the participants. If you want the workshop repeated, the fee would drop to $1,500 if the same content and handouts were used and a mutually convenient schedule could be arranged.

Qualifications

I would be responsible for planning and conducting the workshop. As you can see from the enclosed data sheet, I've had fifteen years of consulting experience in business communications and have spoken and written widely on the topic. You may contact any of the individuals listed in the consulting section of the data sheet to learn their reactions to my previous presentations.

Summary

Previous experience in working with professionals such as your engineers has taught me that they recognize the value of effective business communications and are motivated to improve their writing skills. The course should help your engineers become more effective communicators and more effective managers for Everglades National Corporation.

I wish you much success in your efforts to upgrade the writing skills of your professional staff. Please call me at 555-1036 to let me know your reactions to this proposal.

Sincerely yours,

Anne Skarzinski

Anne Skarzinski, President

mje
Enclosures

5 — Provides enough details to enable the reader to understand what is planned.

6 — Discusses the cost in an open and confident manner.

Highlights only the most relevant information from the enclosed data sheet.

7 — Shows how the reader will benefit from doing as asked.

8 — Closes on a friendly, confident note.

Grammar and Mechanics Notes

5. An alternate format for the page-2 heading is to center it all on one line.
6. "$2,000"—omit the decimal and zeros for even amounts of money.
7. "your engineers has"—uses the singular verb because the subject is *experience*, not *engineers*.   8. "Sincerely yours"—only the first word of a complimentary closing is capitalized.

Citadel, a savings and loan holding company based in Glendale, California, continuously monitors market conditions and interest rate trends in order to maintain their successful operations. Once this market analysis is collected, it can then be included in a business plan. (*Fidelity Federal Bank / Pete Saloutos Photographer*)

6. *Request for funding:* If a request for funding is a part of the business plan, discuss how much money is being requested, how it will be used, and how it will be repaid. Tie each component of the request to a part of your overall operational and marketing strategy.
7. *Supporting information:* Provide in an appendix any supplementary data, including additional background data, detailed tables, and the like that have been referred to in the body of the report.

Software programs can simplify the writing of a business plan.

Various computer software programs are available to help you generate a business plan. For example, *Business Plan Toolkit* (Palo Alto Software, Palo Alto, California) is a set of *Lotus 1–2–3* and *Microsoft Excel* templates that guide you through the detailed analysis of your company, your financial needs, your industry, and your market. The set helps you prepare all the needed statements and forms and also provides a workbook that shows you how to integrate the information into an overall business plan that is created on a word processor. Other development programs, such as *VenturPlan* (Venture Software, Cambridge, Massachusetts) and *Venture* (Star Software Systems, Torrance, California), operate similarly.

The business plan gives potential investors their first look at your proposed venture. Ensure that their first impression is favorable by presenting a report that is physically attractive and free from grammatical and mechanical errors. Show that you take pride in your work, and treat your own property with care. Investors will get the message that you are likely to treat their investment in your firm the same way.

PROMOTIONAL REPORTS

OBJECTIVE 3: Emphasize a particular goal, stress reader needs, and present the facts honestly when writing promotional reports.

Some reports have as their major purposes the promotion of the writer's organization. Examples include news releases, brochures, and annual reports. Three aspects of effective report writing especially pertinent when writing promotional reports are purpose, audience, and ethics.

- *Know what you want to accomplish with the report.* Unless you know exactly what you want your report to accomplish, you will never know whether you have achieved your objectives. For example, specifically what do you want to happen as a result of your news release? Do you want the media to use it in a news story immediately, to file it away for future reference, or simply to note its contents to help them better understand and appreciate the role your organization plays in the industry? Each of these purposes might require different content and a different writing style.
- *Gear the report to the specific needs of the audience.* Since different audiences have different needs and are persuaded by different motives, you must be able to define the audience for whom you're writing. For diverse audiences, you may need to prepare different reports—for example, one brochure for prospective customers and another for prospective investors or lenders.
- *Be honest.* The people who will read your promotional reports—other business people, potential customers, media reporters, and the like—are sophisticated and can easily spot dishonesty and deception. Thus, even apart from any legal and ethical considerations, avoid misrepresentation in order to achieve credibility and therefore achieve the goal of your report. Use objective language, avoid exaggeration, and present evidence to support your statements.

> Consider the purpose, audience, and ethics when writing promotional reports.

To be effective in most business situations, the promotional report must avoid exaggeration not only in the text but also in the design. The overall effect should be one of quiet self-confidence. Exaggerated language, self-serving photographs, or an ostentatious design will have an effect opposite to that intended. Instead, use objective language, a tasteful design, and conservative paper stock.

News Releases

A **news release** is a written report to the news media that contains information you wish publicized about the organization or its employees. It is sent to appropriate newspapers, magazines, and radio and television stations. Sometimes the information is used verbatim, sometimes in condensed form, sometimes as part of a larger story, and sometimes not at all, depending on the amount of time or space the media have available and how newsworthy they judge the story to be.

A news release is usually written on company letterhead stationery or on a special news-release form. Both the current date and the date the story can be released (or, alternately, marked "For Immediate Release") are included, as well as the name and phone number of someone within the organization who can be contacted for further information.

The first paragraph, called the "nut" paragraph, should answer the five *W*'s of journalism: who, what, when, where, and why (or how). Use the remaining paragraphs to provide further details. To increase the chance of the news release's being read and used, ensure that your writing is as concise and as objective as possible. Figure 14.2 provides an example of a news release written in this manner.

> OBJECTIVE 4: Compose promotional reports such as news releases, presentation brochures, and annual reports.

FIGURE 14.2   News Release

Special news-release form is used for immediate recognition.

A talking or descriptive heading is used.

The first paragraph (one sentence long) summarizes the overall message.

The remaining paragraphs provide the background information.

Actual quotations are used for interest.

Provides background information on the organization.

Provides a contact who can provide additional information.

News Release   NASDAQ CWKTF · VSE CWK

TELEPHONE COMPANY "BYPASS" COMES TO CANADA

VANCOUVER, B. C., MAY 18TH, 1988 - Environment Canada, a unit of the Canadian federal government, is the first organization in Canada to utilize CAM-NET's alternative microwave solution rather than the leased lines or cable facilities offered by the telephone company.

CAM-NET, through its Canadian Northstar operations, connected Environment Canada's two local area networks in Hull, Quebec utilizing DEC's METROWAVE™ Bridge and a microwave system supplied by CAM-NET.

CAM-NET provided the engineering, licensing and installation of the system. The Department of Communications approved the licensing thereby paving the way for many other applications across Canada.

"CAM-NET's solution to connect the networks was not only the most cost-effective method but also the most practical as the transmission speed of 10 megabits per second is far superior to the 1.54 megabits per second one would have had to settle for with a telephone company leased line", said Mike Magar, Director of Informatics Management, Environment Canada.

"The installation team from Digital Equipment of Canada and CAM-NET worked together in a very professional way and completed the installation ahead of our deadline. The system has performed flawlessly since. The total package cost approximately $100,000 and is a prime example of Digital Equipment and CAM-NET's networking expertise." stated Mr. Magar.

CAM-NET anticipates completing numerous microwave installations across Canada now that the licensing of hundreds of potential applications are feasible.

Cam-Net Communications Network Inc., is a Canadian company providing alternative long distance service and through its Northstar subsidiaries provides telecommunications engineering and private network facilities utilizing microwave, fibre optic, and satellite transmission to business users throughout North America. Revenue for 1987 was up 380% over 1986.

For further information contact:
        Daryl Buerge
        Vice President Corporate Relations
        (604) 684-4111

™ METROWAVE is a trademark of Digital Equipment Corporation

News releases present the organization's side of both good news and bad news.

Although most news releases are written to publicize positive information about the company, it is just as important to ensure that all the relevant facts are known when negative events at the organization are deemed newsworthy. If such information is going to be reported, you at least want it to be reported accurately and to have your organization's viewpoint represented.

Presentation Brochures

Although sales brochures are typically written by advertising specialists, managers throughout the organization will occasionally need to prepare a **presentation brochure**—a written report that highlights the work of an

CSX Corporation, an international, multimodal
transportation company based in Richmond, Virginia, has
developed humidity-controlled ocean containers used in
shipping. To highlight the work on this and other projects,
CSX utilizes presentation brochures.
(*Source: Reprinted with permission of CSX Corp.,*
Richmond, VA)

organization, department, or project and that is distributed to prospective
employees, customers, suppliers, investors, lenders, or other interested
groups. For example, almost every company, especially small or new
enterprises, should have a presentation brochure that introduces the company and explains its background, mission, products, and other relevant
information.

When developing a presentation brochure, avoid built-in obsolescence.
Because brochures are expensive to produce, omit information that changes
frequently; for example, names of officers, financial or sales figures, and
photographs that will quickly become dated. If such information is central
to the purpose of your brochure, then design the brochure in such a way
that revisions will be easy and inexpensive. One way to do so is to design
a cover that will remain more or less permanent. Then the inside copy can
be updated quickly and inexpensively.

Also, avoid using an awkward format. The most convenient size for a
brochure is 8½ by 11 inches, printed sideways (called a landscape orientation, as opposed to the portrait orientation of most documents) and on
both sides and then folded to form three panels. Assuming that two of the
panels will be the front and the back covers, this format provides four
columns for copy and art, each column about 3½ inches in width. Such a
document can easily be inserted into a standard size No. 10 business
envelope and is easy for the reader to file.

Devote enough time and resources to the cover design to gain the reader's
attention. Inside, highlight the most important points, stating them in terms
of how they will benefit the reader and providing sufficient supporting
evidence. Use photographs where appropriate but avoid "visual clichés"—
photographs that are so obvious and uninteresting they add nothing to the
clarity of the text.

> Design your brochure in
> a simple, easy-to-update
> format.

Annual Reports

Annual reports are complex documents that require the expertise of many people.

It is unlikely that you, or any other one person, will ever write a complete annual report. An **annual report** is usually a collaborative communication that details the organization's financial activities, operations, and plans for the future. Thus, you may be asked to write the section that discusses your own particular area of responsibility within the firm. As with other collaborative writing projects, someone is then designated to serve as the editor, to make sure the complete document is consistent and unified.

Although corporations whose stock is publicly traded are required by law to furnish an annual report to their stockholders, many other organizations, including professional, civic, and charitable organizations, are increasingly providing such reports as a convenient way to inform members and others about their performance.

Because annual reports have legal implications, make sure that the sections you write are accurate and complete. Although you will naturally wish to highlight the most positive aspects of performance, it is not permissible, legally or ethically, to ignore negative aspects and therefore mislead the reader. Use confident, but objective, language.

If you are responsible for putting the entire report together, make sure the merged report exhibits coherence and smooth transition when moving from one topic to another and that the same format and writing style is used throughout. Also make sure the report has appropriate emphasis, with all important areas receiving an appropriate amount of space.

▼
OBJECTIVE 5: Compose policies and procedures using simple language, practical content, and logical organization.

POLICIES AND PROCEDURES

Policies are broad operating guidelines that govern the general direction and activities of an organization; **procedures** are the recommended methods or sequential steps to follow when performing a specific activity. Thus, the organization's attitude toward promoting from within the firm would constitute a policy, and the steps to be taken to apply for a promotion would constitute a procedure. Policy statements are typically written by top management; procedures are typically written by managers and supervisors involved in the day-to-day operation of the organization.

Avoid making policies so general that they are of little practical help.

Begin a policy statement by setting the stage for the policy; that is, justify the need for a policy. Your justification should be general enough that the policy covers a broad range of situations but not so general that the policy has no real "teeth." Ensure that the reader knows exactly who is covered by the policy, what is required, and any other needed information. Finally, show how the reader, the organization, or someone benefits from this policy.

Write procedures in a businesslike, step-by-step format.

Write procedures in a businesslike, but not formal, manner, using contractions and the active voice. Imagine that you are explaining the procedure orally to someone. Go step by step through the process, explaining what should not be done as well as what should be done. Try to put yourself in the reader's shoes: How much background information is needed, how much jargon can safely be used, what reading level is appropriate? Anticipate questions and problems. Show and tell; that is, use pictures and diagrams as appropriate.

Don't assume that the reader knows anything about the process, but likewise don't assume that the reader is completely ignorant. Since it would be impossible to answer every conceivable question, concentrate on the high-risk tasks—those that are difficult to perform or that have high safety or financial implications if performed incorrectly.

Minimize the amount of conceptual information included, concentrating instead on the practical information. (Remember that a person can learn to drive a car safely without needing to learn how the engine actually propels the car forward.) Usually, numbered steps are appropriate, but a narrative approach may be used if it seems to be more effective.

After you have written a draft, have several employees (who are typical of those who will use the document) read and comment on it. If the document is a policy, ask them questions to see if they really understand the policy. If it is a procedure, have them follow the steps to see if they work. Revise as necessary.

> Have typical users review and edit drafts of policies and procedures.

Examples of both a policy and a procedure are shown in Figure 14.3. Could you follow this procedure and get the desired result?

Specialized reports often go one or more steps beyond the purpose of common reports. For instance, while a common report (such as a routine management report or a one-time situational report) might inform, analyze, or recommend, a specialized reports (such as proposals, business plans, promotional reports, and policies and procedures) often have the additional purpose of persuading or teaching. (*Source: © Lou Jones / The Image Bank*)

FIGURE 14.3A   Policy

Heading provides the necessary background information for filing and locating the policy.

Tells who is affected by the policy.

Introduces the topic and provides a setting.

Uses an appropriate balance between general and specific language to describe the policy.

Shows a caring attitude by closing with a discussion of reader benefits.

(seal)	**STANDARD PRACTICE GUIDE**	SUBJECT: Alcohol
		EFFECTIVE DATE: May 1, 1989
CENTRAL MICHIGAN UNIVERSITY		NUMBER: U-803 PAGE 1 OF 1

SUBJECT: Alcohol

APPLIES TO: All Faculty, Staff, and Student Employees

Central Michigan University (CMU) is committed to providing a workplace which is free from the unauthorized or unlawful manufacture, distribution, dispensation, or possession of beverage alcohol.

It is the intent of CMU to provide a healthful, safe, and secure work environment. No employee will report to work evidencing any effects of alcohol consumption. Use of beverage alcohol is limited to those locations approved by CMU policy or licensed by the State of Michigan. Violations of this policy will result in disciplinary action, up to and including dismissal pursuant to university procedures relating to employee discipline.

All university employees will, as a condition of employment, abide by the terms of this policy.

CMU supports programs aimed at the prevention of alcohol abuse by its employees. CMU's Employee Assistance Program provides preventative programs, counseling for employees experiencing alcohol dependency problems, and assistance for problems related to alcohol abuse. Such counseling is confidential and unrelated to performance evaluations. Leaves of absence to obtain treatment may be obtained under the medical leave provision of the appropriate labor agreement, employee handbook, or policy.

Procedure

FIGURE 14.3B

Procedure for Hiring a Temporary Employee

Actor	Action
Requester	1. Requests temporary employees with specific, specialized skills by filling out Form 722, "Request for a Temporary Employee."
	2. Secures manager's approval.
	3. Sends four copies of Form 722 to buyer of special services in the Purchasing Department.
Buyer of Special Services	4. Sends one copy to the labor analyst in the Budget Control Department.
Manpower Analyst	5. Checks overtime figures of regular employees in the department or section.
	6. If a question, contacts manager to learn of any upcoming increased workload.
	7. If satisfied that the specific people and skills are necessary, checks budget.
	8. If funds are available, approves Form 722, returns three copies to buyer, files the fourth copy.
Buyer of Special Services	9. Notifies temporary help contractor by telephone and follows up the same day with a confirming letter.
	10. Negotiates a mutually agreeable effective date.
	11. Contacts both Personnel and Furniture/Equipment sections by phone, telling them of the number of people, the effective dates, and the equipment requirements.
Personnel	12. Notifies Security, Badges, and Gate Guards.
	13. Returns one copy of Form 722 to the requester.
	14. Provides a temporary I.D.
Contractor of Temporary Help Services	15. Furnishes assigned employee or employees with information on the job description, effective date, and the individual to whom to report.
Temporary Employee	16. Reports to receptionist one half-hour early on effective day.

Uses a descriptive title.

The procedure begins with the act that starts the process and ends with the final result.

Contains only essential information.

The format used is optional. This procedure uses a "playscript" format that clearly specifies what role each person plays in the process.

Clearly and concisely details what steps are necessary and in what order.

Complete sentences are not necessary, so long as parallel structure is maintained; verb clauses are used here.

Source: Adapted from Leslie H. Matthies, "Writing Your First Procedure—How to Go About It," *Journal of Systems Management* (November 1987), pp. 25–29.

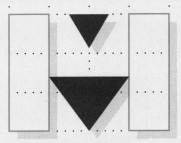

MICROWRITING A PROPOSAL

The Problem

You and your colleagues who teach business communication at Valley State College are interested in setting up a business writer's hotline—a telephone service that will provide answers to grammar, mechanics, and format questions from people who call in. You see this as a way of providing a much-needed service to local business people, as well as a way of providing positive public relations for your institution.

Each faculty member is willing to donate time to answer the phones, but you will need funds for telephone lines, answering machines, reference books, advertising, and the like. You decide to apply for a grant from the A. C. Reynolds Foundation to fund the project for one year. After that, if the hotline is successful, you will either reapply for funds or ask the Valley State College administration to fund the continuing costs. For requests less than $3,000, the foundation requires a simple narrative report explaining and justifying the request.

The Process

1. What is the background of the problem?

   Every writer has occasional questions about writing
   style but may not have a reference book or style manual
   available to answer the question. We know there is a
   need for such a service because we frequently get calls
   from people on campus with these questions. Although
   many grammar hotlines operate nationally, none is
   available within a 200-mile radius of Portland.

2. What will be the outcome of the project?

   A telephone service that will be available free of
   charge 24 hours a day to answer any question regarding
   business writing.

3. Describe the audience for this report and the implications for structuring your report.

   The A. C. Reynolds Foundation is a small foundation
   located in Portland. It makes grants to nonprofit
   organizations in the Portland area mostly for small
   projects of less than $10,000 each. The foundation
   takes a personal interest in each grant awarded.
     Because of the foundation's small size and personal
   orientation, a direct and personal writing style should
   be used rather than a scholarly style. This approach is
   also consistent with the principles of effective business writing.
     Since there is no reason to expect that the foundation
   holds a negative attitude toward this project, the
   request for funds will be made at the beginning of the
   report.

4. Describe how the hotline will work.

    a. A faculty member will answer phoned-in questions
       each weekday from 10 A.M. until 2 P.M.
    b. Questions phoned in at other times will be recorded
       on an answering machine, with a telephone response
       guaranteed by the end of the next working day.
    c. A phone line with a call-forwarding feature will be
       installed. Faculty members can have the calls for-
       warded to their offices so they can work on other
       matters when no hotline calls are being received.
    d. The faculty will agree on which books should serve
       as the standards of reference.
    e. The faculty will attempt to answer any reasonable
       question about grammar, mechanics, format, and the
       like, but will not review or edit anyone's writing
       and will not answer questions requiring extensive
       research (such as, "What is the most popular style
       of business letter in Fortune 500 companies?"

5. What are the advantages of this project, and where should they be
   presented in the report?

    a. Enhancing the college's reputation as an asset to
       the community.
    b. Providing a genuine service to business writers.
    c. Aiding business productivity by decreasing
       communication problems.
    d. Helping the business communication faculty stay
       abreast of their fields.

    These advantages should be discussed under the section
    detailing the outcomes of the project as a way of
    emphasizing the importance of these outcomes.

6. What will the project cost?

    The faculty members are willing to donate their time.
    Two copies of each of the reference books needed will
    cost $123.50. The telephone line will cost $61.30
    monthly, and long-distance charges for returning calls
    are estimated at $55 monthly. An answering machine with
    the features we need costs $119.50. Monthly advertise-
    ments in the campus newspaper and in the local
    newspaper are estimated at $62.50.

7. What are the qualifications of those involved in this project?

    Each of the 12 faculty members has a doctoral degree,
    with an average of eight years of teaching business
    communication and related courses.

The Product

THE BUSINESS WRITER'S HOTLINE

A Proposal Submitted by Professor Steve Harland
Valley State College of Portland, Oregon
March 15, 19--

All business writers have occasional questions about writing
style. Indeed, the business communication faculty at Valley State
College frequently receives calls asking questions about punctuation, subject-verb agreement, the correct format for business
correspondence, and the like. Although many grammar hotlines
operate nationwide to answer such questions, none is presently
available within a 200-mile radius of Portland.

Thus, the business communication faculty of Valley State
College requests that a grant for $2,388.60 be awarded for the
purpose of establishing and operating a Business Writer's Hotline
for one year to benefit the Portland community and Valley State
College students, faculty, and staff.

Outcome of the Project

The project will fund the establishment and operation of a
Business Writer's Hotline in which qualified business communication faculty members answer telephone inquiries from business
writers on the subject of grammar, mechanics, and format. The
service will operate at no cost to users and will be available
each day that Valley State College is in session.
    The advantages of the Business Writer's Hotline are that it
will

1. Increase business productivity by lessening the chance that an
   error in writing will cause communication problems, needless
   delays, or even incorrect decisions.
2. Provide a genuine service to business writers (including
   college students, faculty, and staff; business people; and
   others) who presently have no effective and convenient way of
   getting their questions answered.
3. Enhance the college's reputation as an asset to the local
   community.
4. Help the faculty consultants keep abreast of the kinds of
   writing decisions that are causing problems for the university
   and business community.

Procedures

When school is in session, a faculty member will be available to
answer any phoned-in questions every weekday from 10 a.m. until 2
p.m. Questions phoned in at other times will be recorded on an
answering machine, with a telephone response provided by the end
of the next working day.
    A dedicated telephone line with a call-forwarding feature
will be installed. Faculty members on duty can simply have the
calls forwarded to their offices so that they can work on other
matters when no phone calls are being received.

2

   Faculty consultants will attempt to answer any reasonable
question regarding grammar, mechanics (including punctuation and
spelling), document format, and the like. They will not review or
edit anyone's writing and will not be available to answer questions that require extensive research. Three books will serve as
the standard references: The Chicago Manual of Style, The
Associated Press Stylebook and Libel Manual, and The American
Heritage Dictionary, 2d College Edition. Other references will be
consulted as needed.
   The hotline will begin operating the first day of the school
year after the award of the grant and will continue for one year.
A small ad announcing the availability of this service will be
placed monthly in the Valley State Voice and in the Portland
Herald.
   A detailed log will be maintained showing the amount of use
and types of questions answered. These records will show whether
the service is fulfilling a need and whether a need exists for
additional collegiate education or industry training in business
writing.

Budget

The following budget is projected for the Business Writer's
Hotline for the first year of operation:

Purchase of two copies each of the three standard
reference books 123.50
Purchase of one telephone-answering machine 119.50
Rental on one telephone line (12 mo. @ 61.30) 735.60
Long-distance charges (12 mo. estimated @ 55) 660.00
Newspaper advertisements (12 mo. @ 62.50) 750.00

   Total 2,388.60

Note: The faculty consultants will provide their time at no cost
to the project.

Personnel Qualifications

Each of the 12 faculty members who will act as a voluntary
consultant has a doctoral degree and an average of eight years of
teaching business communication and related courses. Thus, the
faculty members have had much experience in answering the types of
questions likely to be encountered.
   The curriculum vita of each instructor is provided in
Appendix A.

Summary

The establishment of a Business Writer's Hotline will increase the
communication skills and the quality of writing of the local community. The recurring yearly cost of $2,145.60 is less than $10
per day and 40 cents per hour for the 45 weeks of 24-hour service.
This cost is a small amount to pay for the benefits that will be
provided to area business writers, the college, and the faculty
volunteers.

Summary

Proposals are persuasive reports and may be solicited or unsolicited. Each proposal should contain background information, objectives of the project, procedures, personnel or organizational qualifications, a direct request for approval of the project, and any needed supporting information. The writing style should be objective, with ample, credible evidence provided to support any claims and to justify the request. Reader benefits should be identified and emphasized.

Business plans are a specialized form of proposal that are written primarily to secure funding for a proposed venture. Complete, detailed information should be included that describes the company, the market, the promotional plans, and appropriate financial statements.

Promotional reports include news releases, brochures, and annual reports. The important considerations for such reports are specifying what the report is intended to accomplish; gearing the content, organization, and writing style to the needs of the specific audience; and being honest.

Policies and procedures are written in a businesslike, but not formal, manner. Practical, as opposed to conceptual, information is emphasized, with an appropriate balance between generality and specificity. To ensure that such reports achieve their purpose, typical users should be asked to review and edit them.

Key terms

Annual report— A written report that details the organization's financial activities, operations, and plans for the future.

Business plan— A written report that describes a proposed for-profit venture and often solicits financing for that venture.

News release— A written report to the news media that contains information the writer wishes publicized about the organization or its employees.

Policy— A broad operating guideline that governs the general direction or activities of an organization.

Presentation brochure— A written report that highlights the work of an organization, department, or project and that is distributed to prospective employees, customers, suppliers, investors, lenders, and the like.

Procedure— The recommended methods or sequential steps followed when performing a specific activity.

Proposal— A written report that seeks to persuade a reader outside the organization to do as the writer wants.

Review and discussion

OBJECTIVE 1
OBJECTIVE 1
OBJECTIVE 1

1. Give an example of a solicited proposal and an unsolicited proposal.
2. What are the legal implications of a proposal?
3. What sections are typical in a proposal?

4. What is meant by the statement "In a business plan, focus on the market—not on the product"?

OBJECTIVE 2 ◄

5. Why is honesty such an important characteristic of promotional reports?

OBJECTIVE 3 ◄

6. Write the nut paragraph of a news release announcing the selection of a new president for your firm.

OBJECTIVE 4 ◄

7. What steps can you take to make a presentation brochure economical and convenient for the reader?

OBJECTIVE 4 ◄

8. Why might a nonprofit organization issue an annual report?

OBJECTIVE 4 ◄

9. Give an example of a policy and a related procedure. Which one would you most likely be asked to write in an entry-level position?

OBJECTIVE 5 ◄

10. How much detail should be given in a procedure?

OBJECTIVE 5 ◄

EXERCISES

1. **Proposal—Planning a Research Project**   You are a research associate at We Find Out, Inc., a market-research firm located in Bloomington, Minnesota, which has a population of 82,000. Your firm employs ten people (the president, a business manager, a secretary shared by the president and business manager, four research associates, and three clerical workers) and has been in business in Bloomington for seven years. Although you specialize in market research, your firm has conducted several research projects for both the city of Bloomington and the state of Minnesota.

OBJECTIVE 1 ◄

You've just received a copy of an RFP from the Bloomington City Council asking for a proposal as follows:

The City of Bloomington solicits proposals to conduct a survey of residents of Bloomington regarding their opinions of Bloomington's municipal parks. Using appropriate survey and sampling techniques, the awardee shall determine the extent and types of recreational uses made of parks; measure knowledge of and satisfaction with such factors as appearance, location, service, amenities, and the like; secure suggestions for improvements; and gather such other data as may be relevant and useful to the Parks and Recreation Department in managing the park system. Please submit a three- to five-page proposal to the Budget Director, City of Bloomington, 5700 Green Valley, Bloomington, MN 55437.

Your boss has asked you to prepare a proposal in formal report format in response to this RFP. In establishing a budget, use actual cost estimates. Assume that you will be conducting the study; your own time is currently billed at $40 per hour; clerical and research assistant time is billed at $15 per hour. Use whatever information you know about conducting such a research project, plus any specific additional information that may need to be collected. You may assume whatever data is reasonable. Submit your report in typed format, with double-spacing and an appropriate cover sheet.

2. **Business Plan—University Hosts**   Assume that you're the president of the Hospitality Services Association, a campus organization comprised of students planning careers in hotel or motel management, tourism, and the like. HSA wants to start a business, tentatively named University

OBJECTIVE 2 ◄

Hosts, which would provide local services and organize various events for campus visitors.

For example, when the Admissions office lets your firm know that a prospective student and his or her family will be visiting the campus, you would immediately contact the family and offer to arrange such events as a campus tour; a meal at a local restaurant or in a campus dining hall with a faculty member; a tour of the town; tickets to campus or local events; and interviews with any desired campus officials, real estate agents, bank loan officers, and the like. In addition, you would arrange hotel reservations, automobile rentals, check-cashing privileges, and transportation to and from the airport. In short, you would provide any reasonable service to help campus visitors enjoy their stay and receive a favorable impression of the institution.

You foresee that your service would be especially helpful to potential students and their families, alumni, donors, prospective faculty and staff members, visiting legislators, and others.

Personnel time (to be supplied by student members of HSA) would be billed at $10 per hour; a 10% surcharge would be added to the actual cost of all services provided; automobile expenses would be billed at 22 cents per mile; and other charges would be billed at actual cost.

The only way that your venture could be successful is if you receive the endorsement of the University; that is, you want the Admissions Office, Alumni Association, Development Director, and others to let potential visitors know about your service and to promote it to the external campus community. In addition, University Hosts will place ads in the campus newspaper and in the local newspapers of the largest cities in the state.

The venture will provide both revenue for the service projects sponsored by HSA and practical work experience for HSA members.

Develop a business plan that will be submitted to the vice president for student affairs. The purpose of the plan is to get the University's agreement to promote this plan as a service to campus visitors; you are not asking the University to commit any funds to the project. You may assume any reasonable information needed to complete this project.

▶ OBJECTIVES 3–4

3. **News Release—Course Article** Most local newspapers are happy to publish news articles of interesting happenings on campus; after all, the college is an important part of their community. The news bureau at your college sends out news releases about campuswide happenings; however, it is likely that in a class this term you've experienced something that might be of interest to the local community—an interesting speaker, an unusual assignment, some type of interaction with local business, or some other project.

Write a news release to submit to the local newspaper, publicizing an actual event taking place this term in one of your classes. With your instructor's approval, submit this news release to the local newspaper. How successful were you in achieving your objective?

▶ OBJECTIVES 3–4

4. **Collaborative Writing—Annual Report** Assume that your group of three to five managers has been asked to compare your firm's annual report with those of similar organizations and to recommend improvements. Collect the latest annual reports from four Fortune 500 firms

that are in the same industry. (Your library should have either actual
or microfilm copies of these annual reports.) Assume that your group's
firm is the one first in alphabetical order.

OBJECTIVES 3–4 ◀

Critique your firm's report, and compare it with the other four
reports on such factors as the following (you should be able to think
of other comparison factors as well):

a. Effectiveness of the overall format
b. Clarity of the writing style (conduct a readability study of each
   report)
c. Credibility
d. Treatment of negative information
e. Unity, coherence, and good transitions
f. Use of emphasis and subordination

Write a two- to three-page memo report to your instructor presenting
and analyzing your findings and recommending any appropriate improvements to your firm's annual report.

5. **Procedure—Giving Directions**   As director of the student union at
   your institution, you frequently receive calls from both profit and
   nonprofit organizations inquiring about reserving a room for special
   meetings. Sometimes these organizations want food service such as a
   meal or refreshments, sometimes they want a cash bar, and other times
   they simply want an attractive meeting room. Of course, they're also
   interested in the cost, availability of parking, use of audiovisual
   equipment, deadlines, forms that need to be completed, and the like.

OBJECTIVE 5 ◀

   Prepare a procedure that can be distributed to inquirers that will
   answer their most frequent questions and that will take them through
   the procedure from initial inquiry through paying the final bill (if there
   is one). Use the actual practices in effect at your institution. Decide on
   an effective format for the written report.

6. **Policy—Using University Facilities**   See Exercise 5. Assume that your
   institution is establishing a policy that only nonprofit organizations
   may reserve meeting rooms on campus and that reservations by any
   on-campus groups take precedence over those from off-campus groups.
   The reason for this policy is to avoid competing with local commercial
   establishments and to prevent overcrowding of campus facilities.
   Prepare a policy statement (University Policy No. 403) for the board
   of trustees to consider at its next meeting.

OBJECTIVE 5 ◀

CASE PROBLEM ━━━━━━━━━

The Copy Cat

Larry Haas has been surprised to learn when examining the quarterly
departmental statements that photocopying costs have more than doubled
from the previous quarter. In talking over the problem with others, he has
learned that some workers photocopy nearly everything on their small
departmental photocopier (there are five of these convenient, but relatively
inefficient, copiers at headquarters) and other workers copy only small jobs

OBJECTIVE 5 ◀

on the small copiers and send larger jobs to the copy center, one of the departments managed by Eric Fox.

Jobs that are too big or too complicated for even the copy center to manage are sent to a local print shop. Some departments do this on their own; others rely on the copy center to do it. Regardless of where the copying is done, the individual department is charged for the job. From a company point of view, however, Larry is interested in ensuring that each job is completed in the most cost-effective way possible.

An additional problem Larry discovered is that the company's lax attitude about using the departmental photocopiers has perhaps given the erroneous impression that employees have permission to photocopy personal documents. He heard of many instances regarding the copying of personal insurance forms, recipes, sports stories, even kids' homework.

In speaking with the manager of the copy center, Larry learns that departmental copiers are designed for small jobs—no more than 30 copies of an original and no more than 20 originals per job. Any larger job should be sent to the copy center, which will decide whether to do the job in-house or send it to a print shop.

Generally, the in-house center will handle any one-color job on 8½-inch or smaller paper and up to 2,000 copies. Any job requiring more copies, more than one color, special binding, photographs, and the like are sent to the print shop.

Larry decides that a policy is needed on photocopying. And several specific procedures need to be established to accomplish the legitimate photocopying efficiently.

1. Write a policy statement (General Guideline 72) on the topic of photocopying. You may assume any reasonable information needed.
2. Once jobs are submitted to the copy center, a procedure must be in place to decide whether to do the job in-house or send it to a print shop. Write a procedure that covers the situation from when the job reaches the copy center until it is returned to the requester.

WORD WISE
- The longest novel ever published is *Men of Good Will* by Louis Henri Jean Farigole. It was published in fourteen volumes between 1933 and 1946.
- The most overdue book recorded in America was a book on febrile diseases checked out in 1823 from the University of Cincinnati Medical Library and returned in 1968. The $2,264 fine was waived.
- An estimated 27 million Americans are functionally illiterate.

Oral
Communication

Business Presentations

After you have completed this chapter, you will be able to

1. Understand the important role that business presentations play in the organization.

2. Plan a presentation by determining its purpose, analyzing the audience, and determining the timing and method of delivery.

3. Write a presentation by collecting the data and organizing it in a logical format.

4. Develop effective visual aids for a presentation.

5. Practice a presentation to develop an effective speaking style.

6. Deliver a presentation in a clear, confident, and efficient manner.

7. Plan and deliver minor presentations, including impromptu remarks, introductions, and special recognitions.

8. Make collaborative and video presentations.

Few industrial ventures arouse public anger as reliably as a new oil drilling operation. And few oil drilling operations arouse anger as those situated in environmentally sensitive areas. Therefore, when the Shell Oil company decided to go ahead with the plan to drill for oil on a Southern Florida Indian reservation, public relations expert Richard Hansen took on one of the toughest challenges of his career. As Shell's Public Affairs Manager for Exploration and Production, Hansen had the nearly-impossible task of persuading every party who could stop the project that the drilling operation was in their best interests. Hansen placed those target parties into three categories: the critics, the politicians, and the press. His goal was to create a presentation that would best address the concerns of each of the three audiences.

"The idea here was to see the company and the project as the outside world saw us," says Hansen. "Before we began, we asked ourselves questions: What's our plan? (We want to drill a well.); Will there be opposition? (Yes, especially from environmental groups.); What will be their complaints?; Are they valid?; How can we address their complaints? We composed an internal working document that defined what we were doing and proposed a plan of action. In the course of the communication plan, we considered using press releases and fact sheets externally. The facts have to be right and you have to be honestly doing the right thing. The worst mistake a public relations person can do is try to deceive the public," admonishes Hansen.

Richard Hansen, Public
Affairs Manager for
Exploration and Production,
Shell Oil, Houston, Texas

With the South Florida well, the Shell public relations team worked closely with the technical team. They identified every environmental problem possible and then designed a procedure to address the problem. Once they felt they could drill the well without negative environmental impacts, they proceeded with their communications plan.

"The communication process has to include contingencies, and it has to anticipate how the audience will receive the message. The key is to be credible and to be honest. When you give a presentation, you're under a microscope. What you say has to be what is really happening."

"We took two years to plan," says Hansen. "We worked with technical people to see what environmental studies we should do to illustrate the anticipated minimal negative impact. We assembled the right cast of characters— environmental scientists, a Native American representative, Shell representatives—and we chose the right materials, the right graphics for example, to make the presentation. We then drafted a message to a specific area and said, 'Your community is concerned with water quality' or 'Your community is concerned with tax revenues' and so on. You shape the message to the receiver."

After planning his presentation, Hansen mapped out a response to likely questions. "You *can* plan for crisis." says Hansen. "There are a number of things that can go wrong in any situation, so write them down, one through 10 with a corresponding 'What do we do?' The idea is that when a crisis hits, you open up to chapter three and there you find your answer to crisis number three."

Finally, Hansen called in Shell's media trainer who spent a morning working with Hansen and others. Then Hansen and his team took the show to Washington.

"We went to 12 senators and congressmen, and by the time we got to the last four, we were pretty good." Then Hansen went to Florida to talk to the press.

"The *Miami Herald* gave us a major article. They reported every argument we made. It's always been sort of 'open season' on oil companies in the media, but the article was much more sympathetic than we expected."

Shell's presentation also disarmed local critics of the drilling operation. Hansen won all three rounds of his fight, and Shell Oil won permission to drill. While Hansen attributes the victory to his careful preparation, he adds one bit of counsel. "Of course," he says, "you need some luck too." ▼

IMPORTANCE OF BUSINESS PRESENTATIONS

Anyone who plans a career in sales or marketing expects to make many oral presentations to customers and potential customers each week. What you may not realize, though, is that just about everyone in business will probably give at least one major presentation and many smaller ones each year—to customers, superiors, subordinates, or colleagues. Here are some typical business presentations and examples:

- *Sales pitches* (why you should purchase our products)
- *Status reports* (how we're progressing on our network conversion)
- *Briefing sessions* (what I learned at the OSHA workshop last week)
- *Proposals* (why you should adopt my idea)
- *Training* (how to operate the new communication software)
- *Explanations of policies, procedures, and plans* (how our new insurance plan will affect you and your family)

As many as 11 million meetings are held each day in this country,[1] and many of them involve oral presentations. Thus, it is not surprising that the ability to speak effectively is considered a strategic managerial skill.

Unfortunately, some managers don't have this skill. In one recent survey of vice presidents in the nation's largest corporations, 44% described most presentations they heard as "boring," and only 3% described them as "stimulating." Furthermore, 40% admitted that they had dozed off while listening to a presentation.[2] It is clear, then, that many executives who are highly competent in their fields never learn how to present orally what they know.

The costs of ineffective presentations are immense. With many top executives earning $100,000 or more a year, a presentation that discusses ideas incompletely and inefficiently wastes time and money. Sales are lost, vital information is not communicated, training programs fail, policies are not implemented, and profits and efficiency drop.

Written Versus Oral Presentations

Written reports and oral presentations both play an important role in helping an organization achieve its objectives. An oral presentation may be made either in conjunction with or in place of a written report. Effective communicators must recognize the advantages and disadvantages of presenting business information orally.[3]

Advantages   Probably the most important advantage of oral presentations is the *immediate feedback* that is possible from the audience. Questions can be answered and decisions can be made immediately. In addition, the speaker can pick up cues from the audience regarding how well they understand and agree with his or her points and adjust content and delivery accordingly.

A second advantage concerns *speaker control*. A written report may never even be read, let alone studied carefully. But speakers have a captive audience. They can control the pace of the presentation, question the audience to ensure attention and understanding, and use nonverbal cues such as pauses, gestures, and changes in voice speed and volume to add

OBJECTIVE 1: Describe the important role that business presentations play in the organization.

Oral presentations provide immediate feedback, allow speaker control, and require little work of the audience.

emphasis. In addition, visual aids used in an oral presentation are often more effective than those used in a written report.

A third advantage of the oral presentation has to do with the listener: presentations are *less work for the audience.* Listening is simply less strenuous work, and often more enjoyable, than reading. The written word presents mostly verbal clues, whereas the oral presentation is filled with a variety of verbal and nonverbal clues to make comprehension easier and more enjoyable.

Disadvantages   Considering the advantages of immediate feedback, speaker control, and reduced audience effort, why isn't *all* business information communicated orally? The first reason is that oral presentations are *impermanent.* They disappear, and much of the information presented is forgotten within hours of delivery. Also, listeners have only one opportunity to understand what they're hearing. And, although much of what is read is also forgotten within hours, the written report provides a permanent record that can be reread and referred to in the future.

Oral presentations may also be very *expensive.* It is much more cost effective to have 1,000 managers scattered around the country read a written report than to have them hear the same information in a mass meeting. The sheer logistics of assembling such a large group can be overpowering. In addition, the visual aids used in oral presentations are often more expensive than those used in written reports (that is one reason why they're typically more effective). For example, a color slide of a graph costs many times more to produce than a black-and-white paper copy printed directly from the computer.

It's not surprising, then, that many presentations include both an oral and a written component. As a business communicator, you'll need to weigh a number of factors when you decide whether to communicate orally or in writing: the complexity of the material, the size of your audience, your need for immediate feedback, and the cost of the presentation, among others. We'll have more to say about these factors in Chapter 16.

THE PROCESS OF MAKING A BUSINESS PRESENTATION

The presentation process requires planning, organizing, developing visual aids, practicing, and delivering the presentation.

As you will remember, we followed a specific process when learning to communicate business information in written form; the process consisted of planning, writing, revising, formatting, and finally proofreading the written document. We follow a similar logical process for making an oral presentation:

1. *Planning:* determining the purpose of the presentation, analyzing the audience, and determining the timing and method of delivery
2. *Organizing:* collecting the data and outlining it in a logical order
3. *Developing appropriate visual aids:* selecting the appropriate type, number, and content
4. *Practicing:* rehearsing by simulating the actual presentation conditions as closely as possible and paying special attention to the use of simple language, correct diction, effective voice qualities, and appropriate body language

5. *Delivering:* dressing appropriately, maintaining friendly eye contact, speaking in an effective manner, and answering questions confidently

The process of making a business presentation is outlined in Checklist 14. Each stage is discussed in more detail in the sections that follow.

PLANNING THE PRESENTATION

When assigned the task of making a business presentation, your first impulse might be to sit down at your desk or computer and begin writing. Resist this temptation because, as in written communications, several important steps precede the actual writing. These steps involve determining the purpose of the presentation, analyzing the audience, planning the timing of the presentation, and selecting a delivery method.

In addition to helping you decide what to include in your presentation, these planning tasks will give you important information about the degree of formality appropriate for the situation. The more formal the presentation, the more time you'll devote to the project. In general, complex topics or ones that have high stakes demand more formal presentations, with well-planned visuals, a carefully thought-out organization plan, and extensive research. Also, the larger the audience (and especially if there is need to repeat the presentation) and the greater the audience's opposition to your ideas, the more formal the presentation should be.

OBJECTIVE 2: Plan a presentation by determining its purpose, analyzing the audience, and determining the timing and method of delivery.

Purpose

Most business presentations have one of these four purposes:

- *Persuading:* convincing the listener to purchase something or to accept an idea you're presenting
- *Reporting:* bringing the audience up to date on some project or event
- *Explaining:* detailing how to carry out a procedure or how to operate a piece of new equipment, for example
- *Motivating:* inspiring your listeners to take some action

Most presentations seek either to persuade, report, explain, or motivate.

During the planning and writing of your presentation, keeping your purpose uppermost in mind helps you decide what information to include and what to omit, in what order to present this information, and which points to emphasize and which to subordinate. Assume, for example, that you have been asked to make a short oral presentation of the written report presented in Figure 10.2, on the topic of absenteeism at the Limerick Generating Station.

If you're speaking to the management committee, your purpose would be to *report* the results of your research. Use a logical organization, discussing the effects of the problem, its causes, and possible solutions; and give about equal time to each topic. An overhead transparency outlining your presentation might look like this:

Absenteeism at the Limerick Generating Plant

- Extent of the problem
- Causes
- Solutions

The Oral Presentation Process

Planning

1. Determine if an oral presentation will be more effective than a written report.

2. Determine your purpose: what response do you want from your audience?

3. Analyze your audience in terms of demographic factors, level of knowledge, and psychological needs.

4. If possible, schedule the presentation to permit adequate preparation and to avoid rushed periods for the audience.

5. Select an appropriate delivery method, such as speaking from notes, reading, or memorizing.

Organizing

1. Brainstorm: Write down every point you think you might cover in the presentation.

2. Separate your notes into the opening, body, and ending. Gather additional data if needed.

3. Write an effective opening that introduces the topic, discusses the points you'll cover, and tells the audience what you hope will happen as a result of your presentation.

4. In the body, develop the points fully, giving background data, evidence, and examples.
    a. Organize the points logically, using a plan appropriate to your audience and topic.
    b. To maintain credibility, discuss any important negative points and be prepared to discuss any minor negative points.
    c. Pace the presentation of data; avoid presenting so many facts and figures that the audience can't understand them.

5. Finish on a strong, upbeat note by summarizing your main points, adding a personal appeal, drawing conclusions and making recommendations, discussing what needs to be done next, or using some other logical closing. Leave your audience with a clear and simple message.

6. Use humor if it is appropriate and if you are effective at telling humorous stories.

7. Make sure your visual aids are needed, simple, easily readable, and of the highest quality.

Practicing

1. Rehearse your presentation extensively, simulating the actual speaking conditions as much as possible, and using your visual aids.

2. Use simple language and short sentences, with frequent preview, summary, transition, and repetition.

3. Stand tall and naturally, and speak in a loud, clear, enthusiastic, and friendly voice. Vary both the rate and volume of your voice.

4. Use correct diction and appropriate gestures.

Delivering

1. Dress appropriately—in comfortable, businesslike, conservative clothing.

2. Use a microphone effectively.

3. Maintain eye contact with the audience, including all corners of the room in your gaze.

4. To avoid anxiety, practice extensively, develop a positive attitude, and concentrate on the friendly faces in the audience.

5. Plan your answers to possible questions ahead of time. Listen to each question carefully and address your answer to the entire audience.

If you were speaking to the union personnel, however, your purpose might be to *motivate* the employees to reduce their absenteeism. You might then briefly discuss the extent of the problem, devote your major efforts to showing how the employees ultimately benefit from lower absenteeism, and finally introduce the monthly recognition program. An overhead transparency outlining this presentation might look like this:

> *All in Favor, Say "Present"*
> - How we stack up
> - Full attendance = full employment
> - And the winner is . . .

After your presentation is over, your purpose provides a criterion—the only important criterion—by which to judge the success of your presentation. In other words, did the management committee understand the results of your research? Were the union members motivated to reduce their absenteeism? No matter how well or how poorly you spoke and no matter how beautiful or ineffective your visual aids, the important question is whether or not you accomplished your purpose.

Audience Analysis

In addition to identifying such demographic factors as the size, age, and organizational status of your audience, you will also need to determine their level of knowledge about your topic and their psychological needs (values, attitudes, and beliefs). These factors provide clues to everything from the overall content, tone, and types of examples you should use to the types of questions to expect, and even the way you should dress.

The principles by which you analyze your audience are the same as those we discussed in the chapters on writing letters, memos, and reports (for

> Analyze the audience in terms of demographics, level of knowledge, and psychological needs.

example, in Chapter 7 on persuasive messages). Consider the effect of your message on your audience and your credibility with them. The key is to put yourself in your audience's place, anticipating their questions and reactions. The "you attitude" applies to oral as well as written communication.

The larger your audience, the more formal your presentation will be. When you speak to a large group, speak louder and slower and use more emphatic gestures. Your visuals must be larger. Usually, allow questions only at the end of your talk. If you're speaking to a small group, you can be more flexible about questions, and your tone and gestures will be more like those in normal conversation. Furthermore, when presenting to small groups, your choice of visual aids increases.

If your audience is unfamiliar with your topic, you will need to use clear, easy-to-understand language, with extensive visual aids and many examples. If the audience is more knowledgeable, you can proceed at a faster pace. Suppose, however, that you have an audience composed of both novices and experts. One option, of course, would be to separate the two groups and give two presentations—each geared to the level of that particular audience.

If the gulf in understanding is not quite that wide, you should determine who the key decision maker is in the group—frequently, but not always, the highest-ranking member of that group—and then provide a level of detail necessary to secure that person's understanding. Take time especially to understand this decision maker's needs, objectives, and interests as they relate to your objective.

The audience's psychological needs will also affect your presentation. If, for example, you think your listeners will be hostile—either to you personally or to your message—then you'll have to oversell yourself or your idea. Instead of giving one or two examples, give several. In addition to establishing your own credibility, you may need to quote other experts to bolster your case.

In the first presentation on absenteeism (given earlier), the audience is the management committee. They have very high organizational status and probably expect a somewhat formal presentation. Although they may not be very familiar with the specific problem, they are very familiar with the organization overall and are probably quite interested in the bottom-line implications of the problem.

Regarding the second presentation, the union members are probably a more heterogeneous group than the management committee. Thus, you must make sure the language and examples used are appropriate for a broad range of knowledge, interests, and attitudes. In addition, you'll probably want to use a more informal, conversational style for the presentation.

Once you've identified your audience, it is often helpful to meet with key people before your presentation, especially to meet informally with the key decision makers. These meetings can help you predispose the audience in favor of your recommendations or, at the very least, help you discover sources of opposition. Knowing ahead of time about their concerns will let you build in relevant information in your presentation to address those concerns.

Timing of the Presentation

Often the timing of the presentation is beyond your control. If you've been asked to update the management committee about the absenteeism problem and the committee typically meets at 2 P.M. on the first Tuesday of each month, that is when you must be available.

Sometimes, however, you will have some flexibility. For example, if you want to present a proposal for a pet project to several managers whose cooperation is crucial for your success, you would be in charge of scheduling the meeting.

Consider two factors when scheduling presentations. First, allow yourself enough time to prepare—including gathering data, writing and revising, producing visual aids, and practicing the presentation. Second, consider the needs of your audience. Avoid times when they will be away or so occupied with other matters that they will not be able to concentrate on your presentation. In general, early or midmorning presentations are preferable to late afternoon sessions. Try to avoid giving a presentation immediately before lunch, when the audience may be hungry or eager to make lunch appointments, or, worse, immediately after lunch, when the audience may be late or not very alert.

> Time the presentation to allow adequate preparation and to avoid rushed periods.

Delivery Method

At some point during your planning, you must decide on your method of delivery—that is, will you memorize your speech, read it, or speak from notes? (Impromptu speaking—speaking without formal preparation—is covered later.) Your choice will be determined by the answers to such questions as How long is your talk? How complex is the content? How formal is the presentation? And what method (or combination of methods) are you the most comfortable with?

Memorizing Unless a presentation is very short and very important, memorizing an entire speech is risky and very time-consuming. You always run the risk (a very real one when you're nervous) of forgetting your lines and thus ruining your entire presentation if you have no notes to fall back on. In addition, memorized presentations often sound mechanical and do not let you adapt the material to the needs of the audience. However, memorizing the first or last section of your presentation, a telling quotation, or a joke may be very effective for presenting important parts of your talk.

Reading Reading speeches is quite common in academic settings, where a professor or researcher might be asked to read a paper at a professional conference. Writing out a speech and reading from the prepared text is helpful if you're dealing with a highly complex or technical topic, if the subject is controversial (making a statement to the press, for example), or if you have a lot of information to present in a short time. Such delivery is not recommended for most business settings because the presenter's eyes are typically on the paper and not on the audience, because spontaneity and flexibility are lost, and because, after all, if the speech is going to be read word for word, why not just duplicate and distribute it to the audience for them to read at their leisure?

Speaking from Notes By far the most common method for business presentations is speaking from prepared notes, such as an outline. The notes contain key phrases rather than complete sentences, and you compose the exact wording as you speak. Although you may occasionally stumble in choosing a word, the spontaneous, conversational quality and the close audience rapport that result are generally superior to that of other presentation methods. The notes help ensure that all the material will be covered and in a logical order; yet this method provides enough flexibility that you can adapt your remarks in reaction to verbal and nonverbal cues from the audience.

The specific content and format of the notes is not important; choose whatever works best for you. Some people use a formal outline on full sheets of paper; others prefer notes jotted on index cards. Use either complete sentences or short phrases; and, if desirable, include notes to yourself, such as when to pause, what phrases to emphasize, and when to change a slide or transparency.

Whether you use full sheets or index cards, number each page (in case the pages are dropped). For ease in moving from sheet to sheet or card to card, write on just one side and do not staple. Typed copy is better than handwritten copy and large type is better than small type. Type your notes in standard upper- and lowercase letters rather than in all capitals, which is more difficult to read because each letter is the same size.

A comparison among an excerpt from a written report, an oral presentation using a complete script, and an oral presentation using outline notes is shown in Figure 15.1. The excerpt is from pages 2–3 of the formal business report presented in Figure 13.5. Note several things about the content and format of the excerpts from the oral presentation:

- Both the complete script and the outline notes are typed in larger type for ease of reading, and both contain prompts showing when to display each visual aid (transparency).
- The complete script is written in a more informal, conversational style than the written report and uses a shorter line length and extra spacing between paragraphs.
- The outline notes contain mostly phrases, with each subtopic indented to show its relationship to the main idea.

Of course, some combination of these methods is also possible. Some people, especially those who give speeches only occasionally, do best by writing the entire speech out and then practicing it until they can recite whole paragraphs or thoughts with ease, thereby enabling them to maintain eye contact with the audience. Some even insert delivery cues, indicating when to pause, smile, make a gesture, display a visual aid, slow down, and the like.

Some professionals start off by writing out the entire speech and then practice extensively from the prepared script. Only after they are thoroughly familiar with their verbatim script do they condense it into an outline and then speak from the outline. Whatever method you use, the key to a successful delivery is practice, practice, practice.

> Of the three common methods of presentation (memorizing, reading, and speaking from notes), the last is the most common.

Using a Complete Script Versus Outline Notes

FIGURE 15.1

        The staff employees were asked to rate their level of fa-
miliarity with each benefit. As shown in Table 1, most staff
employees believe that most benefits have been adequately communicated to them.
        At least three-fourths of the employees are familiar with
all major benefits except for long-term disability insurance,
which is familiar to only a slight majority. The low level of
knowledge about automobile insurance can be explained by the
fact that this benefit had only been in effect for six weeks at
the time of the survey.
        In general, benefit familiarity is not related to length
of employment at ASU. Most employees are familiar with most
benefits, regardless of their length of employment. However, as
shown in Figure 1, the one benefit for which this is not true
is life insurance. The longer a person has been employed at
ASU, the more likely he or she is to know about this benefit.

Excerpt from Written Report

        We asked our employees how familiar they are
with our benefits. (<u>TRANSPARENCY 1</u>) As you can see,
most employees know about most of our benefits.

        At least three-fourths of them are familiar
with all but two of our benefits, and those two are
long-term disability and automobile insurance. Only
a slight majority know about our long-term disability insurance, and slightly more than a third know
about our automobile insurance. As you may remember, we began offering automobile insurance just
six weeks before conducting this survey.

        In general, there's no correlation between how
long employees have worked here and how familiar
they are with our benefits. Most employees are familiar with our benefits, no matter how long
they've worked here. The one exception is life insurance. (<u>TRANSPARENCY 2</u>) The longer a person has
worked for us, the more likely that person is to
know about our life-insurance program.

Excerpt from Oral Presentation—Complete Script

Familiarity with benefits--<u>Transparency 1</u>
    --Most know about most benefits
 + 3/4 know about all but 2 benefits:
    --Long-term disability: slight majority
    --Auto insurance: +1/3 (begun 6 weeks before
      survey)

No correlation between employment length &
familiarity
    --Not true for life insurance--<u>Transparency 2</u>
    --Life insurance: Longer employment → more
      familiarity

Excerpt from Oral Presentation—Outline Notes

┌───

S P O T L I G H T   ON INTERNATIONAL ISSUES

PRESENTING ABROAD

Increasingly, managers are being required to make presentations abroad to nationals from other countries. Many of the principles discussed in this chapter continue to apply. However, those discussed in Chapter 3 regarding international communications are also relevant. Because each culture is different, broad generalizations cannot be made. The following discussion, then, simply points out some factors you will need to be aware of as you try to make your presentation appropriate for the specific country.

Planning the Presentation

Planning the presentation should really begin with deciding *who* should make the presentation. In the Japanese culture, age is highly respected and the credibility of a young presenter, regardless of his or her expertise or communication skills, may be questioned by an older audience. Similarly, female presenters may experience difficulty in some Middle Eastern countries.

The culture also affects the content and organization of your presentation, and you should adopt a strategy that will help you accomplish your goal. In their text, *Managing Cultural Differences,* Harris and Moran recommend a dual strategy—one that reflects both cultures (yours and the host country's):

1. Describe the problem as understood by both cultures.
2. Analyze the problem from two cultural perspectives.
3. Identify the cause(s) of the problem from both viewpoints.
4. Solve the problem through cooperative strategies.
5. Determine if the solution is working multiculturally.

Well-planned visual aids and printed handouts are especially desirable in helping an audience for whom English is a second language follow your presentation. The use of examples and frequent summary and review is also helpful.

Know the customs and attitudes of your audience. For example, beginning a presentation with a joke is frowned on in Japan, discussing incidents from one's private life would probably be considered inappropriate in France (where there is a rather complete separation of a person's public and private life), and a question-and-answer period would be expected in many countries but would yield only an awkward silence in France, where questions are generally asked on a one-to-one basis after the speech. German audiences typically focus on the technical aspects, and Swedish audiences focus on the theoretical aspects of the presentation.

Giving the Presentation

In many cultures, a formal presentation will be expected, with the presenter speaking from a full script and using elaborate visual aids. Some audiences may misinterpret an extemporaneous speech given from notes as implying the speaker didn't respect the audience enough to prepare his or her remarks fully.

Writing out your remarks in full beforehand will also help you plan your choice of words carefully. Restrict your vocabulary to the most common English words and your word meanings to the most common ones, and avoid using figures of speech such as jargon, slang, and clichés.

Speak slowly and clearly, using short, simple sentences and keeping gestures to a minimum. Do not be surprised if some audiences do not look at you directly as you speak. Eye contact is not as important in Middle Eastern cultures as it is to many Americans. If possible, try to include some phrases from the local language in your remarks.

An overall attitude of sensitivity, empathy, and flexibility will help you achieve success in giving presentations—both here and abroad.

Sources: Philip R. Harris and Robert T. Moran, *Managing Cultural Differences,* 2d ed. (Houston: Gulf Publishing, 1987); Robert T. Moran, "Tips on Making Speeches to International Audiences," *International Management,* April 1989, p. 59.

───┘

ORGANIZING THE PRESENTATION

OBJECTIVE 3: Write a presentation by collecting the data and organizing it in a logical format.

For most presentations, the best way to begin is simply to brainstorm; that is, to write down every point you can think of that might be included in your presentation. Don't worry about the order or format—just get it all down. During the next several days, carry a pen and paper with you so that you can jot down random thoughts as they occur—during a meeting, at lunch, to and from work, or in the evening at home.

Later separate your notes into three categories: opening, body, and ending. As you begin to analyze and organize your material, you may find that you need additional information. You may need to retrieve records from files, consult with a colleague, or perhaps visit your corporate or local library to fill in the gaps.

Avoid saturating your presentation with so many facts and figures that your audience won't be able to absorb them. Regardless of their usefulness, statistics will not strengthen your presentation if the audience is unable to assimilate the data. A more effective tactic is to prepare handouts of detailed statistical data to distribute for review at a later time.

The Opening

The purpose of the opening is to capture the interest of your audience, and the first 90 seconds of your presentation are crucial. The audience will be observing every detail about you—your dress, posture, facial features, and voice qualities, as well as what you're actually saying—for clues about you and your topic, and they'll be making preliminary judgments accordingly.

> Your opening should introduce the topic, identify the purpose, and preview the presentation.

Begin immediately to establish rapport and build a relationship with your audience—not just for the duration of your presentation but for the long term. If you're making a proposal, you need not only the audience's attention during your presentation but also their cooperation later to implement your proposal. Because the opening is so crucial, many professionals write out the entire opening and practice it word for word until they almost know it by heart.

The kind of opening that will be effective depends on your topic, how well you know the audience, and how well they know you. If, for example, you're giving a status report on a project about which you've reported before, you can immediately announce your main points (for example, that the project is on schedule and proceeding as planned) and go immediately to the body of your remarks. If you're presenting a proposal to your superiors, however, you'll have to introduce the topic and provide background information.

If most of the listeners don't know you, you'll first have to gain their attention with some creative opening. The following types of attention-getting openings have proven successful for business presentations; the examples given are for the presentation to employees on the topic of absenteeism:

> Effective openings include a quotation, question, hypothetical situation, story, or startling fact or visual aid.

- *Quote a well-known person:* "Comedian Woody Allen once noted that just showing up is 90% of the job."
- *Ask a question:* "Our union agreement provides for profit sharing whenever productivity increases by 3%. If we were able to cut our absenteeism rate by half during the coming year, exactly how much do you think that would mean for each of you in your end-of-year bonus check?"
- *Present a hypothetical situation:* "As you were leaving home this morning to put in a full day at work, assume that your son came up to you and said he was too tired to go to school today because he stayed up so late last night watching *Wrestle Mania*. How would you respond?"

- *Relate an appropriate anecdote, story, joke, or personal experience:* "George, a friend of mine who had recently quit one job for another, happened to meet his former boss on the street and asked him whom he had hired to fill his vacancy. 'George,' his former boss said, 'when you left, you didn't *leave* any vacancy!' Perhaps the reason George didn't leave any vacancy was that . . ."
- *Give a startling fact:* "During the next 24 hours, American industry will lose $136,986,301 because of absenteeism."
- *Use a dramatic prop or visual aid.*

Don't apologize or make excuses (e.g., "I wish I had had more time to prepare my remarks today" or "I'm really not much of a speaker"). The audience may agree with you! At any rate, you'll turn them off immediately and weaken your credibility.

Your opening should lead into the body of your presentation by previewing your remarks: "Today, I'll cover four main points. First, . . ." Let the audience know the scope of your remarks. For example, if you're discussing the pros and cons of a plant closing from a strictly dollars-and-cents standpoint, alert the audience immediately that your analysis does not cover political or human-relations considerations. If you don't first define the scope of your remarks, you'll invite needless questions and second-guessing during your presentation.

For most business presentations, let the audience know up front what you expect of them. Are you simply presenting information for them to absorb, or will the audience be expected to react to your remarks? Are you asking for their endorsement, for resources, for help, or what? Let the audience know what their role will be so that they can then place your remarks in perspective.

The Body

Organize the body logically, according to your topic and audience needs.

The body of your presentation conveys the real content. Here you'll develop the points you introduced in the opening, giving background information, specific evidence, examples, implications, consequences, and other needed information. Just as when you are writing a letter or report, choose an organizational plan that suits your purpose and your audience's needs:

- *Direct sequence:* giving the major conclusion first, followed by the supporting details (usually used for presenting routine information)
- *Indirect sequence:* presenting the reasons first, followed by the major conclusion (typically used for persuasive presentations)
- *Chronology:* presenting the points in the order in which they occurred (often used in status reports or when reporting on some event)
- *Cause/effect/solution:* presenting the reasons and consequences of some problem and then posing a solution
- *Order of importance:* arranging the points in order of importance and then posing each point as a question and answering (an effective way of ensuring that the audience can follow your arguments)
- *Elimination of alternatives:* Listing all alternatives and then gradually eliminating each one until only one option (the one you're recommending) is left

Whatever organizational plan you choose, you must make sure your audience knows at the outset where you're going and is able to follow your organization. In a written document, signposts such as headings tell the reader how the parts fit together. In an oral presentation, you must compensate for the lack of such aids by using frequent and clear transitions that tell your listeners where you are. Pace your presentation of data so that you do not lose your audience.

Convince the listener that you've done a thorough job of collecting and analyzing the data and that your points are reasonable. Support your arguments with credible evidence—statistics, actual experiences, examples, and support from experts. Use objective language; let the data—not exaggeration or emotion—persuade the audience. Be guided by the same principles you used when writing a persuasive letter or report.

It will be unlikely that all the data you've collected and analyzed will support your proposal. (If that were the case, persuasion would not be needed.) What should you do about negative information, which, if presented, might weaken your argument? You cannot simply ignore negative information. To do so would surely open up a host of questions that would seriously weaken your position.

Think about your own analysis of the data. Despite the negative information, you still concluded that your solution has merit. Your tactic, then, is to present all the important information—pro and con—and to show through your analysis and discussion that even considering the negative information, your recommendations are still valid. Use the techniques you learned in Chapter 4 about emphasis and subordination to let your listeners know which points you consider important and which you consider subordinate.

> Do not ignore negative information.

Although the important negative information should be discussed, you may safely omit discussion of minor negative points. You must, however, be prepared to discuss these points if any questions about them come up at the conclusion of your presentation.

After you've developed some experience in giving presentations, you will be able to judge fairly accurately how long to spend on each point in order to finish on time. Until then, your most effective strategy is to practice your presentation with a stopwatch. If necessary, insert reminders at each point in your notes indicating where you should be at what point in time. Avoid having to drop important points or rush through the conclusion of your presentation because you misjudged your timing.

The Ending

The ending of your presentation is your last opportunity to achieve your objective. Don't waste it. A presentation without a strong ending is like a joke without a punchline.

> Finish on a strong, up-beat note, leaving your audience with a clear and simple message.

Your closing should summarize the main points of your presentation, especially if it is a long one. Even if the members of your audience have had an easy time following the structure of your talk, they won't necessarily remember all your important points. Let the audience know the significance of what you've said. Draw conclusions, make recommendations, or outline the next steps. Leave the audience with a clear and simple message.

To add punch to your ending, you may want to use one of the same techniques used for opening a presentation. You might tell a story, make a personal appeal, or issue a challenge. However, resist the temptation to end with a quotation. It won't sound dramatic enough. Besides, you want your listeners to remember *your* words and thoughts—not someone else's. Also avoid fading out with a weak "That's about all I have to say" or "I see that I'm running out of time."

Because your audience will remember best what they heard last, your ending might be considered the most important part of your presentation. Finish on a strong, upbeat note. If you've used a slide projector during your presentation, be sure that it's turned off and the room lights are on so that you will be the center of attention. Finally, remember this friendly advice from Toastmaster's International: "Get up, speak up, shut up, and sit down." Also remember that no one ever lost any friends by finishing a minute or two ahead of schedule.

The Use of Humor in Business Presentations

Memory research conducted at San Diego State University showed that when ideas were presented with humor, the audience was not only able to recall more details of the presentation but was also able to retain the information longer.[4]

Most business presenters are not capable of being a Bill Cosby or Roseanne Barr, even if they wanted to be. If you know you do not tell humorous stories well, the moment you're in front of an audience is not the time to try to rectify that situation. Both you and the audience will suffer. If, however, you feel that you can use humor effectively, doing so might add just the appropriate touch to your presentation.

Jokes, puns, satire, and funny real-life incidents are just a few examples of humor, all of which serve to form a bond between the speaker and audience. Humor can be used anywhere in a presentation—in the opening to get attention, in the body to add interest, or in the closing to drive home a point. Humor should, of course, be avoided if the topic is very serious or has negative consequences for the audience.

If you tell a joke, it must always be appropriate to the situation and in good taste. Never tell an off-color or sexist joke; never use offensive language; never single out an ethnic, racial, or religious group; and never use a dialect or a foreign accent in telling a story. Such tactics are always in bad taste. The best stories are directed at yourself; they show that you are human and can laugh at yourself.

Before telling a humorous story, make sure that you understand it and think it's funny. Then personalize it for your own style of speaking and for the particular situation. Avoid beginning jokes by saying, "I heard a funny story the other day about . . . " A major element of humor is surprise, so don't warn the audience a joke is coming. If you do, they're mentally preparing for a funny punchline, and you may disappoint them. If, on the other hand, you're already halfway into the story before the audience even realizes that it's a joke, your chances of success are greater.

Resist the temptation to laugh at your own stories. A slight smile is more effective. Wait for the (hoped-for) laughter to subside; then continue your presentation by relating the punchline to the topic at hand.

> Use humor if it is appropriate and you are adept at telling humorous stories.

Regardless of your expertise as a joke teller, do not use humor too frequently. Humor is a means to an end—not an end in itself. When all is said and done, you don't want your audience to remember that you were funny. You want them to remember that what you had to say was important and made sense.

DEVELOPING APPROPRIATE VISUAL AIDS

Today's audiences are accustomed to multimedia events that bombard the senses. They often assume that any formal presentation must be accompanied by some visual element, whether it is a flip chart, overhead transparency, slide, film, videotape, or actual model. This expectation helps explain why one billion slides are produced yearly in this country, with even more overhead transparencies being produced.[5]

Visual aids help the audience understand the presentation, especially if it includes complex or statistical material. A University of Pennsylvania study found that presenters who used visual aids were successful in persuading 67% of their audience, whereas those who did not, persuaded only 50% of their audience. In addition, meetings in which visual aids were used were 28% shorter than those in which such aids were not used.[6] Similarly, a University of Minnesota study found that the use of graphics increased a presenter's persuasiveness by 43%. Presenters who used visual aids were also perceived as being more professional, better prepared, and more interesting than the group who didn't use visual aids.[7]

OBJECTIVE 4: Develop effective visual aids for a presentation.

Types of Visual Aids

Transparencies for overhead projectors are probably the most commonly used visual aids in business presentations. Relatively inexpensive and easy to produce, they can be used without darkening the room and while you face the audience. Thus, you can maintain eye contact with the audience, and they can take notes if needed.

Although 35-mm slides are best projected in a somewhat darkened room, their high quality adds a distinctly professional touch to a presentation, and they can be used with very large audiences. However, slides lack the flexibility of transparencies; it would be difficult to review an earlier slide or skip forward several slides during a presentation. Slides are moderately expensive to produce and require more preparation time than transparencies. However, the use of computer-generated slides is decreasing both the cost and production time.

Handouts—printed copies of notes, tables, or illustrations—are often important in helping the audience follow a presentation. In addition, they can provide a permanent record of the major points of the presentation and reduce or eliminate the need for note taking. Handouts are especially helpful for presenting complex information such as detailed statistical tables, which would be ineffective if projected as a slide or transparency.

Other types of visual aids often used for business presentations include writing surfaces such as flipcharts and chalkboards, films, videotapes, and models. The appropriate use of each of these types of media is shown in Figure 15.2.

Transparencies, slides, and handouts are the most common visual aids.

FIGURE 15.2

Comparison of Visual Aids

Criteria \ Type of audio-visual aid	Flipcharts, other writing surfaces— usually presenter made	Transparencies for overhead projector	35mm/ 6 x 6 slides	Films	Videotape
Clarity. Resolution	Poor—dependent upon presenter's graphic skills. Crude lettering	Very good— if images are prepared. Can be shown without darkening room	Excellent— but requires that room be darkened for best clarity	Excellent— but requires that room be darkened for projection	Very good— can be viewed in a lighted room
Adaptability to audience size	Poor— limited to small groups	Excellent— can be used with large audiences	Excellent— can be used with large audiences	Excellent— even for very large audiences	Moderate— restricted to small groups. Larger groups require the use of multiple monitors or special wide screen projection
Flexibility. Presenter control	Excellent— can easily be modified by presenter, on the spot	Good— very adaptable. Presenter can mark on visuals during presentation	Fair— if presenter narrates live. Poor— if prepared audiotape is used	Poor— although presenter can stop the projection in order to comment	Poor— although presenter can stop the projection in order to comment
Suitability for repeated use	Poor— susceptible to tears, smudges, etc.	Fair— susceptible to wear and tear	Excellent— but it is important to keep slides in proper order	Excellent— if heavy use is intended, extra prints are advisable to ensure availability	Excellent— if heavy use is intended, extra prints are adviable to ensure availability
Ease of updating	Not applicable— usually created fresh for each presentation	Excellent— transparencies are easily replaced	Excellent— slides can be replaced selectively, and tapes can be dubbed	Poor— editing, splicing, shooting new footage is complicated and costly	Poor— editing, splicing, shooting new footage is complicated and costly
Duplication capability	Poor— not well-suited for duplication	Excellent— extra transparencies can be made from same original	Excellent— slides are easily duplicated: tapes easily copied	Excellent— extra prints are easily made from master	Excellent— extra prints are easily made from master
Realism, image sophistication	Low— usually images are crude and very simple	Good— when made by graphics specialists, but usually poor when made by amateurs	Excellent— high quality and sophisticated, but no motion cability	Excellent— the most realistic audiovisual medium	Excellent— a high degree of sophistication is possible
Production effort	Low—can be produced even during presentations	Fairly low— can be prepared by presenter or by graphics specialist	Moderate— artwork and photography must be well planned and executed	High— requires professional help, and special equipment. Time consuming	High— requires professional help, and special equipment. Time consuming
Dependency upon equipment	Low— requires only stand for pad. A pointer may be desirable	Moderate— requires overhead projector, screen and electrical source	Moderate— requires slide projector, screen and electrical source	Moderate— requires projector and screen plus electrical source	Moderate—requires projector (receiver), and recorder/player for videotape or cassette
Production cost	Low— usually requires only flipchart pad and dark markers	Fairly low— most of cost is associated with artwork and lettering	Moderate— unless extensive location photography is required	High— quality films (sound/colour) are very expensive to produce	High— quality video shows are very expensive to produce
Ease of use (presentation)	Moderate— uncomplicated but requires high input of presenter's energy	Moderate— uncomplicated but requires high input of presenter's energy	Easy— if slides are automatically advanced via tape with advance pulses. Moderate— if slides must be manually advanced	Moderate— threading film can sometimes be complicated. Older projectors subject to malfunction	Easy— if video cassettes are used. Moderate if videotape is used

Source: Scott Inglis and Joanna Kozubska, "Making Presentations," *Management Decision* (May 1987), p. 9. Used with permission.

Desktop Presentations

Desktop presentation software is a special type of software that combines the functions of outline, word processing, and graphics programs into one easy-to-use program that enables you to design overhead transparencies and 35-mm slides easily, as well as produce miniature print copies to use as audience handouts. Because nearly every executive gives oral presentations, industry experts expect desktop presentations to become a much larger software market than desktop publishing.

Two of the most popular presentation programs are Persuasion® by Aldus Corporation and PowerPoint® by Microsoft Corporation. These programs come with slide and transparency templates, or built-in designs that specify such features as background and type colors, the type of border, and the size, type, and position of type. These templates, which can be changed, ensure a professional and consistent appearance for the organization's visual aids.

The outline and word processing features enable the user to type in ideas for the visuals and easily revise and rearrange them. The user can then either create charts or illustrations from within the program or insert charts created in a spreadsheet program. After all the visuals have been created and edited, the program permits easy resorting and updating as needed. When everything is perfect, the user simply uses a modem and communication program to send the data file electronically to a film processing company, which then produces the finished slides and transparencies from the data file and transmits them to the user. Turnaround time is typically 24 hours, at a cost of about $12 per slide. Black-and-white transparencies can, of course, be produced directly from the user's computer on a laser printer if having color transparencies is not an issue.

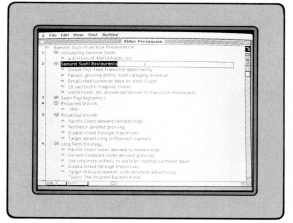

Outline your ideas.

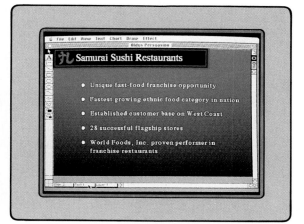

View the finished slides.

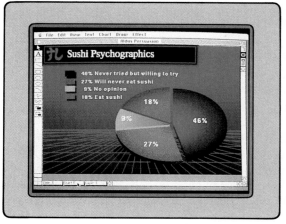

Chart numerical data.

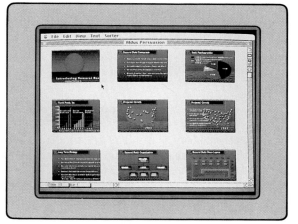

Produce speaker notes and handouts.

FIGURE 15.3   Making Your Visual Aids Effective

Be obvious. You can get a lot of
impact from a large headline and
straightforward text.

Be direct. Using a concise title and
limiting yourself to one idea per slide
helps to make the point stick.

Icons, often more appealing than
text, can be used to tie together
parts of a presentation.

Be sparing in your use of color, and
try to use colors that relate directly
to your subject matter.

Good overheads don't need to be
entirely self-explanatory. They can
reinforce ideas being put forth by
the speaker.

Source: Susanne Waltzman, "Presentations with Power," *ITC Desktop: No. 1.*

Preparing Visual Aids

Visual aids should be
needed, simple, readable,
and of high quality.

The key to effective visual aids is to use them only when needed, keep them simple and readable, and ensure they're of the highest quality.

Avoid using too many visual aids. Novice presenters sometimes use them as a crutch. Such overuse keeps the emphasis on the visual aid rather than on the presenter. Use visual aids only when they will help the audience grasp an important point, and remove them when they're no longer needed. The use of one or two relevant, helpful visual aids is better than an entire armload of irrelevant ones—no matter how beautiful they are.

One of the most common mistakes presenters make in developing visual aids is to simply photocopy tables or illustrations from reports, printouts, or journals and project them on a screen. Print graphics usually contain far too much information to serve effectively as presentation graphics. Using print graphics in a presentation will often do more to hinder your presentation than they will to help it.

Each slide or transparency should contain no more than 40 characters per line, six or seven lines per visual, and no more than three columns of data. Use upper- and lowercase letters (rather than all capitals) in a large, simple typeface and plenty of white (empty) space. Use bulleted lists to show a group of related items that have no specific order and numbered lists to show related items with a specific order.

Establish a color scheme and stay with it for all your visual aids; that is, use the same background color for each slide or transparency. For handouts and overheads, use dark type on a light background; for slides, use light type on a dark background. Figure 15.3 illustrates these principles for developing effective visual aids.

If you do not keep your visual aids clear and simple, your audience can easily become overwhelmed, with their attention drawn to the technology rather than to the content. As always, seek to *express*—not to *impress*. With visual aids, less is more.

The only real way to ensure that your visual aids are readable is to test them beforehand from the back seat of the room in which you will be speaking. If that is not possible, follow this guideline: The smallest image projected on the screen should be 1 inch high for each 30 feet of viewing distance. No one in your audience should be seated farther from the screen than ten times the height of the projected image. Thus, if you're projecting onto a screen six feet high, the back seat should be no farther than 60 feet from the screen, and the projector should be positioned so that the projected letters are at least 2 inches high.

The quality of your visual aids sends a nonverbal message about your competence and your respect for your audience. Just as you don't want your audience's attention distracted by the razzle-dazzle of your slides, neither do you want their attention distracted by their poor quality. If the visual aid isn't readable or attractive, don't use it.

Using Visual Aids

Even the best visual aid will not be effective if it is not used properly during the presentation. Using equipment smoothly does not come naturally; it takes practice and a keen awareness of audience needs, especially when using a slide or overhead projector. If you have the option of positioning the projection equipment (slide or overhead projector) and screen, ensure that the image is readable from every seat and that neither you nor the projector blocks anyone's view (see Figure 15.4).

Confirm that your equipment is in top working order and that you know how to operate it and how to secure quickly a spare bulb or spare machine if one becomes necessary. Adjust the projector so that the image is clearly readable from the farthest seat. However, do not make the image larger than necessary; the presenter should be the focus of attention. The image should be a square or rectangle. Avoid the common keystoning effect (where the top of the image is wider than the bottom) by tilting the top of the screen forward slightly toward the projector.

Practice using your visual aids smoothly and effectively.

FIGURE 15.4   Positioning the Projector Correctly

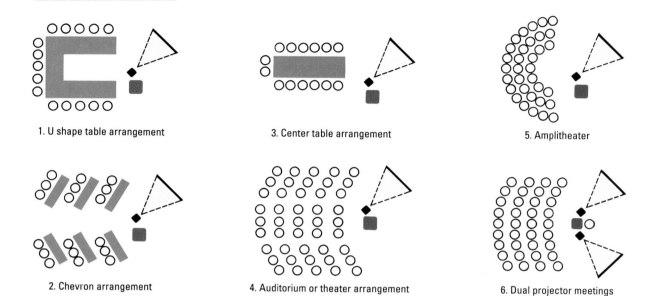

1. U shape table arrangement

2. Chevron arrangement

3. Center table arrangement

4. Auditorium or theater arrangement

5. Amplitheater

6. Dual projector meetings

Source: Robert W. Pike, *Creative Training Techniques Handbook* (Minneapolis, MN: Lakewood Publications, 1989).

When using slide projectors, have a blank opaque slide or a generic title slide as the last slide so that the audience is not suddenly hit with a bright flash of light when you turn off the projector or finish your presentation. And for both types of projectors, avoid walking in front of the projected image.

Try to avoid problems: Lock your slides in place in the tray; number your slides and transparencies so that they can be resorted quickly if dropped; have your film already threaded into the projector; clean the overhead projector glass before using it; tape the clicker used to advance the slides to the lectern to avoid having it tumble off; and have an extra bulb handy. Finally, be prepared to give your presentation without visual aids if that should become necessary.

With practice, you can learn to stand to the side of the screen, facing the audience with feet pointed toward the audience. Then, when you need to refer to some item on the screen, you point with your *left* hand, using either a finger, pointer, or pen. Turn your body from the waist, keeping your feet pointed toward the audience. Doing so enables you to maintain better eye contact with the audience as well as better control of the presentation.

Distribute handouts before your presentation if they contain information the audience will need during your presentation. Otherwise, distribute them at the end of your presentation (to avoid distracting the audience from your remarks). Do, however, alert the audience at the start that you will be distributing a printed summary of your remarks so that people won't take unneeded notes.

PRACTICING THE PRESENTATION

The language of oral presentations must be simple. Because the listener has only one chance to comprehend the information presented, shorter sentences and simpler vocabulary should be used for oral presentations than for written presentations. Presenters have trouble articulating long, involved sentences with complex vocabulary, and listeners have trouble understanding them. A long sentence that can be comprehended easily on paper will leave the speaker breathless when he or she says it aloud. Avoid such traps. Use short, simple sentences and a conversational style. Use contractions freely, and avoid using words that you have trouble pronouncing. Compare, for example, the different styles used in the excerpt from the written report and the oral presentation shown earlier in Figure 15.1.

Use frequent preview, summary, transition, and repetition to help your audience follow your presentation. The old advice to preachers is just as pertinent for business presenters: "Tell them what you're going to tell them, tell them, and then tell them what you told them."

Whether you plan to speak from a complete script or from notes or an outline, begin practicing by simulating the conditions of the meeting room as closely as possible. Always practice standing, with your notes at the same level and angle as a podium, and use any visual aids that will be a part of your presentation.

Videotaping your rehearsal can help you review and modify your voice qualities, gestures, and speech content. If videotaping is not possible, two good substitutes are a mirror and a tape recorder. The mirror can help you judge the appropriateness of your posture, facial expressions, and gestures. Remember that 55% of your credibility with an audience comes from your body language, 38% comes from your voice qualities, and only 7% from the actual words you use.[8] Play the tape back many times, paying attention to your voice qualities (especially speed and pitch), pauses, grouping of words and phrases, and pronunciation.

Speak in a conversational tone, but at a slightly slower rate than normally used in conversation. Vary both the volume and the rate of speaking for interest and to fit the situation, slowing down when presenting important or complex information and speeding up when summarizing. Use periodic pauses to emphasize important points.

Use correct diction. Avoid slurring or dropping off the endings of words (such as *goin* for *going* or *goverment* for *government*). Practice pronouncing difficult names, but also be alert to certain common words that are often mispronounced (such as *libary* for *library, Febuary* for *February,* or *athalete* for *athlete*).

Occasional hand and arm gestures are important for adding interest and emphasis, but only if they are appropriate and appear natural. If you never "talk with your hands" in normal conversation, it is unlikely you will do so naturally while presenting. Avoid annoying and distracting mannerisms and gestures such as jingling coins or keys in your pocket; coughing or clearing your throat excessively; wildly waving your hands; gripping the lectern tightly; nervously pacing; playing with jewelry, pens, or paper clips; or peppering your remarks with "and uh" or "you know."

Practice smiling occasionally, standing tall and natural with body balanced on both feet. Rest your hands on the podium, by your side, or in any

OBJECTIVE 5: Practice a presentation to develop an effective speaking style.

Use appropriate language, voice qualities, gestures, and posture.

Just about everyone in business will give at least one major
presentation and many smaller ones each year. For a
presentation to be effective, you must plan, organize,
develop appropriate visual aids, practice, and then utilize
appropriate delivery techniques while you are making the
presentation.
Source: (© *Ken Kaminski / The Picture Cube*)

natural, quiet position. Your voice and demeanor should reflect professionalism, enthusiasm, and self-confidence.

DELIVERING THE PRESENTATION

OBJECTIVE 6: Deliver a
presentation in a clear, confident, and efficient manner.

Your clothing is a part of the message you communicate to your audience,
so dress appropriately—in comfortable and businesslike attire. Try to dress
just slightly better than the average member of your audience; the audience
will be complimented by your efforts.

If you're speaking after a meal, eat lightly, avoiding heavy sauces,
desserts, and alcoholic beverages. As you're being introduced, take several
deep breaths to clear your mind, walk confidently to the front of the room,
take enough time to arrange yourself and your notes, look slowly around
you, establish eye contact with several members of the audience, and then,
in a loud, clear voice, begin your presentation.

In most environments, a microphone is not needed if you're speaking to
a group smaller than 150 people—10 to 12 rows of people. Your voice
should carry that far. Not using a microphone gives you more freedom to
move about and avoids problems with audio feedback and volume adjustments. If you will need to use a microphone, test it beforehand to see how
it operates and to determine the appropriate setting and height; the
microphone should be four to six inches from your mouth.

You should know your presentation well enough that you can maintain
eye contact easily with your audience, taking care to include members in

all corners of the room. If you lose your place in your notes or script, relax and take as much time as you need to regroup.

If your mind actually does go blank, try to keep talking—even if you repeat what you've just said. The audience will probably think you intentionally repeated the information for emphasis, and the extra time may jog your memory. If this doesn't work, simply skip ahead to another part of your presentation that you do remember; then come back later to the part you omitted.

Stage Fright

For some people, making a presentation is accompanied by such symptoms as these:

- Gasping for air
- Feeling faint or nauseated ("butterflies in the stomach")
- Having shaking hands or legs and sweaty palms
- Feeling the heart beat rapidly and loudly
- Speaking too rapidly and in a high-pitched voice

> To avoid anxiety, practice, develop a positive attitude, and concentrate on friendly faces.

If you have ever been subject to any of these symptoms, take comfort in the fact that you're not alone in experiencing "podium panic." Fear of giving a speech (specialists use the term "presentation phobia") is the Number 1 fear of most Americans. In a recent national poll of 3,000 people, 42% said the one thing they're most afraid of in life is giving a speech—even more so than having cancer or a heart attack.[9]

You have been asked to make a presentation because someone obviously thinks you have something important to say: You should feel complimented. Unless you are an exceptionally good or exceptionally bad speaker, the audience will more likely remember what you have to say rather than how you say it. Most of us fall somewhere between these two extremes as presenters.

Fortunately, behavior-modification experts have found that, of the full range of anxiety disorders, people can most predictably overcome their fear of public speaking.[10]

The best way to minimize any lingering anxiety is to follow the advice of coaches: the best defense is a good offense; that is, overprepare. For the anxious presenter, there is no such thing as overpractice. The more familiar you are with the content of your speech and the more trial runs you've made, the better you'll be able to concentrate on your delivery once you're actually in front of the group. Many presenters routinely memorize the first several sentences of their presentations just so they can approach those critical first moments (when anxiety is highest) with more confidence.

Before your presentation, take a short walk to relax your body. While waiting for your presentation to begin, let your arms drop loosely by your sides and shake your wrists gently, all the while breathing deeply several times. As you begin to speak, look for friendly faces in the crowd, and concentrate on them initially.

Some nervousness, of course, is good. It gets the adrenalin flowing and gives your speech an edge. If you do find that you're exceedingly nervous as you begin your speech, don't say something like "I'm so nervous this morning, my hands are shaking." Probably your audience hadn't noticed, but as soon as you bring it to their attention their eyes will immediately move to your shaking hands, thus creating a needless distraction and weakening your credibility.

Finally, the professional who is anxious about speaking in public should consider taking a public speaking course or joining Toastmasters International (P.O. Box 10400, 2200 North Grand, Santa Ana, CA 92711; phone: 714-542-6793), the world's oldest and largest nonprofit educational organization, with 5,600 clubs in 48 countries. The purpose of this organization is to improve the speaking skills of their members. They meet weekly or monthly and deliver prepared speeches, evaluate one another's oral presentations, give impromptu talks, develop their listening skills, conduct meetings, and learn parliamentary procedure.

Answering Questions

Plan your answers to possible questions ahead of time.

One of the advantages oral presentations have over written reports is the opportunity to engage in two-way communication. The question-and-answer session is a vital part of your presentation; plan for it accordingly.

Normally you should announce at the beginning of your presentation that you will be happy to answer any questions when you are through. Doing so prevents you from being interrupted and losing your train of thought midway through your presentation or possibly running out of time and not being able to complete your prepared remarks. Also, there is always the possibility that the listener's question will be answered later in the course of your presentation.

The exception to a questions-at-the-end policy is when your topic is so complex that a listener's question must be answered immediately, so he or she can follow the rest of the presentation. Another exception is informal (and generally small) meetings, where questions and comments naturally occur throughout the presentation.

As you prepare your presentation, anticipate what questions you might expect from the audience. Make a list of them and think through possible answers. If necessary, make notes to refer to while answering. If your list of questions is very long, you should probably consider revising your presentation to incorporate some of the answers into your prepared remarks.

Always listen carefully to the question; repeat it, if necessary, for the benefit of the entire audience; and look at the entire audience as you answer, not just at the questioner. Treat each questioner with unfailing courtesy. If the question is antagonistic, be firm but fair and polite.

If you don't know the answer to a question, freely say so and promise to have the answer within a specific period. Then write down the question to remind yourself to find the answer later. Do not risk embarrassing another member of the audience by referring the question to him or her.

If your call for questions results in absolute silence, you may conclude either that you did a superb job of explaining your topic or that no one wishes to be the first to ask a question. In the latter case, to break the ice, you might start the questions yourself, by saying something like "One question I'm frequently asked that might interest you is . . ." Or you may ask the program chair ahead of time to be prepared to ask the first question if no one in the audience begins.

After the presentation is over and you're back in your office, evaluate your performance so that you can benefit from the experience. What seemed to work well and what not so well? Analyze each aspect of your performance—from initial research through delivery. Regardless of how well the presentation went, vow to improve your performance next time.

OTHER BUSINESS PRESENTATIONS

In the standard type of business presentation discussed so far, you, the presenter, are the star of the show: you present information that is necessary to conduct the business of the organization, and you prepare your presentation carefully. Occasionally, you may be asked to participate in other types of presentations—ones in which you are a supporting player. Such situations include giving impromptu remarks, making introductions, and making or receiving special recognitions. In addition, you may sometimes be asked to participate in collaborative or video presentations.

> OBJECTIVE 7: Plan and deliver minor presentations, including impromptu remarks, introductions, and special recognitions.

Impromptu Remarks

During the course of a meeting or in conjunction with another person's presentation, you may unexpectedly be asked to come to the podium to "say a few words about" or "bring us up to date" on some topic. In truth, most such situations are not completely unexpected; you can often predict when you may be called on and should prepare accordingly. (Remember the words of Mark Twain: "It takes three weeks to prepare a good impromptu speech.")

Do not be put off by the fact that you may sometimes prepare remarks that will never be given because you were not called on to speak. Reviewing a situation and defining your ideas about it is always helpful, both as a management strategy and as preparation for future speaking opportunities.

> Anticipate and plan for situations when you may be asked to make impromptu remarks.

If, in fact, you truly have no warning, stay calm. You would not have been called on unless you had something positive to contribute. Remember also that the audience knows you are giving impromptu remarks, so they won't expect the same polish as for a prepared presentation. There is no need to apologize. Keep to the topic, limiting your remarks to those areas in which you truly do have some expertise or insight, and speak for no more than a few minutes.

Introductions

When introducing a speaker, remember that the speaker is the main event—not you. All your remarks should be directed at welcoming the speaker and establishing his or her qualifications to speak on the topic being addressed. Avoid inserting your own opinions about the topic or speaking for too long, thereby cutting into the speaker's time.

> Be gracious when introducing a speaker and keep the focus on the speaker.

Before the event, ask the speaker for his or her data sheet. Select from it those accomplishments that are particularly relevant to the current topic, add any personal asides such as hobbies or family information to show the speaker as human, and conclude with a statement such as "We're honored

to have with us Ms. Jane Doe, who will now speak on the topic of _____.
Ms. Doe." Lead the applause as the speaker rises and also when he or she
finishes speaking. Also lead the question-and-answer session if there is one,
and be prepared to ask the first question in case no one in the audience
wants to be first. At the conclusion, extend a sincere thank you to the
speaker.

If you are responsible for seating and introducing a head table, you and
the speaker should be seated on either side of the podium, with the speaker
at the immediate left as you face the audience and you, as master of
ceremonies, at the immediate right side of the podium. When making the
introductions, indicate whether each person should stand when introduced
or remain seated, and ask the audience to hold their applause until everyone
has been introduced. Then introduce each person, saying a few appropriate
remarks about each. Proceed from your extreme right to the podium and
then from your extreme left to the podium.

Give similar types and amounts of information about each person and
ensure that all names are pronounced correctly. Be consistent in identifying
each person—all first names or all personal titles and last names. When
you get to the speaker, introduce him or her in a similar manner, indicating
that a more complete introduction will follow. Lead the applause when all
have been introduced.

Special Recognitions

When presenting an award or recognizing someone for special achievement,
first provide some background about the award—its history and criteria
for selection. Then discuss the awardee's accomplishments, emphasizing
those most relevant to the award. Under such happy circumstances, extensive
praise is appropriate. Lead the applause as the awardee rises.

When accepting an honor, if you're expected to act surprised, do so—
even if you were tipped off beforehand and had an opportunity to prepare
some remarks. Show genuine appreciation and graciously thank those
responsible for the award. You may briefly thank those who helped in your
accomplishments, but do not bore the audience by thanking a long list of
people the audience may never have heard of.

▼
OBJECTIVE 8: Make
collaborative and video
presentations.

Collaborative Presentations

Collaborative presentations are quite common when communicating about
complex projects. For example, when presenting an organization's marketing
plan to management or updating the five-year plan, it is unlikely that any
one person has the expertise to prepare the entire plan and be able to
answer questions about all aspects of it. In such a situation, a cooperative
effort would be most effective.

As discussed in Chapter 2, collaborative presentations, whether written
or oral, require extensive planning, close coordination, and a measure of
maturity and goodwill. If you are responsible for coordinating such efforts,

allow enough time and assign responsibilities based on individual talents and time constraints.

Your major criterion for making assignments is what division of duties will result in the most effective presentation. Some members may be better at collecting and analyzing the information to be presented, others may be better at developing the visual aids, and others may be better at delivering the presentation. Everyone need not share equally in each aspect of the project. As coordinator, you can ensure that all efforts are recognized publicly and equally during the actual presentation, regardless of how much "podium time" each person is assigned.

Just as different people have different writing styles, they also have different speaking styles, and you must ensure that your overall presentation has coherence and unity, that it sounds as if it were given by the same person. Thus, the group members should decide beforehand the most appropriate tone, format, organization, style for visual aids, manner of dress, format for handling questions, and similar factors that will help the presentation flow smoothly from topic to topic and from speaker to speaker.

Full-scale rehearsals—in the room where the presentation will be made and using all visual aids—are crucial. If possible, they should be videotaped for later analysis by the entire group. Critiquing the performance of a colleague requires tact, empathy, and goodwill; and accepting such feedback requires grace and maturity. For the entire presentation to succeed, each individual element must also succeed. And if it does, each individual member shares in the success and any rewards that result.

> Make individual assignments for collaborative presentations based on individual strengths and preferences.

Video Presentations

Increasingly, organizations are videotaping presentations, which can then be presented on a television monitor using a videocassette recorder (VCR). For example, as part of an orientation program for new employees, the president of the organization may have videotaped a welcome speech and a personnel specialist may have taped a presentation of employee benefits. Or a marketing manager may have videotaped a new product announcement to be sent to important customers and the news media around the country. In fact, any presentation that must be given many times is a candidate for videotaping.

Most of the same principles presented earlier apply equally to video presentations. In addition, peculiar effects may result from facing the camera because gazing into the eye of the camera for a long time is such an artificial situation. The only solution is to practice. Fortunately, handheld video camcorders and VCRs are now so common that you can practice easily in the comfort of your own home or office.

> Practice your video presentation using a camcorder and VCR.

The best colors to wear are shades of blue; a light blue shirt or blouse with a blue jacket or blazer is ideal. Avoid contrasting colors and stripes. Makeup is recommended for both men and women to reduce sweat and even out skin tone. When recording, sit or stand straight and look into the camera as long as possible while talking. Always focus your eyes on one of two places—either directly at the camera or at your notes; never gaze off to the side or over the camera. Because television exaggerates movements, stand or sit as still as possible and keep gestures to a minimum.

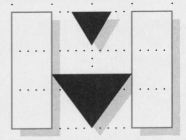

MICROWRITING   A BUSINESS PRESENTATION

The Problem

You are Matt Kromer, an information specialist at Lewis & Smith, a large import/export firm in San Francisco. Your company publishes three major external documents—a quarterly customer newsletter, a semiannual catalog, and an annual report. All three are currently prepared by an outside printing company. However, the decision was recently made to switch to some form of in-house publishing for these publications.

Three weeks ago, your superior asked you to research the question of whether your firm should use word processing or desktop publishing software for these documents. You were asked to make a formal 20-minute presentation of your findings and recommendations in two weeks to the firm's administrative committee.

The Process

1. What is the purpose of your presentation?

   To present the findings from my research, to recommend
   a software program, and to persuade the audience that
   my recommendation is sound.

2. Describe your audience.

   The Administrative Committee consists of the five managers (including my superior) who report to the vice
   president for administration. I have met them all, but,
   with the exception of my own superior, I do not know
   any of them well.
      Their role will be to make the final decision regard-
   ing which type of software program to use. Once that
   decision has been made, the actual users will decide
   which brand to purchase. Four of the five managers are
   casual users of word processing software. They've all
   likely heard of desktop publishing but have never used
   it.

3. What type of presentation will be appropriate?

   This will be a normal business presentation to a small
   audience, so I'll speak from notes and use transparencies. Because I only have 20 minutes to present, I'll
   hold off answering questions until the end—to make
   sure I have enough time to cover the needed
   information.

4. What kind of data have you collected for your presentation?

   I studied each publication's formatting requirements,
   analyzed the features of the most popular word
   processing ("Final Word") and desktop publishing
   ("Personal Editor") programs, and spoke with a

colleague from a firm that recently began publishing its documents in-house.

Based on the criteria of cost, ease of use, and features, I'll recommend the use of word processing software to publish our three documents.

5. How will you organize the data?

First I'll present the background information. Then I could organize my research data by presenting the advantages and disadvantages of each type of program. However, I think it would be more effective to organize my findings by criteria instead; that is, to show how each program rates in terms of (1) cost, (2) ease of use, and (3) features. These were the three criteria I used to make my recommendation decision.

6. Outline an effective opening section for your presentation.

a. <u>Introduction</u>: "Freedom of the Press" (desktop publishing gives us the freedom to publish our own documents at lower cost and with greater flexibility.)
b. <u>Purpose</u>: to recommend whether to use WP or DTP software
c. <u>Organization</u>: by criteria (cost, ease of use, and features)
d. <u>Audience role</u>: to make the final decision

7. How will you handle negative information?

Although I'm recommending word processing software, the desktop publishing program has more features. However, I'll show that (1) we don't need those features, and (2) those features make the program more difficult to learn.

8. What types of visual aids will you use?

<u>Transparencies</u>
Two at the beginning--to preview the topic and to illustrate our three publications
Two in the middle--to compare the costs and features of the two types of programs
Two at the end--to give my recommendation and to show what needs to be done next

<u>Handout</u>
A one-page handout showing miniature copies of the six transparencies--as a summary of my important points and for future reference

9. How will you practice your presentation?

I'll do one or two dry runs in the conference room where I'll be speaking, standing where I'll actually be giving the presentation and using my transparencies. I'll also set up a cassette recorder at the far end of the conference table to tape my practice presentation to ensure that I can be heard, to check for clarity and voice qualities, and to ensure that I'm within my time limits. I'll also practice answering any questions I think I might get.

The Product

Heading contains identifying information—for identification in case of loss and for reference in the future.

Uses an attention-getting opening that is written verbatim for a stress-free start.
Opening gives the purpose, previews the topics, and identifies the audience's role.

Alerts the audience to prevent interrupting questions and unnecessary note taking.

```
              SELECTING DESKTOP PUBLISHING SOFTWARE

10/3/-- Presentation to the Lewis & Smith Administrative Committee
              By Matt Kromer, Information Specialist
                     (Phone: 555-1086)

 I. OPENING
    A. I'd like to talk with you today about freedom of the press--
       specifically, about our recent decision to switch to in-
       house publishing. And though our publications won't be com-
       pletely "free," desktop publishing will provide us with
       more flexibility at a greatly reduced cost.

    B. Purpose of presentation: to recommend whether to use word
       processing or desktop publishing software to publish our
       company's newsletter, catalog, and annual report.
    TRANSPARENCY 1--FREEDOM OF THE PRESS
    C. Comments organized as follows:
       1. Background information
       2. Criteria for decision:
          a. Cost
          b. Ease of use
          c. Features
       3. Recommendation
    D. Your job: to make final decision regarding which type of
       software to support. You will not decide which brand of
       software; that decision will be left up to the users.
    E. Will be happy to answer any questions at the conclusion of
       my remarks. Also have a handout of my transparencies to
       distribute later.

II. BODY
    TRANSPARENCY 2--PUBLICATIONS
    A. Background information:
       1. We publish three major external documents, all of which
          have strategic marketing value:
          a. Newsletter: The Forum, sent quarterly to 2,000 cus-
             tomers; 8 pages; 1-color (black) on ivory stock with
             brown masthead; photos and line art.
          b. Catalog: semiannual; 36-42 pages;
             1-color (black) interior with 4-color cover; 4,000
             copies.

                              1
```

Mechanics Notes

Type the outline in large upper- and lowercase letters, either on individual notecards or on full sheets of paper. Leave plenty of white space (more than is shown here) between sections so that you won't lose your place.

       c. Annual report: annual; 24-28 pages; 1-color (blue) interior on grey stock with 4-color cover; 1,500 copies.

   2. All three presently prepared by Medallion Printing Company.

   3. Research:

       a. Analyzed each publication to determine formatting requirements.

       b. Analyzed features of Final Word, the word processing program we presently support and Personal Editor, the most popular desktop publishing software program (other DTP programs have similar features).

       c. Spoke with Paula Henning from Crown Busch; her company began producing their documents in-house using DTP last year.

B. Criteria:

TRANSPARENCY 3--COST COMPARISON

   1. Cost

       a. Either program will require
         (1) Font cartridge for each user's laser printer; cost--$195 ea.
         (2) One scanner and software to be shared by all users; cost--$1,450

       b. Final Word: $595 list; $475 mail order. But we already own.

       c. Personal Editor: $795 list; $595 mail order; cost for 3 copies--$1,785.

       d. Conclusion: Personal Editor costs $1,800 more than Final Word.

   2. Ease of use:

       a. Final Word:
         (1) Operators already know how to use because they use it every day for routine typing.
         (2) One half-day seminar must be developed to teach advanced features needed for DTP (taught by local community college faculty member); cost $500.

       b. Personal Editor:
         (1) Difficult to learn to use because of its many features; however, once learned, many features are easier to implement than on Final Word.
         (2) Danger of forgetting and having to relearn because Personal Editor will be used infrequently.
         (3) Would need to send three primary users to one-week seminar sponsored by Personal Editor at their Denver headquarters; cost: $450 tuition each plus travel, room, and board; estimated total cost--$3,750.

2

Discusses research procedures to help establish credibility.

Transparency references are well marked for easy identification.

The main part of the speech body is organized by the criteria used for making the decision.

Mechanics Notes

Presentation notes do not have to be in parallel format. No one will see the notes but you. You may need complete sentences to jog the memory for some parts but only partial sentences or even individual words for other parts.

Presents both positive and negative information and discusses the importance and implications of each feature.

Puts the final recommendation and the rationale on transparency—for emphasis.

Closing gives the recommendation and tells what happens next. Ends on a confident, forward-looking note.

Presentation is followed by a question-and-answer session.

```
               c. Considering all costs, Personal Editor costs three
                  times more than Final Word--$5,000 difference.
          TRANSPARENCY 4--FEATURE COMPARISON
            3. Features:
               a. Font flexibility: both have.
               b. Column feature: both have.
               c. Import/manipulate graphics: both have; Personal Edi-
                  tor has more options.
               d. Horizontal and vertical rules: both have; Personal
                  Editor has more options.
               e. Color separations: Personal Editor has; Final Word
                  does not (don't need now; maybe in the future).
               f. Predesigned templates: both have; Personal Editor
                  permits more elaborate designs (not needed).
               g. Ease of revisions (important criterion): Both allow,
                  but easier in Final Word (which has full WP fea-
                  tures). For Personal Editor, must first revise in a
                  WP file; then export to Personal Editor.

     III. CLOSING
          TRANSPARENCY 5--RECOMMENDATION
          A. Recommendation: Final Word
             1. Cheaper
             2. Easier to use/less training needed
             3. Has all the features we presently need
          TRANSPARENCY 6--SCHEDULE
          B. Schedule:
             1. Today: make decision regarding software.
             2. November: purchase and install hardware and software.
             3. December: conduct user training.
             4. January: begin producing three documents in-house.
          C. Our entry into desktop publishing is an exciting project
             because it gives us greater control over our publications
             at less cost. In addition, DTP will open up opportunities
             for even more publishing projects in the future to help us
             better fulfill our corporate mission.

          HANDOUT--SELECTING DESKTOP PUBLISHING SOFTWARE

      IV. QUESTIONS


                                  3
```

Mechanics Notes
The outline actually used for the presentation would undoubtedly have some last-minute handwritten insertions and changes.

Freedom of the Press

1. **Background**

2. **Criteria**
   - **Cost**
   - **Ease of Use**
   - **Features**

3. **Recommendation**

Publications

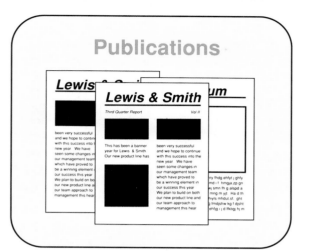

Cost Comparison

	Word Proc.	Desktop Pub.
Font Cartridge	585	585
Scanner	1,450	1,450
Software	—	1,785
	2,035	3,820
Training	500	3,750
TOTAL	**2,535**	**7,570**

Feature Comparison

	Word Proc.	Desktop Pub.
Fonts	Good	Good
Columns	Yes	Yes
Graphics	Good	Excellent
Rules	Good	Excellent
Color	No	Yes
Templates	Good	Excellent
Revisions	Excellent	Fair

Recommendation:
Word Processing

- **Costs $5,000 less**
- **Is easier to use**
- **Requires less training**
- **Includes all needed features**

Schedule

Today	*Make decision*
November	*Purchase and install*
December	*Conduct user training*
January	*Begin publishing*

SUMMARY

Business oral presentations are a vital part of the contemporary organization because they provide immediate feedback, give the presenter full control of the situation, and require less audience effort than do written presentations. However, oral presentations are impermanent and expensive, and the speaker-controlled pace means that some people in the audience may not be able to keep up with the flow of information. Managers need to develop their presentation skills in order to take advantage of these strengths and to avoid these weaknesses.

Planning the presentation requires determining the purpose, analyzing the audience, and planning the timing and method of presentation appropriate for the situation. Organizing the presentation requires developing an effective opening, developing each point logically in the middle, and closing on a strong, confident note. Visual aids should be relevant, simple, easily readable, and of high quality. Practice your presentation as much as necessary. When actually delivering the presentation, dress appropriately, speak in a clear and confident manner, and maintain eye contact with the audience. The final step in the process is evaluating your performance afterward to ensure that presentation skills improve with each opportunity to speak.

Other common types of oral presentations in business include impromptu remarks, introductions, and special recognitions. In addition to giving individual presentations before a live audience, managers frequently give collaborative presentations and occasionally may be called on to make a video presentation.

REVIEW AND DISCUSSION

► OBJECTIVE 1   1. What are the advantages and disadvantages of oral presentations as opposed to written reports?

► OBJECTIVE 2   2. Identify and give an example of each of the four principal purposes of oral presentations.

► OBJECTIVE 2   3. Give an example of a business situation in which it would be appropriate to deliver a presentation (a) by reading the speech and (b) by speaking from notes.

► OBJECTIVE 3   4. What types of information should be presented in the opening section of a presentation?

► OBJECTIVE 3   5. List six possible plans for organizing the body of a presentation.

► OBJECTIVE 3   6. What types of humor are appropriate in a business presentation, and under what circumstances should humor be used?

► OBJECTIVE 4   7. What criteria should be used for deciding to use visual aids in a business presentation?

► OBJECTIVE 4   8. What are the specific advantages of using transparencies, 35-mm slides, and handouts for a business presentation?

► OBJECTIVE 5   9. What type of language is most appropriate for business presentations?

► OBJECTIVE 5   10. What voice qualities are important when presenting business information orally?

11. What are some effective strategies for dealing with stage fright?   OBJECTIVE 6 ◀

12. Why is it best to delay asking and answering questions until the end   OBJECTIVE 6 ◀
of a presentation? Under what circumstances is this strategy not
recommended?

13. Explain the meaning of Mark Twain's observation that "It takes three   OBJECTIVE 7 ◀
weeks to prepare a good impromptu speech."

14. What special considerations must be addressed when preparing a   OBJECTIVE 8 ◀
collaborative presentation?

EXERCISES

1. **Understanding the Role of Business Presentations** Interview two   OBJECTIVE 1 ◀
business people in your community who hold positions in your area
of interest to learn more about their experiences in making oral
presentations. Write a memorandum to your instructor summarizing
what you've learned. You may want to ask such questions as the
following:

   a. How important has the ability to make effective oral presentations
   been to your career?

   b. What kinds of oral presentations do you make in and out of the
   office and how often?

   c. How do you typically prepare for them?

   d. What kinds of audiovisual aids do you use?

2. **Evaluating a Presentation** Attend a presentation given by a business   OBJECTIVE 1 ◀
person, perhaps a speaker at an event sponsored by a campus business
organization or one of the business or professional organizations in
your community. Critique the speaker's presentation in light of what
you've learned in this chapter, and submit a memorandum report to
your instructor.

3. **Planning a Presentation** You decided at the last minute to apply for   OBJECTIVE 2 ◀
graduate school at your institution to work toward an MBA degree.
Even though you have a 3.4 GPA (on a 4.0 scale), you were denied
admission because you had not taken the GMAT, which is a prerequisite
for admission. You have, however, been given 10 minutes to appear
before the Graduate Committee to try to convince them to grant you
a temporary waiver of this requirement and permit you to enroll in
MBA classes next term, during which time you will take the GMAT.
The Graduate Committee consists of the director of the MBA program
and two senior professors, one of whom is your business communication
professor.

   a. What is the purpose of your presentation?

   b. What do you know or what can you surmise about your audience
   that will help you prepare a more effective presentation?

   c. What considerations affect the timing of your presentation?

   d. What method of delivery will you use?

4. **Presenting Research Data** Review the analytical or recommendation   OBJECTIVES 2–6 ◀
report you prepared in Chapter 13. Assume that you have been given
15 minutes to present the important information from your written

report to a committee of your superiors who will not have an opportunity to read the written report.

a. Write your presentation notes, using either full sheets of paper or note cards.
b. Develop four to six overhead transparencies to use during your presentation.
c. Practice your presentation several times—at least once in the classroom where you will actually give it.
d. Give your presentation to the class. Your instructor may ask the audience to evaluate each presentation in terms of the effectiveness of its content, use of visual aids, and delivery.

▶ OBJECTIVES 2–4

5. **Presenting a Proposal**   Review Exercise 2 of Chapter 14, in which the Hospitality Services Association proposes to start a business, University Hosts, that would provide hospitality services for campus visitors. Assume that you have been given 10 minutes to present your proposal orally to the President's Council at your institution. Although you will use an outline for the body of your presentation, you decide to write in full your opening and closing remarks, because of the importance of both the topic and the audience.

a. Write a 1- to 1½-minute opening section for your presentation. Include an attention-getter.
b. Write a 1- to 1½-minute closing section for your presentation.
c. Prepare paper copies of the transparencies you will use for your presentation.

▶ OBJECTIVES 2–6

6. **Presenting Narrative Information**   Locate two journal articles on some aspect of business communication (the topics in the table of contents of this textbook will provide clues for searching). The two articles should be about the same topic. Integrate the important information from both articles, and present it to the class in a 5-minute presentation. Include at least one visual aid in your presentation. Prepare a one-page abstract that synthesizes the important information from both articles and distribute it as a handout to the class after your presentation. Submit to your instructor (1) a photocopy of each article, (2) a copy of your presentation notes, (3) a copy of your visual aids, and (4) a copy of your handout.

▶ OBJECTIVES 2–6

7. **Presenting Negative Information**   Your library probably has copies of the latest annual reports from many Fortune 500 companies. Select an annual report from a company that lost money last year. Assuming the role of that company's CEO, prepare and give a 10-minute presentation to give to a breakfast meeting of the New York Investment Council, a group made up of institutional investors and large private investors. Your purpose is to persuade the audience that your organization is still a good investment. Assume that the audience will have already seen a copy of your annual report. Select two visual aids contained in the annual report, and simplify them for use in your oral presentation.

▶ OBJECTIVES 2–8

8. **Collaborative Presentation**   Divide into groups of four or five students per team. Your instructor will assign you to either the pro or con side for one of the following topics:

- Drug testing should/should not be mandatory for all employees.
- All forms of smoking should/should not be banned completely from the workplace.
- Employers should/should not provide flex-time (flexible working hours) for all office employees.
- Employers should/should not provide on-site child-care facilities for the preschool children of its employees.
- Employees who deal extensively with the public should/should not be required to wear a company uniform.
- Employers should/should not have the right to hire the most qualified employees without regard to affirmative-action guidelines.

Assume that your employee group has been asked to present its views to a management committee that will make the final decision regarding your topic. The presentations will be given as follows:

a. Each side (beginning with the pro side) will have 8 minutes to present its views.
b. There will be a 3-minute period for each side to confer.
c. Each side (beginning with the con side) will have a 2-minute rebuttal—to answer the issues raised by the other side.
d. Each side (beginning with the pro side) will have a 1-minute summary.
e. The management committee (the rest of the class) will then vote by secret ballot regarding which side (pro or con) presented its case most effectively.

Gather whatever data you feel will be helpful to your case, organize it, prepare suitable visual aids, and divide up the speaking roles as you deem best. (*Hint:* It might be helpful to gather information on both the pro and con sides of the issue in preparation for the rebuttal session, which will be given impromptu.)

9. **Presenting to an International Audience** The West Coast manager of Honda has approached your School of Business about the possibility of sending 30 of its Japanese managers to your institution to pursue a three-month intensive course in written and oral business communication. The purpose of the course is to make the Japanese managers better able to interact with their American counterparts.

OBJECTIVES 2–4 ◀

You, the assistant provost at your institution, have been asked to give a six- to eight-minute presentation to the four Japanese executives who will decide whether to fund this program at your institution. The purpose of your presentation is to convince them to select your school.

Because of the care with which you will want to select your wording for this international audience and because of the high stakes involved, you decide to prepare a full script of your presentation (approximately 1,000 words), along with several overhead transparencies. Submit your script and transparency masters to your instructor.

10. **Evaluating Your Oral Communication Skills** Arrange to have an oral presentation that you prepared and gave for this chapter videotaped—either by using your institution's audiovisual services or by having a colleague videotape your presentation using a personal camcorder. Review the tape and evaluate your performance, using each of the 21 criteria given in Checklist 14. Prepare a memorandum to your instructor

OBJECTIVES 2–6 ◀

in which you objectively discuss the strengths and weaknesses of your presentation. Your grade for this assignment will be based on your *evaluation* of your presentation—not on the presentation itself. Submit both the videotape and the memorandum to your instructor.

C A S E   P R O B L E M

The Typists Who Lost Their Touch

▶ OBJECTIVES 2–8

Review the case problems presented at the end of Chapters 11–13, in which Jean Tate asked Pat Robbins to write a report on carpal tunnel syndrome, a neuromuscular wrist injury caused by repeated hand motions such as in typing. Assume the role of Pat Robbins. You have now been asked to present the results of your research in a 20-minute session to the executive committee, composed of Dave Kaplan and the three vice presidents. This is your first opportunity to speak to this high-ranking group, and it is on a topic about which you've developed strong feelings over the past few months as you've researched the topic in depth.

Prepare as many of the following projects as assigned by your instructor. (*Note:* If you did not conduct any primary research for this project, base your presentation on secondary data.)

1. Analyze your audience. Prepare a memo report to your instructor giving the results of your analysis—telling specifically how what you know about each of the executive committee members will affect your presentation.
2. Write your presentation notes, using either full sheets of paper or note cards.
3. Develop five to eight overhead transparencies to use during your presentation.
4. Arrange to have a full-scale practice session of your presentation videotaped—either using the services of your institution's audiovisual department or borrowing a camcorder and having a colleague videotape your practice presentation.
5. View your practice videotape in terms of the guidelines presented in this chapter. Prepare a memo to your instructor critiquing your performance. Submit both your memo and the videotape.
6. Divide into groups of five students, with each student in turn giving his or her presentation. Each presenter should conduct a question-and-answer session immediately after each presentation. Be prepared to ask questions of the presenter and to answer any questions directed to you when you present. Prepare a memo to your instructor critiquing the performance of each presenter.

■ Only one common word can be spelled correctly three ways and have the same meaning: *ketchup, catchup,* and *catsup.*

■ Language experts say that the most widely used word in the world is the word *OK,* spelled variously.

■ Did you hear about the editor of *Roget's Thesaurus* who was fired? He was shocked, horrified, astonished, disturbed, astounded, upset, perturbed, agitated, unsettled, disconcerted, and thrown off guard.

CHAPTER

Business Meetings and Other Types of Nonwritten Communication

Communication Objectives

After you have completed this chapter, you will be able to

1. Plan a business meeting.

2. Determine effective problem-solving strategies for meetings.

3. Conduct a meeting according to parliamentary procedure.

4. Prepare minutes of a meeting.

5. Understand the causes and effects of poor listening skills.

6. Listen effectively in business situations.

7. Use effective techniques for conducting business via the telephone.

8. Dictate business messages.

9. Use business etiquette to maintain effective working relationships.

To meet or not to meet? That's the first question, says Peter Atwood, Vice President of International Marketing and Sales for Newport Technologies, a Rhode Island manufacturer of computer software. Atwood, a former Director of International Marketing for Xerox and an entrepreneur who merged his own software company with Newport Technologies, believes that many corporate managers don't know the answer. He says that many managers are too quick to call their coworkers together for an in-house conference.

"Within a company, two people can get a lot done by phone without getting together face-to-face," says Atwood. "If you do call a group together, your subject had better be important, and you'd better not waste peoples' time."

When, in Atwood's opinion, is a meeting warranted? Atwood calls his staffers together if the subject to be discussed involves a group that must work together. He calls meetings if the subject is so complicated that a question-and-answer session is required to adequately explain it. And he convenes a meeting if there are several different subjects that must be discussed.

But before Peter Atwood calls anyone anywhere, he thinks carefully about *what* he's going to tell them. When he's determined that, he thinks about *how* he's going to tell them.

"If you haven't done your homework, you're dead," says Atwood. "If you're the guy responsible for running a meeting, you not only have to make it useful,

Peter Atwood, Vice President
of International Marketing
and Sales, Newport
Technologies International,
Newport, Rhode Island

you have to make it informative and entertaining. And that is sometimes difficult to do."

Exactly what Atwood prepares depends on who's meeting with whom. "In a sales meeting," says Atwood, "you've got to be very pizzazzy. You need your visuals, your overhead graphics. You may have an account that could be spending $200,000, and they need to feel that they are getting their money's worth while they are there."

On the other hand, says Atwood, if the meeting involved senior management, he would expect to follow a parliamentary procedure. "A meeting of management would be run very much by the book," says Atwood. "Meetings with somebody coming in from outside the company would be more relaxed. Without the bureaucracy of the company itself, the formal atmosphere doesn't apply."

Each year, says Atwood, the decision to meet or not to meet is harder to make, because new technologies like teleconferencing and video conferencing offer us convenient alternatives to face-to-face discourse. And while Atwood appreciates such physical convenience, he tries not to overlook one advantage of people sitting down with people.

"With face-to-face meetings you get better readings in your interactions with people," says Atwood. "You can read a lot as to what is going on around a conference table. You tend to lose that feeling with multi-media. When I'm not in the same room with the person, I have to work harder to make sure that what I heard is not what I *thought* I heard, but what I actually heard. I know from personal experience, on a conference call with five parties, you press the mute button and make a comment about the guy from California, and the rest of them don't know what's going on. Multi-media communication is great, but face-to-face is still the best way to convey that effort. Even with worldwide transactions, that's still the preference. People like to shake hands in the morning and again when they leave at night. People still like face-to-face."

Finally, corporate vice president Peter Atwood advises managers to sharpen the communicating skill that, he says, has remained singularly important throughout his 20 years of business meetings. That skill is listening to what other people at the meeting say. ▼

BUSINESS MEETINGS

In Chapter 15 we discussed oral presentations. As important as such presentations are, most managers spend more of their time communicating in other ways, such as conducting business meetings, listening, using the telephone, and dictating messages. To be effective in such tasks and to maintain effective working relationships, managers must communicate in a polite and appropriate manner. These important topics—conducting a business meeting, listening, using the telephone, dictating, and behaving appropriately and politely in the business environment—are introduced in this chapter.

Meetings serve a wide variety of purposes in the organization. They keep members informed of events helpful in carrying out their duties; they provide a forum for soliciting input, solving problems, and making decisions; and the social interaction promotes unity and cohesiveness among the members.

Considering these important purposes, it is not surprising that as many as 11 million meetings take place each day in America—twice as many as ten years ago. The average executive spends 25% to 70% of his or her day in meetings—and considers about a third of them to be unproductive. No wonder many managers complain that "meetingitis" has become a national plague in American business.[1]

Yet the ability to conduct and participate in meetings is a crucial managerial skill. One survey of more than 2,000 business leaders showed that executives who run a meeting well are perceived to be better managers by both their superiors and their peers.[2]

To use meetings as an effective managerial tool, you need to know not only how to run them but also when to call them and how to follow up afterward. Like so many decisions you will make about communication, your choices will be guided by what you hope to accomplish. See Checklist 15 for guidelines on how to manage business meetings.

> Effective managers know how to run and participate in business meetings.

Planning the Meeting

When you add up the hourly salaries plus fringe benefits of those planning and attending a meeting, the cost can be considerable. Managers must make sure they're getting their money's worth from a meeting, and that requires careful planning: identifying the purpose and determining that a meeting is in fact necessary, preparing an agenda, deciding who should attend, and planning the logistics.

> OBJECTIVE 1: Plan a business meeting.

Identifying Your Purpose and Determining That a Meeting is Necessary   The first step is always to determine your purpose. The more specific you can be, the better results you will get. A purpose such as "to discuss how to make our marketing representatives more effective" is vague and, therefore, not as helpful as "to decide whether to purchase cellular phones for our marketing representatives." The more focused your purpose, the easier it will be to select a means of accomplishing that purpose.

CHECKLIST 15 # Business Meetings

Planning the Meeting

1. Identify the purpose of the meeting.

2. Determine whether a meeting is the most appropriate method for achieving your purpose or whether a memorandum or phone call would achieve your purpose more efficiently.

3. Prepare an agenda for distribution to the participants.

4. Decide who should attend the meeting.

5. Determine the logistics of the meeting—timing, location, room and seating arrangements, and types of audiovisual equipment needed.

Conducting the Meeting

6. Encourage punctuality by beginning every meeting on time.

7. Begin each meeting by stating the purpose of the meeting and reviewing the agenda.

8. Establish ground rules that permit the orderly transaction of business. Many organizations follow parliamentary procedure.

9. Control the discussion to ensure that it is relevant, that a few members do not monopolize the discussion, and that all members have an opportunity to be heard.

10. If your purpose is to solve a problem, adopt an appropriate strategy for reaching a decision, such as using the scientific method, brainstorming, buzz groups, nominal group techniques, the Delphi technique, listening teams, or role-playing.

11. At the end of the meeting, summarize what was decided, what the next steps are, and what each member's responsibilities are.

Following Up the Meeting

12. Before the meeting, assign someone the task of making notes during the meeting. These notes should be objective, accurate, and complete.

13. If the meeting was routine and informal, you may follow it up with a memorandum summarizing the major points of the meeting. However, minutes should be prepared and distributed for more formal meetings.

Meetings are not always the most efficient means of achieving your objective.

Sometimes meetings are not the most efficient means of communication. Very seldom is a face-to-face meeting the most efficient way of communicating routine information. A simple memorandum performs that function more efficiently. Similarly, it doesn't make sense to use the weekly staff meeting of ten people to hold a long discussion involving only one or two members. A phone call or smaller meeting would accomplish that task quicker and at less cost.

However, alternative means of conveying or securing information often present their own problems. Some people don't read written messages carefully or they interpret them in different ways. Time is lost in transmitting and responding to written messages. And information may be garbled as it moves from person to person and from one level to another.

Preparing an Agenda   Once you've established your specific purpose, you need to consider in more detail what topics, and in what order, the meeting will cover. This list of topics, or **agenda,** will accomplish two things: it will help you prepare for the meeting by showing what background information you'll need and it will help you run the meeting by keeping you focused on your topic.

> An agenda helps focus the attention of both the leader and the participants.

Knowing what topics will be discussed will also help those attending the meeting to plan for the meeting effectively—reviewing needed documents, bringing needed records, deciding what questions need to be raised, and the like. The survey of 2,000 business leaders mentioned earlier revealed that three-fourths of the managers consider agendas to be essential for efficient meetings; yet nearly half the meetings they attend are *not* accompanied by written agendas.[3]

Formal, recurring business meetings follow an agenda like this:

1. Call to order
2. Roll call
3. Reading and approval of minutes of previous meeting
4. Reports of officers and standing committees
5. Reports of special committees
6. Unfinished business
7. New business
8. Announcements
9. Program
10. Adjournment

Every meeting will not, of course, contain all these elements. Each item to be covered under these headings should be identified, including the speaker, if other than the chair:

   7. NEW BUSINESS
      a. Review of December 3 press conference
      b. Recommendation for annual charitable contribution
      c. Status of remodeling—Jan Fischer

Deciding Who Should Attend   A great number of ad hoc meetings take place each business day for the purpose of solving a specific problem. If you must decide who will attend a particular meeting, your first concern is how the participants relate to your purpose. Who will make the decision? Who will implement the decision? Who can provide needed background information? On the one hand, you want to include all who can contribute to solving the problem; on the other, you want to keep the meeting to a manageable number of people.

Consider also how the potential group members differ in status within the organization, in knowledge about the issue, in communication skills, and in personal relationships. The greater the differences, the more difficult

> Everyone at the meeting should have a direct reason for being there.

it will be to involve everyone in a genuine discussion aimed at solving the problem.

Consider also any "hidden agendas" of potential group members. If any member's personal goals for the meeting differ from the group goals, conflicts can arise and the quality of the resulting decisions can be impaired. Meeting separately with some of the important participants ahead of time might help to identify sources of problems and provide clues for dealing with them.

Membership in recurring meetings (such as a weekly staff meeting or a committee meeting) is relatively fixed. Even for these meetings, however, the planner must decide whether outsiders will be invited to observe, participate, or simply be available as resource people.

Determining Logistics   It would be unwise to schedule a meeting that requires extensive discussion and creative problem solving at the end of the workday, when members will be drained emotionally and physically. Likewise, it would be counterproductive to schedule a three-hour meeting in a room equipped with uncushioned fold-up chairs, poor lighting, and extreme temperatures.

Instead, facilitate group problem solving by making intelligent choices about the timing and location of the meeting, room and seating arrangements, types of audiovisual equipment, and the like. Doing so will increase the likelihood of achieving the goals of the meeting.

Increasingly, another logistical consideration is whether to hold a face-to-face meeting or a **teleconference**, a meeting in which members in different locations are linked by simultaneous electronic communications, using cameras, projection screens, microphones, and computer equipment (see the "Spotlight on Technology").

Conducting a Meeting

Planning for a meeting goes a long way toward ensuring its success, but the manager's job is by no means over when the meeting begins. A manager must be a leader during the meeting, keeping the group focused on the point and encouraging participation.

An efficient leader begins and ends each meeting on time.

Punctuality   Unless a high-level member or one whose input is vital to conducting business is tardy, make it a habit to begin every meeting on time. Doing so will send a powerful nonverbal message to chronic late arrivers that business will be conducted and decisions made whether they're present or not.

If you wait for late-comers, you send the message to those who *were* punctual that they wasted their time by being prompt. As a result, they will probably arrive late for subsequent meetings. And the chronic late arrivers will then begin arriving even later! Avoid this vicious cycle by beginning (and ending) at the appointed times.

Closing the door when the meeting begins tells late arrivers that they cannot slip in unobtrusively, and they may make a more determined effort to arrive on time. Some meeting planners also arrange the agenda with an eye toward chronic late-comers—placing those items of most importance to late-comers early in the meeting.

S P O T L I G H T   ON TECHNOLOGY

THE ELECTRONIC MEETING

Even before the Persian Gulf War, video conferencing had been enjoying major growth throughout the industrialized world, with 1990 revenues exceeding $500 million. But, with increasing travel restrictions, the increased possibility of airline terrorism, and the increased need to communicate business-plan changes brought about by war conditions, the Gulf War spurred even greater growth in electronic meetings. Several major companies (such as AT&T, MCI, and US Sprint) saw demand triple within a matter of weeks.

The possibility of holding electronic meetings became a reality when American Telephone and Telegraph introduced its Picturephone at the 1964 World's Fair in New York. Since that time, advances in computer and communication technology have made video conferencing more affordable and more effective.

In a video conference, meetings are held in two specially equipped meeting rooms in different parts of the country. These conference rooms may be in the company's own buildings or in public conference rooms at hotels. For example, such large firms as Exxon, Sears, IBM, J. C. Penney, and Hughes Aircraft have installed video conference rooms, as have many Hilton Hotels and Holiday Inns. These rooms contain cameras, projection screens, and microphones that enable participants at one location to see and hear what transpires at the other location or at several other locations.

The major advantages of video conferencing is, of course, the savings in time and cost for executive travel; it may take executives one or more days of travel time to attend a one-hour meeting. Also, because no travel is involved, more executives can participate in video conferences, and as many visual aids can be used as needed. A final advantage, of course, is that most people are more comfortable on their own turf and are more likely to be able to contribute more effectively than if interacting in an unfamiliar environment.

Video conferences have not replaced face-to-face meetings partly because of the cost and partly because of the communication environment. Some managers are uncomfortable in front of a camera and worry about how they look, act, and sound. Also, some managers miss being able to assess nonverbal cues easily and miss the personal chemistry that develops more easily in face-to-face meetings. These self-conscious feelings are likely to diminish as managers become more familiar with the medium and develop more experience in conducting business this way.

Prices are decreasing at the same time that quality and ease of use are increasing. The video conference room that cost $250,000 to equip just a few years ago costs about $50,000 today, with another 50% price reduction projected within a year or two.

Technology is also helping make face-to-face meetings more productive. For example, overhead projectors connected to computers enable everyone to view an image from a small computer monitor on a large projection screen. Chalkboards are being replaced by electronic copyboards, which make photocopies of anything written on their surface for immediate distribution. Brainstorming is made easier by using outlining software programs, which let you expand and contract topics, create and delete headings and subheadings, and organize the information easily.

Another innovation is the use of a "technographer," a specially trained manager who acts as a meeting facilitator. During the meeting, the technographer works with computer equipment to keep track of ideas generated during the meeting, make notes of who said what, help organize the information, and then produce a final document that represents the consensus of the group. Special polling software (such as OptionFinder® by Option Technologies, Inc.) enables group members to be polled electronically, with the results immediately available on a projection screen.

Whether managers meet across the table or across the country, technology is helping them communicate more effectively in meetings.

Sources: "Computers the Key to More Productive Meetings," *Presentation Products Magazine*, August 1989, p. 48; Janet Guyon, "Video Conferencing May Soon Come Alive," *Wall Street Journal*, January 16, 1989, p. B1; Steve Higgins, "OptionFinder 3.1 Aims to Bolster Productivity of Corporate Meetings," *PC Week*, December 11, 1989, p. 43; Carla Lazzareschi, "War Speeds Shift to New Phone Technology," *Los Angeles Times*, January 24, 1991, p. D1; Pamela Sebastian, "Business Bulletin: Video Conferencing Locks on a Market," *Wall Street Journal*, February 7, 1991, p. 1.

Following the Agenda   One of the keys to a focused meeting is to follow the agenda. At formal meetings you will be expected to discuss all items on the published agenda and no items not on the agenda. The more informal the meeting, the more flexibility you have in allowing new topics to be

Ensure that all discussion relates to the purpose of the meeting.

introduced. It's always possible that new information that has a bearing on your problem may come up. To prevent discussion simply because you didn't include the item on your agenda would make it more difficult for you to achieve your purpose. But as leader of the meeting, you must make certain that new topics are directly relevant.

Leading the Meeting Besides following the agenda, there are other steps involved in leading a meeting. Begin meetings with a statement of your purpose and an overview of the agenda. As the meeting progresses, keep track of time. Don't let the discussion get bogged down in details.

Preventing people from talking too much or digressing from the topic requires tact. Comments like "I see your point, and that relates to what we were just discussing" can keep you on track without offending the speaker. You'll also need to encourage the participation of the quieter members of the group with comments like "John, how does this look from the perspective of your department?"

▼
OBJECTIVE 2: Determine effective problem-solving strategies for meetings.

If your purpose is to solve a problem, you should consider ahead of time how you will structure the discussion. There are a number of problem-solving strategies that help groups make decisions:

- *Scientific method:* As a group, identifying in turn the problem, its causes, the criteria for solution, possible solutions, the one best solution, and, finally, the means of implementing that solution.
- *Brainstorming:* Generating as many creative ideas as possible without regard to their feasibility and then evaluating each potential solution in terms of relevant criteria.
- *Buzz groups:* Dividing into subgroups to discuss a particular aspect of a problem or solution and then reporting back to the entire group, with large-group discussion following.
- *Nominal group technique:* Generating individual evaluations first and then merging them into an averaged master list.
- *Delphi technique:* Generating individual evaluations first and then individually revising them based on feedback from the group.
- *Listening teams:* Assigning subgroups a specific listening task (e.g., to listen for any cost implications during the discussion or to listen for any sources of resistance) to avoid losing any information during group presentations and discussions.
- *Role playing:* Solving human-relations or management problems by having participants play other people's roles based on their perceptions of how those people do or should act.

The particular strategy you use will, of course, depend on the nature and importance of the problem and the skills of the group members. For some topics and groups, a simple discussion is all that is needed.

As leader, you'll sometimes have to resolve conflicts among members. Your first step is to make sure all members understand the facts involved and that you and everyone else understand each person's position. You then need to examine what each person's goals are and search for alternatives that will satisfy the largest number of goals.

At the end of the meeting, you should summarize for everyone what the meeting has accomplished. What was decided? What are the next steps? Make sure everyone understands his or her responsibilities.

During the meeting someone should take notes. Either an assistant, the leader, or someone the leader designates should record what happens. That person must report objectively and not impose his or her own biases.

Parliamentary Procedure   Every group needs to adopt ground rules that permit the orderly transaction of business in meetings. The larger the group and the more important their mission, the more important it is to establish written rules of order (called **parliamentary procedure**). Imagine the chaos that could result if a meeting did not follow the basic rule that only one person can have the floor and speak at a time!

The basis for parliamentary procedure is that the minority shall be heard, but that the majority shall prevail. The basic reference for parliamentary procedure—the authority used by governments, associations, and business organizations the world over—is *Robert's Rules of Order*.[4] The rationale for using parliamentary procedure is given in the preface of this reference book:

> The application of parliamentary law is the best method yet devised to enable assemblies of any size, with due regard for every member's opinion, to arrive at the general will on a maximum number of questions of varying complexity in a minimum time and under all kinds of internal climate ranging from total harmony to hardened or impassioned division of opinion.[5] [*NOTE:* This 61-word sentence, incidentally, is probably as good an example as you're likely to find of a long sentence that communicates its message clearly and effectively.]

Robert's Rules of Order was written in 1896 by Gen. Henry M. Robert, a U.S. Army officer who was active in many civic and educational organizations, and has been revised periodically since then. The current edition contains more than 650 pages of rules and procedures; those that are most helpful for running the typical business meeting are summarized in Figure 16.1.

Knowledge of basic parliamentary procedures is a strategic communication skill for managers. Anyone who runs a business meeting, whether at work or in connection with a professional, civic, or social organization, would do well to become familiar with the basic requirements of conducting business in a parliamentary manner.

OBJECTIVE 3: Conduct a meeting according to parliamentary procedure.

Following Up the Meeting

Routine meetings may require only a short memorandum as a follow-up to what was decided. Formal meetings or meetings where controversial ideas were discussed may require a more formal summary.

Minutes are an official record of the proceedings of a meeting; they summarize what was discussed and what decisions were made. Generally, they should emphasize what was *done* at the meeting, not what was *said* by the members. Minutes may, however, present an intelligent summary of the points of view expressed on a particular issue, without names attached, followed by the decision made. Avoid presenting minutes that are either so short they lack the "flavor" of what transpired or that are so long that they tend not to be read.

OBJECTIVE 4: Prepare minutes of a meeting.

FIGURE 16.1   Parliamentary Procedure for Business Meetings

To Do This:	You Say This:	Interrupt the speaker?	Need a second?	Debatable?	Amendable?	Vote needed?
Main Motions						
Make a main motion	*I move that ...*	yes	yes	yes	yes	maj
Secondary Motions						
Adjourn	*I move that we adjourn.*	no	yes	no	no	maj
Amend a motion	*I move to amend by ...*	no	yes	yes	yes	maj
Appeal a chair's ruling	*I appeal the decision of the chair.*	yes	yes	yes	no	maj
Ask a question	*I rise to a point of information.*	yes	no	no	no	none
Call for a secret ballot	*I move the vote be taken by ballot.*	no	yes	no	yes	maj
Call for standing or show-of-hands vote	*I call for a division.*	yes	no	no	no	none
Close debate	*I move the previous question.*	no	yes	no	no	2/3
Close nominations	*I move to close nominations.*	no	yes	no	yes	2/3
Consider parts of a motion separately	*I move to divide the question.*	no	yes	no	yes	maj
Lay the pending motion aside temporarily	*I move to lay the question on the table*	no	yes	no	no	maj
Point out a rule violation	*I rise to a point of order.*	yes	no	no	no	none
Postpone to a certain time	*I move to postpone the question until ...*	no	yes	yes	yes	maj
Postpone indefinitely	*I move to postpone the question indefinitely.*	no	yes	yes	no	maj
Raise a point of parliamentary procedure	*I rise to a parliamentary inquiry.*	yes	no	no	no	none
Refer a motion to a committee	*I move to refer the question to ...*	no	yes	yes	yes	maj
Require that the agenda be followed	*I call for orders of the day.*	yes	no	no	no	none
State a request affecting one's rights	*I rise to a question of privilege.*	yes	no	no	no	none
Suspend the rules	*I move to suspend the rule ...*	no	yes	no	no	2/3
Take a recess	*I move that we take a ... recess*	no	yes	no	yes	maj
Motions That Bring a Question Again Before the Assembly						
Reconsider a previously passed motion	*I move to reconsider the vote on ...*	no	yes	yes	no	maj
Revoke action taken at previous meeting	*I move to rescind the motion relating to ... adopted at the May meeting.*	no	yes	yes	yes	2/3[a]
Take from the table	*I move to take the question from the table.*	no	yes	no	no	maj

[a] Requires a 2/3 vote if no prior notice has been given, majority vote if prior notice has been given.

> The minutes should be accurate, objective, and complete.

The first paragraph of the minutes should identify the type of meeting (regular or special); the date, time, and place; the presiding officer; the names of those present (or absent) if a customary part of the minutes; and the fact that the minutes were read and approved.

The body of the minutes should contain a separate paragraph for each topic. According to parliamentary procedure, the name of the maker of a motion, but not the seconder, should be entered in the minutes. It is often helpful to use the same subheadings as used in the agenda; for example:

Parliamentary Procedure (*continued*)   **FIGURE 16.1**

Miscellaneous Notes

1. Types of motions:
   a. A main motion brings an action before the group. It may be made only when no other motion is pending and must be made and seconded before it can be discussed.
   b. A secondary motion may be made and considered while a main motion is pending and must be acted on before the main motion can be considered further.
   c. A motion that brings a question again before the assembly enables the group to reconsider an action disposed of earlier.
2. Special rules adopted by the group take precedence over *Robert's Rules of Order.*
3. Unless otherwise specified, a majority of the membership constitutes a quorum (the minimum number of members who must be present to transact business).
4. A vote is not required to approve the minutes of the previous meeting. They are simply accepted as read and/or distributed, or they are accepted as corrected.
5. A vote is not required to accept a committee report. However, committee recommendations that require action must be voted on. Motions made on behalf of the committee do not require a second.
6. The purpose of tabling a motion is to enable the group to consider a more urgent matter that has arisen. If the tabled motion is not taken from the table by the next regularly scheduled meeting, the question dies.
7. The purpose of postponing a motion definitely is to defer action until a later date (e.g., when more information has been gathered). The purpose of postponing a motion indefinitely is to avoid taking action on the motion, thereby killing it.
8. The motion to reconsider a previously passed motion must be made at the same meeting as the original vote and must be made by someone from the prevailing (majority) side of the original vote.
9. After a motion has been made and seconded, the chair repeats the motion before calling for discussion and again before calling for the vote.

Review of December 3 Press Conference

A videotape of the December 3 press conference conducted by Donita Doyle was viewed and discussed. Roger Eggland's motion that "Donita Doyle be commended for the professional and ethical manner in which she presented the company's views at the December 3 press conference" was adopted unanimously without debate.

<u>Recommendation for Annual Charitable Contribution</u>

Tinrah Porisupatani moved "that American Chemical
donate $15,000 to a worthwhile charity operating in
Essex County." Linda Peters moved to amend the motion
by inserting the words "an amount not exceeding"
after the word "donate." On a motion by Todd Chandler,
the motion to make a donation, with the pending
amendment, was referred for further study to the Social
Responsibility Committee with instructions to recommend
a specific amount and charity and report at the next
meeting.

The last paragraph of the minutes should state the time of adjournment and, if appropriate, the time set for the next meeting. The minutes should be signed by the person preparing them. If someone other than the chair prepares the minutes, they should be read and approved by the chair before being distributed.

LISTENING

Effective communication requires both sending and receiving messages—both transmission and reception. Whether you are making a formal presentation to 500 people or conversing with one person over lunch, your efforts will be in vain if your audience does not listen.

Listening involves much more than just hearing. Hearing is simply perceiving sound; sound waves strike the eardrum, sending impulses to the brain. Hearing is a passive process, whereas listening is an active process. If you *perceive* a sound, you're merely aware of it; you don't necessarily comprehend it. When you *listen*, you interpret and assign meaning to the sounds.

> There is a difference
> between hearing and
> listening.

Consider the automobile you drive. When the car is operating normally, you're barely aware of the sound of the engine as you're driving; you tune it out. But as soon as the engine begins to make a strange sound—not necessarily louder or harsher, but just *different*, you immediately tune back in—listening intently to try to discern the nature of the problem. You *heard* the normal hum of the engine but *listened to* the strange noise.

The Problem of Poor Listening Skills

OBJECTIVE 5: Understand the causes and effects of poor listening skills.

Listening is the communication skill we use the most. White-collar workers typically devote at least 40% of their workday to listening.[6] Yet, after hearing a ten-minute oral presentation, the average person retains only 50% of the information. Forty-eight hours later, only 25% of what was heard can be recalled.[7] Thus, listening is probably the least developed of the four verbal communication skills (writing, reading, speaking, and listening).

One of the major causes of poor listening is that most people have simply not been taught how to listen well. Think back to your early years in school. How much class time was devoted to teaching you to read and write? How many opportunities were you given to read aloud, participate in plays, and speak before a group? Chances are that reading, writing, and perhaps speaking were heavily stressed in your education. But how much formal training have you had in listening? If you're typical, the answer is not much.

Another factor that contributes to poor listening skills is the disparity between the normal speed of speech and the speed with which our brains can process data; that is, we can think much faster than we can speak— about four times faster. Thus, when listening to others, our minds may begin to wander, and we lose our ability to concentrate on what is being said.

The effects of poor listening skills include such problems as instructions not being followed, equipment broken from misuse, sales lost, feelings hurt, morale lowered, productivity decreased, rumors started, and health risks increased. Still, poor listening skills are not as readily apparent as poor speaking or writing skills. It's easy to spot a poor speaker or writer but much more difficult to spot a poor listener because a poor listener can fake attention. In fact, the poor listener may not even be aware of his or her weak listening skills. He or she may mistake hearing for listening.

Keys to Better Listening

To learn to listen more effectively, whether you're involved in a one-on-one dialogue or are part of a mass audience, give the speaker your undivided attention, stay open-minded, avoid interrupting, and involve yourself in the communication.

OBJECTIVE 6: Listen effectively in business situations.

Give the Speaker Your Undivided Attention   During a business presentation, a member of the audience may hear certain familiar themes, think, "Oh no, not that again," and proceed to tune the speaker out. Or during a conference with a subordinate, an executive may make or take phone calls, doodle, play around with a pen or pencil, or do other distracting things that give the person talking the impression that what he or she has to say is unimportant or uninteresting.

Physical distractions are the easiest to eliminate. Simply shutting the door or asking your assistant to hold all calls will eliminate many interruptions during personal conferences. If you're in a meeting where the environment is noisy, the temperature too cold or hot, or the chairs uncomfortable, try to tune out the distractions rather than the speaker. Learn to ignore those distractions over which you have no control and concentrate instead on the speaker and what he or she is saying.

Mental distractions are more difficult to eliminate. But with practice and effort, you can discipline yourself, for example, to temporarily forget about your tiredness or to put competing thoughts out of your mind so that you can give the speaker your attention.

Just as it is important for the speaker to maintain eye contact, it is also important for the listener to maintain eye contact with the speaker. Doing so sends the message that you're interested in what the speaker has to say, and the speaker will be more likely to open up to you and provide the information you need.

We talk about giving the speaker your undivided attention. Actually, it would be more accurate to say that you should give the speaker's *comments* your undivided attention; that is, you should focus on the content of the talk and not be overly concerned about how the talk is delivered. It is true,

Pay more attention to what the speaker says than to how he or she says it.

of course, that nonverbal clues do provide important information. However, do not be put off by the fact that the speaker may have dressed inappropriately, spoken too fast or in an unfamiliar accent, or appeared nervous. Almost always, what is said is more important than how it is said.

Likewise, avoid dismissing a topic simply because it is uninteresting or is presented in an uninteresting manner. Boring does not mean unimportant. Some information that may be boring or difficult to follow may in fact prove to be quite useful to you and thus well worth your efforts to give it your full attention.

Stay Open-Minded   Regardless of whom you're listening to or what the topic is, keep your emotions in check. Listen objectively and empathetically. Be willing to accept new information and new points of view, regardless of whether they agree with your existing beliefs. Concentrate on the content of the message rather than on its source.

Don't look at the situation as a win-or-lose proposition; that is, don't consider that the speaker wins and you lose if you concede the merits of his or her position. Instead, think of it as a win-win situation: the speaker wins by convincing you of the merits of his or her position, and you win by gaining new information and insights that will help you perform your duties more effectively.

Maintain neutrality as long as possible, and don't jump to conclusions too quickly. Instead, try to understand *why* the speaker is arguing a particular point of view and what facts or experience convinced the speaker to adopt this position. When you assume this empathetic frame of reference, you will likely find that you neither completely agree nor completely disagree with every point the speaker makes. This ability to evaluate the message objectively will help you gain the most from the exchange.

Interrupting a speaker creates a barrier to effective communication.

Don't Interrupt   Perhaps because of time pressures, we sometimes get impatient. As soon as we've figured out what a person is trying to say, we tend to interrupt and finish the sentence for the speaker; this is especially a problem when listening to a slow speaker. Or, as soon as we can think of a counterargument, we tend to rush right in—whether or not the speaker has finished or even paused for a breath.

Such interruptions have many negative consequences. They are considered rude, first of all. Also, instead of speeding up the exchange, such interruptions tend to drag it out, because they often interfere with the speaker's train of thought, causing backtracking. The most serious negative consequence, however, is the nonverbal message such an interruption sends—that I have the right to interrupt you because what I have to say is more important than what you have to say! Is it any wonder that such a message hinders effective communication?

There is a difference between listening and simply waiting to speak. Even if you're too polite to interrupt, don't simply lie in wait for the first available opportunity to rush in with your version of the truth. If you're constantly planning what you'll say next, you cannot listen attentively to what the other person is saying.

Americans tend to have low tolerance for silence. Yet waiting a moment or two after someone has finished before you respond has several positive effects—especially in an emotional exchange. It gives the person speaking

Meetings serve a wide variety of purposes in an
organization. They keep members informed of events,
provide a forum for soliciting input, solving problems, and
making decisions, and they promote unity and cohesiveness
among those attending the meeting. Because the average
executive spends 25% to 70% of his or her day in meetings,
effectively conducting and participating in meetings is a
crucial managerial skill.
(*Source: © 1990 Ed Kashi*)

a chance to elaborate on his or her remarks, thereby drawing out further
insights. It also helps create a quieter, calmer, more respectful atmosphere,
one that is more conducive to solving the problem at hand.

Involve Yourself   As we have said, hearing is passive whereas listening is
active. You should be *doing something* while the other person is speaking
(and we don't mean doodling, staring out the window, or planning your
afternoon activities).

Much of what you should be doing is mental. Summarize to yourself
what the speaker is saying; create what the experts call an internal paraphrase
of the speaker's comments. Because we can process information so much
faster than the speaker can present it, use that extra time for active
listening—ensuring that you really are hearing not only what the person is
saying but the motives and implications as well.

> Involve yourself mentally in what the speaker is saying.

Some listeners find it helpful to jot down important points, translating
their mental notes into written notes. If you do this, keep your notes brief;
don't become so busy writing down the facts that you miss the message.
Concentrate on the main ideas; if you get these, you'll be much more likely
to remember the supporting details later. Recognize also that a detail or
two of the speaker's message might be inaccurate but the major points may
still be valid. Evaluate the validity of the overall argument; don't get bogged
down in trivia.

Be selfish in your listening. Constantly ask yourself, how does this affect me? How can I use this information to further my goals or to help me perform my job more effectively? Personalizing the information will help you to concentrate more easily and to weigh the evidence more objectively— even if the topic is difficult to follow or uninteresting and even if the speaker has annoying mannerisms or an unpleasant personality.

Encourage the speaker by letting him or her know that you're actively involved in the exchange. Maintain eye contact, nod in agreement, lean forward, utter encouraging phrases such as "uh huh" or "I see." Ensure that your mental paraphrases are on target by summarizing aloud for the speaker what you think you're hearing. In a conversation, you can give such feedback as "So you believe . . ., is that true?" or "Do you mean that . . .?" Such feedback enables the speaker to clarify remarks, add new information, or to clear up any misconceptions. Further, it tells the speaker that you're paying attention to the exchange.

COMMUNICATING BY TELEPHONE

▼

OBJECTIVE 7: Use effective techniques for conducting business via the telephone.

There are more than 285 million telephones in the world, with 115 million of them in the United States. That is the equivalent of about one telephone for every two people in this country. American Telephone and Telegraph (AT&T) processes 75 million telephone calls on these phones every single day.[8] No wonder, then, that communicating effectively by telephone is a crucial managerial skill, one that becomes increasingly important as the need for instantaneous information increases. Your telephone demeanor may be taken by the caller as the attitude of the entire organization. Every time the phone rings, your organization's future is on the line.

Telephone Versus Writing

Before you pick up the phone, consider whether you'll accomplish your purpose best by calling or by writing. If your message is long and complicated, it may be easier for your audience to understand in writing, plus the person can refer back to the document when necessary. If you are conveying bad news, a phone call may soften the blow, whereas a letter may strengthen the force of your message. You'll need to have a clear purpose and understand the effect the form of your message will have on your audience.

Written messages, of course, provide a record of communication. Even if you decide to telephone, remember that often a call should be followed by a written note, both to make sure there have been no misunderstandings and to document your communication.

Your Telephone Voice

Your voice is your primary means of accomplishing your objective on the phone.

Much of what you have learned about body language is useless when you're talking on the phone. You cannot maintain eye contact or observe facial expressions and body posture through the phone lines. That is one reason why ear-to-ear communication is often not as effective as person-to-person communication in solving difficult problems.

You are able to make use of such voice qualities as rate of speech and pitch to provide nonverbal clues about the other person (and, of course, the other person is able to make use of the same information about you). But even here, you're not getting a high-fidelity transmission of the speaker's voice characteristics. Most phone lines transmit only a poor copy of a voice; they mask fine shadings of inflection that can change the meaning of the verbal message.

Because the person to whom you're speaking has no visual clues to augment the auditory clues, if your voice is raspy, hoarse, shrill, loud, or weak, it can make you sound angry, excited, depressed, or bored—even if you aren't. Therefore, it is especially important to try to control your voice and project a friendly, competent, enthusiastic image to the other party.

To make your voice as clear as possible, sit or stand tall and avoid chewing gum or eating while talking. If your head is tilted sideways to cradle the phone between your head and shoulder, your throat is strained and your words may sound unclear.

Greet the telephone caller with a smile—just as you would greet someone in person. Your voice sounds more pleasant when you're smiling. An experiment was once conducted in which telephone salespeople were instructed to smile when they talked to their customers on one day and to scowl on the next. The salespeople sold almost twice as much on the days they were smiling.[9]

When the phone rings, pause, shift gears mentally, smile, and then answer the phone. Some firms even attach a sticker to the phone to remind employees to smile. "Smile," the sticker says, "It might be the boss calling."

Your Telephone Technique

Although every office worker will answer phones, the people who answer the firm's central number are vital to the firm's public image. These people must be trained and highly qualified—not the newest or least informed workers, as is often the case. These people's contacts with customers can have more impact on the organization's public image than the best advertising and promotion campaign.

> Answer promptly and courteously, providing as much helpful information as possible.

Always answer the phone by the second or third ring. Regardless of how busy you are, you do not want to give the impression that your company doesn't care about its callers. Answer clearly and slowly, giving the company's name. Remember that even if you give the same greeting 50 times a day, your callers probably hear it only once. Make sure they can understand it.

Be a good listener. Just as you would never continue writing or reading while someone speaks to you in person, neither should such distracting activities occur during phone calls. Pay attention especially to getting names correct and use the person's name during the conversation to personalize the message.

As with most other communication forms, emphasize positive language. Instead of saying, "I don't know," say, "Let me check and call you right back." Instead of saying, "You'll have to . . .," say, "We'll be happy to handle that if you'll just . . . ."

Encourage employees to answer the phones of coworkers who are temporarily away from their desks. If you're answering calls for someone else, take messages graciously, using language such as "Ms. Hall will be attending meetings most of the day but would be happy to return your call tomorrow morning. May I give her your message?" Always give the impression that callers are important (they are!) and that you will do anything you reasonably can to assist them.

If you must put a caller on hold, always ask, "May I put you on hold?" and then give the caller an opportunity to respond. Long-distance callers may prefer to call back rather than to be put on hold. When you get back on the line, do not appear rushed or exasperated. Give the patient caller your complete attention.

Telephone Tag

The telephone would be a much more efficient instrument if we could be assured of reaching our party each time we call. Instead, we're often forced to play the unproductive game of **telephone tag**, in which Party A calls Party B, is unable to reach her, and leaves a message. Party B then returns A's call, is unable to reach him, and leaves a message. And the process continues until the connection is finally made or until one party gives up in frustration.

Only 17% of business callers reach their intended party on the first try, 26% by the second try, and 47% by the third try.[10] Thus, it takes the majority of business callers at least three tries to reach their intended party. As a result, it is estimated that business callers waste at least four work weeks each year on unproductive or unnecessary telephone calls.[11]

Here are some suggestions to avoid unnecessary telephone tag:

Develop specific strategies to minimize telephone tag.

- *Plan the timing of your calls.* Try to schedule them at times when you're most likely to reach the person. (Likewise, make yourself available in the office at established hours so that your contacts will know when they can likely reach you.)
- *Announce when you're returning a call.* If you're returning someone's call and get a secretary on the line, begin by saying you're returning the boss's call. This will clue the secretary that the boss wanted to speak to you. (Incidentally, it's a good idea to get to know the secretaries of those people whom you call frequently. They're often "gatekeepers" who screen their bosses' calls carefully and are more likely to put through your call if they know you.)
- *Explore alternatives.* Find out what time would be best to call back or whether there is anyone else in the organization who can help.
- *Leave effective messages.* Recognize before you even make the call that you might have to leave a message (perhaps on an answering machine), so plan your message beforehand. Be polite and get to the point quickly. Clearly define the purpose of the call and the desired action and always give your phone number—even if the caller has it on file. The calls that get returned the fastest are those that are easiest to make.
- *Make use of technology.* Know how and be willing to use answering machines, voice mail, electronic mailboxes, call processing, and other automated devices that will help you achieve your purposes. If your organization has a network of computers connecting employees, you'll find that electronic mail often eliminates telephone tag. Employees can send and receive mail at their convenience; there's no need for both parties to be available at the same time.

Finally, know when to call it quits. If you haven't reached your intended party after numerous attempts, it is unlikely that further attempts will be successful. When all else fails, stop calling and write a letter.

DICTATING

There are, of course, many input methods for written communication. You can jot a note on a personal memo form and send it through interoffice mail in handwritten form, you can keyboard and format your own message, or you can dictate your message for transcription by someone else.

Dictation is the process of transmitting information orally for subsequent transcription. (**Transcription** is the process of preparing a typed copy of a document from longhand notes, shorthand notes, or machine dictation.) Dictation is usually accomplished either by dictating to a secretary who records the dictation in shorthand or by dictating to a machine that records your message on magnetic media for later transcription.

In the future, it is likely that voice input into a computer will become a third major form of dictation. A **voice-input system** translates human speech into electronic signals that are readable by computer software. Such systems, which are still in the experimental stage for office dictation, let the operator speak rather than type the information into the computer.

Shorthand has lost popularity in recent years because of the added expense of requiring two people for the input phase—the dictator and the secretary. Machine dictation requires the services of a secretary (or other clerical worker) for the transcription phase but not for the dictation phase. As a result, the cost of a typical business letter transcribed from shorthand dictation is $9.89, whereas the cost of a machine-dictated letter is 22% less ($7.67).[12]

Despite the efficiency, convenience, and ease of use of dictation equipment, it is estimated that as many as 30 million white-collar workers who would benefit from using dictation equipment continue to either write their messages in longhand or dictate to a secretary—primarily because they are unfamiliar with the equipment and don't know how to dictate efficiently into a machine.[13]

Preparing to Dictate

Become familiar with the operation of the equipment you'll be using. Dictation systems range from large centralized systems that are accessed via the telephone to battery-operated handheld units 2 inches wide by 3 inches long that can be carried and used anywhere. The operator's manual that comes with the machine will tell you how to use the machine's features for maximum efficiency.

To prepare for a particular dictation session, first gather the resource materials you'll need—copies of past correspondence, notes, files, and the like. Then arrange your dictation jobs in order from highest to lowest priority. That way, if you are interrupted before you finish, you will have the most important jobs dictated and on their way to being transcribed.

OBJECTIVE 8: Dictate business messages.

Machine dictation is more efficient than writing in longhand or dictating to a secretary taking shorthand.

If you're answering a piece of correspondence, mark it up: underline or highlight the important points and jot notes to yourself in the margins. Then make a rough outline of what you intend to say, keeping in mind the purpose of the message and the needs of the audience. Arrange the points in a logical sequence, using one of the organizational patterns you learned in Part III.

Dictating the Message

Dictate any needed instructions for transcribing your message.

Unless the same person transcribes all your correspondence and is familiar with your voice, begin by giving your name, title, department, and phone number. Then identify the document you're dictating, indicating, for example, whether it is a letter, memorandum, or report. If your organization has not adopted a standard style for each type of document, give formatting instructions (e.g., modified-block style) and any special stationery requirements (e.g., monarch stationery). Finally, indicate whether the document is to be a draft or final copy, the number of copies needed, and the turnaround time needed for the typed document. All this information is needed before the transcriber can begin typing the document.

Before beginning to dictate, shut your office door and remove all materials from your desktop except your reference papers so that you can give the dictation your undivided attention. Speak distinctly and at a speed somewhat slower than in normal conversation. Pause between each sentence and at punctuation points. By tone of voice, indicate when you're giving dictation to be transcribed and when you're given special instructions to the transcriber that are not to be transcribed. Avoid eating, chewing gum, pacing back and forth, or making other distractions while dictating. It is to your advantage to be heard clearly and distinctly.

Spell out proper names, and indicate punctuation if needed.

Spell out any proper noun that might possibly be misspelled—Is it *Louis* or *Lewis* (or even *Lois*)? *Lyn* or *Lynn*? *JoAnn* or *Jo Ann* or *Joanne*? It is often helpful to use the phonetic alphabet used by telephone operators when spelling words:

A Alice	J James	S Samuel
B Bertha	K Kate	T Thomas
C Charles	L Lewis	U Utah
D David	M Mary	V Victor
E Edward	N Nellie	W William
F Frank	O Oliver	X X-ray
G George	P Peter	Y Young
H Henry	Q Quaker	Z Zebra
I Ida	R Robert	

For example, you might say, "This letter is to Robert Batz, that's B as in Bertha, A as in Alice, T as in Thomas, and Z as in Zebra."

Unusual punctuation should be indicated. Indicate which words or phrases should be underlined, typed in all capitals, or be enclosed in quotation marks. It is generally unnecessary to indicate the ends of sentences; your voice inflection will provide sufficient guidance for the transcriber. You should, however, indicate each new paragraph (generally, by saying "Paragraph" at the end of a paragraph and in a different tone of voice).

Whether or not to indicate such internal punctuation as commas, semicolons, colons, and apostrophes depends on your own language skills as well as those of the transcriber. If you're confident about your own skills but unsure of those of the transcriber's, your best bet is to insert all punctuation. If you choose not to, you're indicating your willingness to accept the transcriber's judgment.

If your dictation unit is not voice activated, use the pause or stop button to turn the machine off temporarily when you're thinking or searching for information. It would be inefficient to make the transcriber listen to long periods of silence.

Special instructions should always precede the passage to which they apply. If you want a passage indented from each margin or set in all capitals or underlined, tell the transcriber *before* he or she types the passage. Otherwise, the passage will have to be retyped. Complicated sections, such as tables and diagrams, are often best prepared as handwritten rough drafts that are then submitted for typing along with the dictation.

When you make an error or decide to rephrase a passage, do so immediately. Simply reverse the tape to the point where the correction begins and tape over the original version. Or, using a different tone of voice, say something like "Transcriber, let's rephrase that last sentence." If you need to revise an earlier passage or if you omitted instructions that were needed, use the cuing feature of the machine—the function that places a tone on the recording to give special instructions to the transcriber or to indicate where corrections are to be made.

If the same person always transcribes your dictation, it will probably be unnecessary to dictate all the closing lines; typically, a "Sincerely yours," will be enough for the transcriber to know to then insert your name and title as you prefer them. Otherwise, dictate all the closing lines. In either case, don't forget to indicate any enclosures and copy notations, and if necessary, tell where the enclosures may be found. End each session by thanking the transcriber. A sample dictation session might begin as follows:

> This is Betty Johnson, assistant manager, purchasing department, Extension 4056. Please prepare a letter in standard format to Mr. Edward LaPaz; that's capital *L* as in *Lewis*, *A* as in *Alice*, capital *P* as in *Peter* (no space before the *P*), *A* as in *Apple*, and *Z* as in *Zebra*. His address is American General Corporation, ten twenty-six Woodland (one word) Street, Milwaukee, Wisconsin 53172.
>
> Dear Ed: The following items we received from your company on Invoice (capital *I*) 3076 arrived in damaged condition. Operator, please arrange the following items in two columns. The heading for the first column is *Item No.* (abbreviated *N-o-.*) and for the second column *Description*. Please underline each column heading. . . .

The transcribed pages will be returned to you for your approval, signature, and distribution. Proofread each transcribed document carefully before signing it or approving it for distribution. Remember that documents are sent out under your name—not under the transcriber's name. You are responsible for their accuracy and appearance. Whether the mistake was your own or the transcriber's, now is the time to correct it. Use appropriate proofreader's marks to indicate corrections.

OBJECTIVE 9: Use
business etiquette to
maintain effective working
relationships.

BUSINESS ETIQUETTE

Business etiquette is the practice of polite and appropriate behavior in the business setting. It dictates what behaviors are appropriate and under what circumstances; thus, business etiquette is really concerned with interactions between people—not meaningless ritual.

Each organization has its own rules about what is and is not appropriate in terms of dress, ways of addressing superiors, importance of punctuality, and the like. In addition, every country and every culture has its own rules. Generally, these rules are not written down but must be learned informally or through observation. Executives who follow correct business etiquette are more confident and appear more in charge; and the higher you advance in your career, the more important such behavior will become.

Learn what is appropriate behavior in your organization.

Business etiquette differs in many ways from social etiquette. The manager who enumerates all his or her accomplishments to the superior during an annual performance appraisal is simply being savvy, but if the manager does so during a social engagement, he or she is being a boor. You must be sensitive to what is appropriate under any given circumstances.

Good manners are good business; they communicate a strong positive message about you as a person. As Mark Twain once observed about etiquette, "Always do right: You will please some people and astonish the rest."

Making Introductions

The important point to remember about making introductions is simply *to make them*. The format you use is less important than the fact that you avoid the awkwardness of requiring two people to introduce themselves.

Traditionally, a man is introduced to a woman (saying the woman's name first), the lower ranking person is introduced to the higher ranking person (saying the higher ranking person's name first), and other people are introduced to the guest (saying the guest's name first). However, when introducing a newcomer to a group of people, simply mention the newcomer's name first and then go around the group, introducing each person in turn.

The format for an introduction might be this: "Helen, I'd like you to meet Carl Byrum. Carl just began working here as an account manager. Carl, this is Helen Smith, our vice president." Or, in a social situation, you might just say, "Rosa, this is Gene Stauffer. Gene, Rosa Bennett." The appropriate response to an introduction is "How do you do, Gene?" Regardless of the gender of the two people being introduced, either may initiate the handshake—a gesture of welcome.

Use a person's name in the conversation to help you remember it.

To help you remember the name of someone you've met, make a point of using his or her name when shaking hands. And using the person's name again at least once during the conversation will help to fix the name in your mind. If you cannot remember someone's name, when the person approaches you, simply extend your hand and say your name. The other person will typically respond by shaking your hand and also giving his or her name.

Whenever you greet an acquaintance whom you've met only once some time ago, introduce yourself and immediately follow it with some information to help the other person remember—unless he or she immediately recognizes you; for example, "Hello, Mr. Wise, I'm Eileen Wagoner. We met at the Grahams' party last month."

Dining

The restaurant you select for a business meal reflects on you and your organization. Choose one where the food is of top quality and the service dependable. In general, the more important your guest, the more exclusive the restaurant. If a maitre d' (headwaiter) seats you and your guest, your guest should precede you to the table. If you're seating yourselves, take the lead in locating an appropriate table. Give your guest the preferred seat, facing the window with a lovely view or facing the dining room if you're seated next to a wall.

Although customs vary, it is typical for a man to hold the woman's chair as she is being seated and for the nearest man to rise when a woman excuses herself for a moment and again when she returns. Female managers and professionals do not mistake genuine gestures of courtesy as chauvinism. Let common sense and your knowledge of the person's preferences guide your actions.

When making a food recommendation or announcing, when asked, what you intend to order, recognize that your guest will take your choice as a guideline to suitable price ranges. Each guest should order for him- or herself at a business meal. If the waiter mistakenly begins by asking you, the host, for your order, simply tell the waiter, "My guests will order first," thereby letting the waiter also know that you should get the check. In most parts of the country, the usual tip for standard service is 15% of the food and bar bill and 10% of the cost of the wine.

Giving Gifts

Giving gifts to suppliers, customers, or workers within one's own organization is typical at many firms, especially in December during the holiday period. Although such gifts are often deeply appreciated, you must be sensitive in terms of whom you give a gift to and the type of gift selected. Most people would consider a gift appropriate if it meets these four criteria:

- *It is an impersonal gift.* Gifts that can be used in the office or in connection with one's work are always appropriate.
- *It is for past favors.* Gifts should be used to thank someone for past favors, business, or performance—not to create obligations for the future. A gift to a prospective customer who has never ordered from you before might be misinterpreted as a bribe.
- *It is given to everyone in similar circumstances.* Singling out one person for a gift and ignoring others in similar positions would not only embarrass the one selected but create bad feelings among those who were ignored.
- *It is not extravagant.* A very expensive gift might make the recipient uneasy, create a sense of obligation, and call into the question the motives of the giver.

> Avoid giving gifts that are extravagant or personal, or that might be perceived as a bribe.

Although it is often the custom for a superior to give a subordinate a gift, especially one's secretary, it is less usual for the subordinate to give a personal gift to a superior. More likely, coworkers will contribute to a joint gift for the boss, again selecting one that is neither too expensive nor too personal.

Around the Office

Follow the golden rule in your dealings with others at work.

Many situations occur every day in the typical office that call for common courtesy. The basis for appropriate behavior is always the golden rule: "Treat others as you yourself would like to be treated."

Drinking Coffee   If there is a container provided to pay for the coffee, do so every time you take a cup; don't force others to treat you to a cup of coffee. Also, take your turn making the coffee and cleaning the pot if that is a task performed by the group. Although in most offices it is acceptable to drink coffee or some other beverage while working, many offices have an unwritten rule against snacking at one's desk. Regardless, never eat while talking to someone in person or on the telephone.

Smoking   Most offices today have designated smoking areas, and many prohibit smoking anywhere on the premises. If you smoke, follow the rules strictly. If you smoke in your office, do so only when you're alone. Show consideration for your office guests by purchasing an air purifier.

Electronic Mail   Because E-mail is often written "on the fly"—composed and sent as one keyboards the message, there is sometimes a tendency to forget the niceties and to let emotions take over. Such behavior is called "flaming" and should be avoided. Always assume that the message you send will never be destroyed but will be saved permanently on somebody's computer file.

Dealing with the Handicapped   When talking with a blind person, deal in words rather than gestures or glances. As you approach a blind person, make your presence known; and if in a group, address the person by name so that he or she will know when you're talking directly to him or her. Use a normal volume and speed.

When interacting with a physically handicapped person, always ask before providing special assistance, and follow the person's wishes. Most importantly, insofar as possible, forget about the handicap, and treat the person as you would anyone else. That person was hired because of the contributions he or she could make to the organization—not because of the handicap.

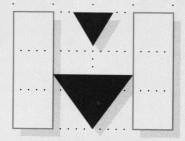

MICROWRITING A PLAN FOR A BUSINESS MEETING

The Problem

You are Dieter Ullsperger, director of employee relations for the city of Columbus, Ohio. The city manager has asked your department to develop a policy statement regarding the solicitation of funds from employees during work hours for employee weddings, retirements, anniversaries, and the like.

Despite the good intentions of such efforts, the city manager questions whether such efforts put undue pressure on some employees and take unreasonable time from official duties. You have already gathered secondary data regarding this matter and have spoken with your counterparts in Jacksonville, Florida; Milwaukee, Wisconsin; and Memphis, Tennessee. You are now ready to prepare a first draft of the policy statement.

The Process

1. What is the purpose of your task?

   To prepare a policy statement on soliciting funds from employees during office hours.

2. Is a meeting necessary?

   Because this policy will affect every employee in city government, it should be developed based on input from representatives of the work force. Therefore, a planning meeting is desirable.

3. What will be the agenda?

   My first reaction is that the meeting agenda is to write the new policy. However, I recognize that it is not reasonable for a policy statement to be written in a meeting. Thus, the real agenda detailed in the following memo is to develop the broad outlines for the policy. The policy will be planned collaboratively, drafted individually, reviewed collaboratively, and finally revised individually.

4. Who should attend the meeting?

   Because I want to ensure broad consensus on this policy, I'll ask the union steward of our two unions to attend. (I'll represent management.) I'll also ask the city attorney to attend to ensure that our policy is legal. Finally, I'll ask Lyn Peterson in Transportation to attend; she is a veteran city employee who is well-respected among her peers and has served as the unofficial social chairperson for numerous fund-raising events over the past several years. I'll telephone each of them to ask for their voluntary participation in this project.

5. What about logistics?

> Since I want the meeting to be informal, we'll hold it
> in the small conference room downstairs, which has an
> oval table. The only audiovisual equipment I'll need is
> a chalkboard to display any ideas we might have. I'll
> ask my secretary to take minutes. Since I was not given
> a specific deadline, I'll delay the meeting for three
> weeks, because two retirement parties are already
> scheduled in the meantime.

The Product

MEMO TO: Betty Haggblade, Union Steward, OPEIU Local 146
          Harold Inacker, City Attorney
          David Ma, Employee Representative, AFGE Local 38
          Lyn Peterson, Chief Dispatcher

FROM: Dieter Ullsperger, Director of Employee Relations *DU*

DATE: December 14, 19—

SUBJECT: Planning Meeting for New Policy Statement

Thanks so much for agreeing to serve on a committee to help draft
a policy statement on soliciting funds from employees during
office hours. As I indicated to each of you, the city manager has
requested such a statement.

Let's plan to meet on Friday, January 9, from 1:30 until 3:30 p.m.
in the downstairs conference room (HG 204). Our agenda will be as
follows:

1. Reviewing the city manager's charge
2. Describing policies in effect in other cities
3. Identifying possible alternatives
4. Evaluating possible alternatives
5. Reaching consensus on the major outlines of the new policy
6. Scheduling assignments and future meetings

Before our meeting, I would appreciate your discussing this matter
with your colleagues so that we might have the benefit of their
thoughts as we develop this policy that will affect each city
employee.

tgh

SUMMARY

Planning a business meeting requires determining your purpose and whether a meeting is the most efficient way of accomplishing that purpose. You must then determine your agenda, decide who should attend, and plan such logistics as timing, location, and room arrangements.

When conducting a meeting, begin with a statement of your purpose and agenda. Then follow that agenda, keeping things moving along. Control those who talk too much, and encourage those who talk too little. Use whatever strategies seem appropriate for solving problems, and try to keep conflicts under control. At the end of the meeting, summarize what was accomplished. After the meeting, send a follow-up memo if needed or distribute minutes of the meeting.

Listening is the most used but least developed of the four verbal communication skills. Whether listening to a formal presentation or conversing with one or two people, you can learn to listen more effectively by giving the speaker your undivided attention, staying open-minded about the speaker and the topic, avoiding interrupting the speaker, and involving yourself actively in the communication.

When communicating by telephone, give the person to whom you're speaking your undivided attention, speak clearly, listen carefully, and treat the other party with courtesy. Take positive steps to avoid the inconvenience of not being able to reach your party (telephone tag).

To dictate a message, first gather your resources and outline what you intend to say. While dictating, avoid interruptions, speak slowly and distinctly, and indicate unusual directions or punctuation. Because the transcribed message carries your name, edit and proofread it carefully.

Business etiquette is a guide to help people behave appropriately in business situations. To be effective in business, learn how to make introductions, conduct business lunches, give gifts appropriately, and maintain good working relationships around the office. Good manners are good business.

KEY TERMS

Agenda— An ordered list of topics to be considered at a meeting, along with the name of the person responsible for each topic.

Business etiquette— The practice of polite and appropriate behavior in the business setting.

Dictation— The process of transmitting information orally for subsequent transcription.

Minutes— The official record of the proceedings of a meeting that summarizes what was discussed and what decisions were made.

Parliamentary procedure— Written rules of order that permit the efficient transaction of business in meetings.

Teleconference— A meeting in which members in different locations are linked by simultaneous electronic communication, using cameras, projection screens, microphones, and computer equipment.

Telephone tag— The communication barrier caused by the repeated inability to reach someone by phone.

Transcription— The process of preparing a typed copy of a document from longhand notes, shorthand notes, or machine dictation.

Voice-input system— A combination of recording, computer, and software technology that translates human speech into electronic signals that are readable by computer software, thereby avoiding the need for keyboarding.

REVIEW AND DISCUSSION

OBJECTIVE 1   1. Under what circumstances is a meeting the most efficient way of accomplishing one's objectives?

OBJECTIVE 1   2. What are some ways of encouraging punctuality at meetings?

OBJECTIVE 2   3. What are seven problem-solving strategies that are effective at meetings?

OBJECTIVE 3   4. What is the difference between a main motion and a secondary motion?

OBJECTIVE 3   5. What is the difference between tabling a motion and postponing a motion?

OBJECTIVE 4   6. What types of information should be included in minutes of a meeting and what types should be excluded?

OBJECTIVE 5   7. What is the difference between listening and hearing?

OBJECTIVE 5   8. What are the major causes of poor listening skills?

OBJECTIVE 5   9. What are some effects of poor listening skills?

OBJECTIVE 6   10. What is meant by "be selfish in your listening"?

OBJECTIVE 6   11. Is a boring presentation necessarily an unimportant one? Explain.

OBJECTIVE 7   12. Why is it important to greet the telephone caller with a smile?

OBJECTIVE 7   13. What are some suggestions for avoiding telephone tag?

OBJECTIVE 8   14. What is the difference between dictation and transcription?

OBJECTIVE 8   15. What steps are necessary before beginning to actually dictate a message?

OBJECTIVE 9   16. How should you introduce your professor and the person who sits beside you in class?

OBJECTIVE 9   17. What guidelines should you follow for giving business gifts?

EXERCISES

OBJECTIVES 1–2   1. **Planning a Meeting**   Assume you are a dean at your institution, which does not now celebrate Martin Luther King, Jr.'s birthday. You are seeking the support of the college's other six deans for making the third Monday in January a holiday for all college employees and students.

a. Will a meeting best serve your purpose? Why or why not?

b. Assume you've decided to call a meeting with the deans. Prepare an agenda, decide who should attend (using your own institution for your decisions) and determine the logistics of the meeting—timing, location, room and seating arrangements, and types of audiovisual equipment needed.

c. What problem-solving strategies would you use for this meeting?

OBJECTIVE 2   2. **Collaborative Communication—Conducting a Meeting**   Divide into groups of five, with each person assuming the role of a dean at your institution (see Exercise 1). Draw straws to determine who will be the dean calling the meeting. Decide beforehand which one of the problem-solving strategies discussed in this chapter (scientific method, brainstorming, buzz groups, nominal group technique, Delphi technique, listening teams, or role playing) you will use to achieve your objectives. Conduct a 15- to 20-minute meeting. Following the meeting, evaluate its effectiveness. Did you achieve your objective?

3. **Collaborative Writing—Conducting a Meeting**   Divide into groups of five, with each member playing the role of a president of one of the five business student organizations on campus. The dean of the school of business has proposed requiring all students to purchase a certain brand of portable computer (student price of $1,450) before being allowed to take upper-division courses. Your group is meeting to either support or oppose this proposal. Draw straws to determine who will be group leader. Each person other than the group leader must either make or amend a motion during the meeting.

OBJECTIVES 2–3 ◄

Conduct a 15- to 20-minute meeting on this topic, following correct parliamentary procedure. Do not adjourn until you have approved a motion one way or the other. After adjournment, evaluate the meeting. Discuss how efficiently it was conducted, how well each person's role was performed, and whether correct parliamentary procedure was followed. Write up your evaluation in a joint memo to your instructor.

4. **Preparing Minutes of a Meeting**   Attend some business meeting on campus this week—either a meeting of some student organization or some faculty or staff meeting (most of them are open to visitors). Take minutes of the meeting, edit them, and turn them in.

OBJECTIVE 4 ◄

5. **Listening**   Your instructor will assign you a television show to watch this week—either a news program, talk show, or documentary. Using the listening techniques you learned in this chapter, take notes of the important points covered in the meeting. Listen for the major themes—not the details. Write a one-page memo to your instructor summarizing the important information you heard. Should every student's paper contain basically the same information?

OBJECTIVES 5–6 ◄

6. **Communicating by Telephone**   Role-play the following situation. Record the conversations for later evaluation. While two students are role-playing, the others in the class should be making notes of what went well and what might have been improved. To help simulate a telephone environment, have the two actors sit back to back so that they cannot see each other or the class members.

OBJECTIVE 7 ◄

Situation: You are Rob Renshaw, administrative assistant for Ronald Krugel, the marketing manager at Kraft Enterprises. Susan Plachta, an important customer whom you've never met, calls your boss with a complaint that an item she ordered two weeks ago does not work as advertised. Your boss won't be back in the office until tomorrow afternoon.

7. **Evaluating Telephone Communications**   Telephone two organizations in your area. Your purpose is to speak to the director of human relations to learn how much time he or she spends in meetings each week and to get an evaluation of the effectiveness of these meetings. Call at least three times if you're not successful the first time. Leave a message if necessary. Keep a log of each person with whom you speak at each organization, and evaluate the effectiveness of that person's

OBJECTIVE 7 ◄

telephone communication skills. Finally, write a summary of what you learned about meetings in that organization. Submit both your log and your summary to your instructor.

▶ OBJECTIVE 7

8. **Leaving Effective Telephone Messages**   Assume that on your third try (see Exercise 7) you were still unsuccessful in reaching the director of human relations by telephone. Instead you got a recording, asking you to leave a message of no more than 30 seconds. Compose the message you would leave.

▶ OBJECTIVE 8

9. **Dictating**   For this assignment, you will need to work with a partner and to have a cassette recorder and blank tape. Set up the tape recorder so that it is ready to record. Your instructor will give each of you in turn a simple letter or memo to write—perhaps a routine message from Chapter 6. You will have 15 minutes to study the assignment, make whatever notations you wish, and then dictate your message using the cassette recorder. Your partner will then do the same thing using his or her assigned problem. After you have both recorded your dictation, exchange cassettes and transcribe the dictation in final format. You may insert any punctuation you feel is needed, but you may not change the dictator's wording. Submit both your transcribed document and the cassette to your instructor.

▶ OBJECTIVE 9

10. **Using Business Etiquette**   Assume that you're the dean of your college. Think of three people to whom it would be appropriate to give a gift during the December holidays and three people to whom it would not be appropriate to give a gift. Identify the person and his or her position, and give reasons for your decision. For the three people for whom a gift would be appropriate, suggest an appropriate gift, along with a suggested cost.

CASE PROBLEM

Don't Let the Smoke Get in Your Eyes

▶ OBJECTIVES 1–4

Marc Kaplan ground his cigarette into the ashtray and thought, "Here go those save-the-earth people again." He had just read a copy of a memo that Neelima had sent to Dave Kaplan asking that smoking be prohibited throughout the premises of Urban Systems—both in Ann Arbor and in Charlotte. Neelima cited health dangers, lessened productivity, rights of nonsmokers, and damage to company property. Marc knew he could cite some arguments also: the rights of smokers, the unfairness of requiring new restrictions that were not in place when the workers were hired, the lessened productivity due to stress from not smoking, and the fact that other health and productivity hazards (such as gross obesity) were not banned. He felt he could enlist the support of O. J. Drew and Wendy Janish also—the other two smokers in the management offices. Arnie McNally, an ex-smoker, was an unknown.

At any rate, Dave Kaplan had decided to hold a special meeting of the executive committee, made up of Dave and the three vice presidents, next week to discuss and resolve this issue. Parliamentary procedure is followed at these meetings.

1. Assume the role of Dave Kaplan. Compose a memo to the executive committee announcing the meeting and giving the agenda.
2. What problem-solving strategies should be used at the meeting?
3. Have four members play the roles of Dave and the three vice presidents, and conduct the meeting. The other members should listen actively, take notes, and be prepared to discuss the events afterward. Each observer should also serve as the secretary and submit a set of minutes for the meeting.
4. Afterwards, discuss the situation. How did each actor feel? Was anyone arguing a position he or she didn't really feel? Was parliamentary procedure followed? Was the meeting successful? Did anyone win? Lose?

WORD WISE

- The word *queueing* (meaning "getting into lines") contains five consecutive vowels.
- The word *facetious* contains the five major vowels in order.
- The longest word that contains just one vowel is *strengths*.
- The longest word that contains just one repeated vowel and no other vowel is *defenselessness*, which contains 15 letters, 5 *e*'s, and no other vowels.

VI

Employment Communications

CHAPTER 17

Developing Your Résumé and Application Letter

Communication Objectives

After you have finished this chapter, you will be able to

1. Analyze your interests, strengths, weaknesses, and preferred lifestyle as the first step in choosing a career.

2. Research possible professions, demographic trends, industries, and prospective employers.

3. Use different types of techniques to locate job leads and secure a job interview.

4. Determine the appropriate length and format for your résumé.

5. Determine the appropriate content for your résumé.

6. Compose solicited and unsolicited application letters.

Once a week Bill O'Grady sits down with his boss, the Chief Executive Officer at Livingston, New Jersey's CIT Group. They talk about organizational issues—such as how to strengthen one of the six operating companies. If a company or department is weak in a certain area—say in technological know-how—they discuss whether or not someone should be hired to provide needed expertise. If the answer is yes, it is O'Grady's responsibility to find the right candidate.

Each day four or five unsolicited résumés show up on O'Grady's desk. The 51-year-old Executive Vice President of Administration said that nearly every unsolicited résumé is from someone looking for an executive position at the company. CIT Group has over $11 billion in assets and employs thousands of people. With those numbers, one may get the impression that an upper-level executive who sends in an unsolicited résumé has a good shot at getting a job there. "But, I have to tell you that out of 100 of those unsolicited résumés we receive, we *might* invite one person in," said O'Grady, who has been in the human resources field since 1965.

The things that O'Grady likes to see in the experienced manager's résumé and cover letter are basically the same things that should be on *any* résumé. Obviously, there should be some differences between what is presented by a recent college graduate and a top managerial applicant—especially in the amount of experience listed—but the fundamentals of how each presents his or her written material are the same.

William O'Grady, Executive Vice President of Administration, CIT Group, Livingston, New Jersey

When a candidate's package comes into O'Grady's office, the first thing he does is look at the cover letter. To get him interested it must be "crisp, precise, and get right to the point, and not be egomaniacal with all kinds of claims, like *I'm your guy*—the hard-sell kind of a cover letter—*I can turn your business around.*"

O'Grady would rather see "a more business-like letter that quickly gets to the point. And again in the résumé, the same thing holds true." If a résumé is more than two pages long, "it's a killer," he said.

One recent trend O'Grady has noticed on résumés, one that he doesn't like much, is that the listing of accomplishments has gotten paragraphs long. What he likes are "merely a couple of bullet points that follow your title that highlight significant things that you got into. Some people," he noted, "get a little bit caught up in writing their own biography in a résumé. It's overwhelming and you lose interest."

Unbusiness-like gimmicks don't impress O'Grady, such as résumés and cover letters written in the third person. He also doesn't like to see photographs attached to a résumé. "That really smacks of an overblown ego."

Finally, a résumé must demonstrate that a candidate has the appropriate experience or educational background for the job he or she is seeking. O'Grady noted that a lot of applicants try to shape their experience or educational backgrounds to fit a position that simply doesn't suit them.

What continues to surprise O'Grady is the number of poorly written résumés and cover letters he sees from experienced executives who should, at this point in their careers, know how to present themselves well on paper. A bad résumé or cover letter might be more easily overlooked if it is composed by an entry-level candidate, but why should anyone take chances?

To put it simply, O'Grady, like most personnel managers, said he likes résumés and cover letters that "just give you the facts." ▼

PLANNING YOUR CAREER

Although we've stressed throughout this text the importance of communication skills for success on the job, one of your first professional applications of what you've learned will be in actually securing a job. Think for a moment about some of the important communication skills you've developed thus far; for example, how to analyze your audience, write effective letters, research and analyze data, speak persuasively, and use nonverbal communication to achieve your objectives.

> Communication skills play an important role in the job campaign.

All these communication skills will serve you well when you begin your job-getting campaign—from researching career, industry, and company information to writing effective résumés and application letters to conducting yourself effectively during the job interview.

To refine these skills further, in this chapter you will learn how to plan your career, develop a résumé, and write application letters. The following chapter covers other important phases of the job campaign: completing application blanks, taking employment tests, interviewing, and writing post-interview letters.

As you begin to think about your career, consider these facts about the American work force:[1]

- Three to four million new jobs are created each year, but job seekers have to beat odds of at least six to one to secure a job because there are typically six candidates equally qualified in terms of education and experience for each vacancy.
- Less than half (41%) of the work force consciously chose their jobs or careers; instead, most got their jobs through chance, by having no other choice, or as the result of pressure from family or friends.
- More than half (51%) of American workers say they would choose a different line of work if they had it to do over again.
- One in four entry-level employees fails to make it through the first year, and nearly one-third of the entire work force expects to change jobs within the next three years.

As these statistics make clear, you must put considerable time, effort, and thought into getting a job if you want to have a rewarding and fulfilling work life. The process is the same, whether you're beginning your first job, changing careers, or returning to the workplace after an extended absence; and it begins with a self-analysis.

Self-Analysis

If you are typical of many students, you have changed your major at least once during your college career. Thus, you've already made many important decisions about your life and career. When it is time to decide how to use your college education, you must do some soul-searching to decide exactly how you wish to spend the working hours of your life. Recognize that during the week you will probably spend as many of your waking hours at the workplace as at home.

> OBJECTIVE 1: Analyze your interests, strengths, weaknesses, and preferred lifestyle as the first step in choosing a career.

Think about your life, your interests, things you're good at (and those you're not), and the experiences that have given you the most satisfaction.

Such introspection will help you make sound career decisions. Take a few moments now to answer these questions:

1. Which courses have you enjoyed most and least in school?
2. Recalling projects on which you've worked in class, in organizations, or at work, which kinds of projects have you been most successful at and enjoyed most? Which have you disliked?
3. Do you enjoy working most with records (reports, correspondence, and forms), people, ideas, or things? Do you enjoy working more with your mind or your body?
4. Do you prefer working independently on a project or with a group?
5. How important to you is being your own boss?
6. In what type of work setting do you function best: a quiet office, an environment with lots of activity and people, or an outside location? Would you most enjoy working in the organization's home office, a branch, while traveling, or at home?
7. What type of work schedule would you prefer: Fixed or flexible? Days, nights, or weekends? How willing or eager are you to work overtime?
8. What is important about the geographical situation of your job in terms of climate, size of metropolitan area, and location (downtown, suburban, or rural)? Do you prefer a particular city, state, region of the country, or international setting? How willing or eager are you to relocate?
9. For what kind of organization would you like to work: Large or small? Established or new? Commercial, government, or nonprofit?
10. What is important about the personalities of the people with whom you will work? Describe your ideal boss, subordinates, and colleagues.
11. How would you like to dress at work?
12. What types of material rewards are important for you in terms of salary, commissions, fringe benefits, job security, and the like?
13. How willing or eager are you to participate in an extensive on-the-job training program?
14. What are your career goals five years from now?

Your answers to these questions will help you identify the type of career that would offer you the most satisfaction and success. Remember that for any particular college major, many jobs are available; and one of them will likely meet your needs and desires.

Research

OBJECTIVE 2: Research possible professions, demographic trends, industries, and prospective employers.

Armed with your self-assessment, you are now ready to secure additional information—about possible occupations, demographic trends, and industries and companies in which you're interested. Many job seekers begin their search for occupational information by interviewing one or more people currently employed in the career or industry in which they're interested. Such sources can provide the current and detailed information you seek, and they're likely to be more objective than a recruiter. Locate such sources by reading the business section of the local newspaper, asking family and friends, or consulting with your college placement office or your professors.

Although the major purpose of such interviews is data gathering, these sessions also advertise your availability for and interest in a position. The interviewee may volunteer information about possible job leads. Avoid, however, turning the informational interview into an employment interview.

Occupational Information   One of the most comprehensive sources of up-to-date information about jobs is the *Occupational Outlook Handbook*, published by the U.S. Department of Labor.

This handbook describes in detail the 225 occupations that account for 80% of all jobs in the U.S. economy. For each occupation, detailed and accurate information is given regarding (1) the nature of the work; (2) working conditions; (3) employment levels; (4) training, other qualifications, and advancement; (5) job outlook (i.e., projected employment levels and factors influencing the future of the occupation); (6) earnings; (7) related occupations; and (8) sources of additional information.

> Learn as much as you can about the occupations in which you're interested.

To illustrate the comprehensive coverage of the *Handbook*, Figure 17.1 shows the listing for the job of actuary, which was recently rated the best occupation in the country based on such criteria as work environment, income, stress, security, travel, and physical demands.[2]

Other sources of job information are your college placement office, professional associations (see the *Encyclopedia of Associations*, published by Gale Research Company of Detroit, Michigan, for a list of professional associations in your area of interest), and business periodicals, such as the *Wall Street Journal*, *Business Week*, and *Forbes*. The latter two publications are especially helpful because each issue contains an index of those companies mentioned in that issue.

Demographic Information   No matter how much you enjoy handwriting and no matter how clear and lovely your lettering is, it is unlikely that you would be able to make a good living today as a scribe (a copier of manuscripts) because technology has preempted that occupation. Smart career choices are dictated not only by personal interests but also by demographic characteristics with which you should become familiar. Some of the demographic trends that the U.S. Department of Labor believes will affect employment through the year 2000 are as follows:[3]

> Study the environment in which you will be working.

- *Population:* There will be a smaller proportion of children and youth in the future and a considerably greater proportion of middle-aged and older people. Blacks, Hispanics, and Asians will make up a larger share of the population. The West and South will grow in population, the Midwest will remain the same, and the Northeast will decline.
- *Labor force:* Blacks, Hispanics, and Asians will account for 58% of the growth in the labor force between 1986 and 2000; women will account for 47% of the labor force in 2000. The fastest-growing jobs will be in executive, managerial, professional, and technical fields—those requiring the highest levels of education and skill.
- *Industrial profile:* Nearly four out of every five jobs in the year 2000 will be in industries that provide services—such as banking, health care, hospitality, and consulting. In the goods-producing industries, only the construction industry is expected to grow; manufacturing, mining, and agriculture will decline.

FIGURE 17.1   Job Profiles

Learn About the Jobs in Which You're Interested

Actuaries

(D.O.T. 020. 167-010)

Nature of the Work

Why do young drivers pay more for automobile insurance than older drivers? How much should an insurance policy cost? How much should an organization contribute each year to its pension fund? Answers to these and similar questions are provided by actuaries, who design insurance and pension plans and keep informed on their operation to make sure that they are maintained on a sound financial basis. Actuaries assemble and analyze statistics to calculate probabilities of death, sickness, injury, disability, unemployment, retirement, and property loss from accident, theft, fire, and other hazards. They use this information to determine the expected insured loss. For example, they may calculate how many persons who are 21 years old today can be expected to die before age 65-the probability that an insured person might die during this period is a risk to the company. They must make sure that the price charged for the insurance will enable the company to pay all claims and expenses as they occur. Finally, this price must be profitable and yet be competitive with other insurance companies. In a similar manner, the actuary calculates premium rates and determines policy contract provisions for each type of insurance offered. Most actuaries specialize in either life and health insurance; a growing number specialize in pension plans.

To perform their duties effectively, actuaries must keep informed about general economic and social trends and legislative, health, and other developments that may effect insurance practices. Because of their broad knowledge of insurance, company actuaries may work in investment, group underwriting, or pension planning departments. Actuaries in executive positions help determine company policy. In that role, they may be called upon to explain complex technical matters to company executives, government officials, policyholders, and the public. They may testify before public agencies on proposed legislation affecting the insurance business, for example, or

explain intended changes in premium rates or contract provisions. They also may help companies develop plans to enter new lines of business.

The small number of actuaries who work for the Federal Government usually deal with a particular insurance or pension program, such as Social Security or life insurance for veterans and members of the Armed Forces. Actuaries in State government are usually employed by State insurance departments that regulate insurance companies, oversee the operations of State retirement or pension systems, handle unemployment insurance or workers' compensation problems, and assess the impact of proposed legislation. They might determine whether the rates charged by an insurance company are proper or whether an employee benefit plan is financially sound.

Consulting actuaries provide actuarial advice for a fee to various clients including insurance companies, corporations, hospitals, labor unions, government agencies, and attorneys. Consulting actuaries set up pension and welfare plans, calculate future benefits, and determine the amount of employer contributions. Consulting actuaries may be called upon to testify in court regarding the value of potential lifetime earnings lost by a person who has been disabled or killed in an accident, the current value of future pension benefits in divorce cases, or the calculation of automobile insurance rates. Actuaries who are enrolled under the provisions of the Employee Retirement Income Security Act of 1974 (ERISA) evaluate these pension plans and report on their financial soundness.

Working Conditions

Actuaries have desk jobs that require no unusual physical activity; their offices generally are comfortable and pleasant. They generally work between 35 and 40 hours a week except during busy periods, when overtime may be required, and they may be required to travel to branch offices of their company or to clients.

Employment

Actuaries held about 9,400 jobs in

1986. Many worked in insurance company headquarters in New York, Hartford, Chicago, Philadelphia, and Boston.

Most of these worked for life insurance companies; others worked for property and liability (casualty) companies. The number of actuaries employed by an insurance company depends on its volume of business and the types of insurance policies it offers. Large companies may employ over 100 actuaries; others, generally smaller companies, may rely instead on consulting firms, accounting firms, or rating bureaus (associations that supply actuarial data to member companies). Other actuaries work for private organizations administering independent pension and welfare plans or for government agencies.

Training, Other Qualifications, and Advancement

A good educational background for a beginning job in a large life or casualty company is a bachelor's degree with a major in mathematics or statistics; a degree in actuarial science is even better. Some companies hire applicants with a major in engineering, economics, or business administration, provided that applicant has a working knowledge of mathematics, including calculus, probability, and statistics. Courses in accounting, computer science, and insurance also are useful. Companies prefer well-rounded individuals with a liberal arts background. Although only about 30 colleges and universities offer a degree in actuarial science, hundreds of schools offer a degree in mathematics or statistics.

A strong background in mathematics is essential for persons interested in a career as an actuary. It is an advantage to pass, while still in school, one or more of the examinations offered by professional actuarial societies. Three societies sponsor programs leading to full professional status in their specialty. The Society of Actuaries gives 10 actuarial examinations for the life and health insurance and pension field; the Casualty Actuarial Society gives 10 examinations for the property and liability field. Because the first parts of the examination series of each society cover similar materials, students need not commit themselves to a specialty until they have taken three examinations. These test competence in subjects such as linear algebra, numerical methods, operations research, probability, calculus, and statistics. These first few examinations help students evaluate their potential as actuaries, and those who pass usually have better opportunities for employment and higher starting salaries.

The American Society of Pension Actuaries gives seven examinations covering the pension field. Membership status requires the passage of two actuarial exams. Fellowship status requires the passage of three actuarial and two advanced consulting exams.

Actuaries are encouraged to complete the entire series of examinations as soon as possible: completion generally takes from 5 to 10 years. Many students pass two or more actuarial examinations before graduating from college. Examinations are given twice each year. Extensive home study is required to pass the advanced examinations; many actuaries study for several months to prepare for an examination. Actuaries who complete five examinations in either the life insurance series or the pension series or seven examinations in the casualty series are awarded "associate" membership in their society. Those who pass an entire series receive full membership and the title "fellow."

Consulting pension actuaries who service private pension plans and certify their solvency must be enrolled by the Joint Board for the Enrollment of Actuaries. Applicants for enrollment must meet certain experience and education requirements as stipulated by the Joint Board.

Beginning actuaries often rotate among jobs to learn various actuarial operations and different phases of insurance work. At first, they prepare tabulations for actuarial tables or perform other simple tasks. As they gain experience, they may supervise clerks, prepare correspondence and reports, and do research.

Advancement to more responsible work as assistant, associate, and chief actuary depends largely on job performance and the number of actuarial examinations passed. Actuaries who have a broad knowledge of the insurance, pension,

and employee benefits fields often advance to top administrative and executive positions in underwriting, accounting, or data processing departments.

Job Outlook
Employment of actuaries is expected to grow much faster than the average for all occupations through the year 2000. Most job openings, however, are expected to arise each year to replace actuaries who transfer to other occupations or retire or stop working for other reasons. Job opportunities should be favorable for college graduates who have passed at least two actuarial examinations while still in school and have a strong mathematical and statistical background.

Employment in this occupation is influenced by the volume of insurance sales and pension plans, which should continue to grow through the end of this century. Shifts in the age distribution of the population will result in a large increase in the number of people with established careers and family responsibilities. This is the group that traditionally has accounted for the bulk of private insurance sales.

As people live longer, they draw health and pension benefits for a longer period, and more actuaries are needed to recalculate the probabilities of such factors as death, sickness, and length of retirement. As insurance companies branch out into more than one kind of insurance coverage, more actuaries will be needed to establish rates. Growth in new forms of protection, such as dental, legal, and kidnap insurance, also will stimulate demand. The increase in the number of mergers and acquisitions and the passage of legislation on tax reform will spur demand for actuaries to evaluate the financial condition and investment portfolios of firms. As more States pass competitive rating laws, many companies that previously relied on rating bureaus for actuarial data may create their own actuarial departments or use the services of consulting actuaries.

The liability of companies for damage resulting from their products has received much attention in recent years. Actuaries will continue to be involved in the development of product liability insurance, as well as

medical malpractice and worker's compensation coverage.

Insurance coverage is considered a necessity by most individuals and businesses, regardless of economic conditions. Therefore, actuaries are unlikely to be laid off during a recession.

Earnings
In 1986, new college graduates entering the life insurance field without having passed any actuarial exams averaged about $19,000 - $24,000, according to estimates by the Society of Actuaries. Beginners who had completed the first exam received between $21,000 and $25,000, and those who had passed the second exam averaged between $23,000 and $26,000 depending on geographic location.

Insurance companies and consulting firms give merit to actuaries as they gain experience and pass examinations. Actuaries who became associates in 1986 averaged between $32,000 and $45,000 a year; actuaries who became fellows during that year averaged between $44,000 and $55,00. Fellows with additional years of experience can earn substantially more—top actuarial executives received salaries of $60,000 a year and higher.

Related Occupations
Actuaries assemble and analyze statistics in their day-to-day work. Other workers whose jobs involve similar skills include mathematicians, statisticians, economists, financial analysts, and engineering analysts.

Sources of Additional Information
For facts about actuarial qualifications and opportunities contact:

American Academy of Actuaries
1720 I St. NW., 7th Floor
Washington, DC 20006

American Society of Pension Actuaries
2029 K St. NW., 4th Floor
Washington, DC 20006

Casualty Actuarial Society
One Penn Plaza
250 West 34th St.
New York, NY 10119

Society of Actuaries
500 Park Blvd., Suite 440
Itasca, IL 60143

Source: U. S. Department of Labor, *Occupational Outlook Handbook, 1988–89* (Washington, DC: Bureau of Labor Statistics), pp. 65–66.

Industry and Company Information   Now that you have analyzed yourself in relation to a career, investigated possible professions, and studied demographic trends, you probably have a good idea of the career you want to pursue. You're now ready to research industry and company information. No organization exists in a vacuum; each is affected by the economic, political, and social environment in which it operates.

Start with the Standard Industrial Classification (SIC) code for the industry in which you're interested. Also helpful are (1) the *U.S. Industrial Outlook*, published by the U.S. Department of Commerce, and (2) *Standard and Poor's Industry Surveys*.

After learning about the industry, pick out a few companies in the industry to explore further. Be guided by your interests—large versus small firms, geographical constraints, and so forth. This research will give you a better framework for evaluating the specific companies at which you will be interviewing.

One handy reference is the *CPC Annual*, a three-volume directory of employment opportunities for college graduates (both two-year and four-year) published by the College Placement Council of Bethlehem, Pennsylvania. This directory, which is available in most college placement offices and libraries, contains narrative information about more than 600 large employers and the types of positions they have available. It is indexed by employer, occupation, and geographical region.

Audience Analysis   As noted throughout this text, the concept of audience analysis is pivotal to every type of communication skill. Learn as much as you can about the employment environment so that you can customize your employment communications to the needs of the employer.

For example, an effective résumé is tailored to the needs of the prospective employer. Analyzing the audience—your potential employer—will show you how to emphasize what you have gained from your education or work experience that will benefit the employer. Employers do not hire you as a reward for what you've accomplished in the past but rather for the promise of what you can do for them in the future. So treat your résumé as an advertisement of good things to come rather than as an obituary of what has already happened.

It currently costs an organization more than $6,000 to hire one executive,[4] so the cost of making a wrong decision is great. And if you multiply your likely salary times three or four years in a job, you'll see that the organization is making a very expensive purchase when it hires you. If you were making that large an investment, wouldn't you go to great lengths to ensure that you'd made the right choice?

To convince the organization that you're worth the investment, learn as much about the organization as possible so that you can then present your credentials in terms of specific reader benefits.

> Analyzing the specific organization enables you to tailor your credentials in terms of the organization's needs.

Job-Getting Techniques

> ▼
> OBJECTIVE 3: Use different types of techniques to locate job leads and secure a job interview.

Do not depend on any single technique for landing the ideal job. Instead, use every technique at your disposal that you feel can benefit you. Some of the more popular ones are networking, using professional employment services, answering advertisements, and advertising yourself.

Networking   In the job-getting process, networking refers to developing a group of acquaintances who might provide job leads and career guidance. The term has been used so much recently that it has perhaps become a buzzword, but it is still an important job-getting tool. Everyone—from the most recent college graduate to the president of a Fortune 500 firm—has a network on which to draw in searching for a job.

Your initial network might include friends, family, professors, former employers, social acquaintances, college alumni, your dentist, family doctor, insurance agent, local businesspeople, your minister or rabbi—in short, everyone you know who might be able to help. Ideally, your network will combine both personal and professional connections. That's one benefit of belonging to professional associations, and college isn't too early to start. Most professional organizations either have student chapters of their associations or provide reduced-rate student memberships in the parent organization.

Certainly, you don't develop a network of acquaintances purely for personal gain; the friendships gained through such contacts can last a lifetime. But don't forget to seek the advice and help of everyone who can be of assistance in this important endeavor.

Professional Employment Services   Professional employment services include your college placement office, the state employment service, private employment agencies, and private career consulting services. The college placement office is generally the first, the most effective, and often the only source of help used by most graduating students. Such offices typically provide career information, critique student résumés, and arrange interviews with campus recruiters.

Your state employment service can provide information on job vacancies, job requirements, training programs available, and local economic conditions. For a fee, private employment agencies seek to match vacancies at a firm with qualified applicants. Their primary allegiance is to whoever pays their fee; the fee is sometimes paid by the applicant and sometimes by the employer. Career consultants charge a fee for the service of helping people identify and promote their own strengths; their services range from helping with résumé writing, to administering interest and aptitude tests, to career counseling.

Answering Advertisements   Any large daily newspaper contains hundreds of classified ads of job openings, and you would be wise to scan them. Often you can pick up important words and phrases that will help you describe yourself appropriately in your résumé and application letter.

Be aware, however, that most jobs are not filled through want ads; in fact, only 14% are. The methods by which all jobs are typically filled are shown here as percentages of the whole:[5]

Networking or personal contacts	70%
Help-wanted ads	14
Executive search firms	11
Mass mailing of résumés	5
	100%

> Seek the help of professional and personal acquaintances in your job campaign.

> Most jobs are filled through personal contacts.

For hiring new college graduates, on-campus interviewing is the major source of jobs, accounting for 42% of all selections, with responses from help-wanted ads accounting for 8%.[6]

If you use want ads, don't rely on them exclusively; follow other leads as well. In addition, to increase your chances respond as soon as you see a suitable position advertised.

Many newspaper ads are "blind" ads; that is, instead of listing a company name and address, they simply provide a box number for responding to the ad. Although most such ads are legitimate, a word of caution is in order. There have been instances of people submitting their résumés in response to these blind ads who have been victimized as a result of harassing phone calls, burglary, or even bodily harm. After all, your résumé often contains your home address, home phone number, and perhaps even the hours when you're most likely to be at home. Anyone expecting to make heavy use of newspaper ads would be well advised to rent a post-office box for this purpose.

Advertising Yourself Suppose you've followed every lead you can find and have still not been able to locate a suitable vacancy. If, for example, you go to college in the Midwest and plan to seek employment in Southern California, you won't be able to make as effective use of your institution's placement service because many of the midwestern recruiters will be interviewing for regional vacancies.

In such circumstances, if you're an aggressive job seeker you go "prospecting"; that is, you begin contacting companies you identified during earlier research and ask if they have openings for which you might qualify. Enclose your résumé with your prospecting (or unsolicited application) letters—letters of inquiry written to organizations that have not advertised any vacancies.

Suppose you have learned, for example, that XYZ Corporation is building an assembly plant in Nogales, Mexico. Wouldn't it be reasonable to expect that they might need a personnel specialist (you) who is fluent in Spanish? Write a prospecting letter to find out. Although "blind" prospecting— simply mailing out hundreds of résumés along with a duplicated application letter—will seldom lead to an interview, using the knowledge from your research to customize your appeal to each company can prove very effective.

Preparing your résumé

A **résumé** is a brief record of one's personal history and qualifications that is typically prepared by an applicant for a job. Although recruiters sometimes refer to the résumé as a *wilawid* ("What I've learned and what I've done"), the emphasis in the résumé should be on the future rather than on the past: you must show how your education and work experience have prepared you for future jobs; specifically, the job for which you are applying.

Right from the start, be realistic about the purpose of your résumé. Very few people are actually hired on the basis of their résumés. (However, many people are *not hired*, because of their poorly written or poorly presented résumés.) Instead, applicants are generally hired on the basis of their performance during a job interview.

GETTING A JOB ELECTRONICALLY

Both employers and job seekers are making increasing use of technology to make the job-selection process more effective and more efficient. Let's follow Robin Gryder, a records-management major, as he begins his job search. Although some of the technology he uses may not be widely available or economical yet, they probably will be within a few years.

Résumé Software

To begin with, Robin purchases the *Résumé Kit*, a software program from Spinnaker Software (Cambridge, Massachusetts), to help him prepare his résumé. The *Résumé Kit* takes Robin through a sequential process that helps him organize his skills, experience, and education into a clear and concise format of his choice. When he selects from the nine different résumé styles available, the spacing, fonts, boldfacing, tabs, and underlining are done automatically for a customized résumé in minutes. In addition, the software program comes with a 100,000-word spelling checker, a word processor for writing cover and interview follow-up letters, and an on-screen calendar system for managing his schedule.

Registering on Line

Using his computer and modem, Robin then logs onto Dialog Information Services to make use of the Career Placement Registry, an on-line job service operated by Plenum Publishing of Alexandria, Virginia. This service, which has been operating since 1981, charges students $12 to post their résumés on line for six months, with an $8 renewal fee each six months.

Interested companies from around the country (or even around the world) can then search those résumés using a variety of criteria. The companies pay an hourly usage fee in addition to $1 for each résumé that meets their criteria and is called up for review and printing. Approximately 500 American companies currently search this database each month, and approximately 4,000 students list their résumés for the 600 or so positions that are filled monthly.

Video Résumés

Recognizing that a printed résumé does little to communicate how he talks, acts, and looks, Robin takes his job search one step further by contacting Res-A-Vue, a video marketing company in Connecticut. For a fee ranging from a few hundred to several thousand dollars, Res-A-Vue will prepare a professionally produced video résumé of a job candidate. Such résumés typically last about five minutes and give the candidate an opportunity to tell about his or her abilities and ambitions before a studio camera. Res-A-Vue then edits the tape to delete any weak or distracting footage and adds on-screen titles and background music. Robin can then send copies of the videotape to prospective employers to give them an opportunity to "meet" him before the job interview takes place.

Scheduling Recruiter Interviews

Using his computer again, Robin bids for an open interview slot with one of the on-campus recruiters. He can do this from the comfort of his dormitory room, 24 hours a day, seven days a week—not just when the placement office is open. He also uploads his résumé to the placement-office computer for the recruiter to review electronically.

As soon as he has scheduled an on-campus interview, Robin logs back onto Dialog Information Services and enters the Disclosure database to learn more about the company with whom he will be interviewing. Disclosure contains detailed information about all publicly held U.S. corporations, including annual reports, 10-K reports, and proxy statements. It costs approximately $20 to print out three years of information about the company, such as income statements and balance sheets; names, ages, and salaries of corporate officers and directors; the management discussion from the annual report; and a description of the products or services the company sells.

Processing Applications

One of the companies that received Robin's résumé was Apple Computer, of Cupertino, California. Every large, multinational firm receives thousands of such résumés each year; Apple, for example, receives 300,000 résumés yearly. It keeps track of them by scanning them into a minicomputer that reads key words from the text.

Employers are also using technology to lower the cost of interviewing candidates—especially for the early round of interviews. For example, one company, Corporate Interviewing Network (CIN), will interview candidates for an employer at one of its locations in every major city in the country. The employer specifies the questions used, and CIN furnishes the company with a videotape of the interview. The employer pays an initial $100 registration fee and $50 per interview—quite a saving from the hundreds of dollars typically required to fly a candidate to headquarters for interviewing.

Sources: "Apple Beats Résumé Flood," *PC Week*, September 18, 1989, p. 74; "Computers Can Make Best Interviewers," *USA Today*, July 17, 1989, p. 6B; William G. Flanagan, "Interview . . . Take One!" *Forbes*, November 18, 1985, pp. 244–245; Claudia Gentner, "Tracking Information," *The National Business Employment Weekly* (College Edition), Winter/Spring 1989, p. 20; Tony Lee, "Landing a Job Online," *The National Business Employment Weekly* (College Edition), Winter/Spring 1989, pp. 19–21.

Thus, the purpose of the résumé is to get you an interview, and the purpose of the interview is to get you a job. Remember, however, that the résumé and accompanying application letter (cover letter) are crucial in advancing you beyond the mass of initial applicants and into the much smaller group of potential candidates invited to an interview.

Résumé Length

Most recruiters prefer a one-page résumé for entry-level positions.

Decisions about résumé length become much easier when you consider that recruiters typically spend no more than 35 seconds looking at each résumé during their initial screening to pare down the perhaps hundreds of applications for any particular position into a more manageable number that will then be studied in more detail.[7] How much information can the recruiter be expected to read in less than a minute? It won't matter how well qualified you are if the recruiter never reviews those qualifications.

As one recruiter for a large corporation has noted, the perfect résumé is "like a Henny Youngman two-liner. No fat. Get to the point and then say goodbye. . . . Remember: You're trying to get us to hire you, not to marry you."[8]

How much is too much? Surveys of employment and human resource executives consistently show that most managers prefer a one-page résumé for the entry-level positions typically sought by recent college graduates, with a two-page résumé being reserved for unusual circumstances or for higher-level positions.[9] True or not, take note of the old placement office saying, "The thicker the résumé, the thicker the applicant."

According to a recent survey of 200 executives from major U.S. firms, the most serious mistake job candidates make is including too much information in their résumés. Their rank listing (in percentages of the whole) of the most serious résumé errors is as follows:[10]

Too long	32%
Typographical or grammatical errors	25
No descriptions of job functions	18
Unprofessional appearance	15
Achievements omitted	10
	100%

A one-page résumé is not the same thing as a two-page résumé crammed into one page by using small type and narrow margins. Your résumé must be attractive and easy to read. Shorten your résumé by making judicious decisions about what to include and then by using concise language to communicate what is important.

Résumé Format

Although the content of your résumé is obviously more important than the format, remember that first impressions are lasting. As pointed out earlier, those first impressions are formed during the less than a minute that is often devoted to an initial reading of each résumé. Therefore, even before you begin writing your résumé, think about the format, because some format decisions will affect the amount of space available to discuss your qualifications and background.

One of your first decisions will be whether to prepare your résumé yourself or to hire someone to do it for you. In years past, it was often advantageous to have your résumé prepared and typeset at a print shop. Although typeset résumés do look professional, the danger is that most résumé-preparation services tend to use the same format and type style for many résumés, so your résumé tends to look like many others. Experienced résumé readers can always spot a professionally prepared résumé and may wonder why the applicant did not feel qualified to prepare his or her own. Recruiters want to learn about you, not about someone else's interpretation of you.

Another problem is that once you've gone to the trouble and expense of having your résumé professionally prepared, you'll probably be reluctant to change it. But as any experienced job seeker can attest, you'll learn things during each interview that will help you sharpen your résumé, and you'll want to revise, add, delete, and reorganize the information.

Thus, a far better option is to design and prepare your résumé yourself. Your college placement office will likely have on file many résumés that you can review for format and content ideas. And consult some of the many employment guides, such as *How to Write a Winning Résumé*, by Deborah Bloch (VGM Career Horizons, 1987); *Your First Résumé*, by Ronald Fry (Career Press, 1989); and *What Color Is Your Parachute?*, by Richard Bolles (Ten Speed Press, 1987).

If you prepare your résumé and application letter on a computer, you can easily customize them for each employment opportunity. In addition, you'll be sending the employer a nonverbal message that you know how to use a computer and word processing software.

If you print your résumé on a laser printer, it will be nearly indistinguishable from a typeset one. With laser printers, you have the option of using different typefaces (such as Times Roman or Helvetica) and different sizes and styles (such as boldface and italics) to make different parts stand out. Consider the two versions of the same résumé shown in Figure 17.2. Although both contain identical information, which one do you think will make the better first impression?

Choose simple, easy-to-read type, and avoid the temptation to use a lot of "special effects" just because they're available on your computer. One or two typefaces in one or two different sizes should be enough. Use a simple format, with lots of white space, short paragraphs, and a logical organization. With type size and style, indentation, bullets, and the like, show which parts are subordinate to other parts.

Format your résumé on standard-size paper (8½ by 11 inches) so that it can be filed easily. Also, avoid brightly colored papers: They'll get attention, but perhaps the wrong kind. Dark colors do not photocopy well, and you want photocopies of your résumé (whether prepared by you or by the potential employer) to look professional. Choose white or an off-white (cream or ivory) paper, of good quality—at least 20-pound bond.

Unless you're applying for a creative position (such as a copywriter of advertising material) and know your intended audience well, avoid being too artistic and original in formatting your résumé. If you are applying for

Design and prepare your own résumé.

Use a clear, simple design, with plenty of white space.

FIGURE 17.2 First Impressions Count

PATRICIA L. BAILEY

(Address until May 10, 1992)	(Address after May 10, 1992)
112 Campus Drive, Apt. B	915 North Jay Street
Bloomington, IN 47401	Indianapolis, IN 46204
Phone: 812/555-9331	Phone: 317/555-0328

JOB OBJECTIVE

Professional position in hotel management in the Chicago metropolitan area

EDUCATION

Bachelor of Science in Business Administration
Indiana University: May 1992
Major: Hospitality Services Administration
Minor: Marketing
Achieved overall grade point average of 3.4 (on 4.0 scale)
Received Board of Regents' tuition scholarship
Financed 75% of college expenses though savings and part-time work.

WORK EXPERIENCE

Assistant Manager, McDonald's Restaur
Bloomington, Indiana: 1988-P
part-time during school year)
Advanced to this position
counter clerk and cook.
part-time employees. De
successful employee ince
able practical experience
handling human-relation
Student Intern, Valley Hideaway
South Bend, Indiana: Septemb
internship sponsored by India
Worked as an assistant t
resort. Gained experienc
management system. Re
and weekly occupancy re
employee newsletter.

PERSON/
Active member of Sigma Iota Epsilon (bu
Treasurer of Hospitality Services Associ
Special Olympics volunteer--Summer 19

REFERENCES AVAILABL

This version of the résumé was typed on an electronic typewriter and arranged in an attractive easy-to-read format. However, the lack of availability of different type styles and sizes limits design flexibility.

Patricia L. Bailey

(Address until May 10, 1992)	*(Address after May 10, 1992)*
112 Campus Drive, Apt. B	915 North Jay Street
Bloomington, IN 47401	Indianapolis, IN 46204
Phone: 812/555-9331	Phone: 371/555-0328

Job Objective
 Professional position in hotel management in the Chicago metropolitan area

Education
 Bachelor of Science in Business Administration   Indiana University—May 1992
 Major: Hospitality Services Administration
 Minor: Marketing
 • Achieved overall grade point average of 3.4 (on 4.0 scale)
 • Received Board of Regents' tuition scholarship
 • Financed 75% of college expenses through savings and part-time work.

Work Experience
 Assistant Manager, McDonald's Restaurant   Bloomington, Indiana
 1988-Present (full-time during summers; part-time during school year)
 • Advanced to this position after only six months as a counter clerk and cook.
 • Developed work schedules for 23 part-time employees.
 • Designed and administered several successful employee incentive projects.
 • Gained considerable practical experience in supervising employees and
   handling human-relations problems.

 Student Intern, Valley Hideaway   South Bend, Indiana
 September-December 1991 (full-time internship sponsored by Indiana University)
 • Worked as assistant to the night manager of 200-room resort.
 • Gained experience in operating GuestServ management system.
 • Responsible for producing daily and weekly occupancy reports.
 • Wrote two articles for employee newsletter.

Personal
 Active member of Sigma Iota Epsilon (business honor society)
 Treasurer of Hospitality Services Association
 Special Olympics volunteer—Summer 1991

References Available Upon Request

This version was typed on a microcomputer using word processing software (Word Perfect 5.1) and printed on a laser printer. It contains the same information as the typewritten version.

the typical business position, the overall appearance of your résumé should present a professional, conservative appearance—one that adds to your credibility. Don't scare off your readers before they have a chance to meet you.

Finally, your résumé and application letter must be 100% free from error—in content, spelling, grammar, and format. Ninety-nine percent accuracy is simply not good enough in seeking a job. Show right from the start that you're the type of person who takes pride in his or her work.

Résumé Content

Fortunately, perhaps, there is no such thing as a standard résumé; each is as individual as the person it represents. There are, however, standard parts of the résumé—those parts recruiters expect and need to see to make valid judgments. For example, one survey of 152 Fortune 500 company personnel indicated that 90% or more wanted the following information on a résumé:[11]

- Name, address, and telephone number
- Job objective
- College major, degree, name of college, and date of graduation
- Jobs held, employing company or companies (but not complete mailing addresses or the names of your supervisors), dates of employment, and job duties
- Special aptitudes and skills

Similarly, items *not* wanted on the résumé (items rated unimportant by over 90% of those surveyed) related primarily to bases for discrimination: religion, race, age, gender, photograph, and marital status. Additionally, most of the employers questioned thought high school activities should not be included on the résumés of college graduates.

The standard and optional parts of the résumé are discussed here in the order in which they typically appear on the résumé of a recent (or soon-to-be) college graduate:

Identifying Information   It doesn't do any good to impress a recruiter if he or she cannot locate you easily to schedule an interview; therefore, your name and complete address (including phone number) are crucial.

Your name should be the very first item on the résumé, arranged attractively at the top. Use whatever form you typically use for signing your name (e.g., with or without initials). Give your complete name, avoiding nicknames, and do not use a personal title such as *Mr.* or *Ms.*

It is not necessary to include the heading "Résumé" at the top, any more than it is necessary to use the heading "Letter" at the top of a business letter. The purpose of the document will be evident to the recruiter. Besides, you want your name to be the main heading—where it will stand out in the recruiter's mind.

If you will soon be changing an address (e.g., from a college address to a home address), include both, along with the relevant dates for each. If you are away from your telephone most of the day and no one is at home to answer it and take a message, you would be wise to invest in an

OBJECTIVE 5: Determine the appropriate content for your résumé.

Display your name, address, and phone number in a prominent position.

answering machine or get permission to use the telephone number where you work as an alternate phone listing. The important point is to be available for contact.

Job Objective   The job objective is a one-sentence summary that lets the reader know of your area of expertise and interest. As indicated, most recruiters want the objective listed so that they will know where you might fit into their organization. Don't force the employer to draw his or her own conclusions about your career goals.

Don't waste the objective's prominent spot at the top of your résumé by giving a weak, overgeneral goal such as the following:

- "A position that offers both a challenge and an opportunity for growth"
- "Challenging position in a progressive organization"
- "A responsible position that lets me use my education and experience and that provides opportunities for increased responsibilities"

The problem with such goals is not that they're unworthy objectives; they are *very* worthwhile. That is why everyone—including the recruiter, presumably—wants such positions. The problem is that such high-flown goals don't help the recruiter find a suitable position for *you*. They waste valuable space on your résumé.

For your objective to help you, it must be personalized—both for you and for the position you're seeking. Also, it must be specific enough to be useful to the prospective employer but not so specific as to exclude you from many types of similar positions. The following job objectives achieve these goals:

- "Position in personal sales in a medium-size manufacturing firm"
- "Opportunity to apply my accounting education and Spanish-language skills in a corporation overseas"
- "A public-relations position requiring well-developed communication, administrative, and computer skills"

Note that after reading these three objectives, you feel you know a little about each candidate, a feeling you did not get from reading the earlier general objectives. If your goals are so broad that you have difficulty specifying a job objective, consider either eliminating this section of your résumé or developing several résumés, each with a different job objective and emphasis.

Education   Unless your work experience has been extensive, fairly high level, and directly related to your job objective, your education is probably a stronger job qualification than your work experience and should therefore come first on the résumé.

List the title of your degree, the name of your college and its location if needed, your major and (if applicable) minor, and your expected date of graduation (month and year).

List your grade-point average if it will set you apart from the competition (generally, at least a 3.0 on a 4.0 scale). If you've made the dean's list or

Don't depend on a single job-getting technique for landing
the perfect job. Utilize techniques such as networking,
professional employment services, answering advertisements,
advertising yourself, and on-campus interviewing.
(*Source: Frank Siteman 1990 / The Picture Cube*)

have financed any substantial portion of your college expenses through
part-time work, savings, or scholarships, mention that. Unless your course
of study provided distinctive experiences that uniquely qualify you for the
job, avoid a lengthy listing of college courses.

Work Experience Today, almost half of all full-time college students are
employed, most of them working between 15 and 29 hours a week.[12] And
most other students have had at least some work experience in the past,
for example, summer jobs. Thus, most students will have some work
experience to bring to their future jobs.

Work experience—*any* work experience—is a definite plus. It shows the
employer that you've had experience in satisfying a superior, following
directions, accomplishing objectives through group effort, and being re-
warded for your labors. If your work experience has been directly related
to your job objectives, consider putting it ahead of the education section
where it will receive more emphasis.

In relating your work experience, use either a chronological or a functional
organizational pattern.

- *Chronological:* In a chronological arrangement, you organize your experience by date, describing your most recent job first and working
  backward. This format is most appropriate when you have had a strong
  continuing work history and much of your work has been related to your
  job objective (see Figure 17.3.) About 95% of all résumés are chronological, beginning with the most recent information and working backward.[13]

> Regardless of which type
> of organizational pattern
> you use, provide com-
> plete information about
> your work history.

■ *Functional:* In a functional arrangement, you organize your experience by type of function performed (such as supervision or budgeting) or by type of skills developed (such as human relations or communication skills). Then, under each, give specific examples (evidence) (see Figure 17.4). Functional résumés are most appropriate when you're changing industries, moving into an entirely different line of work, or are reentering the work force after a long period of unemployment, because they emphasize your skills rather than your employment history and let you show how these skills have broad applicability to other jobs.

In actual practice, the two patterns are not mutually exclusive; you can use a combination. And regardless of which arrangement you ultimately decide on, remember that more than 90% of the employers in the survey cited earlier indicated they want to see on a résumé the jobs held, employing company or companies, dates of employment, and job duties.

Remember that the purpose of describing your work history is to show the prospective employer what you've learned *that will benefit him or her.* No matter what your previous work, you've developed certain traits or had certain experiences that can be transferred to the new position. Based on your previous research into the duties of the job you are seeking, highlight those transferrable skills.

Show how your work experience qualifies you for the type of job for which you're applying.

If you can honestly do so, show in your résumé that you have developed as many of the following characteristics as possible:

■ Ability to work well with others
■ Communication skills
■ Competence and good judgment
■ Innovation
■ Reliability and trustworthiness
■ Enthusiasm
■ Honesty and moral character
■ Increasing responsibility
■ Loyalty
■ Supervisory ability

Use concrete, achievement-oriented words to describe your experience.

Complete sentences are not necessary. Instead, start your descriptions with action verbs, using present tense for current duties and past tense for previous job duties or accomplishments. Concrete words such as the following make your work experience come alive:

accomplished	collected	designed
achieved	communicated	determined
administered	completed	developed
analyzed	conceived	diagnosed
approved	concluded	directed
arranged	conducted	edited
applied	consolidated	established
assisted	contracted	evaluated
authorized	controlled	forecast
balanced	constructed	generated
budgeted	coordinated	guided
built	created	handled
changed	delegated	hired

implemented	operated	revised
increased	ordered	scheduled
instituted	organized	screened
interviewed	oversaw	secured
investigated	planned	sold
introduced	prepared	simplified
led	presented	studied
maintained	presided	supervised
managed	produced	taught
marketed	purchased	trained
modified	recommended	transformed
motivated	reported	updated
negotiated	researched	wrote

Avoid weak verbs such as *attempted, endeavored, hoped,* and *tried,* and avoid sexist language such as *manpower* or *chairman.* When possible, ensure credibility by listing actual accomplishments, giving numbers or dollar amounts. Highlight especially those accomplishments that have direct relevance to the desired job. Here are some examples:

Weak: I was responsible for a large sales territory.
Better: Managed a six-county sales territory; increased sales 13% during first full year.

Weak: I worked as a clerk in the cashier's office.
Better: Balanced the cash register each day; was the only part-time employee entrusted to make nightly cash deposits.

Weak: Worked as a bouncer at local bar.
Better: Maintained order at Nick's Side Door Saloon; learned first-hand the importance of compromise and negotiation in solving problems.

Weak: Worked as a volunteer for Art Reach.
Better: Personally sold more than $1,000 worth of tickets to annual benefit dance; introduced an "Each one, reach one" membership drive that increased membership every year during my three-year term as membership chairperson.

As illustrated in the last example, if you have little or no actual work experience, show how your involvement with professional, social, or civic organizations has helped you develop skills that are transferrable to the workplace. Volunteer work, for example, can help develop valuable skills in time management, working with groups, handling money, speaking, accepting responsibility, and the like. In addition, many schools offer internships where a student receives course credit and close supervision while holding down a temporary job. | Work experience need not be restricted to paid positions.

The résumé has been called "a balance sheet without any liabilities," and readers recognize your right to put your best foot forward in your résumé; that is, to highlight your strengths and minimize your weaknesses. However, you must never lie about anything and must never take credit for anything you did not do. A simple telephone call can verify any statement on your résumé. Don't risk destroying your credibility before being hired, and don't risk the possibility of being dismissed later for misrepresenting your qualifications. | Be ethical in all aspects of your résumé.

As space permits, include other information that uniquely qualifies you for the type of position for which you're applying.

Other Relevant Information   If you have special skills that might give you an edge over the competition (such as knowledge of a foreign language), list them. Although competence in common software programs such as spreadsheets, word processing, and databases was considered a special skill in the past, today employers assume that all business graduates will have such skills; therefore, listing them will not be of special benefit to you. However, nonbusiness majors should list these and any other specific business skills on their résumés.

Include any honors or recognitions that have relevance to the job you're seeking. Memberships in business-related organizations demonstrate your commitment to your profession and should be listed if space permits. Likewise, involvement in volunteer, civic, and other extracurricular activities gives evidence of a well-rounded individual and reflects your values and commitment.

Avoid including any data that can become grounds for a discrimination suit—such as information about age, gender, race, religion, handicaps, marital status, and the like. Do not include a photograph with your application papers. Some employers like to have the applicant's Social Security number included as an aid in verifying college or military information. If you have military experience, include it. If your name stereotypes you as a possible noncitizen and citizenship is important for the job you want, you may want to explicitly state your citizenship.

Other optional information includes hobbies and special interests, travel experiences, willingness to travel, and health status. (However, since it is unlikely that anyone has ever written "Health—Poor" on a résumé, including a health statement may be meaningless.) Such information may be included if it has direct relevance to your desired job and if you have room for it, but it may be safely omitted if space is needed for more important information.

The names of references are generally not included on the résumé.

References   A **reference** is a person who has agreed to provide information to a prospective employer regarding a job applicant's fitness for a job. As a general rule, the names and addresses of references are not given on the résumé itself. Instead, give a general statement that references are available. This policy ensures that you will be contacted before your references are called. The exception to this practice is if your references are likely to be known by the person reading your résumé; in this case, their names should be listed.

Your references should be professional references rather than character references. The best ones are employers, especially your present employer. University professors with whom you have had a close and successful relationship are also valuable references. When asking for references, be prepared to sign a waiver stating that you won't claim that a reference prevented you from getting a job. Many firms are becoming reluctant to authorize their managers to provide reference letters because of the possibility of being sued.

Study the résumé presented earlier in Figure 17.2 and the two presented in Figures 17.3 and 17.4. Note the different formats that can be used to present the data. As stated earlier, there is no standard résumé format. Use

Résumé—Chronological Format   **FIGURE 17.3**

<table>
<tr><td>

Aurelia Gomez

225 West 70 Street, New York, NY 10023
Phone: Days— (212) 555–3079; Evenings— (212) 555–3821

Career Objective   1
Entry-level staff accounting position with a public accounting firm.

Experience

Summer   <u>Accounting Intern</u>: Coopers & Lybrand, New York City

1991   Assisted in preparing corporate tax returns; attended meetings with
          clients; conducted research in corporate tax library and wrote research
          reports; was invited to work again the following summer.

Nov. 1987– <u>Payroll Specialist</u>: City of New York
June 1990   Full-time civil-service position in Department of Administration. Used   2
            payroll software on both DEC 1034 minicomputer and IBM microcompu-
            ters; audited all overtime billing; developed two new forms for requesting
            independent-contractor status that are now used throughout all branches
            of city government; represented 28-person work unit on the department's
            management-labor committee; left job to pursue college degree full time.

Education

Jan. 1985– Pursuing a bachelor of business administration degree from New York   3
Present   University

            Major: Accounting
            Expected graduation date: June 1992
            Attended part-time from 1985 until 1990 while holding a full-time job;
            have financed 100% of all college expenses through savings, part-time
            work, and student loans; plan to sit for the CPA exam in November 1992.

Personal

• Helped start the Minority Business Student Association at New York University and
  served as program director for two years; secured the publisher of <u>Black Enterprise</u>
  magazine as a banquet speaker
• Have traveled extensively throughout the Caribbean
• Member of the Accounting Society
• Excellent health
• Willing to relocate

References Available on Request

</td><td>

Name is in larger type to stand out.

Objective is specific enough to be useful.

Applicant considers her work experience to be a stronger qualification than her education and so puts it first.

Notice the use of action words: *assisted, conducted, wrote, developed,* and so on.

Provides degree, institution, major, and graduation date.

Provides additional data to enhance her credentials.

Actual names and addresses are not included.

</td></tr>
</table>

Grammar and Mechanics Notes

1. Major section headings are in parallel format.   2. To conserve space and emphasize active words, incomplete sentences are used (it would be boring to have so many sentences starting with "I."   3. The side headings for the dates were set up using parallel columns. Note that abbreviations may be used.

FIGURE 17.4   Résumé—Functional Format

Provides both temporary and permanent address.

The three skill areas are introduced in the objective and expanded in the sections that follow.

Note how each item listed relates directly to the desired job.

Provides specific evidence to support each skill.

Note how work experiences, education, and extracurricular activities are all woven into the skill statements.

Doesn't repeat the duties given earlier.

Raymond J. Arnold

15 Turner Hall
Northern Arizona University
Flagstaff, AZ 86001-8134
Phone: (602) 555-9883

Address after June 15, 1992:

801 Benjamin Avenue
Apartment 16-G
Norfolk, NE 68701
Phone: (308) 555-3714

OBJECTIVE   1
   Labor relations position in large multinational firm that requires well-developed
   labor relations, management, and communications skills

LABOR-RELATIONS SKILLS   2
   • Majored in labor relations; minored in psychology
   • Belong to Local 463 of International Office Workers Union (member since
     1989)
   • Was crew chief for second-shift work team at Valley National Bank
   • Served as student member of faculty senate, Northern Arizona University

MANAGEMENT SKILLS
   • Learned time-management skills by working 30 hours per week while attending
     school full-time
   • Was promoted twice in three years at Valley National Bank
   • Sharpened interpersonal and human relations skills while dealing extensively
     with the public as a teller and salesperson
   • Practiced discretion while dealing with financial affairs of others; treated all
     transactions confidentially

COMMUNICATION SKILLS   3
   • Was newsletter editor for Alpha Kappa Psi, professional business fraternity
   • Ran for senior class vice president, requiring frequent campaign speeches and
     impromptu remarks
   • Took elective classes in report writing and business research
   • Know how to use word processing and desktop publishing software

EDUCATION
   Bachelor of Science degree from Northern Arizona University
   Degree to be awarded June 1992
   Major: Labor Relations; Minor: Psychology

EXPERIENCE   4
   Bank Teller, Valley National Bank, Flagstaff, Arizona: 1989-Present

   Salesperson, Penney's, Norfolk, Nebraska: Summer 1987

REFERENCES
   Available from Placement and Career Information Center, Northern Arizona
   University, Flagstaff, AZ 86001-8134; phone: (602) 555-2000.

Grammar and Mechanics Notes

1. Putting the headings along the side and indenting the copy opens up the résumé, providing more white space.   2. Bullets are used to highlight the individual skills; asterisks would have worked just as well.   3. All items are in parallel format.   4. Uses less spacing to separate items within a section than to separate the sections.

these résumés or others to which you may have access (available from your college placement office or from job-hunting books) to glean ideas for formatting your own.

Note also the different organizational patterns used to convey work experience. The résumé in Figure 17.3 is arranged in a chronological pattern (with the most recent work experience listed first), whereas the one in Figure 17.4 is arranged in a functional pattern that stresses the skills learned rather than the jobs held. Note how job descriptions and skills are all geared to support the applicant's qualifications for the desired job. Note also the concise, concrete language used and the overall tone of quiet confidence.

Because your résumé is about you, it is perhaps the most personal business document you'll ever write. Use everything you know about successful communication techniques to ensure that you tell your story in the most effective manner possible. After you're satisfied with the content and arrangement of your résumé, proofread your document carefully and have several others proofread it also. Then have it photocopied on high-quality white or off-white 8½ by 11-inch paper, and turn your attention to your cover letters.

The guidelines for developing a résumé are summarized in Checklist 16 on page 572.

WRITING APPLICATION LETTERS

A résumé by itself is all that is generally needed to secure an interview with an on-campus recruiter. However, you will likely not want to limit your job search to those employers that interview on campus. Campus recruiters typically represent large organizations or regional employers. Thus, if you want to work in a smaller organization or in a distant location, you need to contact those organizations by writing application letters.

An **application letter** communicates to the prospective employer your interest in and qualifications for a position within the organization. The letter is also called a *cover letter*, because it introduces (or "covers") the major points in your résumé, which should then be included with the application letter. A **solicited application letter** is written in response to an advertised vacancy, whereas an **unsolicited application letter** (also called a "prospecting" letter) is written to an organization that has not advertised a vacancy.

Most job applicants use the same résumé when applying for numerous positions and then use their application letter to personalize their qualifications for the specific job for which they are applying. Even so, much of the information in cover letters remains constant; therefore, using word processing software will result in less input time and higher-quality output.

Because the application letter is the first thing the employer will read about you, it is of crucial importance. Make sure the letter is formatted appropriately, looks attractive, and is free from typographical, spelling, and grammar errors. Don't forget to sign the letter, and don't forget to enclose a copy of your résumé.

OBJECTIVE 6: Compose a solicited and unsolicited application letter.

Use the application letter, which is often your first contact with the potential employer, to personalize your qualifications for one specific job.

Writing a Résumé

Length and Format

1. For most entry-level positions, keep your résumé to one page.

2. For maximum impact and flexibility, format your résumé on a computer with word processing software and print it on a laser printer.

3. Use a simple format, with lots of white space, and short blocks of text. By means of type size, indenting, bullets, boldface, and the like, show which parts are subordinate to other parts.

4. Print your résumé on standard-sized, good-quality white or off-white (cream or ivory) paper.

5. Make sure the finished document looks professional, attractive, and conservative and is 100% error free.

Content

6. Type your complete name (without a personal title) at the top of the document (omit the word *résumé*) followed by an address (both temporary and permanent if needed) and a daytime phone number.

7. Include a one-sentence job objective specific enough to be useful but not so specific as to preclude consideration for similar jobs.

8. Determine whether your education or your work experience is your stronger qualification, and list it first. For work experience, determine whether to use a chronological (most recent job first) or a functional (list of competencies and skills developed) organizational pattern.

9. For education, list the title of your degree, the name of your college and its location, your major and minor, and your expected date of graduation (month and year). List your grade-point average if it is impressive, and any academic honors. Avoid listing college courses that are part of the normal preparation for your desired position.

10. For work experience, stress those duties or skills that are transferrable to the new position. Use short phrases and action verbs, and provide specific evidence of the results you achieved.

11. Include any additional information (e.g., special skills, professional affiliations, and willingness to travel or relocate) that will help to distinguish you from the competition. Avoid including such personal information as age, gender, race, religion, handicaps, or marital status.

12. Provide a statement that references are available on request.

13. Throughout, highlight your strengths and minimize your weaknesses, but always tell the truth.

Some personnel specialists say they learn more about the applicant from reading a cover letter than from reading a résumé. According to one recruiter, "A résumé tells what they [job applicants] have done. A cover

Because of the danger that a professionally-prepared
résumé might resemble other applicants' résumés, you
might prefer to design and prepare your résumé yourself.
Preparing it on a computer allows you to customize your
résumé for each employment opportunity. Furthermore, if
you print your résumé on a laser printer, it will be nearly
indistinguishable from typeset ones.
(*Source: Arnold J. Kaplan / The Picture Cube*)

letter tells who they are. I can learn a person's style, poise, confidence,
humbleness, skills, control of the language, and potential from a cover
letter."[14]

Your cover letter is a sales letter—you're selling your qualifications to
the prospective employer. You should use the same persuasive techniques
you learned earlier; for example, provide specific evidence, stress reader
benefits, avoid exaggeration, and show confidence in the quality of your
product.

An application letter should be no longer than one page. Let's examine
each part of a typical letter. Figure 17.5 shows a solicited application
letter—a letter to accompany the résumé presented in Figure 17.3. An
unsolicited application letter is shown on p. 580.)

Address and Salutation

Your letter should be addressed to an individual rather than to an
organization or department. Remember, the more hands your letter must
go through before it reaches the right person, the more chance for something
to go wrong. Ideally, your letter should be addressed to the person who
will actually interview you and who will likely be your supervisor if you
get the job.

Address your letter to a
specific individual in the
organization.

FIGURE 17.5   Solicited Application Letter

This is an example of a solicited application letter (see the corresponding résumé in Figure 17.3).

March 13, 1992   1

Mr. David Norman, Partner
Ross, Russell & Weston
452 Fifth Avenue
New York, NY 10018

Dear Mr. Norman:

Opening identifies the job position and the source of advertising.

My varied work experience in accounting and payroll services, coupled with my accounting degree, has prepared me for the position of EDP specialist that you advertised in the March 9 New York Times.   2
                                                                                   3

Emphasizes a qualification that might distinguish the writer from other applicants.

In addition to taking required courses in accounting and business information systems as part of my accounting major at New York University, I also took an elective course in EDP auditing and control. The training I received in this course in applications, software, systems, and service-center records would enable me to become an immediately productive member of your EDP consulting staff.

Relates her work experience to the specific needs of the employer.

My college training has been augmented by an internship in a large public accounting firm. In addition, my two and a half years of experience as a payroll specialist for the city of New York have given me first-hand knowledge of the operation and needs of non-profit agencies. This experience will enable me to contribute to your large consulting practice with governmental agencies.

Refers to the enclosed résumé and tactfully asks for an interview.
Telephone number may be given either in the body or in the last line of the address block.

After you have had an opportunity to review my enclosed résumé, I would appreciate having the opportunity to discuss with you in person why I believe I have the right qualifications and personality to serve you and your clients. I can be reached by phone at (212) 555-3821 after 3 p.m. daily.   4

                                         Sincerely,

                                         Aurelia Gomez

                                         Aurelia Gomez
                                         225 West 70th Street   5
                                         New York, NY 10023

Enclosure

Grammar and Mechanics Notes

1. This letter is formatted in modified-block style with standard punctuation (colon after the salutation and comma after the complimentary closing). 2. Underline the name of newspapers. 3. Do not capitalize the names of college courses unless they include a proper noun. 4. The word *résumé* may also be properly typed without the accent marks: *resume*. 5. Putting the writer's name and address together at the bottom makes it convenient for the reader to respond to the letter.

If you do not know enough about the prospective employer to know the name of the appropriate person (the decision maker), you have probably not gathered enough data. If necessary, call the organization to make sure you have the right name—including the correct spelling—and position title. In your salutation, use a courtesy title (such as *Mr.* or *Ms.*) along with the person's last name.

Some job-vacancy ads are blind ads; they do not identify the hiring company by name and provide only a post-office address, often in care of the newspaper or magazine that contains the ad. In such a situation, you (and all others responding to that ad) have no choice but to address your letter to the newspaper and to use a generic salutation, such as "Dear Personnel Manager."

Opening

The opening paragraph of a solicited application letter is fairly straightforward. Since the organization has advertised an opening, it is eager to receive quality applications, so use a direct organization: state (or imply) the reason for your letter, identify the particular position for which you're applying, and indicate how you learned about the opening.

Gear your opening to the job and to the specific organization. For positions that are widely perceived to be somewhat conservative (e.g., finance, accounting, and banking), use a restrained opening. For more creative work (e.g., sales, advertising, and public relations), you might start out on a more imaginative note. Here are two examples:

> Mr. Adam Storkel, manager of your Fleet Street branch, has suggested that I submit my qualifications for the position of assistant loan officer that was advertised in last week's *Indianapolis Business*.

> If quality is Job One at Ford, then Job Two must surely be communicating that message effectively to the public. My degree in journalism and work experience at the Kintzell Agency will enable me to help you achieve that objective. The enclosed résumé further describes my qualifications for the position of advertising copywriter posted in the June issue of *Automotive Age*.

For unsolicited application letters, you must first get the reader's attention. You can gain that attention most easily by talking about the company rather than about yourself. One effective strategy is to show that you know something about the organization—its recent projects, awards, changes in personnel, and the like—and then to show how you can contribute to the organization's effort.

> Now that EDS has expanded operations to Central America, can you use a marketing graduate who speaks fluent Spanish and who knows the culture of the region?

Your opening should be short, interesting, and reader-oriented. Avoid tired openings such as "This is to apply for . . ." or "Please consider this letter my application for . . ." Also maintain an air of formality. Don't address the reader by first name and don't try to be cute. Avoid such

Use the direct organizational plan for writing a solicited application letter.

Emphasize how you can help the organization.

attention-grabbing stunts as sending a worn, once-white running shoe with the note "Now that I have one foot in the door, I hope you'll let me get the other one in" or writing the application letter beginning at the bottom of the page and working upward (to indicate a willingness to start at the bottom and work one's way up). Such gimmicks send a nonverbal message to the reader that the applicant may be trying to deflect attention from a weak résumé.

Body

In a paragraph or two, highlight your strongest qualifications and show how they can benefit the employer. Show—don't tell; that is, provide specific, credible evidence to support your statements, using wording different from that used in the résumé. Tell an anecdote about yourself ("For example, recently I . . ."). Your discussion should reflect modest confidence rather than a hard-sell approach. Avoid starting too many sentences with "I."

> *Not:* I am an effective supervisor.
> *But:* Supervising a staff of five counter clerks taught me . . .

> *Not:* I am an accurate typist.
> *But:* In my two years of experience as a student secretary, none of the letters, memorandums, and reports I typed were ever returned with a typographical error marked.

> *Not:* I took a course in business communications.
> *But:* The communication strategies I learned in my business communication course will enable me to solve customer problems as a customer-service representative at Allegheny Industries.

Refer the reader to the enclosed résumé. Subordinate the reference to the résumé, and emphasize what it contains.

> *Not:* I am enclosing a copy of my résumé for your review.
> *But:* As detailed in the enclosed résumé, my extensive work experience in records management has prepared me to help you "take charge of this paperwork jungle," as headlined in your classified ad.

Closing

You are not likely to get what you do not ask for, so close by asking for a personal interview. Indicate flexibility regarding scheduling and location. Provide your phone number—either in the last paragraph or (preferably) immediately below your name and address in the closing lines.

> After you have reviewed my qualifications, I would appreciate your calling or writing to let me know when we can meet to discuss further my employment with Connecticut Power and Light. I will be in the Hartford area from December 16 through January 4 and could come to your office at any time that is convenient for you.

Marginal notes:

Don't repeat all the information from the résumé.

Politely ask for an interview.

Writing an Application Letter

1. Use your application letter to show how the qualifications listed in your résumé have prepared you for the specific job for which you're applying.

2. If possible, address your letter to the individual in the organization who will interview you if you're successful.

3. When applying for an advertised opening, begin by stating (or implying) the reason for the letter, identify the position for which you're applying, and tell how you learned about the position.

4. When writing an unsolicited application letter, first gain the reader's attention by showing that you are familiar with the company and can make a unique contribution to its efforts.

5. In one or two paragraphs, highlight your strongest qualifications and relate them directly to the needs of the position for which you're applying. Refer the reader to the enclosed résumé.

6. Treat your letter as a persuasive sales letter: provide specific evidence, stress reader benefits, avoid exaggeration, and show confidence in the quality of your product.

7. Close by tactfully asking for an interview.

8. Maintain an air of formality throughout the letter. Avoid cuteness.

9. Make sure the finished document presents a professional, attractive, and conservative appearance and that it is 100% error free.

Or: I will call your office next week to see if we can arrange a meeting at your convenience to discuss my qualifications for working as a financial analyst with your organization.

Use a standard complimentary closing (such as "Sincerely"), leave enough space to sign the letter, and then type your name, address, and phone number immediately below. Include an enclosure notation (for your résumé). Even though you may be sending out many application letters at the same time, take care with each individual letter. You never know which one will be the one that actually gets you the interview. Sign your name neatly in blue or black ink, fold each letter and accompanying résumé neatly, and mail.

The guidelines for writing an application letter are summarized above in Checklist 17.

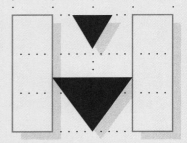

MICROWRITING AN APPLICATION LETTER

The Problem

You are Ray Arnold, a senior labor relations major at Northern Arizona University. You have analyzed your interests, strengths and weaknesses, and preferred lifestyle and have decided you would like to work in some area of labor relations for a large multinational firm in Southern California. Because you attend a medium-sized school in a small Arizona town some distance from Southern California, you decide not to limit your job search to on-campus interviewing.

In your research you learned that Precision Systems, Inc. (PSI), has recently been awarded a $23 million contract by the U.S. Department of State to develop a high-level computerized message system to provide fast and secure communications among U.S. government installations throughout Europe. PSI, which is headquartered in Los Angeles, will build a new automated factory in Cuidad Juárez, Mexico, to assemble the electronic components for the new system.

You decide to write to PSI to see whether they might have an opening for someone with your qualifications. You will, of course, include a copy of your résumé with your letter. (See Figure 17.4 for the résumé.) Send your letter to Ms. Phyllis Morrison, Assistant Director of Personnel for Precision Systems, Inc., P.O. Box 18734, Los Angeles, CA 90018.

The Process

1. Will this be a solicited or unsolicited (prospecting) letter?

   ```
   Unsolicited--I don't know whether PSI has an opening or
   not.
   ```

2. Write an opening paragraph for your letter that gets attention and that relates your skills to PSI's needs. Make sure the purpose of your letter is clear from your opening paragraph.

   ```
   PSI's recently accepted proposal to the State
   Department estimated that you would be adding up to
   3,000 new staff for the Cuidad Juárez project. With
   this dramatic increase in personnel, do you have an
   opening in your human resources department for a
   college graduate with a major in labor relations and a
   minor in psychology?
   ```

3. Compare your education with PSI's likely requirements. What will help you stand out from the competition?

   ```
   --It's somewhat unusual for a labor relations major to
     have a psychology minor.
   --My coursework on my major and minor were pretty
     standard, so there's no need to list individual
     courses.
   ```

4. Compare your work experiences with PSI's likely requirements. What qualifications from your résumé should you highlight in your letter?

```
--The interpersonal and human relations skills
  developed as a teller will be an important asset in
  labor management.
--Written and oral communication skills developed
  through work and extracurricular activities will
  enable me to communicate effectively with a widely
  dispersed work force.
```

5. What other qualifications should you mention?

```
My degree in labor relations, combined with my union
membership, will help me look at each issue from the
perspective of both management and labor.
```

6. Write the sentence in which you request an interview.

```
I would welcome the opportunity to come to Los Angeles
to discuss with you the role I might play in helping
PSI manage its human resources in an efficient and
humane manner.
```

The Product

This is an example of an unsolicited application letter (see the corresponding résumé in Figure 17.4).

Begins with an attention-getting opening that relates the writer's skills to the needs of the company.

Shows how the writer's unique qualifications will benefit the company.

Provides specific evidence to support his claims. *Shows*, rather than *tells*.

Gives the reader the option of phoning the applicant or having him phone her.

```
                                                                    1
        15 Turner Hall
        Northern Arizona University
        Flagstaff, AZ 86001-8134
        February 7, 1992

                                                                    2
        Ms. Phyllis Morrison
        Assistant Director of Personnel
        Precision Systems, Inc.
        P.O. Box 18734
        Los Angeles, CA 90018

        Dear Ms. Morrison:

        PSI's recently accepted proposal to the State Department estimated
        that your organization would be adding up to 3,000 new staff for
        the Cuidad Juárez project. With this dramatic increase in
        personnel, will you have an opening in your human resources      3
        department for a recent college graduate with a major in labor
        relations and a minor in psychology?

        My combination of coursework in business and liberal arts will
        enable me to approach each issue from both a management and a
        behavioral point of view. Further, my degree in labor relations
        along with my experience as a union member will help me consider
        each issue from the perspective of both management and labor.

        During my term as editor of a student newsletter, the Scholastic
        Press Association recognized our publication for its ''original,
        balanced, and refreshingly candid writing style.'' On the job,   4
        dealing successfully with customers' overdrawn accounts, bank
        computer errors, and delayed-deposit recording has taught me the
        value of active listening and has given me experience in
        explaining and justifying the company's position. As detailed on
        the enclosed résumé, these communication and human-relations
        skills will help me to interact and communicate effectively with
        PSI employees at all levels and at widely dispersed locations.    5

        I would welcome the opportunity to come to Los Angeles at your
        convenience to discuss with you the role I might play in helping
        PSI manage its human resources in an efficient and humane manner.
        I will call your office on February 14, or you may call me at any
        time after 2 p.m. daily at (602) 555-9863.


        Sincerely,

        Raymond J. Arnold

        Raymond J. Arnold

        Enclosure
```

Grammar and Mechanics Notes

1. In a personal business letter, the writer's return address may be typed above the date or below the sender's name. 2. This letter is formatted in block style, with all lines beginning at the left margin and in open punctuation, with no punctuation after the salutation and complimentary closing. 3. Do not capitalize the names of college majors and minors. 4. A period goes inside the closing quotation mark. 5. Do not hyphenate a compound adjective followed by a noun (such as "widely dispersed locations") if the first word ends in -ly.

SUMMARY

One of the most important communication tasks you will ever do is securing a rewarding and worthwhile job. The job-seeking campaign thus requires considerable time, effort, and thought.

The planning phase begins with a self-analysis of your interests, strengths, weaknesses, and needs. Then you should gather data about possible jobs, demographic trends, and industries and companies in which you're interested. Use all available sources of information and strategies, including networking, professional employment services, job announcements and advertisements, and self-promotion.

The purpose of your résumé is to get you a job interview. Strive for a one-page document, preferably typed in a simple, readable format on a computer and output on a laser printer. Include your name, address, phone number, job objective, information about your education and work experience, and special aptitudes and skills. Include other information only if it will help to distinguish you favorably from the other applicants. Use either a chronological or functional organization for your work experience, and stress those skills and experiences that can be transferred to the job you want.

You will typically use the same résumé when applying for numerous positions and then construct an application letter that discusses how your education and experience qualify you specifically for the job at hand. If possible, address your letter to the person who will interview you for the job. When writing a solicited application letter, begin by stating the reason for your letter, identify the position for which you're applying, and tell how you learned about the position. When writing an unsolicited letter, you must first gain the reader's attention. Then use the body of your letter to highlight one or two of your strongest qualifications, relating them to the needs of the position for which you're applying. Close by politely asking for an interview.

If your application efforts are successful, you will be invited to come for an interview. Successful interviewing strategies are covered in the next chapter.

KEY TERMS

Application letter— A letter from a job applicant to a prospective employer explaining the applicant's interest in and qualifications for a position within the organization; also called a "cover" letter.

Reference— A person who has agreed to provide information to a prospective employer regarding a job applicant's fitness for a job.

Résumé— A brief record of one's personal history and qualifications that is typically prepared by a job applicant.

Solicited application letter— An application letter written in response to an advertised job vacancy.

Unsolicited application letter— An application letter written to an organization that has not advertised a vacancy; also called a "prospecting" letter.

REVIEW AND DISCUSSION

▶ OBJECTIVE 1

1. Think of two different occupations. How might the answers to the 14 questions on page 552 differ for someone interested in each of these occupations?

▶ OBJECTIVE 2

2. What types of career information are contained in the *Occupational Outlook Handbook*?

▶ OBJECTIVE 3

3. What services does the placement office or career-information center at your own institution provide?

▶ OBJECTIVE 4
▶ OBJECTIVE 4
▶ OBJECTIVE 4

4. What is the purpose of a résumé?
5. How long should a résumé be?
6. What are the advantages of preparing your own résumé rather than having a service prepare it?

▶ OBJECTIVE 5

7. Under what conditions should the education section precede the work-experience section?

▶ OBJECTIVE 5
▶ OBJECTIVE 5
▶ OBJECTIVE 5

8. What kinds of information should *always* go in a résumé?
9. What kinds of information should *never* go in a résumé?
10. What is the difference between a chronological and a functional organizational pattern?

▶ OBJECTIVE 5
▶ OBJECTIVE 6

11. How should references be treated in a résumé?
12. What is the difference between a solicited and an unsolicited application letter?

▶ OBJECTIVE 6

13. When might it be necessary *not* to address the application letter to the specific person who will be interviewing you?

▶ OBJECTIVE 6

14. Assume that you are interested in a position as a personnel specialist. Construct an opening paragraph both for a solicited and for an unsolicited application letter.

▶ OBJECTIVE 6

15. Should the focus of an application letter be on the past or the future? Explain.

EXERCISES

▶ OBJECTIVE 1

1. **Self-Assessment** As a first step in your job campaign, answer the 14 questions given on page 552. Type each question, and then answer it. Although the content of the answer is certainly more important than mechanics and format, use this exercise as a test of your basic writing skills as well, taking care to use complete sentences, correct grammar, and good writing style.

▶ OBJECTIVE 1

2. **Tell Me About Yourself** One of the most common strategies an interviewer uses to start an interview is to ask you to tell him or her something about yourself. Of course, you need to think about this question much earlier than the interview; the start of your job campaign is the time for this self-disclosure. In approximately 250 words (i.e., a one-page double-spaced report), respond to the interviewer's request to "tell me about yourself." Keep in mind your job objective.

▶ OBJECTIVE 2

3. **Audience Analysis—International** Assume that you wish to work in another country upon graduation from college. Select a company headquartered in another country, and research that organization. Learn about its products, economic outlook, employment needs,

politics, organizational climate, and the like. Knowing what you know about the company, what points about your own background might you stress in your application letter and résumé that would be of particular interest to them? Write a two-page memo report to your instructor detailing what you've learned about the organization (and about yourself).

4. **Career Planning**   Select a career in which you might be interested. Using at least four references (one of which should be the latest edition of the *Occupational Outlook Handbook*), write a two-page memo report to your instructor with the following sections:

   a. *Job description:* Include in this section a description of the job, including, perhaps, a definition of the job, typical duties, working conditions, and the kinds of knowledge, skills, and education needed.

   b. *Employment levels:* Nationally, how many people are employed in this type of job? Are employment levels increasing or decreasing? Why? What industries or what parts of the country are experiencing the greatest and the least demand for this job? What are the projected employment levels in the future?

   c. *Salary:* Discuss the latest salary statistics for this job—actual salaries, changes, trends, and projections.

   d. *Expected changes:* What changes are expected in this career within the next ten years or so? Discuss both the expected changes and the factors causing such changes. For example, will technology have any impact on this job? International business competition? Federal or state regulation?

   Provide a concluding paragraph for your memo report that summarizes the career information you've discussed, and then indicate whether your initial opinion about the job has changed as a result of your research.

5. **Collaborative Project—Job-Getting Techniques**   Working in a group of four to five students, complete the following tasks:

   a. Select an occupation. (Perhaps, to be fair to everyone, you might select one that none of you plans to pursue as a career.)

   b. Compose a list of five people any of you know who might provide information about this career or possible job leads. Tell why each person in your network of contacts was chosen.

   c. Interview (either in person or by telephone) a counselor at a nearby private employment service to determine what help the service could provide in securing a job in this occupation.

   d. Review the help-wanted ads in your local newspaper to determine what types of jobs are available in this occupation. Write a memo report to your instructor presenting the results of your research.

6. **Résumé Project**   Assume that you are beginning the last term of your senior year in college. Using factual data from your own education, work experience, and so on (include any data that you expect to be true at the time of your graduation), prepare a résumé in an effective format. Make five photocopies of your résumé on appropriate paper—the kind you would use for your job campaign. Meet with three professionals who have expertise in your career area—the type of people who might be interviewing you for a job. Ask them to critique

OBJECTIVE 2 ◄

OBJECTIVE 3 ◄

OBJECTIVES 4–5 ◄

your résumé for you, commenting both on positive aspects and on any areas that should be strengthened. Revise your résumé based on this feedback. Submit a copy of both your original résumé and your revised version to your instructor, along with a memo explaining what was revised and why.

OBJECTIVES 4–5

7. **Résumé Project—Format**   Review the final résumé you developed in Exercise 6. Using the same information, prepare another résumé in a different format; that is, include the same content but arrange it on the page differently. Which format do you think works better? Why? Submit both résumés, along with a short memo to your instructor, evaluating the format of each document.

OBJECTIVE 6

8. **Application-Letter Project**   This project consists of writing both a solicited and an unsolicited application letter. Prepare each letter in an appropriate format and on appropriate paper. Include a copy of your résumé with each letter. Submit each letter to your instructor folded and inserted into a correctly addressed envelope (don't forget to sign your letter).

   a. Identify a large prospective employer—one that has not advertised for an opening in your field. Using the résumé you developed in Exercise 6, write an unsolicited application letter.

   b. For various reasons, you might not secure a position directly related to your college major. In such a situation, it is especially important that you show how your qualifications (no matter what they are) match the needs of the employer. Using your own background, apply for the following position, which was advertised in last Sunday's *New York Times*:

   MANAGER-TRAINEE POSITION. Philip Morris is looking for recent college graduates to enter its management-trainee program in preparation for an exciting career in one of the diversified companies that make up Philip Morris. Excellent beginning salary and benefits, good working conditions, and a company that cares about you. (Reply to Box 385-G in care of this newspaper.)

OBJECTIVES 1–3

CASE   PROBLEM

"Help Wanted"

When Neelima Shrikhande accepted the position of vice president of administration at Urban Systems, she knew she would have to work closely with Marc Kaplan, vice president of marketing. However, being an ardent feminist, she resented Marc's condescending attitude toward her and his chauvinistic remarks toward female employees in general.

Despite her best efforts, their relationship has now deteriorated to the point that Neelima believes it is adversely affecting her ability to perform her job effectively. Knowing that Marc (one of the two founders of the company) has no plans to leave, Neelima has decided to explore other career opportunities.

Neelima is savvy enough to recognize that she is highly marketable and that many organizations would be eager to create a position for her even if they had no advertised openings. She is interested in finding a position in information management at a large organization located in a metropolitan area. She is free to relocate anywhere in the country. Hoping to avoid the kind of situation she presently faces, she would like to become associated with a progressive organization, preferably one whose top-level officers are active in social and political causes. An organization that has other females in prominent top-level positions who could serve as her mentors would be especially attractive.

Your assignment is to locate three organizations that would be top prospects for Neelima to explore for a career move. Identify the organizations and provide sufficient evidence to show how they would be a good "fit" for Neelima in terms of the criteria just discussed. Present a balanced view of the organizations, providing both positive and negative information. Finally, provide the name, address, and phone number of an appropriate person for Neelima to contact. Organize your information in a logical manner, and present it as a letter report to Neelima.

Note: Although you already know quite a bit about Neelima—both from the background information contained in Appendix D and from the case studies in previous chapters, you may assume any additional reasonable information you need to complete this project.

Studies show the average person has three phobias. Every fear has a name. W O R D   W I S E
Are you the victim of any of the following fears?

- Bibliophobia (books)
- Glossophobia (speaking in public)
- Graphophobia (writing)
- Haphephobia (touching or being touched)
- Laliophobia (talking)
- Onomatophobia (a specific word or name)
- Sophophobia (knowledge)
- Verbaphobia (words)

Note: If you have more than three of these fears, you may be a victim of pantophobia—the morbid fear of everything!

CHAPTER 18

Other Employment Communications

After you have finished this chapter, you will be able to

1. Complete a job-application form.
2. Prepare for an employment test.
3. Prepare for an employment interview.
4. Conduct yourself appropriately during an employment interview.
5. Complete the communication tasks needed after the employment interview.

Ben & Jerry's is a self-proclaimed "left-of-center" ice cream company located in rural Vermont. Many of the company's 350 employees have been interviewed by Elizabeth Lonergan, the Employee Development Manager, who has been with the company in different capacities since 1983. Ben & Jerry's often attracts job candidates who, in Lonergan's words, "think this is a different company." But even a company that has business practices outside of the "norm" must do some things traditionally in order to be successful. "And recruiting," Lonergan said, "happens to be one of them."

The company—which sponsors an annual folk music festival, donates 1% of its profit to charity, and does not have a dress code for its managers—interviews many people who could not imagine working in a "normal" corporate environment. In fact, some candidates believe Ben & Jerry's is the only company they could work for. But while enthusiasm is important, the "only-place-for-me" attitude shows immaturity on a candidate's part. "It's a great company, but it's not perfect. It makes me nervous when people tell me this is the *only* place they want to work," Lonergan said sadly. "I call that the Prince Charming theory, like little girls who think there's only one man they can be happy with in their whole lives. It's simply not true. There are lots of people you can make a good life with, and there are lots of good companies out there."

Lonergan noted that quite a few company employees are former city dwellers who decided that Ben & Jerry's location would help provide them with a change in lifestyle. While the company's country setting gives Ben & Jerry's an almost romantic appeal, it seems to stop some candidates from doing a little basic research on the company's hiring and paying practices. Following an interview,

Elizabeth Lonergan, Employee
Development Manager,
Ben & Jerry's Homemade,
Inc., Waterbury, Vermont

some managerial candidates have left Vermont shaking their heads after Lonergan told them the company has a five-to-one salary ratio with a salary cap of $81,200 a year. That information, Lonergan said, is stated clearly in Ben & Jerry's annual report.

In addition to candidates who are not interested in working for a company with a low salary cap, or those unable to imagine working anywhere else, an interviewee least likely to be hired is one who arrives with a pompous attitude. "I don't mean a healthy, 'I'm the one for the job.' There is a difference," Lonergan said. A candidate bound to be rejected is someone "who doesn't give me the impression that he or she can relate to employees at all levels. I don't like prima donnas. I enjoy the fact that when I walk into the plant there are people at every level whom I know. I feel that's really important, especially when you're hiring managers, that people be able to relate from the board room to the boiler room, so to speak."

Simply because a company is "different" doesn't mean that good manners, during and after an interview, aren't important. In most cases, Lonergan has made her mind up about a candidate soon after the interview is over. But sometimes the decision is especially rough, and a few candidates still under consideration have ruined their chances by calling Lonergan a day or two after being interviewed and treating her assistant shabbily—an indication of pompousness that wasn't evident during an interview. Her assistant, she said, works too hard to be treated as if she didn't matter. "Basically, if they won't tell her who they are or insist they have to speak to only me, they don't get anywhere," she said.

The success of Ben & Jerry's, like any successful company, is due largely to its employees' maturity, enthusiasm, and ability to work with others. And just because a company is "different" doesn't mean Lonergan will hire candidates who don't show they have these qualities when they are interviewed. ▼

COMPLETING A JOB-APPLICATION FORM

Planning your job campaign, developing your résumé, and sending out letters of application are important first steps toward getting a rewarding job, but they are only the first steps. Many organizations, especially large ones, will require you to fill out an application form or undergo some sort of testing, and all will want to interview you before offering you a job. After the interview, you will have many types of letters to write—thanking the interviewer, accepting a job offer, rejecting others, and perhaps resigning from a position. Strategies for completing these communication tasks are given in this chapter.

Most large organizations and nearly all governmental agencies require the job applicant to complete an application form—either before or after the job interview. From the employer's point of view, application forms are important assessment tools. To begin with, they make sure the applicant includes all information relevant to the hiring decision. For example, an applicant who had been convicted of theft could simply omit that fact from the résumé. But the question "Have you ever been convicted of theft?" on an application form requires a direct answer.

Similarly, the application form ensures that the applicant excludes all irrelevant information, thus saving the evaluator's time and protecting the organization from the possibility of a lawsuit based on discrimination. Finally, having the same information in the same place for each applicant makes it easy for the evaluator to compare job candidates objectively and efficiently.

Because you may be asked to complete an application form during the interview process, bring a copy of your résumé with you to the interview. It will probably contain most of the dates, addresses, and similar details requested on the application form. If possible, however, complete the application form after the interview, when you will have enough time to ensure completeness and accuracy.

Ask for two copies of the blank form to guard against making an uncorrectable error. If that isn't possible, you may want to write a first draft on a photocopy. Nothing looks more unprofessional than having to cram two lines' worth of information on one line because you unexpectedly ran out of space. Always read through the entire form before beginning to complete it. You may find that information that you might initially have included in one section more logically belongs in another section.

Type the information if possible, unless of course the directions indicate that your answers should be handwritten. Not only will you avoid the possibility of having your handwriting misread but your form will also look more professional. Don't write "See résumé" for any question on the form, even if you must repeat word for word information already contained in your résumé.

Answer each question completely and accurately. Do not leave any blanks on the form. If some requested information does not apply to you, write or type "N/A" (not applicable) to let the reader know that you didn't simply skip a question. Never lie on your application form. Doing so can be grounds for firing later when the falsehood is discovered. If you believe an honest answer to a particular question would eliminate you from further consideration for the position, and if you believe you can explain the answer adequately in person, simply enter "Will explain" in the space provided. You can be sure you will be asked about the topic during your interview.

Even if an application form is required before your application will be considered, you should also include a copy of your résumé with the

OBJECTIVE 1: Complete a job-application form.

> Application forms ensure that all relevant information is included, irrelevant information is excluded, and all information is in the same place.

application form and letter. Your résumé highlights your specific accomplishments and unique qualifications in a way that is not possible on a standardized form.

TAKING AN EMPLOYMENT TEST

Organizations are increasingly using various types of employment tests as a way to get data to help in employee selection. Such tests include paper-and-pencil tests, performance indexes, and personality inventories. Some organizations administer the tests as part of the interview process; others ask applicants to take the tests before the interview so that they can discuss and explore the test results during the interview.

Paper-and-pencil tests are often used to measure the applicant's basic general skills (such as reading, writing, and computation) or to measure technical skills (such as knowledge of accounting, finance, or computer information systems). In addition, simulations of typical business situations can often be conducted via paper-and-pencil tests.

Common employment tests include paper-and-pencil tests, performance indexes, and personality inventories.

Performance indexes require the candidate to actually perform a task under timed and observed conditions. For example, an applicant for a secretarial position may be given a timed writing or asked to take and transcribe dictation. An applicant for a programming position may be given a short problem and asked to generate the computer code necessary to solve it.

Find out beforehand what types of tests will be administered (employers will often provide a sample of the tests they use) so that you can practice. Doing so will make you better prepared and less nervous on the day of the test. Find out what you will need to bring, if anything, to the testing center, get a good night's sleep, and arrive early.

Read or listen to the instructions for each section carefully. If the test is timed, work at a steady pace and do not spend too much time on any one question. Find out if there is a penalty for guessing. If there is not, do not leave any questions blank. Even if there is a penalty for guessing, if you can eliminate one or two of the alternatives you will increase your score by guessing.

Personality testing is becoming more prevalent because of the increased cost to companies of making poor hiring decisions. Just like societies, organizations have cultures; and prospective employers want to ensure that the applicant's personality meshes with that of the organization. The applicant should view these tests as helpful to him or her also. If an applicant's personality is such that he or she would be unhappy working in a particular type of environment, the time to discover that fact is before accepting a job there.

Personality and other psychological tests are often administered by a trained psychologist. The most commonly used tests (such as the Myers-Briggs Type Indicator or the Strong-Campbell Interest Inventory) have proven validity. Your best strategy is to get a good night's sleep, relax, and answer each question honestly. Only honest answers will provide you with helpful feedback about yourself; in addition, these tests are very sophisticated and inconsistent answers are likely to be discovered.

S P O T L I G H T ON ETHICS

THE ETHICAL DIMENSIONS OF THE JOB CAMPAIGN

Most recruiters have heard the story about the job applicant who, when told that he was overqualified for a position, pleaded in vain, "But I lied about my credentials." When constructing your résumé and application letter, when completing an application form, and when answering interview questions, you will constantly have to make judgments about what to say and what to omit. Everyone would agree that outright lying is unethical (and clearly illegal as well). But when is hedging or omitting negative information simply being smart, and when is it unethical?

Extent of the Problem

Recruiters believe that the problem they call "résumé inflation" has increased in recent years, and there is some research to back them up. One survey of executives found that 26% of them reported hiring employees during the previous year who had misrepresented their qualifications, education, or salary history. By far, the most frequent transgression is misrepresenting one's qualifications.

Acting ethically does not, of course, require that you emphasize every little problem that has occurred in your past. Indeed, one study showed that the majority of Fortune 500 human resource directors agree with the statement "Interviewees should stress their strengths and not mention their weaknesses unless the interviewer asks for information in an area of weakness."

Recognize, however, that many employers have a standard policy of terminating all employees who are found to have falsely represented their qualifications on their résumés. Generally, the employer must show evidence that the employee intentionally misrepresented his or her qualifications so as to fraudulently secure a job. Claiming to have a college degree when, in fact, one does not, would likely be grounds for termination, whereas an unintentional mistake in the dates of previous employment would probably not be.

The Certified Résumé

To combat the problem of résumé inflation, some companies (and some job applicants) have resorted to using a certified résumé—one that has been checked out and substantiated to the maximum extent possible. Either job applicants themselves or prospective employers pay a private firm to investigate the applicant's

résumé. Most private firms will only do this with the full cooperation of the job applicant. They might verify the work history, administer a lie-detector test, secure copies of college transcripts, check for arrests and convictions, and provide whatever additional background checking is deemed necessary for the particular job and that has been approved by the job applicant.

The fee for this background check, which usually amounts to approximately $125, is sometimes paid by the applicant and sometimes by the prospective employer. Some applicants, especially those who must be bonded or who work in positions of high trust, feel that having a certified résumé gives them an edge on the competition when applying for a job. Employers then don't have to wonder about the integrity of the résumé data.

The Ethics of Accepting a Position

For some applicants, another ethical dilemma occurs when they receive a second, more attractive job offer after having already accepted a prior offer. Most professionals believe that such a situation should not present a dilemma. A job acceptance is a promise that the applicant is expected to keep. The hiring organization has made many decisions based on the applicant's acceptance, not the least of which was to notify all other candidates that the job had been filled. Reneging on a promise not only puts the applicant in a bad light (don't underestimate the power of the network in communicating such information) but also puts the applicant's school in a bad light.

If you're unsure about whether to accept a job offer, ask for a time extension. Once you've made your decision, however, stick to it and have no regrets. If you decide to accept the job, immediately notify all other employers that you are withdrawing from further consideration. If you decide to decline the job, move on to your next interviews without looking back. Learn to live with your decisions.

Sources: "Certified Résumés Eliminate Hiring Fears," *Chain Store Age Executive* (June 1987), p. 68; "Creative Résumés," *Dun's Business Month* (June 1985), p. 20; Nelda Spinks and Barron Wells, "Employment Interviews: Trends in the Fortune 500 Companies—1980–1988," *ABC Bulletin* (December 1988), p. 17; "Will Ethical Conflicts Undo Your Career?" *Morning Sun,* May 12, 1988, p. 9.

▼
OBJECTIVE 3: Prepare for
an employment interview.

PREPARING FOR AN EMPLOYMENT INTERVIEW

Ninety-five percent of all employers require one or more employment interviews before extending a job offer, resulting in up to 150 million employment interviews being conducted annually.[1] The employer's purpose in these interviews is to verify information on the résumé, explore any issues raised by the résumé, and get some indication of the probable chemistry between the applicant and the organization. (It is estimated that 90% of all job failures result from personality clashes or conflicts—not incompetence.[2]) The job applicant will use the interview to glean important information about the organization and to decide whether the culture of the organization meshes with his or her personality.

Consider the employment interview as a sales presentation. Just as any good sales representative would never attempt to walk into a potential customer's office without having a thorough knowledge of the product, neither should you. You are both the product and the product promoter, so do your homework—both on yourself and on the potential customer.

Researching the Organization

Learn as much as you can about the organization—your possible future employer.

As a result of having developed your résumé and written your application letters, you have probably done enough general homework on yourself. You are likely to have a reasonably accurate picture of who you are and what you want out of your career. Now is the time to zero in on the organization.

It is no exaggeration to say that you should learn everything you possibly can about the organization. Research the specific organization in depth, using the research techniques you developed in Chapter 11. Search the current business periodical indexes to learn what has been happening recently with the company. Many libraries maintain copies of the annual reports from large companies, either in hard copy or on microfiche. Study these or other sources for current product information, profitability, plans for the future, and the like. Learn about the company's products and services, its history, the names of its officers, what the business press has to say about the organization, its recent stock activity, financial health, corporate structure, and the like.

Relate what you learn about the individual company to what you've learned about competing companies and about the industry in general. By trying to fit what you learned into the broader perspective of the industry, you will be able to discuss matters more intelligently during your interview instead of just having a bunch of jumbled facts at your disposal.

If you're interviewing at a government agency, determine its role, recent funding levels, recent activities, pending legislation affecting the agency, and to what extent being on the "right" side (i.e., the official side) of a political question is important to the agency. If you're interviewing for a teaching position at an educational institution, determine the range of course offerings, types of students, conditions of the facilities and equipment, professionalism of the staff, and funding levels. In short, every tidbit of information you can learn about your prospective employer will help you make the correct career decision.

After you have developed your résumé and written
application letters, you are probably ready to research the
organizations to which you are applying. Learn everything
you can about the organizations by utilizing research
techniques, searching current business periodical indexes,
studying annual reports, and even attending job fairs.
(*Source © Emily Stors / The Picture Cube*)

You will use this information as a resource to help you understand and
discuss topics with some familiarity during the interview. But don't bring
up such information merely to impress the interviewer. No one is impressed
by the interviewee who, out of the blue, spouts, "I see your stock went up
5½ points last week." However, in response to the interviewer's comment
about the company's recent announcement of a new product line, it would
be quite appropriate for the applicant to respond, "That must have been
the reason your stock jumped 5½ points last week."

In short, bring up such information only if it flows naturally into the
conversation. Even if you're never able to discuss any of the information
you've gathered, having such information will still provide perspective in
helping you to understand what the interviewer is talking about and in
helping you to make a reasonable decision if a job offer is extended.

> Avoid "showing off" your knowledge of the organization.

Practicing Interview Questions

Following is a sample of typical questions that are often asked during an
employment interview. Questions such as these provide the interviewer
important clues to the applicant's qualifications, personality, poise, and
communication skills. The interviewer is interested not only in the content
of your response but also in your reaction to the questions themselves and
how you communicate your responses.

Before going for your interview, practice dictating a response to each of
these questions into a cassette recorder. Then assume the role of the

> Practice your responses to typical interview questions.

interviewer and play back your responses. How acceptable and appropriate was each response?

- Tell me about yourself.
- How would you describe yourself?
- Tell me something about yourself that I won't find in your résumé.
- What do you take real pride in?
- Why would you like to work for our organization?
- Why should we hire you?
- What are your long-range career objectives?
- What types of work do you enjoy doing most? Least?
- What accomplishment has given you the greatest satisfaction?
- What would you change in your past life?
- What courses did you like best and least in college?
- How does your education or experience relate to this job?
- What salary do you expect?

These questions are fairly straightforward and not especially difficult to answer if you have practiced them. Not infrequently, however, interviewers may pose more difficult questions—ones that seemingly have no "right" answer. Sometimes they even try to create a stressful situation by asking pointed questions, interrupting, or feigning disbelief in an attempt to gauge your behavior under stress.

> Answer each question honestly, but in a way that highlights your qualifications.

The strategy to use in such a circumstance is to keep the desired job firmly in mind and to formulate each answer—no matter what the question—so as to highlight your ability to perform the desired job competently. You don't have to accept each question as asked. You can ask the interviewer to be more specific or to rephrase the question. Doing so not only will provide more guidance for answering the question but will give you a few additional moments to prepare your response.

Here are examples of some challenging questions you might be asked, along with suggested strategies for answering these and similar questions. Again, you should recognize that the interviewers may be more interested in your reaction and poise under stress than in your actual words, so be aware of the nonverbal signals you are communicating.

- *Tell me about your strengths and weaknesses.* When asked about a strength, mention one of your qualifications that is directly related to the specific job. If asked about a weakness, identify a relatively harmless matter, such as "I tend to work too hard;" "I'm very tenacious; once I've started a project, I won't relax until I've finished it"; or "I tend to ask a lot of questions." Answer the weakness part of the question first, ending with a discussion of some job-related strength. Relate an anecdote or give examples when possible.
- *Suppose you had to pick between two equally qualified subordinates for promotion. One was a black male and the other a handicapped female. Whom would you select?* Whenever you're given a question that has no right answer, avoid answering the question directly. Instead, talk about related issues—in this case, your respect for affirmative-action and equal-opportunity efforts, your interest in working for an organization that had such a wonderful "problem," or some other issue that relates to the question without forcing you to make an unreasonable choice. If you're asked for the "most important" something, you're generally safer to

instead list several items as being very important, without assigning any one of them the top position.

- *What position do you expect to hold in five years?* Avoid telling the interviewer, "your job." He or she won't appreciate it, even if that is an accurate answer. Instead, talk about what you hope to have accomplished by then, the types of increasing responsibility you hope to be given, or the opportunities to make greater contributions to the organization's efforts.

- *Tell me about your personal interests.* Your investigation of the organization should have revealed its attitudes and "personality." Rightly or wrongly, most organizations reflect upper middle-class attitudes and mores. If you wish to fit in at such organizations, you should provide honest, middle-of-the-road responses. When asked your personal interests, for example, then would not be the time to discuss your preoccupation with the occult. Also avoid appearing *too* interested in any outside pursuit. Organizations are looking for well-rounded individuals with outside interests, but who do not have such a consuming interest that it might interfere with their jobs.

- *What do you like most or least about your present job?* For the most-liked part of this question, select an aspect of your present job that you both enjoyed and that is directly related to the new position. For the least-liked part of the question, select an aspect of your present job that you dislike and that will not be a part of the new position.

> *How* you respond to difficult questions may be as important as *what* you respond.

Preparing Your Own Questions

During the interview, many of the questions you may have about the organization or the job will probably be answered. However, an interview is a two-way conversation, so it is legitimate for you to pose relevant questions at appropriate moments, and you should prepare those questions beforehand.

Questions such as the following will provide useful information on which to base a decision if offered a job:

> Ensure that any relevant questions you may have are answered during the interview.

- How would you describe a typical day on the job?
- How is an employee evaluated and promoted?
- What types of training are available?
- What are your expectations of new employees?
- What are the organization's plans for the future?
- To whom would I report? Would anyone report to me?
- What are the advancement opportunities for this position?

Each of these questions not only provides needed information to help you make a decision but also sends a positive nonverbal message to the interviewer that you are interested in this position as a long-term commitment. Do not, however, ask so many questions that the roles of the interviewer and the interviewee become blurred, and avoid putting the interviewer on the spot.

Finally, avoid asking about salary and fringe benefits during the initial interview. There will be plenty of time for such questions later, after you've convinced the organization that you're the person they want. In terms of

> Avoid appearing to be overly concerned about salary.

planning, however, you should know ahead of time the market value of the position for which you're applying. Check the classified ads, reports collected by your college placement service, and library sources to learn what a reasonable salary figure for your position would be.

Dressing for Success

Prefer well-tailored, clean, conservative outfits for the interview.

The importance of making a good first impression during the interview can hardly be overstated. One study has shown that 75% of the interviewees who made a good impression during the first five minutes of the interview received a job offer, whereas only 10% of the interviewees who made a bad impression during the first five minutes received a job offer.[3]

The most effective strategy for making a good impression is to pay careful attention to your dress, grooming, and posture. Dress in a manner that flatters your appearance while conforming to the office norm. The employment interview is not the place to make a fashion statement. You want the interviewer to remember what you had to say and not what you wore. Although different positions, different companies, different industries, and different parts of the country and world have different norms, in general prefer well-tailored, clean, conservative clothing for the interview.

For most business interviews, men should dress in a blue or gray suit with a white or pale blue shirt with a subtle tie, dark socks, and black shoes. Women should dress in a blue or gray tailored suit with light-colored blouse, and medium-height heels. Avoid excessive or distracting jewelry, heavy perfumes or after-shave lotions, and elaborate hairstyles. Impeccable grooming is a must, including clothing free of wrinkles and clean, shoes shined, teeth brushed, and hair neatly styled and combed. Blend in; you will have plenty of opportunity to express your individual style once you've been hired.

Controlling Nervousness

Overpreparation is the best way to control nervousness.

Control nervousness during the interview the same way you control it when making an oral presentation; that is, practice until you're confident you can face whatever the interviewer throws your way. The placement offices at many colleges conduct mock interviews to prepare prospective interviewees. If not, ask a professor or even another student to interview you. Practice answering lists of common questions.

Become so thoroughly familiar with your résumé, application letter, and (if used) application blank that you won't have to search for some particular item or try to remember exactly how you responded to a particular question.

Interviewers know that you may be nervous and will probably begin the interview with some fairly innocuous, easy-to-answer questions to break the ice. It is to their advantage to put you at ease so that the real you can shine through, and they will try to do so. Recognize also that some nervousness is helpful; a bit of nervous energy will keep you alert and give sharper focus to the verbal exchange.

One way to avoid nervousness is to arrive properly equipped—a pen and notebook, a list of questions you want to ask, two copies of your résumé, any past correspondence with the organization, a list of references (including addresses and phone numbers), and, if applicable, work samples.

SPOTLIGHT ON LEGAL ISSUES

THE LEGAL IMPLICATIONS OF APPLYING FOR A JOB

I applied for a job and was told I will be hired if I take a lie-detector test. Must I take this test?

In most states, yes, if you want the job. A few states, however, (including Oregon, Washington, Alaska, Delaware, and Minnesota) prohibit employers from requiring a lie-detector test as a condition of employment.

The computer firm where I want to work requires all job applicants to take a psychological test as part of the application process. Is this legal?

Yes. Aptitude, personality, and psychological tests are legal so long as the results are accurate, are related to success on the job, and do not tend to eliminate anyone on the basis of sex, age, race, religion, or national origin.

I work full time and have been offered a dream job by another employer—if I can start the new job immediately. Do I have to give my current employer a certain number of days' notice?

No, legally you're not required to do so unless the contract you signed specifies how far in advance you must notify the company.

I'm an older student who will be applying for positions along with much younger ones. Can the interviewer ask my age?

No, not unless the employer can show that most people beyond a certain age cannot perform the job competently or safely. If you're worried about the possible impact of your age, you might wish to volunteer certain information to allay the interviewer's concerns, for example, mentioning some vigorous physical activity you habitually engage in.

What types of information may not be asked for on an application form or during a job interview?

- Race or national origin (including origin of a surname or place of birth; however, you may be asked to prove that you have legal authorization to work in the United States)
- Family information (including marital status, plans for marriage or children, number of children or their ages, babysitting arrangements, spouse's occupation, roommate arrangements, and home ownership)
- Handicaps (unless they relate directly to the job)
- Arrests (you may, however, be asked about convictions for serious offenses)

How should I respond to an illegal question during a job interview?

The best response, assuming you want to continue to be considered for the position, is to deflect the question by focusing on how you can contribute to the job. For example, if you were asked about your plans to have children in the immediate future, you might respond, "I assure you that I'm fully committed to my career and to making a real contribution to the organization for which I work." Or you may respond by saying you don't believe such questions are relevant to your ability to do the job, or by asking the interviewer to explain the relevance of the question. You could also, of course, file a complaint with the Equal Employment Opportunity Commission.

Sources: Ronald A. Anderson, Ivan Fox, and David P. Twomey, *Business Law and the Legal Environment*, 14th ed. (Cincinnati: South-Western, 1990); Gordon W. Brown, Edward E. Byers, and Mary Ann Lawlor, *Business Law: With UCC Applications*, 7th ed. (New York: McGraw-Hill, 1989); Gordon W. Brown and R. Robert Rosenberg, *Understanding Business and Personal Law*, 7th. ed. (New York: McGraw-Hill, 1984); Neil Story and Lynn Ward, *American Business Law and the Regulatory Environment* (Cincinnati: South-Western, 1989).

Map out the route you will take to the interview site, and avoid the stress of having to rush to arrive on time. Plan to arrive 10–15 minutes early, but no more than that. Arriving too early makes you appear too eager and may disrupt the interviewer's prior plans. If you're a bit nervous, plan to arrive a half hour early, find your way to the correct office, and then go for a walk. It will release some of the pent-up energy you may have stored on the drive over.

▼
OBJECTIVE 4: Conduct yourself appropriately during an employment interview.

Assume a confident, courteous, and conservative attitude during the interview.

CONDUCTING YOURSELF DURING THE INTERVIEW

Observe the organizational environment very carefully and treat everyone you meet, including the receptionist and the interviewer's secretary, with scrupulous courtesy. Maintain an air of formality. When shown into the interview room, greet the interviewer by name, with a firm handshake, direct eye contact, and a smile.

At the beginning, address the interviewer as "Mr." or "Ms.," switching to a first-name basis only if specifically requested to do so. If you're not asked to be seated immediately, wait until the interviewer is seated and then take your seat. Sit with your feet planted firmly on the floor, lean forward a bit in your seat, and maintain comfortable eye contact with the interviewer. Avoid taking notes, except, perhaps for a specific name, date, or telephone number, if needed.

Recognize that certain parts of the office are off limits—especially the interviewer's desk and any area behind the desk. Do not rest your hands, purse, or notes on the desk and never wander around the office. Show interest in everything the interviewer is saying; don't concentrate so hard on formulating your response that you miss the last part of any question. Answer each question in a positive, confident, forthright manner. Recognize that more than yes or no answers are expected.

Throughout the interview, your attitude should be one of confidence and courtesy. Assume a role that is appropriate for you. Don't go in with the attitude that "You're lucky to have me here." The interviewer might not agree. Likewise, you needn't fawn or grovel. You're applying—not begging—for a job. If the match works, both you and the employer will benefit. Finally, don't try to take charge of the interview. Follow the interviewer's lead, letting him or her determine which questions to ask, when to move to a new area of discussion, and when to end the interview.

Answer each question put to you as honestly as you can, always keeping your mind on the desired job and how you can show that you are qualified for that job. Don't try to oversell yourself, or you may end up in a job for which you're unprepared. However, if the interviewer doesn't address an area in which you feel you have strong qualifications, be on the alert to volunteer such information at the appropriate time, working it into your answer to one of the interviewer's questions.

If asked about your salary expectations, try to avoid giving a salary figure, indicating that you would expect to be paid in line with other employees at your level of expertise and experience. If pressed, however, be prepared to reveal your salary expectations. Although salary figures change yearly, the average starting salaries for 1991 college graduates with different undergraduate majors were as follows:[4]

Engineering	$34,300
Computer	$31,900
Chemistry	$31,100
Mathematics or statistics	$29,900
Accounting	$28,400
Economics or finance	$27,600
Sales and marketing	$26,900
Business administration	$26,200
Liberal arts	$26,100

When discussing salary, talk in terms of what you think the position and responsibilities are worth rather than what you think *you* are worth. If salary is not discussed, be patient. Very few people have ever been offered a job in industry without first being told what they would be paid.

It is possible that you may perceive an immediate rapport problem with the interviewer, either that the interviewer dislikes you or that you dislike the interviewer. In the former situation, take stock immediately of yourself and the verbal and nonverbal signals you're sending out, and try to adjust them to send a more appropriate message.

If your first impression of the interviewer is unfavorable, recognize that first impressions are not always valid. Also, remember that the interviewer may not be your superior or may not be your superior for long. Evaluate the long-term situation before making any immediate decision. At any rate, conduct yourself as professionally and as effectively as possible throughout the interview. You can make a final decision later, after you've had more time to evaluate the situation more clearly.

It is possible that you will participate in a group interview, where several people interview you at once. If possible, find out about this ahead of time so that you can learn the name, position, and rank of each interviewer. Address your responses to everyone, not just to the person who asked the question or to the most senior person present.

It is also likely that you will be interviewed more than once—having either multiple interviews the same day or, if you survive the initial interview, a more intense set of interviews to be scheduled at some later date. Be on the alert for clues you can pick up from your early interviews that might be of use to you in later interviews and be sure to provide consistent responses to the same questions asked by different interviewers. Assume that the different interviewers will get together to discuss their reactions to you and your responses.

When the interview ends, if you've not been told, you have a right to ask the interviewer when you might expect to hear from him or her. You will likely be evaluated on these four criteria:

> You will likely be evaluated on education and experience, mental qualities, manner and personal traits, and appearance.

- *Education and experience:* Your accomplishments as they relate to the job requirements, evidence of growth, breadth and depth of your experiences, leadership qualities, and evidence of willingness to assume responsibility
- *Mental qualities:* Intelligence, alertness, judgment, logic, perception, creativity, organization, depth
- *Manner and personal traits:* Social poise, sense of humor, mannerisms, warmth, confidence, courtesy, aggressiveness, listening ability, manner of oral expression, emotional balance, enthusiasm, initiative, energy, ambition, maturity, stability, interests
- *Appearance:* Grooming, dress, posture, cleanliness, apparent health

COMMUNICATING AFTER THE INTERVIEW

Although you may be exhausted (mentally and physically) from your interview sessions, there are several tasks that remain to be done. Some must be completed immediately after the interview; others must wait until you receive notice of the hiring decision.

> OBJECTIVE 5: Complete the communication tasks needed after the employment interview.

SPOTLIGHT ON INTERNATIONAL ISSUES

WORKING IN THE INTERNATIONAL ARENA

If you wish to secure a position at an American subsidiary of a Japanese firm, you may be wondering how to conduct yourself during the intensive interviewing that precedes a job offer. The best advice is just to be yourself. When you meet with your interviewers, for example, you do not need to bow; neither, however, should you appear to be too effervescent, wildly shaking hands and talking in a loud voice, with exaggerated body language.

If you're the type of person who needs an immediate decision and who dislikes meetings, you will quickly decide that you should look for a job elsewhere. The Japanese style of consensus management means that you will attend lots of meetings where every nuance of every decision is discussed; also, many executives will be involved in the interview process. The advantage of such a strategy is that all issues are raised and discussed, everyone has his or her say, and everyone thus feels a part of the final decision. Therefore, while decision-making may take longer than in an American firm, implementation is often faster and easier.

Job interviews are often very involved and time-consuming. The reason stems partly from the fact that the Japanese operate by consensus management and partly because they assume a job offer is a lifetime commitment. The Japanese view the organization as an extended family and are quite interested in how the applicants as well as their families would fit into the organizational family. They will probably be smart enough not to ask you about your marriage or family plans (since doing so is illegal), but the astute applicant may wish to casually volunteer such information when it fits naturally into the conversation. Look also for an opportunity to show that you are a team member, are eager to work with others, and get along well with your colleagues.

If you pass the initial screening, you'll likely be invited to participate in an intensive assessment-center exercise to further evaluate your ability to fit in. For example: Diamond-Star Motors in Normal, Illinois, is a joint venture of Mitsubishi Motors and Chrysler Corporation that employs 2,900 people. As part of its testing program, applicants for supervisory positions are required to assemble and disassemble a flashlight. Then, working together, each group must find and implement improvements in the assembly process. All the while, the applicants' individual and group behaviors are being assessed and compared to the prevailing corporate culture.

You will likely rise faster and higher in a Japanese-owned firm if you're in the sales or personnel area, which is often headed by an American. Finance, however, which requires close coordination with the headquarters in Japan, is nearly always headed by a Japanese. And the chief executive officer is invariably Japanese. Female managers will often find more resistance to their promotion and less access to information than will their male counterparts.

Although it is not absolutely necessary in all cases, competence in the native language is a very strong qualification—and one that will set you apart from most of your competitors. Only through learning the native language is a person truly able to appreciate a culture, understand how its members think, and become accepted by them. Even if the native business people speak English, as many of them surely will, the fact that you've taken the trouble to learn their language, albeit haltingly and with a pronounced accent, will demonstrate vividly your interest in and respect for them.

The opportunities for important and satisfying careers in the international arena are enormous and growing rapidly each year. Japanese companies alone will soon employ more than 1 million Americans. Companies such as Matsushita Electric, Sony, Nissan Motors, Honda, Toyota, and Konica Business Machines employ thousands of American business people. In addition, American companies, especially financial institutions like Citibank, Chase Manhattan, BankAmerica, Manufacturers Hanover, American Express, and Merrill Lynch have significant international divisions. Finally, don't overlook U.S. government positions, including positions in the foreign service and in such organizations as the U.S. Agency for International Development.

Even small and medium-sized companies are finding a ready market for their products and services on both sides of both oceans. If you are adventuresome, self-confident, independent, flexible, curious, and open-minded, perhaps the world, rather than any particular country, will become your new home.

Sources: Philip R. Harris and Robert T. Moran, *Managing Cultural Differences,* 2d ed. (Houston: Gulf Publishing, 1987); Brian Moskal, "Can You Pass Muster" *Industry Week,* February 15, 1988, p. 20; Bill Powell, "How to Win Over a Japanese Boss," *Newsweek,* February 2, 1987, p. 46.

Following Up the Interview

Immediately after the interview, conduct a self-appraisal of your performance. Try to recall each question that was asked and evaluate your responses. If you're not satisfied with one of your responses, take the time to formulate a good answer. Chances are that you may be asked a similar question in the future.

After the interview, critique your performance, your résumé, and your application letter.

Also reevaluate your résumé. Were any questions asked during the interview that indicated some confusion about your qualifications? Does some section need to be revised or some information added or deleted? If you have composed your résumé on a computer, making the needed changes will be easy.

Determine too whether you can improve your application letter based on your interview experience. Were the qualifications you discussed in your letter the ones that seemed to impress the interviewers the most? Were these qualifications discussed in terms of how they would benefit the organization? Did you provide specific evidence to support your claims?

You should also take the time to send the interviewer (or interviewers) a short thank-you note as a gesture of courtesy and to reaffirm your interest in the job. The interviewer probably spent quite a bit of time with you and spent additional time before and after the interview session and deserves to have his or her efforts on your behalf acknowledged.

Send a short thank-you note immediately after the interview.

Recognize, however, that your thank-you note may or may not have any effect on the hiring decision. Most decisions to offer the candidate a job or to invite him or her back for another round of interviewing are made the day of the interview, often during the interview itself. Thus, your thank-you note may arrive after the decision has been made.

The real purpose of a thank-you note is to express genuine appreciation for some courtesy extended to you; you do not write to earn points. Also avoid trying to resell yourself. You've already made your case through your résumé, cover letter, and interview.

Your thank-you note should be short and may be either typed or handwritten. Consider it a routine message that should be written in a direct organizational pattern. Begin by expressing appreciation for the interview; then achieve credibility by mentioning some specific incident of insight gained from the interview. Close on a hopeful, forward-looking note. The thank-you note in Figure 18.1 corresponds to the résumé and application letter presented in Chapter 17.

If you have not heard from the interviewer by the deadline date he or she gave you for making a decision, telephone the interviewer for a status report. If they have not yet made a decision, your inquiry will keep your name and notice of your continued interest before them as they proceed toward a decision. If they've already selected someone else, you need to know this information as well, so that you can continue your job search.

Handling Rejection

Rejection is a normal part of the job campaign. No one receives job offers for every interview held.

Some job applicants become discouraged at the long wait between mailing out their initial résumés and being invited for an interview. You should recognize, however, that the first responses you will get are the rejections,

FIGURE 18.1   Thank-You Note

The letter should be written within a day or two of
the interview.

In the salutation, address
the person as you did during the interview, using
either "Dear Dave" or
"Dear Mr. Norman."

Begins directly, with a
sincere expression of
appreciation.

Mentions a specific inci-
dent that occurred and relates it to the writer's
background.

Closes on a confident, forward-looking note.

April 5, 1992

Mr. David Norman, Partner   1
Ross, Russell & Weston
452 Fifth Avenue
New York, NY 10018

Dear Mr. Norman: 2

Thank you for the opportunity to interview for the position of EDP
specialist yesterday. I very much enjoyed meeting you and Arlene
Worthington and learning more about the position and about Ross,
Russell & Weston.

I especially appreciated the opportunity to observe the long-range
planning meeting yesterday afternoon and to learn of your firm's
plans for increasing your consulting practice with nonprofit   3
agencies. My experience working in city government leads me to
believe that nonprofit agencies can benefit greatly from your
expertise.

Again, thank you for taking the time to visit with me yesterday. I 4
look forward to hearing from you.

Sincerely,

Aurelia Gomez

Aurelia Gomez
225 West 70th Street
New York, NY 10023

Grammar and Mechanics Notes

1. Use the ampersand (&) in a firm name only if it is used by the firm
itself.   2. Use a colon (not a comma) even if the salutation uses the reader's
first name.   3. "Nonprofit": Most words beginning with "non" are written solid—
without a hyphen.   4. "Again$_1$": Introductory clause.

because it takes less time to eliminate those who are obviously unsuited for a specific position than to evaluate those who might be suitable. Each of us is unsuitable for *some* positions, but that doesn't mean we're unsuitable for *all* positions.

Similarly, don't spend your time after a job interview sitting by the phone waiting word on the hiring decision. You may have to go on several employment interviews at different organizations before being offered a job, so don't waste valuable time. Immediately schedule additional interviews; they can always be canceled if necessary, but they will give you something to fall back on if you're passed over for one position. In addition, the perspective that comes from having interviewed at numerous organizations will help you make an informed decision when a job offer is made.

The job applicant who presents a well-groomed and confident appearance, who is well qualified, and who is well prepared for the interview has an excellent chance of being offered a position. You should know, however, that despite the employer's best efforts, job selection is as much an art as a science. Personal likes and dislikes and good chemistry also play a role.

Although feelings of hurt and disappointment are natural in such circumstances, there is no reason to feel anger at the organization that rejects your application. If there are 200 applicants for the position, 199 of them are going to receive the same letter you did. Instead of getting mad, write a gracious note to the interviewer, such as the following:

The smart applicant sends a gracious note following a rejection.

> Although I'm naturally disappointed that I was not selected for the position, I do appreciate the professionalism and courtesy that you showed me and hope you will keep me in mind if a position for which I might qualify opens in the future.

Such a note speaks volumes about the maturity of the applicant and might open the door for future employment. Besides, it is not unusual for any successful job applicant to receive several offers, all but one of which must be declined. Your gracious note might just put you at the top of the list for a second interview if the chosen applicant declines the job.

Remember that the job campaign is a job itself—perhaps one of the most important jobs you'll ever undertake and maybe even one of the most difficult. Depersonalize any early rejections. Look at them objectively, determine what went wrong, and learn from the experience. As with most endeavors, perseverance, preparation, and a positive attitude will pay off in ultimate success.

Accepting, Delaying, and Refusing a Job Offer

Remember that a job offer is never "official" until it is in writing, so avoid making permanent plans until the confirming letter arrives. Accepting a job offer is easy. An acceptance letter is, of course, a good-news letter and should be written in the direct organizational pattern. Give the good news first, follow it with any necessary details, including salary, starting date, and other contractual details. Close with a positive look to the future. Always accept in writing, so that you and the organization have a permanent record of your decision.

Use the direct organizational style when writing an acceptance letter.

Suppose you receive a job offer from one organization while you still have other job interviews pending. In such a case, you may be unsure whether to accept and need more time to make a decision. Recruiters are certainly aware that you are interviewing at more than one organization; on the other hand, they may be facing deadlines or putting other qualified candidates on hold until you respond, so your request for a time extension must be diplomatic. Your best strategy is to express appreciation for the job offer, tactfully ask for an extension, and close by reaffirming your interest in the job.

> Thank you for your letter of May 30 offering me the position of manager-trainee at a salary of $23,500. This position represents a wonderful professional opportunity for me, and I'm giving it careful consideration.
>
> I had previously scheduled another job interview on June 14, the day before you asked for my acceptance decision. I feel obligated to keep this appointment and would appreciate being able to give you my decision June 21—one week after this final interview.
>
> The position you have offered is an exciting one, especially since you indicated the strong possibility of an overseas assignment after my one-year training program. But because my decision is so important to both of us, I'd be grateful to have one additional week to consider it.

Consider your acceptance of a job as a binding commitment.

Once you've accepted one job offer, you should immediately inform all other organizations at which you're being seriously considered for a position to withdraw your name from further consideration. Similarly, if you receive any subsequent job offers, you should immediately decline them. When withdrawing your name from further consideration for a job or declining a job, you may communicate either by letter or by telephone. Phone calls are faster, but you run the risk of being asked for more details about either the job you've accepted or your reasons for declining the other job than you care to divulge. You have more control of what you communicate in a letter; in addition, letters provide a permanent record—both for you and for the employer.

Your refusal letter should be brief and written in the indirect organizational plan.

Refusal letters are best written in the indirect organizational pattern, beginning on a neutral but relevant note, stating the refusal in neutral or positive terms, and closing on a pleasant, supportive note. Such letters may be brief and need not go into great detail. The important point is to convey the news in a professional manner which the organization needs to complete its search process.

If you accept a job while employed elsewhere, you must resign immediately from your present job. Your resignation may or may not come as a surprise to your employer; either way, it should be in writing. Because you're writing to someone within the organization, an interoffice memorandum is the appropriate type of communication.

Surely, your resignation will be bad news to your superior and should therefore be written in the indirect format. Regardless of your reason for leaving, then is not the time to bring up past injustices or to tell your superior how he or she should manage the organization's affairs. Dwell on the positive—what you've learned on the job and the satisfaction that came from making a contribution to the organization's welfare. Provide any additional details needed and close on a positive note.

Acceptance Letter   **FIGURE 18.2**

```
                         15 Turner Hall
                         NOrthern Arizona University
                         Flagstaff, AZ 86001-8134              1
                         March 17, 1992


Ms. Gladys M. Morrison, Director
Human Resources Division
Precision Systems, Inc.
6171 West Century
Los Angeles, CA 90045

Dear Ms. Morrison:

      I am delighted to accept your offer of a position as EEOC co-      2
ordinator for PSI at an annual salary of $24,600. I look forward
to beginning my new position on July 5.

      Enclosed are the completed medical examination and insurance
forms. I plan to be in the Los Angeles area on May 13-15 to secure
an apartment and would be happy to meet with you then if any           3
further matters related to my employment need to be resolved.

      Thanks, Ms. Morrison, for giving me this opportunity to make      4
a contribution to the Human Resources Division and to Precision
Systems, Inc.

                         Cordially,

                         Raymond J. Arnold

                         Raymond J. Arnold

Enclosures
```

Gives the good news (that you accept the offer) first, where it will receive the most attention.

Provides the needed additional details.

Closes on a friendly, forward-looking note.

Grammar and Mechanics Notes

1. The use of a 9-digit ZIP code is optional.   2. This letter is formatted in the modified-block style with indented paragraphs.   3. "an apartment _and": No comma is needed because the second clause lacks a subject.   4. "Thanks, Ms. Morrison,": Separate nouns of address by commas.

FIGURE 18.3   Rejection Letter

Begins with a supportive, relevant, and neutral opening.

Gives a simple statement of the facts. Providing a reason for the refusal is optional.

Closes with a sincere, gracious statement about the company.

```
                                   15 Turner Hall                       1
                                   Northern Arizona University
                                   Flagstaff, AZ 86001-8134
                                   March 17, 1992


Mr. Stanley Scukanec, Director
Personnel Department
Occidental Life, Inc.
1901 Avenue of the Stars
Los Angeles, CA 90067

Dear Mr. Scukanec:

    I certainly enjoyed meeting with you and your colleagues on
March 3 and was pleased to receive an invitation to join your firm    2
as wage and salary administrator.

    After careful consideration of the offers I've received, I've
decided to accept a position as EEOC coordinator at an electronics
firm. This position will require substantially less travel time
than would have been necessary with the Occidental position.

    I want to thank you and your colleagues for the time you           3
spent with me. As I stated in my letter of March 5, I've always
been impressed with the professionalism of your insurance agents
and look forward to continuing my relationship with Occidental as
a satisfied customer.

                              Cordially,

                              Raymond J. Arnold

                              Raymond J. Arnold
```

Grammar and Mechanics Notes

1. The writer's return address may be given above the date (as here) or as part of the closing lines, immediately below the writer's name. 2. Job titles are not capitalized unless used in place of a personal title (e.g., "Vice President Smith"). 3. "March 5": Use cardinal (rather than ordinal) numbers for dates unless the day precedes the month (e.g., "the 5th of March").

Resignation Memorandum   **FIGURE 18.4**

V A L L E Y   N A T I O N A L   B A N K

★ ★

MEMO TO: Austin Gibson   1

FROM: Ray Arnold

DATE: May 1, 1992

My position as a teller at the Fulton Street branch of Valley   2
National Bank has certainly been a rewarding experience--both in
terms of providing funds for my college education and, just as
important, in terms of the experience I gained in dealing with the
public, learning time-management skills, and handling the confidential affairs of our customers.

These skills will surely be of help to me in my chosen field of
labor relations. Although you indicated to me earlier that a
management position would be available for me at VNB when I
graduate in June, I think you know of my desire to live on the   3
West Coast. Therefore, I've accepted a position as EEOC coordinator for Precision Systems, Inc. in Los Angeles.

My first day of work at PSI will be July 5, and I would like to
terminate my present position on Friday, June 7. The intervening
five weeks should allow sufficient time for you to hire a replacement and for me to provide whatever on-the-job training you might
desire.

I shall always be grateful for the opportunities you provided me,
Mr. Gibson, and will remember my two and one-half years here with   4
great fondness.

c: Personnel Department   5

Fulton Street Branch • Phone (602) 555-3889

Begins indirectly by acknowledging what has been learned from the present job.

Explains in a positive manner the reason for the resignation before actually communicating the bad news.

Provides needed details and offers to help.

Closes on a positive note.

Grammar and Mechanics Notes

1. Memorandums are written from one employee to another within the same
organization. They do not contain a salutation or closing lines.   2. "experience—
both": A dash is comprised of two hyphens with no space before or after.
3. "West Coast": A direction is capitalized only when it is part of a proper name
representing a part of the country.   4. "one-half": Fractions are hyphenated.
5. A copy notation is used to let the recipient know that a copy of the document
has been sent to another party.

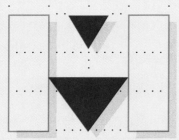

MICROWRITING EMPLOYMENT REJECTION LETTER

The Problem

You are Aurelia Gomez, whose résumé is shown in Figure 17.3. As a result of your application letter to David Norman, partner at Ross, Russell & Weston (see Figure 17.5), you participated in two job interviews at the accounting firm and just received the following letter:

```
Dear Aurelia:

I am pleased to offer you the position of EDP Specialist with our
firm, effective July 1, at an annual salary of $29,400. Your
duties are outlined in the enclosed job description.

This offer is conditional upon your passing a comprehensive
medical examination (see enclosed). In addition, your probationary
period, during which time you may be released with two weeks'
notice, will extend until you receive a passing score on all parts
of the New York State CPA examination.

I look forward to having you join our firm, Aurelia, and would
appreciate receiving a written acceptance of this offer by May 30.

Sincerely,
```

Your excitement at receiving this letter is tempered by the fact that last week you verbally accepted an offer of $27,000 from Modlin and Associates, another accounting firm, and their confirming letter arrived yesterday. Although you've not yet answered this letter, you had planned to do so this weekend. You had also planned to write Ross, Russell & Weston this weekend, asking them to withdraw your name from further consideration.

The Process

1. Which job offer is more appealing to you?

   ```
   In addition to offering a larger salary, another factor
   I like about Ross, Russell is that they are more active
   in city politics than Modlin. If their offer had
   arrived first, I would definitely have taken it.
   ```

2. Since you haven't responded in writing to the Modin offer, are you still free to accept the Ross, Russell offer?

   ```
   No. I definitely did accept the Modlin offer over the
   phone. In addition to the ethical dimension, public
   accounting firms are a very "clubby" group. Partners in
   different firms tend to have frequent contact with each
   other, and it is likely that my action would become
   known to both firms.
   ```

3. Should your rejection letter be written in the direct or indirect organizational style?

   ```
   Indirect. Presumably, they will consider my rejection
   of their job offer as bad news because they will have
   to reopen their search process.
   ```

608

4. Can you leave open the possibility of future employment with Ross, Russell?

Considering the fact that one in four entry-level employees fails to make it through the first year, there is always that possibility. However, any direct reference to future employment would be inappropriate.

5. Should you express regret that you cannot accept their offer?

No. It might invite additional job negotiations from Ross, Russell, which would not be in my best interests. I accepted the Modlin offer because I thought it would be a good career move. Despite the new offer, I still feel I will be happy and productive at Modlin.

The Product

Dear Mr. Norman:

The opportunity to join a progressive accounting firm in New York City, especially one that is active in the political life of the city, is certainly attractive.

I am sure, therefore, that you can appreciate the mixed feelings with which I inform you that I accepted another job offer last week. Your letter arrived before I had a chance to inform you of my decision.

I thank you sincerely for the opportunity I had of learning about your firm, its employees, and its management philosophy. I found the entire process very educational and rewarding, and I look forward to continuing to get to know you and your firm better as my career in public accounting progresses.

Sincerely,

The Employment Interview

Preparing for an Employment Interview

1. Before going on an employment interview, learn everything you can about the organization.

2. Practice answering common interview questions and prepare questions of your own to ask.

3. Select appropriate clothing to wear.

4. Control your nervousness by being well prepared, well equipped, and on time.

Conducting Yourself During the Interview

5. Throughout the interview, be aware of the nonverbal signals you are communicating through your body language.

6. Answer each question completely and accurately, always trying to relate your qualifications to the specific needs of the desired job.

7. Whether you are interviewed by one person or a group of people, you will be evaluated based on your education and experience, mental qualities, manner and personal traits, and general appearance.

Communicating After the Interview

8. Immediately following the interview, critique your performance and also send a thank-you note to the interviewer.

9. Recognize that several interviews at different organizations may be needed before you are offered a worthwhile job, so continue scheduling interviews.

10. When you receive a job offer you want to accept, write the organization an acceptance letter and telephone or write all other employers asking to have your name withdrawn from further consideration.

11. If you need additional time to consider a job offer, write a tactful letter expressing appreciation for the offer, justifying your request, and assuring the organization of your continuing interest in the position.

12. If you receive additional offers, reject them immediately. Similarly, if you are presently employed, write a letter of resignation.

SUMMARY

Request two copies of any job-application form you are asked to complete. Type the information, answering each question completely and accurately. If a question doesn't apply to you, insert "N/A," to indicate that you haven't simply skipped the question.

Different types of employment tests (including paper-and-pencil tests, performance tests, and personality assessments) are being used increasingly in employment selection. Ensure that you understand the directions completely, work at a steady pace if the test is timed, and determine beforehand whether there is a penalty for incorrect answers. For personality tests, answer each question honestly, recognizing that there is no one "correct" answer for each question. For all testing situations, get a good night's sleep, arrive early, and relax.

To succeed at the interview phase of the job campaign, prepare for the interview, conduct yourself appropriately during the interview, and complete the communication tasks needed after the interview. The specific steps are summarized in Checklist 18.

REVIEW AND DISCUSSION

1. Why do many organizations require prospective employees to complete a job-application blank?   OBJECTIVE 1 ◄
2. Should you submit a résumé along with your completed job-application form? Why or why not?   OBJECTIVE 1 ◄
3. Define and give an example of each of the three major types of employment tests.   OBJECTIVE 2 ◄
4. What types of information should you research about the organization with which you will be interviewing?   OBJECTIVE 3 ◄
5. What overall strategy should be used when answering questions during the interview?   OBJECTIVE 3 ◄
6. Describe item by item what articles of clothing and other apparel from your own wardrobe you might wear to a job interview.   OBJECTIVE 3 ◄
7. What should you do if an interviewer does not ask about an area in which you feel you are uniquely qualified for the position?   OBJECTIVE 4 ◄
8. What criteria does an organization generally use to assess the interviewee?   OBJECTIVE 4 ◄
9. Should you ask about salary during the interview? Why or why not?   OBJECTIVE 4 ◄
10. Why should a thank-you note be written after the interview?   OBJECTIVE 5 ◄
11. What organizational patterns should be used for writing job-acceptance and rejection letters and requests for time extensions?   OBJECTIVE 5 ◄

EXERCISES

1. **Completing a Job-Application Form** Secure two copies of a job-application form (from your institution, your present employer, a colleague or family member who works, etc.). Complete the form in terms of your own qualifications.   OBJECTIVE 1 ◄

2. **Preparing for an Employment Test** Select three organizations for whom you might like to work. Telephone someone in the personnel area of each organization to find out what employment tests they use for different types of positions. Ask about the reasons for the tests, what directions they give to the candidates, and what use is made of the results. Then write a memo report to your instructor identifying the source of your information and discussing the results.   OBJECTIVE 2 ◄

▶ OBJECTIVE 3

3. **Preparing for the Interview** Page 594 contains a list of commonly asked interview questions. Prepare a written answer for each of these questions in terms of your own qualifications and experience. Then select two of the stress questions on pages 594–595 and answer them. Type each question and then your answer.

▶ OBJECTIVE 3

4. **Researching the Employer** Refer to Exercise 8 in Chapter 17. Assume that Philip Morris has invited you to interview for the manager-trainee position. Research this company prior to your interview. Prepare a two-page double-spaced report on your findings. You will, of course, concentrate on that information that will be most helpful to you during the interview. As you're conducting your research, some questions are likely to occur to you that you'll want to get answered during the interview. Prepare a list of such questions and attach it as an appendix to your report.

▶ OBJECTIVE 4

5. **Collaborative Project—Mock Interviews** This project uses information collected as part of Exercise 4. Divide into groups of six students. Draw straws to determine which three members will be interviewers and which three will be applicants. Both groups now have homework to do: The interviewers must get together to plan their interview strategy (10–12 minutes for each candidate); and the applicants, working individually, must prepare for this interview.

The interviews will be conducted in front of the entire class, with each participant dressed appropriately. On the designated day, the three interviewers as a group will interview each of the three job applicants in turn (while the other two are out of the room). Given the short length of each interview, the applicant should refrain from asking any questions of his or her own, except to clarify the meaning of an interviewer question.

Following each round of interviews, the class as a whole will vote for the most effective interviewer and interviewee.

▶ OBJECTIVE 5

6. **Accepting a Job Offer**—Assume that you were offered the position of manager-trainee at Philip Morris (see Exercise 8 in Chapter 17) at a salary of $23,500, starting June 15. Write your acceptance letter to Ms. Janice Trimmer, Personnel Manager, Kraft Food Division, Philip Morris Companies, 120 Park Avenue, New York, NY 10017.

▶ OBJECTIVE 5

7. **Rejecting a Job Offer** Assume that you were offered the job in Exercise 6 above. Even though the position is with the Kraft Food Division of Philip Morris, you've had second thoughts about working for an organization so closely allied with tobacco products. You prefer to take your chances on getting another job offer, one with which you will be more comfortable. Write your letter of rejection to Ms. Trimmer.

C A S E   P R O B L E M

Neelima Takes a Walk

▶ OBJECTIVE 5

Neelima Shrikhande has been on two job interviews and is scheduled to go on a third next week. Yesterday in the mail, she received a job offer from Applied Biosystems (James R. Douglas, Vice President, 850 Lincoln Centre Drive, Foster City, CA 94404) to begin work on September 1 as director of management information systems at an annual salary of $73,500. Today, she received a phone call from Anne McKenzie, president of Stride Rite (5 Cambridge Center, Cambridge, MA 02142), offering her the newly created position of Director of Corporate Communications at an annual salary of $67,000, effective at her convenience, but not later than 60 days from acceptance of the job offer.

Despite the somewhat lower salary, Neelima immediately decides to accept the position at Stride Rite. She will report directly to Anne McKenzie, and she feels she will enjoy living in the Boston metropolitan area. She will cancel her interview next week with Victor DeJorgè at Southeast Banking in Miami.

1. Assume the role of Neelima Shrikhande. Write to Anne McKenzie accepting her job offer.
2. Write to James R. Douglas declining his job offer.
3. How should Neelima inform Victor DeJorgè of her decision to cancel that interview?
4. One week later, Neelima received an overnight letter from Jim Douglas. His letter contained a counteroffer: Neelima's salary will be increased to $80,000, and she will be named to head a corporate-wide task force to coordinate Applied Biosystems efforts to increase the role of women in technical and engineering positions within the organization. Write to Jim Douglas, giving your decision.

A word that has two opposite meanings is called a *contronym*. Here are some common examples:

WORD WISE

■ *Buckle:* fasten together; pull apart.

> Please buckle your safety belt.
> The earthquake caused the floor to buckle.

■ *Commencement:* beginning; conclusion.

> A strong economy marked the commencement of his term of office.
> She rented an academic robe for her college commencement.

■ *Gave out:* produced; stopped producing.

> The flashlight gave out a strong beam.
> The flashlight gave out just when we needed it most.

■ *Left:* departed; remaining.

> Three people had left the meeting.
> Three people were left at the meeting.

■ *Temper:* soften; strengthen.

> Please temper your anger with reason.
> Our factories must temper the steel before using it.

Appendix A

L A B   **L A N G U A G E   A R T S   B A S I C S**

Grammar

Suppose the vice president of your organization asked you, a systems analyst, to try to locate a troublesome problem in a computer spreadsheet. After some sharp detective work, you finally resolved the problem and wrote a memo to the vice president saying, "John and myself discovered that one of the formulas were incorrect, so I asked he to revise it."

Instantly, you've turned what should have been a "good-news" opportunity for you into, at best, a "mixed-news" situation. The vice president will be pleased that you've uncovered the bug in the program but will probably focus entirely too much attention on your poor grammar skills.

Grammar refers to the rules for combining words into sentences, sentences into paragraphs, and paragraphs into complete messages. The most frequent grammar problems faced by business writers are discussed below. Learn these common rules well so that your use of grammar will not present a communication barrier to the message you're trying to convey.

ADJECTIVES AND ADVERBS

An adjective modifies a noun or pronoun; an adverb modifies a verb, an adjective, or another adverb. Use a comparative adjective or adverb (*-er, more,* or *less*) to refer to two persons, places, or things and a superlative adjective or adverb (*-est, most,* or *least*) to refer to more than two.

> The Datascan is the fast<u>er</u> of the two machines.
> The XR-75 is the slow<u>est</u> of all the machines.
>
> Rose Marie is the <u>less</u> qualified of the two applicants.
> Rose Marie is the <u>least</u> qualified of the three applicants.

Note: Do not use double comparisons, such as "more faster."

AGREEMENT (SUBJECT/VERB/PRONOUN)

Agreement indicates the quality of having related subjects and verbs (and any related pronouns) refer to the same *number;* that is, all of them singular if they refer to one and all of them plural if they refer to more than one.

Agreement

Use a singular verb or pronoun with a singular subject and a plural verb or pronoun with a plural subject.

The four <u>workers</u> <u>have</u> a photocopy of <u>their</u> assignments.
Roger's <u>wife</u> <u>was</u> quite late for <u>her</u> appointment.
<u>Mr. Tibbetts and Ms. Downs</u> <u>plan</u> to forego <u>their</u> bonuses.
Both <u>the controller and the auditor</u> <u>indicated</u> that <u>they</u> had examined the statements.
Included in this envelope <u>are</u> a <u>contract and affidavit</u>.

Note: This is the general rule; variations are discussed below. In the first sentence, the plural subject (*workers*) requires a plural verb (*have*) and a plural pronoun (*their*). In the second sentence, the singular subject (*wife*) requires a singular verb (*was*) and a singular pronoun (*her*). In the last sentence, the subject is "contract and affidavit"—not "envelope."

Company Names

Company names may be singular or plural so long as consistency is maintained.

Bickley and Bates <u>has</u> paid for <u>its</u> last order. <u>It</u> is now ready to reorder.
Bickley and Bates <u>have</u> paid for <u>their</u> last order. <u>They</u> are now ready to reorder.
Not: Bickley and Bates <u>has</u> paid for <u>its</u> last order. <u>They</u> are now ready to reorder.

Expletives

In sentences that begin with an expletive, the true subject follows the verb. Use *is* or *are*, as appropriate.

There <u>is</u> no <u>reason</u> for his behavior.
There <u>are</u> many <u>reasons</u> for his behavior.

Noun: An expletive is an expression such as *there is, there are, here is,* and *here are* that comes at the beginning of a clause or sentence. Because the topic of a sentence that begins with an expletive is not immediately apparent, such sentences should be used sparingly in business writing.

Intervening Words

Disregard any words that come between the subject and verb when establishing agreement.

Only <u>one</u> of the mechanics <u>guarantees</u> <u>his</u> work. (not *their work*)
The <u>appearance</u> of the workers, not their competence, <u>was</u> being questioned.
The <u>secretary</u>, as well as the clerks, <u>was</u> late filing <u>her</u> form. (not *their forms*)

Note: First determine the subject; then make the verb agree. Other intervening words that do not affect the number of the verb are *together with, rather than, accompanied by, in addition to,* and *except.*

Pronouns

Some pronouns (*anybody, each, either, everybody, everyone, much, neither, no one, nobody,* and *one*) are always singular. Other pronouns (*all, any, more, most, none,* and *some*) may be singular or plural, depending on the noun to which they refer.

> <u>Each</u> of the laborers <u>has</u> a different view of <u>his or her</u> job.
> <u>Neither</u> of the models <u>is</u> doing <u>her</u> job well.
> <u>Everybody</u> is required to take <u>his or her</u> turn at the booth. (not *their turn*)
>
> | | |
> |---|---|
> | <u>All</u> the <u>dessert</u> <u>has</u> been eaten. | <u>None</u> of the <u>work</u> <u>is</u> finished. |
> | <u>All</u> the <u>reports</u> <u>have</u> been filed. | <u>None</u> of the <u>workers</u> <u>are</u> finished. |

Subject Nearer to Verb

If two subjects are joined by correlative conjunctions (*or, either/or, nor, neither/nor,* or *not only/but also*), the verb and any pronoun should agree with the subject that is nearer to the verb.

> Either Robert or <u>Harold</u> <u>is</u> at <u>his</u> desk.
> Neither the receptionist nor the <u>operators</u> <u>were</u> able to finish <u>their</u> tasks.
> Not only the actress but also the <u>dancer</u> <u>has</u> to practice <u>her</u> routine.
> The tellers or the <u>clerks</u> <u>have</u> to balance <u>their</u> cash drawers before leaving.

Note: The first noun in this type of construction may be disregarded when determining whether the verb should be singular or plural. Pay special attention to using the correct pronoun; do not use the plural pronoun *their* unless the subject and verb are plural. Note that subjects joined by *and* or *both/and* are always plural: *Both <u>the actress and the dancer</u> <u>have</u> to practice their routines.*

Subjunctive Mood

Verbs in the subjunctive mood require the plural form, even when the subject is singular.

> I wish the situation <u>were</u> reversed.
> If I <u>were</u> you, I would not mention the matter.

Note: Verbs in the subjunctive mood refer to conditions that are impossible or improbable.

CASE

Case refers to the form of the pronoun that indicates its use in a sentence—either nominative, objective, reflexive, or possessive. (Possessive pronouns are covered under "Apostrophes" in the section on punctuation in LAB 3.)

Nominative

Use nominative pronouns (*I, he, she, we, they, who, whoever*) as subjects of a sentence or clause and with the verb *to be.*

> The customer representative and <u>he</u> are furnishing the figures. (*he is furnishing*)
> Mrs. Quigley asked if Oscar and <u>I</u> were ready to begin. (*I was ready to begin*)
> <u>We</u> old-timers can provide some background. (*we can provide*)

It was <u>she</u> who agreed to the proposal. (*she agreed*)
<u>Who</u> is chairing the meeting? (*he is chairing*)
Mr. Lentzner wanted to know <u>who</u> was responsible. (*she was responsible*)
Anna is the type of person <u>who</u> can be depended upon. (*she can be depended upon*)

Note: If you have trouble determining which pronoun to use, reword the sentence by getting rid of the plural subject or by substituting another pronoun. See the reworded clauses in parentheses above.

Objective

Use objective pronouns (*me, him, her, us, them, whom, whomever*) as objects in a sentence or clause.

Thomas sent a fax to Mr. Baird and <u>me</u>. (*sent a fax to <u>me</u>*)
This policy applies to Eric and <u>her</u>. (*applies to <u>her</u>*)
Joe asked <u>us</u> old-timers to provide some background. (*Joe asked <u>us</u> to provide*)
The work was assigned to <u>her</u> and <u>me</u>. (*she assigned the work to <u>me</u>.*)
To <u>whom</u> shall we mail the specifications? (*mail them to <u>him</u>.*)
Anna is the type of person <u>whom</u> we can depend upon. (*we can depend upon <u>her</u>*)

Note: For *who/whom* constructions, if *he/she* can be substituted, *who* is the correct choice; if *him/her* can be substituted, *whom* is the correct choice. Remember: *who—he, whom—him*. Note the difference in the last sentence under the Nominative and Objective sections: <u>*who*</u> can be depended upon vs. <u>*whom*</u> we can depend upon.

Reflexive

Use reflexive pronouns (*itself, myself, yourself, himself, herself, ourselves,* or *themselves*) to refer to or emphasize a noun or pronoun that has already been named. Do not use reflexive pronouns to substitute for nominative or objective pronouns.

I <u>myself</u> have some doubts about the proposal.
You should see the exhibit <u>yourself</u>.

Not: Virginia and <u>myself</u> will take care of the details.
But: Virginia and <u>I</u> will take care of the details.

Not: Mary Louise administered the test to Thomas and <u>myself</u>.
But: Mary Louise administered the test to Thomas and <u>me</u>.

APPLICATION

Directions   Select the correct word in parentheses.

1. Sherrie Marshall, in addition to James M. Smith, (are/is) in line for an appointment to the Federal Trade Commission. (Who/Whom) do you know on the FTC staff? None of the people I contacted (has/have) heard of them. Smith, I believe, is the (younger/youngest) of the two.

2. Tower and Associates is moving (its/their) headquarters. (It/They) (are/is) selling (its/their) old furniture and equipment at auction. Not only a conference table but also a high-speed collator (are/is) for sale. The facilities manager asked that all inquiries be directed to (her/she).

3. If he (was/were) honest about his intentions, Carl Ichan would talk directly to Ivan and (me/myself). After all, he knows that it was (I/me) (who/whom) made the offer originally. Between the two of us, Ivan is the (more/most) supportive of Ichan's position.

4. Here (are/is) the reports on Hugo's bankruptcy. It seems that (us/we) investors were a little over-confident, but it is generally the early investors (who/whom) make the most money.

5. Neither our savings account nor our long-term securities (are/is) earning adequate interest. Everybody in finance (are/is) trying to improve the performance of (his or her/their) portfolio. Each of the analysts (are/is) trying to maintain quarterly investment goals.

6. There (was/were) several people in the audience (who/whom) questioned whether each of our divisions (was/were) operating efficiently. The CEO asked (us/we) division managers to respond to their questions.

7. Neither Lan Yang nor the two programmers (was/were) able to resolve the problem. In fact, neither of the two programmers (was/were) successful in locating the source of the problem. However, Lan Yang, as well as the programmers, (are/is) continuing (her/their) efforts.

8. John is the (more slower/most slower/slower/slowest) of the two welders. Only one of his jobs (has/have) been finished, so I asked (he/him) to work overtime this weekend.

9. (Who/Whom) will you ask to assist (I/me/myself)? Alex is the (more accurate/most accurate) typist on our entire staff; however, Jill is the type of worker (who/whom) can coordinate the entire project.

10. I wish it (was/were) possible for Ella and (I/me) to ask both Roger and David about (his/their) experience in using temporary help. Getting their answers to our questions (are/is) going to require some real detective work, and it is (I/me) (who/whom) will have to do it.

LAB   LANGUAGE ARTS BASICS

Punctuation—Commas

Punctuation serves as a roadmap to help guide the reader through the twists and turns of your message—pointing out what is important (underscores), subordinate (commas), copied from another source (quotation marks), explained further (colon), considered as a unit (hyphens), and the like. Sometimes correct punctuation is absolutely essential for comprehension. Consider, for example, the different meanings of the following sentences, depending upon the punctuation:

> What's the latest, Dope?
> What's the latest dope?

> The social secretary called the guests names as they arrived.
> The social secretary called the guests' names as they arrived.

> Our new model comes in red, green and brown, and white.
> Our new model comes in red, green, and brown and white.

> The play ended, happily.
> The play ended happily.

> A clever dog knows it's master.
> A clever dog knows its master.

> We must still play Michigan, which tied Ohio State, and Minnesota.
> We must still play Michigan, which tied Ohio State and Minnesota.

> "Medics Help Dog Bite Victim"
> "Medics Help Dog-Bite Victim"

The comma rules presented below and the other punctuation rules presented in LAB 3 do not cover every possible situation; comprehensive style manuals, for example, routinely present more than 100 rules just for using the comma. Rather, these rules cover the most frequent uses of punctuation in business writing. Learn these rules—because you will be using them frequently.

Commas are used to separate ideas and to set off elements within a sentence. When typing, leave one space after a comma. Many writers use commas inappropriately. No matter how long the sentence, make sure you have a legitimate reason before inserting a comma.

Adjectives

Use a comma to separate two or more adjectives that modify the same noun if the adjectives are *not* joined by a coordinate conjunction.

> He was an aggressive, unpleasant manager.
> *But:* He was an aggressive and unpleasant manager.

Note: The major coordinate conjunctions are *and, but, or,* and *nor;* they join elements of equal rank. Do not use a comma if the first adjective modifies the combined idea of the second adjective plus the noun: *Please order a new bulletin board for the conference room.* Do not use a comma between the last adjective and the noun: *Wednesday was a long, hot, humid_day.*

Complimentary Closing

Use a comma after the complimentary closing of a business letter that is typed using standard punctuation.

> Yours truly,
> Sincerely yours,

Note: No punctuation follows the complimentary closing if open (instead of standard) punctuation is used.

Date

Use commas to set off the year in a complete date.

> The note is due on May 31, 1998, at 5 p.m.

Note: Do not forget the comma *after* the year. A comma should not be used after a partial date: *The note is due on August 31_at 5 p.m.*

Direct Address

Use commas to set off a name used in direct address.

> Thank you, Ms. Cross, for bringing the matter to our attention.
> Ladies and gentlemen, we appreciate your attending our session today.

Independent Clauses

Use a comma to separate independent clauses connected by a coordinate conjunction (unless both clauses are short and closely related).

> Mr. Karas discussed last month's performance, and Ms. Daniels presented the sales projections.
> The meeting was running late, but Mr. Mears was in no hurry to adjourn.

> The firm hadn't paid_and John was angry.

Note: Do not confuse two independent clauses (which are separated by a comma) with a compound predicate (which is not separated by a comma): *Mrs. Ames had read the merger report_but had not yet had an opportunity to discuss it with her colleagues.* Examine the clauses on each side of the conjunction; a comma separates the clauses only if *both* of them can stand alone as complete sentences.

Interrupting Expression

Use commas to set off an interrupting expression.

> I believe it was John, not Nancy, who raised the question.
> It is still not too late to make the change, is it?

Introductory Expression

Use a comma to set off an introductory expression (unless it is a short prepositional phrase).

No, the status report is not ready.
When the status report is ready, I shall call you.
To finish the task on time, Frank hired temporary help.
In 1990 we expanded into South America.

Note: An introductory expression is a word, phrase, or clause that comes before the subject and verb of the independent clause. When the expression comes at the *end* of the sentence, no comma is needed: *I shall call you when the status report is ready.* Do not use a comma between the subject and verb: *To finish that boring and time-consuming task in time for the monthly sales meeting was a major challenge.*

Nonrestrictive Expression

Use commas to set off a nonrestrictive expression.

Ann Cosgrave, who has had some experience, should apply for the position.
But: Anyone who has had some expereience should apply for the position.
Those papers, which we had left on the conference table, are missing.
But: Only those papers that we had left on the conference table are missing.
Wagner's latest book, *Merger Mania*, was the topic of the session.
But: The book *Merger Mania* was the topic of the session.

Note: A nonrestrictive expression is a word, phrase, or clause that may be omitted without changing the basic meaning of the sentence. A restrictive expression, on the other hand, limits (restricts) the meaning of the noun or pronoun that it follows; because it is essential to the meaning of the sentence, it is *not* set off by commas. Always examine the noun or pronoun that comes before the expression to determine whether the noun or pronoun needs that expression to complete its meaning; if it does, do *not* use a comma.

In the last pair of sentences, note that an appositive (a noun that renames the preceding noun) is set off by commas only if it is nonrestrictive.

Place

Use commas to set off a state or country that follows a city.

The sales conference will be held in Phoenix, Arizona, on May 13-15.
Our business agent is located in Brussels, Belgium, in the P.O.M. Building.

Note: Do not forget to insert the comma after the state or country.

Quotation

Use commas to set off a direct quotation in narrative material.

The president said, "You have nothing to fear," and I believed him.

"I assure you," the vice president said, *"that no positions will be terminated."*

Note: If a quotation at the beginning of a sentence is a question, use a question mark instead of a comma: *"How many have applied?" she asked.*

Series

Use commas to separate three or more items in a series.

> The committee may meet on Wednesday, Thursday, or Friday.
> Carl wrote the questionnaire, Anna distributed it, and Tim tabulated the results.

Note: Some style manuals indicate that the last comma (before the conjunction) is optional. However, to avoid ambiguity in business writing, this comma should be inserted. Do not use a comma after the last item in a series: *Planning the agenda, preparing the handouts, and recording the minutes are the three jobs left to complete.*

Transitional Expression

Use commas to set off a transitional expression or independent comment.

> You may, of course, cancel your subscription at any time.
> One suggestion, for example, was to undertake a leveraged buyout.

Note: Examples of transitional expressions and independent comments are *in addition, as a result, therefore, in summary, on the other hand, however, unfortunately,* and *as a matter of fact.*

APPLICATION

Directions Insert any needed commas in the following sentences. In the blank at the left, write the abbreviation for the comma rules being applied. If a sentence is correctly punctuated as shown, write a C in the blank.

Examples: _*tran*_ We cannot, therefore, accept your offer.
   _C_ I hoped to receive permission but was disappointed.

_____   1. The contracts to be signed were left on the supervisor's desk.

_____   2. Portland Oregon is a lovely city.

_____   3. Leonard has prepared numerous reports news releases and sales presentations.

_____   4. At the manager's direction we are extending store hours until 7 p.m.

_____   5. I will attend the conference in August and let you know what happens.

_____   6. You may make the slides yourself or you may request assistance from audiovisual services.

_____   7. I assumed as a matter of fact that the project was finished.

_____   8. We signed the original lease on January 1 1990.

_____ 9. I hope you will purchase Lotus 1-2-3 and will make use of it in budgeting.

_____ 10. They must have your answer by June 15 before the board meeting.

_____ 11. The group of co-op students from Los Angeles visited our offices today.

_____ 12. Ross hopes to get the figures to you soon but cannot promise delivery by a certain date.

_____ 13. The consultant was pressed for time to complete the analysis before closing time.

_____ 14. Their software-support department for example handles more than a thousand calls daily.

_____ 15. To end the quarter with a small surplus is the major goal for the division.

_____ 16. Richardson gave a concise reasoned explanation of the process.

_____ 17. You will note Bonnie that your signature appears on the document.

_____ 18. It is not too early I suspect to begin planning our tenth-anniversary sale.

_____ 19. Their catalog states "All merchandise is guaranteed for 90 days."

_____ 20. To end the quarter with a small surplus we must reduce costs by at least 8%.

_____ 21. Everyone please be seated so that President Mary Webler can tell us about her short but interesting conversation.

_____ 22. His attempt to conceal his role in the cover-up of the savings-and-loan scandal was not successful.

_____ 23. Identifying prospects qualifying them and determining their preferences will consume most of the afternoon of June 13 1992 for Anne's group.

_____ 24. I agree with you but do not feel that such drastic action is necessary.

_____ 25. To do your job well you will require some assistance from another department.

_____ 26. To do your job well will require a major time commitment.

_____ 27. A noun that comes before a restrictive expression is followed by a comma but one that comes before a nonrestrictive expression is not.

_____ 28. By working hard we gained approval to hold our conference in Phoenix and not in Springfield.

_____ 29. John drove and I navigated.

———— 30. The fact that Pete Johnson and I both came from San Francisco and had been with the company for a total of 32 years did not persuade the human resources director to approve our request that the retirement plan be modified to permit early retirements.

LAB   LANGUAGE ARTS BASICS

Punctuation—Other Marks

APOSTROPHES

Apostrophes are used to show that letters have been omitted, as in contractions, and to show possession. When typing, do not space before or after an apostrophe (unless a space after is needed to end the word).

Gerund

Use the possessive form for a noun that comes before a gerund.

> Garth questioned Karen's leaving so soon.
>
> Their raising so many questions delayed the adjournment.
>
> Mr. Matsumoto knew Karl and objected to his going to the meeting.

Note: A gerund is the *-ing* form of a verb used as a noun.

Pronoun

Use an apostrophe plus the letter *s* to form the possessive of indefinite pronouns; do not use an apostrophe to form the possessive of personal pronouns.

> It is someone's responsibility.   The responsibility is theirs.
> I will review everybody's figures.   The company used its credit.

Note: Examples of indefinite possessive pronouns are *anybody's, everyone's, no one's, nobody's, one's,* and *somebody's.* Examples of personal possessive pronouns are *hers, his, its, ours, theirs,* and *yours.* Do not confuse the possessive pronouns *its, theirs,* and *whose* with the contractions *it's, there's,* and *who's: It's time to put litter in its place. There's no reason to take theirs. Who's determining whose jobs will be eliminated?*

Singular Nouns

Use an apostrophe plus *s* to form the possessive of a singular noun.

> Al Brown's office   Gil Hodges's record
> brother-in-law's problem   a year's time
> Mr. and Mrs. Smith's home   the CPA's opinion
> Michigan National Bank's assets the boss's contract
> the buyer's and the seller's   Bush and Quayle's administra-
>   signatures   tion

Note: To indicate joint ownership, make only the last noun possessive: *John and Mary's report.* To indicate separate ownership, make both nouns possessive: *John's and Mary's reports.* Add the apostrophe plus *s* to the last word in a compound possessive *(attorney general's opinion).*

Plural Nouns

Use only an apostrophe, without an *s*, to form the possessive of a plural noun (except for a few irregular plurals).

the two companies' agreement	*But:*
both girls' statements	the children's books
the Smiths' home	the men's dressing room
all the doctors' offices	
two years' worth	

Note: Make sure that what comes before the apostrophe is a complete word: *juries'* verdicts and not *jurie's verdicts*. To avoid problems with plural possessives, first make the noun plural; then form the possessive: *child, children, children's shoes; city, cities, the two cities' boundaries.* Do not confuse plural nouns with possessive nouns (singular or plural). Whenever a noun ending in *s* is followed by another noun, the first noun is probably a possessive, requiring an apostrophe; for example, *company's policies* or *companies' policies*; not *companies policies*.

COLONS

Colons are used (1) after an independent clause that introduces explanatory material and (2) after the salutation of a business letter. When typing, leave two spaces after a colon; do not begin the following word with a capital letter unless it begins a quoted sentence.

Explanation

Use a colon to introduce explanatory material that is preceded by an independent clause.

Just remember this: you may need a reference from her in the future.

The fall trade show offers the following advantages: inexpensive show space, abundant traffic, and free press publicity.

Note: An independent clause is a subject-verb combination that can stand alone as a complete sentence. Expressions commonly used to introduce explanatory material are *the following, as follows,* and *these.* The explanatory material may be a listing, a restatement, an example, or a quotation.

Make sure the clause preceding the explanatory material can stand alone as a complete sentence. Otherwise, no punctuation is needed; for example, "The fall trade show offers inexpensive show space, abundant traffic, and free press publicity."

Salutation

Use a colon after the salutation of a business letter that is typed using standard punctuation.

Dear Mr. Jones:
Dear Alice:

Note: Never use a comma after the salutation in a business letter. (A comma would be used in a personal letter.) With standard punctuation, a colon follows the salutation and a comma follows the complimentary closing. With open punctuation, no punctuation follows the salutation or complimentary closing.

ELLIPSES

An ellipsis (three periods, with one space before and after each) is used to show that something has been left out of a quotation. Four periods (the sentence period plus the three ellipsis periods) indicate the omission of either the last part of a quoted sentence, the first part of the next sentence, or a whole sentence or paragraph. Here is an example:

> *Complete Quotation:*
> The average age of homebuyers has risen to 31.5 years from 29.6 years in 1989. This increase is partly due to the rising cost of new home mortgages. Adjustable-rate mortgages now account for 60% of all new mortgages.

> *Shortened Quotation:*
> The average age of homebuyers has risen to 31.5 years. . . . Adjustable-rate mortgages now account for 60% of all new mortgages. [The typing sequence is *years*.(space).(space).(space).(2 spaces)*Adjustable*.]

Omission

Use ellipsis periods to indicate that one or more words have been omitted from quoted material.

> According to *Business Week,* "A continuing protest could shut down . . . Pemex, which brought in 34% of Mexico's dollar income last year."

HYPHENS

Hyphens are used in compound words (such as money-maker), between syllables in some words (such as *quasi-public*), and in word divisions. When typing, do not leave space before or after a regular hyphen. Likewise, do not use a hyphen with a space before and after to substitute for a dash. (Make a dash by typing two hyphens with no space before or after.) Leave one space after a suspended hyphen (see the following section) unless it is followed by a punctuation mark.

Compound Adjective

Hyphenate a compound adjective that comes *before* a noun (unless the adjective is a proper noun or unless the first word is an adverb ending in -*ly*).

> We hired a first-class management team.
> *But:* Our new management team is first class.

> The long-term outlook for our investments is excellent.
> *But:* We intend to hold our investments for the long term.

> The General Motors warranty received high ratings.

> Alice presented a poorly conceived proposal.

> Only first- and second-class mail will arrive on time.

Note: Don't confuse compound adjectives (which are generally temporary combinations) with compound nouns (which are generally well-established concepts). Compound nouns (such as *social security, life insurance, word processing,* and *high school)* are not hyphenated when they come before a noun; thus, *income tax form, real estate agent, public relations firm,* and *data processing center.* In the last sentence, note that when two hyphenated adjectives have a common base you should use a "suspended" hyphen rather than repeating the base word (*class* is the base word in this example).

Numbers

Hyphenate fractions and compound numbers 21 through 99.

> Nearly three-fourths of our new applicants were unqualified.
>
> Seventy-two orders were processed incorrectly.

PERIODS

Periods are used at the ends of declarative sentences and polite requests and in abbreviations. When typing, leave two spaces after a period (or any other punctuation mark) that ends a sentence.

Request

Use a period to end a sentence that is a polite request.

> Would you please sign the form on page 2.
>
> May I please have the report by Friday.

Note: Consider the statement a polite request if you expect the reader to respond by *acting* rather than by giving a yes-or-no answer. "Would you be willing to take this assignment?" is a real question, requiring a question mark, whereas "Would you let me know your answer by Friday." is a polite request, requiring a period.

QUOTATION MARKS

Quotation marks are used around direct quotations, titles of some publications and conferences, and special terms. When typing, do not space after the opening quotation mark or before the closing quotation mark. Type the closing quotation mark after a period or comma but before a colon or semicolon. Type the closing quotation mark after a question mark or exclamation point if the quoted material is a question or an exclamation; otherwise, type it before the question mark or exclamation point. Capitalize the first word of a quotation that begins a sentence.

Quotation

Use quotation marks around a direct quotation.

> "When we return on Thursday," Luis said, "we would like to meet with you."
>
> Did Helen say, "I will represent us"?

Note: Do not confuse a direct quotation with an indirect quotation, which is not enclosed in quotation marks: "Warren said that he wanted to meet with me on Thursday."

Term

Use quotation marks around a term to clarify its meaning or to show that it is being used in a special way.

> Net income after taxes is known as "the bottom line."
>
> The job title was changed from "chairman" to "chief executive officer."
>
> The president misused the word "effect" in last night's press conference.

Title

Use quotation marks around the title of a newspaper or magazine article, chapter in a book, report, conference, and similar items.

> Read the article entitled "Wall Street Recovery."
>
> Chapter 4, "Market Segmentation," of Industrial Marketing is of special interest.
>
> The theme of this year's sales conference is "Quality Sells."
>
> The report "Common Carriers" shows the extent of the transportation problems.

Note: The titles of *complete* published works are underscored. The titles of *parts* of published works and most other titles are enclosed in quotation marks.

SEMICOLONS

Semicolons are used to show where elements in a sentence are separated. The separation is stronger than a comma but not as strong as a period. When typing, leave one space after a semicolon and begin the following word with a lowercase letter.

Comma

Use a semicolon to separate independent clauses that contain internal commas.

> Although high-quality paper was used, the photocopy machine still jammed; and neither of us knew how to repair it.
>
> I slept through my alarm; consequently, I was late for the meeting.
>
> Carmella knew what needed to be done; but because of her illness, a combination of flu and malnutrition, she was unable to do it.

Note: Make sure the semicolon is inserted *between* the independent clauses—not within one of the clauses. Note in the last sentence that a comma goes after, but not before, the introductory expression "because of her illness."

Independent Clauses

Use a semicolon to separate independent clauses that are not connected by a coordinate conjunction.

The president was eager to proceed with the plans; the board was not.

Note: If a coordinate conjunction (such as *and, but, or,* or *nor*) connects the two clauses, use a comma: "The president was eager to proceed with the plans, but the board was not." Do not use a comma to separate two independent clauses that are not joined by a coordinate conjunction (such an error is called a *comma splice*).

Series

Use semicolons to separate items in a series if any of the items already contain commas.

> The personnel department will be interviewing in Dallas, Texas; Stillwater, Oklahoma; and Little Rock, Arkansas, for the new position.

> Among the guests were Henry Halston, our attorney; his wife Edith; and Lisa Hart-Wilder, our new controller.

Note: Make sure the semicolon is inserted between (not within) each item in the series. Even if only one of the items contains an internal comma, separate all of them with semicolons. Do not use a semicolon after the last item in the series: "Our president, Greg Compton; the honoree, Dorothy Cheung; and I attended the award ceremony."

UNDERSCORES

An underscore (or underline) is a line typed under an expression to show emphasis or to substitute for italic type. When typing a title, underscore the spaces between the words, but do not underscore any punctuation after the title. When underscoring individual words, do not underscore the spaces between the words: "Does the author of <u>The Last Dollar</u> spell her name <u>Joanne</u>, <u>Joann</u>, or <u>Jo Ann</u>?"

Title

Underscore the title of a book, magazine, newspaper, and other complete published works.

> Roger's newest book, <u>All That Glitters</u>, was reviewed in <u>The New York Times</u>.

> The Alaco oil spill was the cover story in last week's <u>Time</u>.

Note: Material that was underscored in the original typed copy will be set in italics in the printed copy.

APPLICATION

Directions Insert any needed punctuation (including commas) in the following sentences. In the blank at the left, write abbreviations for the punctuation rules being applied; some sentences will apply more than one rule. If a sentence is correctly punctuated as shown, write a *C* in the blank. Each numbered item is one sentence.

Examples: __poss__ We received our money's worth.
　　　　　　__C__ Your presentation to the president was first class.

_____   1. I plan to attend Judys session Gretchen does not.

_____   2. Doris finished the newsletter on time but in the meantime her other duties were left undone.

_____   3. Mr. McGlynn training director Ms. Little forms analyst and I should be consulted before any action is taken.

_____   4. You must read the article in *Business Week* entitled Japanese Carmakers Flash Their Cash.

_____   5. Chris Overmans updating of the lobbies furnishings was widely appreciated.

_____   6. Will your remarks be off the record?

_____   7. If Agnes intends to go she should let Mark know he will make all the arrangements.

_____   8. They will first paint my office then after five minutes rest they will paint yours.

_____   9. These are the new requirements three years experience and union membership.

_____   10. Those peoples computers are privately owned.

_____   11. They were careful workers nevertheless two errors slipped by them.

_____   12. Its about time your division was given its due share of resources.

_____   13. Dayle is certainly a highly valued employee of ours.

_____   14. Betty wanted to attend the APICS meeting but she was out of town.

_____   15. Mens wallets and womens handbags are featured in this weeks sale.

_____   16. The award ceremony was a never to be forgotten experience for that workers family.

_____   17. You may test up to three fourths of the workers said Mr. Palmer if you notify them ten days prior to the testing.

_____   18. The two dates to remember are March 15 1992 and April 15 1993.

_____   19. It took Mavis only two hours to do the five hour job.

_____   20. The Browns automobile is two years newer than the Wilsons.

_____   21. Bills leaving delayed our new product introduction by two weeks.

_____   22. My superiors wife used the term nonboring to describe their new family life.

_____ 23. Twenty one of the reports were prepared on the secretaries computers.

_____ 24. The inns guests complained about the geeses honking.

_____ 25. Here is the latest development Business Week will feature the company in their next issue.

_____ 26. The mayors voted to coordinate their efforts in attracting the new firm we should be receiving their joint plan soon.

_____ 27. Would you please photocopy the article entitled Green Is the Color of Money that appeared in last weeks Money magazine.

_____ 28. The Secretary of Commerce said We will trim imports by two thirds by the end of the quarter.

_____ 29. You will be meeting our agent in Milan next week but do not forget to visit Rudolpho Angeletti our distributor in Rome on your way home.

_____ 30. John Hague accounting department Margaret Morgan insurance department and Haskell Springer transportation department were all awarded blue ribbons for first place.

LAB LANGUAGE ARTS BASICS

Mechanics

Writing mechanics include those elements in communication that are evident only in written form: abbreviations, capitalization, number expression, spelling, and word division. (Punctuation, also a form of writing mechanics, was covered in LABS 2–3.) While creating a first draft, you need not be too concerned about the mechanics of your writing. However, you should be especially alert during the editing and proofreading stages to follow the common rules that follow.

ABBREVIATIONS

Use abbreviations sparingly in narrative writing; many abbreviations are appropriate only in technical writing, statistical material, and tables. Consult a dictionary for the correct form for abbreviations, and follow the rule "When in doubt, write it out." When typing, do not space within abbreviations except to separate each initial of a person's name. Leave one space after an abbreviation unless another mark of punctuation follows immediately.

Not Abbreviated

In narrative writing, do not abbreviate common nouns (such as *acct., assoc., bldg., co., dept., misc.,* and *pkg.*) or the names of cities, states (except in addresses), months, and days of the week.

With Periods

Use periods to indicate many abbreviations.

No.   8 a.m.
Dr. M. L. Peterson   P.O. Box 45   e.g.   4 ft.

Without Periods

Write some abbreviations in all capitals, with no periods (including all two-letter state abbreviations used in addresses).

CPA   IRS
TWA   UNESCO

Note: Two-letter state abbreviations should be used only when followed by a ZIP code.

CAPITALIZATION

The function of capitalization is to emphasize words or to show their importance. For example, the first word of a sentence is capitalized to emphasize that a new sentence has begun.

Compass Point

Capitalize a compass point that designates a definite region or that is part of an official name. (Do not capitalize compass points used as directions.)

Margot lives in the South.
Our display window faces west.
Is East Orange in West Virginia?

Letter Part

Capitalize the first word and any proper nouns in the salutation and complimentary closing of a business letter.

Dear Mr. Smith:	Sincerely yours,
Dear Mr. and Mrs. Ames:	Yours truly,

Noun Plus Number

Capitalize a noun followed by a number or letter (except for page and size numbers).

Table 3	page 79
Flight 1062	size 8D

Position Title

Capitalize an official position title that comes before a personal name (unless the personal name is an appositive set off by commas).

Vice President Alfredo Tenegco	Shirley Wilhite, dean,
our president, Joanne Rathburn,	The chief executive officer retired.

Proper Noun

Capitalize a proper noun and an adjective derived from a proper noun. Do not capitalize articles, conjunctions, and prepositions of three or fewer letters (such as *a, of,* or *and*). Capitalize *the* only if it is an official part of the title. The names of the seasons and the names of generic school courses are not proper nouns and are not capitalized.

the United States of America	Amherst College
New York City	the Mexican border
the Fourth of July	Friday, March 3,
Sam's Seafood Shanty	*The New York Times*
First-Class Storage Company	Margaret Adams-White
business communication	the winter holidays

Quotation

Capitalize the first word of a quoted sentence. (Do not capitalize the first word of an indirect quotation.)

According to Hall, "The goal of quality control is specified uniform quality."
Hall thinks we should work toward "specified uniform quality."
Hall said that uniform quality is the goal.

Title

In a published title, capitalize the first and last words, the first word after a colon or dash, and all other words except articles, conjunctions, and prepositions.

> "A Word to the Wise"
> *Pricing Strategies: The Link with Reality*

NUMBERS

Authorities do not agree on a single style for expressing numbers—whether to spell out the number in words or to write it in figures. The following guidelines apply to typical business writing. (The alternative is to use a *formal* style, in which all numbers that can be expressed in one or two words are spelled out.) When typing numbers in figures, separate thousands, millions, and billions with commas; and leave a space between a whole-number figure and its fraction.

General

Spell out numbers for zero through ten and use figures for 11 and over. (Follow this rule only when none of the following special rules apply.)

the first three pages	ten complaints
18 photocopies	5,376 stockholders

Figures

Use figures for

1. dates. (Use the endings *-st, -nd, -rd,* or *-th* only when the day precedes the year.)
2. all numbers if two or more *related* numbers both above and below ten are used in the same sentence.
3. measurements—time, money, distance, weight, and percent (Be consistent in using either the word *percent* or the symbol %.)
4. mixed numbers.

May 9 (or the 9th of May)	10 miles
4 men and 18 women	**But:** The 18 women had four cars.
$6	5 p.m. (or 5 o'clock)
5 percent (or 5%)	6¾

Words

Spell out

1. numbers used as the first word of a sentence.
2. the smaller number when two numbers come together.
3. fractions.
4. the words *millions* and *billions* in even numbers.

Thirty-two people attended.	nearly two-thirds of them
three 25-cent stamps	150 two-page brochures
37 million	$4.8 billion

Note: When fractions and the numbers 21 through 99 are spelled out, they should be hyphenated.

SPELLING

Correct spelling is essential to effective communication. A misspelled word can distract the reader, cause misunderstanding, and send a negative message about the writer's competence. Because of the many variations in the spelling of English words, no spelling guidelines are foolproof; there are exceptions to every spelling rule. The five rules that follow, however, may be safely applied in most business writing situations. Learning them will save you the time of looking up many words in a dictionary. (Although it is no substitute for a dictionary, Appendix C contains a list of 1,000 words that are frequently misspelled in business writing.)

Doubling a Final Consonant

If the last syllable of a root word is stressed, double the final consonant when adding a suffix.

Last Syllable Stressed		Last Syllable Not Stressed	
prefer	preferring	prefer	preference
control	controlling	total	totaling
occur	occurrence	differ	differed

One-Syllable Words

If a one-syllable word ends in a consonant preceded by a single vowel, double the final consonant before a suffix starting with a vowel.

Suffix Starting with Vowel		Suffix Starting with Consonant	
ship	shipper	ship	shipment
drop	dropped	glad	gladness
bag	baggage	bad	badly

Final E

If a final *e* is preceded by a consonant, drop the *e* before a suffix starting with a vowel.

Suffix Starting with Vowel		Suffix Starting with Consonant	
come	coming	hope	hopeful
use	usable	manage	management
nerve	nervous	sincere	sincerely

Final Y

If a final *y* is preceded by a consonant, change *y* to *i* before any suffix except one starting with *i*.

Most Suffixes		Suffix Starting with I	
company	companies	try	trying
ordinary	ordinarily	forty	fortyish
hurry	hurried		

EI *and* IE *Words*

Remember the rhyme:

Use *i* before *e*	believe	yield
Except after *c*	receive	deceit
Or when sounded like *a*	freight	their
As in *neighbor* and *weigh*.		

WORD DIVISION

When possible, avoid dividing words at the end of a line, because word divisions tend to slow down or even confuse a reader (for example, *rearrange* for *rearrange* or *read- just* for *readjust*). However, when necessary to avoid grossly uneven right margins, use the following rules. Although other optional word-division guidelines are also sometimes given, these rules are absolute—they must always be followed. Most word processing software programs have a hyphenation feature that automatically divides words to make a more even right margin. When you are typing, do not space before a hyphen.

Compound Word

Divide a compound word either after the hyphen or where the two words join to make a solid compound.

    self- service   free- way

Division Point

Leave at least two letters on the upper line and carry at least three letters to the next line.

    ex- treme   typ- ing

Not Divided

Do not divide a one-syllable word, contraction, or abbreviation.

    straight   shouldn't
    UNESCO   approx.

Syllables

Divide words only between syllables.

    per- sonnel   knowl- edge

Note: When in doubt about where a syllable ends, consult a dictionary.

APPLICATION

Directions *Rewrite the following paragraphs to make sure that all words and numbers are expressed correctly. Do not change the wording in any sentences.*

1. 5,000 of our employees will receive their bonus checks at 4 o'clock tomorrow. According to dorothy k. needles, human resources director,

employees in every dept. will receive a bonus of at least 4% of their annual salary.

2. As of june 30th, nearly ¾ of our inventory consisted of overpriced computer chips. The vice president for finance, o. jay christensen, presented this and other information in figure 14 of our quarterly status report.

3. The public relations director of our firm gave 14 1-hour briefings during the 3-day swing. Then he drove west to columbus, oh, for a talk-show interview.

4. In response to the $4 drop in price that was reported on page 45 of yesterday's newspaper, president ronald bradley said that next quarter's earnings are expected to be 1⅔ times higher than this quarter's earnings.

5. Today's los angeles herald-examiner quoted jason fowler as saying, "we're proud of the fact that 4 of our regional managers and 13 of our representatives donated a total of 173 hours to the hospice project."

Directions *Correct the one misspelling in each line.*

1. phenomenon	hypocricy	assistance
2. liaison	precedant	miniature
3. surprise	harrass	nickel
4. similiar	occasionally	embarrassing
5. concensus	innovate	irresistible
6. benefited	exhaustible	parallell
7. seperately	inadvertent	exhilarated
8. efficiency	insistance	disapproval
9. accidentally	camouflage	alloted
10. criticize	innocence	indispensible
11. accommodate	perserverance	plausible
12. apparent	deterrant	license
13. category	occurrence	wierd
14. recommend	changeable	hairbrained
15. argument	boundry	deceive

Directions *Write the following words, inserting a hyphen at the first correct division point. If a word cannot be divided, write it without a hyphen.*

Examples: *mis-spelled*
            thought

1. desktop	released	safety
2. abundant	rhythm	masterpiece

3. ILGWU   loudly   planned
4. importance   couldn't   senator-elect
5. ahead   extremely   going

 **LAB** **LANGUAGE ARTS BASICS**

Word Usage

The following words and phrases are often used incorrectly in everyday speech and in business writing. Learn to use them correctly to help you achieve your communication goals.

In some cases in the following list, one word is often confused with another similar word; in other cases, the structure of our language requires that certain words be used only in certain ways. Because of space, only brief and incomplete definitions are given here. Consult a dictionary for more complete or additional meanings.

Accept/Except   *Accept* means "to agree to"; *except* means "to leave out" or "to exclude."

> I will <u>accept</u> all the recommendations <u>except</u> the last one.

Advice/Advise   *Advice* is a noun meaning "counsel"; *advise* is a verb meaning "to recommend."

> If I ask for her <u>advice</u>, she may <u>advise</u> me to quit.

Affect/Effect   *Affect* is most often used as a verb meaning "to influence" or "to change"; *effect* is most often used as a noun meaning "result" or "impression."

> The legislation may <u>affect</u> sales but should have no <u>effect</u> on gross margin.

All Right/Alright   Use *all right*. (*Alright* is considered substandard.)

> The arrangement is <u>all right</u> (not *alright*) with me.

A Lot/Alot   Use *a lot*. (*Alot* is considered substandard.)

> We used <u>a lot</u> (not *alot*) of overtime on the project.

Among/Between   Use *among* when referring to three or more; use *between* when referring to two.

> <u>Among</u> the three candidates was one manager who divided his time <u>between</u> London and New York.

Amount/Number   Use *amount* to refer to money or to things that cannot be counted; use *number* to refer to things that can be counted.

> The <u>amount</u> of interest was measured by the <u>number</u> of cards returned.

Anxious/Eager   Use *anxious* only if great concern or worry is involved.

> Jon was <u>eager</u> to get the new car although he was <u>anxious</u> about making such high payments.

Any One/Anyone   Spell as two words when followed by *of*; spell as one word when the accent is on *any*.

Anyone is allowed to attend any one of the sessions.

Between   See *Among/Between*.

Can/May   *Can* indicates ability; *may* indicates permission.

I can finish the project on time if I may hire an additional secretary.

Cite/Sight/Site   *Cite* means "to quote" or "to mention"; *sight* is either a verb meaning "to look at" or a noun meaning "something seen"; *site* is most often a noun meaning "location."

The sight of the high-rise building on the site of the old battlefield reminded Monica to cite several other examples to the commission members.

Complement/Compliment   *Complement* means "to complete" or "something that completes"; *compliment* means "to praise" or "words of praise."

I must compliment you on the model, which will complement our line.

Could Of/Could've   Use *could've* (or *could have*). (*Could of* is incorrect usage.)

We could've (not could of) prevented that loss had we been more alert.

Different From/Different Than   Use *different from*. (*Different than* is considered substandard.)

Your computer is different from (not different than) mine.

Each Other/One Another   Use *each other* when referring to two; use *one another* when referring to three or more.

The two workers helped each other, but the three visitors would not even look at one another.

Eager   See *Anxious/Eager*.

Effect   See *Affect/Effect*.

e.g./i.e.   The abbreviation *e.g.* means "for example"; *i.e.* means "that is." Use *i.e.* to introduce a restatement or explanation of the preceding expression. Both abbreviations, like the expressions for which they stand, are followed by commas. (Many writers prefer the full English wording to the abbreviations, because they are clearer.)

The proposal has merit (e.g., it is economical, forward-looking, and timely). Unfortunately, it is also a hot potato (i.e., it will generate unfavorable publicity).

Eminent/Imminent   *Eminent* means "well-known"; *imminent* means "about to happen."

The arrival of the <u>eminent</u> scientist from Russia is <u>imminent</u>.

Enthused/Enthusiastic   Use *enthusiastic*. (*Enthused* is considered substandard.)

I have become quite <u>enthusiastic</u> (not *enthused*) about the possibilities.

Except   See *Accept/Except*.

Farther/Further   *Farther* refers to distance; *further* refers to extent or degree.

We drove 10 miles <u>farther</u> while we discussed the matter <u>further</u>.

Fewer/Less   Use *fewer* to refer to things that can be counted; use *less* to refer to money or to things that cannot be counted.

Alvin worked <u>fewer</u> hours at the exhibit and therefore generated <u>less</u> interest.

Further   See *Farther/Further*.

Good/Well   *Good* is an adjective; *well* is an adverb or (with reference to health) an adjective.

Joe does a <u>good</u> job and performs <u>well</u> on tests, even when he does not feel <u>well</u>.

i.e.   See *e.g./i.e.*

Imminent   See *Eminent/Imminent*.

Imply/Infer   *Imply* means "to hint" or "to suggest"; *infer* means "to draw a conclusion." Speakers and writers *imply*; readers and listeners *infer*.

The president <u>implied</u> that changes will be forthcoming; I <u>inferred</u> from his tone of voice that these changes will not be pleasant.

Irregardless/Regardless   Use *regardless*. (*Irregardless* is considered substandard.)

He wants to proceed, <u>regardless</u> (not *irregardless*) of the costs.

Its/It's   *Its* is a possessive pronoun; *it's* is a contraction for "it is."

<u>It's</u> time to let the department increase <u>its</u> budget.

Lay/Lie   *Lay* (principal forms: *lay, laid, laid, laying*) means "to put" and requires an object to complete its meaning; *lie* (principal forms: *lie, lay, lain, lying*) means "to rest."

Please <u>lay</u> the supplies on the shelf.   I <u>lie</u> on the couch after lunch each day.
I <u>laid</u> the folders in the drawer.   The report <u>lay</u> on his desk yesterday.
She had <u>laid</u> the notes on her desk.   The job has <u>lain</u> untouched for a week.

Less   See *Fewer/Less*.

Lie See *Lay/Lie*.

Loose/Lose *Loose* means "not fastened"; *lose* means "to be unable to find."

> Do not <u>lose</u> the <u>loose</u> change in your pocket.

May See *Can/May*.

Number See *Amount/Number*.

One Another See *Each Other/One Another*.

Percent/Percentage With figures, use *percent*; without figures, use *percentage*.

> We took a commission of 6 <u>percent</u> (or 6%), which was a lower <u>percentage</u> than last year.

Personal/Personnel *Personal* means "private" or "belonging to one individual"; *personnel* means "employees."

> I used my <u>personal</u> time to draft a memo to all <u>personnel</u>.

Principal/Principle *Principal* means "primary"; *principle* means "rule" or "law."

> The guiding <u>principle</u> is fair play, and the <u>principal</u> means of achieving it is a code of ethics.

Real/Really *Real* is an adjective; *really* is an adverb. Do not use *real* to modify another adjective.

> She was <u>really</u> proud that her necklace contained <u>real</u> pearls.

Reason Is Because/Reason Is That Use *reason is that*. (*Reason is because* is considered substandard.)

> The <u>reason</u> for such low attendance <u>is that</u> (not *is because*) the weather was stormy.

Regardless See *Irregardless/Regardless*.

Same Do not use *same* to refer to a previously mentioned item. Use *it* or some other wording instead.

> We have received your order and will ship <u>it</u> (not *same*) in three days.

Set/Sit *Set* (principal forms: *set, set, set, setting*) means "to place"; *sit* (principal forms: *sit, sat, sat, sitting*) means "to be seated."

> Please <u>set</u> your papers on the table. Please <u>sit</u> in the chair.
> She <u>set</u> the computer on the desk. I <u>sat</u> in the first-class section.
> I have <u>set</u> the computer there before. I had not <u>sat</u> there before.

Should Of/Should've   Use *should've* (or *should have*). (*Should of* is incorrect usage.)

We should've (not *should of*) been more careful.

Sight   See *Cite/Sight/Site.*

Sit   See *Set/Sit.*

Site   See *Cite/Sight/Site.*

Stationary/Stationery   *Stationary* means "remaining in one place"; *stationery* is writing paper.

I used my personal stationery to write them to ask whether the minicomputer should remain stationary.

Sure/Surely   *Sure* is an adjective; *surely* is an adverb. Do not use *sure* to modify another adjective.

I'm surely glad that she is running and feel sure that she will be nominated.

Sure And/Sure To   Use *sure to*. (*Sure and* is considered substandard.)

Be sure to (not *sure and*) attend the meeting.

Their/There/They're   *Their* means "belonging to them"; *there* means "in that place"; and *they're* is a contraction for "they are."

They're too busy with their reports to be there for the hearing.

Theirs/There's   *Theirs* is a possessive pronoun; *there's* is a contraction for "there is."

We finished our meal but there's no time for them to finish theirs.

They're   See *their/there/they're*

Try And/Try To   Use *try to*. (*Try and* is considered substandard.)

Please try to (not *try and*) attend the meeting.

Well   See *Good/Well.*

Whose/Who's   *Whose* is a possessive pronoun; *who's* is a contraction for "who is."

Who's going to let us know whose turn it is to make coffee?

Your/You're   *Your* means "belonging to you"; *you're* is a contraction for "you are."

You're going to present your report first.

APPLICATION

Directions Circle the correct words in parentheses.

1. Please (advice/advise) the (eminent/imminent) educator of the (real/really) interest we have in his lecture.

2. The three workers on the (stationary/stationery) platform (can/may) help (each other/one another) if they are running late.

3. The writer (implied/inferred) that she and her colleagues divided (their/there/they're) time about evenly (among/between) the two projects.

4. (Whose/Who's) convinced that (fewer/less) of our employees (can/may) elect this option?

5. If you (loose/lose) seniority, (your/you're) work schedule might be (affected/effected).

6. Mary Ellen (cited/sighted/sited) several examples showing that our lab employees are (real/really) (good/well) protected from danger.

7. In comparing performance (among/between) the two companies, Brenda noted that our company earned 7 (percent/percentage) more than (theirs/there's).

8. I try (and/to) (complement/compliment) the advertising group for (its/it's) stunning new brochure.

9. When Susan (laid/lay) the models on the table, I was surprised at the (amount/number) of moving parts; (e.g./i.e.), I had expected simpler designs.

10. The reason the (personal/personnel) department (could of/could've) been mistaken is (that/because) we failed to keep them informed.

11. Sherry refused to (accept/except) the continuous-form (stationary/stationery) because it had (fewer/less) absorbency than expected.

12. (Your/You're) being paid by the (amount/number) of defective finished products you (cite/sight/site) while observing on the assembly line.

13. The (principal/principle) reason we're (anxious/eager) to solve this problem is that (a lot/alot) of workers have complained of dizziness.

14. All our customers are (enthused/enthusiastic) about the new pricing (accept/except) for Highland's, which asked for a quantity discount and expected (it/same) to be granted.

15. Be (sure and/sure to) point out to her that the (percent/percentage) of commission we pay new agents is no different (from/than) that which we pay experienced agents.

16. I am (anxious/eager) to see if (its/it's) going to be Arlene (whose/who's) design will be selected.

17. I (implied/inferred) from Martin's remarks that Austin is a (sure/surely) bet as the (cite/sight/site) for our new plant.

18. The (principal/principle) (advice/advise) that Michelle gave was to (set/sit) long-term goals and stick to them.

19. Although (their/there/they're) located (farther/further) from our office than I would like, I believe their expertise will (complement/compliment) our own.

20. (Any one/Anyone) who can (farther/further) refine the (loose/lose) ends of our proposal should come back this afternoon.

21. In the previous shot, Joyce and Kathy (should of/should've) been (laying/lying) next to (each other/one another) on the beach, discussing their plans for the evening.

22. Please (set/sit) awhile and tell them about your experiences in the Foreign Service, (e.g./i.e.), the time you were arrested in Buenos Aires for doing a (good/well) deed for a local shopkeeper.

23. (Theirs/There's) no reason to pry into an applicant's (personal/personnel) life; however, it is (all right/alright) to ask about the applicant's general state of health.

24. (Any one/Anyone) of the stockbrokers, (irregardless/regardless) of his or her philosophy, would (sure/surely) question such a strategy.

25. (Their/There/They're) will be little (affect/effect) on operations from the (eminent/imminent) change in ownership of the firm.

Appendix B: REFERENCES

CHAPTER 1

[1]Herbert W. Hildebrandt, Floyd Bond, Edwin L. Miller, and A. W. Swinyard, "An Executive Appraisal of Courses Which Best Prepare One for General Management," *Journal of Business Communication,* 19 (Winter 1982): 5–15; Beverly D. Sypher and Theodore E. Zorn, "Communication-Related Abilities and Upward Mobility: A Longitudinal Investigation," *Human Relations Research,* 12 (Spring 1986): 420–431.

[2]"CEO Communication with Employees Can Help Bottom Line," *Administrative Management* (April 1988): p. 6.

[3]Robert L. Montgomery, Listening Made Easy—How to Improve Listening on the Job, at Home, and in the Community (New York: American Management Associations, 1981): p. 6.

[4]Albert Mehrabian, "Communicating Without Words," *Psychology Today* (September 1968): pp. 53–55.

[5]Judee K. Burgoon and Thomas Saine, *The Unspoken Dialogue: An Introduction to Nonverbal Communication* (Boston: Houghton Mifflin, 1978), p. 123.

[6]Mark L. Knapp, *Essentials of Nonverbal Communication* (New York: Holt, Rinehart & Winston, 1980), pp. 21–26.

[7]Edward T. Hall, *The Hidden Dimension* (Garden City, NY: Doubleday, 1966), pp. 107–122.

[8]Des Crossan, "A Company Employee Communications Strategy," *Management Decision,* 25 (May 1987): 31.

[9]Donald B. Simmons, "The Nature of the Organizational Grapevine," *Supervisory Management,* 30 (November 1985): 40; Alan Zaremba, "Working with the Organizational Grapevine," *Personnel Journal,* 67 (July 1988): 40; Carol Hymowitz, "Spread the Word: Gossip Is Good," *Wall Street Journal* (October 4, 1988): p. B1.

CHAPTER 2

[1]*The World Almanac and Book of Facts: 1989,* pp. 522, 532; *The 1989 Information Please Almanac,* p. 139.

[2]Retha H. Kilpatrick, "International Business Communication Practices," *Journal of Business Communication,* 21 (Fall 1984): 36; *The 1989 Information Please Almanac,* pp. 225, 522.

[3]Stephen Karel, "Learning Culture the Hard Way," *Consumer Markets Abroad,* 7 (May 1988): 1, 15.

[4]Martin Rösch and Kay G. Segler, "Communication with Japanese," *Management International Review,* 27 (December 1987): 56.

[5]Koreo Kinosita, "Language Habits of the Japanese, *Bulletin of the Association for Business Communication,* 51 (September 1988): 36.

[6]Lennie Copeland, "Making the Most of Cultural Differences at the Workplace," *Personnel,* 65 (June 1988): 52.

[7]Amy Bermar, "Bulletin Boards Can Take Many Tacks," *PC Week,* November 10, 1987, p. 63.

[8]Donald Harris, "A Matter of Privacy: Managing Personal Data in Company Computers," *Personnel,* 64 (February 1987): 39.

[9]Nancy Allen, Dianne Atkinson, Meg Morgan, Teresa Moore, and Craig Snow, "What Experienced Collaboraors Say About Collaborative Writing," *Iowa State Journal of Business and Technical Communication,* 1, No. 2 (1987): 70–90; Lester Faigley and Thomas Miller, "What We Learn from Writing on the Job," *College English,* 44 (1982): 557–569.

[10]John R. Pierce, "Communication," *Scientific American,* 227 (September 1972): 36.

[11]Irving R. Janis, *Victims of Groupthink* (Boston: Houghton Mifflin, 1972).

CHAPTER 3

[1]Scot Ober, "The Basic Vocabulary of Written Business Communications," Research Project 81-902-111-03 (Phoenix: Arizona Department of Education, 1981).

[2] Richard A. Lanham, *Revising Business Prose* (New York: Scribner's, 1981), p. 2.

CHAPTER 4

[1] Robert Gunning, *The Technique of Clear Writing* (New York: McGraw-Hill, 1968), pp. 38–39.

[2] George R. Klare, "A Second Look at the Validity of Readability Formulas," *Journal of Reading Behavior,* 8 (1976), 147.

[3] Gunning, p. 28.

[4] Gunning, p. xiii.

CHAPTER 5

[1] See, for example, "Mind Mapping: Brainstorming on Paper," *Training,* September 1987, pp. 71–76; Sherwood Rudin, "Banishing Writer's Block from Letters, Reports, and Memos," *Personnel,* April 1987, pp. 46–53; Joseph F. Trimmer and James M. McCrimmon, *Writing with a Purpose,* 9th ed. (Boston: Houghton Mifflin, 1988), pp. 28–30.

[2] Marshall Cook, "Seven Steps to Better Manuscripts," *Writer's Digest,* September 1987, p. 30.

[3] Retha H. Kilpatrick, "International Business Communication Practices," *Journal of Business Communication* 21 (Fall 1984): 40–42.

CHAPTER 6

[1] Marj Jackson Levin, "Don't Get Mad: Get Busy," *Detroit Free Press,* March 10, 1989, p. B1.

CHAPTER 7

[1] Abraham Maslow, *Motivation and Personality,* 2d ed. (New York: Harper & Row, 1970), pp. 35–58.

[2] Cynthia Crossen, "You Call It Junk, But Denison Hatch Sees Gold in It," *Wall Street Journal,* September 25, 1989, p. A1.

[3] Ed Cerny, "Listening for Effect," *American Salesman,* May 1986, p. 28.

[4] Herschell Gordon Lewis, *Direct Mail Copy That Sells!* (Englewood Cliffs, NJ: Prentice-Hall, 1984), p. iii.

5 Linda Lynton, "The Fine Art of Writing a Sales Letter," *Sales & Marketing Management,* August 1988, p. 55.

CHAPTER 8

1 For a discussion of the empirical rationale for using an indirect versus a direct approach, see D. Brent, "Indirect Structure and Reader Response," *Journal of Business Communication* (Spring 1985), pp. 5–7; Mohan Limaye, "Buffers in Bad News Messages and Recipient Perceptions," *Management Communication Quarterly,* 2 (August 1988), 90–101; Kitty O. Locker, "The Rhetoric of Negative Messages," *English for Specific Purposes* (July 1984), pp. 1–2; and Douglas Salerno, "An Interpersonal Approach to Writing Negative Messages," *Journal of Advanced Composition,* 6 (1985–86), 139–149.

CHAPTER 9

1 Mark Memmott, "More Firms Stop Giving References," *USA Today,* December 5, 1989, p. B1.

CHAPTER 10

1 John Naisbitt, *Megatrends: Ten New Directions Shaping Our Lives* (New York: Warner Books, 1984), p. 17.
2 Scot Ober, "The Physical Format of Memorandums and Business Reports," *Business Education World,* 62 (November–December 1981): 9–10, 24.

CHAPTER 11

1 *DIALOG Database Catalog—1989* (Palo Alto, CA: DIALOG Information Services, 1989), p. 1.
2 Robert Rosenthal and Ralph L. Rosnow, *The Volunteer Subject* (New York: Wiley, 1975), pp. 195–196.
3 "Food for Thought," *Reader's Digest* (June 1989): p. 102.

CHAPTER 12

1 Jeremiah J. Sullivan, "Financial Presentation Format and Managerial Decision Making: Tables Versus Graphs," *Management Communication Quarterly,* 2 (November 1988), 194–216.
2 Edward Tufte, *The Visual Display of Quantitative Information* (Cheshire, CT: Graphics Press, 1983).
3 Mary Eleanor Spear, *Practical Charting Techniques* (New York: McGraw-Hill, 1969).
4 American Association for Public Opinion Research, *Code of Professional Ethics and Practices* (Princeton, New Jersey, Undated).

CHAPTER 15

1 Michael Doyle and David Straus, *How to Make Meetings Work: The New Interaction Method* (New York: Wyden Books, 1976), p. 4.
2 "Wake Me When It's Over," *Presentation Products,* August 1989, p. 8.
3 Adapted from Leonard F. Meuse, Jr., *Mastering the Business and Technical Presentation* (Boston: CBI Publishing Co., 1980), pp. 2–7.
4 Kerry L. Johnson, "You Were Saying," *Managers Magazine,* February 1989, p. 19.
5 Jerry Cahn, "Presentation Graphics Revolution," *ITC Desktop* (September–October 1989), p. 22.
6 Wharton Applied Research Center, "A Study of the Effects of the Use of Overhead Transparencies on Business Meetings, Final Report," Philadelphia: University of Pennsylvania, September 14, 1981.

7 "Why Presentations?" *MacWorld* (April 1988), p. 143.

8 Albert Mehrabian, "Communicating Without Words," *Psychology Today,* September 1968, pp. 53–55.

9 David Wallechinshy, Irving Wallace, and Amy Wallace, *The Book of Lists* (New York: William Morrow and Company, Inc., 1977), pp. 469–470.

10 Jolie Solomon, "Executives Who Dread Public Speaking Learn to Keep Their Cool in the Spotlight," *Wall Street Journal,* May 4, 1990, p. B1.

1 Michael Doyle and David Straus, *How to Make Meetings Work* (New York: Wyden Books, 1976), p. 4; Marcy E. Mullins, "Are Meetings Worthwhile?" *USA Today,* August 28, 1989, p. B1; E. F. Wells, "Rules for a Better Meeting," *Mainliner,* May 1978, p. 56.

2 "Managing Meetings: A Critical Role," *The Office,* November 1989, p. 20.

3 "Managing Meetings," p. 20.

4 Henry M. Robert, *The Scott, Foresman Robert's Rules of Order, Newly Revised* (Glenview, Illinois: Scott, Foresman and Company, 1981).

5 Robert, p. xlii.

6 Ralph G. Nichols, "Listening Is a Ten-Part Skill," *Nation's Business,* September 1987, p. 40.

7 "Listen Up!" *American Salesman,* July 1987, p. 29.

8 Alan Russell and Norris McWhirter (eds.), *1988 Guiness Book of World Records* (New York: Bantam Books, 1987), p. 418; Tom Heymann, *On an Average Day* (New York: Fawcett Columbine, 1989), p. 185.

9 John T. Molloy, "Dress for Success," *Detroit Free Press,* December 19, 1989, p. 3C.

10 "Only 17% Get Through on First Phone Call," *Office Systems '89,* March 1989, p. 13.

11 "Phone Calls Waste a Month Each Year," *Office Systems '89,* September 1989, p. 14.

12 "6% Increase Posted for Business Letter Cost." *Dartnell Target Survey* (Chicago: Dartnell Institute of Business Research, 1988).

13 "An R_x for the Fear of Dictation," *The Office,* May 1988, p. 154.

1 Karen Ball, "Poll: Chance a Big Factor in Job Choice," *Morning Sun,* January 14, 1990, p. 1C; Selwyn Feinstein, "The Checkoff," *Wall Street Journal,* November 6, 1990, p. A1; Ronald W. Fry, *Your 1st Résumé,* 2d ed. (Hawthorne, NJ: Career Press, 1989), p. 15; "Grass Always Greener for Most in Job Survey," *Office Systems '89,* March 1989, p. 16; "Job Search Data," *Administrative Management,* December 1985, p. 10; L. Patrick Scheetz, *Recruiting Trends 1989–90* (East Lansing, Mich.: Michigan State University Career Development and Placement Services, 1989).

2 Les Krantz, "The 15 Best Jobs for New College Grads," *The National Business Employment Weekly* (College Edition), Fall 1988, p. 4.

3 U.S. Department of Labor, *Occupational Outlook Handbook, 1988–89* ed. (Washington, DC: Government Printing Office), pp. 8–13.

4 Selwyn Feinstein, "Labor Letter," *Wall Street Journal,* October 3, 1989, p. A1.

5 Keith Carter, "Networking Is the Key to Jobs," *USA Today,* August 7, 1989, p. B1.

CHAPTER 16

CHAPTER 17

6 John D. Singleton, "The Economics of the Job Market," in *CPC Annual*, Vol. 1, 32d ed., Bethlehem, Penn.: College Placement Council, 1988, p. 49.

7 Sandra L. Latimer, "First Impressions," *Morning Sun*, May 8, 1989, p. 6.

8 Larry McCoy, "Tell Me About Yourself . . . That's Enough!" *Wall Street Journal*, April 5, 1989, p. A10.

9 See, for example, Jules Harcourt and A. C. "Buddy" Krizan, "A Comparison of Résumé Content Preferences of Fortune 500 Personnel Administrators and Business Communication Instructors," *Journal of Business Communication*, Spring 1989, pp. 177–190; Rod Little, "Keep Your Résumé Short," *USA Today*, July 28, 1989, p. B1; Darlene C. Pibal, "Criteria for Effective Résumés as Perceived by Personnel Directors," *Personnel Administrator*, May 1985, pp. 119–123.

10 "Most Serious Résumé Gaffes, *Communication Briefings*, March 1991, p. 6.

11 Jules Harcourt and A. C. "Buddy" Krizan, "A Comparison of Résumé Content Preferences of Fortune 500 Personnel Administrators and Business Communication Instructors," *Journal of Business Communication*, Spring 1989, pp. 177–190.

12 "Flashcard," *Education Life* (Supplement to the *New York Times*), November 5, 1989, p. 21.

13 Therese Droste, "Executive Résumés: The Ultimate Calling Card," *Hospitals*, March 5, 1989, p. 72.

14 Sandra L. Latimer, "First Impressions," *Morning Sun*, May 8, 1989, p. 6.

CHAPTER 18

1 Lynn Ulrich and Don Trumbo, "The Selection Interview Since 1949," *Psychological Bulletin*, 43 (1965): 100.

2 Shelley Liles, "Wrong Hire Might Prove Costly," *USA Today*, June 6, 1989, p. 6B.

3 Mary Bakeman et al., *Job-Seeking Skills Reference Manual*, 3d ed. (Minneapolis: Minnesota Rehabilitation Center, 1971), p. 57.

4 "Average Starting Salaries," *Indianapolis Star*, March 3, 1991, p. D1.

Appendix C: BASIC SPELLING LIST FOR BUSINESS WRITING

This list contains 1,000 words that are frequently misspelled in business writing. The list is long enough to serve as a useful first reference for checking the spelling of a suspect word, yet short enough for efficient use.*

A

abandon
abbreviation
abscess
absence
accede
accelerated
acceptable
acceptance
access
accessible
accessory
accidentally
acclaim
accommodate
accommodation
accompanying
accomplice
accordance
accountant
accumulate
accuracy
accrual
accrued
achievement
acknowledgment
acquaintance
acquiesce
acquire
acquisition
across
actuary
adapt
address
adequate
adherent
adhesive
adjacent
adjustment
administrative
admirable
advantageous
advertisement

advisable
advisory
aeronautics
affidavit
affirmative
affluent
agenda
aggravate
aggressive
aging
agreeable
agreement
aisle
alien
alignment
alkali
all right
alleged
allegiance
allocate
allotment
allotted
allowable
allowance
almost
alphanumeric
already
altogether
aluminum
amateur
amendment
amortize
analysis
analyze
announcement
annoyance
annual
annuity
anonymous
answer
antagonistic
anticipate
anxiety
anxious

apathy
apologize
appall
apparatus
apparel
apparent
appearance
appliance
applicable
applicant
appointment
appraisal
appreciable
appropriate
approximate
approximately
arbitrary
arbitration
architect
archive
arguing
argument
arrangement
article
articulate
artificial
ascertain
asinine
assassinate
assessment
assignment
assistance
associate
assured
athletic
atrocious
attendance
attention
attorneys
auctioneer
auspices
authorize
automation
autumn

*Scot Ober, *The Spelling Problems of First-Year Typewriting Students.* (Mankato, Minnesota: Delta Pi Epsilon Research Foundation, 1984).

653

auxiliary
available
awkward

B

bachelor
baggage
bankruptcy
bargain
barometer
basically
basis
beginning
believe
belligerent
beneficial
beneficiary
benefited
biased
binary
boisterous
bookkeeping
booster
boundary
breakfast
brilliant
brochure
budget
bulletin
bullion
bureau
bureaucracy
buses
business
busy
buyout
byte

C

cabinet
calculator
calendar
calorie
camouflage
campaign
cancel
canceled
cancellation
candor
cannot
capital
capitol
carburetor
career
carriage
cashier
casualty
catalog
category

cause
cellular
cemetery
census
ceremony
certificate
chairperson
changeable
chaplain
chargeable
chattel
chief
chronological
circumstances
circumstantial
clerical
client
clientele
coding
coincidence
collateral
collator
collectible
colonel
colossal
column
columnar
coming
commentator
commercial
commission
commitment
committee
comparable
comparatively
comparison
compatible
compelled
competent
competitive
competitor
complete
composite
compromise
computer
concealment
concede
conceivable
conceive
concern
concession
concurred
condemn
condenser
conference
confident
confidential
congratulate
congregation
connoisseur
conquer

conscience
conscientious
conscious
consensus
consequence
consign
consignment
consistent
contagious
container
contingent
continuous
contract
controlling
controversy
convenience
convenient
conversion
converter
cooperative
coordinate
cordially
corduroy
corporation
correspondence
courteous
courtesy
coverage
creditor
criticism
criticize
current
cursor
customer
cycle

D

debtor
deceive
decide
decimal
decision
deductible
defamation
defendant
defense
deferred
deficiency
deficit
definite
definitely
dehydrate
delegate
democracy
demonstration
denominator
dependent
depositors
depreciation
descendant

describe
description
desirable
destination
deteriorate
deterrent
detrimental
development
device
devise
dexterity
diagraming
dictionary
difference
differential
digital
dignitary
dilemma
director
disappear
disappointed
disaster
disastrous
disbursement
discernible
discipline
discrepancy
disguise
diskette
dissatisfied
distortion
distribution
docket
document
double
duplicating
duress

E

eagerly
easement
economical
economics
economy
education
efficiency
eighth
either
electronic
elementary
eligible
eliminate
embarrass
embezzlement
emergency
eminent
emphasis
emphasize
employee
employer

emptied
empty
enclosure
encumbrance
encyclopedia
endeavor
endorsement
ensemble
enterprise
enthusiasm
enthusiastic
entree
entrepreneur
entries
enumerate
envelope
environment
equality
equipment
equipped
equity
ergonomics
escalate
escrow
especially
essential
establish
etiquette
exaggerate
exceed
excellence
excellent
excessive
exclamation
excusable
exercise
exhaustible
exhibit
exhilarated
existence
exonerate
exorbitant
expedite
expenditure
expense
expensive
experience
explanation
extemporaneous
extension
external
extraordinary
extremely
eyeing

F

facilities
facsimile
fallacy
familiarize

fascinate
favorable
favorite
feasible
February
fiery
finally
financial
financier
flexible
fluorescent
forbade
forcible
foreclosure
foreign
foresee
forfeit
forfeiture
fortieth
forty
fourteen
fourth
fraud
freight
friend
frustrate
fulfillment
fundamental
furniture
furthermore

G

gauge
genuine
gigantic
glamorous
glamour
government
governor
grammar
grateful
gratuitous
gray
grievance
grievous
grudge
gruesome
guarantee
guardian

H

handled
harassment
hardware
hazardous
hectic
height
heir
hesitant

heterogeneous
hindrance
hoping
hors d'oeuvre
humanitarian
hygiene
hypocrisy

I

identical
illegality
illegible
illiterate
illuminate
immediate
immediately
impasse
imperative
impossible
inasmuch as
incidentally
incontestable
inconvenience
incurred
indebtedness
indelible
indemnity
independence
independent
indispensable
individual
inducement
industry
inevitable
infinite
inflammable
influential
initial
innocence
innocuous
innovation
innuendo
inquiry
insistence
installation
installment
integrated
intelligence
intention
intercede
interest
interfere
interfered
interfering
interim
intern
interpret
interrupted
intestate
inventory

investor
irrelevant
irreparable
irresistible
irreverent
issuing
itemized
itinerary

J

jeopardize
jeopardy
journal
jubilee
judgment
judicious
justifiable

K

kilocycle
kilowatt
knowledge
knowledgeable

L

label
labeled
labeling
laboratory
language
lawyer
ledger
legible
legitimate
leisure
length
letterhead
leverage
liable
liaison
libel
librarian
library
license
lien
lieutenant
lightning
likable
limousine
linear
linoleum
litigation
livelihood
luxury

M

magazine
magnetic

magnificent
maintenance
malignment
manageable
management
maneuver
manifestation
manipulate
manufacturer
manuscript
marriage
material
mathematics
matrix
maximum
mediocre
memento
memorandum
menu
menus
mercantile
merchandise
meticulous
microcomputer
mileage
millionaire
miniature
minimum
minuscule
minutiae
miscellaneous
mischievous
misdemeanor
misspell
modem
modernize
mortgage
motion
motor
movable
murmur

N

necessary
negative
negligible
negotiate
negotiation
neighborhood
neither
nevertheless
nickel
nineteenth
ninety
ninth
nonessential
notice
noticeable
novice
nuclear

nucleus
numerator

O

oblige
oblivious
obsolete
obstinate
obvious
occasion
occasionally
occupant
occupation
occurred
occurrence
occurring
offense
offered
offering
official
offset
omission
omitted
operator
opinion
opportunity
optical
optimism
option
ordinary
organization
organize
original
originator
orphan
output
overconfident
overdue

P

pageant
paid
pamphlet
panic
panicked
paragraph
parallel
paralyze
parenthesis
parochial
partial
partially
participant
participate
particularly
partnership
patience
pastime
patronage

penalize
percent
peripheral
permanent
permissible
permitted
perseverance
persistent
personal
personnel
persuade
persuasion
pharmacist
phase
phenomenal
phenomenon
phony
photocopy
physician
plagiarism
plaintiff
planning
plausible
pleasant
pleasure
pneumatic
positive
possession
practical
practically
practice
precarious
precede
precedent
precision
preferable
preference
preferred
prejudice
preliminary
premium
prerequisite
prerogative
pressurized
prestige
presumptuous
pretense
previous
printout
privilege
probably
procedure
proceed
processing
professor
programmed
prominent
promissory
prompt
pronounce
pronunciation

propeller
proprietor
propulsion
prosecute
psychiatric
psychology
publicly
punctuation
pursue

Q

quantitative
quantity
questionnaire
quorum

R

ratification
reaffirm
realize
reasonable
rebellious
rebuttal
receipt
receive
recently
receptacle
receptionist
recipe
recipient
reciprocate
recognition
recognize
recommendation
reconcile
reconciliation
reconnaissance
recruit
recurrence
reference
referendum
referred
referring
regrettable
reimbursement
reinforce
relevant
remember
reminiscent
remittance
remunerate
rendezvous
renewal
renowned
repetition
repetitively
replica
representative
repudiate

requirement
requisition
reservoir
rescind
resistance
response
responsibility
responsible
restaurant
résumé
retrieval
retroactive
reveal
rhetorical
rhyme
rhythm
ridiculous
rotary
route
rudiment

S

salable
salary
satellite
satisfactorily
scarcity
schedule
scissors
secretary
securities
seize
seniority
separate
sergeant
serviceable
settlement
shipment
shipping
siege
significant
similar
simplified
simultaneous
sincerely
sincerity
sizable
skeptic
skiing
skillful
socialism
solar
sources
souvenir
sovereign
specialize
specialty
specifications
specimen
sponsor

stabilize
statement
statistics
stenographer
stockholder
straight
strategy
strength
strictly
submitted
subpoena
subscriber
subscription
subsidiary
substantial
subtle
subtlety
succeed
successful
successor
sufficient
suing
summary
superintendent
supersede
supervisor
surgeon
surprise
surveillance
susceptible
survey
sympathize
synonymous
synthetic
system

T

tangible
tariff
taxiing
technique
technology
telecommunication
temperament
temperature
temporary
tempt
tenacious
tenancy
tenant
territory
theater
theory
thorough
threshold
throughout
totaled
tragedy
tranquil
transcribe

transferred
transit
transistor
traveler
trivial
truly
turbine
turnaround
twelfth
twentieth
typewritten
typing

U

ultimately
unanimous
undoubtedly
unforgettable
unfortunately
unique
unmanageable
unnecessary
until
unwieldy
upheaval
urgent
usable
usage
usually
usury
utterance

V

vacancies
vacillate
vacuum
valuable
vandalism
variable
various
vegetable
vehicle
vendor
veracity
verbatim
vetoes
vicinity
vicious
victim
visible
vitalize
vocational
void
volume
voluntary
volunteer

W

waiver
warehouse

warranty
wealthiest
weather
Wednesday
weird
whether
whiskey

wholesale
wholly
wield
withhold
witness
workstation
worthwhile

wraparound
writing
wrought

Y

yield

Appendix D:
Urban Systems, Inc.

THE COMPANY

Urban Systems, Inc. (US) is a small, "start-up" company whose primary product is Ultra Light, a new, paper-thin light source that promises to revolutionize the illumination industry. The company employs 178 people at its corporate headquarters in Ann Arbor, Michigan, and in a completely automated manufacturing plant in Charlotte, North Carolina. It is incorporated under the laws of the state of Michigan, with all stock privately held by the founders and their families.

Urban Systems has annual sales in the $30 million range, with a net profit last year of $1.4 million. It is considered a progressive company by the investment community, with good management and good earnings potential. The local community considers US to be a good corporate citizen; it is a nonpolluting firm, and its officers are active in the local chamber of commerce and in community affairs.

THE PRODUCT

Ultra Light is a flat, electroluminescent sheet of material that serves as a light source. It is capable of replacing most fluorescent, neon, and incandescent light fixtures. Physically, Ultra Light is a paper-thin sheet of chemically treated material laminated between thin layers of clear plastic. In effect, it is a credit-card thin light fixture that is bendable and that can be produced in a variety of shapes and sizes. Operated either by battery or wall current, it generates a bright white or colored light.

Ultra Light is cost-competitive with other, more conventional lighting, and its life expectancy is measured in years. All of this, combined with the appeal of its very thin profile, battery operation ("use it anywhere"), the evenly distributed light it produces, and the way it can conform to a variety of physical shapes, makes Ultra Light a new product with a lot of potential.

COMPANY HISTORY

US was founded in 1983 by two brothers, David and Marc Kaplan. David was a chemical engineer at Dow Chemical when he developed the basic concept of Ultra Light while working on another project. Since Dow was not interested in pursuing the manufacturing and marketing of this product, David bought all rights to Ultra Light from Dow and patented it in 1983. Then he and his younger brother Marc, formerly a marketing manager for an advertising agency in Chicago, started Urban Systems in an abandoned warehouse in Midland, Michigan.

The company received start-up funds through personal investments of $50,000 by David Kaplan and $35,000 by Marc and a $68,500 five-year loan from the United States Small Business Administration. Because of Marc's advertising background, the company's five-year business plan focused on marketing Ultra Light initially for advertising purposes—to illuminate signs, point-of-purchase displays, and the like. Later, as the company became better established in the marketplace, plans were to expand into industrial, office, and consumer applications. Hence, a company name—Urban Systems—was selected that was broad enough to encompass a variety of products.

After a somewhat uneven start, US had become profitable by the end of its fifth year of operations and had outgrown its original building. The company recently built an 11,000 square-foot facility in an attractive office park in Ann Arbor, Michigan, to house its administrative, marketing, and R & D functions. The company also moved its manufacturing operations to Charlotte, North Carolina, in a leased facility. The manufacturing facility is completely automated, with state-of-the-art robotics, just-in-time inventory control, and a progressive union-management agreement. The latest three-year agreement expires next year.

PERSONNEL

The organization chart for Urban Systems is shown in Figure D.1. Each position and the person currently occupying that position are described below.

BOARD OF DIRECTORS

The Board is comprised of David J. Kaplan, chair; Marc Kaplan, vice-chair; Judith Klehr Kaplan (David Kaplan's wife), Secretary/Treasurer; Thomas V. Robertson, general counsel; and Eileen Jennings (vice president of U.S. National Bank of Michigan). As required by the articles of incorporation, the Board meets quarterly at company headquarters.

PRESIDENT: DAVID J. KAPLAN

Dave Kaplan, age 49, is a professional engineer-turned-manager. He graduated with honors from the Massachusetts Institute of Technology with a degree in chemical engineering. Upon graduation from MIT, he began working as a chemical engineer in the polymer division at Dow Chemical, where he worked until 1983 when he started US. During his time at Dow, he attended graduate school part time at Central Michigan University, where he received his MBA degree in 1968. Although he was offered numerous management positions at Dow, he elected to continue working as a chemical engineer. His work resulted in numerous profitable patents for Dow, and he was considered a highly respected member of the scientific staff.

Dave has published numerous articles in scholarly journals, has presented papers in his area of specialty at several international conferences, and has served as president of the Michigan Society of Chemical Engineers.

Although he manages his new company effectively, Dave will tell you that some of his happiest times were working in the lab at Dow—pursuing some esoteric research project alone and at his own pace. He will also tell you that the aspects of managing Urban Systems that he dislikes the most are the incessant meetings and having to manage and be responsible for the work of others. At US, Dave is considered a perfectionist and a workaholic. Although not an especially warm person, he is highly respected by his staff.

Dave married Judith Klehr immediately upon graduation from college. They have three children (Jonathan, age 25, a newspaper reporter in Washington, DC; Michael, age 22, a senior at Syracuse University; and Marla, age 16, a sophomore in a private school in Ann Arbor). The family lives in Ann Arbor, where Judy is very active in community affairs.

EXECUTIVE SECRETARY: AMY STETSKY

Amy Stetsky, or "Stetsky" as she is called by nearly everyone, was one of the first people hired by David Kaplan. She is 32 years old, has an associate's degree in office systems, and recently earned the Certified Professional Secretary (CPS®) designation as a result of passing an intensive two-day exam administered by a division of Professional Secretaries, International. She is highly respected and well-liked by everyone in the organization.

VICE PRESIDENT— MANUFACTURING: ARNOLD MCNALLY

Arnie McNally knows the production business from top to bottom. He has been with the company from the beginning, having been hired away from a similar job at Steelcase Corporation. Although only a high school graduate, McNally has earned the respect of both Dave and his subordinates, including the engineers in the Research and Development unit.

Arnie gives his staff wide latitude in running their units. He supports them, even when they make mistakes. He does insist, however, on being kept informed at every step of the way. He is a very direct type of person—you always know where you stand with him. If any of his subordinates have some bad news to convey, they know he wants to know immediately and directly—with no beating around the bush.

Arnie is 60 years old and is looking forward greatly to retirement. Although he gets along well with both Dave and his subordinates, he and Marc Kaplan have had several run-ins during the past five years. Privately, he would tell you that he believes Marc is a "lightweight" who is not particularly effective in marketing the firm's products. Arnie is especially upset that Marc has shot down several new products proposed by Arnie's R&D staff.

VICE PRESIDENT— MARKETING: MARC KAPLAN

People who know both Dave and Marc Kaplan cannot believe they are brothers. Marc, age 42, is the complete opposite of Dave. He is warm and outgoing, with a wide circle of friends both in and out of business. His extensive network of personal and professional contacts has resulted in numerous large and lucrative orders for the firm.

Marc depends heavily on his three managers, especially for in-house operations. He spends a great deal of time away from the office—entertaining customers and prospective customers, attending conventions where US exhibits its products, and making the rounds of golf tournaments and after-hours cocktail parties. Marc is divorced and lives in a high-rise condominium in Ann Arbor, where he has a very active social life.

Marc is aware of Arnie's feelings about him but brushes them aside as normal jealously. He believes that if he could get Arnie to go on a golf outing with him a few times, things could be patched up. As it is, although their relationship is somewhat strained, it is not affecting either's ability to do his job.

VICE PRESIDENT— ADMINISTRATION: NEELIMA SHRIKHANDE

Aged 38, Neelima Shrikhande (pronounced *Nee-LEE-ma Shree-KON-dee*) is from India. She has a master of science degree in management information systems from Stanford University. She was promoted to her present position only last year, having served as manager of the Office and Information Systems (OIS) unit at Urban Systems for four years prior to that.

Neelima is single and an ardent feminist. She is also very actively involved in politics and worked extensively in the unsuccessful campaign of Walter K. Mason, the Liberal Party candidate for governor of Michigan last year.

Neelima manages the division housing both the personnel function and the office function; the office function employs a large number of clerical and secretarial workers (all of whom are female). When Dave Kaplan offered her the promotion to vice president, Neelima informed him that one of her goals would be to institute policies that would upgrade the role of females within the company. Although she gets along well with Arnie McNally, she resents Marc Kaplan's sometimes condescending attitude toward her and what she considers his chauvinistic attitude toward many of the females on his staff.

FINANCIAL DATA

By year's end, assets for Urban Systems totaled $23.2 million, with net income of $1.4 million. Earnings per share for the current year were $1.08; and a dividend of $0.64 per share was paid on the 1.3 million outstanding shares (all of which are held by the two Kaplan families). This and other financial information are contained in the most recent financial statements for Urban Systems, shown in Figures D.2 and D.3.

FIGURE D.1   Organizational Chart

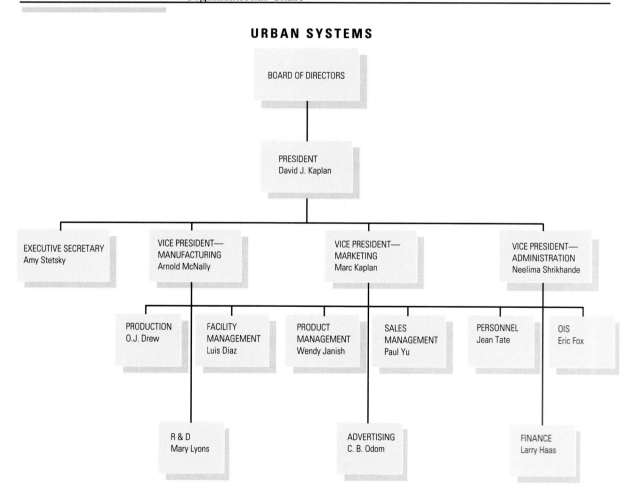

Financial Statement

URBAN SYSTEMS
BALANCE SHEET
December 31, 19--

Assets

Current Assets:

Cash and marketable securities	423,600
Trade receivables	4,942,400
Inventories	5,645,100
Prepaid expenses	307,500
Total Current Assets	11,318,600
Other Assets	5,825,200

Property and Equipment:

Land	255,300
Buildings and improvements	4,291,600
Machinery and equipment	5,749,500
Furniture and fixtures	347,100
Total	10,643,500
Less allowances for depreciation	4,558,600
Total Property and Equipment	6,084,900
TOTAL ASSETS	23,228,700

Liabilities and Shareholders' Equity

Current Liabilities:

Notes payable	3,250,000
Accounts payable	4,971,800
Accrued compensation and taxes	946,100
Other liabilities	952,500
Long-term debt due within one year	205,300
Total Current Liabilities	10,325,700
Long-Term Debt	1,345,600
Deferred Federal Income Taxes	1,800,500

Shareholders' Equity:

Common stock—par value$1.00 per share
  Authorized shares: 3,000,000

Outstanding shares: 1,327,500	1,435,800
Additional capital	7,147,900
Retained earnings	1,173,200
Total Shareholders' Equity	9,756,900
TOTAL LIABILITIES AND SHAREHOLDERS' EQUITY	23,228,700

FIGURE D.3   Financial Statement

URBAN SYSTEMS
STATEMENT OF OPERATIONS
For the Year Ended December 31, 19--

Net Sales	29,750,100
Operating Costs and Expenses:	
Cost of Sales	23,026,400
Selling and Administrative Expenses	2,795,200
Interest Income—Net	(289,500)
Other Income—Net	(97,500)
Total Operating Costs and Expenses	27,434,600
Income From Continuing Operations Before Taxes	2,315,500
Provision for Federal Income Taxes:	
Current	689,900
Deferred	195,400
Total Federal Income Taxes	885,300
Net Income	1,430,200
Retained Earnings:	
Retained Earnings—January 1	1323,600
Dividends Per Share—$0.64	849,600
Retained Earnings—December 31	1,173,200
Earnings Per Share	1.08

Acknowledgments

Grateful acknowledgment is made to the following companies and individuals for allowing their interviews to be included in this book:

Chapter 1 The Home Depot / Deedy Rogers; *Chapter 2* International Business Protocol / Dorothy Manning; *Chapter 3* Frank Sanitate Associates / Frank Sanitate, President, Frank Sanitate Associates, 1152 Camino Manadero, Santa Barbara, CA 93111; *Chapter 4* Gerry Baby Products / Mary Snyder; *Chapter 5* Keep America Beautiful, Inc. / John Kazzi; *Chapter 6* Amway Corporation / Joan Jahr; *Chapter 7* Seva Foundation / Mirabai Bush; *Chapter 8* Digital Equipment Corporation / Alan Pike; *Chapter 9* Ranger Rover / Steve McNight; *Chapter 10* General Electric Company / George Bolin: Published with permission General Electric Company, U.S.A.; *Chapter 11* Della Femina McNamee / Mary Hall; *Chapter 12* OshKosh B'Gosh / Jim Solum; *Chapter 13* Heinz Corporation / Jay Abraham; *Chapter 14* New England Business Magazine / Richard Manning; *Chapter 15* Shell Oil / Richard Hansen; *Chapter 16* Newport Technologies / Peter Atwood; *Chapter 17* CIT Group / William O'Grady; *Chapter 18* Ben & Jerry's / Elizabeth Lonergan

CHAPTER 2
Figure 2.1 "Writing Analysis Software" is reprinted by permission of RightSoft, Inc. Copyright © RightSoft, Inc.

Figure 2.3, "Electronic Revision" is reprinted by permission of Mainstay, Inc.

Figure 2.4, "Solving Problems in Small Groups" is reprinted from Ernest G. Bormann and Nancy C. Bormann, EFFECTIVE SMALL GROUP COMMUNICATION, 4th ed., Burgess Publishing, 1988, pp. 143–144.

CHAPTER 11
"Food for Thought" contributed by J.K. Hillstrom is reprinted with permission from the June 1989 READER'S DIGEST. Copyright © 1989 by The Reader's Digest Assn., Inc.

Figure 11.1, "A Fatty Stock" by Eric k Schmuckler is excerpted by permission of FORBES magazine, June 26, 1989. © Forbes, Inc., 1989.

CHAPTER 12
Figure 12.6A, "US Textile Imports" is reprinted by permission from Standard & Poor's, STANDARD & POOR'S INDUSTRY SURVEYS, 1989, Vol. 2 (New York" Standard & Poors, 1989), p. T64.

Figure 12.6C, "Principal U.S. Oil Basins," is reprinted by permission from STANDARD & POOR'S INDUSTRY SURVEYS, 1989, Vol. 2 (New York: Standard & Poor's, 1989), p. U-20.

Figure 12.7, "Avoiding Varying the Size of Pictograms," from Calvin F. Schmid, HANDBOOK OF GRAPHIC PRESENTATION (New York: The Ronald Press Company, 1954), p. 225 is reprinted by permission of John Wiley & Sons, Inc.

Figure 12-8, "Cheating by Charting," is adapted from Mary Eleanor Spear, PRACTICAL CHARTING TECHNIQUES (New York: McGraw-Hill), 1969, pp. 56–59. Reprinted by permission of McGraw-Hill Publishing Company.

CHAPTER 14
Figure 14.2, "News Release," is reprinted by permission of Cam-Net Communications Network, Inc.

Figure 14.3A "Policy," is reprinted with the permission of Central Michigan University.

Figure 14.3B, "Procedure for Hiring a Temporary Employee," is adapted by permission from Leslie H. Matthies, "Writing Your First Procedure— How to Go About It," JOURNAL OF SYSTEMS MANAGEMENT, November 1987, pp. 25–29.

CHAPTER 15
Figure 15.2, "Comparison of Visual Aids." Source: Scott Inglis and Joanna Kozubska, "Making Presentations, MANAGEMENT DECISION (May 1987), p. 9. Used with permission MCB University press LTD.

Spotlight on Technology, "Desktop Presentations." All images were created with Aldus Persuasion (R). Reprinted with the express permission of Aldus Corporation. Aldus (R) and Persuasion (R) are registered trademarks of Aldus Corporation. All rights reserved.

Figure 15.3, Susanne Waltzman, "Presentations with Power," ITC DESK-TOP: No 1. Reprint permission by International Typeface Corporation, New York, NY. Copyright ITC 1989.

Figure 15.4, "Creative Training Techniques." Used with permission by Robert W. Pike, President, Creative Training Techniques International, Inc., Eden Prairie, MN.

Index